RELIGIOUS DISSENT IN THE ROMAN EMPIRE

Religious Dissent in the Roman Empire is the third instalment in Vasily Rudich's trilogy on the psychology of discontent in the Roman Empire at the time of Nero. Unlike his earlier books, it deals not with political dissidence, but with religious dissent, especially in its violent form. Against the broad background of Second Temple Judaism and Judaea's history under Rome's rule, Rudich discusses various manifestations of religious dissent as distinct from the mainstream beliefs and directed against both the foreign occupier and the priestly establishment. This book offers the methodological framework for the analysis of the religious dissent mind-set, which it considers a recurrent historical phenomenon that may play a major role in different periods and cultures. In this respect, its findings are also relevant to the rise of religious violence in the world today and provide further insights into its persistent motives and paradigms. *Religious Dissent in the Roman Empire* is an important study for people interested in Roman and Jewish history, religious psychology and religious extremism, cultural interaction and the roots of violence.

The notes and full bibliography to accompany the book are available for download at www.routledge.com/9780415161060, under the eResources tab.

Vasily Rudich taught history and classics at Yale University in 1984–1995. He is the author of *Political Dissidence under Nero: The Price of Dissimulation* and *Literature and Dissidence under Nero: The Price of Rhetoricization*. He lives in New Haven, Connecticut.

ROUTLEDGE MONOGRAPHS IN CLASSICAL STUDIES

LATE CLASSICAL AND EARLY
HELLENISTIC CORINTH, 338–196 B.C.
Michael D. Dixon

APULEIUS AND AFRICA
Edited by Benjamin Todd Lee, Ellen Finkelpearl and Luca Graverini

CONSUMERISM IN THE ANCIENT WORLD
Imports and Identity Construction
Justin St. P. Walsh

MENANDER IN CONTEXTS
Edited by Alan H. Sommerstein

DISPLAYING THE IDEALS OF ANTIQUITY
The Petrified Gaze
Johannes Siapkas and Lena Sjögren

ROMAN THEORIES OF TRANSLATION
Surpassing the Source
Siobhán McElduff

ROMAN LITERATURE, GENDER, AND RECEPTION
Domina Illustris
Edited by Donald Lateiner, Barbara K. Gold and Judith Perkins

CHILDHOOD IN ANCIENT ATHENS
Iconography and Social History
Lesley A. Beaumont

PLATO'S DIALECTIC ON WOMAN
Equal, Therefore Inferior
Elena Blair

VIRGIL'S HOMERIC LENS
Edan Dekel

ROME IN THE PYRENEES
Lugdunum and the Convenae from the First Century B.C.
to the Seventh Century A.D.
Simon Esmonde-Cleary

DACIA
Landscape, Colonization and Romanization
Ioana A. Oltean

**PASSIONS AND MORAL PROGRESS IN
GRECO-ROMAN THOUGHT**
John T. Fitzgerald

BETWEEN ROME AND PERSIA
The Middle Euphrates, Mesopotamia and Palmyra
under Roman Control
Peter Edwell

GREEK MAGIC
Ancient, Medieval and Modern
John Petropoulos

UTOPIA ANTIQUA
Readings of the Golden Age and Decline at Rome
Rhiannon Evans

**LIFE AND LETTERS IN THE ANCIENT
GREEK WORLD**
John Muir

**ACTORS AND AUDIENCE IN THE ROMAN
COURTROOM**
Leanne Bablitz

THE EUNUCH IN BYZANTINE HISTORY AND SOCIETY
Shaun Tougher

THE ROMAN GARDEN
Space, Sense, and Society
Katharine T. von Stackelberg

Forthcoming:

LUCIAN AND HIS ROMAN VOICES
Eleni Bozia

ATHENS TRANSFORMED, 404–262 B.C.
From Popular Sovereignty to the Dominion of Wealth
Phillip Harding

THEOLOGY AND EXISTENTIALISM IN AESCHYLUS
Written in the Cosmos
Richard Rader

RELIGIOUS DISSENT IN THE ROMAN EMPIRE

Violence in Judaea at the Time of Nero

Vasily Rudich

LONDON AND NEW YORK

First published 2015
by Routledge
2 Park Square, Milton Park, Abingdon, Oxon OX14 4RN

and by Routledge
711 Third Avenue, New York, NY 10017

Routledge is an imprint of the Taylor & Francis Group, an informa business

© 2015 Vasily Rudich

The right of Vasily Rudich to be identified as author of this work has been asserted by him in accordance with sections 77 and 78 of the Copyright, Designs and Patents Act 1988.

All rights reserved. No part of this book may be reprinted or reproduced or utilised in any form or by any electronic, mechanical, or other means, now known or hereafter invented, including photocopying and recording, or in any information storage or retrieval system, without permission in writing from the publishers.

Trademark notice: Product or corporate names may be trademarks or registered trademarks, and are used only for identification and explanation without intent to infringe.

British Library Cataloguing in Publication Data
A catalogue record for this book is available from the British Library

Library of Congress Cataloging in Publication Data
Rudich, Vasily, 1949-
Religious dissent in the Roman Empire : violence in Judaea at the time of Nero / Vasily Rudich. – First [edition].
pages cm. – (Routledge monographs in classical studies)
Includes bibliographical references.
ISBN 978-0-415-16106-0 (hardback : alk. paper) – ISBN 978-1-315-75079-8 (e-book)
1. Religion and politics–Rome. 2. Religion and state–Rome. 3. Rome–Religion. I. Title.
BL805.R83 2014
200.9'015–dc23
2014029198

ISBN: 978-0-415-16106-0 (hbk)
ISBN: 978-1-315-75079-8 (ebk)

Typeset in Baskerville
by Taylor and Francis Books

Printed and bound in the United States of America by Publishers Graphics, LLC on sustainably sourced paper.

THIS BOOK IS FOR JOANNA AND DANIEL,
GRATO ANIMO, AND FOR PHILIP.

CONTENTS

Acknowledgments   x
Preface   xi

Introduction: Religion and Religious Dissent   1

1   The Vibrant Faith   10

2   The Breaking Point   68

3   The Conquered Land   89

4   The Fragile Balance   154

5   The Zealous Storm   210

6   The Dagger Men   253

7   The Fateful Siege   286

Conclusion   321

Select Bibliography   328
Subject Index   337
Name Index   345

ACKNOWLEDGMENTS

This book would have never been completed without the unremitting help and encouragement on the part of many people. First and foremost, I owe my deepest gratitude to Joanna and Daniel Rose for their generous friendship and faith in my work. Bernard Frischer, a true Renaissance man, was indispensable in sharing with me his knowledge, wisdom and insights. I am indebted to Sir Fergus Millar, Tessa Rajak and the late Yosef Yerushalmi, who supported this project from the start. Victor Bers and Otto Steinmayer spent much time and effort in adjusting my awkwardly literal translations from Greek to readable English. The discussions with Dmitri Panchenko and Marina Kostalevsky helped in clarifying my thoughts on the practice of historiography and its literary dimension. Alexander Poznansky and Ekaterina Chernova greatly alleviated my navigating library facilities and the relevant bibliography. In various respects, I have increasingly benefitted from conversations and exchanges with the late Sir Isaiah Berlin, Shari Berman, Susan Bers, John J. Collins, Jane Crawford, Carolyn Dewald, Louis Dupré, Svetlana Evdokimova, Brian Fuchs, Herb Golder, Donald Kagan, Tatyana Kovalevskaya, Hillel Levine, Shula Levine, Rita Lipson, Ramsay MacMullen, Bill Mullen, the late William Odom, Zlatko Plese, Rabbi James Ponet, Brooks Prouty, Emily Rose Marrow, Gideon Rose, Maria Rybakova, Peter Salovey, Jonathan Spence, Tomas Venclova, the late Robin Winks, and Fareed Zakaria. Last, but not least, I especially appreciate the patience and understanding I have enjoyed, all the way through, in my relationship with Amy Davis-Poynter and Matthew Gibbons at Routledge. Given the long time this project took in coming to fruition, I consider their willingness to tolerate my protracted work pace an example of high professional ethics; the same applies to my editors Andrea Service and Andrew Watts. It goes without saying that all flaws, faults and defects in this book are entirely mine.

PREFACE

This book is the product of a very long, even excessively long, gestation. During the 1990s, I embarked on a project of closely studying the specific, historically and culturally conditioned forms of mentality, which I defined as 'psychology of dissidence', under the early Roman Empire. Since I always felt acutely that history is the process of continuous change, I chose as limited a time span as possible (14 years of Nero's reign) to make sense of my subject matter, rather than generalize on the basis of the existent evidence from chronologically different settings, which is often the case with social historians: after all, dissident sensibilities under Nero differed, I believe, in various respects from those under Vespasian. Consequently, I published two studies throughout the decade: the first, *Political Dissidence under Nero: The Price of Dissimulation* (1993), dealt with the issue of how 'dissident psychology' made itself manifest in the public behavior of its carriers; and the second, *Dissidence and Literature under Nero: The Price of Rhetoricization* (1997), undertook to demonstrate its manifestations in their writings.

Eventually, I came to recognize that by concentrating on political dissidence I eschewed other forms of discontent: social, cultural and religious. But for the period in question, that is, Nero's principate (A.D. 54–68), the evidence on social and cultural dissensions (popular riots at Rome, harassment of Greek philosophers), although extant, still does not provide enough material to make a book. On the other hand, the phenomenon I chose to call 'religious dissent' (to distinguish it clearly from 'political dissidence'), seemed to have been very much in operation around the same time within the Jewish community across Roman Palaestina, and may have contributed (at the very least) to the catastrophic events that brought about the collapse of Second Temple Judaism. This whole development was treated, as I well knew, in the extensive writings of Flavius Josephus, while the outbreak of the Great Revolt against Rome, otherwise known as the Jewish War, occurred two years prior to Nero's downfall (which makes the last chapter in my first book), even though it extended into further three years, having witnessed the succession of four emperors and the emergence of the new Flavian dynasty.

It often happens that one miscalculates the duration of work on a particular project. I confess to have been naïve in my belief that, having specialized in

PREFACE

Roman history, I could handle the political and cultural dynamics of Roman Judaea within a relatively short time. At the very outset I was struck by the sudden realization of how difficult and complex was the endeavor on which I had embarked: I was entering a passionate and multidimensional world, fraught with tension and fascination, which – despite whatever affinities generated by a certain degree of convergence – vastly differed from the traditional vision of classical Antiquity that most of us share. It soon also became clear to me that the broad century-long scholarly consensus on what Second Temple Judaism must have looked like has suffered, in the last few decades, a dramatic and extraordinary breakdown so that experts now disagree not only on the important, but also on the insignificant, issues, even to the minutest detail. It took me several years of active research until I could say that the time had arrived to start producing the earliest drafts. This work-in-progress, however, was delayed and interfered with by various circumstances, for the most part beyond my power, not least the massive flood of publications, sometimes annually numbering in the hundreds, that needed to be taken into account. The manuscript went through a long series of drafts; I can only hope that the result justifies the efforts and that, in its final form, the book's narrative coheres and proves of sufficient interest to the present-day professional as well as lay readers.[1]

The word 'history' in contemporary usage signifies three interconnected notions: history as a process, as a subject of study, and the actual study of and writing on the process – that is, historiography. It is this last enterprise that has increasingly become the target of vociferous attacks by scholars and intellectuals employing 'postmodernist' (as they have come to be called) methods and procedures. In the final analysis, these attacks deny customary historical scholarship, that is to say, an attempt at interpreting the past, based on consensually recognized criteria, its very right to exist. In part, the fault has lain in the actual practitioners of history-as-discipline, who rarely articulate their theoretical and methodological views, while most of them ignore postmodernist objections (as a rule highly abstract and often abstruse), preferring instead to proceed with their usual business. I wish I could follow their example, but it strikes me as disingenuous. If the ongoing critique of historiography is not met and responded to, at least on some basic level, it would mean that this book makes no sense at all, since postmodernist sensibilities have by now begun to permeate the scholarship on Second Temple Judaism.

It is obvious that any meaningful refutation of the postmodernist approach to history (be it a process, a field for study or a written text) needs volumes rather than one short Preface. Fortunately, some such arguments of considerable import have already been produced, a notable example being *In Defense of History* by Richard Evans (1997). But given the current challenge to the historian's profession, I believe that even a special study like mine calls for a clear exposition of the premises on which it is based, and of the authorial attitudes towards major theoretical issues of history and history writing. In what follows, I intend to fulfill, as succinctly as possible, this requirement, together with critical comments at various points on the theories and practices the postmodernists seek to promote.

These remarks will chiefly, though not exclusively concern political history, which I consider my primary field.[2]

One major issue was debated long before postmodernism's advent: is it possible for any historical narration to be entirely objective? By now, the answer seems clear: it is not. In the first place, it must be firmly kept in mind that within the historical process everything influences and is being influenced by everything. The factors, which partake in it, are multiple (theoretically, countless), and they all interact in equally multiple (theoretically, countless) ways. This means that our very process of selecting the empirical material for discussion is implicitly biased, whether we like and realize this or not. Furthermore, there existed presumably numerous facts or factors, in particular, during the pre-modern period, of which we know little or nothing for the lack of evidence. Some such gaps can be filled by exercising creative historical imagination; others cannot. It follows that an entirely objective history, in terms of factual knowledge, can be written only by a superhuman omniscient mind, like God's; in this case, even artificial intelligence will prove of no avail. Later on, I will briefly address how this predicament reflects on the problem of historical causality.

The second point is trivial: the historian, like everyone else, is a child of his, or her, social-political-cultural environment, what the Germans call 'der Zeitgeist'. Again, whether we approve it or not, any history is written from the vantage point of the present that is fraught with 'ideologies', politics, intellectual fads, philosophical tenets and scholarly quarrels, from which no author can be fully free. As E. H. Carr famously phrased it in the still influential book, history means "an unending dialogue between the present and the past". Furthermore, apart from being confined within the historical context one is fated to reflect, a historian necessarily develops a personal worldview that may be coherent or contradictory, but in either case problematic. In a narrower sense, the advanced professional at some point reaches certain (however flexible) positions – theoretical, methodological and moral – in the exercise of his or her craft. Finally, in every historical investigation, the researcher pursues, consciously or not, a particular agenda, which affects his/her procedures, inferences and conclusions. This may work to both the advantage and detriment of historical studies.

R. G. Collingwood's classic *The Idea of History* (1956) persistently emphasizes, although sometimes in abstract quasi-Hegelian terms, that reflection and self-reflection are requirements of the historian's enterprise: historical knowledge, we read, "is not either knowledge of the past and therefore not knowledge of the present, or else knowledge of the present and therefore not knowledge of the past; it is knowledge of the past in the present, the self-knowledge of the historian's own mind as the present revival and reliving of the past experiences". This self-knowledge in a history writer should include not only, as Collingwood proposes, a self-conscious exercise of historical imagination (on which, see below), but also a conscientious effort at soul-searching to recognize the impact upon one's work of one's own *Weltanschauung*, methodological (frequently aprioristic) positions, and the agenda underlying each particular project. I further submit

PREFACE

that it would be a good idea, and a proof of one's intellectual integrity, if the results of this introspection, or self-reflection, are clearly articulated by the author at the outset, so that the reader may take into account its possible bias in appreciating the merits of a given historical study. This especially pertains to a specific agenda that otherwise may remain unconscious: when a historian arrives at the realization that a piece of empirical evidence contradicts the authorial purpose, is incompatible with the chosen interpretive methods and cannot be legitimately incorporated into the narrative, the project must be abandoned rather than the evidence disregarded or casually dismissed. This last condition, commonplace as it seems, is violated more often than one would wish. It may help to recall Sherlock Holmes's dictum: a single detail, which does not fit a crime's potential reconstruction, means that the latter is wrong. Observing this principle, along with articulating his or her bias and agenda, allows a historian, in my view, to approach – as close as is humanly possible – the notion of 'objective history'.[3]

My own *Weltanschauung* has been also shaped under the influence of biographical and cultural factors. Being a matrilineal Jew, I am a lifelong admirer of Jewish tradition; as a convert to Roman Catholicism, I espouse its broadest and universalist interpretation, which is not necessarily in agreement with *all* pronouncements issued by the Holy See. Both of these commitments were bound to affect my perspective on this book's main subject, violent religious dissent, although I have made every effort to reduce their impact to the minimum, not allowing them to interfere with my use of the available empirical data. Having spent my youth in the Soviet Union, I learned on my own the importance of freedom and intellectual pluralism. Forced to leave my homeland because of my participation in the movement for human rights, I was able to observe in person, as an immigrant American, the role played in the Western world by the liberal and conservative points of view. This experience reaffirmed my support of the former, despite substantial problems entailed in liberalism, both in its theory and practice. Since I consider individual human life an absolute value (in so far as one may possibly speak of absolutes), I believe in the need to respect and protect it, which can best be achieved in a pluralist society, based on the principles of political freedom, elective government and the rule of law. I deplore the excesses of liberal doctrine at the points where it condones, implicitly, potentially or explicitly, or for whatever reason, an exercise of violence. So far as I am concerned, violence always (even when necessary, as in the case of defensive wars) begets violence and ultimately results in some disaster. If this attitude seems conservative, so be it. By extension, it pertains to various forms of political radicalism, speaking not of Marxism, with the latter's victims who can be numbered in millions. I happened to learn first-hand the sorry results of the latter doctrine's historical implementation. Its inglorious collapse as a 'scientific' project for the bright future of humanity was not too long ago witnessed by the entire world.[4]

What I called 'theoretical and methodological positions' towards history and history writing primarily concern questions of historical causality, of the moral dimension in historical process and in historical narrative, and of lessons that may or may not be learned from historical experience.

I have always felt, on an instinctive level, that no 'laws of history' can be detected, proved or convincingly argued. The reason is the infinite complexity of human life, including its historical forms, which is not reducible to generalized or formulaic definitions. One contribution made by postmodernists I am happy to acknowledge is their part in demolishing historical determinism, which is implicitly and perforce teleological, irrespective of its guise – providential, progressive, nationalist, Hegelian or Marxist. It is in that respect it differs from causality – the epistemological concept, which is impossible to deny. In history we can at best speak about configurations of circumstances. They may variously resemble each other when operating within different contexts, or betray parallels in their inner logic, but never prove identical, being influenced (as I have earlier suggested) by the multiplicity of factors beyond our ability to calculate. It is the task of a historian, I believe, to take into account as many such factors as one can, and then attempt, through a careful and painstaking analysis, to determine, whenever feasible, their 'hierarchy of importance'. I think it imperative that, in any given case, this should be done on its own individual merits. What we call 'accidents' may prove significant, sometimes decisive factors in the development of events. This includes the personalities of historical agents, exceptional, able or incompetent, who partake in the decision-making process, and thus justify the centuries-long controversy about the role played by 'great men'. All such variables, responsible for history's 'indeterminist constituent', depend on the specific context or predicament and resist all attempts at generalization. In this sense counter-factual history ("what would have happened if"), which has finally achieved professional recognition, offers – provided we possess sufficient data to work with – a helpful analytical tool to appreciate the interaction between the historically inevitable and the accidental. Lastly, an application of chaos theory to historiography that is already underway *may* come up with interesting results. It goes without saying that, given the dynamics within the historical process and historical scholarship, any causative interpretation of past events is perforce provisional.[5]

It is common within the profession (despite exceptions, notably, John Lewis Gaddis) to hold the belief that their métier requires historians to abstain from moral judgments. Even Marc Bloch (1953), although he never hesitates to recognize additional dimensions in historical discourse, denies it the right of ethical inquiry: the historian's business, he insists, is not "judging" but "understanding". In this regard, however, I must proceed against the current. The belief in a historian's moral impartiality is an illusion. Our mind works in such a way that it evaluates human affairs, be it on the individual, societal or global level, in morally hierarchical, though often contradictory terms. This pertains even to science: scientists themselves are divided, for instance, on such issues as ecology or artificial intelligence, not on the grounds of the available scientific data, but according to their own moral conscience. Consequently, historiography cannot remain 'beyond good and evil': if it is not 'moral' it is bound to turn 'amoral', just as it happened in Nazi Germany and the Soviet Union, where its prominent practitioners put their craft in service of demonstrably evil regimes. Furthermore, though rarely explicit, implicitly moral judgment is contained all the time in modern history writing, conveyed through the very language, for the most part, ideologically colored, that it employs: thus, whenever we read that the *ancien régime* in France was 'reactionary', or that Jacobins initiated 'the reign of terror' (which is in both cases true), this already implies a moral wrong. Conversely, if historians contend that brutality, perpetrated by England's Henry VIII or Russia's Peter the Great in the course of their reforms, was historically necessary for some 'pragmatic' and/or 'progressive' purpose; or that in their terrorist policies Jacobins or Bolsheviks were motivated by the common good (notwithstanding the scale of their victims), it signifies moral approval, with the logic ultimately reducible to the Machiavellian maxim of the end justifying the means – which is a moral rather than merely intellectual or political position. The denial of ethical dimension in historiography, given its implicit ideological moralism, amounts to hypocrisy (even if often unconscious). I prefer to have made explicit (as morally 'right' and 'wrong'), rather than ideologically implied, what history writers condone or condemn in the activities of historical agents or groups, and why. This would help the reader to appreciate the authorial perspective, test it against the material at hand, and arrive at his or her own conclusions.

Finally, the alternative of 'understanding' *or* 'judging' is false. For the historian, it is entirely possible to understand *and* judge. Marc Bloch's own fate offers a tragic illustration of this need. An authentic Jewish hero, he found himself evacuated to England after Dunkirk, with good prospects for continuing a successful academic career. Instead, he returned to occupied France, entered the Resistance, was arrested and tortured by the Gestapo, having never betrayed his comrades, and was executed on March 18, 1944. It is not difficult to understand the motives and reasons of the Gestapo in torturing and killing this great man: as exponents of Nazi ideology, they were bound to consider him both enemy and subhuman, to which must be added practical exigencies, like deterring the resistants. But if a historian refuses to state in no uncertain words that his executioners were wholly evil, such a person, so far as I am concerned, should exit the profession.

To my mind, therefore, the historian has a right (if not a duty) of moral judgment on the events and characters from the past. But ethics derives only in part from rational considerations; it is also an aspect of our emotional life. This raises the issue of the role played by feelings, sentiments, passions and so forth in the historical process, and their bearing on historical scholarship, an issue the academic orthodoxy still tends to eschew – although less often, it must be admitted, than was the case in the recent past. The irrational dimension of both collective and individual behavior is huge, as so many terrible events of the last century painfully attest, questioning the entire rationalist legacy of the Enlightenment. *Homo sapiens* turns all too frequently into *Homo emotionalis* or even *Homo irrationalis*. The present book, by centering on religious dissent, which is indeed a powerful expression of irrationalism, is intended as one more step towards clarifying what it does mean and how it historically works.

PREFACE

In any event, it cannot be denied that personal and societal values differ, depending on historical and cultural contexts. Our modern value system may (though by no means always must) contradict those of bygone times, which requires it to be made patent that the historian's axiological pronouncements are rooted in the present, reflecting either its Zeitgeist, or a purely personal viewpoint. This also applies *mutatis mutandis* to the matter of political correctness: moral criticism directed at the behavior by groups or nations centuries ago should not be taken as offensive by their present day descendants.[6]

Cicero claimed that 'history' (*historia*) is "the teacher of life" – *magistra vitae* (*De orat.*, 2, 36). Irrespective of whether he meant the 'process' or the 'narrative', and of the role played by rhetoric in classical historiography, the real concern, both in philosophical and political terms, that made itself intellectually felt throughout centuries, is if it is or is not possible to derive any lesson from studying the historical past. The matter is convoluted, and the debates on it essentially idle. Most authors today would probably contend that there is no such thing as a 'historical lesson' and that history is, despite Cicero, in no sense a 'teacher'. They would point out that history does not repeat itself, and that politicians, governments, movements as well as entire nations commit similar blunders under similar circumstances, notwithstanding all the talk about its educational value. This does not prevent, however, their opponents and the public from searching for and discussing historical parallels in hopes that they can be used as cautionary tales and help to avoid yet another disaster at present or in the future.

It cannot be denied that history knows what I have termed 'configurations', resembling each other in various respects, and sometimes revealing similar situational logic. It follows that – in theory – historical lessons can be learned, but it does not mean that they are learned as often as one would wish, or that it is always done correctly. In other words, the problem lies not in history, or its potential lessons, but in *us*. A case in point helps us appreciate the complexity – and perplexity – of the matter. We know that Russian Bolsheviks were obsessed with the French Revolution and considered its main lesson to have been the emergence of a sole ruler, Napoleon Bonaparte. With the purpose of preventing any such outcome, their leaders conspired to eliminate Leon Trotsky; but they disregarded yet another lesson from the same event – namely, that "revolution devours its own children", and as a result fell victims to Stalinist terror that they failed to anticipate. Although it is not easy to list demonstrable examples of correct decisions (seen as such retrospectively) made by governments or individual politicians on the basis of studying the past, it stands to reason that accumulated historical knowledge often affects, on a conscious or unconscious level, political and institutional deliberations. For instance, it is obvious that the framers of the American Constitution relied to a great extent on what they knew about the operation and deficiencies of the government in the Roman Republic.

In fact, there exists a scholarly discipline that cannot function without comparative historical analysis (though often with mixed results), and that is political science, whatever may be said about its 'scientific' status. Its practitioners discuss 'historical lessons' in a routine manner. At their best, they proceed from detailed empirical study rather than relying on the existent academic dogmas. As Gideon Rose (2010) warns in his recent book on 'how wars end', the lessons thus learned "can serve as cognitive blinders, narrowing the way officials think about the situation they face", but at the same time "they can also guide". Finally, in a paradigmatic sense, many historical phenomena prove recurrent: despotism and popular rule, revolutionary and reform movements, imperialism, the rise and fall of nations, and the like. One such recurrent phenomenon – religious dissent within an established and powerful religion, in the forms it took under the conditions of Roman Judaea – makes this book's central subject: its relevance for our world of today requires no further comment.

I am not concerned with a predictive potential of historical research, or the lack thereof. The belief in it is implicit in theological perspectives on history, philosophical or 'scientific', and – to put it mildly – strikes me as wishful thinking: it took a century to make this clear in the case of Karl Marx, but only two decades for Francis Fukuyama. On the other hand, one may cite occasional episodes of correct forecast, which owes to experience rather than theory, or to insight (a notion as indefinable as 'Zeitgeist') – like Churchill's comment upon the infamous Munich agreement that, having chosen shame to avoid war, the British government will be getting both.[7]

Theoretical and methodological positions as outlined inform much of my agenda in the present inquiry. In the first place, I wished to make it topical, taking of course into account all reservations and qualifications. Although primarily concerned, like many modern historians, with reconstructing the reality of Judaea under Roman rule and the developments responsible for both the outbreak and the failure of the Great Revolt, I remained intensely aware of our own political and cultural predicament: after all, religious dissent turned into violence had been demonstrably operating in various historical contexts. It is not my intent, however, to produce detailed comparisons between the events of 2000 years ago and the present, and even less to indulge in forecasts, however tentative. This would require a very different set of procedures.

On the emotional plane, I was seriously motivated by abhorrence at violent and oppressive constituents of historical behavior. I deeply resent violence in any form, including institutional (such as the death penalty), especially when it leads to a massive loss of human life, whether brought about by the reign of terror under individual or collective tyranny, a bloody war or revolutionary bloodshed, irrespective of slogans or rationales for their justification. In my first two books I explored, on behavioral and psychological levels, the violent effects of an autocratic tyrannical regime; this one deals with the repercussions of self-destructive violence exercised by the masses fallen prey to 'virtual reality' through *sui generis* irrationalism and wishful thinking. In all three cases I have made a conscientious effort not to allow my own intellectual and emotional leanings critically (that is, beyond the range of legitimate interpretations) to interfere with the empirical and textual material at hand.

PREFACE

I do not particularly care whether historical study and history writing are considered the province of science or art. The Greeks intuitively knew that both might receive inspiration from the Muses: in the case of history, she was called Clio, but they similarly revered her sister Urania, the Muse of astronomy. Our modern conception of science is rationalist and experimental, while a historian's enterprise also involves other constituents of creative pursuit: empathy, imagination and, as I have argued, the need for moral appraisal. This relates it to cultural interests that draw on the whole gamut of our abilities in response to reality, intellectual, emotional and instinctive, such as literature, the visual arts and music. This is not to say that history-as-discipline is less rationalist, in terms of logic and argument, than any proverbial science. It is even capable of 'retrospective experimentation', which became possible only in the last century and a half with the arrival of pseudo-scientific doctrines promising to better the human race or human lot. History tells us that these experiments, perpetrated by the Nazis and the Communists, not only failed dismally, but cost the lives of millions. Fortunately, English knows the word (different in meaning from the German '*Wissenschaft*', or Russian '*nauka*') which embraces this blend of the 'scientific' and the 'artistic': the word is 'scholarship', and I am perfectly happy seeing it applied to historiography, indicative of its purpose and its competence. As theorists argued from Ranke to Bloch and beyond, all depends on the historian's craft, the quality of which is to be judged by his or her peers and readers – a matter to which I will later briefly return. Apart from analytical skill, this craft implies the aesthetic excellence that distinguishes the work of all great historians, starting with Thucydides and Tacitus. We do owe to postmodernism the long-delayed appreciation of the literary aspect in history writing. The trouble is that its promoters, as often happens in their discourse, drove a sensible point beyond any reasonable measure. This takes us to the challenge of the so-called 'linguistic turn', and the issues of 'history as narrative', 'metahistory', and the historiographical rhetoric, all of which largely result from the confusion between literary and historical scholarship that postmodernists have produced and propagate.[8]

It remains debatable whether postmodernism continues today to be on the rise, or whether its influence has slowly begun to wane. Be that as it may, the 'linguistic turn', so prominent in the postmodernist agenda, represents the most recent theoretical assault on the whole concept of history writing, even though it is largely ignored within the profession. It emphasizes the ambiguous nature of language, absolutizing the input of rhetoric and employing notions borrowed from literary criticism to undermine the authority of historiographical texts. I bewilder what can be called the 'extremalist' tendency in modern intellectual practice, where a reasonable enough idea, instead of being balanced *vis-à-vis* the contingencies and complexities of human experience and human condition, is driven to its logical (and sometimes illogical) extreme, which turns it absurd. Problematization of language does not mean that the latter should be abandoned or that it makes no sense: otherwise, no communication at all would be possible between individuals, groups and cultures, with the human race inevitably ending up in self-destruction. Ergo: despite all its inherent ambiguities and the random play of the signifiers, language – however imperfectly – continues to work. Rhetoric (understood as the desire to make an utterance compelling) is theoretically present in every speech act, even if only on the unconscious level. Recognized by classical Greeks for a special skill, an instrument to achieve success as a public speaker and politician, or to gain literary prominence, it became an essential aspect of self-expression in Western history and culture. Today we routinely speak of rhetoric not only in oral or written discourse, but also in visual arts, music and even science. When applied to historiography, however, rhetoric was from the outset assigned a subordinate role by its practitioners: it functioned through orchestrating and dramatizing the narrative, elaborating the orations ascribed to historical agents, but – despite modern claims to the contrary – *not* fictionalizing the historical process. Rhetoric helps to represent (or misrepresent) the reality, sometimes obfuscate it, and often embellish it, but does not itself invent events, excepting the occasional historically insignificant detail – a point to which I will return. The ancients were fully aware of the difference between what they considered 'history' and what we would call the 'historical novel': it is sufficient to compare, for instance, the erotic romance *Chaereas and Callirhoe* by Chariton (written in the first century A.D., but explicitly set at the time of the Peloponnesian War) with any historiographical writings from Thucydides onwards. Similarly, the strategies of 'emplotment', postulated by the 'metahistorical' theoretician Hayden White in his influential book, while reflecting their individual perspective and preoccupations, served the historians he considers (Burckhardt, Ranke, Michelet and de Tocqueville) primarily the purpose of organizing their material into coherent narratives, and it does not follow at all that they falsified in any substantial sense the public record or empirical evidence from the past.[9]

Eventually, the literary-critical approach, privileging rhetoric for the sake of rhetoric, was extended to classical historiography by Anthony J. Woodman and his followers, who went so far as to contend that the historical events in Antiquity which we take for granted on the basis of our written sources may have not taken place at all. This is itself a demonstrable – and unsubstantiated – piece of rhetoric, since I am not aware of any example to have proved – or even attempted to argue – that any event of significance (in Greek history, subsequent to Solon, and in Roman, after the conquest of Italy) accepted as historical by scholarly consensus is a mere product of rhetorical invention. In the characteristically postmodernist fashion, which disregards common sense, these revisionists ignore the obvious: that all such developments were a matter of public knowledge, having been at the time of their occurrence witnessed by thousands and often memorialized in state documents. This was bound to impose limits on classical historiographers, their rhetoric and imagination, especially those dealing with history still fresh in popular memory – that is, across one or two generations, such as Thucydides, Polybius, Tacitus and Flavius Josephus. By arguing what they do, these practitioners of what some of them call 'composition criticism' ignore the major tenet in postmodernist literary scholarship – 'the reader's response'. At the time of their writing, the audience might have enjoyed the rhetorical skill displayed by the classical historiographers, but to think that educated contemporary readers are prepared to believe in the events that they knew had not happened, or had happened very differently, is preposterous.

In the course of the last two centuries, history as a field of scholarship has suffered invasions by other disciplines aimed at swallowing it up – the natural sciences (Positivism), economics (Marxism), sociology (Cliometrics), and psychoanalysis (Psychohistory). In each case, while it absorbed methodological components it could profitably employ for its own reasons, it managed to survive by maintaining its independence and integrity. This leads one to expect with confidence that it will also successfully outlast the current onslaught by partisans of literary theory and deconstruction.[10]

In my earlier book (1997) I proposed as an analytical framework what I call 'the hermeneutic triangle', consisting of a text that pertains to and partakes in both author and reader, with none of these components privileged at the expense of others. The historical narrative (as distinct from other forms of narration), I believe, can be profitably approached in terms of a 'historiographical triangle' – that is, the relationship between action, representation and interpretation. I use the word 'action' rather than 'fact' to underscore its human character (since 'event' may be cosmic, like an appearance of a comet, or a natural disaster, like an earthquake), to eschew the controversy on what 'fact' means, and to emphasize the dynamic character of the historical process. It must be remembered that action needs first to occur before it is dramatized, detailed, embellished, manipulated or rhetoricized through representation. The latter mediates between the action and its interpretation by the narrative's author; at the same time, representation being the fabric any such text displays within the 'hermeneutic triangle', mediates between its author and its readers, with their own interpretations, which perforce include modern scholarly arguments. For a history student to navigate the historical narrative from the past requires a professional knowledge of its politico-socio-cultural context, which, more often than not, by sorting out its representative features (realistic, plausible, imaginative, biased, rhetorical, etc.) makes it possible to proceed with coherent assessment. In my examination of Josephus's accounts I repeatedly try to demonstrate how this can be done. The success of one's argument depends on one's intellectual integrity and persuasive force in competing with alternate interpretations. It has to be judged by professionals, but this is precisely the stuff of the historiographical enterprise.[11]

The entire 'historiographical triangle' is, of course, embedded in a historical narrative. The latter word and related notion are as debatable and, in the end, elusive, as 'knowledge', 'ideology' and the like. Narrative is subject to a very abstract philosophizing. The range of its treatments and meanings stretches from the formal analysis of the Prague school, to its problematization by Barthes, deconstructionists and White, to the profound metaphysical discussions of Paul Ricoeur. One can hardly deny, on the other hand, that narrative is the major instrument (in terms of conceptualization and expression) for endowing human experience with meaning, and thus it partakes in every human cognitive and creative activity: the Greeks would have conceived its role as transforming 'chaos' into 'cosmos'. This applies to a diary entry, lyrical poem, landscape painting, scientific tract, musical composition and computer game. An influential view considers life itself a narrative of sorts. Like language and logic, narrative is an imperfect tool in cognition and communication, but we do not possess any better: ultimately, this pertains to the structure and propensities of our consciousness. As a concept, narrative yields multiple definitions and interpretations. In this book, when speaking of 'historical narrative', I mean a representational (but not necessarily chronological) sequence of actions, which may or may not entail – or imply – an interpretive contiguity.

That a successful historical narrative, ancient or modern, involves an exercise of historical imagination cannot be disputed. This is a privilege coming from Clio, Muse of History. But the attempt by 'metahistorians' and other postmodern revisionists to confuse or identify it with a fiction, such as the historical novelist produces, is untenable. The historian's imagination draws exclusively on his or her knowledge of empirical material: when it deals with probabilities, or indulges in speculation (even in the case of classical authors), this is properly qualified, and it never invents agents or action absent from the public record. It is true that a great work of literature may provide one with an even deeper insight into the past than any conventional historiography, but this is beside the point. It has to do with convoluted philosophical and psychological issues, like the nature of creativity and perception that will perhaps never be resolved.[12]

It is not surprising that the rise of postmodernism was met with multiple counter-arguments and philosophical refutations by its opponents, which has prevented – despite claims to the contrary – its triumph in Western academia at large. To sum up my earlier comments, I will briefly list some major objections to it, putting in relief the conflict areas between postmodernism and the humanistic tradition to which historical scholarship intimately belongs. To my knowledge, notwithstanding public noise and abstruse jargon, none of what follows has ever been successfully refuted. First, there is, of course, an inherent and insoluble contradiction in the very epistemology of relativism: if any pronouncement aimed at cognition is relative, this means the relativity itself is relative, and so is the relativity of relativity, continuing *ad infinitum* – and resulting in a vicious circle. Ironically, it makes of postmodernism, which claims to be debunking 'absolutisms', 'totalities', 'great narratives' and the like, a 'master narrative' *par excellence* that denies legitimacy to anything outside itself. It becomes a closed system, increasingly indulging in intellectual aggressiveness and self-congratulation. As Mikhail Bakhtin (1984) memorably phrased it, "it should be noted that both relativism and dogmatism equally exclude all argumentation, all authentic dialogue, making it either unnecessary (relativism) or impossible (dogmatism)". One effect of this condition is reductionism and resort to sophistry, like the notorious claim about 'the death of the author', which the claimers would not (as in many similar cases) apply, however, to themselves and their written production: as perhaps no other intellectual fad, postmodernism invites – and inadvertently encourages – its *reductio ad absurdum*. Next, one cannot ignore the unbridgeable gap, characterizing epistemological agnosticism in any disguise, between abstract theories and practical experience: the fact that humankind continues to survive, interact, cognize and communicate, irrespective of all solipsistic trends in philosophizing, from Protagoras and Gorgias onwards. Finally, the adoption by postmodernists of the 'virtual reality' outlook – that is, privileging 'what goes on in our heads' rather than the world beyond (which has come to permeate even our political and economic vision) – is dangerous, both in theory and in practice. Eventually and inevitably, the 'real reality' will respond to our neglect or ignorance by striking back, with vengeance. So far as I am concerned, this alone justifies, according to its own tenets, the view of the postmodernist discourse as 'fiction', in comparison with which the 'historical narrative' it seeks to fictionalize signifies a genuine quest for truth.[13]

During my work on this project I encountered a series of logistic difficulties, and I cannot be certain that the solutions I have found are the most appropriate. The problems were threefold, pertaining to the character of our sources, the scholarly situation in the field, and the purpose I had in mind for this study. All of it accounts for the peculiarities in the book's shape and structure.

From the outset I wished this narrative to prove accessible to lay educated and interested readers. I wanted the main text to be clear and readable, lacking scholarly references and specific polemics. I felt acutely conscious, on the other hand, that I was a newcomer to a very contested field, fraught with passions, intellectual debates and ideological quarrels. Consequently, I needed to fortify myself as thoroughly as I could against the charges of ignorance and incompetence coming from potential critics. This task I attempted to fulfill with voluminous endnotes, which contain the relevant Greek passages, elaboration on the arguments in the main text, additional information of interest, even though sometimes tangential, on the issues involved, the spectrum of the learned opinions, with quotes, *pro* and *contra* the inferences and procedures I propose, and often detailed and complex polemics regarding some current textual interpretations or historical reconstructions. I have to admit that this huge scholarly apparatus almost went out of control because in recent decades the professional consensus even on major features of Second Temple Judaism has collapsed, and at present all its aspects remain the matter of controversy. Eventually, it became obvious that it was not possible to have both the main text and the lengthy endnotes printed in one volume. As a result, I have gladly accepted the proposal by Routledge to create an accompanying website to be used by the readers. The website provides the entire set of numbered endnotes for each chapter and a full bibliography (my dossier was effectively closed at the end of 2011).

PREFACE

Now, it is important to state what this book is *not* about: it is not about the Jewish War as such, and not about Josephus as such, although both themes figure in it very prominently. As the title indicates, it is about the violent religious dissent in Roman Judaea before and subsequent to Nero's principate. The trouble rests, however, with the character of our sources, especially the literary ones, which not only suffer from major factual gaps, but also – for reasons that I seek to explain – minimize or hush up the evidence that might have elucidated the working of the religious dissent mindset. I came to realize that any analysis of isolated data on this subject outside the context risks becoming incomprehensible, and that any relevant discussion made sense only within a much larger narrative. This would necessarily require, beside the theoretical Introduction, at least two lengthy accounts: the basic, though sufficiently informative, outline of what Second Temple Judaism must have been, and a survey of the developments, including the patterns of religious dissent proclivities in the period from Rome's arrival on the scene under the late Hasmoneans up to the Great Revolt's outbreak. This constitutes my first and third chapters, which perforce exceed in length every other. I must frankly confess that I have placed the discussion of events directly leading to the explosion point in the second chapter for dramatic purposes in order to have the reader plunged *in medias res*, and in a belief that the historical narrative need not to be strictly chronological. Reading the subsequent survey of the previous decades will hopefully allow non-specialists better to assess retrospectively the forces responsible for that seminal action. I apologize if this reverse sequence may cause some readers a momentary disorientation. I also found it reasonable to elect the vicissitudes of the *sicarii*, as closest to the exemplary religious dissenters, for special treatment in the penultimate chapter. The rest of the chapters carry on more or less chronologically, with only a few occasions when the material overlaps. Depending on its relevance, direct or indirect, to the book's main concern, some actions are examined in more detail, while others are compressed or summed up in brief descriptions. At times, it might appear that, against the dramatic realities of the Jewish War as portrayed by Josephus, and recounted or reappraised in this study, the issue of religious dissent has been lost or has almost vanished from sight; but I have made a consistent effort to keep it alive as the central leitmotif, even when it stays beneath the surface: not always visible or transparent, it still must have still affected the intricate relationships and sensibilities the alignment of which we can often only guess.

I employ these somewhat convoluted procedural and narrative strategies in the hope that a more subtle, complex, multifaceted and nuanced representation of religious dissent, its mindset, and its role in the revolutionary upheaval, which transformed Second Temple Judaism, could be achieved. Whether this goal has been reached is for my readers and critics to judge.[14]

Vasily Rudich
New Haven, August 2014

INTRODUCTION
Religion and Religious Dissent

The conceptual term I have chosen for the main subject of this book – 'the psychology of religious dissent' – serves, in the first place, to put it in sharp relief to that of political dissidence, which I discussed extensively in my earlier work. Secondly, I believe the notion of 'religious dissent' is more accurate and valuable, for descriptive and interpretive purposes, than terms usually employed in common parlance, such as 'fanaticism', 'fundamentalism', 'religious extremism' and the like. Finally, I want to dissociate my inquiry from the term and concept of 'ideology'. The latter, in my view, is often misused, and implies certain features specific of modern times. I always preferred to avoid applying it to the ancient world as a potential misnomer.

In the present study I am concerned with religious dissent within an established, vibrant and powerful religion, not merely with a variety of religious attitudes characteristic of a pluralist or secular society like our own – or, for that matter, to a large extent, of the Roman Empire. The religion in question is Second Temple Judaism, which provides, despite the deficiencies of our sources, the only opportunity to examine the operations of religious dissent (in a sense stated above) alongside political turmoil in Greco-Roman Antiquity. To do so, one must start with a series of methodological observations.

The sense of discontent stemming from the contrast of the desirable and the real is, of course, an essential aspect of the human condition. It takes multiple forms, starting with most intimate and private experiences and ending with public outrage at acts of tyranny and injustice. The version of resentment that I call 'dissidence' pertains to a conflict of one's personal ideals and the political realities of the time. This is an approximate definition, used in an almost technical sense, but still distinguishable from other forms of discontent – social, cultural and religious. In other words, the way I employ this term denotes a decidedly political phenomenon, a resentment aimed, first and foremost, at the form of government, carriers and structures of power, or the methods of administration.

In my published work on political dissidence under Nero I argued that the individuals who experienced this state of mind stood in urgent need of accommodating their beliefs to a reality of which they disapproved, so that they could both survive and justify their status and public behavior. In this respect, as in its reluctance to engage in violence, dissident mentality must be distinguished from the social revolutionary mindset which is preoccupied, by definition, with a different agenda.

Furthermore, I have tried to demonstrate that dissident disposition is never a constant: it is in perpetual flux, which not only does not exclude, but assumes the necessity of compromise and opportunism since it becomes otherwise impossible for a dissident individual to develop any strategy of self-adjustment. These strategies may range widely – from a belief that one's own activities, irrespective of one's compliance with an act of injustice, may eventually exercise a beneficent effect on society, to an argument that while in the company of wolves one has no choice but to behave like one.

There is a fundamental difference between conception and perception of dissidence in an open, liberal society like the United States, and within the close confines of a repressive regime, such as Nazi Germany and the former Soviet Union. In America a 'dissident' is usually the one who speaks up; in Communist Russia those who thought of themselves as dissidents more often than not preferred, out of fear and apprehension, to keep silent or emigrate.

In contrast, individuals engaged in religious dissent – within the framework of a dominant and wholesome religion – exhibit no ability or desire to adjust their beliefs to reality, political or otherwise. The reason for this pertains to their conviction of standing in direct and continuous relationship with the divine, while denying the priestly authorities their traditional role as mediators. They conceptualize themselves as carriers of the higher truth, as God's instruments, or both. Consequently, their dissent arises from dissatisfaction with the religious establishment of the day, which they, on whatever grounds, reject and come to denounce for being corrupt and betraying the very foundations of the faith. Thus individual and collective passions and protests come to be identified with God's own will. This condition is bound to problematize the attitudes taken by such people toward reality. As a result, their concerns move in a direction opposite to those of political dissidents – namely, what they seek is accommodating not their beliefs to reality but reality to their beliefs. As in the case of political dissidents, in order to achieve this, they employ a spectrum of available strategies. One option is to misread reality, or to read it selectively and focus on what may appear as signs, like rumored miracles, indicating its imminent change in fulfillment of a divine plan. Next, one may withdraw from reality altogether and exist in a sort of dream world in expectation that some supernatural interference will eventually take place. Finally, there always remains an opportunity to join what one considers the forces of Light and personally contribute to God's work on Earth, thereby achieving a privileged position with God in this world or in the next. In turn, this can be accomplished in word – that is, by the way of preaching, or in deed – that is, by resorting to violence. Sometimes, as we know from history, these two activities are pursued by the same person or group and thus reinforce each other. At the same time, it seems clear that any of these strategies involves, to a greater or lesser degree, the repudiation of reality as such. This form of discontent, as any other, is a subject to fluctuation: its bearers, even within a particular movement, differ in motives, attitudes and behavior, or exhibit a different degree of radicalization. Not to be forgotten are ever-present fringe elements; some, depending on the force of their character and beliefs, prepare for martyrdom, others may defect. It also must be emphasized that the religious dissent mentality – or its elements – is not by necessity socially conditioned and may reach all strata of society, affecting laymen as well as priests, but even the latter in that case have to operate largely outside the existent institutions. In the ultimate sense, religious dissent draws on individual psyches, but taking over the masses and playing on their frustration and aspiration, it acquires identifiable features, as a distinct phenomenon in terms of mentality and its societal or historical function. Furthermore, like anything human, this may lead to constructive results (such as achieved by the reform movements within various denominations) or towards disaster. Everything depends on the attitude of the dissenters – and of their opponents – to violence. As historical experience amply demonstrates, more often than not violence begets violence and therefore – despite the periodic popularity of revolutionary ideas and slogans – it should be, in my view, unequivocally condemned.

This study will concentrate on the violent form of religious dissent, the mentality behind it and its role in a particular historical upheaval.[1]

It is true that throughout history religious and political agendas intertwine, and their relationship takes complex and multiple forms, with the borders between the two sometimes blurred. But at no point can it be claimed that they became entirely one and the same. In the ambience of vibrant faith, politics tends to be subsumed by religion, but it still implicitly continues to influence the decision-making process. Within an environment of declining faith, the opposite would occur. In the final analysis, this is all dependent on the intensity of religious feelings in an individual or a group. In part, this explains why the bearers of religious dissent are often intractable in terms of conventional politics, diplomacy, negotiable settlements and similar pragmatic solutions. They tend to express their sentiments in terms of moral and religious rather than political anger. They find it difficult to comprehend or justify the intricacies of political procedures and the very concept of politics seems to them irrelevant, false or opaque. In other words, if political dissidence involves such variables as pragmaticism and adjustment, religious dissenters partake in privileged knowledge (as they understand it) and wishful thinking – that is, actual or potential absolutes: political and even social issues are made subordinate to, or at best blended with what is considered (at a given point and by a given dissent movement) a religious imperative. This accounts for perhaps the most prominent and apparently irrational aspect of their characteristic behavior – namely, their willingness and ability to proceed against incredible odds such as military forces outnumbering them tenfold or worse, in the confident belief that, at the 11th hour, the Deity – in some miraculous manner – must come to their aid and procure the wholesome destruction of the enemy. By extension, they exhibit a strong sense of self-righteousness and moral superiority even in respect of their nominal co-religionists: for the pure everything is pure. This pertains to a striking paradox of their ultimately relativist approach towards the prescriptions of their own faith, explicitly articulated in the sacred texts: they are prepared to disregard, misinterpret or distort any such injunction, which interferes, in their view, with their immediate agenda, on the assumption that God (that is, the cause) is more important than the Book. (This is one reason to discard, for the sake of the argument, the term 'fundamentalism', which implies the literal observance of the Scriptures.) What often matters is not doctrine, but temperament and sensibilities specific to their mentality, which help them to gloss over or explain away moral or psychological contradictions that might otherwise create for some individuals serious inner problems or make them compromise. As will be seen in subsequent chapters, our sources provide sufficient evidence to demonstrate that all these features are discernable in the conduct of the Jewish religious dissenters up to, during and after Nero's reign.

To be sure, this brief outline is a generalized construct: it presents a religious dissenter *par excellence* – in the same sense as we speak of 'ideal gas' in physics. Politics and other aspects of reality necessarily intrude upon the consciousness of many such persons and in various ways affect their behavior: the demarcation line between its non-violent and violent forms seems also to lie in their attitudes towards power, the issue that inevitably involves a degree of politization. In the latter case, turning militant, the promoters of religious dissent come to disregard human life, including their own, as expendable, and in this respect resemble the extreme manifestations of revolutionary worldview, which in fact mirrors the totalitarian mindset it seeks to uproot. The profitable route of inquiry in each case is to examine it on its own merits. I would suggest that history provides evidence for existence, in various periods, of prominent personages and entire popular movements that resemble closely enough the model of religious dissent I have described.

There is no reliable procedure for generalizing on psychological or circumstantial causes of individual conversions from the traditional or mainstream faith to various forms of religious dissent. One may postulate that such factors as sudden and abrupt hardship, influence of a charismatic figure or self-hypnotization may always play their role, along with a desire to partake in a tightly knit group of like-minded people. Any other factor may intervene, but all of this remains, for the most part, a matter of speculation. So far as I could ascertain, modern sociological and psychological studies of 'religious extremism' do not provide any definitive or indisputable results, more often than not blaming this or that aspect of the environment and ignoring or under-rating the character and importance of religious mentality as such. Even in those cases where a researcher offers some new pertinent data or arrives at interesting conclusions, one must be very cautious in retrojecting any of the modern material or technique on the distant past.[2]

INTRODUCTION

It is imperative for any study of 'extremism' in monotheistic religions to dissociate the operation of religious dissent from the attitudes and agenda of their religious establishment. By its very nature, the 'church' – Jewish, Christian or Moslem (I use this single word for the sake of convenience, in a purely technical sense) – is intensely conservative and resists any change as potentially fraught with trouble. Its primary interests lie in stability and preservation of the status quo. Thus, St. Augustine considers 'peace which procures peace' the beneficent aspect of the earthly condition as decreed from the above:

> Even the heavenly city, therefore, while in this its pilgrimage, makes use of the earthly peace, and guards and seeks the merging of human wills in regard to the things that are useful for man's mortal nature, so far as sound piety and religion permits, and makes the earthly peace minister to the heavenly peace, which is so truly peace that it must be deemed and called the only peace.
>
> (*De civ. Dei*, 19, 17)

As a rule, a religious establishment turns aggressive and violent either at the early expansionist stage of the new faith, in the spirit of conquest, like the early Islam, or in confrontation with what it comes to consider a major threat for its own functioning or even its existence, as was the case with the Catholic Church in the Catharist crisis of the early 13th century as well as at the time of Reformation and its aftermath, when the Inquisition was given free hand to destroy thousands of human lives. Finally, this may happen at historical moments when – apart from other possible reasons – there arises an overwhelming perception that a key sacred object or concept is being profaned, which had allowed to justify religiously the Crusades, and to the present day it accounts for the continuous dispute on the verge of violence between the Jews and the Muslims over the Temple Mount. This last point must be particularly emphasized, given the failure of the modern secular West to appreciate, or even understand, the nature of sacredness and what it means for a believer – despite the formidable efforts in this regard by scholars of religion, from Rudolf Otto to Mircea Eliade to René Girard and Paul Ricoeur. This is the issue to which I will repeatedly return.

Furthermore, by the fact of operating in the society and under temporal authorities, a religious establishment (so long as it persists as such despite whatever internal contradictions) must perforce accommodate itself to whatever political exigencies it may encounter: after all, the earthly powers come from God (cf. Rom., 13). Again, St. Augustine offers an example: notwithstanding his distaste for secular states, which lacked, in his view, true justice, and likening them to "great robber bands" (*magna latrocinia* – *De civ. Dei*, 4, 4), he successfully cooperated with the Imperial regime as required. Therefore, in contrast to religious dissenters, the religious hierarchy in any historical context was bound to understand what politics is about and to develop the gamut of necessary political skills, from dissimulation to blackmail. This also endows them with, for the most part, a sober and adequate view of reality, even though the belief in the possibility of a miracle and divine intervention remains among the central tenets of their faith. In contrast, religious dissenters defy reality; they tend to dream of 'history's reversal' that would restore the presumed primordial innocence and purity of man.

This can be discerned, for instance, in the story of the Crusades: beside such factors as religious fervor or the desire for plunder and conquest, the Roman Church, in inspiring and approving that enterprise, must have considered, along with the secular authorities, whether it was feasible, and concluded that it was, that is to say, that the united force of the European princes was indeed capable, in terms of manpower and military resources, to take over the Holy Land – which, temporarily, it did; while the Children's Crusade, with its expectation of a miraculous victory by the young innocents, originated outside and in spite of the Church and, in one sense or another, directly or indirectly under the influence of the period's religious dissent. It follows that the term 'religious extremism', like 'fundamentalism', is not adequate to describe the phenomenon under discussion.[3]

To place in relief the specifics characterizing the religious dissent at the time, I shall now briefly discuss the relevant aspects of political and psychological environment in Rome under the Julio-Claudians. The senatorial order is, in fact, the only section of Roman society for which we have evidence of dissident behavior ample enough to allow an insight into its motives. The source of discontent lay largely in the incompatible demands exercised on the period's aristocracy, on the one hand, by the *mos maiorum* – traditional code of private and public conduct, perhaps impracticable, but still exercising its spell, and, on the other, by the actual exigencies of survival and self-advancement. Furthermore, a contradiction became conspicuous within the very tenets of the "ancestral customs", *mos maiorum*: between a duty of serving the state and the need to maintain personal dignity. If under the Republic this double concern with *civitas* and *dignitas* could be harmoniously resolved by free play among equals in pursuit of glory and wealth, it ceased to be the case under tyrannical emperors who, like Nero, enjoyed being ostentatiously immoral. Since the emperor began increasingly to be seen as state incarnate, serving the evil one in any capacity could, from the viewpoint of a traditionally oriented senator, amount to a blow at his dignity, *diminutio dignitatis*.

This set of complexities generated a mechanism of psychological mediation that the Romans called *dissimulatio* – a word often used by the authors of the day in political contexts. This was a complex and peculiar state of mind, the result of contradictory forces operating within one and the same person – intellectual, emotional and instinctive. It oscillated between the old behavioral stereotypes and the limits imposed on individual activity by the new power structure. The effect of *dissimulatio* was pervasive. It can be discerned on many levels of society's life and pertains to the gap between *verba* and *acta* which became one of the chief features, recognized by the Romans, of the principate as political system, owing to the contrast of its monarchical nature and republican pretense. As the means of self-adjustment by the dissidents and accommodation of their beliefs to the reality they disapproved, the practice of *dissimulatio* could and sometimes did imply tortuous existence, fraught with attempts, often futile, at self-justification. This transpires, for instance, in the study of Seneca's writings. The extreme outcomes of this predicament would be a personality split, with the concomitant loss of self-identity, or suicide – which, even when enforced, still was styled as an ultimate gesture of protest. The example of utter psychological confusion is the case of Faenius Rufus who at the same time, and apparently without realizing it, behaved as a leading conspirator against Nero and as the praetorian prefect in charge of investigating the very conspiracy he had joined. Even an act of withdrawal from public life, the *secessio*, would not help, as is evident from the prosecution of Thrasea Paetus, who was indicted for treason because he ceased to attend the meetings of the humbled and powerless Neronian Senate. It is not surprising then that, despite their continuous efforts at accommodation, such different individuals as Seneca, Lucan, Petronius and the same Thrasea Paetus were eventually compelled to take their lives, each in a highly stylized manner, aimed at publicizing their moral or intellectual superiority over the tyrannical oppressor.

In the matter of religious toleration, the early Roman Empire, at least in some respects, was not unlike our own society. It embraced a variety of cults without expressing, for the most part, any concern with the substance of their faith. There were, of course, exceptions: Druidism, accused, as it seems, justifiably, of practicing human sacrifices was suppressed; certain orgiastic cults were frowned upon; individual emperors, concerned with the spread of this or that "un-Roman" religion (*superstitio*) among the aristocracy could ban it at whim temporarily, on the pretext of criminal charges (such as fraud), or for purely political reasons, with the purpose of incriminating an undesirable person, or persons, whom otherwise it would have been difficult to impeach. None of this is entirely unfamiliar to us. Our present liberal attitudes notwithstanding, I doubt that today's Americans would welcome a revival of the Aztec or Maya religion that involved daily offerings of human sacrifices. Episodes, like the forced suppression of the Branch Davidian cult at Waco under the Clinton administration, suggest that a certain kind of religious practice is not even now to be tolerated by society. And we continue to hear, from time to time, about the persecution, on various grounds, of Satanist groups and their ilk.

As is well known, Roman official religion was formalist and highly ritualistic. Animist in its origin, it relied on the basically magical procedures and placed minimal value on individual mystical experience. Like Greece, Rome lacked a unified and professional priesthood that could have contended for power with secular authorities. These and other factors account for the relative tolerance regarding religion practiced by both the government and society.

Of course, there was one fundamental difference with our modern view of religious freedom, and it pertains precisely to the official or civic character of

Roman *religio* under the principate. This implied an obligation on the part of every free inhabitant of the Empire to participate in a set of public duties, common to all, irrespective of individual preferences or beliefs. In the Greco-Roman polytheist world this could hardly have caused moral or psychological trouble to a pagan worshipper. On the contrary, it must have been seen as an important condition for securing and perpetuating the *pax deorum* – "peace of the gods".

But there did undoubtedly exist another political reason for the mandatory character of public worship. An autocratic, especially a repressive regime, requires all its subjects to take part in the same ritual as a sign of loyalty and approval. In the final analysis, this means instilling in each participant a sense of complicity with whatever the regime may do, so that if the former refuses or tries to avoid performing properly, this could be interpreted as an act of treason. This accounts for the fact that in public festivities, side by side with the veneration of statues representing Greco-Roman gods, one was expected to worship images of the Emperor. It is of no consequence that this ritual ran the risk of becoming increasingly shallow; what mattered was form, not substance. Thus, in the former Soviet Union a mere presence at various rallies, meetings and demonstrations would suffice. I have mentioned that Thrasea Paetus was charged by Nero with subversion simply for not having attended the gatherings of the Senate.

On the other hand, it seems natural, against such a background, that only Jews and Christians, believing in one and only one God, were bound to experience acute discomfort at the prospect of venerating deities who were for them nothing but empty names or, even worse, evil demons. In their case, this was further aggravated by the injunction of the Third Commandment, literally understood: "Do not worship graven images!" It meant a total refusal, on the part of Jewish and Christian believers, to compromise with the Imperial authorities on that issue. The Jews were eventually excused on the grounds of Judaism's status as an ancient and therefore respectable religion (*religio antiqua*). No doubt, this was also due to the recognition by the Romans of the impossibility to impose their will, in this respect, on an entire nation prepared passionately to resist any such interference: Caligula's attempt to enforce the veneration of his image among Jews almost led to a full-scale Jewish insurrection, prevented by the fact of his murder. This accounts for the largely reconciliatory politics of the Julio-Claudians with regard to Jewish faith, to the point of Emperors sponsoring special sacrifices on their own behalf in the Temple of Jerusalem.

None of these considerations, however, applied to Christians. As "a new superstition" (*superstitio nova*) they could not claim any venerable tradition and were exempt from the allowances granted to Jews. Consequently, they were labeled *religio illicita* ("illegal religion") and harassed for the span of more than 200 years. This was the reason for successive persecutions of the early Church in the second and third centuries, but not for the original one under Nero. At that time they were tried and executed not for practicing illegal worship, or for *nomen ipsum*, "the mere name", as was to happen in later years, but on the charge of incendiarism, which was a matter of political expediency. As Tacitus tells us, Nero's motive was, by providing a convenient scapegoat, to divert public suspicion from himself, and to contravene a rumor that he had deliberately set Rome on fire.

It must come clear now why official Roman policies under the early Empire proved more conducive to generating political dissidence rather than what I have earlier described as religious dissent within the framework of an established and powerful religion. The only environment capable of producing such a phenomenon at the time was that of Judaism. Consequently, I now turn to the basic, although perforce brief, discussion of Second Temple Judaism – arguably, the most contested subject matter of ancient history – and its features, which concern, in one sense or another, our present study. Its socio-political, religious and cultural environment underwent multiple changes throughout 600 years or so between the return from Babylonian exile and the destruction of the Second Temple in A.D. 70. For the purpose of this book I will primarily concentrate on several aspects of the situation as it evolved throughout the Roman period up to the time of the Great Revolt.[4]

1

THE VIBRANT FAITH

I.

This book is concerned with the last stage of the Second Temple's existence, when Judaea, step by step, fell under Rome's domination. The revolt of 167 B.C., led by the Maccabean family, against the Hellenistic Seleucid King Antiochus IV Epiphanes, who attempted to suppress Judaic religion, eventually resulted in the establishment of the independent Jewish state. This kingdom of the Hasmoneans lasted for about a century before it went into decline in the grip of a dynastic war, which precipitated Rome's military interference with the region. The following decades saw its reduction to the status of vassal kingdom ruled by the Herods, until it was finally integrated as a province of the Roman Empire in A.D. 6.

It cannot be doubted that Judaism of the period belonged among the best-organized religions in the ancient world. Josephus describes the traditional Jewish form of government as 'theocracy' (a word that he seems to have coined): "Our legislator / ... / established the government / ... /, relegating all power and rule to God" (cAp., 2, 165). Although at this point Josephus does not explain how the implementation of God's will as revealed in the Torah was to be supervised or interpreted, it comes clear in his subsequent discussion:

> Could there exist anything better or more just than making God the head of the whole, and assigning the management of the most important affairs to the body of priests, and entrusting to the high priest the leadership of all other priests? / ... / Their task was a strict supervision as regards the observance of the law and of other practices, since the priests were made the overseers of all and judges over the disputes and punishers of those condemned.
>
> (185 ff.)

This picture of what perhaps one may better call 'hierocracy' is, of course, idealized. To what extent and in what periods it came closer to reality is another matter. At the very least, Josephus's formulations say something about how the

Jewish religious establishment at his time sought to conceive of itself. But before we advance any further, it is imperative to comment briefly on the current debate on whether Second Temple Judaism, as the wholesome phenomenon, did actually exist.

Under the influence of relativist cultural anthropology and postmodernist argumentative procedures, it has now become fashionable to speak not of Judaism as such, but of many 'Judaisms', depending on the evidence that pertains to various social, cultural and political contexts. I find this phenomenologically untenable. It also defies the rules of logic – namely, the logic of the general and the partial. In the final analysis, it results in the abuse of pluralism as a cognitive approach. It is evident that any rational category usable in a historical (or any other) inquiry does not correspond to the multiform reality in all its aspects. This was clear already to Plato (although one does not need to accept his metaphysical projections, which are a *non sequitur*): there is no such thing as 'tree', since each tree is different from another, but this does not mean that, as a category, 'tree' is wrong. In other words, one and the same phenomenon (which is a generalized intellectual construct) takes in reality a multiplicity of forms, or manifests itself in multiple ways. Thinking otherwise easily lends itself to the *reductio ad absurdum*: thus, in the whole world no two individuals are exactly the same, even among identical twins, but this is not the reason to claim the existence of 5 billion 'humankinds'. It is obvious that with the abolition of phenomenological categories such as meant here, a reasonable discussion in terms of epistemology becomes impossible.

All of this makes sense, of course, provided that there exists the least common denominator to denote the entire phenomenon under discussion. In the case of Judaism, whatever its historical or cultural manifestation, this is obviously the case: any Jew partaking in it as religion recognizes as theological truth Israel's Covenant with God, the revelation at Sinai and the sanctity of the Torah. The religious Jews practice circumcision, celebrate major festivals, attend (although with varying regularity) the synagogue and consider the Sh'ma as expressing the substance of their beliefs. Stressing the essential unity of Judaism does not mean that in all its aspects it was or is harmonious and non-contradictory: no cultural development, including religion, is or ever was. It does not follow, however, that for these reasons Judaism does not exist as a distinct phenomenon, or the Jewish people as a distinct entity. Jews always conceived of themselves and their faith in terms of the common rather than the particular – a fact that cannot be easily dismissed as it sometimes is.

This said, it must nonetheless be recognized that the issue of 'Jewish identity' under the Second Temple is not that simple. Recent scholarly discussions have demonstrated the variety of attitudes, both in Diaspora and in Judaea, as to who then was or could be considered a 'Jew': after all, there happened to exist, it seems, throughout the period 'Judaized gentiles' as well as 'gentilized Jews'. Much depended on time, place and immediate environment. One cannot doubt that religious and ethnic components played a role, as did, although differing in force and degree under the circumstances, political and cultural factors; but a series of questions remains about the status of proselytes, gentile sympathizers and the persons of mixed ethnic origin, even though they all seem not to have been numerous, but rather belonged among the fringe or marginal groups. This further involves a terminological matter: some scholars distinguish between appellations of 'Jews' and 'Judeans', offering various justifications for their usage of this or that term. In this book, for the sake of clarity and convenience, I propose to define the Second Temple 'Jewishness', so to say, 'apophatically': 'Jews' were individuals who refused, or would have refused, to participate in gentile religious rites (or in any other enterprise religiously colored, such as festivals) on the grounds of their commitment to the unique religion of Israel and specific ancestral traditions it entailed. It goes without saying that (as it is now) the absolute majority of persons so described would also prove to be ethnically Jewish. Consequently, I will keep using the terms 'Jews' and 'Jewish' in this very sense, and also since they are more familiar to the reader; most of the developments narrated in this book had occurred on the territory of Judaea under Roman rule, which makes it unnecessary to specify its Jewish population as 'Judeans'; on several occasions when I discuss the Jews of the Diaspora, this is made clear by the context.[1]

It cannot be denied that, at the time of the Second Temple, Judaism took a variety of forms: there was a difference between the realities in Judaea and the Diaspora; in some cases it might have undergone various degrees of Hellenization: as practiced by the Herods, for instance, it differs from its vision in Philo, although Hellenistic influences apparently affected both. The same is true, of course, regarding the three famous "philosophies" or 'sects' within what is often called 'mainstream' or 'common' Judaism – Pharisees, Sadducees and Essenes, portrayed in Josephus and other documents (a matter I will shortly return to), or other groups, of which we know little or nothing.

All of this, however, relates only tangentially to the subject and main argument of this study. My concern is not so much with various beliefs and practices within the 'common' Judaism at the time, but with the attitudes of groups or individuals towards the religious establishment administering the land, at the time of independence in conjunction with the royal Hasmonean family, later on with the Herods, and finally the Roman occupiers. This establishment was by no means always, or necessarily, monolithic, but however quarrelsome it might have been, it still did not disintegrate, or fall apart, until the upheaval of the Great Revolt. It consisted largely of the higher priesthood, usually associated with Sadduceism and centered around the Temple, and lay individuals from the scribal and Pharisaic circles who were willing, for this or that reason, and under these or those circumstances, to cooperate. It can hardly be doubted that this authority provided guidance and spiritual supervision for the vast majority of the populace by defining and perpetuating, in terms of their abilities, what some scholars aptly named 'convenantal nomism'. Our interest, on the other hand, lies with those who tended to challenge or reject this establishment as illegitimate and corrupt.

One difficulty in any assessment of Second Temple Judaism, apart from the fact that it kept changing in various respects from the time of Nehemiah and Ezra onwards, is that it continues to be a subject of passionate scholarly controversy, which affects the basics as well as the details. In recent decades its descriptive and interpretive paradigms have changed and shifted rapidly, sometimes almost annually, questioning nearly every aspect of extant evidence, including such major issues, long considered beyond doubt, as the existence at the time of the Sanhedrin and the Oral Torah, the origin and dating of the synagogues, the role and meaning of Phariseism, the provenance of the Qumran documents, the historicity of the Mishnaic traditions, the origin of the Yavneh Academy, and so forth. On a number of important issues learned opinions are mutually exclusive, and at the moment no consensus seems possible. Later in this chapter I will attempt to tackle the current critique of our sources that sometimes verges on the excessive and, I believe, largely unproductive hypercriticism. At this point, it is imperative to realize that the matter must be handled with great caution. In the following effort at presenting a broad outline, I will first concentrate on what Jewish religious/cultural life in Palaestina seemed to look like during the Roman period; and, second, I warn the reader that, since in various arguments, I either side with a particular school of thought or provide a view of my own, some positions stated hereafter remain debatable.

Even if one allows for exaggerations on the part of our sources, it cannot be denied that, at the time we are interested in, the absolute majority of the Jewish people considered legitimate the supervision of the cult, centering at the Temple in Jerusalem, by the hereditary priesthood and the body of the Levites, subordinate ministers, traditionally held as descended from the tribe of Levi. The duties at the Temple involved the performance of daily sacrifices, other rituals and public prayers; the same priestly establishment must also have been responsible for the proper conduct of the religious festivals in the capital, the chief of which had been Passover (Pesah), Pentecost (Shavuot) and Sukkot (the Feast of the Tabernacles), requiring the pilgrimage of all Jews to worship in Jerusalem; as well as Yom Kippur (Day of Atonement), when the high priest enters the Holy of Holies. It must be mentioned at this point that the accumulation of the crowds in the capital during the three above-mentioned and biblically mandated holidays (*Shalosh regalim*) was bound to cause particular apprehension to the Roman authorities who feared potential political trouble, and these fears, as will be seen, sometimes proved justified.

Finally, the priests provided essential guidance in the proper religious life of the population at large. Even upon the revolt's outbreak, the high priestly group temporarily succeeded in taking over the leadership of the so-called 'first regime' and was followed by the majority of Jerusalem's population for more than a year until its overthrow through the zealot *coup d'état*. It is, however, most unlikely that their motivation had anything in common with what this study recognizes as the 'psychology of religious dissent'. They were people well versed in politics due to their dealings with the Roman authorities for decades, capable of dissimulation, if needed, and of compromise. Their behavior was largely determined by the pressure of circumstances, power struggle and, one assumes, some wishful hope for national independence. It must also be remembered that some of their colleagues chose to oppose the insurrection or eventually sided with the Romans.

There is no compelling reason to doubt that virtually all Jews in Judaea, as well as in the Diaspora (one should, of course, allow for individual exceptions and apostates), willingly followed the fundamental precepts of the Torah, such as the dietary laws and observation of the Sabbath. One assumes that much of the rural populace remained illiterate, but there seems to have existed a kind of network (although the details are difficult to establish) across the country, consisting of ordinary priests, Levites and scribes (and perhaps some local Pharisees) to instruct the masses on the main tenets of the Law. The essence of the faith came through the regularity of public and private prayers, while the Torah was being read and discussed at both informal gatherings and in the synagogues.[2]

One can say with some confidence that the Judaism of the time did not know the concept of 'heresy' in Christian and medieval terms. (The Samaritan problem is more complex and altogether different in origin and in substance, and will be briefly addressed later.) We know that, within the mainstream, Josephus distinguishes three 'sects', or schools of thought: Sadducees, Pharisees and Essenes. In several digressions he attempts to characterize their role and their views (*BJ*, 2, 162 ff.; *AJ*, 13, 171 ff.; 18, 11 ff.), with a varying degree of detail and reliability that depends on his personal bias we can only guess at. Furthermore, in his treatment Josephus borrows from the philosophical vocabulary, current within the Roman Empire at the time, to stress what he sees as similarities between Greek and Jewish wisdom. In his view, it would presumably have helped his gentile audience to understand the unfamiliar material; but this was also bound to entail simplifications and distortions, often difficult to unravel. There is no evidence that any of the three sects, as a body, did oppose, in principle, the centrality of the Temple or considered entering a violent conflict with the priestly establishment. Even the controversial schismatics in Qumran, who did reject the *current* Temple as profaned through inappropriate practices, which were bound, in their view, to be reconfigured in future, seem to have still followed, by virtue of their own secession (and their eschatology notwithstanding), a non-violent path of religious dissent. Only the adherents of what Josephus calls the "fourth philosophy", whom he sets apart, exemplify the violent, revolutionary type, both in theory and in practice: preaching a sort of 'religious anarchism' through their denial of any authority other than God, they attempted an insurrection early in the Roman period and proved instrumental in the outbreak of the Jewish War. The available evidence on this and similarly disposed groups will be repeatedly scrutinized in the course of this book.

It is not my intent here to enter, in any significant manner, multiple debates on the role, composition and persuasions regarding any of the three 'sects' as evidenced in our sources. Most of the material is fragmentary, contradictory and biased. More importantly, none of the three, as a body, or a wholesome movement, provides for the case of violent religious dissent (the Essenes may be viewed as representing its non-violent form), which is my chief concern in this book. Similarly, it cannot be demonstrated that any of these groups as such (unlike their individual members) took part in the revolt, pursuing some specific revolutionary agenda. This is why in what follows I will limit my treatment to a broad outline, trying to draw, as far as possible, on those elements in scholarly positions which admit at least some degree of consensus.[3]

Of the Sadducees we know the least. They disappeared from the historical scene (or at least from the literary record available) soon after the destruction of the Temple; the references to them in our extant sources (Josephus, New Testament and the rabbinic writings) are unsatisfactory and, for the most part, hostile. Given the fact that a considerably larger body of evidence we possess on the Pharisees and the Essenes has produced an ongoing heated controversy, with no hope for even a basic scholarly agreement, it is not surprising that the lesser attention given to the study of the Sadducees could not have resulted in any certainty on our part about almost any aspect of their historical existence. It is generally assumed that they belonged to the dominant social and political class, which would largely mean the priestly and secular aristocracy; but this is clearly not enough to define them as a coherent movement or a distinct strand within the Judaism of the time. Even if we accept that the Sadducees were influential within the Jewish religious establishment, it does not follow that any Temple priest was a Sadducee, or that any Sadducee was a Temple priest; their actual number cannot be ascertained. In fact, we know of only one high priest explicitly called such by Josephus (*AJ*, 20, 199): that was Ananus b. Ananus, who eventually came to preside over the first revolutionary government. The origin of the group is obscure, and even the etymology of their name is a subject of disputation. It is debated whether the Sadducees could have actually (or allegedly) descended from the biblical priest Zadok of Aaron's direct line; if so, in the earlier stage of their history, they may have related to the hereditary Zadokids, who chose to stay in Jerusalem and cooperate with the Hasmonean rulers rather than emigrate to Egypt with the high priest Onias III (or IV), or withdraw to the desert as (presumably) did the sectarians at Qumran. According to Josephus, they achieved political prominence during the Hasmonean period under John Hyrcanus I (*AJ*, 13, 293 ff.), only to be replaced in that role by the Pharisees under Salome Alexandra (ibid, 405 ff.; cf. *BJ*, 1, 110 ff.). Later on, their relative fortunes and influence might have varied; but with the rise of Herod and, even more, after the Roman annexation of Judaea, they became increasingly subordinate to the royal, prefectorial and procuratorial regimes.

Josephus explicitly insists that the Sadducees refused to recognize the Pharisaic customs, or practices received through "ancestral succession", but "which are not written in the laws of Moses [i.e. the Torah]" (*AJ*, 13, 297; cf. 18, 17). This statement used to be understood as meaning the rejection of the Oral Torah, having evolved out of the *halakhas*, based on the Written Torah's exegesis by the Pharisees, and considered mandatory by the latter. This view has been challenged in recent decades to the point of denying the very existence of the Oral Torah throughout the Second Temple period (it is first mentioned in the rabbinic writings only in the second century after Christ). Be that as it may, it seems fair to propose, in view of the current scholarly debate, that the Sadducean and Pharisaic perspectives on, or interpretation of, the Pentateuch must have significantly diverged.

Their presumed literalism may, at least in part, elucidate Josephus's remarks on 'theology' held by the Sadducees, which I regard as particularly baffling. According to him, they refuted the notion of both afterlife and fate, while "placing God beyond any deed and sight of evil", and professed the doctrine of free choice (*BJ*, 2, 164 f.). I find it difficult to square the disbelief in the soul's immortality, ascribed to them by Josephus (only in loc. cit.) with any variant of a monotheist religion. It seems true that in Judaism definitive ideas about the afterlife, with rewards for the virtuous and punishments for the sinners, came to be shaped only in the post-exilic period; and that the earlier texts in the Hebrew Bible do not offer insights into this matter, comparable with the New Testament, the Koran or even Homer, apart from the vague references to the 'Sheol' (e.g., *Ps.* 6: 4 f.; 18: 5 ff.; 86: 13; 139: 8; *Job*, 7:9; *Jonas*, 2:2). But even there we read of King Saul summoning the shade of prophet Samuel though necromancy by the Witch of Endor (*I Sam.*, 28), which makes it clear that upon one's death a soul does not altogether disappear, but continues to exist in some, perhaps unfathomable, condition. Consequently, it seems to me unlikely that the Sadducees, who did accept scriptural traditions, could have denied a soul's immortality as resolutely as Josephus makes it appear. Rather, they may have been refuting the non-traditional Pharisaic beliefs (also found in many Pseudepigrapha) on rewards and punishments in the afterlife and specifically their doctrine on the resurrection of the dead – the dispute for which we also possess evidence from the synoptic Gospels (*Mk.* 12: 18 ff.; *Mt.* 22: 23 ff.; *Lk.* 20: 27 ff.) and the *Acts* (23: 7 ff.). Josephus's motives for simplifying, or distorting, the Sadducean position on this subject may have involved his intent to discredit this 'sect', which he apparently disliked, in the eyes of his pagan audience by comparing it *implicite* to the Epicureans, given the fact that he explicitly associated two other Jewish 'philosophies', the Pharisees and the Essenes, with their supposed Greek counterparts – Stoics and Pythagoreans, respectively (*Vita*, 12; *AJ*, 15, 371). It is known that the followers of Epicurus utterly denied the soul's survival after death, and they came to acquire a bad name in the mainstream quasi-philosophical parlance of the day.

Mutatis mutandis, similar motivation might have existed in Josephus's statement on the allegedly Sadducean 'theological' anti-determinism, although in that case the matter appears even more complex – or confused. In the first place, the concept of 'Fate' (*eimarmene*) as an impersonal principle is decidedly non-Jewish, and is clearly employed here (and elsewhere) to the benefit of Josephus's gentile readers. As regards the view absolving God from any involvement with evil, this formulation needs not to be taken, although it often is, as the disclaimer of God's interference with human affairs. This last reading militates against, and is incompatible with, the scriptural (largely Deuteronomist) 'theology of history', including its central events, such as the Exodus and the Revelation at Sinai. Consequently, what Josephus might have had in mind is that the Sadducean God, being the Supreme Good (not unlike the Stoic *summum bonum*), cannot be held responsible for any manifestation of evil, which is in every case a product – or abuse – of human freedom. By a stretch of imagination, one may further read into this passage an idea – although it is not actually spelled out – that, upon the return from the Babylonian exile, God ceased directly interfering with Israel's destiny and allowed his chosen people a free exercise of choice, for good or for bad. This position would have, on the other hand, enhanced the distrust of the self-styled prophets (claiming to have been the conveyers of God's will) and the hostility towards their Messianic (or quasi-Messianic) agitation, which was current (as it seems manifest from the New Testament and the Pseudepographa) within various societal strata in Judaea and the Diaspora at the time. The Sadducees may have been especially concerned with the preservation of the *status quo* that could have been threatened by individuals and groups usurping the divine authority to interfere with matters political or/and religious. Finally, this 'indeterminist' stance Josephus ascribes to the men he felt little sympathy for might have again reminded his reader of the often maligned Epicureans, with their 'atomist' gods, who exist in blissful condition, totally aloof from all human tribulations.[4]

Compared to the Sadducees, the material we possess on the Pharisaic movement seems abundant: the Pharisees are visibly present in Josephus, who also digresses on them at greater length; they often appear in the New Testament and are apparently celebrated in the Tannaitic corpus. The problem is that the two latter sources are demonstrably biased: the New Testament authors treat them largely (although not always) with polemical hostility, while the later rabbis, as is now recognized by most scholars, tended to retroject on the period of the Second Temple their own expectations and concerns and even to indulge in historical fantasies. As for Josephus, his summaries and occasional pronouncements on the Pharisees (with him claiming to have been one of them – *Vita*, 12) came to be increasingly questioned for their accuracy and even veracity, while the motives behind his assumed historical distortions remain elusive.

The spectrum of social, political, historical and religious issues relating to the Pharisees is so vast, and the current debate on them so complex, that it does not allow here even a brief survey along the lines I have devoted to their Sadducean rivals. In consequence, I will deal with only a few select aspects of the problem, more relevant to this book's main topic – for the most part, with the controversy over the alleged Pharisaic 'doctrinal' domination inside the religious establishment of the Second Temple and their influence on the people at large, which further pertains to their political activities or lack thereof; and with the matter of ritual purity, one of their conspicuous characteristics, its religious implications and potential misuse.

It appears that what Josephus says in his digressions on the Pharisaic basic moral and 'theological' tenets (*BJ*, 2, 162 f., 166 f.; *AJ*, 13, 171 ff., 297 ff.; 18, 12 ff.) largely makes sense (despite his comparing them with the Greek Stoics – *Vita*, 12, which may be seen as somewhat misleading) and is often in agreement with what we know from elsewhere. Their adherents are described as mild in character, modest in lifestyle and eschewing luxury, observing not only the laws of the Torah but also those "traditions of the fathers", which they saw fit, believing in the interaction between Providence and free will, in the immortality of the soul, posthumous rewards and punishments (resurrection of the dead, one of the major Pharisaic tenets, is never explicitly mentioned). What has actually caused a major controversy is Josephus's claims of their domineering influence over the urban populace (*AJ*, 18, 14 f.; cf. 13, 298) to the point that even the Sadducean aristocrats, he writes, upon taking office, were compelled to "obey, although involuntarily and perforce, what a Pharisee says, since otherwise they would become unacceptable to the masses" (ibid, 18, 16). This comes close to (although is not fully identical with) the view propagated in the Mishnah and I do not find anything in the New Testament material substantially to contradict Josephus's insistence on the Pharisaic prominence in religious and social affairs.

It is not surprising then that for a long time this portrayal of the Pharisees' role in society was considered, in its main features, historically reliable. A more recent and influential argument, however, intends to refute it as a big exaggeration, if not outright fiction. The scrutiny of Josephus's own text, contend its promoters, does not justify his summaries and leads to the conclusion that it was the priesthood rather than the Pharisaic movement who provided most experts in the Law and religious guidance to the people. Furthermore, in this view, upon their brief period of supremacy under Salome Alexandra (76/75–67 B.C.), and, in particular, with the advent of the Romans, the Pharisees tended to withdraw from public life and concentrate on their own affairs. In the narrowest formulation (which is polemically opposed even to this revisionist perspective), they confined themselves exclusively to table fellowship within the framework of their movement. Much of this may well be right, although two moments, I believe, should serve as a (moderate) caveat. In the first place, it must be remembered that when Josephus wrote (especially, the *Bellum*), the situation he described must still have been a living memory. This means that, to maintain his credibility, he was not in a position excessively to fictionalize or deviate too far from what his Jewish audience felt prepared to believe in. Consequently, there must have been among his readership of Greek-speaking literate Jews, both in the Diaspora (and, closest to his interests, the Jewish community in Rome), but also in Judaea, those who shared the same vision of the Pharisaic prominence – irrespective of whether it did or did not reflect the realities of life. Some degree of wishful thinking inevitably features in religious psychology, and may reach a point of obsession, as we will see, in the case of religious dissent. Secondly, their episodic re-emergences under Herod and the fact that the priests found it imperative to consult them upon the termination of the Imperial sacrifices at the revolt's outbreak (*BJ*, 2, 411) suggest that they could have continued expressing an undercurrent of interest, or even partaking in the affairs of state. In any event, it is hard for me to imagine that at moments of crisis, such as under Pontius Pilate, or at the time of Caligula's projected desecration of the Temple, they would not have joined the priestly establishment in pleading the Jewish cause before the occupier. Still, it must be emphasized that so long as they peacefully interacted with the Temple and priestly elite and partook in 'common' Judaism, as a movement, they cannot be (in our terms) considered religious dissenters. Individuals, however, could be different: we are told (*AJ*, 18, 4) that Saddok the Pharisee was a co-founder, with the more famous Judas the Galilaean, of the "fourth philosophy" rebel group, which represents the clearest example of the violent religious dissent. The Pharisaic participation in the earlier stage of the revolt is well attested, and their eminent teacher Simon b. Gamaliel played an important role in the first revolutionary regime (*Vita*, 190 ff., cf. *BJ*, 4, 159).

A special problem on which much depends is Josephus's personal stand towards the Pharisees and their traditions. Scholars came up with opposite arguments that often tend to kill each other. In many cases, the problem is that they look for a simple solution, whether positive or negative. I believe that in this respect, as in others regarding Josephus's idiosyncrasy as historian (to which I will repeatedly return), the issue is more complex. I find it difficult to explain away his unequivocal statement in the *Vita* that by his 19th year he "came to enter public life following the school of the Pharisaic school" (12) as some sort of sham. His circle of Jewish acquaintances was, one presumes, sufficiently wide and would know whether this was true; for him, to lie on such a sensitive subject would have been taking a needless risk. It is an altogether different matter what Josephus may have meant by this pronouncement. A professed adherence to a certain culturally or historically defined *Weltanschauung* does not necessarily mean that one approves of it in its entirety or its details, especially since all such movements entail a variety of attitudes, inner conflicts and arguments, which prevail or fail to prevail depending on the circumstances. This was certainly true of the historical Pharisees, with their continuous disputes between the houses of Hillel and Shammai, on which see shortly below. Furthermore, the depth of commitment and enthusiasm also individually varies and pertains to such imponderables as temperament, capacity for introspection and experience. The fact remains that both the *Bellum* and the *Antiquitates* contain explicit praise of the Pharisaic movement, of its mores and its outlook, – in contrast to censuring the Sadducees; and if their author shows or implies his disapproval of their particular action, characteristic or an individual Pharisee, it does not need to detract from the overall sense of endorsement: thus, American Democrats feel free to criticize this or that behavior of a Democratic president or a Democratic Congress without withdrawing their support or party membership. On the other hand, Josephus was a partially Hellenized Jew, consorting with the Herodian royalty and Flavian Emperors, who might have felt no obligation to force any 'sectarian' Jewish perspective on his readers. For this reason, a search for pro- or anti-Pharisaic bias may lead to some interesting and nuanced results, but it should hardly affect, I believe, our basic appreciation of the Josephan narratives.

A further puzzle is Josephus's total silence on such major issues as the controversy between Hillel's and Shammai's schools within Phariseism as well as the Yavneh Academy and the rise of early rabbinism. With this, we enter even more uncertain grounds. The fact is that, apart from his apologetic concerns, both patriotic and personal, little or nothing can be said about the vagaries of his mind, including his motives for disregarding things which we – or even his readership – might have found important. One point is clear: we must not expect him strictly to follow the procedures of what we understand as historiography, even in its Greco-Roman form, despite his efforts in imitating the Thucydidean model. His many silences could have depended on a plethora of factors, which are, due to the lack of evidence, beyond our grasp. This is why scholarly attempts to fill these gaps through speculation often strike one as unconvincing. At this point I propose that, facing this peculiar feature of Josephus's discourse, it may be advisable, rather than speculating without minimal factual data, or piling supposition on supposition (*petitio principii*), or abusing the *argumentum ex silentio*, simply to confess in each such case our ignorance and impotence and put the matter at rest.

The absence of reference in Josephus to the houses of Hillel and Shammai and their disagreements throughout the late Second Temple period, on the other hand, may be explained, at least in part, by his apologetic agenda: namely, the implicit tendency to eschew, so far as possible, mentioning the conflicts of religious nature within the mainstream Judaism, since it might otherwise have played into the hands of the gentile Judophobic publicists, eager to portray the religion and traditions of the Jews as troublesome, disorderly and subversive by their very nature; on the other hand, he might have felt that the substance of these disputes would make little sense to non-Jews. The historian's silences, however, give us no reason to deny the existence of the Hillelite–Shammaite controversy at the time, the echoes of which are prominent in rabbinic texts: one school of thought having been more universalist, in accordance with their master's famous pronouncement: "That which is hateful to you, do not do to your fellow. That is the whole Torah; the rest is the explanation; go and learn" (*bShab.*, 31a); and another more exclusivist. I find it inconceivable that the phenomena of this magnitude could have been a mere product of later rabbis' historical imagination. It will be argued that the Shammaite argument and constituency may have influenced the decision to terminate Imperial sacrifices at the Temple and thus contributed to the outbreak of the great revolt.

Another point of contention pertains to the material on the judiciary body (or bodies) known in Hebrew as *Sanhedrin* (Greek *Synedrion*). Today one must accept that the elaborate and idealized picture of it and its workings in the Mishnaic tractate of the same name (*mSanh.*) is essentially a historical fiction, and recognize the fact that Josephus's references to it are rare and sometimes obscure. On these grounds, it has been argued that in the late Second Temple period there was no such permanent court, but it could have been summoned *ad hoc* and in an arbitrary manner by the current high priest; and that it was the echo of such irregular meetings, which found its way into the New Testament. Although in this connection the argument from silence is forcefully invoked, it seems to me counter-intuitive to think that, given the complexity of Jewish religious life, there was no standing institution of some sort to pronounce on the perceived moral or ritual misconduct by a person or a group, at least within the confines of Jerusalem. If this was so, then it might have been indeed called Sanhedrin and included both Sadducees and Pharisees: after all, the *Acts* (5:34 ff.), written towards the end of the first century A.D. (that is, roughly contemporary to Josephus and 100 years earlier than the Mishnah), speak of the famous Pharisaic sage R. Gamaliel (I) the Elder (incidentally, a teacher of St. Paul; ibid, 22:33) as its prominent and 'liberal' member.

Although the concept of Oral Torah, as it is present in the Mishnah, may not have been a definitive reality during the period under discussion, there is no reason to doubt the existence of the Pharisaic *halakhas* issued and transmitted across generations, but perhaps meaningful and mandatory largely for the members of that movement. It is impossible to ascertain to what extent the Pharisees had been listened to by the population at large. The frequent references in the Mishnah to an *am ha-aretz* ('rustic'), considered unclean and ritually ignorant, suggest that the majority of country residents did not observe (at the very least) the prescriptions of purity which the Pharisees and later the rabbis considered particularly important. There is no reason to think that in any earlier period it might have been different from the time of the Mishnah's composition. This brings us to the issue of ritual purity on which I can comment here only briefly.

In the first place, it must be emphasized (however trivial the point might now seem) that, despite the continuous claims of all and sundry anti-Semites, the religious concept of 'chosen people' has nothing to do with any racism. The reason is simple: while racism is, by definition, a biological proposition (that is, one cannot enter a race by choice), it was and is possible for any person to partake in Judaism through conversion upon performing certain rituals and procedures, even if it may involve (for males) some physical discomfort: thus, we are told, for instance, of St. Paul's decision to have his disciple Timothy circumcised and make him thereby a *bona fide* Jew (*Acts* 16:3). (It must be specified, however, that the extent to which circumcision was considered mandatory, and by whom, during the Second Temple remains uncertain and constitutes the subject of the ongoing scholarly debate; the same is true about the variety of attitudes towards proselytes in different Jewish communities at the time as well as in their own self-identification.)

On the other hand, the notion of ritual purity (intimately relating to the idea of the sacred and taboo practices) seems well embedded in the human psyche and is, in one sense or another, characteristic of many religions: for instance, the strictures imposed in Rome on the priest of Jupiter (*flamen Dialis*) were no less severe (and more bizarre) than those observed by the Jerusalem Temple priesthood.

This said, one still must concede that the degree of commitment to purificatory piety within Judaism, especially in its Pharisaic, Essenic and rabbinic mold, extends beyond most other cultures and compares perhaps with only some traditions in Hinduism. Its centrality is evident already in the Torah, starting with the dietary laws, and the treatment of this issue in the Tannaitic texts reaches the heights of sophistication and refinement. In principle, this entails nothing improper, but rather may contribute to individual and collective health, physical as well as spiritual. Furthermore, it has been powerfully demonstrated that the rabbinic perspective on purity involves metaphysical implications of a high order. At the same time, it can hardly be denied that this pervasive concern with purity and purification does enhance the exclusivist aspect of the Jewish faith. As history repeatedly proves, in the hands of religious dissenters bent on violence any such premise could easily turn into both a motive and an instrument for destruction. One starts with self-purification, first of the body, then of the soul, which is all well and good. Next, in the grip of spiritual ardor and wishful thinking about their relationship with the divine, a person or persons proceed to 'purify' others, often out of existence, and consider this a sacred duty. Some noxious developments, like Stalin's party purges, or ethnic cleansing, may be legitimately viewed as secular and political venues for similar urges felt and fulfilled by the self-proclaimed 'carriers of Truth'. Later in this book I will examine a peculiar paradox manifest in the behavior of the Jewish religious insurgents: on the one hand, their campaign for purity, and, on the other, their willingness to perform defilement of the sacred by internecine slaughter at the very Temple, invoking – as they understood it – God's very will.

Unlike their Saducean rivals, the Pharisees seem to have eventually triumphed – and ceased to comprise a 'sect'; at the very least, their many teachings and positions found expression in the later rabbinic material. They must have succeeded in regrouping upon the Temple's destruction and, under the leadership of remarkable individuals, such as Rabban Johanan b. Zakkai, and with the Roman fiat, founded the scholarly center at Yavneh (the development left unmentioned in the Josephan narratives), which in the course of time came largely to formulate the Judaism that we know today. They were conscientious men who contributed, in various ways, to the emergence of exegetical literature on an astounding scale for the benefit, as they saw it, of their people. The bad reputation the name 'Pharisees' had acquired in European languages is historically undeserved. It is owed to the polemics against them on the part of the early Christian authors, the reasons for which are beyond the scope of this book.[5]

We are familiar with the pejorative phrase "scribes and Pharisees", which derives from the polemical pronouncements in the Gospels. Owing to Josephus and other sources, we have at least some basic idea (irrespective of the present debate on their role in the society of the time), of who the Pharisees were (as well as the Sadducees and the Essenes), and that they did not deserve the contempt piled on them throughout centuries in the Christian world. Regarding the scribes, there is less certainty about who they were or might have been. The

Gospels' formula, on the one hand, affiliates them with the Pharisees (which suggests that at least some portions of the populace must have envisaged them that way); on the other, it makes clear that they were seen as a separate group. Furthermore, there is a striking discrepancy concerning scribes in our three main sources. Josephus refers to them almost exclusively as officials and lower administrators (apparently, in the Greek sense of the word); the New Testament authors portray them as part of the Jewish political and religious establishment, the teachers of the people; in rabbinic texts (and the extant papyri) they emerge as writers and legal experts. It seems that the only way to harmonize this material is to suggest that whatever role men thus designated may have played in the biblical and early post-exilic periods, or in writing, editing and canonizing the Scriptures, at the time under discussion, they did not represent a well-defined category in the eyes of their contemporaries. Furthermore, the multilingual environment of Roman Palaestina contributes to our confusion about them and their status. The meaning of the Greek term is narrow compared to Hebrew, which suggests that although many 'scribes' could have indeed been local officials or private secretaries, like their Greek counterparts, they possessed legal and writing expertise (along with, as seems likely, their interest in wisdom literature, traditionally associated with the 'sages'). Some of them, by virtue of their origin, wealth or personality, might have reached the higher echelons of society and exercised influence in political and religious affairs. And, of course, as is the case with the Pharisees, their lasting proverbial condemnation is equally undeserved.[6]

With all its complexities, passions and disagreements, the current scholarly debate on the role and character of the Pharisaic movement during the Second Temple period looks almost like child's play when compared with the controversy over the third of the Josephan 'sects' or 'school of thoughts' – the Essenes. Until the mid-20th century the evidence we possessed of that group was limited to the written accounts of them, largely by Philo (chronologically, the earliest: *Quod omnis*, 12, 75 ff.; *Hypothetica* ap. Eus., *Praep. Evang.*, 8, 11) and Josephus (*BJ*, 2, 119 ff.; *AJ*, 13, 171, 298; 15, 371; 18, 18 ff.; *Vita*, 10 f.). Although by no means devoid of inner contradictions, this material nonetheless provides a fairly consistent picture of extremely pious sectarians and their ascetic lifestyle based on communal existence, a lengthy trial period, collective property, celibacy, subordination, and ritual purity, occasionally to the point of excess. These sources celebrate the Essenes for their benevolence (even though they are said to have practiced the death penalty for blasphemy), wisdom (some of it secret), scriptural knowledge and prophetic gifts. Josephus explicitly compares them with the Greek Pythagoreans (*AJ*, 15, 371) and elsewhere expands on their belief in Fate's omnipotence, the soul's immortality, posthumous punishments and rewards as well as on their extraordinary endurance of physical pain. Philo (*De vita cont.*, 1) links them to the Therapeutae, a sect existent in the Jewish Diaspora, especially, in Egypt, who placed an even greater emphasis on contemplation and the union with the divine. By and large, these portrayals contain many features characteristic of groups carrying on the non-violent religious dissent (or simply looking for individual salvation) that recur in the history of different cultures: primitive communism, strict control of sexuality, (quasi-) egalitarianism coupled with the sense of exclusivity, rejection of the official worship practices, considered insufficient, profane or corrupt as well as of the priestly establishment, responsible for their perpetuation – in brief, an effort at withdrawal from the reality that is being strongly disapproved. One is struck by the resemblances between the descriptions referred to above and the multiple testimonies we possess about the way of life in medieval monasteries (even if in both cases the reports betray, arguably, a degree of idealization). It is not surprising then that the early scholars showed a tendency to derive the social organization of the nascent Christian church directly from the Essene communities.

This sense of consistence and continuity was irreparably shattered by the discovery of the Dead Sea Scrolls in 1947 near Qumran. That find generated a storm of arguments and refutations, fraught with scandals, charges of conspiracy, lawsuits, Internet harassment and even criminal convictions, as well as the literature on a huge scale, both popular and professional, which at the present point seems to be getting virtually beyond control. The disagreements range from the relationship, or lack thereof, between the Qumran sectarians and the Essenes as known to us from Philo and Josephus; to the provenance of the Qumran texts; to the origin and even actual existence of the sectarian Qumran community in a form other than wishful thinking; and so forth, not to mention the chronological conundrum involved. The situation has been aggravated by recent archaeological expeditions: their results are difficult to harmonize, especially with some statements found in the scrolls. Much of this discussion requires specialized knowledge I cannot claim. In consequence, here (as I will do in all similar cases) I present a brief and very general outline of what could be (and has been) said on the matter with various degree of certainty, and add a few comments, which may (or may not) be relevant to the main concerns of this study.

It seems to me that there is no need to deny the basic reliability of the Essene accounts by Philo and Josephus on the grounds that they were written by the outsiders who also (allegedly) drew on the earlier sources. Josephus insists that he had personal experience with all three 'schools of thought' (*Vita*, 10 f.; he adds that he spent three years in wilderness with a hermit, one Bannus – ibid, 11, who may or may not have been formally an Essene, but must have possessed some reliable information about them), and until this possibility is thoroughly disproved, it cannot be easily dismissed as it sometimes is. Irrespective of whatever (presumed to have been Hellenistic) written source he could have used, he might have sought opportunities for talking to the members of the movement and put the material thus acquired, as well as his personal insights, in his report. Although the latter is undoubtedly rhetorical, this is not a reason to reject it as thereby unhistorical. Contrary to the currently fashionable view, so far as history writing is concerned, rhetoricization does not *eo ipso* mean fictionalization. Any good writing is rhetorical by definition (rhetoric, after all, is concerned with how to write or speak *well*). It certainly may (and does) affect the presentation or interpretation of the facts, but it by no means requires *inventing* them. Thucydides and Tacitus – or, if you wish, Gibbon and Mommsen (and any other great historian!) – all wrote rhetorically (that is to say, beautifully), and all pursued their own intellectual or 'ideological' agenda; but it does not follow that the events they described had not happened or the realities appearing in their narratives did not exist. One problem with the present day historical scholarship is that it proves often *not enough* rhetorical and, as a result, is poorly written and boring. Thus we cannot deny that Josephus's (and Philo's) portrayal of the Essenes is idealized and, in certain respects, follows the conventions of Hellenistic 'ethnography'. But again, this simply means that some features of their lifestyle were emphasized and embellished, some omitted (because of authorial ignorance or bias), but hardly any invented out of whole cloth. The length of the excursus on the Essenes in the *Bellum* is inordinate and cannot be fully explained; it remains one of the Josephan minor puzzles. In any event, his (and Philo's) treatment must have been in essential agreement with the perception of them by their Jewish readership at large (though perhaps not well informed of what went on inside their communities or about the specifics of their beliefs). The argument that Josephus indulged in idealizing and fictionalizing the Essenes for apologetic purposes in order to convince his gentile audience of the goodness, piety and peaceful character of Jews at large, incapable of subversion and revolt, unless misled by crazy revolutionaries, is undercut by the fact, made patent in the narrative, that Essene sectarians represented a very small minority of the entire Jewish population; furthermore, they are linked directly to the events of the revolt by celebrating their endurance under tortures inflicted on them by the Romans (*BJ*, 2, 152 f.) – a passage I will discuss shortly. Finally, it must be stressed that, all reservations aside, Josephus still provides enough important parallels, including even details, with material found in Qumran (which, a scholarly majority continues to believe, is ultimately of Essene extraction), to be regarded as a trustworthy contemporary witness.

To Josephus and Philo must be added Pliny the Elder, who in his brief reference to the Essenes (*NH*, 5, 73) emphasizes their solitude and uniqueness, absence of women within their ranks and their ascetic lifestyle. From the descriptions by outsiders they thus emerge *prima facie* as an example of religious dissent in the very terms I have argued. This impression must be largely correct: they did, for the most part, separate themselves from the practices of the period's 'mainstream' or 'common' Judaism that centered on the cult at the Temple, which they must have considered, at the very least, not entirely 'kosher' (cf. *AJ*, 18, 19). Since, as all other Jews, they recognized the sacredness of the Scriptures (Josephus reports that some of them, endowed with a gift of prophecy, were "brought up on the holy books and various purifications" – *BJ*, 2, 159), postulating the Temple worship as religious duty, their isolationism can be explained only by their belief that the sanctuary was being profaned and for that reason should be eschewed by the truly pious. The last point must apply even more forcefully to the Temple priesthood, seen as *a priori* responsible for the sorry state of affairs, and to the religious leadership at large. (The Qumran texts, such as *The Temple Scroll* and *The Damascus Document*, powerfully testify to their respective authors' dream of constructing a new and perfect Temple in the eschatological future, and to the hatred of the official priests, 'men of the pit' – e.g. 1QS, 10:17 f.; cf. 9:16 f., 22 f.) The Essenes, as have other similar communities throughout history, also claimed the possession of esoteric knowledge and writings hidden from the rest of the world (*BJ*, 2, 142) and the ability to prophesize.

Perhaps one reason for scholarly disagreement regarding the Essenes is the unspoken assumption that their 'sect' was homogeneous in terms of attitude, outlook and behavior. This, however, never happens. To the contrary, any religious, political or ideological movement develops, often from the outset, a variety of forms, strands and colors, which may peacefully coexist throughout its historical existence or experience periodic conflicts; otherwise, this could result in brutal suppression or an irreparable split. It suffices to recall such phenomena as the Mahayana and Theravada schools in Buddhism; the Shiite and Sunnite split in Islam (with numerous sects within each of the larger groups); the differences between Roman and Irish churches in the early Medieval period; the Protestant Reformation, ending in the multiplicity of fully autonomous denominations; the story of Marxism, with its century-and-a-half-long quarrel between revolutionists and reformers, and so forth. We have seen above that this also applies to the Pharisees, in view of the Hillelite–Shammaite debate, involving at times issues of considerable importance, such as the relationship with the gentiles. Likewise, in the *Bellum*, Josephus explicitly recognizes that along with the Essenes practicing celibacy, there existed yet another 'order' under their name "of the same mind with the rest as regards the way of life, behavior and rules, but differing in their view on marriage" (2, 160). That some such division within the same movement could have taken place is supported by the Qumran material (whatever the provenance of individual texts might have been): the two major documents (CD and 1QS) speak, respectively, of different – married and celibate – communities. There might have also been some difference of nuance in the religious beliefs among the Essenes, perhaps concerning eschatology, but on this Josephus, following his customary strategy, is silent. Otherwise, his statement on the Essene 'theology', when stripped of 'Hellenizing' trappings, makes sense: they are said to have considered the human soul imperishable and immortal and subject to posthumous rewards in the case of the virtuous and eternal punishment for the wicked (153 ff.). (This last point implies a strict moral dichotomy, which Josephus, as we have seen, also attributes to the Pharisees. The Qumran writings, however, divulge it in extreme form, and more exclusivist than one finds in the rabbinic corpus or in the extant Pseudo-epigrapha, approaching what may be called – colloquially – 'Manichaeism' *avant-la-lettre*: a small minority, called 'Sons of Light', consisting, as it seems, only of the writers themselves and their following, will survive and triumph in the eschatological war under divine leadership against the rest of humanity, labeled 'Sons of Darkness', who are going to perish, physically and spiritually, forever.)

Taken alone, the material in Philo and Josephus makes it difficult to specify the origin and character of the Essene religious dissent. For the lack of the evidence to the contrary, it must be assumed that they constituted a non-violent movement which chose to withdraw, as far as they could, from the corrupt reality, rather than transform the latter through the use of violence or even public preaching, irrespective of whatever eschatological expectations they might have entertained. In other words, similarly to both the Sadducees and the Pharisees, the Essenes did not partake in the revolt against the Romans *as a body*, though it does not exclude that individual members of the sect could have joined the rebels' ranks. (I will discuss one such possible case, of a man called by Josephus "John the Essene", in a later chapter.)

One passage from the Essene digression in the *Bellum*, however, requires special attention:

> The war with the Romans altogether tested their souls, in the course of which, while twisted and sprained, burned and broken, and suffering every instrument of torture meant to make them blaspheme against their lawgiver or eat something improper; they did no such thing, never flattering their tormentors or crying out. But smiling in their agony and deriding those responsible for their tortures, they cheerfully released their souls, so that they could recover them again.
>
> (2, 152 f.)

Although Josephus praised in similar language the endurance of the conspirators against Herod and his Pharisaic opponents (*AJ*, 15, 288 ff.; 17, 152 ff.; cf. *BJ*, 1, 653) as well as the *sicarii* executed in Egypt (*BJ*, 7, 416 ff.), the quote just cited provides one of his strongest anti-Roman statements. Read in the context, it portrays these unidentified Essenes as innocent and pious victims fallen into the hands of a cruel enemy subjecting them to mockery and physical affliction, who nonetheless triumph spiritually by virtue of their creed. It follows that Josephus meant implicitly to condemn the occupiers by reporting their persecution even of the Jews, who *a priori* could not have joined the revolt due to their withdrawal from the world. Envisioning these particular people as insurgents would have diminished the power of his rhetoric, and it is unlikely that here he was celebrating any revolutionary militants, whom he learned to hate and hold in contempt.[7]

If it is true that outside reporters, like Philo and Josephus, do not provide enough information for a deeper inquiry, one is tempted to say that what is considered by many 'inside' sources – namely, the Dead Sea Scrolls – coupled with the archaeological findings offer too much of it. As I have stated above, this material seems increasingly contradictory and resists harmonization. Two factors, however, look fairly certain: influential experts still hold that the totality of the data points towards the Essene origin of the entire complex, or – phrasing this more cautiously – that it signifies a variety (or varieties) of Essenism:

objections to this, or alternative explanations, have so far proved less persuasive. Despite various discrepancies, the similarities between Josephus's Essene digression in the *Bellum* and the whole gamut of features, characterizing life within the Qumran community, prevail – pointing, at the very least, to the close interdependence, which defies stricter definition, of these two kindred 'sects', with their boundaries somewhat blurred.

Next, the discovery of the scrolls in close proximity to the settlement at Qumran strongly suggests that the former belonged to the latter. But it does not follow that all these manuscripts must have been produced on the spot. Sometimes they reflect divergent views on aspects of communal existence and other matters, indicating that a number of them could have been written elsewhere and purchased or brought in by the successive membership in the group.

At present, several facts complicate a coherent interpretation of the material at hand. As I have mentioned, two major Qumran texts describe different types of religious communities. Some details of New Covenant in the so-called *Damascus Document* (CD), also known as *The Zadokite Fragments*, are said to address the entire Israel (presumably, in eschatological perspective), while other particulars in the same text involve a closer, currently existent association, distinct from the rest, but family-based and pursuing an ever more pious and chaste lifestyle. Furthermore, this document claims that the movement it represents originated "in the land of Damascus" (A.6:5, 19; 7: 14 f., 16 ff.; 8: 21; B.19: 33 f.; 20:12) and was eventually given shape by a figure famously called the Teacher of Righteousness, who entered into a conflict with a Wicked Priest and an apostate Man of Lie (or the Liar); on the identity of both, scholars endlessly speculate. In contrast, the so-called *Community Rule*, or *Manual of Discipline* (1QS), which is a sort of charter, postulates a tightly organized elite community of men (*yahad*), practicing celibacy and extreme ritual purity, with no women or children ever mentioned. The question is whether and how these two different collectives could have coexisted on the same grounds or even belonged to the same religious movement – although Josephus testifies, as we have seen, that the Essenes considered legitimate both ways of life, marital and celibate. In any event, it is clear that the break with the Temple at Jerusalem was carried out by both the Essenes and Qumranites: the latter community actually seems to have conceived of itself spiritually as a Temple.

Other problems result from archaeology, which has demonstrated that some structures and artifacts, most recently excavated at Qumran, do not square with requirements articulated in the scrolls. Among these findings are a few luxury objects, in contradiction to the claims of asceticism; the proof that the inhabitants of the site were engaged in pottery production, a fact the extant writings never cite; and – perhaps, most tellingly – the earlier discovery of the toilet (Locus 51), despite strict injunctions against any such thing on residential territory in several texts (*1QT*, 46:13 ff.; *1QM*, 7:6 f.), indirectly confirmed by Josephus (*BJ*, 2, 148 f.). To this must be added the currently insoluble (and highly controversial) puzzle of the Qumran cemetery, which exhibits inconsistent burial customs and, although predominantly male, still includes women's remains – altogether scarce, as it seems, to accord with the *Damascus Document*, but too many for fitting the *Community Rule*. It is not surprising that specialists came to wonder what kind of settlement Qumran was, and whether it could actually have been Essene, otherwise sectarian, or even religious.

It seems to me nonetheless that, unless further contradictory material is uncovered, the hypothesis should be preferred which considers Qumran a community of religious dissenters (most likely, related to the Essene movement), who voluntarily withdrew from ordinary life, regarding it as sinful, who repudiated customary worship as profaned, believing themselves to have been the recipients of a secret revelation and a promise for a special dispensation by God. Although it still does not remove a series of minor problems, this interpretation makes greater sense than the alternative proposals (Qumran as a rustic villa, a pottery factory or a military fort), which are less plausible on a variety of grounds and weakly argued. There is no reason to deny the possibility for peaceful coexistence, within the essentially same sectarian movement, of two groups holding similar 'theological' views, but with different attitudes toward marriage and procreation. History offers such examples: for instance, the Cathars (likewise, the practitioners of religious dissent) in the medieval Languedoc, where a large married population, the *credentes* ('believers'), embraced and revered the ascetic elite called the 'perfect' (*perfecti*). Conversely, the Qumran sect might have started as homogeneous, accepting women and recognizing formal marriage, but later transformed into the narrower *yahad*, with its exclusive membership of celibate men – in which case the *Damascus Document* must have predated the composition of *Community Rules*. Further (and much smaller) discrepancies between the scrolls can be explained either in terms of different chronology or by their different provenance. They could have been written at various moments throughout the sect's history – and history is always a process of change; or produced at diverse locations and environments. In fact, both the *Damascus Document* and the *Community Rule* imply that they address not an audience confined in one specific place, but clusters of the faithful across the entire land. The texts might have originally belonged to individual members before they joined this particular branch of the sect and then accumulated as a common property. The argument that the scrolls had originally been the product of the Jerusalem priests, and then hurriedly hidden by the latter in caves to avoid their falling into Roman hands, does not hold: many pronouncements they contain are directed precisely against the Temple leadership, who thus would not have been interested in their preservation.

The discovery of luxury items at Qumran does not necessarily undercut the Essene hypothesis either: like some scrolls, it could signify bequests or contributions by members upon entering the commune and considered the property of all. On the other hand, I cannot fully rule out that the group might have undergone stages when the enforcement and observance of the rules slackened (humans are known for often not living up to their ideals), and such luxury objects were tolerated, perhaps for their aesthetic or sentimental value.

The pottery production at the settlement is equally explicable: no such community could subsist exclusively on agriculture; some form of limited trade, or bartering, had to be expected. In fact, Josephus implies that the Essenes did possess a variety of skills (*BJ*, 2, 129). Again, the European Middle Ages provide a possible parallel: monasteries, despite their ascetic practices and the ban on private ownership, could still amass a considerable wealth and engage in trade and crafts.

Finally, the Qumran cemetery still remains largely unexplored, in part, owing to the religious sensibilities of the present day inhabitants in the area, Jewish and Islamic. The dating of individual graves is very difficult, and the matter is further aggravated by the later intrusive burials, many of them Moslem. In summary, until and unless the cemetery is thoroughly excavated, the material it may contain cannot be interpreted with any degree of confidence.

Despite several hints (which require decoding) in the scrolls, next to nothing can be said about the events of Qumran's history. We are not even certain that the place had been inhabited continually by the same people or sect. It cannot be established whether the latter originated in exile at Damascus, as is implied in CD (for example, 8, 21), or whether this is a foundational myth. The causes of the sect's secession remain equally unclear. An earlier theory that the break came through the usurpation of the high priesthood by Jonathan Maccabaeus (153 B.C.), and that it was initiated by the hereditary Zadokite priests, who withdrew to Qumran, seems now undermined, largely by the argument from silence, since the extant scrolls never mention *explicite* any such issue; as for their references to "the sons of Zadok" (for example, *1QS* 5), the expression is not necessarily meant to be literal, but honorific. The archaeological and paleographical data do not support this early date, and suggest the end of the second and the beginning of the first century B.C. as a starting point. If it were so, the original dispute might have been caused by differences over matters of law, ritual and calendar and then extended into 'theological' and moral condemnation. In this view, the conflict between the Teacher of Righteousness and the Wicked Priest represents just one historical episode (regrettably, absent from Josephus) that could have occurred at some point in his career. In any event, it appears that the peak of the Qumran sect's activity, including the production of the scrolls, falls in the late Hasmonean or early Herodian period, around the mid-first century B.C. One major text, however, seems to have been directed specifically against the Romans, on which I will comment shortly. No coins were discovered at the site later than A.D. 68, and archaeology makes it clear that it was violently destroyed, no doubt by the Romans in the course of the Jewish War.[8]

Two major Qumran documents – *The Temple Scroll* (*11QT*) and *The War Scroll* (*1QM*) – not only demonstrate in full their authors' (whoever they might have been) religious dissent, but also reveal its strikingly imaginative qualities as well as the wishful thinking on the scale that, as it will be seen, could defy, along with the socio-cultural reality, the principles of nature. Both texts represent visionary utopias, peaceful and militant, respectively, taking place prior to or during the eschatological crisis. They combine the aspiration to restore and magnify Israel's former glory and for the supernatural interference that would change the very order of human life. This is not, however, a place to analyze these two compositions in detail. The first document (very poorly preserved) offers, beside the material on law, ritual and kingship, a remarkably specified blueprint for constructing an enormous and perfect Temple to replace the current one, so that it could meet the highest requirement of ritual purity and provide a worthier dwelling for the Almighty – a project patently directed against the existent priesthood and their practices. This vision is largely, but not wholly, derived from the Torah, with the characteristic use of first person speech as addressed by God to Moses, even when it involves altering the third person biblical passages. This interference with the scriptural text, although merely stylistic, seems nonetheless to imply that the author(s) thought to be transmitting a special revelation. According to the scroll, the supreme purity should also reign, by extension, in the entire holy city Jerusalem, which houses the sanctuary where God resides. This requires, we read not without some sense of astonishment, relegating men and women outside the walls for the performance of marital duties, and – furthermore – building toilets beyond its confines "with the minimum distance from the city of three thousand cubits [i.e., about 1.5 kilometers! – V.R.]" (46:13 ff.; cf. 45:11 f.). Thus, the mentality of religious dissent chose to ignore, in pursuit of the desirable, even elementary physiological needs.

No less surprising is the second document (also known as *The War of the Sons of Light against the Sons of Darkness*), the provenance and dating of which (as is usual with Qumran) is debated, although many believe that the name *Kittim*, applied to some eschatological adversaries in this text, signifies the Romans. Filled with biblical and prophetic imagery, it describes, in minute detail, the battle order and organization of the triumphant and pious sectarian army ("the exiles of the wilderness" – 1:2), led, on one hand, by the priests, and, on another, by the angels into a sort of Armageddon. Their enemies, "sons of Belial" (apparently, all other nations – cf. 4:12; 6:6; 11:13, 15 *et passim*), include "those, who violate the covenant" (one assumes, the Jews not belonging to the sect – 1:2), and are doomed all to be defeated, exterminated, or enslaved (cf.1:5 ff., 10 f.). This text's strict moral and theological dualism, as well as the motif of ultimate confrontation between Good and Evil, recurs in many Pseudepigrapha (and in the Book of Revelation). But its blend of visionary fantasy, bordering on the supernatural, and concrete military thinking, makes it virtually unique. It has been argued that the author(s) utilized not only biblical references and precedents, but also the gentile manuals on tactics. One is particularly impressed by the utter and pervasive conviction on the part of the only few hundred (at best) sectarians that they were specifically chosen to fulfill, even if only in some indeterminate future, God's own ultimate intent – as it transpires, for instance, from the following:

> For the battle is yours! With the might of your hand their corpses have been torn to pieces with no-one to bury (them) / ... / For the battle is

yours! And it is from you that power comes, and not from our own being. It is not our might nor the power of our own hands which performs these marvels, except by your great strength and by your mighty deeds.

(11:1 ff.; cf. 1:10 ff.; 3:2 ff.; 9:8 ff. *et passim*)

It is left unclear in both scrolls how the grandiose developments they envisage could be practically achieved, given the huge effort needed to mobilize the masses to construct the colossal new Temple, or fighting the epic battle with the 'nations', and altogether the absence of references to missionary or propaganda activities in the Qumran texts. Perhaps they did not even try rationally to bridge this gap: two issues, 'theoretical' and 'practical', might well have partaken in different compartments of the sectarian mindset that interacted through the all-powerful leap of faith.

The War Scroll may appear seriously to question Josephus's and Philo's portrayal of the Essenes (or the quasi-Essene kindred groups, one of which must have been the Qumranites) as peaceful and non-violent religious dissenters. But this is not necessarily so. In the first place, there is no reason to read into this text some sort of 'ideology' typical of the entire Essene movement. I find it difficult to envisage people as withdrawn from the world, as were the majority of the Essenes, living in perpetual suspense and expectation of the immediate warfare on so grand a scale in which they would be required to participate *en masse*; rather, the text reflects the aspirations of a much smaller group, consisting of its author(s) and his/their following, who may or may not have resided at Qumran. It may characterize just one, perhaps even an aberrant, strand within the broadly conceived 'Essenism'. Next, it is clear that one deals here with a 'futurological' fantasy, not real, but potential violence and in the end totally unrealistic. Finally, the emphasis in the scroll is placed on the divine nature of the whole enterprise that, by definition, cannot be initiated by mere humans, however pious. It implies that, before taking up arms, "the exiles of the wilderness" were to wait for an unequivocal signal from God that the time for the final battle had arrived; how to recognize and correctly interpret any such thing remained a problem. A penchant for misreading reality in terms of omens and the desire for miracles seems to have permeated the period, as is famously observed by the Apostle: "For Jews demand signs (*semea*) and Greeks seek wisdom" (*1 Cor.*, 1: 22). Consequently, Paul felt much preoccupied with 'distinguishing between the spirits' (ibid, 12:1 ff.; cf. *I John*, 4:1: "Beloved, do not believe every spirit, but test the spirits to see whether they are of God; for many false prophets have gone out into the world," etc.). Commonsense suggests that this was a matter of concern for not only the incipient Christian movement, but (*mutatis mutandis*) for any passionate believer, especially since a number of self-proclaimed prophets at the time failed to demonstrate that they had indeed been endorsed by God. In sum, *The War Scroll* is, first and foremost, a remarkable testimony to the power of wishful thinking, a major psychological trait inherent in both violent and non-violent religious dissent. But it still does not justify – given the lack of evidence for their actual and voluntary involvement in any bloodshed – placing the Essenes, or even the Qumranites, in the same category as the revolutionary zealots, *sicarii* and their ilk, with whom this book is primarily concerned.

This said, the Essene movement (so long as we associate it, directly or not, with the Qumran texts) must have been substantially Messianic, irrespective of Josephus's choice to omit this fact. Furthermore, the scrolls provide for the eventual arrival of two Messiahs, the royal and the priestly (e.g., *1QS*, 9:11 – "the anointed of Israel and Aaron"), accompanied by yet a third (and elusive) figure, an eschatological Prophet (ibid). The candidates for some such role had been also cropping up in society at large. In the course of this study I will repeatedly refer to the Messianic (or quasi-Messianic) episodes, recorded by Josephus, and other aspects of the same phenomenon. It is difficult, however, if not impossible, to establish a direct link between visionary products, such as *The War Scroll*, or some apocalyptic Pseudepigrapha, and the emergence of individual pretenders with their following, who were bent on the immediate revolution. The violent imagery and allegory these writings contain, coupled with the alleged divine promises, may have served, directly or indirectly, an inflammatory purpose. But this is as much as one can say without indulging in unwarranted speculation.

I find it fair to assume that all writings from the scrolls constituted, in one sense or another, the stuff of sectarian beliefs, soliciting their response, both intellectual and passionate, to the ideas, imagery and symbolism they contained. As I have earlier suggested, it seems unlikely that they were bothered by what we consider contradictions or inconsistencies in these texts: the religious mind operates differently from prescriptions of scholarly logic, and there hardly exists a major document in world religions, which is entirely devoid of contradictory elements. Furthermore, we know from history that various religious, quasi-religious and 'ideological' movements tend to subsume texts or ideas, which preceded them, even differing in details, sometimes substantial, in terms of *Weltanschauung* – provided they can be claimed to have anticipated, in one sense or another, some important tenets of the sect's or movement's current position. In that case, such material is incorporated in the latter group's special thesaurus, while the points of contradiction are ignored, or (more or less awkwardly) explained away. The relationship of the Old and New Testaments makes, in fact, a prominent example.

The present day Qumran scholarship being fraught with multiple problems, perhaps the most difficult issue is a 'mysterial' or 'esoteric' aspect of the sect's world outlook. The term 'esotericism' implies, first and foremost, the transmission of some special knowledge, orally or in writing, within a close group of privileged individuals who are willing and allowed to receive it because of their spiritual and moral worth. This usually involves secrecy, several stages of initiation and a feeling of mystical communion with the divine. By definition, sharing esoteric knowledge with outsiders (the *profani*) is prohibited, and its adepts (in theory) voluntarily submit to strict discipline. Thus broadly understood, the phenomenon of esotericism, often signifying some variety of religious dissent, recurs in various cultures and historical periods to the present day and, as a term, remains a convenient tool for academic inquiry. Josephus insists on secrecy among the Essenes (*BJ*, 2, 141 f.) and informs us of the initiatory period they practiced (137 ff.). Similarly, the Qumran material provides ample evidence meeting the basic criteria of esotericism: the scrolls repeatedly refer to 'secret knowledge' and the need for separation from the rest (e.g., *1QS*, 4:5 f.; 8: 13 ff.; 9:16 ff.; 10, 24 f.; cf. *CD*, 6:14 f.; 13:14 f.), and several are encrypted (the most well known is the so-called *Horoscope: 4Q186Cryptic*). Any effort to penetrate the sect's 'secrets' or 'mysticism' requires a very close scrutiny of all available texts from Qumran, and comparison with closer parallels in other historical and cultural settings. This special scholarly endeavor has already begun. For the present study, it is sufficient to point out that the emphasis on teaching and interpreting the scripture, on meditation and contemplation, supports the view of the Qumran community (despite the *War Scroll*'s militant eschatology) as essentially non-violent and withdrawn to consider any immediate action. This would be in accord with most, though by no means all, esoteric movements in history. It seems that they were living in a time continuum where the past, in the form of scriptural precedents and prophetic pronouncements, by exegetical application, could govern the present and be projected into the future. This belongs among characteristic features of religious dissent, whether exoteric or esoteric. Regarding the notion of mysticism, I suggest that, in the latter case, as it was with the Qumranites, the sense of union with God could have been achieved by the fusion of individual or group meditative/contemplative (and, possibly, ecstatic) experience and secretly transmitted knowledge taken for ultimate truth, with the two components enhancing each other.

The existent evidence, in my view, does not allow any inference as to whether the sectarian writings found at Qumran influenced the attitudes and behavior of outsiders. We know that the community guarded its secrets, which must have included the texts they saw as close or equivalent to Scripture, the content revealed to them by God's special dispensation. We cannot say with any certainty what scrolls would have fallen into that category – the *Damascus Document*, the *Temple Scroll*, the mysterious *Book of Hagi* or any other? Is it possible, for instance, that the *War Scroll* circulated in society at large and contributed to the growth of religious and political violence? We do not know. If at least some of this material found its way out of Qumran, my guess is that it might have aroused interest across narrow 'sectarian' or social boundaries. Two small facts, though, deserve some attention. The document known as *The Halakhic Letter* (*4QMMT*, almost certainly exoteric) repudiates the gentile offerings and sacrifices at the Temple (8 ff.) and, as it will be shown, the termination of the Imperial sacrifices by the dissenting priestly group in A.D. 66 served as a formal *casus belli* for the Jewish War. On the other hand, this may have been a separate development, indicating that this issue was becoming a matter of concern also elsewhere in society.

Similarly, it might be of some significance that the copy of the Qumranic hymn (*4QSongs of the Sabbath Sacrifice*) was found during the excavations at Masada.

The most enigmatic Qumran text concerns, ironically, an earthly rather than celestial mystery. This is the *Copper Scroll* (*3Q15*), which purports, in code, to convey information about locations with hidden treasure. It is an artifact of unknown provenience and almost certainly did not belong to the sect's original collection; nor is it possible to ascertain whether the treasure it describes is reality or a piece of folklore, if not some elaborate hoax. This has not, however, prevented several attempts to discover the alleged valuables following the directions in the scroll with, so far, no result, reminding one of other futile quests for the Cathars' gold, the Templars' gold or the Holy Grail.[9]

At this point, two developments should be mentioned, the characters of which (in terms of this book) are debatable: whether they can be categorized as forms of religious dissent within Judaism, as separate religions, or as borderline cases – namely, Samaritanism and the incipient Christian church. Neither group used violence, in any regular sense, as a method of self-assertion, a route to domination, or a means to implement the – supposedly – divine will; therefore, they are essentially outside the confines of the present inquiry. Still, some basic comments on both are required, first, to complete this survey of the religious (non-pagan) environment in Judaea during the late Roman period, and, second, to establish, if only approximately, their status *vis-à-vis* 'mainstream' Judaism.

The Samaritans of the Second Temple period claimed to have descended from the people who inhabited the Northern Kingdom of Israel (with Samaria as its capital) before it was taken over by the Assyrians in 722 (or 720) B.C. Although the matter is still a subject of controversy, it appears that, while the local elites were deported by the conquerors (who at the time practiced large-scale forced transfers of peoples) to Mesopotamia, much of the grassroots population was left intact and partially intermingled with the new settlers from the various ethnic origins.

It seems certain that upon receiving permission from the Persian authorities to return to Judaea from the Babylonian exile (late 16th century B.C.), the repatriates eventually entered a conflict with the remnants of the Israelites still inhabiting the land, and the former denied the latter religious fellowship on the grounds of their assimilation and intermarriages with non-Jews (*1Ezra*, 4:1 ff.; *Neh.*, 13:23 ff.; cf. 10:30). Similarly, they were refused the access to and worship at the Second Temple (which the returnees had started to erect), an act that the Samaritan tradition attributes to the biblical figure of Ezra (they called him "Ezra the Cursed"), who allegedly re-established in the former Judah the primacy of the Torah and Law; among other things, he is said to have initiated mandatory divorce proceedings between Jews and their non-Jewish wives (*1Ezra*, 9:1 ff.). Consequently, the rejected "people of the land" (ibid, 4:4) chose for their sacred place of worship, as different from Jerusalem, Mount Gerizim, where they built their temple, in the neighborhood of the ancient city Shechem, long venerated in the earlier Northern Kingdom.

One should, however, keep in mind, as regards our sources, especially, Josephus, an important terminological problem – that is, distinguishing between the 'Samarians', the people of various descriptions living in the territory that had belonged in the past to the Kingdom of Israel, and the 'Samaritans', the practitioners of the Samaritan religion as it exists to the present day; sometimes this is difficult or even impossible to achieve. The original quarrel may have resulted in the foundation of the sanctuary on Mount Gerizim, but this did not mean that the Samaritan 'sect', with its specific religious and cultic characteristics, was already active, since that process took several centuries. It seems telling, however, that they did not participate in the Maccabean revolt (167–164 B.C.) against the Hellenistic rule of the Seleucids; only after the military campaign of the Hasmonean ruler John Hyrcanus (I), who conquered their country and burned down their Mount Gerizim settlement and their temple (between 113 and 110 B.C.), did the schism become irrevocable and final. The subsequent mutual hostility accounts for the consistent anti-Jewish stand taken by the Samaritans at times of trouble: they sided with Herod I against his rebellious Jewish subjects, and then with the Romans, until the outbreak of the Great Revolt, in which they finally participated, to their detriment.

Upon his assumption of kingship, Herod I rebuilt the city of Samaria, on the model of the Greek polis, and renamed it Sebaste to honor Augustus. Its population quickly became mixed, and it is impossible to ascertain the percentage of (religious) Samaritans living there. Nor can one even speculate on their number (if any) among the infamous 'Sebastenian' troops created by Herod from the non-Jewish populace, who were sometimes used to suppress riots and certainly contributed to ethnic and religious strife in the region. Although the problem of differentiating the 'Samarians' (as an ethnic/geographical entity) from the Samaritans proper remains, the context makes it clear that the specific episodes of their conflicts *vis-à-vis* the Jews or the Romans in this period as recorded by Josephus refer to practitioners of the Samaritan faith.[10]

The Samaritan religion, so far it can be ascertained during the Roman period, differed from ordinary Judaism primarily in two respects: the texts considered Scriptures and the location of the sacred grounds in which God was believed to dwell. For a religious mind, both aspects are hugely significant – a fact the secular imagination finds increasingly difficult to appreciate. Despite scholarly efforts, initiated by authors such as Mircea Eliade, the modern Western liberal intellect largely refuses to recognize the psychological reality of the sacred for those who believe in it. For them, this reality is absolute and transcendental, partaking in the divine; individual and collective destinies depend on it both in this life and thereafter. Word and Space, transfused with this sense of sacredness, thus often become major objects of passionate veneration.

The Samaritans recognized as Scripture only their own idiosyncratic version of the Pentateuch, which contains about 6000 variations from the Masoretic Text, a significant number reflecting Samaritan historical, ritualistic and theological concerns (thus, for instance, the mention of Mount Gerizim is inserted even in the Decalogue – *SP, Exod.*, 20:17). They did not acknowledge the rest of the Hebrew Bible (*Tanah*) as sacred, although revering (but not as Scripture) the so-called *Samaritan Book of Joshua*, substantially different in both content and perspective from the biblical prototype. The Qumran sectarians (and, presumably, the Essenes) never denied the sacredness of the grounds on which the Jerusalem Temple stood: their objections pertained to it having been ritually profaned by the corrupt priesthood, and – as we have seen – they envisaged its perfectionist reconstitution towards the End of Days on exactly the same place. Samaritans, on the other hand, completely repudiated the legitimacy of Jerusalem as the holy city and its Temple as God's chosen seat of residence, replacing it with their shrine on Mount Gerizim.

These divergences might provide for considering the two religions separate, but it is no less important that this was how *both* communities regarded each other, in terms of self-identification, for over two millennia, and continue to the present day, with about 600 Samaritans living as a cluster in Israel and still practicing animal sacrifices on Mount Gerizim. Religious phenomena often resist strict criteria for categorization. They fluctuate, depending on historical and cultural contexts, in their tendencies towards exclusivity or interaction; they may remain a fringe case (or 'heresy') within a larger development or turn into a new and full-scale religious movement: relatively modern examples of this diversity in form and stages would be the Mormons, the Rastafaris and the Bahais. This accounts for the legitimate lack of consensus among scholars on the status of Samaritanism as a religion: I am inclined to describe it, at least, in Antiquity, as intermediate (or 'borderline') between a 'sect' and a 'church'. What matters, however, is the essentially non-violent character of their dissent, perhaps owing to the very paucity of its carriers.[11]

Within the format of this study I will not be able to discuss, even on a most superficial level, the origin and early history of Christianity during its formative period, the so-called Apostolic generation. Apart from the question of the historical Jesus, his mission, career, trial and crucifixion, the cluster of issues, any aspect of which, one fears, will never cease generating scholarly controversy and conflicting passions, ideological and methodological bias on all sides, be they Catholic, Protestant, Jewish, atheist or postmodernist, make any such enterprise exceedingly problematic. Although I realize that my eschewing this material is to an extent artificial, and that no firm demarcation can be postulated for much of Antiquity between the historical vicissitudes of Jews and Christians, any deeper foray into their interaction requires a separate and laborious endeavor. One fact, furthermore, places this theme beyond my immediate concerns here: the pronouncedly non-violent character of Christian dissent within Judaism in the period under consideration. In later chapters, however, I will briefly dwell on a few episodes largely taken from the *Book of Acts*, to illustrate the point.

One delicate matter still needs a comment. The procedures of the form and style of critical school notwithstanding, one cannot simply dismiss as fiction evidence from the *Acts* (and partly Josephus) on the initial harassment of the incipient Christian communities and their leaders by Jewish religious authorities, nor that this must have contributed to the bringing upon the nascent Church censure and persecution on the part of the Romans: without these pressures Christianity would not have realized or shaped itself the way it did.

In view of the subsequent tragic relationship of the two religions over the course of millennia, it is hardly becoming to insist that the original blame must be placed on one side only. To my mind, history, both as a process and a study, is an ethical enterprise, and the discrimination against the Jews, starting almost as soon as Christianity became the Roman Empire's dominant religion (speaking not about their full-scale persecutions throughout the entire Middle Ages up to the horrors of the Holocaust), cannot be ignored. I prefer not to seek condemnation of or apology for either side, but consider their earliest conflict as one of most painful examples in the history of internecine strife.

The intensity of the conflict is nonetheless surprising, given the toleration within Second Temple Judaism of its various forms and practices, the absence of the concept of 'heresy' (in the ecclesiastical sense) and the basic compliance of the nascent Christian communities towards religious and secular authorities – in sharp contrast, for instance, to the bearers of "fourth philosophy" and similar movements indulging in violent attacks upon the establishment. Without arguing this at any length, I would suggest that it was the decree of the first Apostolic Council at Jerusalem (*Acts*, 15), relieving the new Christian proselytes from most prescriptions of Mosaic Law as regards ritual, dietary code, various purity requirements and, last but not the least, circumcision, which proved, in the final analysis, a breaking point and ultimately generated hostility between two religions, the old and the new. Christian universalism, Messianic aspects, even the attitude towards the Temple and the claim of divinity for Christ, must have played their role, but it all was subordinate, in my opinion, to the abandonment of major Torahic traditions and what is often referred to as Pauline replacement of Law with Grace. Not only for the Temple authorities, but also in the eyes of lay pious Jews these developments were tantamount to a breach of the Covenant and threatened the welfare of Israel. From that point onwards Christianity changed from being a form of religious dissent within Judaism into a different missionary movement with an unforeseeable future.[12]

I do not intend here to engage in the longstanding debate on the missionary dimension within Judaism of the Second Temple period. One can discern in it various attitudes towards proselytism: for the most part, it appears that the converts were welcome, provided that legal and ritualist proprieties were observed, but were not sought or encouraged with particular zeal, and it remains unclear in which cases they could or could not have been considered the *bona fide* Jews. On the other hand, individual gentiles, seeking higher spirituality against the background of the traditional Greco-Roman religion that entered the period of decline, could have found a special appeal in the robust and vibrant Jewish monotheism and felt prepared to embrace even those aspects of it they might have considered idiosyncratic. The requirement of circumcision constituted a major obstacle in the case of Greek and Roman males, but other Near Eastern people had been practicing it, in one way or another, for centuries; furthermore, there was nothing like it to endure in the case of women.

There was at least one spectacular episode of conversion to Judaism (ca. A.D. 41–47) by the entire royal family of Adiabene under King Izates II, which Josephus describes in detail, not without a sense of pride (*AJ*, 20, 17–54). The recent neophytes showed, as often happens, inordinate enthusiasm regarding their new faith and co-religionists: thus Queen Helena, while visiting Jerusalem at the time of famine, undertook a considerable relief effort to feed the needy (51 ff.); and a few decades later, members of the royal clan took part in the Jewish revolt against Rome (*BJ*, 2, 520). It is clear that the Adiabene conversion was voluntary and genuine: in the way Josephus portrays it, even the initiative came from the would-be proselytes. An opposite example is the conquest of Idumaea in 104–103 B.C. by the Hasmonean ruler John Hyrcanus I, with the imposition of the Mosaic Law on its inhabitants and, according to Josephus, their forced circumcision (*AJ*, 13, 257 ff.). It does not seem, however, that this compulsory conversion proved particularly successful: as will be seen, the worship of tribal gods persisted among the Idumaeans, and there is evidence that they were not considered by many Jews legitimate Israelites, which caused problems for the half-Idumaean upstart Herod I throughout his reign. It is true that they joined the anti-Roman uprising, but so did the Samaritans; in both cases the motives would have been other than religious solidarity. Finally, Galilee represented a sort of a middle ground. On the one hand, the inhabitants venerated the God of Israel and followed basic Torahic requirements, such as observance of the Sabbath, participating in religious festivals and collection of tithes; on the other, due to several centuries of foreign rule they preserved a variety of local traditions, were involved in local conflicts, and regarded the Temple authorities in Jerusalem as remote and not too relevant. I will occasionally comment on certain aspects of these environments further in this book's narrative.

Lastly, but not the least, one must take into account the complexity of the relationship between the Jews and their gentile – that is, Greco-Syrian neighbors in Palaestina. Apart from Jerusalem, and predominantly (sometimes perhaps exclusively) Jewish towns and villages, there existed across the country many cities with an ethnically mixed population, organized as the Hellenistic *poleis*, such as Caesarea Maritima, Ptolemais or those of the Decapolis. There must have been some among those gentiles, attracted to the Jewish faith, the so-called "God-fearers", who accepted certain precepts of Judaism, short of a full-scale conversion; their number would be altogether small. Conversely, the process of Hellenization among the educated Jews, and especially the Herodian royalty, did not fully stop either, but its effects seem to have been insignificant, as compared with the situation that preceded the Maccabean crisis.

None of this could have counterbalanced the continuous tensions generated by the two communities, gentile and Jewish, despite the need for side-by-side coexistence, trade and mutual accommodation. These tensions, often breaking into conflicts, took multiple forms and were caused by many factors, among them, gentile xenophobia, Jewish exclusivism, local power struggles, the issue of equal civic rights (*isopoliteia*) and so forth. Since the Romans, for political and cultural reasons, tended to support Greco-Syrians at the expense of the Jews, it is not surprising that the predicament proved disruptive, sometimes dramatically so, contributing to the deterioration of the status quo. This will be taken note of in what follows, when required.[13]

II.

As we have repeatedly seen, the major problem for any in-depth study of Second Temple Judaism, especially during the Roman period, arises from the condition of our sources, with their specific priorities, concerns and procedures: the mentality they represent is different from ours. Furthermore, we possess, in the final analysis, only fragments of information on different scales rather than a historical continuum: a collection of bones, some of them big, but still insufficient to fully reconstruct an antediluvian organism. This vitiates the efforts to produce a historical interpretation of the period, as regards both the detail and the basic paradigms that would be logically and methodologically satisfying, and to work towards the achievement of scholarly consensus. The literary evidence at our disposal is heterogeneous, from Josephus's historical and apologetic writings, pervasively biased because of his complex agenda; to Philo's philosophical/theological/exegetical tracts, written in the spirit of Jewish universalism; to the New Testament and the Tannaitic texts, the value of which for historical developments prior to the destruction of the Temple by the Romans is increasingly questioned; to the Pseudepigraphic visionary narratives that survived in different languages, often with subsequent Christian interpolations and which, for the most part, are difficult to date. All this material is fraught with huge factual gaps and has been repeatedly challenged by new archaeological findings.

The situation is further complicated by the gamut of argumentative strategies that have become prevalent among students in the field during recent decades, which – with all due respect for their many accomplishments – seems to have led to the current interpretative chaos. A number of these procedures, some following the characteristic tendency of postmodernist thought to simplify the complex and complicate the simple, are methodologically flawed. Below is the list of those to which I particularly object.

The most obvious, perhaps, is the abuse of the argument from silence.

It is often implied that if a piece of evidence or a fact is mentioned in one source but not supported elsewhere, it must perforce be discarded. Given the fragmentary nature of most of our data, this seems to me a fallacy. There could be multiple reasons, of which we have not the slightest idea, for a particular author, such as Josephus, or the compilers of the Mishnah, to omit or ignore this or that information, and our guesswork at exactly why, more often than one would wish, only obfuscates the issue. In consequence, I believe, the *argumentum ex silentio* should be applied most judiciously only upon a close scrutiny of context, both literary and historical, and it may be wiser sometimes to confess ignorance rather than speculate on possible motives for this or that omission. Less apparent but occasionally troublesome are problems involved in inductive reasoning, which is known to cause errors even in mathematics. On the one hand, it seems legitimate to use details or individual examples, militating against summaries or generalities, found in our sources, and thus debunk the latter; on the other hand, such particulars may constitute exceptions that, at least in some cases, ultimately confirm the rules. One must also remember that if our source had been offering a generalization on some contemporary issue, bound to become a matter of common knowledge, or at least be preserved within living memory, then the audience, or some parts of it, must have taken such statements as acceptable, since otherwise the author in question would seriously undercut his own credibility – the point I will expand on later in this section. Like the argument from silence, inductive procedures should be employed with considerable caution, observing the law of the least common denominator, which is, regrettably, not always the case. Further, one feels surprised by how many current scholars are extremist in their formulations and thus *implicite* exclusivist: more often than not, their arguments tend to kill each other. The experience suggests that, for the most part, the reality lies somewhere in the middle. Given our insufficient data, it does happen that *tertium datur* and the historical process is altogether too complex to be treated only in terms of binary oppositions, as the Hegelians, Marxists and structuralists would have wished. This pertains to a phenomenon, recurrent throughout intellectual history: a powerful inquisitive mind discovers an aspect of human existence previously ignored or underrated, and attempts to account for everything from this unique, newly found standpoint, to the detriment of all others. Modernity offers a series of such 'one-dimensional' developments (Marx and Freud among the most conspicuous), sometimes resulting in national, and even global, disasters. By extension, this could compel the original thinkers and their epigones to treat reality selectively (on the narrower scale of historical scholarship it involves selective reading of the source material): they recognize the facts and features which fit their agenda, and disregard those that do not, often without even taking the trouble to explain why. In addition, there exists a peculiar irony permeating much of modern scholarship. On the one hand, some authors, perhaps unconsciously, project the present-day mental habits upon the ancients, which is fraught with over-interpretation or 'over-sophistication'; that is to say, we should not read into our sources what is not there, nor expect from them what they could not deliver. On the other, today's scholarly debate provides for instances of flawed logic, such as taking *pars pro toto, petitio principii*, violating the least common denominator law (mentioned above), and so forth. Those of the ancients, who had read Aristotle's logical tracts, would have been surprised. Finally, postmodern literary theories, privileging manner over matter (one example would be 'form and style criticism'), when applied to the work of history writers, often prove counter-productive: if consistently pursued, they would abolish historical study as a meaningful intellectual enterprise. (I will return to this issue shortly, in connection with Josephus.) With all this said, I do not want, however, to appear a self-righteous rigorist: *errare est humanum*, and I possess no confidence that, despite every effort to avoid it, I have not myself fallen throughout this book's narrative into any logical or methodological trap. This is for my readers and critics to decide.

The voluminous writings by the Jewish statesman and historian Joseph b. Matthias, better known as [T.] Flavius Josephus (37–ca. A.D. 100), represent the largest source of our information on Judaea during the late Second Temple period. Without this material, we would have only scraps of evidence on the historical events of the time, and next to nothing (apart from short and succinct notices in Tacitus, Suetonius and Dio) about the circumstances of the Great Revolt against Rome. Josephus belongs, however, among the most controversial ancient authors as regards his personality, career and literary output, having generated in the course of centuries arguably more passion and contention than any classical (that is, Greek or Roman) historiographer. The amount of modern scholarship on Josephus is virtually beyond grasp and is fraught with irreconcilable contradictions. I will limit myself to a series of observations on Josephus's strengths and weaknesses, so far as it may help to elucidate some problems, which surround this incredibly complex figure, and facilitate our judgment on the reliability of what he has to say.

Of the four compositions that survive under Josephus's name, the *Bellum Judaicum* (*The Jewish War*) begins with surveying Judaea's history from the Maccabean times onwards, but the bulk of it gives a vivid account of the liberation war waged by the Jews against Rome that the author not only witnessed but in which he took an active part. I would not hesitate to call it, from both the historical and literary viewpoint, a masterpiece, however flawed. It must have been published between A.D. 75–81 – that is to say, when the events of the actual war narrative (which starts in *BJ*, 2, 184) still lingered within living memory. Even though much of the material apparently came from the author's personal experience and his interviews with actors on both sides, it stands to reason that he may have used other contemporary written sources, one possibility being the official *Commentarii* (*Hypomnemata*), drafted by both Vespasian and Titus that Josephus mentions elsewhere (*Vita*, 342, 358; *cAp.*, 1, 56); it goes without saying that, as any other ancient historian of contemporary events, he must have also often relied on rumor and hearsay. His is a powerfully written history, imbued with a heightened sense of drama, which, despite authorial bias, recreates the events in their complexity and sometimes offers acute insights into individual and collective behavior. Given the range of the author's agenda, it makes a coherent and, in its basics, a legitimate treatment of what happened. Josephus's opus magnum, *Antiquitates Judaicae* (*The Antiquities of the Jews*), on the other hand, does not live up to the literary merits of its predecessor. It was published 20 years later (in A.D. 93–94), and was explicitly intended to acquaint the gentile audience with Jewish historical and religious heritage. In the first half of this lengthy tract

Josephus retells the stories that we know from the Hebrew Bible, sometimes with significant variance as regards the rhetoric of representation, but never violating the essential content of the biblical narratives, their message and perspective. In the second half of the *Antiquitates* (books 11–20) Josephus proceeds to cover the Hellenistic, Hasmonaean, Herodian and Roman periods in greater (and sometimes more confusing) detail than in his earlier work. Much of this text is tedious, lacking the poetical and visionary brilliance of the Old Testament. It suffers from obscurities and repetitions, and one wonders why Josephus chose to write the Maccabean–Roman part again, having cogently done so in the *Bellum*. Moreover, it appears that, in the course of his work on it, he failed to consult his own earlier account or to harmonize the two narratives, which at times contradict each other. The third of his extant writings, the so-called *Vita* (*The Life*) was presumably meant as a sort of appendix to the *Antiquitates*. The title is somewhat deceptive, since its content concerns only a short stretch in Josephus's life, attempting to account for his revolutionary pursuits: from the outbreak of the revolt and his appointment by the rebels as governor of Galilee to the fall of Jotapata and his surrender to the Romans. Intended, in part, as a memoir, and for this reason of lesser reliability, the *Vita* is aggressively apologetic, containing (among other things) the author's direct polemic (336–367) against his contemporary opponent and critic, one Justus of Tiberias. This is the least satisfactory of Josephus's literary efforts, often incoherent to the point of rambling, sometimes self-contradictory as well as contradicting on several points the parallel treatment of the same events in the *Bellum*. Reading the *Vita* or, for that matter, the later books of the *Antiquitates*, it is hard to avoid the impression that these are products of a declining mind, slowly drawn into senility. This impression, however, does not square with the superiority of Josephus's last surviving text, *Contra Apionem* ("Against Apion"), in which he vigorously defends Judaism against its gentile detractors. This work of keen intellect and integrity, well constructed and well argued, must have been published shortly after the *Antiquitates* (referred to in *cAp.*, 1, 1 ff., 54, 127; 2, 136, 287). I find it very difficult to reconcile the poor quality of the *Vita* with the excellence of the *Contra Apionem*, written by the same writer and roughly at the same time. It remains one of Josephus's numerous puzzles on which one may speculate infinitely with no tangible results. At least, in part, tensions in his narratives come from the conflict of Greek historiographical and Jewish traditions: his project inevitably entailed communication gaps, which Josephus tried to bridge with different measure of success.[14]

The crucial episode of Josephus's career, responsible for the negative treatment he is often given within mainstream Jewish tradition and even scholarship, was his surviving the collective suicide of his comrades upon their flight from Jotapata, fallen to the Romans, his subsequent surrender and siding with the enemy for the rest of the war. There are those who, even 2000 years later, find it impossible to forgive him for what they construe as his betrayal of the national cause. I submit, however, that the conscientious reading of Josephus's work makes it clear that his choices and vicissitudes owed to the reality, which was singularly complex, and cannot be judged in simplistic – and dualistic – terms of morally right and wrong.

Despite much scholarly attention paid to his personality and self-representation, the man Josephus remains in many respects as elusive as ever. This makes him one of the most complicated – and therefore fascinating – intellectuals and historical agents that we know of from the period under discussion, either on the Jewish or gentile side. Predictably, he portrays himself, in accord with the current rhetorical fashions, as heroic and brilliant as he could. Literary conventions had been certainly exploited: for instance, reading about Josephus's activities in Galilee and the multiple ruses he employed against his foes, the gentile readers were reminded of Odysseus, the man "of many tricks and turns"; the Jews, on the other hand, might have thought in the same context of deceptions shrewdly practiced by Jacob, Israel's great forefather, known from the Bible. None of this, however, succeeded in concealing Josephus's own character faults, the most prominent being perhaps extraordinary vainglory and almost utter lack of self-criticism. His virtues are less obvious but no less real: keen intelligence, capacity for compassion, certain generosity of spirit that allowed him to admire even his worst enemies, and the inner strength which explains, in the final analysis, the personal stand he was able ultimately to maintain *vis-à-vis* all political forces he happened to have been involved with. Elsewhere in this book I will expand on various aspects and events of his life. At the present stage I propose that the totality of Josephus's writings offers irrefutable proof of his pervasive identity as a Jew and of his lifelong commitment to the welfare and interests of his people, even though, depending on the circumstances, he could have seen these in different lights.

Working on his revolt account in the *Bellum*, Josephus must have pursued a threefold agenda. In view of his two audiences, Jewish and gentile (on which I will elaborate shortly), he was bound to adopt certain apologetic strategies towards each belligerent nation *vis-à-vis* the other and present them both in the best possible light. This required portraying Jews as essentially peaceful and pious people, by no means subversive, and their revolt, at the very worst, as a tragic error, the work of misguided, vicious or godless demagogues, and ultimately a misunderstanding. Similarly, the Romans had to be shown justified in their reprisals, however brutal, and, in the final analysis, concerned with the salvation of Jews. Furthermore, it was imperative for the author to defend his own political conduct (and, to a lesser extent, at various points, that of his peers) by implying or arguing that it concurred with *both* Jewish and Roman interests; and, above all, he needed to justify himself in the eyes of God. This was all a formidable task: the modern critic must pause and appreciate its difficulty and magnitude before blaming Josephus, given his delicate predicament as both patriot and renegade, for this or that willful omission, inconsistency or other narrative faults. That the latter are numerous is not surprising; many of them also reflected sensibilities and expectations of Josephus's readers (less logic, more rhetoric), which I have elsewhere called 'rhetoricized mentality'. What earns him considerable credit, however, is the fact that all his priorities, prejudices and peculiarities notwithstanding, the story he tells conceals neither the valor displayed by the Jewish rebels whom he came to hate, nor the atrocities practiced by his Roman masters whom he came to serve. The classical historians we admire most for the quality of their writing are authors with manifestly divided or conflicting loyalties: Thucydides, patriot of Athens and Athenian exile; Polybius, Greek hostage and Roman propagandist; Tacitus, Imperial collaborator and senatorial dissident. All three found themselves 'in between'; but it was this 'intermediate' status which endowed them with room for intellectual maneuver, perceptive commentary and fairer judgment, for implicit, or even explicit criticism of both camps. By the same token, Flavius Josephus belongs to this select group.

We know that Josephus also produced an Aramaic version of the *Bellum* (*BJ*, 1, 3; 6); but since it did not survive, we can learn virtually nothing about its character. As regards the war narrative in Greek that we do possess, the audiences it sought to reach must have matched the historian's agenda outlined above. As an apology for the Jews, it was clearly intended to address educated gentiles, especially those administering the Roman Near East: elsewhere Josephus takes care to announce that the work has been read and approved by both Vespasian and Titus (*Vita*, 361 f.; cf. *cAp.*, 1, 50 f.). As a sort of 'apology' for the Romans, its objective would have been to influence numerous Jews in Judaea and the Diaspora, who spoke and read Greek, to recognize the madness of armed struggle against Rome and to reconcile with the Imperial regime, which might improve their lot in some future. Finally, owing to his own precarious status in Rome, Josephus needed favorable recognition on both sides: as the Empire's loyal servant from the Palatine, and as a trustworthy *bona fide* Jew within the city's Jewish community, which made his immediate environment. This last factor is of major psychological importance (too often underrated and even ignored), and it helps to account for Josephus's anxious efforts in upholding his credibility as a history writer. This was a *conditio sine qua non* to achieve the status and stature he patently aspired for – that of a mediator between the Jewish and Greco-Roman worlds. We do not know much about Rome's Jews and their vicissitudes immediately upon the revolt's suppression, but there is no evidence that they suffered reprisals, which might have affected their number. There is equally no reason to assume that the regular communicating practices between Judaea and across the Diaspora ceased to operate. The literate and interested Jewish audience both in the capital and throughout the Empire must have known the major events of the recent upheaval and could have impeached Josephus's reportage for any serious or patent falsification. As a former revolutionary politician and at present Imperial associate, he was bound to attract considerable curiosity not only among the gentile circles, but also on the part of his local co-religionists. It would have threatened his social and public interests to alienate them further by indulging in detectable mendacity as a chronicler of the Great Revolt. (Even 20 years later he thought it imperative to produce the *Vita*, a polemical apology, which deals with obscure events in Galilee, hardly of interest for an average gentile reader, but of obvious significance for both the Roman and Judaic establishment at the time, with whom he used to interact.)[15]

Josephus's concern with his credentials as a writer of history is made manifest already at the outset, in the Prologue to the *Bellum*, with criticism aimed at the inadequacy and partiality of his predecessors:

Some of them, not having participated in the events, brought together from hearsay random and conflicting tales, which they wrote down in the manner of sophists; while others, who were in attendance, either to flatter the Romans, or from their hatred of the Jews, falsified the facts, alternating accusation and eulogy, with no historical accuracy at all.

(*BJ*, 1,1f.; cf. 6; also *Vita*, 336 ff.; 361 ff.)

Thereupon, he establishes himself as eyewitness, both a participant in and observer of the developments he plans to describe (3). Later on, Josephus argues (which – given the practices of classical historiography – is entirely reasonable) that it is much more difficult and requires a greater intellectual commitment, to produce an account of contemporary events, rather than to revisit and rewrite affairs of the distant past "as if they had not been excellently recounted by ancient writers" (13). Obviously having in mind authors such as Thucydides or Polybius, he stresses their own participation in the events they describe, which elucidates their report, while "lying means to fall into disgrace in the eyes of those who know" (14). The last clause is the key for this passage. It leaves no doubt that Josephus fully realized the risk he would run if he patently falsified the evidence which was a matter of public record or still preserved in living memory. This set a limit to his potential manipulation of historical material: the details could have been twisted, orchestrated or embellished to fit his agenda and 'ideological' bias; the narrative could be rhetoricized and dramatized for the enjoyment of his readers; the significant facts, however, although being sometimes subject to misrepresentation, obfuscation and willful interpretation, were not to be invented. The picture was no doubt more complex than he makes it, but it does not follow that his portrayals are for this reason all wrong. The attitude towards Josephus adopted by hypercritics (of whatever description) proves, in the final analysis, misguided and counter-productive, even when it concerns the veracity of episodes some readers may find uncomfortable, such as the slaughtering of Jerusalem's garrison by the rebels on the Sabbath day, or the factions' reign of terror at the capital under siege. One has to distinguish between his factual reportage and his descriptive and interpretive procedures, an issue that he was perfectly aware of: "I shall recount with accuracy the actions taken on both sides, although in discussion and arrangement of the events I make room for my own feelings to lament the misfortunes of my homeland" (9). On balance, Josephus's own judgment on his work makes better sense than many of his modern interpreters are willing to admit:

> Providing a record of what has not so far been related and putting together the matters of one's own time for the benefit of those who are yet to come is worthy of praise and commendation. One shows diligence not by altering the order and arrangement of what had been done by another, but by offering a new material and producing a historical composition, of one's own. Being myself a foreigner, with hard work and expense, I present to the Greeks and Romans this memorial of their achievements.
>
> (ibid,15 ff.)

The mode of reasoning so far argued militates against the currently fashionable approach to Josephus (as well as other ancient history writers) known as "composition criticism", which privileges the literary aspects of their narrative at the expense of their historical value. In view of its practitioners, the rhetorical tropes pervasively employed by classical historiographers perforce undercut the factual veracity of their reportage. Applied to Josephus, the extreme position claims that one cannot reconstruct history on the basis of his writings without outside corroboration – and, since the latter is minimal, it follows that the only appropriate method of dealing with them is as if they were purely literary artifacts, like historical novels. This argument draws, in part, on the use (and misuse) of the ideas proposed by Hayden White over 30 years ago and expounded by his followers. On the other hand, it also resulted from transferring some interpretative methods, taken from the 'form and style' school of thought in New Testament studies, onto the material found in Josephus. I have no intention to partake in the ongoing debate on these issues, except to make a few general comments. First, any piece of writing, whether a newspaper article or even a scientific tract, is rhetorical by definition since its purpose is to persuade the reader that what it says makes sense or has some other inherent value. It does not follow that on these grounds alone such artifacts are to be denied factual veracity. Phenomena such as 'composition criticism' of historiography largely derive, in my view, from the intrusion by linguistics and literary analysis into territories beyond their legitimate claims. This also may relate to our penchant for engaging with virtual reality and projecting it onto the distant past. Rhetoric and even 'ideology' *per se* do *not* generate historical fiction. They provide a historian with the instruments for interpreting or manipulating the facts, but not inventing them – so far as the latter represent public record that is accessible to the reader. The practice of modern totalitarian regimes, like the Nazi Reich or the Soviet Union, demonstrates that information can be controlled and fabricated to the exclusion of any undesirable item by a powerful modern state bureaucracy. Nothing, however, even remotely similar to it could have operated in ancient societies: thus, when their historians, from Herodotus onwards, include into their contemporary accounts an episode we consider implausible (for instance, a miracle), it is rarely, if ever, a product of their own imagination, but rather is based on popular rumor, already in existence, and could therefore be taken for 'fact' by its recorders. This intimately pertains to the difference between the narrative strategies taken up by the New Testament authors and Josephus. The former addressed audiences in small scattered enclaves, transmitting material that by the time of composition was already unverifiable, a subject of belief rather than inquiry, and drawn on reminiscences, or wishful thinking, within one or several obscure groups across at least a generation. This explains the role and amount of what can be called its 'fictional' component (although the term still must be qualified), especially, as it pertains to its central message – the hope for salvation through faith, the 'good news'. The form and style in which these stories were told acquire primary significance for any attempt at their historical interpretation. The audiences Josephus's *Bellum* sought to reach would be vastly dissimilar, both in character and in scale. Although, as it will be argued, he considered (but for different reasons and in different sense) the issue of religion, perhaps, no less important, his priority was to establish himself as a reliable reporter of developments that were recent, public and tragic, a veritable historical upheaval. This is why he could not afford, in substance, any significant fictionalizing, except for details, rhetorical or dramatic, and as a result of a genuine error. This is also why the analytical principles formulated by the New Testament 'form and style' critics, for the most part, do not apply to Josephus's history of the Great Revolt, which is our primary concern.[16]

It follows, especially in view of its topicality with his contemporary Jewish audience, that Josephus's *Bellum* provides much greater historicity than the recent scholarship is prepared to grant it, irrespective of whether or not his narration could have been controlled by any 'ideological', 'compositional' or 'conceptual' framework. The *Vita*, which elaborates on Josephus's Galilaean campaign, previously described in the *Bellum*, is different. It was written 20 years later, when excitement about the Jewish War was bound to fade in public memory. Being ostensibly a polemical piece of the author's autobiography, it deals with obscure episodes of minor significance. It provided Josephus with a greater room for license in handling the facts, perhaps even for fabricating some, although it is difficult to determine when obfuscation, pervasive throughout the *Vita*, was intentional to confuse his readers, or resulted from increasing negligence on his part. The *Vita*, apart from sometimes exhibiting self-contradiction, disagrees at several points with the parallel narrative from the *Bellum*: apparently, working on the former, Josephus never bothered to consult the latter and correlate the two. All of these features remain enigmatic: to my mind, none of the current explanations are sufficiently persuasive. I fear we should better recognize our inability to penetrate the deeper recesses of Josephus's mind, rather than speculate endlessly on certain peculiar procedures he adopts and the motivations behind them.

Finally, I must briefly comment on Josephus's treatment of the written sources for the portions in the *Bellum* (that is, his Hasmonean, Herodian and, in part, Roman narratives) and in the *Antiquitates*, where he could not draw on his own experiences or on the immediate oral transmission of the evidence. It has been recently proposed that he actively interfered with earlier accounts rather than merely reproducing the work of his predecessors. This may be true, but it does not follow that he would have significantly modified the *factuality* of their data, or invented past events out of cloth, for rhetorical, 'ideological' or some other purpose. So far I have not encountered, apart from suppositions, any convincing argument to that effect. On the contrary: it appears that archaeological and epigraphical material, scarce as it is, tends to support information provided by Josephus; even the Qumran texts do not substantially contradict his overall portrayal of a secessionist sect, such as the Essenes; nor have I discovered any major *factual* conflicts in Josephus with the historically reliable components of the New Testament and the Tannaitic corpus.[17]

My general disagreement with the 'composition criticism' approach notwithstanding, its methods are helpful as regards particulars and may often (though not always) account for apparent (largely minor) contradictions, dependent on the context, between parallel versions of the same events in the *Bellum* and the *Antiquitates*, or the *Bellum* and the *Vita*, as well as for some inconsistencies, within each work. The rhetorical, dramatic or other narrative aims could indeed have been responsible for the author's choice of emphasis, selection or omission of details, and for a nuance, or even reversal, of the authorial judgment. In each case critics must apply such procedures with caution and consider them hypothetical, allowing for alternative explanations, be they apologetics, 'ideology', the historian's genuine change of mind, attitude or perspective, acquisition of new evidence, and so forth. There are, furthermore, many discrepancies within Josephus's individual texts and between them, which yield simpler explanations – like negligence – rather than some specific narrative strategy. One must not project our modern expectations of logical consistency on the ancients. Even nowadays the strict rules of logic are not always observed as regards scholarship in any area of humanities. The ancient writers and, by extension, their audience must have paid, however, much less attention than we do to the argument's coherence, specifics and differences in detail, provided that it met their criteria of good style. I believe that these observations may help to explain some incongruities in Josephus's work, with the caveat that at times the logic of his narrative choices remains beyond our comprehension. Elsewhere I discussed at length the effects of rhetoricization on Silver Age Latin literature, leading to inconsistencies, in both ideas and imagery, in Seneca's moral discourse, Lucan's historical epic and Petronius's satirical fiction. At the outset of this book I have suggested that fully objective (and, one may add, fully consistent) history writing is not possible, and rhetoric is indeed one of the venues allowing individual subjectivity to become manifest. Even so, I find it imperative to reiterate that, since it deals primarily with reportage rather than creative imagination, historiography is better equipped to resist the invasion of rhetoric when the latter threatens to undermine the very enterprise it is engaged in. This is especially true of Josephus, given the utmost topicality of his concerns – a national tragedy that continued deeply to affect the lives of all his compatriots and co-religionists as well as his own.

The wholesome study of Josephus's literary techniques, based not on selected passages, but on the totality of his oeuvre, constitutes a separate and painstaking enterprise that is yet to be done. Here it suffices to note that his abilities as a writer are formidable but flawed. In rhetorical terms, his narratives are uneven, especially when compared with his Greek contemporaries (for instance, Plutarch), and his use of language is sometimes awkward and even obscure. This is not surprising: after all, he wrote not in his native tongue, and there is no evidence that he underwent rigorous training in rhetoric, as did the same Plutarch, or – on the Latin side – Tacitus, Suetonius and their likes. This alone would make me feel skeptical toward the claims that rhetorical and similar literary concerns made the dominant principle of his historical narration, which ultimately cannot meet such criteria: it is all too often poorly structured, fraught with gaps and allows for many loose ends. At the same time, Josephus's Hasmonean and Herodian accounts are well balanced in terms of *pro et contra*. To this he provides a clue by evoking, on the one hand, his Hasmonean origin and, on the other, his close relationship with the house of Herod (*AJ*, 16, 187). His polemics with his primary source, Nicolaus of Damascus (ibid, 183 ff.), makes it clear that he felt fully aware of his disagreements with the latter's assessments and moral judgment on particular persons and events, but there is no sign that he sought to impeach the veracity of the actual facts that they both had to deal with. I suppose his engagement with his other sources (of which we know or can guess only few) was similar: he would have accepted their data but reserved a freedom to interpret them in accordance with his views, and orchestrate the details, emphasizing some and omitting others as he saw fit.[18]

Among Josephus's agenda and bias, other than literary, it is his apologetics of Judaism that acquires primary importance in any effort at making sense of what he says – or does not say – about the Jewish religious dissent. Implicit in his writings, especially *Contra Apionem*, is the author's concern with the charge often proffered by the anti-Jewish pagan polemicists, that the Jewish monotheist faith, and the exclusivist practices it entails – what we call, *in toto*, 'Judaism' – in itself constitutes a perpetual source of trouble and subversion. Against the background of the recent revolt, even a hint of the link between religion and disobedience might have entailed negative repercussions. This accounts for Josephus's treatment of the matter: on the one hand, he is proud of the Jews' unique adherence to their ancestral beliefs, laws and customs, even if this involves martyrdom (e.g., *BJ*, 1, 653; 2, 152 f.; *AJ*, 12, 256; 17, 152 ff.; *cAp.*, 2, 232 ff.); on the other, he persistently emphasizes Rome's wisdom and benevolence in not interfering with the religious affairs of the nations they conquered (cf. esp., *cAp.*, 2, 73 ff.). This strategy helps him to impress on the reader that if allowed freely to worship their God and observe their sacred laws, Jews prove as peaceful and obedient subjects of the Empire as any other. Consequently, he endeavors to minimize disagreements in matters of religion among Jews as allegedly pertinent to violence, charging instead their Egyptian antagonists with religious warfare (ibid, 66). In contrast, the Jewish religiosity is portrayed as monolithic:

> It is because of this, first and foremost, that we achieved our remarkable unanimity. Having one and the same view of God, and not differing in

the way of life or in habits, results in the most beautiful concord among human characters. With us alone one will not hear contradictory arguments about God, which happens a lot with other peoples, and not just from anybody to whom passion puts this on the lips, but even boldly attempted by the philosophers, some attacking with arguments, in order to abrogate, the whole nature of God; others depriving him of providence over humankind; only with us one perceives no difference in pursuit of our lives, but with us all things are alike, as regards the notion about God, which is in agreement with our law, saying that he is overseeing all.

(ibid, 179 ff.)

This picture is, of course, simplified and ultimately misleads (tellingly, Josephus here ignores even his own earlier reports in the *Bellum* and the *Antiquitates* that the Sadducees disagreed with the Pharisees precisely on the providential aspect of the Deity, as well as on other issues). But one can understand why: so far as Josephus's pagan, especially Roman, readers were concerned, any religious conflicts were no good, since they impeached on the *pax deorum*, "the peace of gods." This is also why Josephus, somewhat twisting the evidence, insists that the Torah teaches tolerance towards alien gods and believers in them (ibid, 236). This would not do, however, for his lengthier historical texts, the *Bellum* and the *Antiquitates*: the existence of Saducean–Pharisaic controversy must have been known to the gentile educated class in Judaea and the Roman administrators and could not be concealed. Therefore, Josephus takes care to represent (or misrepresent) the two sides as competing philosophical movements, a familiar phenomenon in Antiquity, and in so doing employs the language of Greek philosophy rather than that of the Septuagint. Thus, he succeeded, with the view of the reader, in divorcing their quarrel from practical politics, although, as his own accounts testify, the Sadducees and the Pharisees did enjoy at various times significant political clout. But Josephus's reluctance in revealing disagreements even within the same 'school of thought', such as Phariseism, might explain, at least in part, his bewildering silence about the debate between the houses of Hillel and Shammai: if expanded on, it would have exposed in the latter a strong exclusivist trend within common Judaism that was bound to influence those religious dissenters bent on revolt.

Another technique employed by Josephus to obfuscate the religious dimension of the upheaval is his purposeful and deceptive 'psychologizing' of the motives of the insurgents. In his attempts at psychological inquiries (which combine representation and interpretation), Josephus is occasionally most insightful, but also – more often than not – suspect. He consistently portrays the rebels as conscious and impious blasphemers, while in reality they considered themselves, as religious dissenters always do, the paragons of piety, for whom the cause (that is, God) was more important than tradition, written or oral, in governing social behavior. This is apparent when one recognizes the device of 'polemical reversal', employed by Josephus, when he imposes opposite meanings on the revolutionary vocabulary and arguments: for instance, 'freedom' from Rome turns, under his pen, into 'freedom' from the tyranny of the rebel factions and their leaders, and 'zeal for God' into fight against God's own providence. This explains his ascribing to them the lowest possible motives, such as lust for power and violence, which also helps him to dissociate the rebel leadership and rank-and-file from the rest of the Jewish nation as well as from Judaism as he wanted it to be understood by his readers. These practices are, of course, rhetorical, revealing Josephus's ability to borrow from and manipulate the material and concepts found in classical historiography, especially in Thucydidean analysis of socio-political crisis.

Similar concerns with the potential charges against the Jewish religion must have also prevented Josephus from expanding on such aspects as contemporary Messianism, eschatological expectations, or the tenets and beliefs specific to the adherents of "fourth philosophy", apart from the brief and usually abusive pronouncements. This strategy of omission constitutes a major difficulty for a study such as the present: every known episode (and there are not many), where religious dissent mentality was, or could have been, at work cannot be taken and reviewed in isolation, but must be placed in the narrow context within Josephus's narrative and also examined against its general background.

In other cases, his motives for omissions (or lack of explanations) remain unfathomable: among the outstanding examples are Josephus's total silence on the Rabban Johanan b. Zakkai, his (assumed) negotiations with Vespasian and the latter's permission to establish the rabbinic academy at Yavneh; his failure to mention what had happened in the end to such important figures as Eleazar b. Ananias, the prime mover of the revolt, and the zealot leader Eleazar b. Simon, as well as the inability to explain why the Romans chose to spare the life of yet another major revolutionary, John b. Levi of Ghischala. We simply do not possess enough evidence on the author's relationship with individuals and groups to interpret meaningfully his figures of silence. Although it is always tempting to speculate on such issues, and on a few occasions I will myself indulge in some conjectures, my basic belief is that this is largely a waste of effort and they should be better laid to rest. The profusion of gaps, not only in Josephus but in our other sources, such as the Tannaitic corpus and the New Testament, accounts for the widespread scholarly recourse to the argument from silence, sometimes to the point of abuse. The results, I suspect, are often counterproductive and may ultimately distort historical reality. It is imperative to remember that, unlike the invention of events, their omission does not undermine a historical text's validity in the eyes of readers, even if they recognize that something may be amiss: no historian can cover or know all that has actually taken place and is bound to operate selectively. The experience of modern historiography demonstrates that scholars sometimes may ignore even major factors (such as religious psychology) if they do not fit their agenda.

I further propose, in a tentative manner, since this requires additional research and detailed argument, that Josephus's strategies, including omissions, may have been influenced to some extent by biblical discursive procedures. That he considered Greco-Roman historiography, especially Thucydides, as his model cannot be doubted. On balance, however, he fell short of their achievements precisely in terms of coherence and consistency in his presentation (and explanation) of the facts. It is rare, for instance, that in the known works of classical historians a significant personage is introduced without some preliminary background or disappears into nowhere, or altogether fails to show up, but this does occur in the narratives about the past from the Hebrew Bible: even upon a superficial reading of the Kings and the Chronicles, one wonders what ultimately happened to such important figures as the prophets Nathan, Isaiah (the story of whose martyrdom at the hands of King Manasseh is a later and non-biblical tradition) and Jeremiah (the latter is, surprisingly, not even mentioned in *2Kings*). One possible explanation pertains to the 'theological' perspective of these narratives which are primarily concerned with Israel's history providentially charted by God rather than with its individual agents *per se*, who merit a reference only in appropriate contexts and so far as they partake in the divine plan. Some of this reasoning *may* apply also, *mutatis mutandis*, to Josephus.

The God of Israel is pervasively present in the *Bellum*, not only when directly referred to, but as an active principle of its 'theological', or 'historiosophical', framework that characteristically emphasizes the collective over the individual. It attributes Rome's victory in the Jewish War to the anger of God at the Jews (largely meaning the rebels) for their sins and crimes (sacrilege, fratricide and so forth); in consequence God sided with the Romans, turning them into instruments of divine punishment. This vision was clearly based on the biblical precedent of the Babylonian captivity, which likewise involved the Temple's destruction. At the same time, it must have arisen from Josephus's personal experiences during the revolt, and I find no reason to question his sincerity in these beliefs, scandalous as they may seem. In any event, they provide our author with the room for his pro-Roman apologetics that is further explicit in his persistent exculpation and idealization of Titus (to whom, one must remember, as well as Vespasian, he owed his life).

Like any other ancient historian, one cannot expect Josephus further to elucidate issues we find important, but which were of little or no interest to him and his audience – namely, Roman Judaea's social, economic and institutional structures. His treatment of the latter is particularly exasperating. Josephus does not employ any technical or uniform vocabulary, which would make clear to the reader who exactly were the nameless "elders", "rulers", the "notable" and "powerful" participants in the events, what their actual status in society was, or what office, if any, they might have held. These and similar terms are used interchangeably, and it is hardly possible to sort them out. Either Josephus's readership found no problem in identifying such agencies as a matter of routine and public knowledge, or simply did not care to do so. The last, but regrettably not the least, deficiency of his writings must have been inherent in his very mental process. Josephus's mind, in many respects powerful and profound, largely lacked a capacity for accuracy and precision, which we associate with intellectual vigor and value in the reportages of a Thucydides or a Julius Caesar. Hence, his habit of negligence on the details that require explanation (which worsened with the passage of time), of leaving loose ends, his inexplicable failure, while working with the same material later in life, to consult his earlier narrative and attempt harmonization. The examples are multiple and, coupled with his character traits, such as signs of megalomania and wishful thinking, sometimes make studying and interpreting Josephus a very precarious enterprise. I submit, however, that – despite all its serious faults listed above – we must feel indeed fortunate for possessing Josephus's oeuvre rather than some other source of lesser quality or none at all: it was created by a remarkable and complex individual, ardent patriot with a guilty conscience of a betrayer, keen observer, witnessing a major cataclysm in his people's history and desperately trying to make sense of it without losing his faith.[19]

III.

The remaining written source material, apart from the Qumran scrolls, and compared with Josephus, offers scant information on the violent religious dissent in Roman Judaea until the destruction of the Temple. This material consists of rabbinic writings from the Tannaim period (up to the end of the second century A.D.), mostly codified in the Mishnah; the New Testament; and the collection of random visionary (and largely undatable) texts known as Pseudepigrapha. For the purpose of this study, each category requires a comment, however brief.

Unlike earlier scholarship, which took the reliability of the rabbinic corpus at face value, current expert opinions come close to a consensus that the contents of the Mishnah reflect the historical, cultural and psychological context of the Jewish communities in Palaestina at the time of its compilation, rather than any earlier period, and cannot be taken as a dependable source on the events prior to the fall of Jerusalem in A.D. 70. This can be explained by the workings of collective historical memory, which continuously strives to compensate for national disaster and is known in some cases to transform the historical record beyond recognition. Two examples may suffice. Many hundreds of Russian heroic folk ballads (the '*byliny*') ignore three centuries under Mongol yoke and consistently celebrate imaginary victories over the Mongol invaders. The Persian tradition, culminating in Ferdowsi's monumental poem *Shahnameh* ("The Book of Kings', 10th to 11th centuries), portrays Alexander the Great ("Iskandar") as a legitimate ruler of the East, son of the Persian king and a Macedonian princess. The framers of the Mishnah did not reach that degree of fictionalization, but they tended to ignore much of the relatively recent historical past altogether, or to impose their own vision on it, often demonstrably distant from the reality. Thus, for instance, the detailed description of the pre-A.D. 70 Sanhedrin, its structure and function, in the Mishnaic treatise bearing the same name (*mSanhedrin*) seems to be a much idealized retrojection of how that body operated, under totally different conditions, a century later after the Great Revolt.

Like Josephus, although for different reasons, the rabbis proved reticent on anything relative to the mentality of violent religious dissent. First and foremost, this was not a matter of their immediate concern: they saw their task in systematization of the *halakhas*, based on their understanding of the Torah, with the purpose of regulating the conduct of ordinary life among their co-religionists in accordance with God's will. Further, even upon the suppression of the second revolt in Judaea by Hadrian (A.D. 136), anything pertaining to the resistance against the Romans must have for a long time remained a very sensitive issue for the Jewish communities at large, and the Tannaim had to take this into account: expressing sympathy for the liberation agenda was politically dangerous and potentially fraught with yet another catastrophe; openly criticizing it, on the other hand, would have made them liable to the charge of opportunism and collaboration. In consequence, the Mishnah editors chose, almost consistently, to keep silent. One suspects that such choice was not that easy, given – for instance – the public stand of the great Tannaitic sage R. Aqiba, who had endorsed Simon bar Kokhba's claim as the Messiah and was martyred by the Romans. We moderns must appreciate these strategic difficulties as I have also suggested regarding Josephus's pursuit of his own complicated apologetic agenda.

I believe it is possible nonetheless to extract some pieces of telling data about at least a few episodes from the period under scrutiny, provided that one recognizes the layers of later interests, imagining, polemics or wishful thinking in their (mis)representation. In other words, an echo of an event, individual or collective action, though much altered in the process, could have found its way into the Mishnah and occasionally even reached the Talmud. Consequently, although in principle I adopt a 'minimalist' position on this issue, I am prepared, in the chapters that follow, to consider any such historical (or quasi-historical) reference and allusion in the rabbinic texts, if it may throw, even inadvertently, an additional light on our main theme.

The contents of the Gospels are of little help on the matter of violent religious dissent at the break of the millennia, even though the mention of Simon the Zealot, the brigand Barabbas, as well as scattered signs of popular discontent, may call for attention. They concentrate on the mission undertaken by Jesus of Nazareth and, to a lesser extent, that of John the Baptist, and emphasize the non-violent character of both which I believe is historically accurate. Within the mainstream or common Judaism, both represented dissenting movements, as did the sectarians at Qumran, but there is no evidence that violence in any practical sense entered their message. On the other hand, the very fact of strong emphasis on repentance, charity and self-perfection rather than armed resistance (cf. of the Baptist: "Repent, for the kingdom of heaven is at hand!" – *Mt.* 3:2; and of Jesus: "Love your enemy and pray for those who persecute you so that you may be sons of your Father who is in heaven" – *Mt.* 5:44 f.) certainly suggests the existence of many in their audience who would have preferred to act the opposite.

The *Book of Acts* is, of course, much less a history than the work of Josephus. It is controlled by theological, apologetic and literary concerns, which makes it a more appropriate subject for 'form and style' or 'composition' criticism than the latter. Apart from various omens, such as prophetic dreams (16:9; 18:9 f.; 23:1; 27:23), it recounts the immediate supernatural intervention (like the release of the apostles Peter and John from prison by God's angel – 5:19 f.), which would not have been possible, say, in the *Bellum*. At the same time, it does mention individual religious dissenters, both violent and not, whom we also know from Josephus: Judas the Galilaean, Theudas, the unnamed Egyptian prophet. And the story of St. Paul's vicissitudes and peregrinations betrays some signs of what may be linked to or reflect the mindset we are interested in. It is no less essential to stress the Pauline doctrine of all secular authority as established by God (Rom., 13), which directly contradicts the tenets of the revolutionary "fourth philosophy". In my subsequent narrative this will require comments on a few passages from the Acts, on Nero's persecution of the Christians, and the Christian community at Jerusalem under siege; I will attempt, however, to make them as cogent and brief as I possibly can.[20]

Finally, one cannot altogether ignore in the Second Temple Judaism the dimension variously called 'apocalyptic', 'eschatological' or 'Messianic', which has been receiving greater or lesser scholarly attention dependent on the fashion of the day. These three terms (as applied to mindset and conduct, or literary products) presume different though often interrelated meanings: the term 'visionary' may cover most of these phenomena, although it does not do justice to emotional and spiritual power, or compelling imagery that is sometimes involved; in all cases, however, 'wishful thinking', or what psychologists call 'omnipotence of thought' (particularly characteristic of religious dissent), must have played a major role. To simplify matters, I designate 'apocalyptic' the constituents of texts and behavior conditioned by references to some special revelation(s) other than those eventually codified in the Hebrew Bible; 'eschatological' are those that derive from the belief in the impending end of the world; and 'Messianic' are texts and movements looking forward to the emergence of a Deliverer figure (human, divine or semi-divine) who will liberate Israel from its current woes and might extend (as is often implied) his beneficent rule of peace and justice over the entire humankind.

Apart from the prophetic parts of the Old Testament (most prominently, the Book of Isaiah), and the Dead Sea Scrolls, the visionary material is contained in a considerable body of heterogeneous writings known as Pseudepigrapha. The word indicates their authors' customary self-identification with the famous biblical characters from the past. The positivist scholarship that dominates the field today tends to interpret apocalyptic narratives exclusively in literary and/or theological terms, denying their authors any degree of autonomy or authenticity in their visionary experience: their performance, we are told, is determined by language and 'structures', which leaves open the question of the inspirational impetus that compelled them to write what they did in the first place. Following this logic, one cannot honestly avoid a conclusion (equally applicable to any other mystical discourse) that all such artifacts must have resulted from some sort of self-conscious forgery. This position is not, however, left unchallenged. Major experts on or historians of religion, from William James to Karl Kerenyi to Mircea Eliade to Eric Dodds to Gershom Scholem, recognize that the carriers of mystical experience in manifold forms are able to merge the dynamics of their psyche and what they perceive as the transcendental, and thus to create a reality that embraces both. This is the experience that resists any authentic verbal articulation and is perforce expressed in the language and imagery of the immediate cultural environment. I subscribe to this view: in other words, the Jewish visionary texts from the Second Temple represent, I believe, a complex fusion of genuine mystical ecstasy (resulting from self-hypnosis or some sort of trance) and engagement with the period's theological/literary/cultural conventions, which is responsible for considerable similarity between many such texts that significantly obfuscates their original or individual characteristics.

Pseudepigraphic texts are not unknown within the extant Greco-Roman literature (including faked inscriptions, oracles and occult magical tracts). They may be explained in various ways, as an ascription of authorship to the earlier anonymous texts by the Alexandrian and subsequent scholars, as a form of rhetorical exercise, or by other reasons. (For a number of cases, the debate on the attribution continues to the present day.) The motivation of most such authors or editors in classical Antiquity must have pertained to the literary and sometimes philosophical or political interests; the historical or cultural significance of these artifacts is, at best, marginal. The Jewish Pseudepigrapha, on the other hand, since they concern the matter of religion, represent an entirely different phenomenon. It is difficult to determine a psychological mechanism that might have accounted for a visionary author's full identification with some famous prophetic figure from the past. The easiest explanation of this as deliberate fraud is wrong. Religious psychology, and even more so, the psychology of religious dissent, defies any such rationalism, which is also at odds with the compelling emotional power these texts possess. I am inclined to allow that more often than we are prepared to admit they betray the 'extra-conscious' proceedings of their authors, when the latter operated in a state of ecstasy or trance, with the boundaries between their self-awareness and what they experienced as visionary experience blurred, so that the issue of who has been actually writing the document becomes irrelevant. Modern methods of scientific psychology might further elucidate this problem, but I have encountered no data that could be of such use.

A study in depth of the Pseudepigrapha, with their different provenance (many of them exist only in translation into other languages: Syriac, Ethiopian, Arabic, Armenian, Old Slavonic, and so forth), great difficulties in dating and often obscure imagery, is a complex and somewhat arcane enterprise; it should be conducted by experts. I will dwell only on a few issues relevant to our interest: these texts as a possible source about historical events; their features, construable as manifesting the religious dissent mentality; and their potential role in the revolutionary activity by religious dissent groups.[21]

The Pseudepigrapha predictably employ the vocabulary and nomenclature of the Old Testament. Since their authorship is ascribed to biblical characters, it places their narratives *sub specie aeternitatis*, beyond the immediate experience of time, embracing (or blending) as a continuum – in a specific sense, alien to our modern rationalist mindset, – the past, the present and the future (although in other respects, including some peculiar imagery, they may strikingly differ from the biblical models). In consequence, the dating of the individual texts is exceedingly problematic. The same is true of attempts to discern in them any reflection of actual events, so that at this stage of our knowledge it is difficult, for the most part, or even impossible to identify historical adversaries figuring in various contexts either under names of Israel's past foes, drawn from the Scriptures, or more generally, like 'sons of Belial': the Hellenistic kingdoms or the Roman occupier. It is very rare that this material allows for factual precision, as for instance, in the pseudepigraphic *Psalms of Solomon*, where the description of death suffered by the unnamed foe ("the sinner"), whose body was "carried over the waves, and there was no one to bury him" (2: 26 ff.), clearly indicates Pompey; or the figure of the cruel "wanton king", not of priestly family, from the *Testament of Moses*, exterminating Israel's leaders, and "showing mercy to none" (6: 2 ff.), as an obvious portrayal of Herod I. It can sometimes be surmised whether the text had been written prior to or in the aftermath of the Temple's destruction: thus, for instance, the (*Syriac*) *Apocalypse of Baruch* (known also as *2 Baruch*), with its lamentation over immediate disasters (e.g., 5:1 ff.), belongs among the latter. It is imperative to remember that compositions such as Pseudepigapha could have been revised or rewritten at all stages during their existence, even before they were interfered with by the Christians. Finally, any such text may have contained nuances, hints and allusions, recognizable to its immediate or contemporary audience but not to us. This means that the Pseudepigraphic corpus is of little value as a source for the actual history of the Second Temple, except in the broad sense betraying the socio-politico-religious sensibilities of individuals and groups throughout the period, of whose numbers, membership and circumstances nothing further can be ascertained.

It is important to note that all visionary Pseudepigrapha profess to offer a special (and sometimes secret) revelation other than 'biblical'. Although the codification of the Hebrew canon extended for several centuries, ending only with the rise of rabbinic Judaism, its basic parts, such as the Law and major Prophets, must have been widely considered among the Jews in the late Second Temple period as both possessing unimpeachable divine authority and requiring an exegesis. Thus any ascription of these to extraneous compositions would have appeared, at the very least, suspect in the eyes of the current religious establishment: their mystical aspects alone placed these writings outside the mainstream. The authors of such materials as well as their sympathetic readers must have conceived of themselves as entering into direct communication with the divine, and thus standing in no need of mediating services from the priesthood or anyone else. I suggested at the start that such mindsets belong among the main features of religious dissent. Similarly to the Dead Sea scrolls, one can trace in some Pseudepigrapha the signs of quarrels with the Temple over chronology and calendar – as in the *Book of Jubilees* (known at Qumran), which is attributed to Moses (its narrative is distinct, however, in a number of ways, from the one in the Pentateuch). These disagreements may seem trivial to a modern mind, but when it is realized that for those concerned they represented the aspects of the sacred, then any deviation from mainstream Judaism in the form observed by the priesthood is significant. More importantly, reminding us again of Qumran, certain pseudepigraphic narratives exhibit passionate hostility towards the men who supervised the spiritual life of Israel. Thus, for instance, the *Psalms of Solomon* charge the members of the religious elite with moral and social corruption:

> Why are you sitting in the council of the devout, you, profaner?/ And your heart is far from the Lord,/ Provoking the God of Israel by law-breaking; / Excessive in words, excessive in appearance above everyone,/ he who is harsh in words in condemning sinners at judgment. Is the man severe in speech when he condemns sinners in judgment?/ And his hand is first one against him as if in zeal,/ yet he himself is guilty of a variety of sins and of intemperance./ His eyes are on every woman indiscriminately;/ His tongue lies when swearing a contract./ At night and in hiding he sins as if no one saw:/ With his eyes he speaks to every woman of illicit affairs./ He is quick to enter graciously every house as though innocent./ May God remove from the devout house those who live in hypocrisy;/May his flesh decay and his life be impoverished.
>
> (4:1 ff.)

This and similar passages make patently clear that the Jerusalem leadership is accused of having betrayed the very foundations of the faith, which constitutes, as we know, a major principle in religious dissent. As guilty of such betrayal, they were to be rejected by God and men, and consequently wiped from the face of the Earth. Given their extra-temporal character, it follows that each text of this kind could have been applied by the engaged readers to the reality of which they disapproved, and to the current socio-politico-religious situation at any point in time. By definition, corrupt priests and religious teachers must also be included in eschatological texts among those who are generally labeled 'sinners' destined, together with all unbelievers, for destruction and eternal perdition at the end of the world as a result of God's wrath. Passages to that effect are numerous in the pseudepigraphic corpus and almost always display the same strict religious/moral dualism we have seen at Qumran. Necessarily, these texts assume that their authors, as well as their target audience (that is, readers sharing their vision and attitudes), belonged among the righteous. It must be acknowledged, however, that in contrast to the overtly militant document such as the Qumran *War Scroll*, the extant Pseudepigrapha do not dwell, by and large, on human participation in the projected purge of sinners and infidels. The cleansing of the world from vice and evil is envisioned primarily in terms of cathartic divine intervention. It does not follow that individual readers could not have interpreted this as an implicit call for joining in and contributing to God's work on Earth; but it suggests the disregard, or contempt, for practical politics, which again characterizes the activities of religious dissenters.[22]

It stands to reason, therefore, that the pseudepigraphic material, especially in its apocalyptic, eschatological and messianic aspects, would have influenced the mentality of religious dissent, including what might have been construed as a call for violent action decreed by God. The problem is that we know next to nothing about the transmission of such texts, or of their potential audience: it may have consisted of single unrelated individuals, more coherent groups, or even tight communities, like that of Qumran, or any other, simply unrecorded in our sources. As a result, the mechanism of their function and absorption within Palestinian Judaism remains elusive to the point of unfathomable; even literacy was by no means conditional: these works, or their parts, could have been orally read, interpreted and discussed by any self-appointed teacher or preacher. All depended on the intensity of feelings, sense of anger and frustration, among individual or collective readers or listeners, and their willingness and ability to apply the contents to the current reality, and to draw practical inferences as to what had to be done.

On a few occasions Josephus mentions some ancient prophecies, or 'oracles', placing them directly in the context of the Great Revolt, which it is, however difficult, and perhaps impossible, to identify within the traditional biblical canon. Thus, in describing the terror perpetrated by the zealots, the historian reports:

> They trampled on every human ordinance, every divine matter was laughed at, and they mocked the predictions of the prophets as tall tales from the conjurers. They had foretold, however, a great deal about virtue and evil, which the zealots transgressed, thus achieving the fulfillment of prophecies detrimental to their homeland. For there was an ancient pronouncement by the divinely inspired men that the city would be sacked, and the most holy place [i.e. the Temple] burned down by the right of war, if it fell prey to sedition and native hands desecrated God's sanctuary; although the zealots did not disbelieve these prophecies they made themselves the tools of their realization.
>
> (*BJ*, 4, 386 f.)

This is one of Josephus's major insights into the mind of religious dissenters: although in exaggerated manner, he articulates the inherent paradox of the entire phenomenon: their preference for act over word, and for God's cause over God's book. I will return to this passage and issue in later chapters.

Elsewhere in the *Bellum*, one reads of the by far more famous ancient oracle, to which Josephus attributes particular weight:

> But what stirred them most of all towards the war, was the ambiguous prediction, similarly found in their sacred writings, that at this time someone from their land will come to rule the inhabited world. They took this to mean someone of their own, and many of their wise men were misled in this judgment; but the oracle in fact revealed the authority of Vespasian, proclaimed Emperor in Judaea.
>
> (6, 312 f.)

In this case, attempts have been made to track it to some text in the Hebrew Bible, but it seems likely that the Josephan reference, like the other just quoted, meant one or several, currently unknown, Pseudepigrapha.

As a matter of principle, a religiously dissenting reader might have been affected, in terms of his motivation and conduct, by any prophetic narrative promising transfiguration of the world as befits God's justice, with the consequent deliverance of the righteous and punishment of the wicked. This would obviously include relevant passages from the Old Testament prophets, despite their essential vagueness. Although it is clear that the biblical material was the major source of inspiration for the pseudepigraphic authors, the latter's focus on bizarre images (horned animals, dragons and other monsters, rivers of fire, and so forth) and the multiplicity of detail render them particularly compelling. The apocalyptic in these visionary accounts takes two distinguishable forms: the 'cosmic apocalypse', a celestial journey in which a seer is guided by a divine messenger, typically, an angel, who shows and explains to him the mysteries of the Universe; and the 'historical/eschatological apocalypse' – that is, a *post factum* prediction of events to come, although known to the reader (but presumably not to the pseudepigraphic narrator, relegated to the distant past), which is often extended into eschatological vision, projecting into the remote future cataclysmic occurences that result in the salvation of Israel and the triumph of God's justice. The apocalyptic cosmology is of relevance to our concerns only so far as it may portray the blessed posthumous existence of the virtuous and the sufferings of the wicked; its elaborate descriptions, however, provided the framework for the later development of Jewish mysticism. Some 'historical apocalypses', even apart from their eschatology, may prove more telling, since any citation of a confrontational episode between Israel and its many adversaries from the biblical tradition could have been conceivably applied at the time, by whoever wrote or read them, to their contemporary reality, whether having in mind Hellenistic oppressor or Roman occupier. Furthermore, certain passages in this type of the apocalyptic may reflect, one way or another, on the specific concerns shared among the dissenting-turned-revolutionary groups. For instance, the 'historical apocalypse' in the *Testament of Levi*, while justifying and glorifying the role of the Levites, the patriarch's descendants in Israel's 'future' as the servants in the Temple's cult, provides for a divine sanction (totally absent in *Gen.*, 34:1 ff.) for the notorious scriptural episode in which Levi and his brother Simeon massacred the entire male population of Shechem on the grounds that their prince had seduced Jacob's daughter Dinah, although he then consented to marry her:

> Then the angel led me back to the earth; and he gave me a shield and a sword and said to me, Perform vengeance on Shechem for the sake of Dinah, your sister, and I shall be with you, for the Lord sent me. At that time I put an end to the sons of Hamor, as it is written in the tablets of the fathers.
>
> (*T. Levi*, 5:3 f.)

As I will discuss in a later chapter, the biblical violent acts, such as this one, must have been considered admirable examples of 'zeal for God' during the Great Revolt, and served as models to the radical zealots and their like.[23]

The eschatological aspects of the apocalyptic visions in the Pseudepigrapha raise further questions about Second Temple Messianism (outside of the Qumran community), its character and manifestation, although not all such texts involve a figure (or figures) of Deliverer: in many cases, the triumph of the righteous, be it in the form of Israel's liberation, or as the result of some cosmic upheaval happens through God's intervention, with no intermediary – human, superhuman or divine – being mentioned. The issue of the period's messianic (or quasi-messianic) movements remains as controversial and heatedly debated as almost everything in the field. Although one cannot deny the existence at the time of strong messianic aspirations, traceable to the experience of Babylonian exile, their political, social and religious role in Roman Judaea remains, for the lack of reliable evidence, obscure. Depending on the fashion or the focus of scholarly interests in the course of the last century, as well as on the agenda of individual authors, it tended to be exaggerated, or understated, with the balance of probabilities shifting one way or another, and perhaps even impossible to ascertain. In consequence, I will limit myself to a brief review of the available data and a few comments on their potential significance for our concerns.

It is clear that messianic sensibilities (at any historical time) are due to the increasing sense of frustration and discontent with the status quo, which takes the form of religious protest against the powers-that-be. So far they fall under the working definition of religious dissent I offered at the outset. It becomes more complicated, however, if such sentiments are shared at least to an extent by the religious establishment, as might happen, for instance, because of foreign domination (like Roman) or tyrannical regime (as under the Herods). It seems fairly certain that some sort of expectations for a messianic scenario, even though they proved vague and vastly different in detail, were widespread among Jews under Roman rule. One must distinguish, however, between the hopes for the near end of the foreign yoke, which overthrown, with aid from God, by a powerful national leader to come, will be and for the End of Days, in the 'millenarian' sense (which is not the same as 'messianic' or even 'eschatological', the belief in the world's imminent transformation through some supernatural agency with the resultant deliverance of the righteous and punishment of the wicked. Putting it otherwise (and thus simplifying matters), the expected 'Messiah', in any *practical* sense, would have been a lay military figure (like Judas Maccabaeus), a king (another David) or a miracle worker intimately partaking in the divine. Several prophecies construable as promising the advent of a Deliverer belonged to the revered scriptural tradition. They were forcefully expressed and must have been accepted as authoritative by the priesthood, including the Temple, and Pharisaic lay teachers. This was well and good as long as the messianic liberator remained a prospect for the distant future. When, however, a charismatic individual emerges, exhibiting even an element, or a sign, of what might be called 'the Messiah complex' (a notion to which I will return), such a person was usually hunted down by the royals or the Romans, with the consent and even support of the religious elite: this was the fate of different, in terms of their mission or agenda, historical agents such as Judas the Galilaean and Theudas, John the Baptist and Jesus of Nazareth. In fact, the only messianic pretender, who reportedly received endorsement from what could be considered religious authority, as represented by the major mishnaic sage R. Aqiba, was Simon b. Kokhba, the leader of the last Jewish revolt against Rome (A.D. 132–135).

The issue is complicated by the fact that during this period the image, or concept, of the Deliverer never crystallized to the point of being accepted, or believed in, by a majority of Jews. This is true, furthermore, as regards the number of expected Messiahs: some Qumran material speaks of two such figures ("Messiah of Israel" and the priestly "Messiah of Aaron"), or even three (if one adds the "eschatological Prophet"). The projected saviors also differ in their function, nature or substance: human royal warrior; God's suffering servant; beneficent ruler of the world; divine or semi-divine personage, obscurely portrayed; angel or archangel; or combining any of these characteristics. They appear under various titles (apart from 'Messiah' – that is, literally 'the Anointed One'), such as Son of God, Son of Man, Elect One, Righteous One, Prince of Peace, Prince of Light and so forth – or remain altogether unnamed; even in an allegorical animal form, like Lion, Bull or Lamb; and finally may be designated metaphorically by inanimate objects: Star, Scepter and Rod. Perhaps the only matter of general agreement, conditional for a messianic candidate, was his Davidic origin (also tellingly ascribed to Jesus), but even that is not fully certain. There are Messianic texts that do not mention Davidic descent, and the Qumranic priestly 'Messiah of Aaron' would not have claimed it by definition (Aaron belonged to the tribe of Levi, and David to that of Judah); nor, of course, could it apply to the supernatural agents. Last but not least, there seems to have existed a sort of demarcation, sometimes blurred, between the image of the Messiah as (in one sense or another) superhuman agent and as a mortal person (king, warrior, prophet), even if he had been posturing or perceived as a miracle worker: it is this latter notion that will be of occasional concern throughout this book.

One way to handle the conundrum, I believe, is to recognize and isolate the elements of 'Messianic complex' – that is to say, those that could have pertained to what we call 'Messianism' in the eyes of the contemporaries, with full understanding that a historical 'messianic' claimant (or one publicly perceived as such) may not have needed to possess the totality of them. Even one such element could be emotionally compelling, enhance the stature he might (or was thought to) have aspired to, and could create public excitement and expectations that the promised delivery is finally at hand. The claim of Davidic origin must have certainly (but not necessarily or always) been among such requisites: sometimes even a semblance, biographical or otherwise, to David might work: assumption of or struggle for kingship, perhaps in some superior form of special relationship with the divine, and accompanied by outward attributes, like purple or white dress; insistence on prophetic gift, or behavior suggesting old prophecy (prophecies) being fulfilled; imitation of or call for replicating some biblical precedent (for example, Exodus); reputation as a miracle worker; exceptional personal charisma. And any rumor of supernatural occurrence could, of course, only help. As I suggest in the chapters that follow, one may detect during the Herodian and Roman periods and throughout the Great Revolt a series of individuals who meet at least one or more of these requirements.

The earliest clearly Messianic post-exilic passages are found in the composite product – the (canonical) *Book of Daniel* (7 ff.): they seem to reflect the 'Hellenistic' crisis surrounding Antiochus IV's seizure of the Temple and the subsequent Maccabean wars. Perhaps in their most outspoken and articulate formulation, politically relevant at the time, the pronouncements of the coming 'earthly' Deliverer occur in the *Psalms of Solomon*, hitting at both the last Hasmoneans, engaged in fratricidal warfare, and the first Roman occupier, Pompey:

> See, o Lord, and raise up for them their king,/ the son of David, to rule over your servant Israel/ in the time known to you, O God./ Undergird him with the strength to destroy the unrighteous rulers,/ to purge Jerusalem from gentiles/ who trample her to destruction;/ in wisdom and in righteousness to drive out / the sinners from the inheritance;/ to smash the arrogance of sinners/ like a potter's jar;/ To shatter all their substance with an iron rod;/ to destroy the unlawful nations with the word of his mouth;/ At his warning the nations will flee from his presence;/ and he will condemn sinners by the thoughts of their hearts.
>
> (17: 21 ff.)

This is followed by promises to the righteous and the pious: the Messiah will bring "holy people" together and "distribute them upon the land according to their tribes": "For he shall know them/ that they are all children of their God" (ibid, 27). Meanwhile, "he will have gentile nations serving him under his yoke" (30):

> And he will purge Jerusalem/ (and make it) holy as it was from the beginning,/ (for) nations to come from the ends of the earth to see his glory,/ to bring as gifts her children who had been driven out,/ and to see the glory of the Lord/ with which God has glorified her./ And he will be a righteous king over them, taught by God./ There will be no unrighteousness among them in his days,/ for all shall be holy,/ and their king shall be the Lord Messiah./ (For) he will not rely on horse and rider and bow,/ Nor will he collect gold and silver for war./ Nor will he build up hope in multitude for a day of war./ The Lord himself is his king,/ the hope of the one who has a strong hope in God.
>
> (30 ff.)

The same and similar motifs continue, recurring until the end of the psalm.

Compare this with the 'eschatological' Messiah from the *Second (Syriac) Baruch*, written already after the destruction of the Temple by Titus:

> And it will happen that when all that which should come to pass in these parts has been accomplished, the Anointed One will begin to be revealed. And Behemoth will reveal itself from its place, and Leviathan will come from the sea, – the two great monsters which I created on the fifth day of creation and which I shall have kept until that time. And they will be nourishment for all who are left. The earth will also yield fruits ten thousand-fold / ... / And those who are hungry will enjoy themselves and they will, moreover, see marvels every day. For winds will go out in front of every morning to bring the fragrance of aromatic fruits and clouds at the end of the day to distill the dew of health. And it will happen at that time that the treasury of manna will come down again from the high, and they will eat of it in those years, because these are they who will have arrived at the consummation of time.
>
> (29)

It is under these circumstances that the Messianic figure will come to punish Israel's last foe:

> The last ruler who is left alive at that time will be bound, whereas the entire host will be destroyed. And they will carry him on Mount Zion, and my Anointed One will convict him of all his wicked deeds and will assemble and set before him all the works of his hosts. And these things he will kill him and protect the rest of my people who will be found in the place that I have chosen. And his kingdom will last forever until the world of corruption is ended and until the times which have been mentioned before have been fulfilled.
>
> (40)

It is not my intent to argue, as in the past, that the messianic expectations, or aspirations, were a decisive factor for the development of events in Roman Judaea, resulting in the Great Revolt. Our evidence is meager (although this might be owing to the accident of their survival) for making such bold statements. This said, one must nonetheless recognize that the existence of those sentiments, however vague and ill defined, must have contributed to the emergence of the specific politico-religious wishful thinking within certain groups across the Jewish Palaestina. In turn, this was bound to affect, in one sense or another, the larger public space, even though we are not in a position to detail or to appreciate the extent of that influence. At the same time, it stands to reason that the apocalyptic, eschatological, or/and messianic imagery, so far as we know it from the Second Temple Pseudepigrapha, did possess considerable, for some individuals, perhaps, compelling emotional power, rooted further in their engagement with scriptural tradition. This could not have failed to add to the atmosphere of popular anxiety, with its mixture of hopes and fears, that seems to have been an undercurrent throughout much of the period, providing a convenient breeding ground for the spread of religious dissent in both its non-violent and violent forms. For our purposes, it is essential again to emphasize the belief among religious dissenters, with their denial of mediation by the religious establishment, that they uniquely represented the cause of God, implementing God's very will, resulting in their utter reliance on God's help and their own ultimate salvation. In psychological terms, this may or may not pertain to various elements of the 'messianic complex' as defined above.[24]

It must be clear now that the Jewish society in Roman Palaestina by the time of Nero's Imperial succession experienced the whole variety of tensions. In the chapters that follow I will also expand on its ethnic and social aspects; at this point it is imperative to emphasize its religious dynamism, which our sources, even though often insufficient, still allow us to ascertain. Much of this dynamism pertained to the interaction between the priestly establishment, the large population observing general precepts of 'common' or 'normative' Judaism, and the individual or collective carriers of religious dissent. Of this latter group, some manifestations seem to have been pacifist, such as among the Essenes and related or similar groups, as well as in the case of the early Christians, but others were fraught with potential violence. What proves really important is that there continuously existed a strong, however obscure, undercurrent of popular anxiety, rooted in both spiritual and practical discontent, which provided a breeding ground for occasions of public disorder. It is essential, however, to recognize that despite those disturbances, first Herod I, with Roman help, and then the Imperial authorities succeeded in maintaining control over Judaea for 130 years: it will be seen later in this book that during the most of this period, the province remained relatively quiet and that the occupiers attempted sometimes considerable concessions, especially in religious spheres, to the benefit of the occupied. In history, however, even reconciliatory policies by the powers-that-be often matter less in the eyes of the conquered or oppressed than the fact that the conqueror or oppressor continue to exist. This confronts us with the major issue of Jewish 'nationalism' (at the time under discussion it meant overthrow of the Roman yoke) and its relationship with what this book defines as religious dissent. As with much else in the Second Temple Judaism, it is hardly possible to disentangle these two strands in protest movements or revolutionary attitudes: their common characteristics remained primarily emotional and ranged from wishful thinking to passionate impatience, which – dependent on circumstances – can become a historical force. This said, one still needs to observe some difference in terms of mindset: the nationalist cause does not provide *per se* a belief in final victory; religious, especially in the form of the dissent religiosity, which identifies human and divine will, does. Furthermore, if nationalism aimed at achieving political freedom first tends to unite its adherents of various descriptions, religious dissenters may contribute, in contrast, to internecine strife on exegetical, ritualist and sectarian grounds, or due to their diverging interpretation of God's will. To my mind, this at least partly explains the continuous infighting between factions in the revolutionary Jerusalem, even under Roman siege, which otherwise seems incomprehensible. Apart from the definable religious dissent movements, peaceful or militant, of which we are informed by our sources, there must have existed many people with similar psychological characteristics, but less formed, less conscious, and varying in specifics. Of them we know nothing. It can be surmised, however, that this particular mentality developed, strengthened and spread, with its violent impulses growing proportionately to the increase of corruption and harassment practiced by the Roman provincial administration. This factor was variable, which accounts for the stretched periods of order mentioned above. Theoretically, that could have continued *ad infinitum*, but history cannot be predicted: at any point intensified oppression might result in an upheaval. In this case, a particularly nasty character and conduct of a corrupt procurator triggered the expansion of the religious dissent mentality, with its blend of anger and confidence, beyond and across societal boundaries. Intimately linked to the hope of national liberation, this engendered public frenzy and hit at the very center of the priestly establishment – the Temple. It is now time to inquire *in medias res* as to when and how it happened.[25]

2

THE BREAKING POINT

The event, which signified the actual outbreak of Judaea's revolt by providing the Romans with the *casus belli*, took place in the form of terminating the customary sacrifices at the Temple in Jerusalem on behalf of the emperor that was decreed at some point in late May/early June, A.D. 66 by the Temple priests and their leader Eleazar, son of the former high priest Ananias b. Nedebaeus. At the time, that young man served as the captain of the Temple Guard. This occurred, according to Flavius Josephus, in the 12th year of Nero's principate, and the 17th of King Herod Agrippa II's reign in (parts of) Judaea (*BJ*, 2, 284; cf. 555), with Matthias b. Theophilus holding the office of high priest (*AJ*, 20, 223). As will be seen, this measure proved a culminating point in the dramatically growing tensions across Palaestina under the rule of Gessius Florus, the last Roman procurator of Judaea (A.D. 64–66).

In the *Bellum* we read:

> At the same time at the Temple Eleazar son of Ananias the high priest, a most audacious young man, and then the Temple captain, persuaded those who conducted worship not to accept offering or sacrifice from any alien.
>
> (2, 409)

Josephus unequivocally states that this event "laid the groundwork for the war with the Romans" (ibid), and there is no reason to distrust his judgment. The action must be seen as tantamount to repudiating the oath of allegiance that Augustus and his successors required from their Jewish subjects and could be legitimately considered – given the central role of the Temple worship in the period's Judaism – a gesture of defiance on the part of the entire nation. The formulation Eleazar b. Ananias chose to adopt does not name the emperor explicitly: the decision was to outlaw any acceptance of a gift or a sacrificial offering from a stranger (that is, a non-Jew; ibid), which, incidentally, was bound to diminish the Temple's revenues and alienate at least some gentile sympathizers of the Jewish faith.[1]

Josephus's narrative does not suggest that the issue was debated prior to this event in any kind of popular gathering. It implies that the judgment was made by a particular group of the priests and officials of the Temple. The text says that the "chief priests and the most notable Pharisees" argued with Eleazar's followers that their decree contravenes tradition:

> ... declaring that their forefathers adorned the sanctuary largely at the expense of the aliens and always accepted the donations from outside peoples, and that they not only never hindered anyone's sacrifices, which is a most impious thing, but they consecrated votive offerings around the Temple remaining there for so long time and still to be seen.
>
> (412 f.)

All of these efforts, however, proved reportedly in vain: "the readiest of the revolutionists", Josephus tells us, supported the measure, looking towards the leadership of the Temple's captain (410). Nor did it help when the pro-Roman members of the Jewish elite convoked upon a popular meeting with the purpose of denouncing the cessation decree (411). They produced the experts on the tradition, presumably out of both Saducean and Pharisaic 'sects' (the former are implied by the text, the latter explicitly mentioned; 411), to address the people and argue that their ancestors, who had established the practice, not only did not prohibit the foreigners offering gifts and sacrifices at the Temple, but actually encouraged this kind of practice (412 ff.). Eleazar and his followers were accused of "introducing a strange religious innovation" (414); apart from running a risk to provoke a war with the Romans, they were also guilty of committing impiety since they wished to exclude any other nation but Jews from the right of religious sacrifice and worship (ibid). Knowing what we do about the operations of the religious dissent, it may be surmised that the argument of the radical (or reactionary, depending on one's viewpoint) priests must have been the opposite – namely, the need to *restore* the practices from time immemorial, *before* alien gifts and sacrifices had been introduced (presumably, under the Persian rule) by renegades or opportunists. The outcome of their decision would be – so runs Josephus's rhetoric, with the benefit of hindsight – that "once they abolish the sacrifices for the Romans, they might not be allowed to continue sacrifices even for themselves" (416), that is to say, the ritual will be altogether suppressed by the victorious enemy. But although this argument made sense, both historically and politically, it was apparently at too much variance with the popular mood of the moment and came to be rejected even by the 'ministers' (presumably, ordinary priests and Levites) of the Temple (417). Whatever we make of the details offered by Josephus, and irrespective of precedential or exegetical arguments that could have been offered on each side, one fact stands clear: in this whole development, the course of behavior taken by a defiant group betrays the religious dissent mentality as understood in this book: the traditions revered and upheld by the priestly establishment – and, *eo ipso*, the establishment itself – are repudiated as incompatible with the original spirit of the faith.[2]

At the same time, it must be realized that the moment chosen by Eleazar b. Ananias and his confederates for their secession was, in practical and political terms, hardly propitious. The Romans had just achieved an impressive success in war with Parthia, which forced the latter's King Vologeses I to recognize the Roman protectorate over Armenia: his own brother Tiridates was to travel to Rome with the purpose of receiving the Armenian crown from Nero personally (Tac. *Ann.*, 15, 17 ff.; 16, 23 f.). Under such circumstances, the chance that the Parthians could have supported any uprising in Judaea against Rome must have been negligible; and there was no other force around to offer it military or material help of any real consequence. In fact, the only foreigners who came to aid the insurgents were the royal family of the small neighboring kingdom of Adiabene, several members of whom had converted to Judaism few years earlier – their story is told in much detail by Josephus (*AJ*, 20, 17 ff.); they joined the rebel forces, some fought with valor, and others surrendered eventually to Titus (cf. *BJ*, 2, 520; 6, 357).

Given the specifics of the mindset, characteristic of religious dissenters, one wonders, however, whether such or similar political considerations had been even entertained by some of them at the exalted moment (or any time before that) when they proclaimed that the Imperial sacrifices must cease – and if they thought of this at all, then how seriously. There is no means, of course, to measure the extent or intensity of their feelings, but it seems reasonable to assume that, confronted as they were with the prospect of standing up against the gigantic military machine of the Roman superpower, they must have been ultimately relying, rather than upon pragmatic or military calculations, upon the beneficent support coming from God, the upholder of the righteous, to whose cause, as they must have by then been convinced, they would readily give up their lives.[3]

Josephus's account creates an impression that the chief motives of Eleazar b. Ananias and his group were nationalist: namely, that they sought by their action to make Judaea's breach from Rome irreversible, with the purpose of ultimately liberating the land. In his capacity as apologist of Judaism, however, the historian consistently tended to downplay the significance in decision-making of the religious factor, which was, within the Roman Judaea's context, inseparable from the 'nationalist' project; but it must and can be ascertained. It is true that the rabbinic material should be treated with great caution so far as it concerns the historical events prior to the destruction of the Temple. This is, however, one of those few occasions where some particular information derived from the Tannaitic texts might conceivably elucidate, at least to some extent, what must have been a passionate religious debate behind the sacrifices issue that Josephus chose to ignore. This concerns the famous episode of the Eighteen Halakhoth, when the followers of Shammai are said to have overruled, with the use of force, the Hillelites and promulgated a series of decrees strictly prohibiting the whole variety of intercourse with non-Jews, including the acceptance of their gifts (*mShab.*, 1:4).

The later tradition places this event 'in the upper room of R. Hanania b. Hezekiah b. Garon' (who may or may not have been identical with Eleazar's father Ananias b. Nedebaeus), and there can be little doubt that it would have occurred shortly before or shortly after the demarche at the Temple on the matter of the Imperial sacrifices. One reads that the violence broke down and six men who belonged to R. Hillel's school were put to the sword by the angry Shammaites (*jShab.*,1:4h-i). It does not seem likely that the incident so disruptive and of so great halakhic significance could have been invented by the rabbis out of cloth; even though much embellished or in part fictionalized, this story must reflect – although very much in retrospect – the heated passions surrounding the outbreak of hostilities. The Tosefta observes: "And that day was as harsh for Israel as the day on which the golden calf was made" (*tShab.*, 1:16). This is a very strong statement indeed, but it does make sense: the moment of supremacy enjoyed, within the Pharisaic movement, by the narrow minded and often prejudiced Shammaite creed, was bound to reinforce the irrational behavior among the religious dissenters of various descriptions, and contributed to the subsequent national disaster.

With the cessation of the Imperial sacrifices at the Temple, the payment of the tribute to Rome also stopped (cf. *BJ*, 2, 403 f.). We are told that the collaborationist group, sensing that the trouble was unavoidable, hastened to dispatch envoys to procurator Florus and King Agrippa II with the request for reinforcements (418 f.). Nowhere does Josephus suggest that one of their motives could have been any genuine sympathy for, or sense of duty towards, the conquerors. This may, or may not – apophatically – imply that they did harbor certain genuine patriotic or religious sentiments which were in conflict with the pragmatic needs for pretense and dissimulation; but it seems idle to further speculate on what else could have gone on in the minds of these men. Indeed, Josephus states that they acted in fear of falling first victims to Rome's vengeance and thus were eager to exonerate themselves in advance (*BJ*, 2, 418 f.), which stands to reason, so far as we may imagine, under the circumstances, how at least some such people might behave. But all of this is still a far cry from a belief that the Jewish ruling elite as a group was disloyal to their Roman masters and bears the main responsibility for the revolt – or from categorizing all of them as traitors to their nation. In historical predicaments like this, human motives and conduct, individual or collective, are never simple, but more often than not betray contradictory components. (At least one major Pharisaic sage, although unmentioned by Josephus, Rabban Johanan b. Zakkai, seems to have acted as a pacifist on the matter of principle.)

As it appears, the procurator did not deign even to give a reply to the Jewish emissaries (420); but the King sent to their aid 2000 horsemen (421). It is worth noticing that, in contrast to his treatment, just discussed, of Jerusalem's collaborationists, Josephus takes care to emphasize Agrippa's commitment to Roman interests: he "felt concern equally for the insurgents and for the people with whom they were coming into war, desiring that the Jews would be saved for the Romans, and the Temple and their capital for the Jews" (ibid.).[4]

The figure of Eleazar b. Ananias belongs among the most enigmatic in Josephus's entire narrative. What the latter says about this "most audacious young man"

(409) is by no means sufficient to make any coherent picture of that man's personality and ideas. Like most of the faction leaders in Judaea's politics, before and after the outbreak of the revolt, he was a member of the priestly establishment, and even more than that, a son of the former high priest Ananias b. Nedebaeus, who had exercised a formidable influence on public affairs in Judaea during the first half of the 60s. That up to a point he must have enjoyed the full trust of his father and those of his father's fellow collaborationists with the Romans is apparent from the position he presumably held – the captain of the Temple (*sagan*), an official who in the hierarchy ranked next to high priest. His candidacy for that office had to be approved by all powers that be, both Jewish and Roman: after all, the Temple grounds made, politically speaking, the most sensitive area in the city of Jerusalem since it often provided causes, or pretexts, for popular disturbances. From the *Antiquitates* we also learn that, during the previous procuratorship of Lucceius Albinus, Eleazar's own secretary had been kidnapped by the terrorist *sicarii*, with whom, ironically, Eleazar himself later chose to forge a short-lived alliance against the Romans. Very much in the manner of the present day practitioners of terror, the kidnappers demanded in exchange for their prisoner the release of their own ten confederates who were put in jail by the Roman administration. We are told that Eleazar's father Ananias negotiated with the procurator regarding this request and eventually obtained (perhaps not without some sort of bribery) the latter's consent (20, 208 f.). It did not take him much time, however, to learn the bitter lesson which is familiar to us moderns: that the terrorist demands must, unfortunately, never be met, even at the cost of human life. Josephus writes:

> This was the start of greater evils: for the brigands contrived in all sorts of ways to seize some members of Ananias' household and keeping them in confinement, would not release them unless they get some of their fellow *sicarii* back. Becoming not inconsiderable in number, they turned audacious and began inflicting injury on the entire land.
> (210)

This reads like rhetorical exaggeration, but as in many such cases it does not mean total fictionalizing: at the time, this action by the kidnappers must have been well publicized, and Josephus's Jewish audience knew that this sort of thing could and did happen.

One may only speculate what exactly might have been responsible for Eleazar's change of heart and his adoption of the rebel cause. In part, the answer may lie in the conflict of generations, of fathers and sons. It seems possible that Eleazar's elder brother, Ananus b. Ananias, who preceded him as the captain of the Temple, has been also in some way involved, under the procurator Ventidius Cumanus, with the violent hostilities between the Galilaeans and the Samaritans which almost resulted in the national Jewish uprising, a prefiguration of the Great Revolt in A.D. 66 (*BJ*, 2, 232 ff.; *AJ*, 20, 118 ff.). In any event, Ananus, together with his father, the powerful Ananias b. Nedebaeus, whom his son's attitudes or activities might have drawn into trouble, were sent to Rome by the governor of Syria Ummidius Quadratus; and, according to Josephus, only the intervention of the young king Agrippa II prompted Claudius to render a verdict in favor of the Jews, which allowed them to return home (*BJ*, 2, 243 ff.; *AJ*, 20, 131 ff.).

Eleazar could have been inspired by nationalist fervor and genuinely sought Judaea's liberation from the Roman yoke. To this may be added personal ambitions and hunger for power, major characteristics of most revolutionaries throughout ages. Whether he also proved genuinely susceptible to the sentiments of religious dissent, requiring the break with customary practices they considered corrupt, we do not know, although his conduct as portrayed by Josephus suggests that he did; alternatively, he could have played on such sensibilities in pursuing whatever agenda of his own. But one can hardly doubt that the mindset, characteristic of religious dissenters, motivated most of his priestly followers at the Temple in rising up against both the establishment and tradition; this confirms that it easily crossed over social and sectarian borders. On the other hand, Eleazar was brought up in the environment well attuned to the Imperial politics, fraught with rivalries, bickering and so forth. Thus he may have needed to exercise a measure of dissimulation (before the break) in his relationship with the Romans, his father and other collaborationists – as, later on, with the *sicarii*: for the latter's terrorist conduct and their hereditary leader Menachem b. Judas he could have hardly felt, as the events have proved, any true sympathy. Their abortive alliance can be satisfactorily explained by practical exigencies. One cannot determine, for the lack of evidence, what effect on him might have exercised the theocratic/anarchic "fourth philosophy" founded by Judas the Galilaean (discussed at length in the chapters to follow), which uncannily blended religious and nationalist extremism under the caption of "zeal for God and for the law": it became the driving force behind much of the revolutionary activities at the time. At the very least, Eleazar must have been aware of its existence and appeal. Nor do we hear from Josephus, in contrast to some other dissenters, that Eleazar b. Ananias ever considered himself a vessel of divine grace or a special instrument of God's will. In any event, by formulating the cessation decree as they did – in the spirit of the Shammaite anti-gentile doctrine (that is, banning all alien, and not just Imperial sacrifices) – he and his partisans had also betrayed a characteristic disregard for reality: as I have already pointed out, this was bound notably to affect the Temple's revenues and create a variety of further complications. It may be argued that the broader formula they used implies an element of political calculating. It could have been hoped to subsume the effrontery as aimed specifically at Rome and the emperor; if so, its framers had intended a careful gesture of defiance rather than provoking the full-scale hostilities with the occupier. The subsequent suspension of the tribute payments, however, speaks against this. Josephus is silent on any possible links to have existed between Eleazar b. Ananias and the group of zealots around his namesake

Eleazar b. Simon, who later on took control temporarily over the capital. It is true that the termination of the Imperial sacrifices coincided in time with the capture of the fortress Masada by a different group of insurgents and with Menachem's subsequent march on Jerusalem (*BJ*, 2, 408; cf. 425), but to hold this as a proof of a prearranged conspiracy, with no further supportive evidence, would mean going too far.[5]

Eleazar's actions (so far as they can be construed from the *Bellum*) in the immediate aftermath of his move abolishing the Imperial sacrifices seem to have followed pragmatic needs. We read that for the duration of the entire week he successfully defended the Temple against the troops sent by King Agrippa II under the command of his trusted general Philip b. Jacimus and one Darius, the hipparch (421 ff.). The requirements of the moment resulted in Eleazar's joining forces, against the common enemy, with the 'sicarian' leader Menachem b. Judas, who entered Jerusalem, with all his bodyguards, "like a king" (434) – the description that *may* have related to what I have called, for the sake of convenience, 'the messianic complex'. Together, they proceeded to capture the upper city, formerly in the hands of the loyalists (cf. 422), except for several fortifications at the royal palace that for a time continued to be held by the enemy (425 ff.; 438 ff.) – violating in the process, Josephus says, the feast of wood carrying, when it was customary to bring wood to the Temple's altar so that the sacred flames would never cease (425). Eleazar's apparent connivance with setting the public archives on fire (ca. August A.D. 66) that held the moneylenders' bonds (427) was bound to increase his popular following of whom he stood in strong need: even though this act might have been essentially symbolic, it still betrayed social tensions and anxieties of the common people of which, regrettably, there is little to know. And, finally, his role in the assassination of Menachem (442 ff.; cf. *Vita*, 21) – who by that time is said to have assumed an overall leadership of the rebels (*BJ*, 2, 434) – put an end to the rule of terror introduced by the latter, at the same time offering Eleazar a prospect of an even greater prominence. This signified his resolute rupture with the *sicarii*, many of whom suffered Menachem's fate (446). To this brief interlude, played by the *sicarii* in Jerusalem during the early stage of the revolt, I will return.

Those of them who had survived fled the capital and, under the command of the dead man's relative Eleazar b. Jairus withdrew to Masada (447), where they appear to have remained, not interfering in the affairs at Jerusalem until their famous suicidal stand against the Romans two years after the Flavian triumph, in A.D. 73.

No doubt, the murder by Menachem and his partisans of Eleazar's own father, the former high priest Ananias, and his uncle Ezechias (441) must have deeply affected the son's resolve to get rid of the *sicarii* and their chief. But it cannot be denied that the assault on the latter, committed by him and his adherents at the holy place, however politically expedient, or psychologically explicable, meant the desecration of the sanctuary: it provides an early example from the revolt of the Jewish dissenters violating a fundamental law of their faith.

One may imagine that, irrespective of political antagonism, which seems to have evolved by then between the father and the son, the tragedy had a sobering effect on Eleazar, undermining his moral fiber and his will to struggle for leadership. His hold over his own followers began to slacken. This may explain the butchery of the garrison from the royal palace upon its final surrender – despite the solemnly sworn pledge of their security by the rebels that must have involved the invocation of the gods' – and God's – names:

> So long as they [surrendering soldiers – V. R.] remained armed, no one of the rebels laid a hand on them or betrayed any sign of treachery; but when, in accordance to the treaty, they all put down their shields and swords, and made to leave, still suspecting nothing, men of Eleazar rushed at them, and surrounding them, put them to death, while [the latter], neither resisting nor pleading, only cried out appeals to the treaty and the oaths.
>
> (452 f.)

The episode constitutes therefore a second violation of the basic religious law by the revolutionary dissenters, occurring so quickly after the first: namely, the breach of the sacred oath. Even worse, Josephus emphasizes (and particularly laments) that this slaughter happened on the Sabbath day: "a day on which they abstain even from sacred activities" (456) – a point of significance, not much appreciated in modern scholarship. It is inconceivable that Josephus could have invented any of it: Jerusalem's entire populace was bound to witness what has happened. Furthermore, charging his coreligionists with a sacrilege of such magnitude that in reality did not occur would have fatefully undermined the historian's self-definition as a *bona fide* Jew and utterly destroyed his credibility in the eyes of his entire Jewish audience, including the Jewish community in Rome.

This was the first act of collective atrocity after the war had openly broken out, and it must have left a bitter and pervasive imprint upon the occupiers: during times of trouble, memories of this kind are bound to last long. It is apparent that no such thing could have ever been performed by the traditionally pious Jews, the observance of the Sabbath day being among their religion's central commandments (*Exod.*, 20:8 ff.; 31,13 ff; *Deut.*, 5:12 ff.). Many such individuals surely felt shocked at the perpetrated major – and double – blasphemy (breaking oaths and violating God's Sabbath), even though one allows for much exaggeration in Josephus's comment that the city plunged into public mourning (*BJ*, 2, 455). This violent and ostentatious abuse of the Fourth Commandment, constituting a crime against the Law, required a different set of sensibilities, which we associate with the deep-seated religious dissent, that would allow, in belief of thus fulfilling the divine will, grossly to violate the chief prescriptions of one's own faith. The same mixture of disdain towards religious proprieties, coupled with the enthusiasm in regard to their religion as such, is a strikingly recurrent feature of both individual and collective behavior among the radical insurgents throughout the entire upheaval.

It does not seem likely that the massacre was initiated, or even approved, by Eleazar, who – one assumes – had acquired at least some experience in politics under the auspices of his father to learn what is desirable, permissible or achievable – a quality that would have been alien to the majority of his radical adherents. We are told that only the garrison's commander Metilius managed to save his life by promising to convert into Judaism and even undergo circumcision (454). One wonders what happened to him thereafter.

The amazing fact is that, from this point on, the name of Eleazar b. Ananias virtually disappears from Josephus's narrative of the war. Even if he is identical with a general later selected by the rebels to govern Idumaea, who is referred to in the *Bellum*'s manuscripts as Eleazar, son of Neos (2, 566), and never mentioned again, the puzzle deepens: this would have meant his surprising demotion from prominence in leadership to a lower and subordinate role, especially since he had hardly ever undergone any military experience. Nor does he figure in Josephus's autobiography, the *Vita*. There exists not the slightest hint at his subsequent fate. This is, indeed, a riddle, which may reflect on our author's descriptive, and sometimes unfathomable, procedures – or relate to his contradictory feelings (or lack thereof) about the man whom he must have personally known. So much on the first identifiable leader of the Jewish revolt.[6]

It is now imperative to review a series of disturbances that immediately preceded the cessation of the Imperial sacrifices. Josephus blames the ethnic disorders in Caesarea Maritima for originating the trouble, and irrespective of what we think about the veracity of their representation in his narrative, their very fact cannot be denied, and it must have contributed to the growing trouble. Given the vast divergences in attitudes and patterns of behavior, it is not surprising that socio-politico-cultural tensions between Jews and the gentiles (that is to say, Greeks as well as the Hellenized Syrians, both in Judaea and in the Diaspora) were intermittent: due to xenophobic propensities of human nature, with its fear and suspicion of the 'Other', it could hardly have been different. In the cities of Palaestina, they were often living side-by-side and were thus compelled daily to interact, with varying periods or degrees of reciprocity and discord. Caesarea Maritima, the headquarters of the Roman procurator, became particularly renowned for recurrent inter-communal conflicts, especially over the issue of citizen rights. (Known as Strato's Tower, it was originally founded by the Phoenicians and used by the Greeks largely as the trade outpost; it was fundamentally rebuilt by Herod I and renamed by him in honor of Augustus.) An additional factor to aggravate the problem proved the presence in that city of the so-called 'Sebastenian' cohorts (the word comes from Sebaste, the Roman name for Samaria), consisting of the Samaritan and Syrian recruits, the latter enlisted across the land, who were pervasively hostile towards the local Jews. A few years prior to the revolt, riots in that city (ca. A.D. 59–60) led to the bloody clashes between the Jews and the gentiles, which were suppressed by the procurator Antonius Felix. The delegation representing both sides had been sent to Nero, who eventually ruled against the Jews (*BJ*, 2, 266 ff; 284; *AJ*, 20, 182 ff.). This verdict certainly could not have pacified the local Jewish radicals, and the renewed disturbances there in the spring of A.D. 66 (*BJ*, 2, 285–92) came to engender a chain of events that, among other factors, indirectly led towards revolutionary explosion. Although – in contrast to the cessation of the Imperial sacrifice – this cannot be considered as providing an official *casus belli*, Josephus, in following perhaps Thucydidean precedent, calls it "an insignificant pretext" (*BJ*, 2, 284) for the subsequent disaster. The historian tells us (and there is no reason to disprove this as fact) that the initial bone of contention happened to be a piece of land, owned by a Greek, and adjoining the Jewish synagogue, which the Jewish community sought to purchase. We are told that the owner stubbornly refused their very generous offers and, furthermore, went on with the plans to erect yet another building on the very site the Jews wished to obtain: a conflict of interests not uncommon even now, as for instance between local communities and realtors, with the difference that today carefully crafted legal mechanisms allow for regulating such problems. In response, some young hotheads, in Josephus's words, attacked the builders, which led to Roman intervention ending the violence. At this point, several Jewish notables, led by one John the tax collector, took upon themselves, as it by then became customary, to bribe the current procurator Gessius Florus and offered him eight talents so that he would interfere on their behalf and order the new construction works to stop. Florus accepted the money, did nothing and immediately left Caesarea Maritima for Samaria, providing, Josephus observes, "a free opportunity for sedition, as if he sold the Jews license to do the fighting" (288). The next day, which was a Sabbath, saw a spectacle of mockery offensive to Jewish sensibilities, both ethnic and religious. One of their Greek or Syrian foes performed, at the entrance of the synagogue, a sacrifice of birds on the pot turned upside down (289) – possibly (but not necessarily) an allusion to an old slander that the Jews were driven from Egypt at the time of Exodus for having been lepers. (The Mosaic Law requires that as a sacrifice for a leper, birds are to be killed in an earthen vessel – *Lev.* 14, 4 ff.; 49 ff.). Even though as an insult it may appear slight, the Jews, with their heightened sense of the sacred, considered this an act defiling their place of worship and felt outraged: in this case, it was a predictable and natural response by pious believers, and not any specific manifestation of religious dissent.

The ensuing confrontation, in which both sides came to blows, could not be quieted down even with the arrival of the Roman cavalry commander Jucundus. The gentiles were, apparently, having an upper hand so that the Jews eventually withdrew to Narbata, at some distance from Caesarea Maritima, reportedly taking their Torah with them – one assumes in fear of another blasphemy. Twelve of their number, with the same tax collector John at their head, came to lay their complaints and grievances before Florus at Samaria, with the most unexpected results. Josephus indicates that, while seeking his assistance, they "respectfully" reminded him of the eight talents they had paid him earlier (*BJ*, 2, 292). If this was, indeed, the case, it is an example of poor diplomacy, however carefully conceived. The procurator did not appreciate the reminder and promptly had the delegation arrested on the ridiculous charge of having removed their Books of Law from the city (ibid). This accusation sounds very bizarre: the Roman policies towards Jews followed, for the most part, the principle of non-interference in their religious affairs. Although we do not know enough about the legal boundaries within Roman provincial jurisdiction, it still seems dubious that this measure, taken by Florus, could be justified even in terms of *coercitio*, his right to exercise, under critical circumstances, arbitrary justice, however broad it might have been. On the other hand, Florus's penchant for offensive actions and illegal violence throughout his career in Palaestina was, as will be seen, conspicuously undeniable.

Be that as it may, the conflict that started in one city on purely material, or economic, grounds (rivalry over a plot of land) rapidly acquired cultural and religious dimensions (sacrilege perpetrated in front of the synagogue; removal of the Torah) originating in some turmoil that a hostile Roman administrator could have politically identified as sedition (*seditio*). This is the view, it seems, that Florus took from the outset, which must have determined most of his subsequent decisions.[7]

The repercussions of this affair, Josephus suggests, soon began to be felt in Jerusalem, although its inhabitants, according to him, tried to restrain their anger (*BJ*, 2, 293). It has been argued that the historian made every effort to exonerate the Jewish establishment, to which he belonged, from the responsibility for the outbreak of the revolt, having also overemphasized the repressive policies of the procurator. Still, the latter's subsequent moves, which must have been the matter of public record, speak for themselves. Florus began by sending his agents to forcefully appropriate 17 talents from the Temple's treasury, "referring to the needs of Caesar" (ibid). Even if one believes that there had been legitimate grounds (such as the delay in the payment of tribute; cf. 403, 405) to demand this money, the manner in which it was extracted was clearly reprehensible. It appears that at the time the Herodian royalty, and not the procurators, exercised formal control over the Temple's treasury (cf. *AJ*, 20, 15 f., 222). It seems unlikely, however, that Florus managed to receive in advance (and Josephus chose to suppress the fact) an approval from King Agriipa II, who was then visiting Egypt (*BJ*, 2, 334). Otherwise, various participants, as well as the crowds, would have behaved differently, and the king branded as collaborator from the outset. This is not what happened: the king retained enough influence to communicate later on meaningfully with rulers and people of Jerusalem, and some of his advice, as will be seen, might have even been listened to by the latter before he was finally made to withdraw from the capital.

One of the sad lessons history offers is that all too often it is form we adopt in conducting politics, rather than substance, that matters. Florus's expropriation shocked the people of Jerusalem to the extent that they proceeded *en masse* to remonstrate, "crying out piercingly Caesar's name and called on him to liberate them from Florus' tyranny" (294), a sign that the procurator's activities were widely seen as illegal, while the appeals to Nero – and there is no reason to deny that at least some people in the crowd did in fact loudly invoke his name – testified to their mood of loyalty towards Rome. Nor is this impression contravened by a "bad joke" at the expense of Florus that a group of protesters came to indulge in: we are told that certain individuals, who shouted "most scornful" abuses at the procurator, also mocked him by carrying around a basket, asking for alms on his behalf as if he were a penniless pauper (295) – yet another episode too specific to be invented by Josephus. Again, the target of the joke was not Rome or its emperor, but one particularly corrupt official, since it implied that he took money from the Temple's treasury not on his master's command or behalf, but for the purpose of self-enrichment.

In any event, Florus vastly overreacted. Instead of returning to Caesarea Maritima, where (Josephus points this out) the riotous discontent continued to brew, he marched, with at least one cohort (cf. 332), to Jerusalem in order personally to punish the offenders (296). The very fact that a joke, however bad, could elicit that kind of response is indicative of diverse and extraordinary tensions that developed by this time in Roman Palaestina. Upon his arrival, the procurator took residence in the palace, convoked the tribunal and demanded that the members of the Jewish establishment hand over to him all those who dared to insult him in public (301). Josephus's narrative implies that it was harsh punishment, perhaps even death, that he intended to visit upon the culprits, and this may explain prevarication on the part of the influential Jews who were reluctant to comply. It has been sensibly suggested that the main reason for their resistance could be participation in the joke of some young men, belonging to their own class, perhaps including sons of at least some among those who were summoned by Florus. It might account for various pretexts they supposedly offered, against submitting to the procuratorial order; but this attitude does not signify, as it has been sometimes argued, that Jewish aristocracy, or the majority of it, was prepared, or inclined, to take the road of revolt. At the same time, Florus's proceedings in terms of Roman law strike as increasingly questionable, even if one takes into account the frequent disregard of legal niceties at the time, particularly when it concerned the provincials: strictly speaking, the young men could hardly have been accused with treason (*maiestas*) unless it was demonstrated that in the person of the procurator they sought to slander the emperor. It also remains uncertain whether prosecution on private grounds, such as for libel, could actually fall within boundaries of the procuratorial prerogative, or inquiry, called *cognitio extra ordinem*. Be that as it may, any prudent public official, conscious of the critical situation in the land, would have resorted at that point to diplomacy in order to achieve some sort of compromise, dissolve the strain and avoid further trouble.

Florus, poor dissimulator that he was, chose to do the opposite. He ordered his soldiers to carry out pogroms and massacres (which resulted, according to Josephus, in 3600 victims – 307) – an act justifiable in view of Roman practices elsewhere perhaps only in the case of a full-scale insurrection. Josephus states specifically (308) that the extent of Roman cruelty on this occasion was without precedent, and it seems likely that it was so. The procurator had the Jews of equestrian rank scourged and crucified, which in theory did constitute illegal outrage: the equestrian rank (*dignitas*) implied the possession of Roman citizenship which entitled its bearers not only to a fair trial, but also to seek appeal at the court of the emperor. Finally, Florus committed a grave diplomatic blunder by not only disregarding an attempt at intercession on the part of Agrippa's sister, the would-be-famous Berenice, Queen of Chalcis, but even by placing her very life in danger. Josephus claims that the soldiers of the procurator tortured and murdered their captives under her eyes and, furthermore, they "would have killed her as well, had she not first escaped to the palace, where she spent the night with her guards fearing the attack of the soldiers" (312). His rhetoric notwithstanding, any of this was certainly *not* what routinely used to happen even under the worst of the procurators; and, apart from his infringements of the earlier (and traditional) Roman practices, it is in this respect – in his absolute disregard for proprieties – that Florus betrays *qualitative* difference from all his predecessors, which some modern interpreters fail to recognize. It is known that Josephus's manuscript was read and approved both by Titus and King Agrippa, as well as by other members of the royal house (*Vita*, 362 ff.). In consequence, the whole episode in question is to be considered largely authentic.[8]

The events of the next few days as shown in Josephus's narrative must be briefly summarized. The pacifist, or collaborationist, members of the Jewish establishment, "influential men and chief priests" (*BJ*, 2, 316), undertook to placate the angry crowds, much incensed against Florus and the Romans, and temporarily seemed to have succeeded. For proof of their acquiescence, the procurator demanded that the inhabitants of Jerusalem make procession and greet two more cohorts that were to arrive from Caesarea Maritima (318 f.), an order aimed at their further humiliation. (Josephus describes rather pathetically the efforts on the part of the pro-Roman Jewish leaders in convincing the mob to comply even with this offensive wish; 321 ff.). This led, however, only to another clash with dramatic consequences: a great number of the locals were killed, or trampled upon by horses, or just perished in the crush at the gates. But the Romans failed to seize the Temple or the fortifications and were driven into retreating to their camp in the neighborhood of the palace (329). As a result, the insurgents cut communications between the Temple and the palace. This measure, according to the *Bellum*, was intended to forestall Florus's plan of raiding the Temple's treasury (331). Thereupon, we are told, having realized that the coveted gold, at least for the present, was out of his reach, the procurator consulted with the priestly authorities and the city council, who undertook to restore order, and withdrew from the city. He returned to his headquarters at Caesarea Maritima, leaving behind a cohort that did not participate in the original massacre and was deemed by both sides as a sufficient garrison against any further revolutionary unrest (332). It appears more likely, however, that Florus, conscious of how vulnerable his troops must have been in front of the superior numbers joining the rebels, and that the entire predicament may indeed explode into a national uprising, tried to shift responsibility and look for reinforcements. At any rate, some order was temporarily restored, largely owing to the efforts of Jerusalem's ruling elite, which undermines a modern argument that these very men, for the most part, were themselves the carriers of the revolutionary sentiments.

Having simultaneously received the procurator's report, in which the latter, predictably, blamed Jews for all that had happened, and the petitions from Jerusalem's elders and Queen Berenice, telling him their side of the story, the governor (legate) of Syria, C. Cestius Gallus (A.D. ?63–66), must have felt particularly perplexed. It seems that, in contrast to Florus, not only did he realize the politically precarious character of the situation, but also that it required an exercise of special caution. Therefore, instead of going in person to Jerusalem with an army, as it was reportedly advised by some of his officers, the governor chose to send his trusted emissary, the military tribune Neapolitanus, so that the latter could undertake an impartial inquiry and collect evidence. We are told that Neapolitanus encountered King Agrippa II at Jamnia, finally returning from Egypt (334 f.). It is there that the king was apprised of the recent events both by Neapolitanus and by the delegation of the Jewish notables who came from Jerusalem to welcome him back?

Josephus goes out of his way in order to justify in the *Bellum* Agrippa's subsequent course of action. This is understandable given the personal relationship between two men at the time (one recalls that Agrippa was a privileged reader of this very history Josephus was working on) and the outcome of the deliberations at Jamnia. The very rhetoric of the historian's narrative suggests that the king, well versed in the intrigues at the Imperial court, knew how to practice dissimulation. In a particularly convoluted twist of argument, Josephus asserts that although at the depth of his heart King Agrippa felt solidarity with his people against the procurator, he pretended to have disbelieved them in order "to turn them away from vengeance" (337). It stands to reason that behind his behavior at that point lay the desire to avoid any kind of involvement in the crisis, fraught, as he might have sensed, with incalculable repercussions.

This attitude of the king was further challenged, however, when he and Neapolitanus met with the crowds of the Jerusalemites outside the city, demonstrating against the slaughter and desolation inflicted on it by Florus. Josephus states that, after having examined the evidence, the Roman tribune felt sufficiently impressed: he is said to have commended the multitude for their loyalty to Rome and sermonized on the need to preserve peace (341). We are even told that he paid devotions at the Temple's Court of the Gentiles (ibid; we remember that all this had taken place before the Imperial sacrifices stopped). Given the public character of any such gesture, it could have hardly been invented by Josephus. It remains, however, still a matter of speculation whether, upon his return, Neapolitanus's account to the governor Gallus was indeed as patently favorable towards the Jews as the historian wanted his readers to think.

Josephus reports the proposal by Jews for sending a delegation to Nero with complaints against Florus (342 f.). We do not know who exactly advocated that plan – the text seems to imply that this was the wish of popular majority (342); but under the circumstances this does not sound right. Still, even though Josephus's language betrays his apologetic concerns, this is not the reason to deny that there could well have been present at the gathering a group of strong collaborationists who saw the only sensible course of action in direct negotiating with the Emperor. But in practice, this involved a series of problems. Traditionally, any such project needed the procurator's authorization (in this case, of course, from the very man who was to be indicted – a procedure favored by many bureaucracies), although whether such requirement was formal or mandatory remains uncertain. Furthermore, it was not legally possible for provincials officially to denounce at Rome their current administrator until the expiration of his term in office. There did, however, exist an alternative – namely, to petition Syria's governor Cestius Gallus forcefully to interfere, with the purpose of ultimately bringing the matter to the emperor's attention. With luck, this might have resulted in Florus's recall, upon which they could legitimately charge him of extortion. The precedent under Claudius must have still been fresh in memory, when a similar course of action ultimately led to the removal and disgrace of another offensive procurator. Those in the crowd pressuring for dispatching an embassy might not have been aware of all these legal or quasi-legal niceties, but King Agrippa surely was, and he could have advised them how properly to proceed. This he never did.

Nor did governor Gallus, unlike some of his predecessors, take initiative to rectify Florus's abuses and thus dissolve the crisis. Perhaps even a temporary suspension of the abuser might have sealed the matter. This seems to have been the issue on which the development of the events fatefully hinged. In practice, if not perhaps not in theory, Gallus was in a position to dispatch the procurator to Rome so that he could stand trial before the emperor on the charge of maladministration. Two such precedents were created by his predecessors: L. Vitellius, in A.D. 37 (the last year of Tiberius) thus dismissed Pontius Pilate upon hearing the Samaritan complain about the massacre the latter had committed on Mount Gerisim (*AJ*, 18, 89); and in A.D. 52, under Claudius, Ummidius Quadratus visited with the same kind of treatment the offensive Ventidius Cumanus (he grossly mishandled the Jewish–Samaritan conflict – *BJ*, 2, 244; *AJ*, 20, 132), with the result that the latter was disgraced and sent into exile by the emperor, who eventually ruled in favor of Jews; this last episode must have still been well remembered.

The reasons behind Gallus's failure to act are not known. The study of history suggests that while multiple factors – economic, social, political – contribute to society's descent into crisis, what really matters is the response to it by a relatively small group of individuals who participate in the decision-making process. This means that, among other things, one must thoroughly consider interpersonal relations within that very group, which is, for the most part, very hard – if not impossible – to do, earlier than during the modern period, for the lack of reliable documentation, such as the discussion minutes, confidential papers, diaries and private correspondence. We repeatedly hear of divisions among Gallus's advisers, both prior to (*BJ*, 2, 334) and after (531) the outbreak of hostilities as regards the appropriate course of conduct, although the option of suspending Judaea's current procurator is not even mentioned. Be that as it may, Cestius Gallus's motives cannot be ascertained and his behavior appears erratic: it could have resulted from conflicting influences, lack of character, simple negligence, or something else.

As regards King Agrippa, Josephus's effort at elucidating the reasons for his opposition to the embassy idea seems lame. Any attempt at their reconstruction will remain necessarily speculative. He might have been concerned with the procedural issues stated above, but he still could have offered his good services *vis-à-vis* Syria's governor, or even the emperor, as he had repeatedly done, imitating his father, in the past. It seems logical, on the other hand, to explain Agrippa's attitude by his possession of some privileged knowledge about the change in Nero's stance towards Jews upon the death of his wife Poppaea Sabina, a theme to which I will return. Whatever the case, his avoidance of any direct mediatory role strongly implies that the current situation at the Neronian court must have been altogether adverse to Jewish interests. In any event, given the attitudes taken by Syria's governor and the King, and after the idea of electing the envoys had been buried, nothing could have precluded, as one comes to realize, the development of the events in the direction they took.[9]

The speech addressing the popular rally at Xistus on the current state of affairs, which is attributed to King Agrippa (*BJ*, 2, 345–404), belongs among the lengthiest in Josephus's oeuvre. That the king actually spoke to the people of Jerusalem cannot be doubted: he was too conspicuous a figure, and his actions were still imprinted on public memory, for Josephus to invent or grossly misrepresent them. What he said is, of course, another matter. It is hardly possible to establish how much Josephus's version owed to his own recollection, his hindsight and his agenda at the time of writing, or to rhetorical embellishment. Furthermore, it seems clear that this speech reflects much of the historian's own views, similarly expressed by him elsewhere (cf. esp., *BJ*, 5, 365 ff.) – the views, that is to say, of Flavius Josephus, the Jewish renegade and the Imperial courtier, and not those of Joseph b. Matthias, a young and ambitious Jewish politician, who upon return from his first trip to Rome chose to join the nascent revolutionary turmoil, and may have even been present among the crowds which gathered at Xistus to hear the king.

It is not my purpose to analyze Agrippa's speech here in any detail. Most of the arguments are obvious, and a summary should suffice. In Josephus's version, the king appeals to the "most honest" (*BJ*, 2, 345) portion of the community, who by this very virtue, he implies, must be in favor of peace. Then, not without resorting to some sophistry, he tries to distinguish between the motives of those bent on war: did they want to avenge injustice or achieve liberty? In the first case, he argues, freedom is not an issue; in the second, it is irrelevant whether the masters are good or bad (348–349). But the "irrational hope" (346) for victory – what nowadays one might have been called 'impatience becoming a historical force' – is then appropriately condemned. The speaker further suggests, in pragmatic terms, that it is no good to antagonize the procurators. By fighting one such man they will be rising against the emperor and the entire Roman Empire, while the emperor, who is far away, may not even know of the wrongs visited upon them. (This claim stands, however, in contradiction with Agrippa's own reported disapproval of sending an embassy to inform Nero about the current misrule). Moreover, the same procurator does not stay forever and may well be succeeded by a better man (351–355). Next, the speaker is made to assert that it is too late to start fighting for freedom: their forefathers, who submitted themselves to Pompey, were to blame, and their own submission became hereditary: "the one, who has been once subdued and then revolts, is an insolent slave, not a lover of freedom" (356). This is followed, predictably, by a formidable list of nations, some of them in the past very powerful, which nonetheless failed to resist the military might of Rome and were made its subjects (358–387). (One wonders how much meaning these historical examples – Athens, Sparta, Macedon, Carthage and the like – could have held for the Jewish audience at large). It is stated correctly that the martial resources of all Judaea, on the one hand, and the Roman war machine, on the other, are incommensurable (361–362). The king's listeners are further warned that if they rebel, they will find no allies, not even from the neighboring Adiabene whose royal house recently converted to Judaism; the Parthians will prevent any move from that quarter that might violate their truce with Rome (388–389). And, finally, they are assured – and this is the historian's own favorite argument (cf. e.g., *BJ*, 1, 390; 3, 293; 5, 367; 412; 6, 110) – that there will be no forthcoming help from God since he is evidently on the side of the Romans: "Without God's help so great hegemony [of the Romans] could not exist" (*BJ*, 2, 390). More than that, the very religion of the Jews militates against the possibility of their victory in the war: the observance of the Mosaic code, such as the law of Sabbath, will perforce interfere with their fighting: "But if in this war you transgress the ancestral law, I do not know with what purpose you will continue the struggle, since your only concern is not to allow the dissolution of your fathers' customs" (393). This is (presumably) an enlightened view of the not-wholly-Jewish royalty (Agrippa's great grandfather Herod I was Idumaean), who did not passionately care about the God of Israel (elsewhere in the speech, Rome's preeminence is ascribed not to God, but to a combination of military might and Fortune or Luck; cf. 360, 373). However logical, this was hardly a kind of argumentation to convince the audience of the true believers. In conclusion, the king is made to warn the people that if they revolt and their revolt is crushed, as it surely will be, they should not expect any mercy from the Romans – it would even be better to commit collective suicide (395): "To make you a lesson to other nations, they will put your holy city on fire and destroy your entire race" (397). Furthermore, a catastrophe will befall on the Jewish population in the Diaspora (399).

Agrippa's practical advice (which, according to Josephus, he gave after first having wept) was to keep quiet, pay the tax to Caesar that was in arrears, and restore the parts of fortifications that the Romans used to control (402 ff.); under the circumstances, this may well have been the gist of what he actually proposed. If we accept, as I have suggested, that at the moment the king thought any direct negotiating with Nero useless, this made a reasonable recommendation of a politically competent individual. But the mass of insurgents and many of their leaders were not politicians. Even though the historian insists that some followed Agrippa's lead and went to work on the buildings (one wishes to know who these men were and how many), while some officials attempted to levy the tribute (the figure given is 40 talents) in the villages (405), the respite was short lived. After the king made yet another try to persuade the crowd that they needed to obey Florus until Nero sent a replacement, the popular mood definitely turned against him: we are told that he became the subject of verbal abuse, which was followed by an attempt at stoning him, and finally by a proclamation of his banishment from the city (406) (although it remains unclear what particular citizen body would have pronounced such a verdict). Of course, passions ran deeper than a mere momentary anger at the sermonizing king, of whom everyone knew that he was only a little more than a puppet in Roman hands. But Josephus chose the episode to imply that by this point things went utterly out of control. Agrippa sent the elders to Florus at Caesarea Maritima with an ostensible purpose of continuing the collection of tax, while he, apparently in the absence of a viable alternative, withdrew to the territories under his own rule.[10]

The cessation of the Imperial sacrifices at the Temple, which provided the *casus belli*, occurred shortly after. One wonders whether the estimate of the status quo Josephus ascribes to the king was realistic, or some further energetic diplomacy on his part could have changed the tide. This warrants a brief inquiry into this dilemma on the basis of the little evidence we possess.

Gessius Florus is said to have come from Clazomenae in Asia Minor (*AJ*, 20, 252), but of his previous career we know nothing, and there is a peculiar irony in what Josephus reports as a fact – namely, that he owed his sudden appointment to the influence of Poppaea Sabina, who was considered a patron and protector of Jews (ibid; cf. 195; *Vita*, 16): it appears that she was friendly with Florus's wife Cleopatra, said to have been *au par* with her husband in wickedness (*AJ*, 20, 252). One should also recognize that the above-mentioned Nero's verdict, a few years prior to the Great Revolt's outbreak, in favor of the local Gentiles upon the resolution of the first crisis at Caesarea Maritima, did not signify any special turn in Imperial policies towards Jews or some special anti-Jewish sentiments on his part. Thus, we know that later on he supported the Jewish priesthood in their dispute over the Temple's new wall (which the latter wished to put down), not only against King Agrippa II, but also against his own procurator Porcius Festus (195). According to Josephus, the emperor took this decision in deference to his wife's pro-Jewish sympathies (ibid). One may speculate, of course, that Nero's attitudes changed to the worse in the aftermath of the Great Fire in Rome for which the

Christians, that is to say, a religious sect of Jewish extraction, were blamed (Tac., *Ann.*, 15, 44), and this is why the new procurator of Judaea might have felt safe while indulging, without restraint, in rapacity and extortion. More relevant, however, must have been Poppaea Sabina's death in the summer of A.D. 65 (ibid, 16, 6), roughly within a year or so after Florus took his office. It stands to reason that in the course of the next year, when both the procurator's iniquities and the popular resentment in Judaea reached a critical point, Nero paid little or no attention to the affairs of Palaestina; he was either in a state of grief over accidentally killing his own wife or in preparation for, and then embarking on, his Greek Grand Tour. In any event, Josephus insists that, in comparison with Florus, his predecessor Lucceius Albinus, himself by no means a man of probity, could be seen by the Jews as a paragon of goodness (*BJ*, 2, 277) and even 'a benefactor' (*AJ*, 20, 253).

The historian's description of indignities visited by the last Roman procurator upon the Jews in Judaea is consistent both in the *Bellum* and the *Antiquitates* and is done in the same or similar language of outrage: it does not concede any mitigating circumstance as regards that man's policies of abuse. Thus, in the *Bellum* we read that he behaved like a hangman sent to punish the condemned and did not leave out any form of plunder and violence (*BJ*, 2, 279).

This leads to the rhetorical climax:

> He was cruelest in regard to the pitiable, and most shameless concerning shameful things. No one more than he disbelieved truth; no one invented craftier means of mischief. To get profit from individual persons seemed to him a trivial matter; he pillaged whole cities and ruined entire populations, and all but proclaimed throughout the land that all could engage in banditry, provided that he would get his share of the loot.
>
> (*BJ*, 2, 278; cf. *AJ*, 20, 254 f.)

Despite its dramatic thrust and obvious stylistic ornaments, there is no genuine reason to question the basic veracity of this portrayal. One can hardly doubt that the last procurator's activities made the Romans increasingly hated within all strata of the Jewish society. In the *Antiquitates*, the author unequivocally concludes: "Florus forced us into starting the war with the Romans because we thought it that we be destroyed all together, rather than bit by bit" (20, 257). Tacitus's opinion does not seem much different (cf. *Hist.*, 5, 10).

What should, then, be made of Josephus's repeated insistence that the this corrupt individual deliberately drove Judaea's Jews to revolt so that he could divert the attention of the central authorities from his own rapacious pursuits (*BJ*, 2, 282 f.; 293; 318; 333; 420)? This is an *interpretation*, to which he, like any other history writer, is fully entitled. Whether this makes sense is a matter of opinion. It does appear implausible to some, but – when appropriately qualified – it may not be very far from truth: it is difficult to disregard the accumulated effect of his recorded *actions* (even if they are, in one sense or other, misrepresented by Josephus, which is not always, or by no means, obvious) as suggesting their perpetrator's intent further and further to aggravate the situation. As I have proposed, soon after his arrival to his province, Florus might have felt that he was allowed a sort of *laissez-faire* approach, given the demise of Poppaea Sabina and, possibly, Nero's lack of special interest in or even the latter's hostility towards the Jews. This was, however, bound to change after the multitude complained about the procurator's oppression to the governor of Syria, Gallus, during the latter's Passover (A.D. 65?) stay in Jerusalem (280; cf. 6, 422 ff.), two years or so after Gessius Florus's appointment. On that occasion (obviously historical), a huge crowd reportedly "pleaded him to have mercy on the misfortunes of their nation and cried out that Florus was their country's destroyer" (2, 280). According to Josephus, in response, Gallus pledged that he would take upon himself to insure the greater moderation on the part of the procurator in the future (281). This promise, which seems predictable under the circumstances, was never honored. Nor do we hear of any attempt on the governor's part to restrain Florus in the aftermath of Neopolitanus's mission, as described above. This tends to confirm the conclusion that Cestius Gallus bears a considerable share of responsibility for the subsequent disaster – owing to his inactivity. It is arguable that an action against Florus, if taken by Gallus on the grounds of the earlier precedents, coupled perhaps with another personal visit to Jerusalem in the midst of disturbances, might have still saved the situation. Furthermore, upon the termination of their offender's term, the Jewish authorities would have been able to charge Florus with extortion (*de repetundis*) before the emperor in Rome.

Still, nothing of the sort happened. One may speculate that after the charges had been brought against him in Judaea's capital, Florus became largely dependent on the good will of Gallus, who was his superior both in stature and status. In Roman politics no such attitude was ever a point of constancy, a truth he eventually came to learn by experience. This did not, however, prevent the procurator from pursuing his extortionist policies, whereas the governor did nothing to stop him. Could that mean that the former exercised some form of blackmail over the latter? We will never know. But as a whole, such predicaments, seen in political terms, would support (although this cannot be proved without direct documentary evidence) Josephus's insistence that Florus must have possessed strong motives and a personal stake in bringing about a violent explosion – "the only way by which to cover up his lawlessness" (282).

We already know how Florus responded to the riots in Caesarea and to the consequent developments, in the way that his every move resulted in the new escalation of the conflict. The cessation of the sacrifices for Rome, apparently meant as a response to the growth of the procuratorial harassment, formally signified that the revolt and the concomitant civil war had been *de facto* already in progress.

Finally, one hears from Josephus of the procurator's intrigues later on in the Roman camp during Gallus's march against the rebellious Jerusalem: he is said to have prevented a direct action by bribing the camp prefect, one Tyrannius Priscus (531). This particular piece of information makes, however, little sense and strikes as possibly a calumny; but it does suggest that there was "something rotten" in the higher Roman military command. The last time Florus is mentioned by Josephus in connection with Gallus's alleged resolve, upon his disastrous defeat by the Jews at Beth-horon (November, A.D. 66), is to place the blame for the revolt on the odious procurator (558). Strange as it may seem, there is not a single other word about Gessius Florus in the rest of the *Bellum*'s narrative. This truly repugnant character disappears from history's scene without a trace as suddenly as he arrived on it out of nowhere.[11]

3

THE CONQUERED LAND

I.

The story of Rome's involvement in the affairs of Palaestina is long and convoluted, and it began more than 120 years prior to the Great Revolt. It is not my intention in this book to deal with it in any depth, but for the purpose of the argument it is essential to provide a historical outline, with an emphasis on those aspects of the process or episodes which might, in one way or another, pertain to the peculiar dynamics and psychology of religious dissent.

It is arguable, and almost certainly true, that the Roman encroachment upon Judaea was inevitable, given Rome's imperialist drive and the rivalry between the military strongmen in the last century of the Republic. Furthermore, territorial expansion would have brought the Romans sooner or later into conflict with Parthia, and in order to secure their eastern borders they would have needed to create a system of buffer states and provinces – as they eventually did. It is hard to imagine that Judaea, with its strategic importance, could have escaped the fate it was actually to suffer.

This said, it must be recognized, however, that (as frequently happens in history when some group, or a movement, starts negotiating with an outsider bent on interference in the other nation's domestic struggle) the divisive Jewish leadership of the period supplied the invader not only with the pretext, but also with the direct opportunity to intervene.

The trouble began with the illness and death of the Queen Salome Alexandra (76–67 B.C.), whose rule is portrayed in the rabbinic tradition as the golden age, the last surge of Hasmonaean glory and civic peace. The conflict immediately arose between her two sons, the elder John Hyrcanus (II), whom she had appointed high priest, and his younger brother Judas Aristobulus (II), who managed to seize royal power as well as high priestly office by force (*AJ*, 14, 4, ff.; cf. 7, 41, 97; 15, 41; 20, 243 f.; *BJ*, 1, 120 ff.), an event which, within the span of only a few years, led to an irremediable disaster. Hyrcanus's energetic and devious strongman, the Idumaean Antipater (I) – father of Herod I – stirred up an insurrection against Aristobulus and eventually proceeded to besiege him and his forces on the Temple Mount (*AJ*, 14, 13 ff.; *BJ*, 14, 123 ff.). Both claimants appealed to Pompey, who by 65 was rounding up his Eastern conquests, and upon complex negotiations (which involved, we are told, a series of bribes), the partisans of Hyrcanus won the Roman general's personal support (*AJ*, 14, 29 ff.; *BJ*, 1, 127 ff.) and allowed the Romans to enter Jerusalem so that they could, in a joint effort with the foreigners, defeat their opponents. Those latter by now occupied the Temple Mount, under siege, which lasted over two months (*AJ*, 14, 46 ff.; *BJ*, 1, 133 ff.), defiling the holy grounds with the slaughter of Jews by their own compatriots (*AJ*, 14, 65 ff., 70; *BJ*, 1, 148, 150).

The Temple fell on a festive day at some point by the middle of the year. What happened next might have appeared an insignificant and even trivial matter in the eyes of Pompey and his entourage, but it left an indelible imprint upon the Jewish national memory. The Roman commander, accompanied by several men, not only ventured to enter the Temple's interior, forbidden to the Gentiles, but also penetrated the Holy of Holies, barred to anyone except the high priest, and to him only on the Day of Atonement. As Josephus puts it, "Nothing in the catastrophes of that time afflicted the nation so much as the exposure by the aliens of the sacred place, which up to then had been hidden from view" (*BJ*, 1, 152; cf. *AJ*, 14, 71). Indeed, this act engendered the deep-seated and persistent sense of outrage among Jews within and without Palaestina: one would not exaggerate by suggesting that the long story of Jewish resistance to the Roman authority, which culminated in the Great Revolt and the destruction of the Temple, began on that day. It is by no means certain that Pompey realized the full impact of what he had done. On Roman standards, he might have considered the treatment he visited upon Jews fair, even lenient: after all, he did abstain from plundering the Temple's treasure and, furthermore, ordered the sanctuary to be purified and the customary sacrifices resumed (*AJ*, 14, 73; *BJ*, 1, 152). This apparent disproportion between Pompey's act, most likely motivated by simple curiosity – he might have similarly examined any other foreign cultic edifice (it was widely rumored among the Greeks and the Romans that in the Holy of Holies Jews worship an ass) – and its interpreting by Jews as deliberate and abominable blasphemy reveals one aspect of what it is nowadays fashionable to call 'the clash of civilizations': much of the subsequent trouble owed to this communicational gap. The Romans, for the most part, were not particularly interested in appreciating subtle and not so subtle differences among the societies they came to confront and their own – to them, the concept of cultural sensitivity must have been alien. As Virgil tells us: *tu regere imperio populos, Romane, memento / (hae tibi erunt artes), pacique imponere morem, / parcere subiectis et debellare superbos* ("Roman, remember by your strength to rule/ Earth's peoples – for your arts are to be these:/ to pacify, to impose the rule of law, /to spare the conquered, and battle down the proud" – *Aen.*, 6, 851 ff.) – to me this recalls, *mutatis mutandis*, President Grover Cleveland's famed pronouncement 'America's business is business'. As history had demonstrated, in both cases the dictums proved remarkably short sighted. This is to say that the lesson to be derived from the story of Pompey and the Jews is by no means irrelevant, as the recent developments show, to our immediate concerns, and not only for the sake of political correctness (that is, the desire not to offend sensibilities among various social and cultural groups). The Romans, at least, knew the notion of the 'sacred' (which relates to the issue or object of absolute and transcendent value) even though their view and perception of it vastly differed from the attitudes among Jews. We, on the other hand, have almost entirely lost the very idea of what that word – or the reality behind it – might mean, and feel surprised when we are reminded about this by a sudden outbreak of violence. In any event, one can hardly doubt that the memory of Pompey committing sacrilege at the Temple remained deeply entrenched in the Jewish mind and must have been later taken on, both as a source of inspiration and a propaganda device, by the religious dissenters.

Pompey's settlement of Palaestina included restoring Hyrcanus II to high priesthood, although he denied him the royal title (*AJ*, 14, 73, cf. 20, 244; *BJ*, 1, 153), imposing tribute on the country and Jerusalem, and annexing Coele-Syria, as well as a number of Greek cities, formerly under Jewish rule, to the Roman province, with the right of self-government (*AJ*, 14, 74, 77; *BJ*, 1, 155 ff.). Josephus squarely – and rightly – places the blame for submission to the foreign power on the warring Hasmonaean princes (*AJ*, 14, 77). In this respect, the words he puts in the mouth of King Agrippa II, addressing on the eve of the revolt the crowds bent on liberation, make sense, when he attributes Jewish "hereditary submission" to the behavior of "the forefathers and their kings" at the time of Pompey (*BJ*, 2, 356 f.). One may indeed speculate whether a different outcome was conceivable under the circumstances, even if the nation's leaders had provided a united front against the Roman threat. It is true that the growing trouble at home (63 B.C. was the year of the Catilinarian conspiracy) could have compelled Pompey to hasten back; and that for the next decade or so, and particularly after Crassus's debacle at Carrhae at the hands of the Parthians, the Roman warlords paid attention to the affairs in the Near East, for the most part, only so far as their immediate, or individual, interests required. It can therefore be imagined that, by intelligent political maneuvering throughout several rounds of civil strife under the late Republic, Judaea might have still preserved for a while an independent, or quasi-independent, status. This, however, would have certainly come to an end upon the arrival of Augustus, highly conscious of the need to fortify the Empire's eastern border against the Parthian, and concerned with stabilization of his power.[1]

To contrast it with Pompey's conduct, it seems worth mentioning the treatment of the Temple ten years later by the triumvir Crassus, envious of his predecessor's Eastern conquests. In order to finance his ill-fated Parthian campaign in 54 B.C., according to Josephus, Crassus extorted from the Temple's treasurer 2000 talents in gold and a further 8000 in precious objects (*AJ*, 14, 105 ff.; *BJ*, 1, 179). It is telling, however, that although Crassus set out, in the words of the historian, "to strip the shrine / ... / of all its gold" (*AJ*, 14, 105), his name, unlike Pompey's (who had, as we know, abstained from plundering the sanctuary) meant little or nothing for the subsequent generations of Jews. Apparently, in their eyes, an involuntary sacrilege, perpetrated by the former, came to signify a much harsher offence than the latter's robbery on a grand scale: another lesson one should keep in mind. I find it notable that even Josephus, contrary to his usual practices, chose not to comment, as one might expect, on the subsequent Roman disaster at Carrhae, and on Crassus's own ignominious death at the hands of the Parthians, in terms of divine retribution for his seizing the Temple's funds.[2]

After some attempt at administrative experimentation in Judaea, the Romans came to rely on the collaborationist forces among the Jewish elite and, above all, on the Idumaean family of Antipater, who remained the major and most powerful presence in the local politics. This inaugurated the rise of Antipater's ambitious second son Herod, who after having performed many valuable services for the Romans, was within a decade proclaimed by the latter King of the Jews. In the course of these years the country underwent a series of the Hasmonaean uprisings, and even though in the end they were all successfully dealt with, their very fact demonstrates that, despite all internal divisions and dissension, its people were by no means prepared to accept with ease the encroachment that was *de facto* becoming alien rule. Against the civil wars background of the late Republic, with the rapid changes of fortune among the fighting parties, Antipater and the Antipatrids demonstrated a remarkable dexterity in each case finding themselves allied with the winner: by timely changing sides, while preserving a show of loyalty, they had consecutively enjoyed the support of Pompey, Julius Caesar, the Republican 'tyrannicide' Cassius, Mark Antony and, finally, Caesar Augustus.[3]

Herod's rise to power was fraught with multiple adventures, which resemble the shifting vicissitudes, say, of Alcibiades or Gaius Marius in the latter's conflict with Sulla. In the process, he had lost his father to a poisoner, and a few years later his beloved elder brother Phasael to their enemies' vengeance. Having at one point (ca.47 B.C.) barely avoided condemnation by the Sanhedrin, he was eventually forced to escape first from Jerusalem, and then from his homeland, upon the invasion by the Parthians, who succeeded in temporarily installing the Hasmonaean pretender Mattathias Antigonus as king (40–37 B.C.).

Herod returned to Palaestina from Rome after having been officially granted kingship by the Senate, that is to say, in reality, by Antony and and Octavian, two remaining members of the Second Triumvirate, and took in marriage, further to enhance his royal claims, the Hasmonaean princess Mariamne (*BJ*, 1, 344; *AJ*, 14, 466), granddaughter of both Aristobulus II and Hyrcanus II. But it was not until 38 B.C. that C. Sosius, appointed by Antony a new governor of Syria, provided Herod with full military cooperation so that he could, as it had been promised, *de facto* institute his rule. This was achieved through yet another Roman–Jewish (by the joint forces of Sosius and Herod) siege of Jerusalem, second after Pompey's. It must have lasted from three to five months, and its description by Josephus makes it, in some respects, a sort of rehearsal for Titus's siege 100 years later. As in the latter case, the historian emphasizes the profusion of oracular utterances, desperate courage, as well as resourcefulness of the defenders, their hope for the divine interference, prompt rebuilding of the demolished wall portions and the use of the subterranean passages (*BJ*, 1, 347, 349 ff.; *AJ*, 14, 470 ff.; 474 ff.). Of course, they had no chance to defeat an army, superior both in numbers and military training. The city was captured in the fall of 37 B.C., followed by the wholesale massacre, in which the pro-Herodian Jews took part on equal footing with the Romans (*BJ*, 1, 351 f.; *AJ*, 14, 478 ff.), although Josephus's account suggests that those who found refuge in the Temple were spared and the sacrilege avoided. Herod would have well remembered the effects of Pompey's indiscretion and prevented, not without difficulty, all foreigners from entering the shrine. Writes Josephus:

> Having brought under his control those who were then his enemies, Herod looked to controlling as well his foreign allies, since the alien crowd rushed to view the sanctuary and the sacred objects in the temple. Some he exhorted, others he threatened, and there were still others whom he repulsed by armed force; he regarded victory as more difficult than defeat, if they saw any of those things that were not to be seen.
>
> (*BJ*, 1, 354; *AJ*, 14, 482 ff.)

Eventually, he must have persuaded the Roman commander to end the plunder with a promise of lavish remuneration, which was apparently fulfilled (*BJ*, 1, 352, 355 ff.; *AJ*, 14, 480, 484 ff.). We even read that, prior to his withdrawal from Jerusalem, Sosius dedicated a golden crown to God in the Temple (*BJ*, 1, 357; *AJ*, 14, 488). The last Hasmonaean king surrendered and was sent in chains to Antony, who put him, on Herod's urging, to dishonorable death (*AJ*, 14, 488 f., cf. 481; *BJ*, 1, 353, 357).[4]

Even though by now firmly entrenched as king, Herod continued to experience serious problems for the rest of the decade, both in domestic and foreign policy. As regards the latter, it largely concerned the need to resist the expansionist ambitions of Cleopatra. At home after the new king, with a short campaign of terror, had silenced the last of the Hasmonaean opposition, the nation appeared temporarily pacified, exhausted as it was by foreign invasions and protracted civil warfare; but troubles began to brew within the royal family that would keep haunting Herod until the end of his life. In the years to come, this would lead him to killing his brother-in-law Aristobulus (III), the last Hasmonaean high priest, the old Hyrcanus II – his wife's grandfather – as well as various other relatives, and to judicial murders of his own wife Mariamne (I), whom he passionately loved, and – several decades later – of his three sons.

Octavian's decisive naval victory at Actium in 31 B.C. placed Herod's position and future in jeopardy, owing to the latter's friendship with and patronage by Antony. But his audience next year with Octavian, soon to become Caesar

Augustus, on the island of Rhodes turned into unqualified success: in its timeliness, it represents his last – and greatest – diplomatic coup. Not only all his earlier arrangements with Rome were fully confirmed, but the Jewish king's status was raised to a new level, and a sort of special relationship came to be forged between the Julio-Claudian family and the Idumaean royalty (cf. *AJ*, 15, 187 ff.; *BJ*, 1, 387 ff.). Octavian, a cool pragmaticist, must have understood that what really mattered were not Herod's personal qualities, his claims at integrity or his conduct in the past, but the absence of alternative to him, if the Roman interests in the Near East were served. As a result, the Rhodes settlement introduced in Judaea a long era of relative foreign peace and domestic tyranny.[5]

In terms of our main interest (that is, the problem of religious dissent), only two episodes within this whole period of turbulence may require further attention. One concerns the police operation circa 47 B.C., performed by young Herod, aged 25, whom Antipater appointed governor of Galilee, against one Ezechias, in Josephus's language, "brigand chief" (*AJ*, 14, 159; *BJ*, 1, 204). This man may or may not have been the father of Judas the Galilaean, a founder of the "fourth philosophy" and a primary religious dissenter at the time – a problem I will take up again elsewhere. At this point, it needs mentioning that a group of "leading Jews", presumably representing the anti-Idumaean opposition, attempted to impeach Herod before Hyrcanus II (then still the high priest) and the Sanhedrin on the charges of putting a fellow Jew – Ezechias – and some of his followers to death without a proper trial (*AJ*, 14, 163 ff.; *BJ*, 208 ff.). This suggests that they saw no 'religious deviance' in an executed man and may have even sympathized with his cause. The prosecution led eventually to nothing, although Herod found it prudent to temporarily withdraw from the capital (*AJ*, 14, 172 ff.). The second affair dates by winter 39/38 B.C., when Herod, upon his triumphant return from Rome, needed again to suppress Galilaean 'brigands', many of whom dwelled 'in the caves' of Arbela (*BJ*, 1, 304 ff.; *AJ*, 14, 415 ff.). Who were, in fact, these latter is not clarified: their desperate, sometimes literally suicidal, resistance (it required quite a special effort to put them down) might have betrayed the mindset characteristic of religious dissent; but lacking any further evidence, no such inference can be safely drawn.[6]

II.

There is no proper way to discuss almost 40 years of Herod's reign, or even its salient points, within the framework of this book. I will therefore confine my very brief treatment only to those aspects of it which provide the basic historical context, or may pertain, even if indirectly, to this book's main subject.

Josephus offers us two Herod narratives: one, relatively succinct, in the *Bellum*, and another – lengthier, but also less coherent – in the *Antiquitates*. Both the actual history of that period and Josephus's accounts of it constitute a field of continuous and lively scholarly debate. For the purpose of our discussion, however, it suffices to observe that, stripped of excessive rhetorical dramatization and psychologizing, the latter provide, for the most part, fairly reliable historical material: it must be reiterated that, dealing with ancient historiography, and Josephus in particular, it is essential to distinguish between the actions on the record and the authorial agenda as reflected in their selection, representation, coloration, interpretation, or various forms of innuendo. It appears that in this case our historian set out conscientiously to explore both negative and positive sides of Herod's character and performance, and reach some kind of balance. It must be finally remembered that Josephus's narratives are, in fact, the only consistent histories of the time we possess, and one must be grateful that their quality is no poorer than it is.[7]

The resentment felt against Herod's rule in various strata of the Jewish populace – despite the growth (notwithstanding occasional setbacks) of the material prosperity in the land – could not be doubted. In the final analysis, however, the evidence suggests that the dependence of his power on Rome must have been among the less important causes generating discontent. For the duration of his reign the Romans did not interfere in Judaea's internal affairs (although Herod sought to involve them in the resolution of his own family troubles), nor did they station there any sizable troops, or impose any inordinate tribute. Only towards the end of Herod's life did the Roman presence in the region begin to bear on popular disturbances, but even then because of the king's own misguided initiative. Other reasons for antagonisms proved considerably more important: Herod's origin as an Idumaean – that is, non-Jewish commoner – remained an issue, despite some scholarly efforts to argue Idumaea's full integration within Judaism; his pronounced Hellenistic cultural sympathies and the lack of genuine traditional piety (very discreditable characteristics in the eyes of many and perhaps most of his Jewish subjects); and last but not least the burden of an exceedingly repressive regime, justly described as tyranny, with periodical outburst of terror, harassment and extermination of political opponents. Further spice was added by Herod's slaughter of his own immediate relatives, including his wife and three sons. Although those family disasters may have been of lesser impact upon the nation's political sensibilities than other factors, they were still bound to engender compassion among the masses for his victims and helped in shaping a predominantly hostile public view of Herod both as a man and a ruler.[8]

Herod's foreign policy troubles largely ended with the demise of Cleopatra, who was a prime mover of the earlier conspiracies against him, including that of Costobar (I), his sister Salome's second husband, whom he had appointed governor of Idumaea (*AJ*, 15, 253 ff.). According to Josephus's report, the latter plotted to secede, but was exposed and eventually executed (256 ff.). What this episode makes clear is that upon their conquest and forced conversion to Jewish faith by John Hyrcanus I (ca. 129 B.C. – *BJ*, 1, 63; *AJ*, 13, 255 ff.; cf. 15, 254), the Idumaeans, or at least some portion of them, might still have felt uncomfortable within the environment of the Palestinian Judaism. Conversely, they were not fully recognized by Jews as compatriots (or coreligionists), which explains the problems Herod must have experienced on that same account – a step clarified by his need to invent for himself fictional genealogy, purely Jewish (*AJ*, 14, 9).

Out of his settlement with Augustus at Rhodes, Herod emerged as undoubtedly the most influential royal personage in the region, and he continued to entertain extraordinarily warm 'special relations' with the emperor, his family and his associates, even being capable financially to support the neighboring princes. Towards the end of his rule, this last circumstance, together with his attempt to suppress the brigand activity on the border, made him engage in the war with the Arabs (12–19 B.C.; *AJ*, 16 271 ff.), resulting in a complicated scandal that seriously risked souring his relationship with Augustus, since the latter felt annoyed with what he had construed as Herod's offensive show of independence (289 ff.; 293 f.; 298). It required persistent diplomatic efforts to remedy the situation (*AJ*, 16, 286 ff.; 335 ff.; 351 ff.; 17, 54 ff.; *BJ*, 1, 574 ff.).[9]

It has been seen that, within his own family, Herod's plight began upon his marriage into the Hasmonaean dynasty. The subsequent developments and court intrigues, as portrayed by Josephus, could have provided, in their complexity and dramatics, a plot worthy of Shakespeare – or, at the very least, Alexandre Dumas, and in fact became a subject of several important literary endeavors. In the number of family members killed by him, Herod's story rivals the bloody vicissitudes of the Julio-Claudians under Tiberius, Claudius and Nero. All of this seems to confirm the old adage that the easiest victims of a tyrannical individual are usually those who exist within his close range. Be that as it may, Herod's murderous activities against his own kin might have in the end been rooted, paradoxically, in his exceptional, however unpredictable, commitment to at least some of his immediate relatives, such as his wives, siblings and children, resulting in his twisted and deeply ambivalent relationship with his brother Pheroras, his sister Salome (I), his wife Mariamne (I), his two sons born to him by her, Alexander and Aristobulus, as well as – in particular – his eldest son from the earlier marriage, Antipater (II). In any event, after several crises in their relationship, Herod ordered his Hasmonean wife Mariamne put to death (ca. 29/28 B.C.) on the apparently slanderous charges of adultery with the very person whom he had appointed to watch over her behavior (*AJ*, 15, 202–236; *BJ*, 1441–1444); the execution of her mother Alexandra quickly followed (*AJ*, 15, 247). This same fate visited eventually her two sons, after the protracted and most convoluted sequence of moves and counter-moves by various personages and – presumably – factions at Herod's court, where each was prepared to betray today's allies on the morrow. The two young men were repeatedly accused by Herod and sundry others of parricidal designs, and at one point (12 B.C.) had even been made to stand examination in Rome, with Augustus himself present, who found them innocent (*AJ*, 16, 90 ff.; *BJ*, 1, 452). This did not help, however, in saving their lives: later on, their half-brother Antipater (II) orchestrated yet another campaign of slander, in result of which Herod, no doubt bent on putting an end to the affair, came to convoke a court at Berytus, with the participation of Roman officials, to try them in absentia (*AJ*, 16, 361 ff.; *BJ*, 1, 538 ff.). Both youths were formally condemned and strangled at Sebaste (7 B.C.; *AJ*, 16, 394; cf. *BJ*, 1, 550 f.). The final blow to the aging king was dealt by that very son Antipater, whom he had designated, upon the demise of his half-brothers, the heir to the throne (*AJ*, 17, 52 ff.). Josephus portrays the latter (and I find no reason to deny the basic veracity of this portrayal) as an unscrupulous and resourceful man, still impatient of his chances so long as his father lived, seeking to conspire against the latter and eliminate him, and at the same time trying to get rid of all other potential rivals. But his plots – both in Judaea and in Rome, where he would dwell for protracted periods of time, ostensibly, on a diplomatic mission – must have proved too ambitious and vast, and he himself was fatefully unpopular with both the military and the Jewish masses at large. Antipater's designs were exposed through a series of accidents; eventually, he was apprehended, tried and – with Augustus's consent arriving in time – executed only five days before Herod died at last in torment (*AJ*, 17, 93 ff., 182 ff.; *BJ*, 1, 620 ff., 661 ff.), amidst considerable popular unrest.[10]

As I have indicated, Herod's status as Rome's client king must have in itself made a lesser issue within the politically conscious Jewish community, both in Palaestina and in the Diaspora: after all, this form of dependence appears a relatively small price for putting an end to almost 30 years of internecine strife; nor was the Roman presence at the time especially visible or oppressive. Furthermore, it could not be denied that the Idumaean had been instrumental in negotiating with the Romans some legal enactments to enhance the position of the Jews *vis-à-vis* the gentiles in the Eastern Mediterranean (cf. *AJ*, 16, 29 ff.). Herod's cultural and religious attitudes, on the other hand, proved quite a different matter. His pronounced Hellenistic sympathies inevitably caused substantial resentment among ordinary Jews in Judaea (*AJ*, 15, 267 f., 274 ff., 281, 288, 291, 365; 17, 150 f.; 176; *BJ*, 1, 648 ff.; cf. 654 f. and 2, 6) and, above all, among the Pharisees with their emphasis on traditional piety – which, in turn, increasingly annoyed the king, who construed any disapproval as potential treason. Thus, on both sides, persistent hostility and suspicion came to reinforce each other. Herod's interest in, and enthusiasms for, the Graeco-Roman culture seem genuine, even though they might have also betrayed vanity or political calculation: witness, for instance, his expensive campaign to become the president of the Olympian Games (*AJ*, 16, 149; *BJ*, 1, 426 f.). By the same token, his prodigious generosity towards many foreign cities, including Athens (*AJ*, 15, 326 ff.; 16, 146 ff.; *BJ*, 1, 422 ff.), was directed at soliciting as much good will abroad as he could: given the complexities of regional politics, this was a prerequisite for securing the stature he had come to achieve and maintaining his influence with Rome.

To a large extent, the same accounts for Herod's protectionist policies towards pagan populations in Judaea proper, which found ultimate manifestation in his founding (or re-founding) of two major cities, in accordance with the Hellenistic constitutional principles, and intended as largely non-Jewish: Sebaste (former Samaria – *AJ*, 15, 342; *BJ*, 1, 404 ff.) and Caesarea Maritima (formerly, Strato's Tower – *AJ*, 15, 331 ff.;16, 136 ff.; *BJ*, 1, 408 ff.), later to become the residence of the Roman prefects and procurators. At the same time, it must be recognized that these ethnically mixed enclaves, and legal arrangements instituted for them by Herod, subsequently became a source of particular trouble, breeding social, cultural and political conflicts, and contributing to the eventual outbreak of the Great Revolt. More hazardous, and not contingent on the immediate political exigencies, was Herod's penchant for introduction and promotion in Judaea of the customs, contravening the native practices and the Mosaic law, such as public entertainments in pagan style, including gladiatorial combats with wild animals (*AJ*, 15, 273 ff.). Seen as offensive by the vast majority of his Jewish subjects, and reminiscent of similar tendencies, encouraged by the Hellenizers prior to the Maccabean revolt, such procedures, irrespective of Herod's motives, were politically perilous and fraught with potential disaster. An intelligent statesman, he knew, however, when to retreat or offer proper reassurances to the people (*AJ*, 15, 277 ff., cf. 365 f.; 17, 161 ff.). One such example is his removal of forbidden images from the trophies celebrating Augustus's victories (278 f.). It was only towards the very end of his rule, as we will see (when the old king, terminally ill, seemed to have a weakened grasp of reality), that popular anger at what had been perceived as his connivance with foreigners burst out. And, indeed, Herod's major effort to acquire the good will of all Jews transpires in his reconstruction, completion and celebration of the Temple (*AJ*, 15, 380 ff.; 421 ff.; *BJ*, 1, 401), which – at least in part – could be meant or taken for a gesture of atonement (cf. *AJ*, 17, 161 ff.).[11]

None of this, however, sufficed to endear Herod to those who saw their priority in sustaining traditional Jewish beliefs. Add to this the annoyance at his willful appointments of the high priests, and possibly at the total eclipse during his rule of the Sanhedrin, which (although the evidence of the latter's purpose and operation is scarce) may have been properly functioning under the last Hasmonaeans. Aware not only of the vociferous but also of the silent opposition, Herod made his subjects take oaths of allegiance to him, which revealed a substantial number of conscientious objectors ripe for punishment (*AJ*, 15, 368 ff.; 17, 42). At least one reason for such attitudes must have been their determination not to violate the fourth commandment: "You shall not take the name of the Lord your God in vain" (*Exod*: 20, 7).

In his treatment, with some details, of one conspiracy against Herod (*AJ*, 15, 281 ff.; date unknown), Josephus unequivocally asserts the religious motives for the participants: some of them we are told:

> ... remained disgusted with the foreign practices, both because, regarding the dissolution of ancestral ways as the beginning of great evils, they thought it more holy to make a desperate venture than to seem, when their civic life had been altered, to acquiesce in Herod's

forcible introduction of alien practices – Herod, king in name, but in fact the manifest enemy of the entire nation.

(281)

And upon the exposure of the affair, the historian makes the plotters profess that their intent was "noble and pious" and that they acted "not for the sake of gain or because of personal passions", but – which is a greater thing – on behalf of communal customs, which "the men of worth are to preserve or die for" (288). They are said to have died heroically after being tortured (289), in the manner of the Maccabean martyrs. Their sentiments (apart from resorting to violence), rooted as they were in the centuries of tradition, may well have been shared by the majority within both the priesthood and the larger populace – in contrast to the religious dissenters of the later period, who developed their own idiosyncratic sensibilities.

It is not surprising then that, due to Herod's explosive character and to his penchant for paranoia (despite his occasional effort at restraint), the tensions between the ruler and the ruled kept growing, not only at the court, or within the establishment, but also among the commons and in the army. In addition to the court purges (*AJ*, 16, 235 ff.; *BJ*, 1, 492 ff.), we learn about the prohibition of gatherings, the network of spies, the pervasive surveillance over the citizens and their behavior, as well as the physical, sometimes secret, elimination of the dissidents (*AJ*, 15, 366 f.) – in other words, all the familiar features of the terrorist regime.[12]

It was shortly before Herod's death that the precedent was created for popular discontent to develop into what is portrayed by Josephus as a serious public disorder. This was the 'affair of the golden eagle' – a costly image erected on the king's orders over the Temple's great gate (*AJ*, 17, 152 ff.; *BJ*, 1, 648 ff.). Herod's motives remain uncertain, although he might have just sought by this symbolic gesture (after all, the eagle – *aquila* – did connote the Roman military standard) further to enhance his recently restored friendship with Augustus. Nor could he anticipate the depth of his subjects' resentment at this act, which indeed is not fully explicable: it must have derived, at least in part, from the broader interpretation of the Second Commandment – "You shall not make for yourself a graven image" (*Exod*: 20, 4), although it is known that at the time the representations of the non-human living beings were sometimes tolerated by the Jewish populace, especially within the Diaspora, even in religious contexts. For Jews, the eagle as a symbol did not necessarily imply *per se* anything wrong: it could have even connoted God's omnipotence and protection for Israel; more obviously, it emblematized royal power. This last aspect may have played a role, but it seems likely that the eagle's function as the Roman legionary *signum* proved responsible for the particular sense of outrage among both the learned and ordinary Jews. Two of the former group timely emerged as leaders, Judas b. Sariphaeus (or Sepphoraeus) and Matthias b. Margalothus (or Margalus), "the most erudite among the Jews and the superior interpreters of the Law"

(*AJ*, 17, 149; cf. *BJ*, 1, 648). There is nothing to suggest that they represented any sectarian group of religious dissenters with the agenda of their own, as for instance the later *sicarii* did; rather, to the contrary, in Josephus's words, they had exercised large intellectual and educational appeal (*AJ*, loc. cit.; *BJ*, 1, 649), and their attitudes, rooted in the study of the Torah, found sympathy with the masses. Encouraged by Herod's rapid decline in health, and then by the rumor of his demise, the two scholars ordered their young followers to remove the offensive image from the Temple's gate, with the predictable outcome: some 40 persons were placed under arrest, including both the perpetrators and the instigators of the deed (*AJ*, 17, 152 ff.; *BJ*, 1, 651 f.). Although Josephus in part exploits, to the benefit of his gentile audience, the classical *topos* – the desire for the heroic posthumous glory (*AJ*, 17, 152 ff.) – he leaves no doubt about the paramount importance of their religious and traditionalist concerns as he has them to declare before the king:

> That which we have thought and that which we have done we have thought and we have done with the manly virtue that most befits men.
>
> We are entrusted with the cause to support by God's judgment of our worth and we heed the law's wisdom. It is no marvel if we held that the laws, which Moses bequeathed, inscribing them at the dictate and teaching of God, are more worthy of observance than your teachings. We will endure death and whatever punishment you might impose, not in the service of unjust action, but in love of piety.
>
> (*AJ*, 17, 158 f.)

As phrased by the author, this passage additionally implies the sense, on the part of the speakers, to have been divinely chosen for a mission, which makes one think about the elements of the religious dissent mindset.

Public pressure on Herod must have been so strong that he thought it expedient, before ordering the death of the guilty, to speak on the issue to Jewish officials, gathered in the amphitheater at Jericho, with an argument for his own piety – despite the critical condition of his health (160 f.). Furthermore, he was apparently made to compromise by inflicting mild penalties on most of the imprisoned – another sign of apprehension, – while two ringleaders and their companions were burned at the stake, even then an excessively cruel and unusual punishment (*AJ*, 17, 164, 167; *BJ*, 1, 655).[13]

One must still address the most shocking of Herod's arrangements as told by Josephus: this concerns his alleged plan to exterminate the Jewish notables, summoned on his orders from all parts of the land, and shut up in Jericho's hippodrome, so that the nation, the historian explains, would be plunged into mourning, instead of rejoicing over the tyrant's death (*AJ*, 17, 174 ff.; *BJ*, 659 f.). We read that the king's instructions to that effect were countermanded by his relatives after he had expired (*AJ*, 17, 193; *BJ*, 1, 666). One is not surprised that most scholars feel skeptical about this story: it duplicates a similar episode preserved in the Jewish tradition about the Hasmonaean king Alexander Jannaeus, and it seems particularly repellent to our modern sensibilities. Still, it would defy probability to believe that any such thing had been just invented by Josephus or his source for the sake of spite: it rarely happens in history that an event, thus attested within only two generations, is made up entirely out of the blue. There must have been at least some concrete reason why the tale did, in fact, enter public circulation, even though it might later have been thoroughly exaggerated or revised: for instance, Herod's actual arrest and keeping hostage a number of prominent Jews to provide his successors with the means of political blackmail or room for a maneuver after his death. Any such thing could have easily spurred immediate rumors that he was ready to finish them off in the case of need. To my mind, it is even conceivable that, owing to the vagaries of popular memory and imagination, this might reflect on the eventual emergence of the Massacre of the Innocents legend found in the Gospels (*Mt*: 2, 16).

Herod I (known as the 'Great') died, at the age of 70, after a long and particularly painful illness in the spring of 4 B.C. (*AJ*, 17, 191 ff.; *BJ*, 1, 665 f.), succeeded in power by Herod Archaelaus, his son from Malthace. The matter of Herod's greatness is, however, debatable. He was indeed a complex character and, as becomes clear from the story of his extraordinary career, one cannot doubt his intelligence, resourcefulness or political skill. Nonetheless, I believe, it may help if we disabuse ourselves of the habit, all too often found in modern scholarship, to pronounce judgments on the actors in the historical past only in terms of what they achieved (for the most part, in 'practical' sense), while ignoring the human and moral cost of these achievements. Seen in this latter perspective, Herod – a tyrannical ruler, suffering from paranoia, who had alienated the masses of his subjects, a wife-slaughterer and filicide – seems to have deserved that very reputation as a proverbial evildoer, which he still enjoys in the mainstream of both Jewish and Christian traditions.[14]

III.

In his last will the deceased had named as his heir Herod Archaelaus, one of his remaining sons still eligible for succession. Although at first it appeared that things were under control, the transfer of power occurred by no means smoothly and with unexpected results. We read that Archaelaus began to exercise his authority at once, even though declining to assume the royal title until (as stipulated by the terms of Herod's will) it was confirmed by Augustus in Rome (*AJ*, 17, 202; *BJ*, 2, 2). The troubles that followed were, on the one hand, rooted in the repercussions of the recent 'golden eagle affair', and on the other, in the resentment towards the new ruler within his own family. After the popular unrest culminated during the Passover festival in a rally at the Temple, Archaelaus must have lost his nerve and committed a fateful blunder, ordering the dispersion of the malcontents by force. The violence broke out in the midst of the sacrificial ritual and led to a massacre, with some 3000 persons, according to Josephus, having been killed (April, 4 B. C.: *AJ*, 17, 210 ff.; cf. *BJ*, 2, 8 ff.). Archaelaus emerged in the eyes of all devout Jews as a blasphemer and defiler of the sacred grounds, no less vicious or impious than his father. His next step, even though perhaps inevitable, only helped the crisis further to deteriorate: concerned with personally, and in the speediest manner, getting from Augustus the confirmation of his kingship, he embarked upon the journey to Rome, surrounded by his relatives and associates, and left further turmoil behind (*AJ*, 17, 219 ff.; *BJ*, 2, 14 ff.).

In Rome, Archaelaus's mission ran into difficulties as the Herodian family proceeded with a concerted campaign intent on his impeachment – through the charges of incompetence, brutality, impiety and the lack of filial respect. Consequently, Augustus kept postponing the decision on the royal succession (*AJ*, 17, 248 ff.; *BJ*, 2, 37 f.). The matter became further aggravated with the arrival of yet another delegation, presumably sent by the Jewish nobility, and backed by Rome's Jewish diaspora, requesting altogether to abolish the Herodian monarchy and to bestow autonomy on Judaea within the confines and jurisdiction of Roman Syria (*AJ*, 17, 304 ff.; *BJ*, 2, 80 ff.). When the emperor eventually made up his mind, he confirmed Archaelaus – despite whatever hostile arguments were proffered against him – as his father's heir, but with the lower rank of ethnarch, not king, and the promise of elevating him to full kingship should he behave; this was followed by the appointment of Herod Antipas and Philip (the new ruler's half-brothers) as tetrarchs, each with considerable territory to administer (*AJ*, 17, 318 ff.; *BJ*, 2, 94 ff.). One may only speculate as to why, given the pretext of the formal Jewish appeal, Augustus had judged at the time against Judaea's annexation: perhaps, in the immediate aftermath of the widespread unrest, he thought any such idea premature.[15]

While the Herodian clan kept squabbling in Rome over the issue of succession, the affairs in Judaea continued to deteriorate. One reason for this seems to have been the discrepancy between public actions, or intents, of the gubernatorial and procuratorial authorities. That the tandem of two appointments, one senatorial and another equestrian, in provinces could have often been fraught with tensions, and sometimes even open conflicts, was a well-attested and persistent feature in the administrative history of the principate. At this stage, in Judaea the rank of 'procurator' did not signify, as it did later, the highest Roman official in the land, but merely a financial officer, appointed by and responsible to the emperor, and entrusted with supervision of the latter's estates within the area, the Imperial 'domain'. It was reportedly on his own initiative, and against the judgment held by his superior, Syria's governor (7/6–4 B.C.), P. Quinctilius Varus, that the current procurator of that province, one Sabinus, proceeded in seizing the estates left by Herod's will to Augustus, without waiting for that will's ratification in Rome, and acting, or at least Josephus implies this, not so much in the emperor's interests but rather his own (*BJ*, 2, 16 ff., cf. 41 ff.; *AJ*, 17, 252 ff.). This, and his attempt to take over the citadels and the royal treasury in Jerusalem, led to insurgence during the feast of Pentecost, joined by most of the

Herodian troops (end of May, 4 B.C.). More fighting broke out on the Temple grounds, with the result that the Romans found themselves under siege in the royal palace (*BJ*, 2, 42 ff.; *AJ*, 17, 254 ff.). Only upon Varus's eventual arrival to Jerusalem, as a part of his campaign to pacify the country, did the bloodshed cease, while the procurator hastened secretly to leave the scene (*BJ*, 2, 74; *AJ*, 17, 294). In this context, one may observe that the strained Varus–Sabinus relationship as described, given its flaws and consequences, seems to have foreshadowed, at least in some respects, a similar pattern of interaction in the decades to come between the prefects (later procurators) of Judaea and Syria's governors, with often more enlightened and moderate attitudes on the part of the latter.

The events in Jerusalem, provoked by Sabinus's ill-considered behavior, represented only one episode of what Josephus describes as a vast – although uncoordinated – uprising (*AJ*, 17, 269 ff.; *BJ*, 2, 55 ff.), which in several respects appears to be a prefiguration of the Great Revolt some 70 years later. The royal soldiers mutinied (*AJ*, 17, 270; *BJ*, 2, 55). The pretenders, whom the historian predictably treats as brigand chiefs, propped up in various parts of the country, claimed supremacy and were probably inspired by the story of the biblical David, who rose from robber-band leader to King of Israel:

> Thus Judaea became filled with brigandage, and anyone, if he happened to side with the insurgents, might emerge as king and act to the detriment of the commonwealth, causing some small distress to a few Romans, but leading to the greatest carnage of their own people.
>
> (*AJ*, 17, 285)

One such individual seems to have been the royal slave called Simon, active in Peraea, plundering the rich estates and even managing to burn down the Herodian palace at Jericho. He was defeated in the battle and killed shortly after (*AJ*, 17, 273 ff.; *BJ*, 2, 57 ff.; cf. Tac. *Hist.*, 5, 9). More lasting proved, in Judaea proper, one Athronges, a shepherd by trade, surrounded by four formidable brothers. According to Josephus, they waged war equally against the Romans and the royalists, to be eventually suppressed one by one (*AJ*, 17, 278 ff.; *BJ*, 60 ff.). The historian's statement that both Simon and Athronges sought royal title (in the case of the former, supported by Tacitus – *Hist.*, 5, 9) may or may not suggest that they could have concurrently claimed Davidic descent, which in turn was bound to imply at least an element of what I have earlier called 'a Messianic complex'.

Further, we read about Judas, son of Ezechias – that is, of the very man ("arch-brigand", specifies Josephus – *AJ*, 17, 271; *BJ*, 2, 56) who was suppressed and executed, without an appropriate trial, by Herod in the days of latter's youth. His son is said to have stirred trouble at Sepphoris in Galilee by breaking into the arsenal, became involved in plunder, as well as with other rebel factions, and also aspired to royal rank (*loci citati*). Whether this Judas b. Ezechias was identical with the famous Judas the Galilaean, founder of the "fourth philosophy", is a matter of continuous scholarly dispute. If that were the case, this would make the earliest discernable evidence for the existence of religious dissent as a specific phenomenon in terms of this book's argument. I will, however, relegate the whole discussion of this particular problem to a special chapter.

Varus must have been responsible for the general conduct of operations in curbing various seats of resistance – hence the common reference to this campaign as 'Varus's war.' He acted with efficiency (cf. *AJ*, 17, 286 ff.; *BJ*, 2, 68 ff.), and could have arguably succeeded in pacifying the country with, perhaps, the minimum of human loss, but for his reliance on, apart from the Herodian and Roman armies, the allied Arab troops, who inflicted a series of particular atrocities (which they would likewise perform at the time of the Great Revolt) against the Jewish civil population (*AJ*, 17, 289 f., cf. 296; *BJ*, 2, 69 f., 76).

Lastly, upon the establishment of the ethnarchy, there emerged an imposter, claiming that he was Alexander, Herod's son from Mariamne (I), who had miraculously escaped death ordered by his father (*AJ*, 17, 324 ff.; *BJ*, 2, 101 ff.). The real identity of that individual is not reported, except that he was a native Jew. One reads with amazement that he went on to undertake a journey to Italy, claiming public recognition as Herod's legitimate heir, and even to Rome, where he was unmasked, in accordance with at least one version, personally by Augustus, who spared his life after the man's voluntary confession (*AJ*, 17, 327 ff.; cf. *BJ*, 2, 103 ff.).[16]

Ten years of Archaelaus's ethnarchy (4 B.C. – 6 A.D.) receive short shrift in Josephus's narratives, except references to his arbitrary replacements of high priests (*AJ*, 17, 339, 341). The historian characterizes his rule as cruel and intolerable (*AJ*, 17, 342; cf. *BJ*, 2, 111), although without offering specifics on the alleged misdeeds. Last but not least, the son obviously lacked his father's able and powerful personality.

In any event, the circumstances of Archaelaus's sudden deposition by Augustus are left largely unexplained. We only learn that both Jewish and Samaritan embassies had lodged yet another complaint against him before Augustus, who had ordered summoning the ethnarch from Palaestina (*AJ*, 17, 342 f.; *BJ*, 2, 111) – to the latter's apparent embarrassment (*AJ*, 17, 342 f.; *BJ*, 2, 111). The Samaritan factor might well have been crucial: they were traditionally pro-Roman and pro-Herodian as well as anti-Jewish, so it appears that the grievances capable to make inveterate foes join forces must have indeed been grave. Be that as it may, in Rome after listening to the charges against himself, and having failed, despite the opportunity, to disprove them convincingly, Herod Archaelaus was stripped of his title as ethnarch, with his property confiscated, and banished to Gaul (*AJ*, 17, 344; *BJ*, 111), where he may have died around A.D. 18. The territory of his ethnarchy – Judaea, Idumaea and Samaria – was consequently taken over by the Imperial authority and added to the Roman province of Syria. The equestrian officer, one Coponius, ranked prefect, and possessing the right of capital punishment (*ius gladii*), was sent to administer it (*BJ*, 2, 117; cf. *AJ*, 17, 355), with Syria's governor P. Sulpicius Quirinius as a sort of potential supervisor.[17]

It is not known who kept lobbying in Rome for the abolition of the Herodian monarchy and Judaea's transfer under direct Roman rule. One assumes that the anti-monarchical sentiments were shared – at least in certain quarters – by the Sadducees and the Pharisees alike: the former probably dreaming about the restoration of the high priestly authority, drastically reduced by Herod; and the conflicts of the latter with the Idumaean ruler are well attested. Furthermore, within ancient Judaism, attitudes towards kingship were traditionally ambivalent, much depending on the political context of the time.

Be that as it may, if the native politicians, whoever they might have been, seeking Judaea's 'autonomy' within the Roman province of Syria, hoped for the return to the post-exilic status quo, a sort of 'theocratic aristocracy' (that is, essentially the rule by the priestly nobility with no interference from the outside), they must have felt disappointed soon enough. The eventual administrative organization of the land was complicated and inherently unstable, fraught with inner conflicts, which could only facilitate the lingering unrest that never became fully eradicated; at the same time, the impression of the Roman Judaea as having existed in some sort of perpetual turmoil is clearly wrong. It must be recognized that, due to the character of our sources, we do not possess a clear or consistent picture of the ways in which the local government worked under the Romans: Josephus's narratives often contain gaps and are terminologically mixed up; the rabbinic material (and, to a certain degree, the New Testament data) cannot usually be applied to the periods earlier than those of their composition. Several aspects in the relationship between different power structures, as regards the extent and the limits of their competence, remain obscure, given the variables and imponderables often in operation. The scholarly controversy over almost every issue related to this subject did not so far yield conclusive or reliable results, with modern interpretations for the most part tending to cancel each other, and allowing us no certainty even about such important matter as, for instance, the role of the Sanhedrin. To me, the evidence at hand suggests, in the final analysis, the inadequacy of whatever (if any) formal or legal specifications as well as the importance of the *ad hoc* arrangements, which fluctuated and could bring about unpredictable effects, sometimes threatening to get out of control. At any rate, a closer institutional study of Roman Judaea is beyond both the format and intent of the present inquiry. I will limit myself only to very basic information with the purpose of underscoring the complexity of the matter.

It is true that, in a broad practical sense, the land continued to be ruled by the Jewish aristocratic elite virtually until the outbreak of the Great Revolt. The office of the high priest, however, had lost – owing to the precedents set by Herod – a measure of its public prestige: during the period under discussion high priests were appointed and removed at whim by the prefect or procurator, sometimes by the Herodian princes, and their tenure did not, for the most part, last long. (Even the high priestly vestments – a painful issue for the Jews – were left, more often than not, in the hands of the Romans.)

One presumes that this collaborationist nobility was largely of the Saducean persuasion. This does not exclude, on the other hand, their political support by those Pharisaic groups or individuals, whose primary concern would be with the preservation of stability and peace, and there is no reason to believe they were insignificant or small in number: one such highly influential person apparently was the great Johanan b. Zakkai, who might have quarreled with the Sadducees over religious or ritualist matters, but at the same time kept opposing open resistance to the Romans.

Because of the contradictory evidence at our disposal, the traditional assumptions about the Sanhedrin became increasingly questioned. The detailed portrayal of its structure and functions in the Tannaitic texts (especially the treatise *Sanhedrin*) is now considered by many experts a result of largely wishful thinking. The debate continues as regards that body's (or bodies', if they were more than one institution thus designated) composition, competence, purpose and so forth, although it is unlikely to produce a *communis opinio* in the foreseeable future. I find it safe, however, to assume that whatever Jewish court would have included priestly members, appropriately trained in law, with perhaps some participation of lay experts. To this must be added that the important territories (such as the restless Galilee) fell under the jurisdiction of the tetrarchs, whose relationship, in juridical terms, with the Sanhedrin (or Sanhedrins) cannot be ascertained.

Nor does it seem easy to fully appreciate the interaction between the Jewish authorities and the Roman occupier. What becomes clear, nonetheless, is that it would be a methodological mistake to generalize for the entire period upon one or even several particular episodes or details. The priestly establishment was aware of the need to make compromises and did so – an attitude contrary to the behavior of religious dissenters, such as their stand against negotiations and their incapacity for any such diplomacy. On the whole, the interaction between the ruling Jewish elite and the Roman officialdom in the region must have been flexible, with much depending on the circumstances and personalities involved. It is true that the prefects/procurators of Judaea (residing, however, in Caesarea Martima, and not Jerusalem) were endowed with broad discretionary powers, which included capital punishment and, for the lowest classes of criminals, summary execution. By resorting to procedures such as *cognitio extra ordinem* and *coercitio* they could feel free to take whatever harsh measures they saw fit in preventing or suppressing sedition. On the other hand, all Roman citizens, of whatever origin, were legally entitled to a fair trial and even to making appeals to the emperor (the right of *provocatio*) that, as we know, had been exercised by St. Paul (Acts 25:11 f.). The evidence leaves no doubt that the Roman administrators (despite few exceptions to be seen) took considerable effort not to interfere, so far as it was possible, with the religious affairs of the Jews. One issue, on which much ink has been spilt, is whether Jewish legal bodies could implement the death penalty without Rome's official approval. Although the narratives of the Gospels suggest this must be the case (*Mt* 27; *Mk* 15; *Lk* 23; esp. *Jn* 18:31), one cannot claim in full confidence that, even if a similar stipulation had been indeed formalized, it was regularly sustained or enforced: the contrary argument may cite the stoning of Stephen (*Acts* 7:58 ff.) – with apparently no legal reprisal visited on the perpetrators (between A.D. 31–35), or in A.D. 62 the execution of Christ's brother, James the Just (*AJ*, 20, 200 ff.). In other words, under certain junctures, when the exigencies so required, it was thought that any such principle could be effectively and conveniently ignored – a feature in itself characteristic as regards the operation of the Imperial justice during the period: the view, still occasionally found in literature, which interprets the Roman Empire in strict terms of law, is demonstrably misguided: with a threat of public nuisance, whether political dissidence or any other form of discontent, legal niceties often ceased to matter.

Finally, it must be taken into account that the prefects and procurators of Judaea, even though they were appointed or deposed only by the emperor, in the final analysis, must have relied on their support by the proconsuls of Syria. The latter could intervene with them at the points of crisis and were apparently authorized to suspend them for maladministration if they judged their behavior had overstepped the boundaries, however ill defined, of what could be permitted or desired: in six decades preceding the Jewish War such drastic action, as we will see, was taken twice.[18]

There is no compelling evidence to postulate specifically anti-Jewish policies in Judaea or across the Empire on the part of the central government under the Julio-Claudians, – excepting, of course, Caligula's megalomaniac attempt at introducing his personal cult into Jerusalem's Temple. Otherwise, Jews suffered the same fate as all other provincials equalized as Roman *subjects* – and were even privileged (in a sense) through consideration shown by the authorities for their religious practices, customs and traditional ways of life. (Such toleration was not, for instance, extended – and rightly so – to the Druidic cults in Gaul involved with human sacrifices.) There are reasons to believe that Roman political establishment, both within the central and the provincial administration, was – in practical terms – informed, at least regarding the basics, on the tenets and customs of Judaism, which they may have thought opaque, or exceedingly peculiar, but at the same time, from necessity, were bound to respect. This accounts for a series of edicts (quoted, even though in mangled form, in Josephus – *AJ*, 14, 185–267; 305–22; 16, 160–78) by Julius Caesar and Augustus recognizing the religious freedom of Jews throughout the Empire. It does not mean, however, that this 'legislation' (or any other similar enactment) was uniform or could have been uniformly enforced; in part, this pertained to the precedental nature of Roman law, and in part it reflected the discrepancy between legal formulas and their implementation concerning politically sensitive areas of life, which belonged, as I have mentioned above, among the characteristic features under the principate. Still, one cannot seriously contest that *de facto* Jews, both in Judaea and across the Empire, did enjoy under the Romans the spectrum of rights (some of them common for other cultic communities, but the rest obviously privileges) in 'following their customs and laws'; otherwise they would have been driven into the state of permanent revolt, which – despite some modern opinions to the opposite – had not been the case. Jews were allowed to observe the Sabbath, irrespective of the pressures within their immediate environment, to collect money for the Temple throughout the diaspora, and to practice their faith without interference as long as this did not threaten public peace; objects of their cult, such as the Torah scrolls, were considered sacrosanct. More importantly, they were the only subject people exempt from observing the official religious rites (which included the cult of the goddess Roma and the Imperial cult) and – for the most part – from the duty of service in the Roman army. (The short-lived attempts under Tiberius and Caligula to curtail these last privileges made exceptions, which confirmed the rule.) Lastly, the emperors showed their respect towards Judaism by ordering daily sacrifices on their behalf at the Temple and consenting to the immediate punishment with death of any gentile, even a Roman citizen, who might violate the sacred grounds. Given the close ties between the members of the royal Herodian family and the Julio-Claudians, one assumes that their constant interaction helped further to enhance the awareness about the Jewish ways and beliefs among the upper echelons of the government and at the Imperial court. The Jewish princes and collaborationist aristocrats traveling to or living in Rome were available for consultation, especially at the moments of crisis, and we know that Herod Agrippa I and his son Herod Agrippa II were often successful in playing advocates for their people. One even recalls prominent senatorial politicians who showed special interest in Jewish affairs. Still, it is difficult to imagine an average Roman bureaucrat capable of appreciating, say, the language and wisdom of the Prophets, even if he were reading the Septuagint in Greek. Furthermore, nothing like sensitivity programs had ever existed in the Roman world. This means that the attention paid to the Jewish sensibilities by the provincial administrators at all levels differed, and in each case depended on their individual characteristics: a wider gap in communication, or a mere lack of good will, could occasionally lead to real trouble; but measures were sometimes taken, almost until the end of the period, to have such matters rectified.

Popular disturbances within Judaea, which repeatedly mark the period, proved unexceptional. Despite the often-praised efficiency (sometimes even called beneficence) of the Roman rule, it must be recognized that the provincial administration throughout the Empire was fraught with deep-set corruption, manifest in extortionist behavior by many officials and unprovoked acts of harassment, which could have only led to widespread discontent among the natives. The first century after Christ saw the entire spectrum of this discontent: from the clandestine resistance to guerilla movements to local riots anywhere – and the full-scale revolts as in Gaul, Numidia and Thrace under Tiberius, or in Britannia under Nero.

It is equally true that, tracing the changes in the Imperial attitudes towards the Eastern client, or vassal, principalities (to which Palaestina in part belonged, given the existence on its territory of the Jewish tetrarchies and even kingdoms), one discerns a clear, if slow, trend towards centralization, which meant gradual curtailing of their 'autonomy' with an aim of eventual annexation. This was by no means a straightforward development, having undergone several setbacks, and largely relevant to the vagaries of factional politics at the Imperial court. And again, Judaea was no exception: the same approach operated, for better or worse, on the whole range of the Eastern nations, from Armenia to Thrace.

The rapport between the ruling Jewish elite and Roman officialdom constituted yet another factor that must have affected, in one way or another, the workings of Judaea's government. Predictably, relationships underwent periods of tension (especially under Caligula) and relative relaxation, contingent on the immediate circumstances. The caveat must be repeated: it is methodologically unwise to generalize on the basis of a few individual episodes. One matter appears, however, certain: the members of the royal clan, their reciprocal intrigues notwithstanding, stood invariably loyal by their Roman masters, even if their ambitions might have prompted them to overstep what the latter considered proper limits for their involvement in political affairs. As tetrarchs and occasional kings, the Herodian princes had under their command a sizable and dependable armed force: after Varus's pacification of the country, we do not hear of any defection *en masse* from the royal troops, even during the turbulence of the Great Revolt.

The degree of collaboration on the part of the (presumably or largely) Sadducean establishment and perhaps some pragmaticists within the Pharisaic movement is more difficult to ascertain. But the fact that for the next six decades the province remained governable strongly suggests not only their compliance with the occupier but also their continuous effort to keep people in check. The Roman military presence in Judaea (except at the moments of crisis, when it seemed expedient to bring in the forces from neighboring Syria) was minimal: one legionary cohort stationed in Jerusalem, and the auxiliary troops – the so-called 'Sebastenians' (originally created by Herod I and recruited from the non-Jewish populace) in Caesarea Maritima – where, as we will see, they became a factor in the subsequent ethnic strife. This strategic limitation means that in the ordinary conduct of politics the Romans did rely on the native aristocracy, as it was indeed their custom elsewhere in the Empire. But it does not follow that the relations were not uneasy: the short terms in office for most high priests may be explained, at least in part, by the official disapproval of their performance. In fact, some among them suffered punishment or humiliation at Roman hands. Problems were aggravated by the internal latent conflicts that at times broke open: between the royalists and their opponents, between the sects, and within the priestly nobility itself. All of this contributed to the eventual disintegration of society. According to one view, the paramount cause of the Jewish revolt proved to have been precisely the massive disenchantment of the Jewish elite in the Roman rule and their heartfelt adoption of the revolutionary agenda – a contention which I will discuss later at some length.[19]

IV.

The first Roman prefect of Judaea Coponius (A.D. 6–9) is otherwise unknown and left virtually no mark on Jewish history or memory, except possibly the name for one of the Temple's gates, which – if it was so – may suggest that, at least he had not generated especially hard feelings among his subjects. This cannot be said about his superior, Syria's governor P. Sulpicius Quirinius, who appears in both Jewish and Christian sources against the background of the (in)famous census he conducted on Augustus' orders in A.D. 6. By doing so he precipitated the rise of what Josephus calls the "fourth philosophy", propagated by Judas the Galilaean, the first fully identifiable example of the religious dissent movement, as understood in terms of this book, and attacking what its practitioners must have considered an illicit compromise at the expense of ancestral religion between the current establishment and the conqueror steeped in idol-worship.

The outburst of indignation brought about by the census among the Jewish populace thus owed not only (or perhaps not even predominantly) to the economic or financial aspects, but to what must have been construed by them as yet another (after Pompey's entrance into the Temple) violation of their sacred principles: conducting a census, if it had not been explicitly ordained by God, was prohibited in the Scriptures (*Num*: 1 ff.; cf. 2 *Sam*: 24, 1 ff.). This rage at an impious duty, forced upon them not even by their native ruler, but the foreign master, played into the hands of the Galilaean rebel, who effectively exploited it with his slogan, stipulating that Jews should be obedient solely to the Lord, but not any mortal masters (*BJ*, 2, 118; cf. 433; 7, 253; *AJ*, 18, 23). This must have presumed the return to some form of 'theocracy', perhaps not unlike in the epoch of the Judges when it was written that God directly communicated with an individual he had called upon to rule over his people (*I Sam.*, 2:18, 3:9 f., 6:12 ff. etc.) (It might well have been that the leader of this movement fancied himself one such.) In any way, the proper discussion of the "fourth philosophy", of its founders, its vicissitudes and subsequent fortunes belongs to a special chapter.

We learn nothing from Josephus about the suppression of Judas's revolutionary activities, whether the date or the details. From the New Testament reference (*Acts*, 5: 36), however, one may surmise that the turbulence did extend beyond Coponius's prefecture, and perhaps also those of his successors Marcus Ambibulus (A.D. 9–12) and Annius Rufus (A.D. 12–15), about whose administration, for reasons we cannot fathom, the Jewish historian provides virtually no data (cf. *AJ*, 18, 31). The next prefect Valerius Gratus (A.D. 15–26) is commented upon by Josephus only for the rapid succession of high priests under him: five individuals *in toto* (ibid, 33 f.).[20]

The arrival of Gratus's successor Pontius Pilate (A.D. 26–36/37) signified a series of new troubles. They are often suggested to be related to a set of measures taken under Tiberius against the Jewish community in the city of Rome (A.D. 19), although any such connection seems by no means obvious. Within the framework of this book, those developments in Rome cannot be properly discussed, but there are reasons to believe that they fell within Tiberius's policies aimed at the suppression of the 'un-Roman' religious cults – and may have manifested the concern felt by the authorities over the spread of 'Judaizers' (that is, sympathizers with Judaism, among Rome's lower and upper classes). It is true that Philo charges Tiberius's strongman Sejanus with the nefarious designs to embark upon the wholesome harassment of the Jews, but according to the same author, because of that man's timely downfall, such policies had never been implemented (*Legat.*, 159 ff.). The troubles in Judaea proper under Pontius Pilate, however, were each linked to particular events and do not seem to manifest a consistent program of anti-Jewish policies. The procurator not only survived Sejanus's fall, but was allowed to stay in office for another five years or so, which would have hardly happened had he been the latter's creature.[21]

The fact that Pontius Pilate belongs among the best-known historical names results, of course, from his role in the Crucifixion. Here I cannot afford even the tiniest comment on this most debated event, except to point out that the mention in the Gospels of the 'brigand' Barabbas, who was charged with sedition, but released on popular demand by Pilate, may suggest the continuation under the latter of religious dissent, most likely in the same fashion as practiced by Judas the Galilaean.

Among the judgments on Pilate from the period, Philo's is particularly harsh. Josephus, on the other hand, refrains from any strong language and concentrates on Pilate's acts rather than his character; finally, one recalls the latter's ambivalent portrayal in the Gospels. As we will see, notwithstanding what various sources tell us of his personality, this controversial administrator proved capable of backing off to avoid violence, under pressure from his subjects – and in the last turbulence that cost him his position, he had to deal with Samaritans rather than Jews.

Two episodes are reported, however, in our sources (one by Josephus, another by Philo) demonstrating – especially the first of them – Pilate's lack of sensitivity towards the native populace, and what might have even been the display of ill-will, aimed at provocation. Josephus tells us that at the beginning of his rule the prefect "dared to subvert Jewish customs" by introducing in Jerusalem – significantly, at night – military standards, which carried the medallion-busts of the emperor, the objects of cultic worship among Roman troops (*AJ*, 18, 55 ff.; cf. *BJ*, 2, 169 ff.). Surely a matter of public record, this was an act without precedent: Pilate's predecessors abstained from any such move, respecting the Mosaic prescription against the graven images (*Exod*: 20, 4). The Jewish response was predictable: the burst of indignation, not only among the townspeople, but also in the countryside. Crowds gathered in the capital for protests, and then followed Pilate to Caesarea where, according to the *Bellum*, they pleaded with him not to violate their law, and upon his refusal cast themselves flat on the Earth and thus stayed face down near his residence "for five days and nights without movement" (2, 171; cf. *AJ*, 18, 57). The prefect's argument that the removal of the standards would be tantamount to the offence against the emperor (that is to say, the crime of *maiestas*) sounds indeed lame and had no effect on the supplicants. Exasperated, he opted for the use of force and, on the pretext of giving them a formal hearing before his tribunal at the city's stadium, reportedly ordered to have them surrounded with soldiers and threatened to kill them all unless they complied and left (*BJ*, 2, 172 f.; *AJ*, 18, 57f.). At this point, Josephus tells us, "throwing themselves prostrate and exposing their throats for the slaughter, they declared that they would gladly prefer death rather than dare overstep the wisdom of their laws" (*AJ*, 18, 59; cf. *BJ*, 2, 173 f.). Stunned by this extraordinary manifestation of faith, the prefect gave in and the standards were taken back to Caesarea (*AJ*, loc. cit.; *BJ*, 2, 174).

In its pattern, this event resembles the 'affair of the golden eagle' under Herod (even though with a different outcome). In both cases, the collective anger resulted from the encroachment upon one of the nation's most powerful traditions, deeply entrenched in the popular mind. What strikes us in the present narrative is the non-violent, 'Gandhi-like' form of the protest, which we call today 'civil disobedience', strongly suggesting a mindset different from the one common among the religious dissenters, who as we know had been already in existence, with their belief in revolutionary action: it appears that at this initial stage the latter, for whatever reason, failed to influence significantly the behavior of the masses.

Another, not dissimilar development towards the end of Pilate's stay in office, and strangely missing in Josephus, is referred to by Philo (*Legat.*, 299 ff.) – as it appears, with a pointed political purpose, within the context of the argument (from the memorandum, ascribed to Herod Agrippa I) against Gaius Caligula's plans to install his statue in the Temple. This time, the prefect is said to have set up in the royal palace at Jerusalem, "with the intention of annoying the Jews rather than honoring Tiberius", the golden shields inscribed with the name of the emperor and his own as dedicator (299). The negative impact this act made on the Jewish masses is described as almost no less powerful than it was, according to Josephus, in the case of the legionary standards. Pilate's reluctance to yield reportedly led to the complaint sent directly to the emperor. The text claims that Tiberius responded immediately – without even waiting until the next day! – with a strong admonition to Pilate, "reproaching and rebuking him a thousand times for his new-fangled audacity and telling him to remove the shields at once and have them taken from the capital to the coastal city of Caesarea [Maritima – V.R.] / ... / to be dedicated in the temple of Augustus" (305).

Neither Philo's display of such opportune rhetoric, nor Josephus's silence on the 'golden shields' episode (there are numerous omissions in his narratives which, given the present state of our knowledge, cannot be explained) warrant questioning its basic historicity. Here applies what I have argued for Josephus: irrespective of details in representing or orchestrating the action they chose to narrate, both he and Philo could not have afforded an outright lie since they wrote for the consumption of their contemporaries, who would have known better. What seems really striking in Philo's story is not only the extent of the people's anger, but the very reason for it: the text makes it patently clear that the shields shown up by Pilate were aniconic and did not carry any images offensive to the Jewish beliefs. It is true that, by now, especially in Jerusalem, the population might have felt increasingly resentful about the prefect: the earlier affairs of the military standards and of the aqueduct (to be discussed next) were fresh in memory; but as the epigraphic evidence from Judaea testifies, the honorary and dedicatory inscriptions were, in principle, not disputed. This opens the possibility that the issue lay specifically in the names of the emperor and the prefect, and if so, one may suspect the involvement in popular agitation on the part of the dissenters, practicing the "fourth philosophy", for whom any such reminder about a foreign occupier would have been intolerable, given their refusal to recognize no man's power but the Lord's.

Between the crisis of the standards and the crisis of the shields, there had occurred yet another crisis under Pilate, which graphically reveals the communication gap between the Jewish and Roman mindset. It pertained to the prefect's project of constructing an aqueduct in Jerusalem in order to improve the city's sanitary conditions. As was often Roman practice, he sought to have it financed (perhaps only in part) by the local source, and chose to appropriate the needed funds from the Temple (*BJ*, 2, 75 f.; *AJ*, 18, 60 ff.). In itself, this does not necessarily signify a deliberately offensive anti-Jewish measure. It is true that the Temple tax was treated as sacrosanct by the Romans, but at the same time, according to the Mishna, the surplus Temple money could have been spent on various purposes, including the city's needs (*mShek.*, 4, 2) – presumably if the priestly authorities decided. One assumes then that Pilate acted without the approval from the latter. Furthermore, it seems that the money he had taken belonged to a special coffer, which contained the collection used for the purchase of sacrificial animals – in which case, and provided that he was aware of the fact's significance, one must suspect, on the prefect's side, some real malicious intent.

In any event, this reportedly provoked Pilate's bloodiest showdown with Jews during his tenure. At the time of his visit to the capital, indignant crowds (tens of thousands, in Josephus's words) surrounded his tribunal and demanded to stop the construction. Upon their refusal to withdraw, he is said to have dispersed plainclothes guards with clubs hidden under their garment, and by a prearranged signal ordered them to attack the rioters so that many Jews perished on the spot and others were trampled upon in the subsequent panic (*AJ*, 18, 62; cf. *BJ*, 2, 177). This Jewish response to the aqueduct project still appears an overreaction, which – once again, as in the affair of the shields – may have been due to the influence of some group or groups practicing religious dissent.

Ironically, Pilate's recall (A.D. 36) was due to his trouble not with Jews, but with Samaritans. In the *Antiquitates* (the *Bellum* omits the entire episode as well as the mention of Pilate's recall), Josephus writes of a self-styled prophet from their midst, who urged his compatriots to gather at Mount Gerizim so that he could produce for them the sacred vessels, supposedly hidden there in ancient times by Moses himself. Suspicious of the fact that the man's followers had arrived armed, Pilate apparently dispatched some troops to prevent (in his view) a prospective uprising with the result that the battle was fought, many were killed, others were taken prisoner, and the leaders and notables put to death by the prefect (*AJ*, 18, 85 ff.).

The episode is obscure: we do not know enough of the Samaritan beliefs at the time to interpret it with any certainty, although it suggests an incipient (and *sui generis*) Messianic movement among them, with the figure of a charismatic prophet (unnamed, whose exact fate remains unknown) as perhaps Moses reincarnate. It may be telling, however, that – if we trust Josephus's account – the Samaritans, when complaining about Pilate's action to the governor of Syria, rather than referring to their prophet and sacred vessels, sought to explain their behavior as an attempt to escape the tyranny imposed by Pilate (ibid, 88); this made some scholars even speculate that a kind of genuine exodus might have been contemplated.

Be that as it may, the governor L. Vitellius took the Samaritan complaint seriously, ordered Pilate personally to account for the matter in Rome before the emperor, and installed, the text says, one Marcellus as his temporary replacement (ibid, 89). This decision might have been prompted by the traditional and consistent loyalty of the Samaritans towards Rome (which, of course, cannot be told about Jews), so that an offence against them, unless it was rectified, was capable of imperiling an already delicate power balance in the region. But Pilate is reported to have reached Rome only after Tiberius's death (ibid), and of his subsequent fate – from the sufficiently reliable ancient sources – we know nothing.[22]

In Tacitus, L. Vitellius has largely a bad press: he is portrayed as an informer and unprincipled intriguant. The tradition, on which Josephus must have drawn, considered him, in contrast, an able statesman, one of two senior Roman officials (the other is P. Petronius, on whom more later), friendliest to the Jewish needs. In any event, as governor of Syria (A.D. 35–39?), he made an effort to make up for Pilate's rough policies. We are told that he had visited Jerusalem at least twice, and each time received an enthusiastic welcome: on the first occasion, he abolished all city taxes on agricultural produce and, most importantly, in the dispute over the custody of priestly vestments, ruled in favor of Jews (*AJ*, 18, 90 ff. cf. 15, 404 f.); on the second, he even personally sacrificed to God at the Temple during the Passover (18, 122 f.). Furthermore, in the interval between these two visits, he took – given the arrogance habitually associated with the Romans – an unprecedented step, yielding to the appeals from the Jewish establishment, and changing his plans for the military campaign against the Nabataean Arabs ordered by Tiberius. Instead of traversing Judaea with the army that carried the iconic standards offensive in the eyes of the Jews, he proceeded along the circuitous route across the largely non-Jewish territory (ibid, 121 f.): this was a public matter that must have impressed on the memory of, at least, the Jewish elite. It is not surprising then that after the news of Tiberius's demise had finally arrived, Vitellius succeeded in administering the oath of loyalty to the new Emperor Gaius Caligula throughout the province with no trouble at all (124).

In contrast to his brother Philip, tetrarch of Bashan, whose rule over the largely gentile populace seems to have been uneventful (cf. ibid, 106 ff.), Herod Antipas, in his Galilaean tetrarchy, came to experience his own share of troubles. Even apart from the problems created by the Messianic movements he had to deal with, the purists among Jews grumbled over the animal representations in his palace at Tiberias (*AJ*, 19, 65), the city that the tetrarch had built as Galilee's capital (ibid, 37; cf. 18, 36 ff.). Antipas's character may have been questionable, on which Josephus and the Gospels agree, but the very length of his tenure suggests at least some ability of maneuvering between Roman interests and his restless subjects.

Only the third Gospel has him involved in the trial of Jesus (*Lk* 23:7 ff.). But Josephus basically supports (*AJ*, 18, 116 ff.) the New Testament accounts (*Mt* 14:3; *Mk* 6:17 ff.; cf. *Lk* 3:19 f.; 9:9) regarding his earlier showdown with, and the subsequent execution of, John the Baptist – even though the historian offers no details found in the Gospels. The nature of the Baptist's teaching and the movement he initiated remains subject to debate, although on balance, given his emphasis on repentance leading towards spiritual rather than social or political revolution, he seems to have practiced the peaceful form of religious dissent. In any case, Josephus mentions a tradition, indicative of the sufficiently widespread resentment among the people, which ascribed the tetrarch's subsequent military defeat at the hands of the Nabataeans to the "divine and just" vengeance on him for the murder of the Baptist (*AJ*, 18, 116).

Antipas's downfall shortly after Tiberius's death pertained, as it seems, both to his own political ambitions and personal enmities. While coming to Rome in hope for further elevation of his tetrarch status, he was charged with treason before the young emperor by his own brother-in-law, Herod Agrippa (I), Caligula's friend and confidant, as well as recently the recipient from him of a royal title. Whatever the truth, Antipas was stripped of his dignity as tetrarch and, together with his stubborn wife Herodias, sent into exile (*AJ*, 18, 252 ff.; cf. *BJ*, 2, 182 f.).[23]

During the entire period of Roman domination between Pompey's entry in Jerusalem (63 B.C.) and the cessation of the Imperial sacrifices in A.D. 66, it was only at one point, and for a brief length of time, that there emerged in violation of the established practices a real threat to Judaism's existence, comparable with the developments, which preceded the Maccabean revolt under Antiochus IV Epiphanus. This was, of course, Gaius Caligula's attempt (spring A.D. 40) to introduce his own colossal golden statue, in the guise of Jupiter (Philo, *Legat.*, 347), into the Temple, which would have desecrated the sanctuary and undoubtedly caused the nationwide uprising against the occupier. This affair alone would suffice, despite some revisionist argument to the contrary, in demonstrating Caligula's political incompetence, ultimately rooted in his character problems to which all our sources testify. This dangerous initiative failed, however, owing to the felicitous accumulation of circumstances, by no means necessarily predetermined, among them the remarkable self-restraint shown by the Jewish authorities and people at large *vis-à-vis* the emperor's blasphemous design; the intelligent and responsible performance on the part of Syria's governor P. Petronius; the courageous demarche by King Agrippa I; Caligula's own prevaricating and, last but not least, his timely murder on January 24, A.D. 41.

We possess three basic accounts of the crisis: one by Philo of Alexandria (*Legat.*, 186–348), who was a witness of and, to some extent, a participant in the events, and two by Josephus, with the most coherent (but the least detailed – it lacks a crucial story of King Agrippa's intervention) found in the *Bellum* (2, 184–203), and the more extended, even though perhaps less reliable (containing, as will be seen, some folktale elements), in the *Antiquitates* (18, 261–309). The last two are at certain variance with each other, while the difference between the narratives in Philo and Josephus is considerable, and at several points they cannot be reconciled. This creates a series of difficulties, but one feels little doubt that Philo – as a contemporary and eyewitness – should be given preference, provided that we recognize his immediate bias. The basic actions he reports must be historical and valid, but not necessarily their representation or interpretation. In pursuit of his apologetic philosophical and didactic agenda, Philo resorted to the whole variety of devices, which involved skillful rhetoric, omission of the otherwise known pertinent data, willful speculation on the motives and psychology of the dramatis personae and, implicitly, subtle manipulation of chronology.

On the balance of evidence, it appears that two episodes must have alerted Caligula to the fact that Jews at large will by no means tolerate the worship of him as a divine figure he persistently sought to introduce amongst all his subjects. In the first place, this concerned considerable public disorder that at the time (A.D. 38) broke out in Alexandria, apparently with the connivance of Egypt's prefect A. Avilius Flaccus, and is often considered the first recorded anti-Jewish pogrom in history. It was a complex trouble that resulted from the longstanding quarrel between Alexandria's Jewish and Greek communities over civic rights and public status, various aspects of which still remain elusive and subject to debate. Since this book centers on Judaea, with only occasional interest in the affairs at the Diaspora, a thorough discussion of Alexandria's Jews and their vicissitudes falls beyond its confines. Although the tensions at that city must have been growing for quite a while, it appears that the pretext for the riots was provided by King Agrippa I who visited the city, which is said to have caused jealousy amongst the gentiles (*Flacc.*, 27 ff.). The latter proceeded to mock the illustrious visitor by publicly offering royal honors to a local madman, with the prefect reportedly reluctant to interfere (36 ff.), even though this encouraged the mob to forcibly install Caligula's statues at the synagogues with the purpose of their desecration (ibid, 41 ff.; cf. *Legat.*, 134 ff.). For whatever reason, Flaccus not only sided with the crowds, but, even worse, published an edict where, according to Philo, he called Jews "foreigners and aliens." Thereupon many were resettled, in a sort of 'forced ghettoization', from elsewhere in the city, into the Delta quarter the rest of them used to reside in for generations (*Flacc.*, 53 ff.). This was accompanied by plunder and cruel bloodshed, which Philo powerfully portrays, as for instance:

> For wherever they met with or caught sight of a Jew, they stoned him, or beat him with sticks, not at once delivering their blows upon mortal parts, lest they should die speedily, and so speedily escape from the sufferings which it was their design to inflict upon them / ... / And the most merciless of all their persecutors in some instances burnt whole families, husbands with their wives, and infant children with their parents, in the middle of the city, sparing neither age nor youth, nor the innocent helplessness of infants.
>
> (ibid, 66 ff.)

We read that 38 Jewish elders were scourged, some to death (74 ff.), and that the Roman troops also came to be involved in further harassments (86 ff.).

The city's Jews resented – predictably and passionately – the sacrilege against synagogues no less, it seems, than physical outrage inflicted upon them. It must have belonged among the chief grievances that prompted them to dispatch an embassy to Caligula, with Philo as its leader. In turn, their enemies hastened to represent Jewish anger at this abuse of religious freedom they had been granted by Julius Caesar and Augustus, as proving their irreparable disloyalty to the Imperial regime and, in particular, the current ruler (ibid, 165 ff.; cf. *Flacc.*, 41 f.).

The other development took place in Jamnia (Yavneh), Palaestina, a community of mixed population (and by then a part of the Imperial domain). In that case, as it follows from Philo, the blame should be placed on Jews rather than their opponents. Some radicals from their midst, perhaps religious dissenters of the type we are by now familiar with (the adherents of the "fourth philosophy" or any other such group), went to demolish an altar, built by the local gentiles (*Legat.*, 201 f.). This was certainly not within their rights, but offered an example of belligerence and fanaticism that sometimes marred the generally more reasonable behavior of most Jews regarding their neighbors: such actions could have been only detrimental to Jewish interests, and there are reasons to believe that the most far-sighted teachers, like the great Rabban Johanan b. Zakkai, had opposed them. It is not surprising, on the other hand, that the Jamnian gentiles complained to the procurator (meaning in this context supervisor of the Imperial property) C. Herennius Capito, who chose, for his own reasons, to portray in his letter to Caligula the motives and conduct of the offensive Jews in the worst possible light (202 f.).[24]

Be that as it may, the available narratives, when stripped of contradictory elements, suggest a clear pattern taken by the events that followed. Philo's Jewish embassy from Alexandria learned about Caligula's decision to install his statue in the Temple while still waiting for the promised audience with the emperor on the subject of their earlier grievances (ibid, 186 ff.). The instructions about the statue were sent from Rome to the attention of Syria's governor (A.D. 39–42), P. Petronius, who must have belonged among the ablest provincial administrators throughout the period. Philo even credits him with some knowledge of Jewish "philosophy and religion" (245), which makes him an interesting example of a Roman dignitary displaying intellectual curiosity beyond the customary educational procedures. (The fact that the governor of Syria, rather than Judaea's prefect, was put in charge of implementing the project suggests the latter's transient position: his name and prerogatives, left unclear in our sources, are debated by scholars.)

On what followed, Philo and Josephus basically agree: the governor approached with two legions the frontiers of Judaea where he was met by the masses of Jews, highly agitated as a result of rumors spread about the statue (*Legat*, 225 ff.; *AJ*, 18, 262 ff.; *BJ*, 2, 187, 192 ff.). As if in remembrance of their similar demarche under Pontius Pilate, they proceeded with yet another extraordinary display of the non-violent civil disobedience (almost in John Rawls's sense): the assembled Jews declared that they were better to die at the hands of the Romans than to allow their sanctuary to be blasphemed and their sacred laws violated, an attitude insisted upon by the establishment as well as people at large (*Legat.*, 223 f., 229 ff.; *AJ*, 18, 264, 266 ff.; *BJ*, 2, 195, 197 f.). They are said to have addressed the governor with an exhortation, making clear their intent never to comply. It does not seem that Josephus's rendering of their position deviated much from the truth, as for instance:

> If it is imperative for you by all means to carry in and install that image, punish us [by death] first before implementing that decision. For we will not be able to live on and watch doings prohibited to us by the decree of both our lawgiver and our forefathers, who voted this as pertaining to virtue.
> (*AJ*, 18, 264)

Or:

> We will endure any ill fortune in maintenance of our ancestral customs, with the knowledge that for those who are prepared to face danger there is even hope for prevailing, since God will support us while we welcome terrors in his honor.
> (267; cf. Philo, *Legat.*, 223 f.; 229 ff.)

Upon entering Galilee and reaching Tiberias, Petronius was to confront yet another mass demonstration, eventually joined by prominent figures, who continued pressuring him to desist (*AJ*, 18, 269 ff.; *BJ*, 2, 199; Philo seems to have contracted two Jewish demarches into one). Their message remained one and the same: "On no account would we fight, but we will die before we transgress our laws" (*AJ*, 18, 271). The fact that no violence broke out (as it did 30 years later, and on a slighter provocation, inaugurating the Great Revolt) strongly suggests the failure of revolutionary agitators, such as the promoters of "fourth philosophy", to capture at the current stage the popular imagination and, even less, to spread their dissent within society's upper echelon.

After a series of consultations, governor Petronius came to a courageous decision, which might have cost him not only his career, but – given Caligula's practice of political terrorism – even his life. In Josephus's words, he "while observing the perseverance of the Jewish stand, thought it terrible to drive into death such a great multitude of men in servicing Gaius' madness, and consider them guilty for their piety towards God" (277). Consequently, he made arrangements for construction of the statue at Sidon, but embarked at the same time, and under various pretexts, upon the course of procrastination. As the last resort, he must have decided that by writing him a letter, based on purely pragmatic arguments, he might persuade Caligula to retreat. (One such reason, both Philo and Josephus tell us, would be the threat of famine in the area if Jews extend their disobedience, as they could have done, into refusing to cultivate the land and collect the harvest with the resultant shortage of produce; *Legat.*, 249 ff.; *AJ*, 18, 274; *BJ*, 2, 200.)

At this point, Philo's and Josephus's narratives diverge. Chronological inconsistencies within and between them account for the confusion regarding the order and contents of the subsequent correspondence between the emperor and his governor. All in all, it appears that for a time the issue remained uncertain. Our two authorities also differ on the crucial episode in the entire sequence – namely, King Agrippa's intervention, which had – at least, temporarily – saved the day. Josephus's version seems to have come straight from a folktale: we read that the emperor felt so pleased with his royal friend at a lavish banquet, thrown by the latter, that he made a momentous offer to grant any of his requests (*AJ*, 18, 289 ff.). As the reader could expect, the king seizes the opportunity and implores Caligula to rescind the order on the statue's installation (296 ff.). The latter, in fear of publicly losing face, was compelled to yield so that the author could commend the remarkable courage of the only Herodian whom he had clearly admired (298 ff.). The novelistic character of this story suggests that it might have been at some point concocted inside the royal clan.

Philo's treatment, no less dramatic, but perhaps more credible, makes the king physically collapse after first hearing of the blasphemous project against the Temple from Caligula's own lips (263 ff.), and upon his recovery produce a lengthy and well-reasoned memorandum with the purpose of persuading the emperor to drop it (269 ff.). It is unlikely, given the procedures of the ancient historiography, that this argument, presented by Philo in Agrippa's own voice, and made a part of the *Legatio*'s discourse (276–330), was rendered verbatim (it also contains some of that author's own characteristic bias), but it must have preserved the substance of the actual message: by the force of circumstances, the king and the Jewish ambassador from Alexandria were bound to stay in close contact, and it has even been proposed that Philo might have had a hand in drafting the document.

This action by Agrippa I, reinforcing Petronius's letter, at the very least, made Caligula ponder, but both our sources insist that even though he seems to have complied on the surface, in reality his intent was to continue pursuing the same designs by less direct means. According to Josephus, upon his consent to Agrippa's request, the emperor nonetheless instructed Petronius that if the statue had been already installed, it should be left in place (*AJ*, 18, 301), and later on, in another letter, implicitly threatened him with death (304; cf. *BJ*, 2, 203). Philo suggests, on the other hand, that in one such missive Caligula insisted on encouraging the gentiles in Judaea outside of Jerusalem to establish altars or statues in his honor – which, in the view of our author, would have been "nothing, but a source for risings and civil wars" (*Legat.*, 335). Furthermore, one reads next about Caligula's wish to produce yet another colossal statue of him, this time in Rome, so it could be secretly shipped by sea to Palaestina and put up in the Temple as a shocking surprise (337).

Be that as it may, the crisis, fraught with, one easily imagines, exceptional anxieties and tensions, came abruptly to an end as a result of Caligula's assassination on January 24, A.D. 41. Interestingly, Philo does not mention this in the extant text, ending it with the description of the audience given by that emperor shortly before to the Jewish embassy from Alexandria under Philo's own leadership – a painful affair for the envoys, who were mocked by those present, and with an uncertain outcome (349 ff.). Josephus tells a dramatic tale of Petronius's rescue from his master's wrath, predictably attributing it to the act of divine justice: we are told that Caligula had actually issued a death sentence on his disobedient governor, but the messengers carrying it were delayed for three months by the stormy sea and arrived at Judaea after the news of the Imperial succession (*AJ*, 18, 305 ff.; *BJ*, 2, 203). Although it is true that this story is suspect as a historical prop or literary ploy, there is perhaps no need to reject it as wholly fictional on these sole grounds: sometimes life does imitate art.

In any event, through the efforts of individuals, groups and the masses at large, this time the disaster was averted but by no means forgotten: even though unrealized, it made palpably clear the precarious nature of the Empire's government, where the will of one man could quite literally impeach upon the fates of nations and religions. In Judaea, this was bound to have further fertilized the soil for the growth of the increasingly violent religious dissent.[25]

V.

The major role played by Herod Agrippa I in the aftermath of Caligula's murder as mediator between the Senate, bent on restoring the Republic, and Claudius, proclaimed emperor by the praetorian guard, was responsible for the temporary return of Judaea to the status it enjoyed under Herod I – namely, of the formally independent vassal kingdom (A.D. 41–44). One may only speculate whether Caligula's bestowal of the royal title on his Jewish friend was meant as a mere honorary gesture, or whether it actually made a change in Palaestina's power structure. If the latter was the case, it could explain the gloss in our sources over the activities during the recent crisis (and even that person's exact name) of whoever became, as prefect, Pilate's successor in Judaea proper: it was the higher official, Syria's governor Petronius, who enjoyed (if that word is appropriate) both the responsibility and the limelight.

Be that as it may, Claudius publicly demonstrated his appreciation of Agrippa's services through a solemn treaty of alliance with him (*AJ*, 19, 275), presumably modeled on the one made between Augustus and old Herod, thus recognizing him as 'Great King, Friend of Caesar and Friend of Rome'. The prefectorial system was abolished, Judaea and Samaria, as well as other lands, were placed under royal authority (ibid, 274 f.; cf, *BJ*, 2, 215) so that the territories the new king was to rule now extended beyond even the earlier Herodian kingdom.

Although one might assume that Claudius's subsequent settlement at Alexandria would be owing, at least in part, to Agrippa's advice, in reality his influence on the Imperial policies towards the Jewish diaspora appears limited – contrary to what Josephus sought to persuade his readers. The authenticity of the two pro-Jewish edicts on that matter he cites (*AJ*, 19, 280–285 and 286–291), especially the first one (which condemns in strong language Caligula's 'madness') had been questioned by some modern scholars. Josephus admits that trouble in Egypt's capital had continued after Gaius's death, with Jews taking up arms, bent on vengeance against their earlier harassers (ibid, 278), which undoubtedly brought about the publication of Claudius's *Letter to the Alexandrians* in the fall of A.D. 41, documented on papyrus (*CPJ* 153). The thrust of its argument is impartial, but the language seems more favorable regarding the gentiles (which could be expected since it was written in response to their complaints) and harsher towards the Jews. This text makes it apparent – despite the recent challenge to the scholarly consensus regarding the matter – that Claudius chose, upon consideration, to restore the *status quo ante*: the Jews of Alexandria won so far as their faith, as *religio licita*, was promised further protection by the highest authority; but their long-term effort to acquire fuller civic rights was undone.

Upon his departure back home later in A.D. 41 (and he was never again to visit Rome), King Agrippa nonetheless continued advocating the protection of Judaism against abuse outside Palaestina. Thus we read that when yet another attempt had been made by the young pagans to install the statue of Claudius at the Jewish synagogue in the Phoenician city Dora, he took swift action by informing P. Petronius (still Syria's governor at the time) of the incident (*AJ*, 19, 300 f.). This prompted the latter to address the citizens of Dora in writing with a strong reprimand, pointing out that a Jewish synagogue is by no means a proper place for the emperor's image, and demanding that the offenders be sent to him for investigation (303 ff.).[26]

Herod Agrippa I enjoys, for the most part, favorable press in the rabbinic writings (cf. *mSotah*, 7,8; cf. *AJ*, 19, 293 f.), perhaps due to his reportedly punctual observance of the law (cf. *AJ*, loc. cit.) and, one assumes, his partly Hasmonaean descent; but he is given negative treatment in the New Testament for the reason of his reported attacks on the incipient Church – the execution of St. James, brother of John (ca. A.D. 42–43), and the imprisonment of the Apostle Peter (*Acts*: 12, 1 ff.; cf. 19 ff.). Both appraisals need to be qualified: pious, as he must have been, in his dealings with Jews, he acted as a Hellenizer, when out of their reach, an attitude reflected in his secular pursuits, such as attending the theater, erecting statues to his daughters, and even in his coinage; similarly to his grandfather old Herod, he also took pride in playing benefactor towards the pagan cities beyond his own realm (*AJ*, 19, 328, 330, 335 ff.). The rapid succession of three high priests in as many years also hints at some obscure problems he must have encountered within the religious establishment on which we have no further data to consider. Likewise, the narrative about James and Peter in the *Acts* – being the only tangible evidence for suppression of religious (and, in this case, non-violent) dissent that comes from the first Agrippa's reign – constitutes our sole source on that affair, making it impossible to ascertain why and under what circumstances it could have occurred.

It has been suggested that after a short moment of relaxing Rome's grasp over the Eastern vassal principalities, Claudius had embarked on the strategy of centralization, in a manner more vigorous and consistent than any of his predecessors, and that the new kingdom of Judaea under Agrippa I became one of the first to suffer from that political change. One cannot rule out, however, that certain of Agrippa's own actions might have precipitated, or at least provided, the pretext for tightening the Roman hold. The pattern is familiar: any attempt on the part of the Herodian princes to show even a slight independence of mind that might conceivably affect or disrupt the power balance in the region would immediately result in Imperial displeasure, and sometimes in dire consequences: this was the case, as we have seen, with Herod Antipas, and – temporarily – even with old Herod himself.

Agrippa's ambitious project to build yet another defensive wall around Jerusalem was interpreted as misconduct by Petronius's successor as governor of Syria Vibius Marsus (A.D. 41/42–44/45), who eventually denounced the king, charging him with revolutionary intent in a letter to the emperor. Although the charge does not seem likely, Claudius chose to reprimand his friend and ally with the order to desist, which Agrippa could not afford ignoring (*AJ*, 19, 327; *BJ*, 2, 218 f.; 5, 147 ff.; cf. Tac., *Hist.*, 5, 12). This was the typically Roman preventive measure: Josephus helps to appreciate the new governor's concern by stating that if the wall were completed, it would have been able to withstand the siege laid on the city by the Romans during the Great Revolt (*BJ*, 2, 219). This was followed by yet another gesture of the king, fraught with political indiscretion, and it remains unknown whether it betrayed any ulterior designs (the man having been an adventurer by temperament), or merely a persistent desire for showing off – one recalls an exceptional dinner he is said to have thrown for Caligula. This time, he invited several fellow client princes to a banquet at

Tiberias with, as it seemed, no other ostensible purpose than the expression of good will – but in the eyes of an outsider it could well have looked like some sort of secret conference (*AJ*, 19, 328 f.). In itself, this episode might have been ignored by Claudius, mindful of the services Agrippa had rendered him in the recent past; but the legate Vibius Marsus seized upon it as allegedly subversive of Rome's interests. His sudden arrival interrupted the lavish entertainment the king had been offering his royal guests (330 f.). This official, in contrast to his diplomatic predecessor, proceeded with a display of rudeness: according to Josephus (and I find no reasons to question this piece of evidence), he issued orders to Agrippa's visitors, demanding that they withdraw from the city (341). This method of interference was obviously offensive and uncalled for: it humiliated the arguably most influential native leader in the area, and one is not surprised to read that the relationship between him and this particular wielder of Roman power deteriorated (ibid). If allowed to continue, this negative development might have led to the recall of the governor or, more likely, further trouble for King Agrippa, but any such thing was prevented by the latter's dramatic death in A.D. 44, at the age of 54 (346 ff.).

Compared with other Herodian princes, Herod Agrippa I strikes us as having been both charismatic and resourceful. At least some features of his character, as well as the twists and turns of his life story (Josephus rightly makes him say of himself that he had lived "not in the ordinary fashion" – 347), remind us, *mutatis mutandis*, of his grandfather, Herod I, but in a much milder version, lacking the other man's cruelty, treachery and paranoia, while similarly capable of rare displays of courage. At the same time, there remain enough ambiguities and obscurities in the record we possess as regards his circumstances, conduct and motivation; some of them, from a lack of further evidence, cannot be persuasively clarified. Perhaps the most baffling piece of information about him given by Josephus – and, interestingly enough, confirmed in the *Acts* – is the report that during the festivities at Caesarea Maritima he was acclaimed as god (! – even Claudius, unlike his predecessor, felt reluctant to accept such honors; cf. Dio, 60, 5, 4) by the local gentiles, at which point, still attending a theatrical production, he was visited with an attack of mortal illness that within five days carried him away (*AJ*, 19, 344 ff.; cf. *Acts*, 12: 21 f.). The Jewish historian then proceeds to say that when news of the king's death was made known, the same residents of Caesarea, who had just celebrated his presumed godhead (and also, he adds, the Samaritans at Sebaste), turned immediately around and began to pile insults on him and his family in the most outrageous manner (*AJ*, 19, 356 ff.). In each case their behavior, first adulatory and then exactly opposite, is left unexplained. (One tentative, and perhaps not entirely implausible, hypothesis might be that some gentile troublemakers, counting on the implacable antagonism felt by Jews towards any such practices, sought by pretending divinization of their king to generate unrest among them, which might be exploited by the radical religious dissenters, and might bring about yet another showdown between the Jews and the Romans – and upon the failure of the ruse due to the king's death, the same gentiles made their true feelings towards the latter manifest.)

In any event, upon the death of Herod Agrippa I, the newly created Kingdom of Judaea, after having been in existence for only three years, came to an abrupt end.[27]

In retrospect, Claudius's decision to place Judaea, after the death of King Agrippa I, back under direct Roman rule may be seen as the starting point of the developments that led to the ultimate disaster. And yet, it is not entirely clear why it should have been so. The evidence we possess does not allow any precise diagnosis, and the scholarly views differ as much as ever. Apparently, the whole variety of factors conspired, some of them inherent, some accidental, to provide for social and political deterioration. I will mention here at the outset, however, only what might have had at least some bearing on our chief topic.

It happens in history that nominal, or symbolic, trappings – such as titulature, phraseology, public façade and the like – leave a deeper imprint on the popular mindset than the bare realities of life. So long as people at large believe that they live under their own rulers, even if disagreeable and forcibly imposed upon them by the conqueror, their anger and discontent tend to target primarily such collaborators rather than the occupying power. This seems to have been the state of affairs with Herod I, Herod Archaelaus and Herod Antipas, in contrast to the patently anti-Roman unrest in the time of Varus, Quirinius, Pilate or Caligula. The largely benevolent, although short lived, reign of Herod Agrippa I offered the populace, fraught with continuous anxiety, a welcome respite, augmented by the fiction of 'semi-independence': once again, it appeared that they lived in a 'kingdom', governed by a native monarch, 'a friend and ally of Rome', who endeavored to respect their mores and traditions. A sudden abolition of these 'psychological privileges', upon their resultant return to the status as 'subjects' rather than 'allies', must have caused considerable frustration, at least in some quarters, among Judaea's Jews – despite the fact that, in terms of practical politics, it made little difference. This, in turn, could have spurred the more rapid growth of religious dissent, both in its non-violent and violent forms – which became almost immediately felt.

The matter was repeatedly aggravated by Rome's unfortunate choice of procurators (the officials who now replaced the earlier prefects) to preside over the newly reconstituted province. With a few exceptions, individuals thus appointed during the last two decades before the Great Revolt had proven that they were not up to their task. Claudius and Nero may have personally exercised poor judgment, or the fault lay with their freedmen 'secretariat': the appointment and long tenure of Antonius Felix, brother of the notorious and unpopular secretary *a rationibus* Pallas, testifies to the power enjoyed by that group (cf. Tac. *Ann.*, 12, 54). In any event, apart from the apostate Jew Tiberius Alexander (and possibly Porcius Festus), each of the five other Claudian and Neronian procurators had shown little, if any, sensitivity to or appreciation of Jewish customs, in painful contrast with outward piety recently practiced by King Agrippa I.

THE CONQUERED LAND

The re-annexation of Judaea tallies well with the next stage of Claudius's Eastern policies, characterized by what has been called 'new imperialism', that is to say, tightening the authority and control from the center over the vassal princes: those reluctant to comply ran a risk to be dethroned and their territories incorporated into the Empire. In the case of Judaea, at least some proprieties were formally observed: the late king's heir, Herod Agrippa II (M. Julius Agrippa), aged 16, and then receiving his education at the Imperial court, was politely advised that he was still too young for taking up the responsibilities of kingship (*AJ*, 19, 362); it is very likely that he was promised some sort of restoration upon achieving adulthood (that would have paralleled, *mutatis mutandis*, Augustus's treatment of Herod Archaelaus). If that had been the case, his expectations were partially fulfilled when, five years later, he was created king of Chalcis to succeed his uncle Herod (V). It must be emphasized, however, that although the land under his jurisdiction kept growing, he was never considered a formally independent allied monarch, as was his father, and his authority remained limited all the time, both in territory and in substance. The new 'procuratorial' province proved considerably enlarged in size upon the pre-Claudian 'prefectorial' one by absorbing territories of the former tetrarchies. Despite the territorial increase, however, no further measures were, as it seems, taken to step up Roman military presence: the subsequent events made clear that this amounted to a strategic mistake.[28]

In the *Bellum*, Josephus writes approvingly of the first Claudian procurator Cuspius Fadus (A.D. 44–45) that he did not interfere with the Jewish ancestral customs and thus maintained peace in the land (*BJ*, 2, 220). The material found in the *Antiquitates*, however, suggests a different picture of him as – at least in some respects – another edition of Pontius Pilate. One learns that upon his very arrival to Judaea, he was confronted with the quarrel over the border between the Jews of Peraea and the Graeco-Syrian city Philadelphia. According to our source, although the Jews might have felt some legitimate grievances, it was they who initiated violence "despite the judgment of their first men" (*AJ*, 20, 2 f.). Consequently, the procurator proceeded against them and took captive three of their leaders, one to be executed and other two sent into exile (4).

Next, Fadus came dangerously close to producing yet another crisis by a sudden demand to transfer the high priestly vestments back under Roman custody (20, 6 ff.; cf. 15, 403 ff.), thereby infringing upon the settlement on that issue, reached by L. Vitellius, with Tiberius's approval, in the previous decade – a move which is difficult to interpret otherwise than as a provocation. That Syria's governor, C. Cassius Longinus (A.D. 44/45–50), found it imperative personally to enter Jerusalem with a military force signals the seriousness of the situation and the extent of Roman fear about the Jewish potential response (cf. *AJ*, 20, 7). The motives behind Fadus's uncalled for gesture of interference are hard to fathom, especially given the fact that Vitellius, the man responsible for the earlier settlement, became one of the new emperor's most influential advisors. Whatever the case, the sound judgment on each side won over, and the tensions began to relax when both the legate and the procurator authorized the request by the Jewish leaders for dispatching an embassy to Rome and seeking the Imperial arbitration, but only after the envoys had agreed to deliver their children as hostages: another sign that the Romans took the trouble seriously (*AJ*, 20, 7 f.; cf. 15, 407). It was then that young Herod Agrippa (II) may have taken the first step in his own political career and intervened with Claudius on behalf of his coreligionists, with the result that the dispute was resolved in their favor (ibid, 9; cf. 15, loc. cit.). There is no reason, as it seems, for questioning the authenticity of the emperor's letter cited by Josephus, which reaffirms the right for the nations "to practice their religion in accordance with the ancestral customs" (*AJ*, 20, 13).

Josephus's claim that, owing to the foresight and concern shown by Fadus (5), the whole country was rid of robber-bands, is clearly rhetorical and substantiated only through the reference to a certain Tolomaeus, 'an arch-brigand', working mischief in the South, who was then seized and put to death (ibid). Nothing else is known about the man, and the modern tendency to identify, without further ado, whatever mention of brigandage in the sources with social discontent, religious unrest or 'freedom fighting' should be resisted. This said, it must have been under Fadus that religious dissent, in its purer – and non-violent – facet, again made itself manifest, first time (so long as one relies on the available evidence) since Pilate. We learn of the false prophet Theudas, who, in Josephus's words, convinced 'a great mob' to follow him, with their possessions, towards the Jordan river, which would part at his command and allow them an easy passage (*AJ*, 20, 97) – as for the question 'where to hence?', the text leaves it unanswered. In itself, this *modus operandi* recalls Moses and the Exodus, while the immediate destination, the River Jordan, makes one think of John the Baptist. Fadus, however, "did not allow them to profit from their folly" (98 – one of Josephus's exasperatingly illogical phrases, since what kind of profit, we may ask, could 'their folly' have achieved?) and dispatched a cavalry squadron, which put the whole adventure to an end by killing and capturing many, among the latter Theudas himself, who was subsequently decapitated (ibid). This same episode is also alluded to in the *Acts*, where the speaker Gamaliel places it anachronistically before the revolt of Judas the Galilaean: "For before these days Theudas arose, giving himself out to be somebody, and a number of men, about four hundred, joined him; but he was slain and all who followed him were dispersed and came to nothing" (5:36). Even combined, this information is too scarce to conclude on the character or purpose of Theudas's movement, though the New Testament quote suggests a Messianic element. A miracle is promised, but in contrast to the mission of John the Baptist or Jesus of Nazareth, we do not hear anything about the need for repentance or moral regeneration in order to be saved.[29]

Unlike his uncle Tiberius, who had preferred long prefectorial terms, Claudius exhibited at first a tendency to replace his procurators in Judaea every few years, apparently irrespective of their performance. Thus, after only two years since his arrival to the province, Cuspius Fadus was succeeded by Tiberius Julius

Alexander (ca. A.D. 46–48), nephew of the philosopher Philo, and the only Jew we know of who had achieved major administrative positions in the first century Roman Empire, which may have even included the highest equestrian office, praetorian prefecture. In most cases, the reasoning behind the procuratorial appointments cannot be determined for the lack of relevant data; one suspects that much depended on the pressures and factional rivalry at the Imperial court. In any event, the choice of Tiberius Alexander must have belonged among Claudius's intelligent decisions. Coming from an influential Alexandrian family, this Jewish Hellenizer, intimately familiar, despite his personal apostasy, with the tenets of Judaism, would have known how to spare, whenever it was possible, the sensibilities of his compatriots.

It is said that during his tenure the land was in peace (*BJ*, 2, 220), despite severe famine. One finds it telling, on the other hand, that Josephus was not able to avoid mentioning, for the first time since Quirinius's census, the resurgence of the "fourth philosophy" movement, which represented, as we have seen, the violent form of religious dissent. The inevitable inference is that throughout the intervening years that movement continued to exist, apparently in a sort of underground, although the trouble they might have caused proved insufficient to draw the historian's attention. It clearly broke out at the time of Tiberius Alexander – perhaps in protest against that Jewish renegade? – who is credited by Josephus with capturing and crucifying two sons of the sect's founder Judas the Galilaean, called Simon and James (ibid, 101 f.): this suggests that by then they were already seen as a public threat. In any event, from that time on, the adherents of this same creed, broadly known as the *sicarii*, came eventually to practice individual terrorism and made a recurrent feature of Judaea's political scene. Their convoluted story, however, requires and will receive special treatment later in this book. Further on, when describing the events that occurred under that procurator's successor, Josephus speaks of yet another prominent troublemaker, one Eleazar b. Deinaeus, "who was a bandit for many years and operated in the mountains" (*AJ*, 20, 121; cf. *BJ*, 2, 235); elsewhere it is specified that his career as outlaw ran for 20 years, no less (*BJ*, 2, 253), which would mean it had already begun during Tiberius Alexander's term. This man may or may not have been practicing any form of religious dissent as defined in this book, and might have basically been a common brigand, although not devoid of nationalist sentiments shown by the fact that he later joined forces with the anti-Roman rioters. As we will see, he was eventually captured by the procurator Antonius Felix.[30]

A.D. 48/49 saw several changes in Judaea's political scene. The young Herod Agrippa II succeeded his uncle (and brother-in-law) Herod (V) as king of Chalcis (*AJ*, 20, 104); he chose to stay in Rome, however, for at least another two years rather than going immediately to Palaestina. Sometime earlier Herod of Chalcis had persuaded Claudius to grant him the authority over the Temple in Jerusalem and the rights of appointing high priests (ibid, 15 f.). Upon his predecessor's death Agrippa II inherited all these privileges, which must have also endowed him with potential clout in the affairs of state.

A quandary in regard to the next procurator, Ventidius Cumanus (A.D. 48–52), is created by the contradictory data found in Josephus and Tacitus. If the former unequivocally describes him as Tiberius Alexander's sole successor (*BJ*, 2, 223; *AJ*, 20, 103), the latter states that the province had been divided in two parts, so that Galilee was administered by Cumanus, and Samaria by Antonius Felix, brother of Claudius's powerful freedman secretary Pallas (*Ann.*, 12, 54). It is not immediately clear what version is to be preferred: on the one hand, Josephus is an obvious authority on the history of Judaea; on the other, it seems unlike Tacitus, who had apparently used the Imperial archives, – even though he could be sometimes guilty of a minor factual mistake – to have so grossly erred. One possible way to make sense out of these ostensibly irreconcilable reports is to assume that Felix was given a subordinate appointment under Cumanus at some later stage and eventually came to equal him in authority, *de facto* if not *de jure*, perhaps resulting from the trouble between the Jews and the Samaritans yet to be discussed. After all, as in the case of Tiberius Alexander's appointment, Claudius might have continued experimenting, and we know that Josephus was not above omitting or misrepresenting this or that particular occurrence for reasons of his own.

Be that as it may, Cumanus's procuratorship proved a disaster. The contrast between his lack of sensitivity and his predecessor's expertise in Judaism must have further frustrated not only religious dissenters, but the general public at large, which became increasingly attuned towards any offence or provocation, deliberate or inadvertent, coming from the Romans. Two occasions are recorded on which this led to substantial disturbance: on the first, a sort of uprising had actually happened; on the second, it was barely prevented. Both episodes intimately involved the notion of the sacred, in the specifically Jewish sense alien to the Romans, once again reminding us of our present failure to comprehend any such thing at all, as is testified by the Danish caricature scandal and other similar affairs which cannot be appreciated in full solely through the prism of political correctness.

Josephus tells us that on the fourth day of the Passover festival A.D. 49, a Roman soldier placed, among others, to stand guard on one of the Temple's porticos (a routine procedure during Jerusalem's religious festivities, aimed at maintaining order) performed in public an obscene gesture, which was immediately – and predictably – taken as blasphemy against God by the crowds (*AJ*, 20, 108; *BJ*, 2, 224). In the *Antiquitates* it is said that the latter began to abuse verbally the troops and the procurator (109 f.), while the *Bellum* also speaks of the young Jewish hot-heads and 'revolutionary hopefuls' initiating the fight (225). In any event, Cumanus, seized – one assumes – by both fear and anger, must have overreacted and sent for reinforcements ("the entire army", – says Josephus), whose arrival spread panic among the rioters, prompting them to flee: we are told that, owing to the narrowness of the exits, most of them had perished, in belief that they were pursued by the enemy, from having been trampled upon one another (*AJ*, 20, 11; *BJ*, 2, 226 f.). Although Josephus's figures – between

10,000 and 30,000 casualties (they differ in his two accounts and also in the manuscript readings) appear exaggerated, it can hardly be doubted that the death toll was considerable. And we do not hear of any punishment inflicted on the offender. Our author concludes with a pointed pronouncement, expressing and regretting the truth, which history recurrently confirms, even though it may take different manifestations, irrespective of other political, social or economic forces operating at the time: "Such were the calamities caused by the obscene conduct of a single soldier" (*AJ*, 20, 112).

The second reported act of sacrilege, fraught with even greater perils, evokes a comparison, although not yet on the same scale, to the happenings under Gessius Florus. It started with the robbery by some 'brigands' or 'rebels bent on revolution' of a slave, who had belonged to the Imperial household, near Beth-horon, the very location where the army of Cestius Gallus will be defeated a decade and a half later (*BJ*, 2, 228; *AJ*, 20, 113). Although the reasons for this are not specified, the affair must have been of some official importance, since we are told that Cumanus did at once dispatch soldiers to sack the neighboring villages and bring their elders into his presence in chains (*BJ*, 2, 229; *AJ*, 20, 114). While thus engaged, one legionary had ostentatiously destroyed a copy of the Torah. The effect of this outrage seems as described, and despite all rhetoric, believable: it suggests the remarkable degree of tensions across the land, reminding us of Pompey desecrating (however unwittingly) the Holy of Holies, or Caligula competing in his folly with the God of Israel. "The Jews, – says Josephus – rose up as if their entire country were set on fire" (*BJ*, 2, 230). Following the same pattern as when they dealt with Pilate and Petronius, Jewish crowds confronted the procurator in Caesarea Maritima and demanded the crime against God be avenged; in Josephus's words, they insisted that otherwise – and this also strikes a familiar note – it was pointless for them to continue living "since the laws of their ancestors were thus abused" (*AJ*, 20, 116; cf. *BJ*, loc. cit.). This must have sobered the Roman, with the recent riot at the Temple fresh in his memory, and compelled him to yield:

> Cumanus, alarmed at the thought of yet another revolution of the masses, after having consulted with his friends, beheaded the soldier who had outraged the laws and thus prevented the sedition when it was on the verge of breaking out a second time.
>
> (*AJ*, 20, 117; cf. *BJ*, 2, 231)

This public act as an outcome of the crisis suggests that, depending on circumstances, even the truly hostile, but still ultimately pragmatic, Imperial official could have been made to compromise.[31]

Yet the subsequent events were to demonstrate that this particular procurator failed in properly learning the earlier lessons. We possess three accounts of the showdown in A.D. 51–52 that had effectively ended Cumanus's career – two by Josephus (*BJ*, 2, 232 ff.; *AJ*, 20, 118), again with an occasional telling divergence;

and one in Tacitus (*Ann.*, 12, 54) that offers, however briefly and vaguely, a somewhat different story. This reminds us of a similar problem with our sources, Philo and Josephus, on Caligula's attempt to desecrate the Temple. Tacitus belongs, regrettably, among classical authors who exhibit a strong dislike for Jews. Apparently, he was not familiar with Josephus's work, and his source on the episode may have been an equally brief statement in the writings of some predecessor. Owing, on the other hand, to his own service in the provinces, Tacitus must have known better than Josephus the realities of Roman administrative routine (and this is why I am inclined to accept his claim that *both* Ventidius Cumanus and Antonius Felix were involved in the trouble); and it is for the same reason that his testimony, as we will see, on the depth of corruption within Roman officialdom in Judaea, turns particularly valuable.

Not unlike in the case of Pilate, the Samaritans proved the ultimate cause of Cumanus's debacle. Their enmity towards Jews was common knowledge and, as Tacitus wryly observes, by the time under consideration, the latter felt "less restrained than ever from the contempt of those who ruled over them" (that is, Cumanus and Felix – loc. cit.). The senatorial historian proceeds to draw the picture of the conflict, but in most general terms, and with an emphasis on the illicit conduct by the Roman officials in charge tantamount to criminal complicity:

> Consequently, they [Samaritans and Galilaeans – V.R.] plundered each other, sending in bands of brigands, forming ambushes, and sometimes engaging in battles, and carrying spoils and booty to the procurators, the latter rejoicing at first, but with the growth of the mischief, they interfered with the military force, which was routed.
>
> (ibid)

At the very least, such persistent tensions required constant and careful supervision, and this was precisely what Ventidius Cumanus failed to implement. According to Josephus, the Samaritans killed a number of Galilaean pilgrims on their way to a religious festival in Jerusalem (*BJ*, 2, 232 f.; *AJ*, 20, 118). Cumanus turned down the request by the Galilaean elders to seek out and punish the culprits (*BJ*, 2, 233; *AJ*, 20, 119).

The resultant sense of indignation among Jews would be predicted. This time the offence, as it seems, affected nationalist rather than religious sensibilities; they were spurred on by the angry Galilaeans and made others to feel that – in Josephus's words – though "slavery in itself is a bitter lot, with 'hybris', it becomes altogether unbearable" (*AJ*, 20, 120). We read that the masses in Jerusalem, defying an attempt on the part of the Jewish establishment to mollify them with promises to increase pressure on the procurator, had called for aid from the notorious 'brigand' (treated as such by Josephus) Eleazar b. Deinaeus, already spoken of. As a result, some villages on Samaria's borders were reportedly burned and their inhabitants slaughtered (*BJ*, 2, 235; *AJ*, 20, 121). To retaliate,

Cumanus is reported to have taken over a cavalry squadron of the Sebastenians, traditional enemies of Jews, four infantry cohorts (out of five at his disposal) and – insult added to injury – joined by the armed Samaritans themselves. Thus equipped, he marched against the hastily collected Jewish forces. According to Josephus, many of the latter perished or were taken captive (*AJ*, 20, 122; cf. *BJ*, 2, 236). Those who fled and thus survived, we are told, chose to embrace the arguments of the Jewish establishment, put down their arms and dispersed, while the 'brigands' withdrew to their strongholds so that "thereupon all Judaea was filled with bandits" (*AJ*, 20, 124; cf. *BJ*, 2, 238 f.). Although at this point the historian's logic somewhat falters, this newest massacre must have further contributed to the gradual breaking up of law and order in the land.

Meanwhile the Samaritan delegation approached in Tyre Syria's current governor (ca. A.D. 50–60) C. Ummidius Durmius Quadratus to seek redress against Jews for the ravages inflicted on their territory. The emphasis of their argument, writes Josephus, lay in the claim that even if the Samaritans were guilty in what they had been accused of, the Jews, rather than waging war on them, should have petitioned the Roman authorities for arbitration, while by behaving as they did, they had shown their contempt towards the Imperial nation (*AJ*, 20, 125 ff.). If this had indeed been said, it was patently false: it must have been known at the time (as the emperor's final verdict in their favor implies) that, upon the perpetration of the crime, Jews went to seek justice with the procurator, who had ignored their plea. This was in itself an act of civil disobedience, even though some militants among them might have already embarked upon their own exercise of vengeance. Predictably, this was what the Jewish envoys, including the former high priest Jonathan b. Ananus, are said to have pointed out to the governor. Insisting that the Samaritans had originated the trouble, they rightly placed the burden of responsibility for its consequences on Cumanus (*BJ*, loc. cit.; *AJ*, 20, 127).

Tacitus credits Ummidius Quadratus, in the context of this episode, with having prevented a full scale war in Judaea (loc. cit.). Be that as it may, this very official, although his actions ultimately led to Cumanus's disgrace, does not seem to have shown, unlike L. Vitellius or P. Petronius, acting under similarly critical circumstances, any sympathy towards the offended. The impression of his impartiality is deceptive, given his callous treatment of Jews, irrespective even of their social standing. After having deferred judgment in order to conduct proper investigation, Quadratus entered Judaea and reportedly gave the case two hearings with representatives of both sides present: one in Samaria (as in the *Antiquitates*) or Caesarea Maritima (according to the *Bellum*), and another at Lydda. During the first, he is said to have concluded on the guilt of the Samaritans (*AJ*, 20, 129), but crucified both the culprits from their ranks and the Jews captured by Cumanus (ibid, cf. *BJ*, 2, 241). On the second occasion, when the Samaritans identified a Jew called Doetus as the one who had roused the 'mob' to proceed against them and the Romans, he and his 'revolutionary' associates were, on the governor's orders, similarly put to death (*AJ*, 20, 130). The same attitude transpired in Quadratus's rough handling of Jewish notables: we have already seen that he went so far as to dispatch to Rome (so that they could be acted upon by the emperor) the current high priest Ananias b. Nedebaeus, his son Ananus, who served as the Temple's captain, and several others – in chains; and the same action (but without the reference to chains in our source) was taken with regard of the Samaritan leaders (*AJ*, 20, 131 f.; cf. *BJ*, 2, 243). If the narrative of the *Antiquitates* is to be trusted, this last measure (that is, putting in chains men from the uppermost echelon within the priestly establishment) seems uncalled for and peculiar to the point of puzzlement. The only reason that could have justified such humiliation would have been incontrovertible proof of their complicity in recent disturbances; but as we know, that was not the case. In any event, Josephus – another instance of his sometimes irksome habit – leaves this matter entirely unexplained. In a separate move, the governor suspended Cumanus from his procuratorial office and ordered him, together with a military tribune called Celer (presumably, a key participant in the crisis), to set off likewise for the capital and there account for themselves (*BJ*, 2, 244; *AJ*, 20, 132). This was, on Quadratus's part, a drastic step (the only precedent being Pilate's dismissal by Vitellius), and clearly taken under exigency, indicating the seriousness of the situation. His anxiety became further betrayed, says Josephus, in his visit to Jerusalem, which he reportedly found at peace, celebrating the Passover, with no sign of potential violence (*AJ*, 20, 133; *BJ*, 2, 244).

One may only speculate on what could have exactly happened at the Imperial court to bring about Claudius's verdict in favor of Jews. According to Josephus, the faction opposing them failed to win for the reason that the young Herod Agrippa II (at the time, in the capital) once again had intervened on Jewish behalf (*AJ*, 20, 135; cf. *BJ*, 2, 245) – in the later version, through the agency of Agrippina, urging her to make her husband "consider the case as befits his sense of justice and punish the originators of the revolt" (*AJ*, loc. cit.). As Claudius used to deliberate privately *in cubiculo* (cf. Tac. *Ann.*, 11, 2), the Jewish cause might have also gained backing from the secretary *a rationibus* Pallas, Agrippina's ally and reputed lover, laboring to secure the appointment of his brother Felix as successor to Cumanus – a candidacy, as we learn later, that had also been supported (to his subsequent detriment) by the former high priest Jonathan b. Ananus. Be that as it may, in his ruling the emperor squarely put the blame on the Samaritans, sentenced to death three of their leaders and sent Cumanus into exile (*BJ*, 2, 245; *AJ*, 20, 136). The military tribune Celer (chosen, one suspects, as a scapegoat) was to be dragged in public view around Jerusalem and executed: a punishment inordinately severe, even though the nature of the man's crime remains enigmatic – another example of Josephus's exasperating silences.

As regards the high priest Ananias b. Nedebaeus, if he had been made to endure the ignominy of chains, this did not seem to affect his loyalty to Rome, suggesting that it is wrong to assume, despite the recent efforts to do so, that any act of mistreatment by the occupiers would have necessarily led a Jewish noble to consider revolution. Upon his return home, he continued to exercise substantial (and pro-Roman) influence on the domestic scene. He knew how to enter profitable relationships with a procurator and, as we have seen, on the eve of the great revolt, he kept stubbornly counteracting the secessionist policies of his own son Eleazar, only to be killed, together with his brother Ezechias, by the sicarian dissenters.[32]

On the last Claudian procurator of Judaea [M.] Antonius Felix (A.D. 52 – ca. 60) we possess more information than on any other within the entire period, except possibly Tiberius Alexander. This is owing, of course, to his being brother of the Imperial secretary Pallas whose career and standing under Claudius and Nero were bound to spur interest in his sibling. Irrespective, however, of various pressures at the court that can be easily imagined, the decision to appoint a freedman as Judaea's chief Roman official offers another example of Claudian administrative experimentation.

A few details found in Josephus and the Book of Acts allow to recognize in Felix a character of some complexity which might have affected his policies in Judaea: on the one hand, clearly extortionist; and, on the other, striving, and not entirely without success, to maintain public peace. He must have possessed both some proven abilities and significant charisma, responsible for an extraordinary fact our sources report – namely, that he happened to marry three Eastern queens in a row (Suet. *Div. Cl.*, 28). Felix appears as the only known governor of Judaea (Tiberius Alexander naturally constitutes a special case), who may have acquired useful administrative experience in that country prior to his procuratorial tenure, and even temporarily succeeded in winning the good will of the Jewish establishment, manifest through the support for his candidacy by Jonathan b. Ananus. Still, the mechanism of his appointment through a court intrigue, in which he might himself have participated, and aimed at impeaching Ventidius Cumanus, leaves little doubt that he owed it ultimately to the influence of his powerful brother.

As we have seen, Tacitus treats Felix with considerable contempt, which is not surprising, given his pronounced hostility towards the Imperial freedmen and their role in the government. Elsewhere he singles him out, even among Judaea's Claudian procurators, as the one, who "through all kinds of savagery and lust exercised the right (*ius*) of a king in a manner of a slave" (*Hist.*, 5, 9). To the extent that it was true, this charge could not obviously pertain to Felix's conduct in Judaea before Cumanus's recall, otherwise the preference shown towards him at the time by Jews would be inconceivable. Josephus is silent on Felix's policies in the two remaining years of Claudius's rule; presumably, nothing much had happened. His stay in the office was, however, extended under Nero into another half decade – that is to say, as long as his brother Pallas remained influential. Consequently, Felix's administrative record, fraught with the mixture of energy and deep corruption, will be discussed in this chapter's last section.[33]

Altogether, in the course of his reign, Claudius's own policy exhibited both pro-Jewish and anti-Jewish tendencies: the Romans would have called it fair. On the one hand, he had reaffirmed, as we have seen, Jewish religious freedom and published at least one edict to that effect; on two occasions (the matter of the priestly vestments and the disturbances under Cumanus) he had ruled in favor of the Jews; and in Rome he went on with prosecuting violent Alexandrian anti-Semites as we know from the so-called *Acts of the Pagan Martyrs*. On the other, he twice took measures against the Jewish population at the capital, the evidence for which is obscure and still the subject of much controversy.

It is possible, of course, to interpret these oscillations as resulting from the balance of influences at the court, assuming that Agrippina had inherited pro-Jewish and pro-Eastern attitudes favored by her grandmother Antonia, and postulating the existence of a faction, which opposed them, especially in view of the apparent clash among Claudian courtiers over the Cumanus affair; nor should one disregard the role of the two Agrippas, emphasized by Josephus, as Jewish champions. It seems equally plausible, however, due to the modern re-evaluations of Claudius's administrative record, that in each case the emperor acted pragmatically, in accordance with his own understanding of what should be done.

In any event, under A.D. 41 – that is, the first year of Claudius's rule – Dio reports, without actually supplying any further clues, that the new emperor ordered Jews, "while continuing their traditional way of life, not to hold meetings" (60, 6, 6). On the surface, the statement seems self-contradictory: the prayer gatherings in the synagogues were indeed a part of the Jewish traditional way of life. Dio specifies that Claudius resorted to that measure because the number of Jews in Rome had again dramatically increased, and an attempt at their banishment (a clear reference to the wholesome expulsion of the Jews from the capital in A.D. 19) would have been too problematic (ibid). Could Claudius, in fact, have then considered following that precedent under Tiberius (which I have briefly discussed in the earlier section), and if so, why? As it seems, Dio indirectly implies that the latter intended to curtail Jewish proselytizing; this time, in the aftermath of Caligula's sacrilegious project, it could have hardly been the case. Next, the measure occurred when King Agrippa I was at the height of his influence and engaged in advocating Jewish interests elsewhere; why then did he not try (or at least we do not hear that he did), while still in Rome, to dissuade his august friend from this anti-Jewish move? Finally, if the ban had not concerned public prayers in the synagogues, what kind of meetings had been forbidden? I find most plausible a conjecture that the trouble, though – one presumes – relatively mild, must have been political, on the wave of Jewish agitation across the Empire generated by the pogroms in Alexandria and Caligula's claims at the Temple worship. Ironically, Claudius's position on religious freedom might have added to the fire: it does happen sometimes that a small victory leads those who had won it towards even greater anxiety and demands. As recently proposed, the prohibition known from Dio sought to prevent the activity of crowds threatening law and order. Although Agrippa I may have helped to mitigate the Imperial displeasure, this could still account for a sense of annoyance at the current Jewish behavior which some interpreters read into Claudius's *Letter to the Alexandrians*.[34]

Much ink was spilt to elucidate Suetonius's brief statement that Claudius banished from Rome "Jews, constantly in tumult, compelled by a Chrestus" (*Div. Cl.*, 25, 4) and whether this refers to the event mentioned by Dio. But the latter explicitly denies any expulsion of the Jews at the time, which means that we are dealing with two separate episodes. I am inclined to accept the identification of Suetonius's 'Chrestus' with Christ for the simple reason that, in my view, any other interpretative procedure violates the Occam razor principle. If so, this reference makes our earliest evidence about the Christian activity in the capital, perhaps relating to St. Peter's (legendary) first stay in Rome, claimed by the later ecclesiastical tradition. The dating remains unclear, although Aquila and Priscilla are portrayed in the *Acts* (18:2) as having come to Corinth "because Claudius had commanded all the Jews to leave Rome". It seems that they had suffered from the same harassment, even though the words 'all the Jews' exaggerate, since such wholesale banishment, that is to say, inclusive also of Roman citizens, would not have been possible on legal grounds.

As for Paul's first public encounter, the historicity of which I find no reason to dismiss, with a ranking Roman administrator, this must have happened ca. A.D. 51/52 in Corinth, at the court of L. Junius Gallio, Seneca's brother, and then proconsul of Achaia, where he was taken by the resident compatriots on the charge of "persuading men to worship God contrary to the law" (*Acts*, 18:13). Gallio, however, had dismissed the suit for falling outside of his jurisdiction (18:14 ff.). This agrees well with what we know of the Imperial policies towards the Diaspora: a conscientious Roman statesman would indeed seek to observe Jewish religious freedom by not interfering with their internal conflicts as long as they concerned solely the issues of faith.[35]

VI.

Given the fact that the Great Revolt broke out under Nero, and the latter's reputation within the Roman elite, one might expect Josephus to speak harshly of him in the *Bellum*; the more so, since at the time of its composition, his name was hardly in favor with the first two Flavians. But compared to the pronouncements on Nero by Josephus's two younger contemporaries, Tacitus and Suetonius, the little that he has to say in that work about that notorious Emperor sounds laconic and even mild:

> As regards acts that Nero committed against Fortune out of 'hybris' when an excess of good luck and wealth drove him out of his mind, namely, or how he destroyed in turn, his brother, his wife and his mother; and how afterwards he turned his savagery against the most noble persons; and how finally out of insanity, he rushed onto the theatrical stage, since this is universally bruited about, I will pass it over, and turn to what took place under him in the affairs of the Jews.
>
> (*BJ*, 2, 250 f.)

This restraint and the implicit rhetorical *recusatio* may have at least in part pertained to Josephus's personal and, as it appears, positive experience with the ambience of Nero's court during his first stay in Rome when, as a young man, he went there on a mission to deliver from the Imperial custody certain Jewish priests who were falsely accused of unspecified misdeeds (*Vita*, 13 ff.). Through the agency of the Jewish actor Aliturus, he was given an audience by Poppaea Sabina; as a result, his request was granted and his mission was a success (ibid, 16). Still, it is worth taking note that he passes over an opportunity to place blame for Jewish misfortunes on the (then) unpopular 'artistic tyrant'.

In the *Antiquitates*, written decades later, Josephus – as does Tacitus (cf. *Ann.*, 1, 1; *Hist.*, 1,1) – recognizes the display of *animus nocendi*, the 'malicious intent', by some historians who wrote about the Julio-Claudian emperors: "But it must be allowed to those who are not worried about truth, to write whatever they wish since they seem to take pleasure in doing so" (*AJ*, 20, 156). This accounts for his pledge to provide an objective and balanced narrative: "We intend truth as our aim" (*AJ*, 20, 157), even though it is qualified by the statement that the doings in Rome (which must include, by implication, Nero's crimes and antics) are merely incidental to his interest which concentrates on the fates and affairs of the Jews (ibid). Regarding those latter, however, we read that no hesitation will be shown by the author in demonstrating both their calamities and their blunders (ibid), a promise comparable with Tacitus's famous formula *sine ira et studio* – "without anger and partiality".

We know that neither Josephus, nor Tacitus, succeeded in keeping up with that promise: to the modern eye, their bias is patently clear. But it is an altogether different matter as to whether they or their contemporaries thought about the pursuit of historical truth in the same clear-cut and transparent – or sometimes cynical – terms that we now do.

In any event, for the Jewish people *en masse* the immediate problem was, as we came to know, not the character of the emperor, a remote and, perhaps, august figure residing in a faraway place, but the repercussions of Roman presence in their own land – and, more specifically, the behavior of Roman administrators at any given time representing the central government. This brings us back to Antonius Felix, still a Claudian, not Neronian appointment.

One of Nero's first acts in Palaestina was to enlarge the territory under King Agrippa II, now to include the important city of Tiberias in Galilee, as well as Tarichaeae and two others (*BJ*, 2, 252; *AJ*, 20, 159); this naturally meant at least some diminution of the overall procuratorial authority. Josephus treats Felix's tenure in terms of increasing corruption on his part and continuous decline of law and order throughout the land: "the country came again to be filled with brigands and impostors, who were deceiving the mob" (*AJ*, 20, 160; cf. *BJ*, 2, 253, 258). At the same time, he acknowledges the procurator's energy, manifest in an effort to suppress what he calls banditry (*BJ*, 2, 253; *AJ*, 20, 161; cf. *Acts*, 23:2), and no doubt seen as such not only by the Romans but also by Josephus's many well-to-do compatriots. Both the *Bellum* and the

Antiquitates describe how Felix succeeded in finally capturing the notorious 'brigand' survivor Eleazar b. Deinaeus – under false pretexts, through offering him safe conduct; instead, the man was detained and dispatched to Rome (*AJ*, 20, 161; cf. *BJ*, 2, 253), where he was surely executed. As I have already had occasion to point out, one cannot ascertain whether that individual was merely a felon with some nationalist inkling, or a practitioner, in whatever form, of religious dissent.

Josephus's claim regarding the extortionist character of Felix's administration is supported, as we have seen, by Tacitus. The scale of corruption must have soon enough gone beyond what the Jewish collaborationists could silently tolerate. This resulted in breaking up the alliance between the procurator and the former high priest Jonathan b. Ananus, who had earlier championed his appointment, and now, according to Josephus, was in fear of being attacked, for that very reason, by the people at large (*AJ*, 20, 162). Felix, we read, found Jonathan's repeated censure so injurious ("for those, who wish to do wrong, constant rebuke is painful"; ibid) that he resorted to arranging the latter's physical removal. That Josephus was able even to conceive such a motive is not without interest; it suggests that, in his view, at least some Roman officials could experience concern over their *existimatio* among the Jewish elite. In any case, in the *Antiquitates* (but not the *Bellum*) the procurator is alleged to have secretly negotiated to have the other man killed with the revolutionary *sicarii* (20, 163 f.). (The latter are specifically mentioned by Josephus as first appearing under that name on the political scene around this time – *BJ*, 2, 254.) I will resume, at some length, the discussion of these events in a later chapter.

Prima facie, Felix's behavior (as thus charged) seems to contradict his vigorous campaign to exterminate the militants; but it is well in tune with the Tacitus statement, cited above, on the procurators' complicity with the rebels. The corruption within the province's administration must have run deep to ensure such a phenomenon recurred. Nor were the Romans, in this respect, unique: the same kind of tradeoff, even in critical moments, can be found in many societies, including those of the present day: witness the Russian generals in the Caucasus who were clandestinely selling their military equipment to Chechen insurgents.

As regards the 'impostors', or 'false prophets', Josephus's material on them at this juncture is contradictory, both in his evidence and in his judgment. The discrepancies in significant details between the *Bellum* and the *Antiquitates* are, as often happens, particularly tiresome. The former asserts that the 'brigands' (which may mean the *sicarii* – or a larger spectrum of the discontented prone to violence) and the 'imposters' joined forces in pursuit of the anti-Roman and nationalist cause, threatening to kill the collaborators, and also proceeded to plunder the rich (*BJ*, 20, 264 f.). In the latter's similar context, however, the emphasis is only on the 'brigands'; while the involvement of the 'impostors' in violent acts is altogether absent (cf. *AJ*, 20, 172). Described generally as individuals, trying to achieve the exodus of their adherents into the desert by relying on divine, and not human, agency, they resemble what we know about the practitioners of non-violent dissent, following the patterns taken earlier by Teudas, and perhaps even John the Baptist:

> They said that they will show obvious marvels and signs to be produced in accordance with God's design; many were persuaded and paid penalty for their madness, after having been brought before Felix, who punished them.
>
> (ibid, 168; cf. *BJ*, 2, 259)

An episode Josephus sets apart, with regard to this generalization, as if for the purpose of illustrating, is again treated differently in his two accounts. This concerns an unnamed Egyptian 'false prophet' (one assumes, a Jew from Egypt), who also briefly figures in the *Acts*: at the moment of Paul's arrest after his eviction from the Temple, the Roman tribune is made momentarily to confuse him with that other man (21:38). In the *Bellum*, the Egyptian 'adventurer' is said to have amassed 30,000 followers (2, 261, an obvious exaggeration compared with 4000 in the *Acts*) and led them, by the way of the desert, towards the Mount of Olives, purporting, the text says, to break into Jerusalem, suppress the Roman garrison and set himself up as 'people's tyrant', surrounded by the bodyguard (*BJ*, 2, 261 f.). The *Antiquitates* states only the Mount of Olives as the destination point of the movement, but nothing about its leader's violent and tyrannical plans: instead, we read that the Egyptian had promised his adherents that Jerusalem's walls will just collapse at his command and thus allow them to enter the capital (20, 170). It is interesting, however, that the single sentence on the matter in the *Acts* (loc. cit.) seems to reflect *both* traditions about this Egyptian: on the one hand, the exodus into the desert, characteristic of peaceful dissenters, is mentioned; on the other, it in fact refers (even though in this case, as it seems, misguidedly), using that very term, to the violent *sicarii*. In any event, Felix did apparently anticipate some further action on the part of these dissenters whatever it might have been: with a large Roman force (the *Bellum* claims that the 'whole populace' had joined him – 2, 263), he proceeded against them and must have achieved an easy victory, "killing four hundred of them and taking two hundred prisoners" (*AJ*, 20, 171). It is worth observing that in both accounts the enigmatic Egyptian is said to have escaped and disappeared (loci cit.), which is supported by (and provides an authentic historical ring to) the story of Paul's arrest as told in the *Acts*: it explains how the Apostle could have been confused with the Egyptian troublemaker by the tribune, who for a moment thought that the latter had resurfaced.

As a matter of principle, the further material (fictional or not) on Felix in the *Acts* does not contradict the evidence coming from Josephus. In fact, it exemplifies what both the latter and Tacitus denounced as his rapacity. We are told that, recognized as *civis Romanus* upon his arrest, Paul was taken over by the occupying authorities and properly transferred to Caesarea Maritima, where

Felix held his court (24:1 ff.). By this time Paul's opponents must have realized that purely religious issues, such as infringement of the Mosaic Law, were not sufficient in prosecuting him under Roman law on a capital charge. This must have accounted for their attempt, as stated in the *Acts*, to amplify the indictment by implicitly adding to it the crime of *seditio* (of which Greek *stasis* – "riot" – is a close approximation); it possessed sinister political connotations and thus fell within the governor's competence within the system of *cognitio extra ordinem*: the ultimate purpose of that procedure was indeed maintenance of public tranquility and suppression of those who sought to disrupt it. Given the procurator's reputation, his decision to adjourn Paul's trial *ad infinitum* is nothing unusual and may indeed be explained, just as text does, by his expectation of a bribe (24: 26). The charges against Paul, despite their new political implication, remained vague and unproved, and some goodwill, or lack of interest, in a judge would have sufficed to dismiss them altogether – as happened on the earlier occasion at the court of Gallio. Conversely, a corrupt official, such as Felix, might have expected material benefit in belief that, if Paul has been as influential a leader of the sect as he seemed to be, his brethren will not hesitate to collect a ransom for setting him free. This would make sense of his two-year stay in custody (*Acts*, 24:27) until Felix had to vacate the office. I find no reason to deny that, in terms of action rather than representation, this reflects what historically happened. If so, it suggests that the repeated attempts on the part of the Jewish authorities to resolve their religious quarrel with the Christians by involving the Romans could have proved ultimately self-defeating since they inadvertently encouraged the occupiers to infringe upon that very 'non-interference' principle, on which their policy of religious toleration towards the Jews had been based.[36]

Of various events under Nero, prior to Gessius Florus's appointment, Josephus singles out the emperor's ruling in favor of the gentiles from Caesarea Maritima in their first dispute with the local Jews over the control of the city (*BJ*, 2, 266 ff.; 284; *AJ*, 20, 173 ff.; 182 ff.). This conflict had served as a sort of rehearsal for a major clash a few years later, which triggered, as we have seen, the developments leading to the outbreak of the Great Revolt. The first confrontation seems also to have resulted in terminating Felix's tenure (ca. A.D. 59/60). It must be admitted, however, that Josephus's two versions of this affair and its effects are especially confusing due to textual problems, facts, plausibility and logistics. This is a pity: after all, this episode occurred already within the historian's lifetime, and the obscurities or incongruities that vitiate his narratives must have derived from unknown factors.

In summary, the Jewish–Gentile debate at a major city in Palaestina certainly reflected the growing tensions between two groups and concerned, as in some other localities across the Roman East, the definition of a Hellenistic polis. It is anybody's guess whether Jewish resentment at Caesarea Maritima towards their Graeco-Syrian neighbors further extended, from the outset, against the Roman masters: Josephus is silent, as he also is on the possibility that religious factors might have played a role in this initial disorder – which they did, according to his own report, in the final crisis that again broke out under Gessius Florus to precipitate an insurrection on a national scale.

One observes that in the former case both the *Bellum* (*implicite*), and the *Antiquitates* (*explicite*), place the blame on Jews. The procurator must have thought the same. After violence had been attempted, the punitive measures taken by the city magistrates failed to restrain the troublemakers, and Jews apparently gained the upper hand. As a result, it appears that Felix had no choice but to interfere: he is said to have descended upon them with an armed force, killing them and arresting, and even allowing soldiers to pillage their property (*BJ*, 2, 269 f.; *AJ*, 20, 177 f.) – although, according to the *Antiquitates*, he came to consider the pleas of the Jewish 'moderates' and restrained his troops (178). In any event, the bloodshed failed to finish the matter: by the force of circumstances, and in accordance with the earlier precedents, the procurator chose authorizing both sides to dispatch their embassies for Rome and to seek the emperor's arbitration (*BJ*, 2, 270).

That Nero eventually ruled in favor of the gentiles cannot be doubted, but much else in Josephus's reportage can. In the *Antiquitates* (the *Bellum* does not say a word on this particular intrigue), he wants us to believe that the Syrians offered a large bribe to one Beryllus (an enigmatic and otherwise unknown figure), who is described as Nero's former tutor and his secretary *ab epistulis Graecis* (*AJ*, 20, 183). It is said, with emphasis, that this Beryllus pressured the emperor and eventually obtained from him the rescript denying civil rights to Caesarea's Jews (ibid). This sounds biased and is obviously insufficient to make out what must have realistically taken place. Even more obscure is Josephus's account concerning Felix's replacement as procurator, which may or may not have pertained to the same set of incidents. We read that "the leaders of Jews residing at Caesarea" (a group different from those whom Felix had earlier approved as members of the Jewish embassy?) went up to Rome and charged him with extortions (*AJ*, 20, 182). If one follows Josephus, this must have occurred even *prior* to Nero's ruling against the Jews in their conflict with the Caesarean gentiles – which is hardly possible, given the imperial practice against permitting the provincials to bring charges against their current administrator until the latter steps down. Furthermore, the text says that Felix would have been penalized had not Nero consented to the appeals on his behalf by his brother Pallas, "whom at the time he treated with greatest honor" (ibid); but this does not really square with what we know about the decline of Pallas's influence in the late 50s. Be that as it may, Felix was ultimately recalled and perhaps reprimanded; but – given the balance of power behind the scene, which must have still been delicate enough – and unlike the case of Ventidius Cumanus under Claudius, scandal was avoided that would have inevitably followed his public disgrace. If all of this happened, as I propose, *after* Nero's verdict on the Caesarean affair, Felix's dismissal from his office could be taken (and in part so intended) for a minor gesture of concession towards Jews, by then clearly angry at and tired of that procurator, a way to sweeten the pill.

Seen impartially, Nero's judgment on the citizenship issue at Caesarea Maritima did not, in fact, deviate from the principles of Imperial policy, formulated by Claudius in his *Letter to the Alexandrians*, meaning that, as a minority, Jews were expected to be satisfied with the autonomy of their own community, the *politeuma*, which provided for their religious freedom, but not aspire towards full citizenship in the *polis*. It is true that Josephus repeatedly insists on seeing in Nero's pronouncement the ultimate cause of the Great Revolt (*AJ*, 20, 184; cf. *BJ*, 2, 284); but the historian does not even attempt to substantiate such a position, and the link he postulates between the two events remains unclear. On the other hand, his statement can be read as merely suggesting that this rescript further contributed to the exasperation of both sides.[37]

The next procurator of Judaea Porcius Festus (A.D. 60–62) seems to have been among very few intelligent appointments made by Nero. From Pilate onwards, he is the only one, besides Tiberius Alexander, who is not censured by Josephus, but rather approved of, for his measures against the radicals to restore public order (*BJ*, 2, 271; cf. *AJ*, 20, 185). In the *Acts* (25 f.) he is also portrayed with equanimity, as tough but fair, which must have been a reflection of his personality kept by at least one local tradition. Only two years long, Festus's tenure saw, however, outbreaks of both violent and non-violent religious dissent, the former represented by the *sicarii*, whose numbers and activity apparently grew, as well as the numbers of their victims (*AJ*, 20, 186 f.); and the latter by the movement of yet another unnamed 'false prophet', and by the incipient Christian Church in the person of St. Paul. Of the anonymous 'impostor' (third in Josephus's list, after Theudas and the 'Egyptian adventurer'), we merely learn that he had taken a familiar pattern, promising his adherents "salvation and the end of evils", if they follow him into the wilderness (188), and was slain by soldiers on Festus's orders together with his flock (ibid).

One unusual episode (A.D. 62) occurred during Festus's stay in office, when Nero's ruling against his own procurator, whatever hidden motives or interests might have been behind it, objectively correlated with the Imperial pledge to honor religious autonomy of Jews. We read in the *Antiquitates* (20, 189 ff.) of the feud that broke out between King Agrippa II, the champion of Jewish piety, and the Roman procurator – which Josephus would have never dared to make up. It evolved around the king's building project to extend his palace in Jerusalem with a large chamber adjoining the colonnade. Since the residence, we are told, was eminently located and provided an excellent view of the whole city: "Loving the view, as he reclined, the king would look down from there at the proceedings in the Temple" (190). This is said to have angered the 'elders' as being contrary to the tradition: the Temple rituals, and especially the sacrifices "were not to be spied on" (191). In consequence, a high wall was erected on their order, upon the arcade at the West side in the inner Temple, which blocked the view not only from the new royal chamber, but also from the shrine's outer Western portico, where the Romans used to station their guards through the festivals with the purpose of maintaining public order (191 f.). Whether there were in existence by that time any deeper reasons for resentment between the two parties is left unstated; but we read that the king, apparently taking this as effrontery directed at him, felt indignant – and "even more so" the procurator, who ordered Jews to have the wall demolished. The latter refused, however, to comply on the grounds (comparable with their attitude towards the Temple during the crisis under Caligula) that "they could not continue living if any part of the sanctuary is destroyed" (193). To his credit, Festus granted their request to yet again approach the emperor on the matter, and authorized an embassy to be dispatched and led by the high priest Ishmael b. Phiabi. Nero chose to pronounce in their favor – allegedly, under the influence of Poppaea Sabina, whom Josephus portrays as a Jewish sympathizer (195); if so, his report that it was she who allowed most of the envoys to return, but detained the high priest and the treasurer "as hostages" (ibid), does not make much sense, unless she might have wanted them to instruct her in Jewish faith or customs.[38]

Festus' procuratorship signified the new stage of the Apostle Paul's tribulations, although the format of this study does not allow any substantial comment. It seems that, in pursuit of his apologetic strategy, the *auctor ad Theophilum* made a great effort to obfuscate the nature of what actually had happened at the procuratorial court in Caesarea. But, despite embellishments, implausibilities and contradictions, the gist of it may be discernable. One can infer that at some point a further grave charge – of *crimen maiestatis* (*asebeia*) – had been brought by the Jewish priestly authorities, which changed the character of the case. This is implied in the statement ascribed to Paul: "Neither against the law of the Jews, nor against the temple, nor against Caesar have I offended at all" (*Acts*, 25: 8). Otherwise, his sudden 'appeal to Caesar', resorting – in his capacity as Roman citizen – to the mechanism of *provocatio* cannot be properly explained or understood. This charge of treason, the moment it had been introduced, was bound to transform him, in the eyes of the law, from a religious dissenter within Judaism, and thus of little consequence, into a potential political offender, not to be ignored by any Imperial official, particularly under the tyrannical regime of Nero. This was a juncture, when even personal sympathy, if it existed, on the part of that official would have been of no avail: the outcome of the deliberations became predictable. At this point the prisoner must have realized that to exercise his right of (preventive) appeal was the only means left for him in avoiding condemnation now and then. The crucial fact is indeed that he chose to do it before and not after the pronouncement of the sentence.

The obvious question arises regarding the nature of the evidence for the *maiestas* charge pressured by his enemies. My belief is that it intimately related to "the semantic breakdown" or "communication gap" which existed between the early Christians and Roman officialdom and resulted in the whole spectrum of misunderstanding: we have noticed that this had created considerable difficulties for the Romans even *vis-à-vis* traditional Judaism. The problem could have easily pertained to the customary apostolic appellation of Jesus as King. Even if one presumes that by some effort of intellect and imagination the procurator managed to penetrate the arcana of the Christian message and arrive at the truth in regard to the transcendental nature of Christ's kingship, he would have hardly taken the risk of declaring the defendant in public innocent of treason and setting him free.

Since Festus was left with virtually no other course of conduct except to grant Paul's request for an appeal, the elaborate scene, which follows in the *Acts*, of his consultation with King Agrippa II, as well as his second hearing of the case in the king's and the latter's sister Berenice's presence (25:23 – 26:32), is superfluous and might well be fictional. Still, as it stands, it plausibly illustrates semantic frustration arising from Graeco-Roman and Judeo-Christian minds trying to interact – and with an inadvertent humorous touch:

> " ... To this day I have had the help that comes from God, and so I stand here testifying both to small and great, saying nothing but what the prophets and Moses said would come to pass: that the Christ must suffer, and that, by being the first to rise from the dead, he would proclaim light both to the people and to the Gentiles." And as he thus made his defense, Festus said with a loud voice, "Paul, you are mad; your great learning is turning you mad."
>
> (26:22 ff.)[39]

Porcius Festus happened to die in office (*AJ*, 20, 197, 200). The brief 'interregnum' between his death and the arrival of his successor Lucceius Albinus saw another event of A.D. 62 pertinent to the early ecclesiastical history – martyrdom of James the Just, brother of Christ, and the first bishop of Jerusalem (*AJ*, 20, 200 ff.). As in few other such cases (deaths of Stephen and James b. Zebedee) between the Crucifixion and the trial of Paul, there is no evidence that the Romans had been involved. James, known also from the New Testament (*Mk.*, 6:3; *Mt.*, 13:55 f.; *Acts*, 12:7; 15:13 ff.; 21:17 f.; *Gal.*, 1:18 ff.; 2:9 ff.; cf. 1 *Cor.*, 15:3 ff.), was a formidable figure and led the predominant Judaist wing of the early Christian community. Practicing the non-violent form of religious dissent, he appears to have presided over what is sometimes called a 'Christian Sanhedrin', consisting of the elders. It alone could have caused him trouble with some within the Temple hierarchy. As described by Josephus, his was a judicial murder, undertaken on the initiative of the recently appointed high priest Ananus b. Ananus, whose motives are not stated. Josephus (who must have been in his early 20s when this happened) tells us that the latter had convened the Sanhedrin (an indication that some such body did, in fact, exist at the time), charged James 'and certain others' with transgressing the law and achieved their condemnation to death by stoning (ibid, 200). The historian further reports that the execution of James, famous for his saintly way of life, forced several prominent Jerusalemites to lay complaint with both King Agrippa II and the newly arrived procurator Albinus on the impropriety of what had happened. In result (one presumes), Ananus was deposed after only three months in office (201 ff.).

This episode underscores yet another development, the beginning of which Josephus dates by Felix's procuratorship – namely, the growth of divisions within the Jewish priestly and lay authority. In his account, the trouble began around A.D. 59 when the king had Ishmael b. Phiabi appointed high priest (*AJ*, 20, 179) – the one later detained in Rome by Popaea Sabina. The picture found in Josephus of the discord between 'high priests', simply 'priests' and the 'foremost among people' at Jerusalem (180) remains obscure. *Each* faction, it is said, recruited a band of 'most daring revolutionaries' (radicals in the service of the 'high priests'?) and 'acted as their chief' (ibid) – whatever this might mean. The conflicting groups would break into occasional violence – with full license due to the lack of control by the authorities (ibid). One concrete fact is nonetheless mentioned: the powerful high priests came, by dispatching slaves for that purpose, to deprive their ordinary colleagues of the tithes they were entitled to by the law so that, as the historian puts it, the poorer among them would starve to death (181; cf. 206 f.). And, he concludes, in a rare outburst of indignation against his own class: "Thus did the violence of the rivaling factions destroy all justice" (ibid). The echoes of the period's social conflicts as reported in the *Antiquitates* must have eventually found their way into the Tosefta:

> Concerning these and people like them and people similar to them and people who do deeds like their deeds did Abba Saul b. Bitnit and Abba Yosé b. Yokanan of Jerusalem say, "Woe is me because of the house of Boethus. Woe is me because of their staves. Woe is me because of the house of Quadros. Woe is me because of their pen. Woe is me because of the house of Elhanan. Woe is me because of their whispering. Woe is me because of the house of Ishmael b. Phiabi. For they are high priests, and their sons, treasurers and their sons-in-law, supervisors and their servants come and beat us with staves.
>
> (*tMen.*, 13:21)

The rivalry between the 'high priestly' and aristocratic factions further deteriorated under the penultimate procurator, Lucceius Abinus. The new high priest Jesus b. Damnaeus, was soon replaced by a namesake, Jesus b. Gamala (who was, incidentally, a relative and associate of Ananus b. Ananus and came, like the former, to partake in the first revolutionary regime). The two, Josephus tells us, did not hesitate to build bands of personal adherents and promptly proceeded towards street violence (*AJ*, 20, 213). The well-known Ananias b. Nedebaeus is described as achieving pre-eminence through lavish distribution of bribes (ibid; cf. 205). This behavior on the part of those carrying, or having carried, the highest religious office had been imitated by members of the royal Herodian clan. We read that two relatives of the king, brothers Saul and Costobar, favored by the loyalists, built up street gangs of their own, ready "to plunder those who were weaker" (214).

The gradual breakdown of the Jewish dominant elite during the 60s had been recognized and discussed in recent scholarship. By their very nature, their political alignments could and did realign prior to and in the course of the Great Revolt, although our information on that is scarce. But the very existence of those entrenched and mutually hostile groupings militates against the thesis that almost the entire Jewish establishment, with the declaration of war against Rome, chose – hurriedly and *en bloc* – to embrace the revolutionary cause.[40]

Lucceius Albinus, the immediate predecessor of Gessius Florus, is the only procurator of Judaea (ca. A.D. 62–64), apart from Tiberius Alexander, on whom we possess some data for his subsequent career. Upon the expiration of his term, he was transferred, in the same rank, to Mauretania Caesariensis by Nero, and there perished in the turmoil during the Year of Four Emperors (Tac. *Hist.*, 2, 58 f.). Once again, Josephus's report on his tenure suffers from contradictions, sometimes to the point of bafflement. The *Bellum* portrays him exclusively in black, expanding on Albinus's alleged connivance with the malefactors:

> There remained not one evil thing he failed to perform. Not only did he steal and plunder, through official means, private property and burden the entire people with [presumably, new – V.R.] taxes, but he would release, upon receiving a payment of ransom from their relatives, those who were imprisoned for brigandage by the local authorities or previous procurators; and only those men who did not pay the jailers were left there as criminals.
>
> (*BJ*, 2, 273)

Furthermore, he is accused by Josephus of complicity with the 'revolutionaries' in Jerusalem, whether the zealots or the *sicarii* or whoever else are meant: their chiefs, we read, had obtained the immunity from the procurator for their subversive activities, also with the help of bribes, while "among the populace, the element that did not rejoice in tranquility turned towards Albinus' associates" (274). The resultant picture, in the historian's words, comes close to anarchy: each 'villain', he insists, presiding over the company of followers, came to behave like an 'archbrigand' or 'tyrant', using his bodyguard to harass and rob the peaceful civilians (275): "Generally, freedom of speech was cut away and there was tyranny throughout, and thereafter the seeds of future conquest were sown" (276) – the last clause offering one of Josephus's several pronouncements at various points within his narratives on when the nation's descent into a catastrophe turned, in his view, irreversible.

An assessment as to what extent this description, fraught with rhetorical hyperbole, may be relied upon is problematic. Some sort of collusion between Imperial administrators and the outlaws in Judaea must have existed in the not so distant past: as we have seen, Tacitus insists on similar charges against two of Albinus's predecessors. Still, the scale of the latter's pecuniary operations proposed by Josephus would have been both treasonable and counter-productive, threatening the public order in the province, on which his hopes for a subsequent career must have depended.

The difficulty is amplified by comparing this material with the different account (and the reason for that difference, as is often the case with Josephus, can hardly be fathomed) of the same man's procuratorship in the *Antiquitates*, where he is praised for a successful campaign, upon his arrival, against subversion – by "exercising every effort and method to pacify the land and having destroyed many of the *sicarii*" (20, 204). *Prima facie*, this flatly contradicts what is said in the *Bellum*, but the negotiations with the 'sicarian' sect are still mentioned, although not in the context of the procurator's extortionist misdeeds. This concerns the episode I have earlier commented upon – the kidnapping by the *sicarii* of the secretary under the Temple's captain Eleazar b. Ananias (208 f.), the future revolutionary leader and prime mover of the Great Revolt. His notorious father Ananias b. Nedebaeus is at this juncture presented by the historian in no less contradictory terms: a powerful figure, popular for the reason of his largesse towards the masses, he at the same time closely collaborates and ingratiates himself with the governor (205), while his servants, like those of his other colleagues, bully poorer priests to get hold of their tithes (206; cf. 181).

As we have seen, Ananias and Albinus's deal with the *sicarii* to obtain the release of the kidnapped man in exchange for their ten fellow radicals kept in jail led – predictably – to further similar attacks on the same household with similar outcome (210): as result, those dissenters, growing in numbers and in strength, we read, "felt again emboldened and damaged the entire countryside" (ibid). If this had been so, Josephus's last statement on Albinus seems particularly puzzling:

> When he heard that he was going to be succeeded by Gessius Florus, Albinus wished to acquire a reputation for some service among the residents of Jerusalem. Thus he led out those prisoners, who had obviously merited death and condemned them to be executed, but those who were put in jail for run-of-the-mill offenses, he released for a bribe. Thus the prison was cleaned of the prisoners, but the land filled with the brigands.
>
> (*AJ*, 20, 215)

It is true that Albinus might have been concerned, as a careerist, with his reputation among his subjects, capable of complaining about him to the higher authorities, in Antioch or even Rome. But this pertained only to the upper crust of Jewish society, to whom the Romans would listen, and it is difficult to imagine why the mass amnesty of petty criminals should have pleased any such group. Nor is it exactly clear how the release of common and minor felons could have contributed to the dramatic upsurge, if we believe the historian, of brigandage. On the other hand, if we assume that many such offenders carried religious dissent of the kind we are interested it, then Albinus's measure gave them a free hand in widely propagating their anxieties; and this may have proved critical in creating the passional powder box, which needed only Gessius Florus's brutally incompetent performance to explode. Whatever the truth, it appears that things were going on behind the scenes (and/or in Josephus's mind), which we, for lack of further evidence, are not properly able to comprehend.

The 'minor offenders' set free by Albinus might well have included one Jesus b. Ananias, a man of peasant origin and a self-styled prophet. He appears to represent a very rare case of such practitioners, whose predictions came true. The history of ancient Israel knew many religious dissenters who turned inspired preachers in great belief that the power of their words could, indeed, change reality and thus participate in the realization of God's work on Earth. A major leitmotif in the writings of the Old Testament prophets was an admonition to people that God, because of people's wicked ways, will soon visit them with some terrible disaster. The most recent – and far more famous – example of such individuals had been, of course, John the Baptist. Josephus reports that Jesus b. Ananias had embarked upon his mission four years or so prior to the Great Revolt (that is, at the time when St. Paul might have still been alive). He is said to have suddenly shouted at the Festival of the Tabernacles about hearing "a voice from the East, a voice from the West, a voice from the four winds, a voice against Jerusalem and the Temple, a voice against the bridegrooms and the brides [this is borrowed from Jeremiah – *Jer.*, 7:34 ff.], a voice against all the people" (*BJ*, 6, 301). We read that he kept preaching the same message in public ever since, day and night (especially at the festivities), ignoring all threats from as well as punishments by the powerful and, even when scourged on Albinus's orders, "neither begged for mercy, nor cried", but would "change his voice into most doleful and respond to each stroke with 'Woe to Jerusalem'" – with the result that the procurator declared him insane and let him go (ibid, 304 f.). Thereafter, claims the text:

> Until the time of the war's outbreak, he neither approached nor was seen talking to any citizen, but day after day, as if practicing a prayer, he kept crying out in lament 'Woe to Jerusalem!' He would neither curse those who beat him every day, nor bless those who gave him food, but for all, this sad invocation was his sole reply. At the festivals, he would wail the loudest.
>
> (306 f.)

Apparently, the man went on with his dirge for the duration of seven years and five months, into the siege of Jerusalem by Titus, "his voice never failed, his strength never weakened", until – at the moment when he added to his habitual lament over the city, the people and the Temple, "and woe also to me" – he was struck by a stone and killed on the spot (308). Predictably, Josephus concludes:

> Pondering on these things, one will discover that God takes care of human beings and by all sorts of means does indicate to his people what is their salvation, while they perish under the sway of folly and the evil they choose themselves.
>
> (310)

The story of this little known preacher of the apocalypse (a public figure, whom Josephus could not have simply invented) is remarkable by identifying yet another strain in non-violent religious dissent, with the message contrary to the eschatological expectations, whatever form they took, of zealots, *sicarii* and their like; the insistence on the catastrophe awaiting Jerusalem and the Temple curiously resembles the words ascribed in the Gospels to his namesake, Jesus of Nazareth (cf. *Mt.*, 23:37 f.; 24:2; *Mk.*, 13:2; *Lk.*, 13:34 f.; 19:41 ff.; 21:6, 20).

It was, indeed, A.D. 64 – the very year when Gessius Florus became procurator of Judaea – that saw in Rome the first and most famous persecution of the Christians, the *Institutum Neronianum* (Tert. *Ad Nat.*, 1, 7), known to us, so far as the contemporary material is concerned, almost exclusively from one brief chapter in Tacitus's *Annales* (15, 44). This text became a subject of studies and speculation on an enormous scale and cannot, of course, be treated meaningfully here and now. It is well known that the Christians were accused by Nero's regime of setting the capital on fire – presumably, as some modern authors sought to argue from hindsight – in order to speed up the arrival of the Judgment Day and God's Kingdom on Earth. While it cannot be ruled out (although not a shred of evidence to that effect actually exists) that a few misguided or unstable individuals within the new confession might have been involved in arson, one should not question the fundamentally non-violent character of Christian religious dissent. The writings of St. Paul (claimed by the Church as, together with St. Peter, the Neronian persecution's most illustrious martyr), who sought to create the code of the righteous private and public behavior for his co-religionists, leave no doubt that such was the case. Paul's views on secular power clearly transcend the notion of political dissidence. Some tension between temporal and eschatological aspects of his religious sensibilities may occasionally be traced, but it never develops into any real conflict. For him, politics does not exist apart from metaphysics, and in those terms his only direct pronouncement makes perfect sense: "Let every person be subject to the governing authorities. For there is no authority except from God, and those that exist have been instituted by God. Therefore he who resists the authorities resists what God has appointed, and those who resist will incur judgment" (*Rom.*, 13: 1 f.). This commandment cannot be interpreted, however, as *moral* justification of tyrannical rulers such as Nero. One presumes that the entire passage is ultimately derived from Jesus's dictum: "Then render to Caesar the things that are Caesar's and to God the things that are God's" (*Lk*, 20, 25; *Mt*, 22, 21; *Mk*, 12, 17), and it presents a theological framework for the *function* of secular power, not an *ethical judgment* upon the characters of its individual carriers. This and only this context makes explicable Paul's acknowledgement and, by extension, acceptance of political reality as a temporal phenomenon. That he must have conceived of himself, within the limits imposed by the spirit of faith, as a loyal citizen is manifest, among other things, by his willingness to exercise his civil rights. Thus far Paul's eschatological expectations and his submission to the temporal (literally) authorities seem to be effectively combined, without causing him or, one assumes, any other fellow believer inner discomfort – in sharp contrast to the Stoically oriented Roman dissidents who never succeeded in reconciling their desire to serve the state and their concern for individual dignity. A man with Paul's beliefs, unlike Seneca's, would not have suffered from *dissimulatio* to the point of potential paralysis of will or personality split.

One final episode that had occurred around the same time must be taken into account: namely, a mission that Joseph b. Matthias, the future Flavius Josephus, then aged 26, was able to accomplish in the Empire's capital. According to his report, it concerned Jewish priestly prisoners of his acquaintance, who had been, still under Antonius Felix, charged (as the *Vita* tells us) with "small, trifling offence" and sent to Rome in chains (13). It appears that several years later they continued to languish in jail awaiting trial, which was by no means anything exceptional within the Imperial legal system. It is left unstated whether Josephus undertook to extricate these individuals (whom he extols as *kaloikagathoi*, "fine and good", emphasizing their abstention all the time from gentile food, while they sustained themselves solely on figs and nuts – 14) out of their predicament on his own initiative, or – which is more likely – he had been commissioned to do so by whatever body or political group in Jerusalem. Nor is it made clear whether he acted alone, or as one among official, or semi-official, envoys. He claims to have been given an eventual audience with Poppaea Sabina, upon which not only was he granted his request, but also, the reader is assured, rewarded by her with many gifts (16). Despite all of these details the story remains characteristically obscure: we are kept ignorant regarding the nature of the charges against the men in question, the circumstances of their arrest, or the arguments in favor of their release. Furthermore, the episode does not fit any context or material found in the *Bellum* and the *Antiquitates*, so that one may only wonder why the historian, always prone to expand on his own merits, chose not to mention it within either of those major narratives. In any case, coming back home, Josephus had already found there, to quote his own words, "the beginnings of the revolution and many with high expectations for secession from the Romans" (17).[41]

It is one of history's ironies that the Second Temple, the construction of which had begun centuries earlier, was finally completed (*AJ*, 20, 219 ff.) under the supervision of King Agrippa II in the year of the Great Fire in Rome, A.D. 64, only to be burned and razed to the ground six years later, with the defeat of the Great Revolt. Rounding up this lengthy survey, which covers 130 or so years of Rome's presence in Palaestina, it seems advisable to reiterate and amplify a number of inferences drawn from what has been said.

In the first place, we must not forget that our evidence, despite Josephus's continuous narratives, remains fragmentary in a sense that it almost entirely depends on what the historian chose to say or not. There are gaps which, for the lack of any further data, simply cannot be filled. With this caveat, one has to recognize that, apart from the short period under Caligula, the Imperial authorities, by and large, sought to honor Julius Caesar and Augustus's promise of protecting the religious freedom of Jews. Despite their deficient sensitivity in such matters, the Romans came eventually to recognize that Jews adopted a mode of life that in many respects differed considerably from that of other peoples and, if the *pax Romana* was to be maintained, they required a whole series of concessions or special arrangements. Until Gessius Florus, prefectorial and procuratorial measures, which ran the risk of antagonizing the Jewish populace *en masse*, rather than just the relatively small groups of extreme pietists or religious dissenters, were as a rule retracted, and individual perpetrators of offensive actions penalized. As we have seen, in the disputes between the locals and provincial authorities, the emperors, including Nero, repeatedly (although of course not invariably) favored Jews. At least two hostile officials in charge of the province suffered some form of disgrace owing to the interventions by Syria's governors. All of this means that the outbreak of the revolt was preceded by a long period of various attempts at accommodation. This does not mean that the Imperial regime followed these practices out of some special sympathy towards Jews; but it is equally wrong to think that it sought to implement any consistent anti-Jewish policies. The reason was purely pragmatic and well understood by the emperors or their intelligent advisors (in the end, even Caligula came close to compromise): it concerned the preservation and perpetuation of public order and the *status quo*, which would have been impossible if the masses of Jews in Palaestina and, even more so, in the Diaspora were irreversibly antagonized. This is made quite explicit by Philo, and it must have been recognized before and after he wrote:

> Consequently the whole population of the empire, even if not instinctively well-disposed towards the Jews, was afraid to temper with any Jewish practice in the hope of destroying it.
>
> (*Legat.*, 159)

The reason for this, as Philo makes clear later in the narrative, was:

> ... the vast numerical size of the Jewish nation, which is not confined, as every other nation is, within the borders of the one country assigned for its sole occupation, but occupies almost the whole world / ... / Heaven forbid that the Jews everywhere should unanimously come to the defence! That would produce an impossible military situation.
>
> (214 f.)

To be sure, in Roman Judaea corruption ran deep; but this was no less true elsewhere within the Empire, sometimes causing substantial disturbance in its various parts.

It is certainly true that Pompey's thoughtless intrusion in the Temple in 63 B.C. had generated lasting resentment among Judaea's Jews against the Romans and their collaborators, which was bound to accumulate in the course of the Herodian, prefectorial and procuratorial periods, while such features as nationalist aspirations, ethnic/cultural tension and social discontent continued, and their role probably increased. Nonetheless, we lack any sizable evidence that this presumed overall resentment brought about a consistent popular movement aimed at Israel's liberation from the foreign yoke. The groups of revolutionary enthusiasts, such as those who followed the "fourth philosophy", were reduced to operating underground, existing on the margins of society and/or getting involved in brigandage, a widespread and rampant phenomenon across the Roman world. As regards both the Jewish establishment and masses of common people, their resistance tended to stay passive and not violent – up to a point; but their behavior at moments of crisis testifies that, in their desire to preserve domestic peace, or for any other reason, they were prepared to extend their patience beyond what might have been our own expectations. This is evident in the civil disobedience they chose to display under both Pilate and Caligula, although in the latter case the very basics of Judaism were threatened – when commoners as well as aristocrats demonstrated, with remarkable unanimity, that they would prefer to perish rather than have their customs or sanctuary blasphemed. It must be remembered that over 120 years elapsed between Pompey's capture of Jerusalem and the eruption of an anti-Roman revolt: for most of this period the country remained relatively quiet. One can, indeed, cite peoples in history who suffered for centuries from an alien occupier without any attempt at insurrection, Jews themselves being an example: they survived the Babylonian, Persian and Macedonian yoke patiently, provided that their religious practices were not interfered with. In fact, they remained a part of Hellenistic kingdoms for a longer period than the one between the invasion of Pompey and the revolt under Nero.

It goes without saying that Roman rule took a psychological, and not merely material, toll on the people of Judaea. But the situation was not all equally, or uniformly, bad: even though most of the prefects and procurators seem to have been bigoted extortionists, they also numbered a few fair-minded officials, such as Tiberius Alexander and Porcius Festus. Furthermore, Judaea's status as a province was not invariable: Claudius made it for a while a formally sovereign kingdom under Herod Agrippa I, who enjoyed popularity among his subjects. In the final sense, all depended on the intelligence of the man in Rome who held the purple – but only insofar as it concerned his ability to make accurate character judgments about his appointees. Thus, Josephus recognized (not necessarily from hindsight) – and made King Agrippa II articulate the point – that there always existed room for hope: a better man could replace a bad guy as procurator (*BJ*, 2, 354 f.) – and also, by extension, as emperor.

It is obvious that Roman occupation of Judaea could not have continued *ad infinitum*: in history, whether we like it or not, everything has a beginning and an end, and sooner and later, when the Empire would have begun to disintegrate (as happened, in fact, during the third century crisis), Jews might – or might not – have taken the opportunity to successfully secede. But in theory, the ongoing situation, however stressful, could have still lasted indefinitely, and the question is why popular resentment broke out beyond repair at the time it did.

The historical process, in its intricate complexity, is affected, of course, by multiple factors that range from socio-economic to the individual and collective psychology (speaking not of accidents), some of which – in retrospect – we are often not even able to ascertain due to a lack of knowledge. The crisis may come spontaneously, and its components often cannot be compartmentalized. Still, at particular junctures when – as a man at the cross-roads – society is put first before several alternatives, a few factors, as a rule, are more critical than others and eventually help to determine the outcome. (This is the problem which the newly made legitimate discipline of counter-factual history concerns itself with).

Thucydides tells us (1, 23) that one must distinguish between 'ultimate' and 'immediate' causes of historical events. While, as regards the Jewish revolt, the very fact of Roman military presence undoubtedly constitutes the former, it has been shown that the latter (that is, yet another outburst of recurrent clashes between Jewish and Graeco-Syrian residents at Caesarea Maritima) could have related only indirectly to the occupier's power and administration. Within – chronologically – the Neronian context, three coincidental developments conspired, in my view, to trigger the massive insurrection against Roman rule. One such must have been the decay and corruption within the Jewish establishment that became manifest around this time in the form of rivalries and infighting, which undermined its hold over the minds and conduct of common men; I will elaborate on the controversial issue regarding the role of the native elite in a later chapter. Next, the particularly nasty misrule, practiced by Florus, proved – as Josephus rightly insists – of crucial importance in bringing about the disaster. As I have sought to demonstrate, there are reasons to accept in this, as in some other cases, and despite modern objections, most of the analysis he offers. I find it very significant that Josephus's thesis is implicitly supported by Tacitus ("the patience of the Jews did endure up to the procurator Gessius Florus, under whom the war began" – *Hist.*, 5, 10); this judgment was presumably based on the latter's own reasons and information. The failure on the part of Syria's governor Cestius Gallus to interfere must have further stimulated the upheaval.

Finally, I wish to emphasize the resurgence, starting with the later years under Antonius Felix, of the militant religious dissenters, whose acts of violence must have shaken the public mind, and whose propaganda, as we have seen in the previous chapter, could reach even the highest echelons of the Jewish upper class. That they pursued the national liberation agenda cannot be doubted. But the specifics of their mentality, affecting their individual and group behavior, and their direct reliance on divine help proved in the end, as will be shown, fatefully counter-productive. This blend of anarcho-theocratical utopianism, exemplified by the "fourth philosophy" and the *sicarii*, with the isolationist trend one observes, for instance, in the Shammaite tradition, and colored by the array of eschatological aspirations, produced what can be called a powerful psychological vector, manifest in multifold group or individual forms and shades. This particular mindset strongly encouraged violent activity so that it and the growth of procuratorial harassment reinforced each other: an interaction, which finally succeeded at that but not at any earlier point in provoking popular fury, bound to break down the existent order.

Before we examine further this kind of religious dissent and its impact upon the events to come, it makes sense to briefly look again into Josephus's statements on Nero and to assess the role that the emperor might or might not have played in the impending cataclysm. Be that as it may, both the *Bellum* and the *Antiquitates* exhibit a certain tendency to diminish Nero's own blame for that, with the purpose of shifting it onto his procurators, most notably Florus. This could even have represented Jewish popular opinion during the time, at least in some strata or circles of society (perhaps ultimately responsible for a relatively mild view of Nero found in the later Talmudic tradition).

Moreover, one must appreciate that there was little the emperor could have done, even if he wished, by way of interference, short of recalling and punishing the procurator, as his predecessor did, and provided that he possessed reliable information about what went on. Accordingly, Josephus's report of those people in Jerusalem who insisted on sending an embassy to Nero with formal complaints about the outrages perpetrated by Florus (*BJ*, 2, 342) is worth remembering: this demand must have reflected more or less collaborationist sentiment within certain segments of the Jewish populace. The tide, however, worked against any effort at appeasement, and the euphoria grown out of the victory at Beth-horon determined the nation's descent into warfare, construable – depending on one's own individual perspective – as hopeless, insane or heroic.[42]

4

THE FRAGILE BALANCE

I.

The massacre of the Roman garrison by the followers of Eleazar b. Ananias made irreversible the course of events triggered by the cessation of Imperial sacrifices. If perhaps only theoretically, the restoration of the status quo might still have not been impossible – provided that both sides take measures to achieve compromise: the Romans, for instance, by recalling Gessius Florus, and the Jews by punishing those responsible for the cessation decree and the subsequent riot. Now it was out of the question. This is properly recognized by Josephus in the *Bellum*:

> The Romans suffered little, for out of their immense force, few men perished; but this did seem a prologue to the ruin of the Jews. Aware that the causes of the war were now beyond correction, and that the city was tainted by so great a stain, from which it was natural to expect divine wrath, even if not retaliation from the Romans, they engaged in public mourning. The city was filled with dejection, while everyone among the moderates felt troubled that he will be personally punished on the account of the insurgents.
>
> (2, 454 f.)

This passage was written with hindsight by a survivor. One doubts, however, that an ambitious young man, ready to join the rebel ranks at the outset of the glorious fight for liberty, as it must have looked at the time, would have also felt that way. Within the ambience of popular euphoria, or hysteria – and at the moments of high historical drama– these two mental conditions mean very much the same: many individuals tend to suppress their characteristic beliefs and condone behavior they would have otherwise strongly disapproved. In their eyes the blow dealt to the Romans by slaughtering their garrison might well have outweighed for a moment a terrible fact of sacrilege – violation of both the Sabbath and the solemn pledge to spare enemy lives. In any event, public mourning cited by Josephus must have been declared over the Jewish dead, fallen in fighting, rather than due to their sense of guilt as his text implies. Still, the historian's allusion to God's imminent wrath should not be dismissed too lightly, even though this same argument – that God had sided with the Romans in order to punish the Jews for their own crimes – he invokes repeatedly as a part of his apologetic agenda. This said, it still does not seem plausible that truly pious Jews could have easily gone along with the escalation of blasphemies committed by the radical insurgents. Such persons or groups must have witnessed it with a growing sense of outrage, and in fear of supernatural retribution. This circumstance, I submit, largely accounted for the fact that militant religious dissenters known as zealots – to be discussed properly and at length later – failed to amass, at this initial stage of the uprising, enough popular support to take over the government. True nationalist and religious feelings often went together; but in many cases they could no less effectively function apart from, and even in opposition to, each other – depending on their carriers' views about their relationship with the divine. This points to a major and recurrent feature of the Jewish revolt: similarly (in this respect) to the Maccabean uprising, it was also fraught from the very start with religious warfare – a factor non-existent, outside Judaea, in political, social or ethnic conflicts of classical Antiquity.

Josephus insists that on the same day (and even at the same hour!), when the Romans, upon their surrender, were put to death at Jerusalem ("as if it were by the design of the divinity" – *BJ*, 2, 457, a further intriguing reference to the supernatural) – yet another anti-Jewish pogrom broke out in Caesarea Maritima, in the course of which that city's Jewish population was either exterminated by the local gentiles or arrested by the Romans (ibid). This was followed by the general Jewish uprising across Palaestina, directed, as the historian is predictably careful to emphasize, against the Syrians rather than Romans (ibid, 458 ff.). (Whether this last contention is accurate remains largely irrelevant: in reality, it would not have mattered.) Inevitably, the violence reached the Jewish Diaspora in Syria proper (ibid, 461 ff.; 477 ff.; cf. *Vita*, 24 ff.) as well as Alexandria, where the Roman prefect of Egypt Tiberius Alexander, as we know, himself an apostate Jew, was compelled to make bloody use of Roman force upon his own Jewish compatriots (ibid, 487 ff.).

It would be a mistake, however, to assume the universal character of resentment against Rome among Jews in Palaestina. It was precisely this lack of universality in feelings and motives that accounted for the prominence of civil warfare at every stage of the Jewish revolt – a predicament not uncommon in the struggle for national liberation. There were many reasons for pro-Roman sentiments within various groups of the Jewish populace, including entire cities such as Sepphoris in Galilee – which for a long time had resisted the rebel takeover and ultimately welcomed Vespasian – but at least one fully understandable pragmatic factor is to be singled out: the desire for stability in the need of survival. Josephus emphasizes this point in his treatment of the events at Scythopolis, immediately upon the outbreak of the hostilities throughout the province, and it carries weight irrespective of the author's rhetoric or the veracity of particular details. The Jews of the city, he says, had sided with its Greco-Syrian residents and fought their rebel brethren "considering their own safety more important than common kinship" (*BJ*, 2, 466). Nonetheless, they were treacherously massacred by their pretended allies. This testifies to the extent of the xenophobia that plagued ethnic relationships in the region. Josephus's explanation sounds lame – according to him, the gentiles did this in fear that Jews would recant and stab them in the back, thus making amends to the rebels for their earlier defection (467). The experience suggests, however, that in the moments of upheaval, xenophobia does not need a plausible pretext, but easily transforms itself into a murderous mass frenzy striking at both friends and foes. A glimpse into a kind of drama, that the necessity of making choice might have poignantly afflicted the mind of an ordinary individual, is provided in the story of one Simon b. Saul, told by Josephus with considerable verve (*BJ*, 2, 469 ff.). Whether any such person really existed (although I find no reason to question that) is ultimately irrelevant: the historian may have rhetorically generalized on predicament and experience shared by a variety of individuals, including himself, and he knew that his Jewish audience would have considered this account credible. In any event, we read that Simon b. Saul belonged to what is called, by modern standards, the upper middle class (his father is described as "someone not without distinction" – 469), endowed with both courage and physical power (ibid). He is said to have valiantly fought on the side of the Scythopolitans against the Jewish insurgents. But on the night when Scythopolitan Jews were attacked and slaughtered, and upon belated recognition of the gentile treachery, he first butchered his entire family (his father, his mother, his wife and his children) and then committed suicide, all of this in order to prevent their death at the hands of the enemy and to expiate what he saw as his crime against his own people. To Simon b. Saul Josephus attributes a rhetorically ornate speech that the real man in question would have been hardly able to deliver. But there is no need to doubt the gist of the argument, in terms of plausibility, or its pertinence to a moral and psychological quandary shared by many of Judaea's Jews at the time. First, Josephus makes him recognize the justice of his punishment (472) for fighting his fellow Jews: those who commit so impious a crime against their kin deserve the perfidy of the aliens (that is, gentiles); it is appropriate that they, who are thus cursed, die by their own hand rather than at the hands of the enemy. This is at once a fitting retribution for what they have done and, on their own part, a proof of courage (473). It is worth observing, however, the absence of direct reference to the divine: Josephus chose to portray Simon b. Saul as repentantly professing his ethnic rather than religious kinship with the rebels. He concludes the episode as follows:

> And so a young man who deserved pity, owing to of his physical strength and ardor of his soul, suffered and perished accordingly because of his trust in the aliens.
>
> (476)

One wonders how ironically the account of this affair might have reflected on Josephus' own sensibilities as a 'renegade' Jew.[1]

The extant record of the events makes it clear that the revolution in Judaea was not carefully planned – an indirect sign that the chief factor motivating at least some among its originators lay in the hope of divine aid. In any event, it is apparent that the group around Eleazar b. Ananias, who announced the cessation of the Imperial sacrifices, had little idea of how to proceed. Their secessionist act was followed by disparate developments and *ad hoc* arrangements, which were bound to reflect upon the whole character of subsequent struggle. It was, however, the disastrous and unexpected defeat of Cestius Gallus at the pass of Beth-horon on November 25, A.D. 66 that provided the insurgents with a further powerful motive: it appeared that the belief in the heavenly support has been justified and the liberation of Israel was indeed at hand. This must have induced many of those, who had hitherto been hesitating or even opposing it, to join the revolt, and this involved, presumably, all strata of society. Finally, the rebels could now afford a respite to be used for an attempt at organizing some kind of united front against the Romans as well as a ladder of political authority and military command. This opportunity was used and misused.

Gallus's strategy in the conduct of that campaign remains a puzzle which, given the available evidence, can hardly be solved to one's full satisfaction. He started with successfully defeating the Galilaean rebels at Mount Asamon (*BJ*, 2, 510 ff.) and, despite the initial setback (517 ff.), advanced into Jerusalem as far as the inner city and the outskirts of the Temple (528 ff.). This must have exercised a frightening effect on the city populace (cf. 529) and there is no reason to doubt Josephus's report that some of the elders (533), on the initiative of one Ananus b. Jonathan, sent the Roman commander a promise to open the gates before him (ibid). For whatever reason (Josephus offers anger, disdain and distrust), Gallus chose not to accept that offer immediately, until the insurgents thwarted the whole plot by driving the would-be traitors from the city walls back into their homes (ibid).

The historian attributes the dramatic retreat of Roman forces from Jerusalem to Gallus's failure in appreciating the sense of despair among the rebels under siege and the actual mood of the populace. In consequence, we are told, "he suddenly recalled his troops and, having suffered no reverse, abandoned hope, and withdrew from the city" (540). It seems more likely that the Roman decision was owing to conflicting pieces of information (or disinformation) Gallus had received and the disagreements within his *consilium*. Be that as it may, it happened in the course of this retreat – of which the strategic purpose remains unclear – that the Roman army was attacked and routed by the insurgents (546 ff.). This proved to have been the only real victory achieved by the rebels over the occupier in the course of the revolt.

Josephus contends that after the news arrived of the Roman defeat, many prominent Jews (ibid, 556) left the city "as if it were a sinking ship" (ibid). In recent decades, a considerable scholarly effort occurred with the purpose of identifying Josephus's political bias and rectifying his narratives, especially when it concerned his tendency of minimizing the role of the Jewish elite, to which he belonged, in the outbreak and perpetuation of the revolt. This role is by no means unusual. One recurrent feature of the historical process is that, in various periods and cultures, some individuals or even groups within the ruling classes, for numerous reasons, and despite their own relatively comfortable existence, embark upon competition for leadership in revolutionary movements, particularly in their early 'moderate' stages – the examples range from Marquis de Lafayette or Count Mirabeau, and even Duke of Orleans, Philippe l'Egalité, to Prince Georgii Lvov, the first head of Russia's provisional government upon the abolition of monarchy in February 1917, and the Tsar's cousin Grand Duke Kirill Vladimirovich, who had publicly supported it. This, however, is a far cry from saying that in France or Russia national nobility chose to side with revolutionary regimes. That the majority of rebel leaders in A.D. 66–70 came from the Jewish establishment is an undeniable fact, but it still does not follow that the revolt against Rome enjoyed support by every aristocrat, or even by aristocracy as a group. One must remember the long series of moves made by the Jerusalem leaders in order to negotiate or intercede with the procurator before the cessation of the Imperial sacrifices. Many of them must have acted in good faith and in hope that by common effort, and through persuasion, the crisis could be peacefully resolved. All of this testifies, at the very least, to the reluctance and hesitation on the part of the Jewish rulers at the prospect of entering open hostilities with Rome. This is not surprising in light of their long-time political experience of dealing with the Romans and their recognition both of the latter's ruthlessness and omnipotent military machine. On the other hand, it stands to reason (and is implicit in Josephus's narrative) that many were joining the rebel ranks in fear of destruction at their hands: the example of carnage performed by the followers of Menahem b. Judas (cf. *BJ*, 2, 440) was all too obvious and might have indeed frightened a number of the "powerful" into joining the revolution.

Although Josephus's simile of "sinking ship" must have been misleadingly exaggerated, disregarding his statement as a mere lie would run against commonsense. From the very outset we hear of active and prominent collaborationists, opposing the measures that were bound to antagonize the Romans, such as the cessation decree; and even of those who planned opening the city gates to Cestius Gallus. It is unrealistic to expect all of them to have immediately changed their minds after the rebels' first (and only) victory. Three men (Saul, Costobar and Philip b. Jacimus), named by Josephus as having fled from Jerusalem (loc. cit.), did not and could not exhaust all persons of standing who, for one reason or another, sought safety in the Roman camp. That only a few such individuals are mentioned does not mean others did not exist: thus the *Bellum* is silent on the eventual defection to the Romans of Rabban Johanan b. Zakkai, which (as I will argue in the last chapter), if one disregards the legendary adornments, was likely historical. There must have been a plethora of reasons, personal or 'ideological', mostly unfathomable, due to the lack of evidence, for Josephus's selectivity in recording or suppressing particular facts, and only a few such cases allow legitimate speculation. Furthermore, as regards desertions, he did not even need to provide a larger list of names, since the steady flow of refugees and defectors from the rebel ranks, and from all parts of the civil populace throughout the war, would be a matter of common knowledge, natural and predictable in a political, social and religious conflict on that scale.[2]

In order to put into relief specific features of mentality and behavior associated with religious dissent, it is imperative to examine two groups of individuals who did not share in it, or if they did, only marginally. These were persons and groups, involved in the variety of relationships with the occupier, ranging from diplomacy to complicity. One such group is the direct collaborationists with Rome. Like any form of opportunism in public life, collaboration pertains – psychologically speaking – to the dynamics inherent in *dissimulatio* as practiced by political dissidents rather than in the wishful thinking characteristic of religious dissenters. More complex is the case of those whom Josephus labels 'moderates' (I will comment on this term later). It merits a lengthier treatment, since they constituted most of the leadership under the so-called 'first revolutionary regime', which lasted for about a year until it was overthrown through a violent coup.

In practical terms, at least one segment within the ruling class in Judaea had little choice but to collaborate with the occupier – the members of the Herodian royal house. Irrespective of their personal attitudes or sentiments regarding the events, they knew well that their status in the society, with all attendant privileges, depended on Rome's good will. This was predetermined by the crafty policies of the first Herod and the special relationship that had been forged between his clan and the Julio-Claudian family. On the other hand, the Herodians must have felt increasingly uncertain as to the support they could expect at the time of crisis from their Jewish subjects. Being Idumaean and Nabataean by origin, and thoroughly Hellenized, this royalty generated contradictory feelings among the populace. Their legitimacy was dubious; their observance of the law often seen as perfunctory; and they could have been easily construed by radical dissenters not only as the connivers with the Roman conqueror but – together with some high priests, whom the Herodian kings kept appointing and deposing – as those who betrayed the very foundations of Jewish faith.

In the *Bellum*, Josephus's treatment of King Herod Agrippa II and his sister Julia Berenice is predictably flattering: at the time of its composition they were both alive and in favor with the Flavians. In the *Antiquitates*, written decades later, the historian is less restrained: for instance, he reports the rumor of incestuous relationship between the king and his sister (20, 145) and mentions the latter's malice towards her other sister Drusilla (ibid, 143), as well as her general reputation of licentiousness (ibid, 146). On balance, the last Jewish king seems to have been a competent but not prominent statesman, lacking both the spirit and political ingenuity of his father, Herod Agrippa I.

It is hard to ascertain the extent of Agrippa II's authority, beyond the right, granted to him by the Romans, to appoint high priests and his formal supervision of the Temple's treasury. It may be assumed that responsible Roman officials, such as governors of Syria and procurators of Judaea, were at least expected to consult with him on politically sensitive matters. But, for the most part, he appears to have reigned, not ruled, conducting himself and his affairs in a manner that had to be agreeable to the Romans and minimally offensive to the Jews. He must have well remembered the fates of his uncles Archaelaus and Antipas, who were deposed and disgraced for having caused Roman displeasure. His very position vis-à-vis Romans as well as vis-à-vis Jews was bound to compel him towards exercising *dissimulatio*, in forms not unlike those practiced by political dissidents among the Roman senators. His conduct must be understood not as consistent policies, but rather the *ad hoc* responses, based on the circumstances of the moment, with the priority of his own physical and political survival. He well might have been concerned, as Josephus implies (e.g., *BJ*, 2, 337, 402 ff., 421), and as his several actions suggest, with the plight of the Jews under the procuratorial system – in terms of compatriotism, one suspects, rather than religion. But he was allowed little political room to operate. Thus he could intercede on behalf of the Jews when expecting support from a powerful personage or a court faction, but chose to abstain at the most crucial moment prior to the revolt, most likely in the belief that this time nothing of the sort would be possible. This behavior was in sharp contrast with his father's, who took great risks for the sake of Jews under Caligula, and proved instrumental in advocating their interests under Claudius. This reflects not only on their respective characters, but also on the circumstances they found themselves in. Unlike Caligula and Claudius towards Agrippa I, Nero did not owe any favors to his son, and treated him inconsistently, first enlarging territory under his jurisdiction, but then rebuffing him over the affair of the wall. The consequent sense of apprehension might reasonably account for the king's sudden and fervent activities in Caesarea Philippi: he renamed that city Neronias, enlarged and embellished it with new constructions which, according to Josephus, only increased the animosity against him among the Jews, who resented that it was done at their expense (*AJ*, 20, 211 ff.). All of this, followed by the death of the Jewish patroness Poppaea Sabina, Nero's gradual divorce from reality, and perhaps other considerations we do not know of must have influenced the king's decision for taking at the moment of crisis the stand that he did. As regards Agrippa II's religious sensibilities, there is no evidence that they much differed from his father's. Similarly Hellenized, he seems to have lacked any genuine zeal as regards customary morals and the ritual: this might have been responsible for offensive rumors, such as the allegation of incest. We know that he repeatedly quarreled with the priesthood over issues, which – at least, from his point of view – meant hardly more than trifles. And, of course, one can find nothing in his character and activities that could even remotely resemble the mentality of religious dissent. After the failure of his conciliatory speech at Xistus, and the subsequent public outrage, the king – in the absence, as it appears, of any safe alternative – definitively took the side of the Romans and joined his forces with those led by Cestius Gallus against the insurgents (cf. *BJ*, 2, 500). The royal troops fought with and were defeated by their fellow Jews at the pass of Beth-horon, where the Roman army, as we know, was routed after its sudden retreat from Jerusalem. Until the end of military action, King Agrippa did not waver in his allegiance to the Roman cause. His response to and survival of the attempted putsch by his regent Noarus/Varus testifies to his political dexterity. Josephus also takes care to emphasize his efforts as peacemaker, willing to parley with the rebels (ibid, 2, 523 ff.; 3,14) and on one occasion having been actually wounded for his labors (3,14). Still, his behavior towards his coreligionists was by no means blameless. Josephus reports an episode (perhaps thus betraying his own ambivalent sentiment towards the man) of his selling into slavery Jewish prisoners, handed over to him by Vespasian after the fall of Tiberias (ibid, 541). He was apparently held in high esteem by the Roman commander-in-chief who, following his accession to the purple, made various concessions to him as proofs of goodwill (ibid, 461, 540 f.). We learn that Agrippa accompanied Titus on the latter's abortive mission to Galba. Although halfway to Rome, at the news of the latter's assassination, the young man chose ("under a divine impulse", says Josephus) to return to his father, the king proceeded, undaunted, towards the capital, presumably with the purpose of meeting Otho (ibid, 4, 501). Whether he acted as he did in Vespasian's or his own interests remains unknown, but nothing seems to contradict an impression that this monarch with no realm, for the most part, continued to enjoy favor at the Flavian court after the suppression of the revolt and until his death.

Despite her earlier humiliation at the hands of Gessius Florus, Agrippa's sister, Queen Berenice of Chalcis, followed the same course as her brother. Apparently, she also saw nothing that she could gain in opposing the Romans. A few years later, this colorful and remarkable woman was to experience a passionate affair with Titus Caesar and come very close to becoming a Roman empress – a story that earned her a kind of immortality in great works of literature, art and music. If she seriously considered any such project, she did it in total disregard of Judaism's basic precepts: it was indeed a folly to expect that the Imperial heir apparent could have converted to the Jewish faith, as the Law required. The only other solution would be her own apostasy, the perspective testifying to the quality of her own religious commitment.

The behavior of this royal couple suggests that although they sometimes might have manifested signs, genuine or not, of patriotism, their nationalist sentiments and religious scruples were minimal and unable to prevent their full-scale collaboration with the Romans. This places them miles apart not only from ardent dissenters, like the zealots, but even from the majority of their own class – who, regardless of their own political leanings, thought of themselves, first and foremost, as Jews, the followers of the Law. This also seems to justify, at least to some extent, the view found in a variety of Jewish sources, which treat the whole house of Herod and the Herodian faction – in contrast to the Hasmonaean dynasty – as an imposition alien to the nation's cause.[3]

Occasionally, we hear about members of the Herodian clan other than the king and his sister, who were involved in political strife, and of whom two brothers, Saul and Costobar, seem to have been most conspicuous. In the *Antiquitates* they are mentioned only once in a negative context (20, 214): as the ringleaders of the faction in Jerusalem which deteriorated, during the procuratorship of Lucceius Albinus, into a street band and proceeded to terrorize the populace – rivaling the violence exercised by the similar factions turned gangs led by the ex-high priest Jesus b. Damnaeus and his successor Jesus b. Gamala (ibid, 213). Josephus is careful to point out that because of their Herodian lineage those two brothers enjoyed favor, presumably, with their following (which suggests that there must have existed individuals or groups among Palestinian Jews who were not resentful of their Idumaean royalty); but his judgment, apparently justified, on their characters and activities is harsh: they are accused of plundering the weaker (214). Saul's and Costobar's motives, however, remain indistinct – perhaps, they were merely driven by a desire for self-promotion, with a vague hope of some profit from the ongoing social and political turmoil. It seems unlikely that they acted with any approval from the king, whose main interest must have been to maintain stability, law and order. This suggests that Agrippa II was not able fully to control the behavior of his own extensive family, famous for their vicious infighting.

In the *Bellum*, written decades earlier, Saul and Costobar are treated in neutral rather than pejorative terms. They figure as the members of the delegation sent from Jerusalem by the pro-Roman Jewish notables, after the Imperial sacrifices at the Temple had been discontinued, to King Agrippa, asking for reinforcements (2, 418 f.). They apparently chose to stay in Jerusalem until Cestius Gallus's retreat from that city and his subsequent defeat at Beth-horon, and then fled to join the Romans (556). (They had been hiding in Herod's palace and survived its siege by the rebels, which cost the life of their old political rival and recent ally, the ex-high priest Ananias b. Nedebaeus – cf. 429.) Finally, we read that Saul and his companions (558) were, at their own request, dispatched by Gallus to Nero in Greece. They were supposed to inform the emperor of what had happened and lay upon Florus the responsibility for the revolt (ibid, 557 ff.); whether this last is a fact or just a rumor recorded by Josephus is not possible to say. I will comment on three further members of the Herodian clan, who chose to stay in revolutionary Jerusalem and eventually perished there at the hands of zealots, in a different context later in this chapter.

Contrary to several modern opinions, it does not follow from Josephus that the delegation sent to Nero also included another prominent figure within the loyalist camp (although not related to the royal family), the prefect Philip b. Jacimus, who is first introduced in the *Bellum* as the commander of the forces sent by the king to relieve the collaborationists besieged in the royal palace at Jerusalem by the revolutionary forces (2, 421). In the *Antiquitates* (17, 23 ff.) we read that he descended from a man called Zamaris, the leader of several hundred Babylonian Jews, whom the first Herod, late in his reign, settled in Batanea for reasons of his own. Like his father, Philip served as the master of the king's bodyguard but was promoted to a general, and later on became the commander-in-chief of the royal army (*BJ*, 4, 81). In the *Bellum*, and especially in the *Vita*, Josephus offers an inordinate amount of information, often contradictory, about this curious figure. The reasons for the historian's special interest in this particular individual are difficult to ascertain. The basic outline suggests that, upon his failure to relieve the Roman garrison and pro-Roman Jewish faction in Jerusalem from the rebel siege, Philip b. Jacimus succeeded at some point in leaving the city and joining the Romans (*BJ*, 2, 421; 556). The *Vita*, however, implies that, in the interval between his flight from the capital and his arrival at Cestius Gallus's camp, he came to be embroiled in a complex intrigue the details of which remain obscure. That affair centered on yet another associate of Agrippa II (and Philip's rival) by the name of Noarus (*Bellum*) or Varus (*Vita*), whom the king installed as regent in Caesarea Philippi for the duration of his own visit to meet with Gallus at Antioch (*BJ*, 2, 481). Allegedly, this man Noarus/Varus contemplated, on the grounds of his august (but not Herodian) lineage (cf. *BJ*, 2, 487; also 248), some sort of coup with the purpose of reaching supremacy. The regent's plot, who saw Philip as a competitor, is said to have involved interception of his letters to the royals, murder of his messengers, spreading false rumors about him and his master, as well as the massacre of the 'Babylonian Jews' at Batanea, who must have constituted Philip's power base and the whose remains found refuge in Gamala (*Vita*, 48 ff.; cf. *BJ*, 2, 481 ff.). According to the *Vita*, Philip b. Jacimus thwarted the plot by arriving in the latter city and rejecting the appeal of its inhabitants, who pressured him into a war against Varus/Noarus and his Syrian supporters (59, ff.; the *Bellum*'s much shorter account of the same events does not even mention Philip's name). Soon after, Agrippa II reportedly learned of what had happened, deposed the regent (but spared his life on the grounds of his ancestry) and replaced him with one Aequus Modius (*Vita*, 61; *BJ*, 2, 483). The activities of Noarus/Varus, among other things, helped to create the impression that Philip b. Jacimus had disappeared, with the resultant rumor of his defection to the rebels (cf. 182 f.).

Much later in the *Vita* his story is resumed (179 ff.) to tell us that with the appointment of Modius (who is described as his own old friend and companion), Philip b. Jacimus succeeded in finally reaching the royals by letter and thus exonerating himself from the suspicion of treachery. On the king's summons he came to Berytus and was there instructed to secure the evacuation of the royal household from the restive Gamala, resettle the 'Babylonian Jews', and prevent, in general, any possible further trouble in that city (182 ff.). This last task, as it appears, he had failed properly to accomplish since in a short time Gamala rose up against the king and the Romans. We are told that in the whole revolutionary turmoil, several relatives of Philip perished as well as those of his kinsman by marriage, Justus b Pistus from Tiberias, who was to become Josephus's literary nemesis (177, 186).

The final installment related to Philip b. Jacimus and his vicissitudes comes towards the very end of the *Vita* (407 ff.), where the Tyrians, inveterate enemies of the Jews, are portrayed as attempting to accuse Agrippa II of disloyalty before

Vespasian. Allegedly, they argued that it was on the king's orders that his general Philip had betrayed the Roman garrison in the royal palace at Jerusalem, to be slaughtered by the rebels. The ploy, however, did not work: Vespasian warned the accusers not to slander "a man who was both a king and a friend", but at the same time advised that the latter should send Philip b. Jacimus to Rome with the account for Nero of everything that had happened (408). According to Josephus, however, the two never met: Philip came back to Judaea without having talked to the emperor, since his arrival in the capital, we are told, had coincided with the disturbances which led to the outbreak of civil war and Nero's downfall (409).

This web of incongruous information makes it virtually impossible to appraise even tentatively this man's motives or those of others like him. Still, there is no evidence to suspect a strong religious constituent in their behavior – even if we allow that at some point they might have felt a temptation for siding with the rebels. Like most of the Herodian adherents, he – or for that matter his antagonist Noarus/Varus – was, in the first place, a politician and acted in terms of political exigencies. They were concerned with their own interests, at best pertaining to the sense of loyalty, and at worst enhanced by the desire for self-aggrandizement. It also stands to reason that, having been better experienced in the state of affairs throughout the Empire, they knew all too well that, despite any temporary success, the revolt was sooner or later to be crushed in a horrifying bloodbath.

We do not hear in any of Josephus's accounts about the royal troops changing sides in any substantial numbers (it also does not necessarily mean that no such thing ever happened: the historian could well have chosen to stay silent). Among the king's officers, two defections of relative importance are reported: Silas the Babylonian, who fought bravely on the rebel side and perished during the attack on Ascalon, and the capable Niger of Peraea, whose activities and eventual terrible death at the hands of zealots will be treated elsewhere in this narrative.[4]

II.

Although the variety of problems engendered by Josephus's texts is notorious, one feels especially exasperated by their gaps and inconsistencies with regard to the emergence, membership and operations of what is often called the revolutionary 'coalition government', or 'first regime', under the ex-high priest Ananus b. Ananus. It is true that the historian was confronted with a difficult and delicate task to handle. It was, after all, the very leadership that appointed him governor of Galilee where, irrespective of his relationship with his superiors in Jerusalem, he prosecuted a vigorous military campaign against various foes until the fall of Jotapata and his own surrender to Vespasian. As we know, he stood in dire need of portraying his career as a rebel in the most favorable light for the benefit of his Graeco-Roman audience and, on the other hand, did not want to entirely alienate his potential Jewish sympathizers. In other words, he had to persuade the reader that all the way through he was a subject of double loyalties: to his own people and to their conquerors, that at one and the same time he was and was not fighting Rome or, at the very least, did it reluctantly, or under pressure from the fanatical 'brigands'. The question arises, of course, as to how plausible this self-presentation is, and the majority of modern scholars insist that it is not. This is the matter I will repeatedly return to. The same point also applies to Josephus's treatment of the leaders presiding over the 'first regime', whose official appointment he accepted, their motives, attitudes and behavior, and – by extension – of the entire social group, that is, Jewish priestly and lay nobility, to which both they and he prominently belonged. So much for the *Bellum*. The *Vita*, with its often incoherent composition and specific aim of countering criticism by the author's opponents, such as Justus of Tiberias, offers an even less comprehensible picture. Thus, as will be seen, only in the *Antiquitates* is one occasionally able to have at least a glimpse into the historian's true feelings towards certain individuals and groups other than the radical revolutionaries whom he must have hated unabashedly from the very start.

Despite Josephus's sustained effort to minimize their participation in the revolt against Rome, it is now demonstrated that at the outset it was largely dominated by the members of the Jewish establishment. These people were accustomed to govern, and many of them, who did not doubt that they have every right to it, were not prepared to yield that privilege under any circumstances. After all, they learned how to exercise a considerable share of power even under the occupation, within the complex structure of the political authority in the Roman Palaestina. Many of them came to recognize the irreversible character of the events and tried preserving their supremacy in times of trouble, especially when threatened, though they might have exaggerated it, with the possibility of social revolution. In practice, this meant siding with the anti-Roman insurgents, irrespective even of their personal preferences and ties, and preventing a takeover by the socially inferior whom, as is evidenced in Josephus, they feared and tended to treat as mere 'brigands'.

This still does not prove that *all*, who belonged to society's upper echelon, or even the upper class as a group, sympathized with the anti-Roman rage or with the prosecution of the war, although it does help to explain and appreciate some of Josephus's numerous omissions and distortions. But none of it, however, can satisfactorily account for a total absence in his work of even scanty information on several major issues which would not have interfered with his personal agenda, for instance, such as the structure of the new government; its mode of deliberation; its relationship with the traditional bodies of the Jewish polity: the judiciary (whether the Sanhedrin or any other court of justice), the city council, the assembly and so forth.

It appears that, as was the habit of many ancient historians, Josephus chose to provide the material only for what would have interested him or his projected readers within a particular context, and without giving a thought to the interpreters from the future. On the other hand, the state of evidence found in his narratives might have reflected, at least in some respect, a kind of formlessness shown by the 'coalition regime', its inner incoherence, which would not be without historical parallels: under revolutionary circumstances things tend to happen in terms of *ad hoc* arrangements and improvised resolutions.

The evidence gleaned from the *Bellum* and the *Vita* suggests that the rebel leaders, returning to Jerusalem after the pursuit of the defeated Cestius Gallus, proved instrumental in setting up the first 'coalition' regime. They are said to have brought over to their side those who remained still pro-Roman, either by force or by persuasion (*BJ*, 2, 562). This does not signify, of course, that no collaborationists remained in the city, but under the circumstances they must have kept quiet.

We learn of at least two military men who had by then earned distinction in fighting the Romans: Silas the Babylonian and Niger of Peraea (ibid, 520; cf. 3, 11). It is a telling touch, however, that none of them received a major appointment; one can only speculate why: perhaps their exploits had spurred jealousy in others, or they were not sufficiently trusted due to their former allegiances. Of Silas one does not hear at all until the Jewish attack on Ascalon at the end of the year (ibid, 3, 11) in which he perished (ibid, 19); as for Niger, he received the command in Idumaea, not on his own authority, but as a subordinate to two other men (2, 566), neither of whom is referred to as military. Nevertheless, and despite his apparent failure to pacify Idumaea, Niger the Peraean must have served the 'first regime' faithfully, to the extent that he fell among the early victims in the reign of terror instituted by zealots after their *coup d'état* of spring A.D. 68 (ibid, 4, 359 ff.).

When, after the defeat of Gallus, the anti-Roman leaders from the Jerusalem establishment met on the Temple grounds with the victorious rebel commanders to deliberate on the common effort against the enemy (*BJ*, 2, 562 ff.), they were faced with harsh problems. In the *Vita*, Josephus (who must have been in attendance) sensibly outlines their main concern:

> The principal men of Jerusalem, observing that the brigands together with the revolutionaries were well provided with weapons, feared that having no arms they would be at the mercy of their opponents – as it eventually happened.
>
> (28)

This made compromise a necessity. Based on the fact, however, that it occurred, at least two inferences can be drawn: on the one hand, this meant that the rebel commanders (many of whom, owing to Josephus's figures of silence, remain anonymous), as newcomers on the political scene, lacked a power base, or the ability, or both, to gain the upper hand in the course of the negotiations – despite their possession of men, arms and much of the finances, as well as their control over the Temple. On the other hand, the achievement of compromise implies that Jerusalem's nobles won because of their superior skill in diplomacy and public relations – even though their factional strife plagued Judaea's politics for decades. One assumes that most of them were familiar, and some perhaps even popular, figures in the capital, consummate politicians and opportunists, hardened by the exigencies of their dealings with the Romans, the city populace and with each other – and, consequently, the masters of dissimulation. It stands to reason that in order to succeed, the rival factions of the nobility must have united at that stage, if only temporarily, around the ex-high priest Ananus b. Ananus. In consequence, they were allowed to obtain supreme authority and place the rebel military into subordinate positions.

Their most immediate accomplishment, a sort of diplomatic coup, was the exclusion from any real power of two Eleazars – Eleazar b. Ananias, known as the author of the cessation decree and thus a major player in the revolt's outbreak; and Eleazar b. Simon, the priestly head of the zealots who, as a group, only at this point first appear in Josephus's narrative.

It has been mentioned that the fate of Eleazar b. Ananias, after the Roman garrison's surrender, is almost entirely obfuscated by Josephus. He may or may not have been appointed one of the rebel generals in Idumaea – depending on an emendation in the manuscripts. In any event, there is not the slightest evidence that he participated in or influenced the events to come. One way of explaining that man's rapid eclipse is a supposition that by then he came to alienate most of the individuals who comprised the competing factions. The radicals might have been resentful of his role in the murder of Menahem b. Judas and the departure of the *sicarii* from the capital; those whom Josephus calls 'moderate' (persons who might have been originally neutral or even pro-Roman, but were made to join the revolt "by force or by persuasion") could have silently blamed him for originating the entire trouble in the first place, and the very fact of his earlier cooperation with the extremists would have compromised him in the eyes of the latter's opponents; finally, the truly orthodox within the rebel ranks, even some of the zealots, conceivably held him responsible for a double sacrilege – the slaughter of the Roman garrison on the Sabbath day and violating a solemn pledge for their safety. I have also speculated that the feeling of remorse over his father and uncle's brutal deaths weakened his resolve, thus contributing to his apparent withdrawal from the fray. Be that as it may, it seems improbable that, with Eleazar b. Ananias out of the picture, any group of his adherents continued to function as a single body within the coalition. They must have dissolved among other groups according to individual preferences.

As regards the elimination (temporary, as it happened) of another Eleazar – b. Simon – Josephus comes up with a reasonable account of why it was wished, but not of how it was done. The dominant group, the historian implies, chose not to entrust that man with an office (*BJ*, 2, 564) because they suspected him as potential tyrant (ibid); in addition, he was surrounded by the loyal partisans who behaved like a bodyguard (ibid). Even his appropriation of Roman spoils and his control over a large part of public treasure (ibid) did not help, which suggests that at this point the zealot influence in the capital was yet insufficient to provide them with a leverage not only to justify but also to enforce their claims. This, however, was gradually to change, and the historian warns us that the activities (in his view, predictably, "beguilements"; ibid, 565) of Eleazar b. Simon, combined with financial exigencies, came to enhance and increase his influence, so that the people in the end yielded him the authority in all matters (ibid) – thereby dramatically anticipating the events of the zealot *coup d'état* more than a year later (*BJ.*, 4, 135 ff.). I see no reason to doubt this basic Josephan information.

Thus, the results of temporary compromise, which made the coalition possible, proved initially advantageous to the nobles rather than the militant rebels. The former faced the task of organizing the hastily made up troops into a regular army, and of still preserving the supreme power over their commanders; they were also allowed access without hindrance to the Temple, at the time, still in the hands of the radicals. The benefits acquired from the compromise by the latter were less obvious to assess: one may argue that they felt satisfied by forming a united front, however fragile, against the common enemy, the Romans; they also won a place, as well as standing, within the framework of the Jerusalem politics which allowed them a room and all sorts of opportunities to work towards eventual takeover.

Perhaps the most constructive facet of the 'first regime' is precisely the recognition by its leaders that at the moment unity was, in pragmatic terms, a matter of uppermost importance. To their credit, they managed, notwithstanding the intermittent factional conflicts, to abstain, almost until the very end of their rule, from destroying fellow Jews *en masse*. One, however, suspects that already at this early stage the shrewdest minds in both camps recognized the fragile nature of the compromise: it offered only a respite, and the coalition was doomed because of irreconcilable differences in outlook, motives and agenda. The real issue was who will outwit or overpower whom, and when, so it seems almost a wonder that the 'first regime' lasted as long as it did.[5]

The former high priest, Ananus b. Ananus, a scion of a powerful clan, should be rightly considered, following the eclipse of Eleazar b. Ananias, the next major leader to carry on the revolt. No detail of his rise to power is known other than Josephus's brief statement that at the Temple meeting he and one Joseph b. Gorion were chosen "to wield sole rule over all affairs in the city, especially to fortify its walls" (*BJ*, 2, 563). There is no mention of an assembly or some other authoritative body to have convoked or conducted the conference. It cannot be ruled out that the historian intentionally omitted any such fact, although in this case it would be difficult to fathom his motives. Consequently, it seems that the 'provisional' government came to be formed by a relatively small number of the meeting's participants, presumably the old city politicians and the newly risen military commanders, that is to say, in conventionally legal terms (if one can speak of conventional legality at the time of revolution), it was self-appointed.

The new Jewish leader strikes us as a gifted political player who was able to withstand and even control, at least for a while, the rapid growth of threatening odds, both from within and without. He belonged to a family famous for wealth, power and greed, his father having been (most likely) the high priest Annas (Ananus b. Sethi, in office A.D. 6–15), known from the Gospels (as is his brother-in-law, Joseph Caiapha, the chief persecutor of Christ; furthermore, Josephus tells us that all five sons of the elder Ananus achieved high priesthood – "a thing that had never happened to any other of our high priests"; *AJ*, 20, 198).

Even though in the war narrative and elsewhere Josephus pays him considerable attention, Ananus b. Ananus largely remains a no less elusive personage than Eleazar b. Ananias, though for different reasons. His case represents perhaps the most flagrant example of inconsistent and contradictory judgments on the same subject that are so maddening for any careful reader of Josephus, and which at times makes it difficult and even impossible to reconstruct a coherent picture of either the latter's own attitudes or the facts he narrates.

Ananus figures in all three of Josephus's historical works now extant, and the harshest verdict on him is to be found in the *Antiquitates* written more than 20 years after his death. There the historian describes the man as "rash in temper and of unusual audacity" (20, 199) and seems to link his harshness to his membership among the Sadducees, "who are more severe in judgment than other Jews" (ibid). This is written in the context I have discussed on the earlier occasion: the martyrdom of James the Just, brother of Christ. We remember that it was, according to Josephus, the work of Ananus b. Ananus as a newly appointed high priest (successor to Joseph Kabi b. Simon), who cleverly chose a moment in the interval between the death of one procurator and the arrival of the next to destroy that widely respected man (ibid, 197 ff.). His motives are not specified. I find it possible that, having been a son and brother-in-law of men who must have been closely involved with the Crucifixion (one cannot dismiss their portrayal and role in the Gospels as fiction simply because one does not like it), he found it imperative to continue persecuting Christ's relatives and followers, a sort of 'family feud'. We recall that for impropriety of this action Ananus b. Ananus had been denounced by the group of respectable citizens before the new procurator and the king who deposed him after only three months in office (ibid, 201 ff.). As it has been noted, this whole episode was bound to further the deterioration of the high priesthood and of the general status quo: Ananus's successor Jesus b. Damnaeus was soon replaced with Jesus b. Gamaliel (or b. Gamala), and the two of them began an armed quarrel fraught with violence: "they often descended from verbal insults to throwing stones [at each other]" (213).

That Ananus b. Ananus could not only survive the scandal and subsequent disgrace but even emerge as a head of the rebel government implies that the groups which had opposed him, past and present, in the end proved less influential, perhaps because they were perceived as too closely linked to the Romans. (Inadvertently, this also suggests the lack of sympathy for Christian dissenters on the part of the masses.) It seems plausible that the humiliation he suffered at the hands of the procurator and the king, in the final analysis, prompted him to support the insurgents, and allowed him cleverly to manipulate his image as

Rome's victim in the interests of self-aggrandizement. If this was the case, Josephus's attempts to represent his political 'moderation' as an offshoot of some allegedly secret pro-Roman tendencies indeed look suspect. This pertains to the issue of the historian's encomiastic attitude to Ananus b. Ananus in the *Bellum*, especially in his obituary (4, 319 ff.), standing in stark contrast with the negative judgment on his character quoted above from the *Antiquitates*. In the earlier text he is praised as the exemplary 'moderate' statesman, who:

> … was honorable in every respect, and most just; with all the dignity of his origin, his rank and the office that he obtained, he liked to treat the humblest as if they were his equals; an exceptional lover of freedom and democracy, always preferring the common welfare to his own interest, and above all, he strove for peace.
>
> (ibid, 319 f.)

And it continues, emphasizing Ananus's reluctance to fight the Romans and, at the same time, his abilities as a military leader (320 ff.), to all of which, as well as his alleged democratism, I will return. This glorious characteristic contradicts not only the one in the *Antiquitates* but also what is said about the man in the *Vita*. In other words, we are dealing with an incontrovertible example of an author demonstrably lying – at least on this occasion – about his true feelings towards the subject of his discourse. It stands to reason that in the choice between the later and earlier pronouncements as reflecting Josephus's genuine sentiment about Ananus, we should opt for the former, which is to say, the one from the *Antiquitates*, written at the time when political, or personal, exigencies that had in the past affected the author of the *Bellum* ceased to be relevant. The nature of those exigencies, however, is unclear. It goes without saying that one cannot explain the emphatically favorable treatment of Ananus b. Ananus throughout the war in terms of the Imperial or Flavian propaganda: any negative portrayal of him would have served it better. A supposition that Josephus wrote the *Bellum* (at least in part) to misrepresent, justify or exculpate the revolutionary behavior among the members of the Jewish elite to which he belonged, and thus went on celebrating their leader whom in fact he loathed, sheds some light on the matter; but this, as well as mere rhetorical and literary reasons, does not fully account for the extent of the false enthusiasm shown in the text. One cannot but suspect an ulterior motive: in the *Bellum*, by interpreting the role and character of Ananus b. Ananus as he did, the historian sought to invite a parallel of that man's alleged predicament and his own, to wit, a secret pacifist, man of integrity and hater of the rebels, playing an uncannily perilous game.

In the *Vita*, written upon the completion of the *Antiquitates* (cf. *AJ*, 20, 266), Josephus comes closest to betraying the reason of his resentment against Ananus, by now made palpable. We learn that while the future historian, as the governor of Galilee newly appointed by the rebels, had been taking energetic measures to gain control over that area, he ran a risk of being impeached through the intrigue his enemies perpetrated in Jerusalem behind his back (*Vita*, 189 ff.; cf. *BJ*, 526 ff.). Stated briefly, it concerns the alliance between the reputable Pharisee Simon b. Gamaliel, who apparently held a position of influence within the 'first regime', and Josephus's nemesis, a local Galilaean politician, John b. Levi of Gischala, destined later to become one of three chief rebel leaders in Jerusalem under Roman siege. One reads that the two made an effort to remove Josephus from his command or – using the latter's own phrases – "cut off" his "growth" by "not permitting" his "fame ever to reach its peak" (*Vita*, 193). Simon is even alleged to have threatened Ananus and his associates that, if they delayed Josephus's recall, the latter would hear of their deliberations and march on Jerusalem (ibid). Reportedly, Ananus at first resisted Simon's pressure, arguing that so far Josephus proved an able general, and that one cannot be impeached without good reason (194), but he eventually gave up – according to the *Vita*, after his group was offered gifts:

> In the end, Simon achieved what he sought: for Ananus and those with him were corrupted by the bribes and consented to expel me [i.e. Josephus] from Galilee, with no one in the city knowing of it.
>
> (ibid, 196)

This resulted in sending an official five-member delegation in Galilee, with a mandate to either unseat or even kill Josephus (193, 202): later I will return to his reportage about their activities and tribulations. Finally, we are told that when, owing to Josephus's counter-maneuvers, people in Jerusalem learned of the plot against him, they felt indignant at the clandestine activities conducted by the factions around Simon b. Gamaliel and Ananus b. Ananus (the *Vita* even claims that there were attempts to set their houses on fire, which sounds less than probable), and his command of Galilee was publicly confirmed (309 f.).

Whatever share of truth this story contains, even its bare outline does not square with Ananus's portrayal in the *Bellum* as an incorruptible leader whose priority was common good, although the charge of bribery motivating his behavior is no doubt gratuitous: he must have been affluent enough not to be tempted by that kind of thing. It was almost certainly an offer of some tradeoff, inevitable in a power coalition, that made him change his mind and act against Josephus – any politics entails a display of opportunism. Be that as it may, the *Vita*'s account sheds some light on the causes of the historian's discrepant judgments, in various contexts, on one and the same man: it seems apparent that at the time of writing the *Bellum*, the author's political and apologetic concerns overrode his personal bad feelings, and only in the works written much later was he able freely to manifest his resentment. On the other hand, while Josephus's reasons were personal, one cannot rule out that this discrepancy might have also indirectly reflected the divergent opinions of Ananus b. Ananus held in various circles of Jewish society or by the individuals with whom the historian was in touch.

We are told explicitly that the leader of the first regime "followed the school of the Sadducees" (*AJ*, 20, 190). This rules out any possible element of religious dissent in his motivation. The Sadducees were the dominant group within the priestly elite and, according to Josephus, believed in the exercise of free will and did not regard God as a participant in the affairs of men (*BJ*, 2, 165; *AJ*, 13, 173). This seems to preclude the notion of any direct individual communication with the divinity, which – as I have argued – constitutes a major component in psychology of religious dissenters. The religious policies of Ananus b. Ananus seem to have been conventional and believable, irrespective of rhetoric, which permeates Josephus's narration. He is portrayed as drawing on both exigencies and custom: attacking in his speech the zealots' violation of the Temple's grounds (*BJ*, 4, 163, 171 f., 183 ff.), and invoking divine wrath against the miscreants (190; in some contradiction with the above-mentioned Saducean doctrine) as well as professing his own willingness to die for the sake of God and his sanctuary (191 f.). One conspicuously pious action performed by his regime was ordering Josephus, who promptly complied, to destroy Herod Antipas's palace in Tiberias, which contained animal images prohibited by law (*Vita*, 65), but this might well have been done under pressure from his Pharisaic allies or zealots.

The precariousness of the position held by Ananus b. Ananus required a substantial effort to be spent on political and diplomatic maneuvering, which may account for the lack of military action against the Romans during the period when he ran the government. It is true that Josephus emphasizes, in general terms, his efforts to fortify Jerusalem so that it could withstand an eventual Roman siege (*BJ*, 2, 248 ff.). But outside of the city's walls, and apart from Josephus's own exploits in Galilee (where he soon became *de facto* an independent player), we hear only of the futile Jewish attack on the Graeco-Syrian city of Ascalon, which cost them some of their ablest commanders (*BJ*, 3, 9 ff.).

There still remains a question as to whether such an experienced pragmatist as Ananus b. Ananus, well familiar with the power of the Roman military machine (recently made manifest in a difficult a war with Parthia over the Armenian succession), failed to recognize that the revolt was doomed and its suppression was merely a matter of time. Could he, like radical revolutionaries, have fallen under the spell of euphoric optimism in the aftermath of Cestius's defeat? Although nothing can be said on the matter with certainty, it is still conceivable that Ananus (and his likes) underwent the moments of both inspiration and despair. He might have also acted out of hope against hope, a mixture of make-believe and self-persuasion, which one would expect any historical agent to live through under circumstances like these.

In his eulogy, which follows the account of the zealot coup, Josephus insists that the fallen 'moderate' leader:

> ... was concerned above all with obtaining peace: he stood in awe of Roman invincibility, but having been forced by necessity into war, took

care that, if the Jews would not have reconciled with the enemy, they could carry on the fight with better skill.

(*BJ*, 4, 320)

This statement is clearly fraught with contradiction, but it still makes sense so far as it reflects psychological dichotomy, by no means unknown at the times of trouble or socio-political conflicts, and in this context probably involving specific features. The claim in the second clause, namely, that under his leadership, the struggle might have been conducted more efficiently, is not that implausible: it appears that Ananus b. Ananus, unlike the religious dissenters who succeeded him, had chosen to rely primarily on practical and military measures rather than hope for divine intervention. The chief problem lays in Josephus's first clause which implies that the Romans could have offered Jewish rebels terms other than unconditional surrender and spared their leaders' lives – a very questionable proposition to be further discussed towards the end of this chapter.

In any event, the *Bellum* presents the heroic stature of Ananus b. Ananus as increasing in the same measure as his and his faction's conflict with the zealots escalates: he is attributed an eloquent speech urging the populace of Jerusalem to take up arms and suppress the Temple's radical occupants (4163–4192), presides over the ensuing bloodshed, and is finally killed by the Idumaean allies of the zealots (ibid, 314 f.).[6]

All three major 'sects' or 'schools of thought' within the Second Temple Judaism may have been represented in the rebel leadership of the 'first regime' – Sadducees, Pharisees and Essenes. The presence of the latter could be noteworthy given their tendency to withdraw from public life. Of the only person on record often counted among them (if Josephus's adjective does not mean simply "from the town Essa"), one John the Essene, nothing is known as regards his circumstances and background. If we assume this man to have been an Essene, his form of religious dissent, unlike in the (presumably) majority of his fellow sectarians, took a radical turn and made him an active revolutionary fighter. We learn that he was appointed a general in the toparchy of Thamna, which included Lydda, Joppa and Emmaus (*BJ*, 2, 567); and that, as one of three commanders (the other two being Niger of Peraea and Silas the Babylonian), "prominent for courage and intelligence" (ibid, 3, 11), he had led the Jewish force in an abortive attack on Ascalon and there perished in action (ibid,19).

Josephus's treatment of Jesus b. Gamala (the rabbinic Joshua b. Gamaliel), yet another ex-high priest and thus supposedly a Sadducee, who became Ananus's closest associate, follows the same bewildering and discrepant pattern as that in the case of the latter. The *Antiquitates* portray this man (incidentally, the second to last to hold the high priestly office – cf. *AJ*, 20, 223) unfavorably: he is said to have quarreled, in A.D. 63, with his predecessor Jesus b. Damnaeus to the point that each of them came to recruit a loyal band of thugs (ibid, 213), engaged in mutual verbal abuse and street fighting. This was promptly imitated by the royal relatives Saul and Costobar, with their own gangs of rogues (214), which led the historian sadly to conclude: "It was from about this time in particular that our city had fallen sick and everything began turning to the worse" (ibid). Perhaps this reputation of a troublemaker, which could have hardly endeared him to the Romans, proved a decisive factor in his eventual siding with the insurgents.

Similarly to that of Ananus, Josephus's harsh judgment on Jesus b. Gamala in the *Antiquitates* is hardly compatible with the eulogy of him in the *Bellum*, upon his and Ananus's murder by the Idumaeans during the zealot coup (4, 322 ff.). There he is made to share much, but not all, of Ananus's glory: in the words of the historian, "though not comparable" to his great fallen colleague, he still "stood out far above the rest" (ibid, 322). Their obituary ends with rhetoric striking as excessive and therefore suspect: "I think that virtue herself bemoaned these men, lamenting that she was so defeated by evil" (325).

The reader's perplexity is further magnified by the contradictory role played by Jesus b. Gamala in the *Vita*, written, as we know, after the completion of the *Antiquitates*. On the one hand, in it he is called the author's own "friend and companion" (204) who warned Josephus, through the agency of his own father Matthias, about the trouble brewing for him in Jerusalem; on the other, we are told explicitly (cf. 193) that he belonged to the faction which tried to drive the future historian out from his command in Galilee. In the final analysis, however, this may not be particularly bewildering: in politics, and even more pronouncedly at the time of crisis, individual betrayals occur as a matter of fact; Josephus's divergent appraisals of the second-in-power in the coalition government must have been motivated by the same reasons as his treatment of the regime's leader. In the *Bellum*, Jesus b. Gamala, like Ananus, was needed to provide the author with a respectable parallel to his own character and behavior; in the *Antiquitates*, when that need ceased to exist, Josephus could afford to vent out his dislike for him, caused, or intensified perhaps, because of the earlier betrayal by a man who was a former friend.

Despite his obvious public influence, it is not clear whether Jesus b. Gamala held any formal office during the revolution: at one point he is simply called "most senior among the archpriests after Ananus" (*BJ*, 4, 238). He is not mentioned in connection with the Temple meeting. It appears that he belonged among those politicians who prefer to exercise their power from behind the scenes. In any event, his authority seems to have eclipsed that of one Joseph b. Gorion, originally elected, together with Ananus b. Ananus, to preside over the conduct of the warfare (ibid, 2, 563)

Perhaps in order to emphasize that the role played by Jesus b. Gamala was by no means inconsiderable, Josephus attributes to him in the *Bellum* a major speech on the eve of the first regime's overthrow (4, 239–269). He is made to address the armed force of the Idumaeans, whom the zealots, reportedly at the instigation of John b. Levi of Gischala, had summoned to the capital as potential allies against Ananus and the latter's 'moderate' supporters (216 ff.). The fact of this speech may well have been historical, but of course not its highly rhetorical version given by Josephus (who by that time had been already in Roman captivity). He makes Jesus b. Gamala start with the praise of the Idumaeans while vilifying his own zealot foes. He calls it the Fortune's "evil turn" when "a whole nation is armed on behalf of the bunch of villains" (*BJ*, 4, 243). Next follows the denial of the charge, pressed by zealots, that Ananus b. Ananus and his group have contemplated treason through communicating secretly with the Romans (245 ff.). The gist of the argument ascribed to Jesus b. Gamala claims that it was too late for any hope of peace negotiations since the 'moderate' leadership at Jerusalem chose to reject the earlier options "either to abstain from revolting altogether, or after having revolted, promptly to recant" (248). It is further pointed out that there was no evidence whatsoever of the alleged treasonous intent and that allegation was in itself of recent origin, that is to say, it was first made up only after the coalition created at the Temple meeting had collapsed and zealots began preparations for their coup (252 ff.). They are accused of initiating the reign of terror (259 ff.) and desecrating the Temple (261 ff.) as well as inciting fratricidal bloodshed: "In their insolence, they are willfully trying to bring people against people, city against city to enlist the nation to strike at its own entrails" (263). By implication, zealots do not represent the residents of the capital but constitute the mixed bad lot, transferring their "brigand-like audacity" (261) from the countryside, and smaller towns, to the very center of national life (ibid).

The speech proceeds to present Idumaeans with three options: they are invited to join the 'moderates' in their fight against the zealots (264); or enter the city as arbitrators (265 f.); or not to enter at all, but to stay outside the walls, maintain neutrality and leave both parties to their own devices (267). In this last case, they would protect the capital both from the Romans and any attempt at treason (268 f.). If they were not willing to adopt any of these options, the speaker is made finally to proclaim, they should not "be surprised that the gates are barred" to them as long as they carry arms (269).

In a rare attempt to follow Thucydides's precedent by presenting a set of speeches argued from two opposite viewpoints, Josephus provides a rebuff to Jesus b. Gamala, allegedly delivered by an Idumaean officer, one Simon b. Cathlas (272–282), which is, predictably, shorter and cruder in its expression. In substance, it reiterates the charge against Ananus and Jesus's faction of treasonous intent and celebrates zealots as champions of freedom (cf. 272).

Irrespective of its historicity, this exchange places into relief the contrast the historian sought to convey between the intransigence shown by those whom he considered radical and the regret that bridges had been burned, with its potential for eventual negotiation, which was present, according to him, in the minds of so-called 'moderates'. How far all of this might have reflected reality makes a troublesome issue. The developments which followed are well known: at some point, zealots managed to open the gates of Jerusalem and, by joining their forces with the Idumeans, insured the success of their coup. Both Ananus b. Ananus and Jesus b. Gamala were killed in the process.[7]

We are told by Josephus that, upon the cessation of the Imperial sacrifices, the 'chief priests' were joined by leading Pharisees to deliberate on the state of affairs (*BJ*, 2, 411). At the Temple meeting, which set up the government under Ananus b. Ananus, some of them were to attain positions of leadership. Of them the most famous, if one follows Josephus, turned out to be Simon b. Gamaliel, son of the renowned *Rabban* from the Talmudic tradition (who also figures in the *Acts of the Apostles* – 5, 34 ff.), and the father of the Patriarch Gamaliel II. This is yet another personage on whom the historian passes contradictory judgment in different narratives, depending apparently on his own personal agenda at the time. The *Bellum* mentions Simon b. Gamaliel only in passing, and in honorable context: side by side with other 'moderate' leaders, he protests the zealots' desecration of the Temple and their appointment of a high priest by lot, shortly before the fighting between factions broke out in Jerusalem. We read that on this occasion he exercised his influence both through public speeches and private visits, urging people to punish the "destroyers of freedom" (that is, zealots) and "purge the sanctuary of the butchers" (4,159).

The *Vita*, however, treats Simon b. Gamaliel at greater length with somewhat puzzling results. We have seen that in the cases of Ananus b. Ananus and Jesus b. Gamala, their portrayals by Josephus, although differing in terms of positive or negative coloration, are still relatively consistent within the frame of each narrative. Here, on the other hand, Simon b. Gamaliel is first highly praised for his character and achievements, and then described as having initiated and pursued an ugly intrigue, which involved bribery and character assassination, in the same textual sequence. One cannot escape the impression that either the historian continued to entertain divided feelings about the man at the time of this writing, or that he wrote what he did for some ulterior purpose.

Simon b. Gamaliel must have enjoyed considerable prestige as the teacher of Law which in fact found its reflection in the Mishnah, where he figures as a Torah expert and a sage (cf. e.g., *mAvot*, 1:17 f.), which – if we accept the material from the *Vita* – went along in his case with the taste for political scheming. Simon's learning is properly emphasized by Josephus, next to his illustrious origin and his adherence to the school of the Pharisees, within whose ranks, we are told, he stood out because of some particular skills: "full of insight and ability to reason, he was able, by dint of his own wisdom, to rectify situations turning bad" (192). The statement is (consciously or not) ironic, perhaps inadvertently so. The thrust (whether right or wrong) of Josephus's own narrative implies that Simon's political maneuvering, in the first place, his association with John b. Levi of Gischala, eventually led not only to the political and military mess in Galilee, but to the collapse of the 'moderate' rebel government he was himself a part of, and even – by extension – to the ultimate disaster, Jerusalem's fall: a peculiar proof indeed of one man's wisdom!

Be that as it may, even such apparently encomiastic rhetoric did not prevent the historian from making this very man responsible for the intrigue in Jerusalem aimed at Josephus's impeachment as Galilee's revolutionary governor. It must be noticed, however, that in the *Vita*'s narrative, Simon's motives for the campaign he is said to have conducted against his young colleague remain obscure (tellingly, the corresponding portion of the *Bellum* leaves his name out). But Josephus is careful to specify that it was "then" – which implies "not always" – when Simon b. Gamaliel "was at variance" with him (*Vita*, 192), although the nature of their disagreement is never explained. We lack evidence even to attempt reconstructing the balance of power, or power dynamics, within the leadership of the 'first regime', but the accounts offered by Josephus, fraught with contradictory statements and omissions, strongly (and predictably) indicate that the relationships between different personalities were shifty, uneasy and complex. Even though the *Vita* suggests that Simon b. Gamaliel acted at the instigation of John b. Levi of Gischala, an "old and close friend" (ibid), who became Josephus's chief antagonist, it was not intended, however, in the eyes of the historian to serve for Simon as a mitigating circumstance: rather, the contrary.

From the *Vita*'s report (taken, in its basics, at face value), one infers that Simon b. Gamaliel was not in a position to act at his own pleasure or initiative. His status within Ananus's leadership is left unclear and we are not told whether he held any formal appointment. According to the text, Simon acted in the interests of John b. Levi, who denounced Josephus, one presumes, as either a failure or a potential tyrant (cf. *Vita*, 260; *BJ*, 2, 626). We read that he made an attempt at convincing Ananus b. Ananus and his associates (*Vita*, 193) on the need for his recall from Galilee – in the midst of Josephus's attempts to pacify the area, and before he had any an opportunity to act against the common foe, the Romans. Having been unable to achieve this purpose by persuasion, Simon reportedly advised those, who sought Josephus's disgrace, to make use of bribery (195), which resulted in a success: the delegation of four respectable individuals was sent to Galilee with the purpose of securing the governor's dismissal (196 f.).

At least three of its members seem to represent the Pharisaic constituent of the 'first regime'. This, however, involves considerable trouble, textual and onomastic. One called Ananias figures both in the *Vita* (197) and in the *Bellum* (2, 628) – the latter specifies that he was a son of Sadok. Two other names differ: Jozar "of the priestly family" from the *Vita* (loc. cit.), in the *Bellum* (loc. cit.) is called Joesdrus, son of Nomicus; and the *Vita*'s Jonathan (the text states that he and Ananias belonged to the common people – loc. cit.), whom it portrays as the delegation's leader, is entirely absent in the *Bellum*, where he is replaced with one Judas, son of Jonathan, otherwise unattested. The *Vita*'s Ananias, Jozar and Jonathan are there explicitly treated as Pharisees (loc. cit.). The fourth man, Simon, figures in both versions, but while in the *Vita* (which refers to him as "the youngest" – 197) he is attributed the high priestly descent (ibid), the *Bellum* makes him, like the above-mentioned Judas, another 'son of Jonathan' (loc. cit.). Now, if the *Bellum*'s Judas is identical to the *Vita*'s Jonathan (above), this Simon also must have come from the common stock. This conundrum is insoluble: Josephus could have hardly forgotten the names of the opponents, who relentlessly tried to unseat, and perhaps even kill, him during his tenure in Galilee; on the other hand, it seems disproportionate to ascribe this confusion, fraught with the whole series of onomastic misplacements, solely to the scribes.

In any event, the delegates were apparently instructed just to remove Josephus from his office rather than replace him with John b. Levi, as the latter and Simon b. Gamaliel must have hoped; the historian also claims that they were told to kill him in case he offered any resistance (*Vita*, 202; cf. *BJ*, 2, 628). The *Vita* further insists that the revolutionary authorities at Jerusalem provided the envoys with very substantial amounts of money from public funds (199), which is remarkable, in terms of inappropriate expenses at the moment of crisis, and in light of preparations needed for the prosecution of war against Rome. Moreover, a Galilaean 'brigand' named Jesus (possibly the same individual, already used, as will be seen, by the pro-Roman Sepphoris against Josephus – 105 ff.) was hired, 600 armed men under his command, to escort the party, their salary for three months paid in advance (200). This seemed not enough: yet another 300 enlisted in expectation that they should maintain themselves throughout the mission (ibid); lastly, John's brother followed up with a further 100 (201 f.). Altogether, this must have made a formidable force (the *Bellum* cites an exaggerated number of 2500), capable of taking military action if needed.

Although the information we possess is hardly satisfactory, and a series of questions must remain unanswered, it cannot be doubted, as a matter of fact, that the delegation failed to achieve its purpose. It seems that this was owing in part to the complexity and instability of the political status quo across Galilee, and in part to Josephus's successful counter-maneuvering. One learns from both the *Vita* and the *Bellum* that they did approach various Galilaean cities and constituencies, sometimes (though perhaps not always) supported by John b. Levi, but only with partial, or temporary, success. They also attempted to negotiate with Josephus (as the latter claims, each time planning some treachery – 216 ff., 236 ff., 271 ff.), and at least once – so far as we are told – played the religious card: at one point, when two parties were to discuss their differences at Tiberias, a member of the embassy proclaimed a public fast, with the provision that the partakers assemble unarmed, at the same time appealing to John for reinforcements (290 ff.). Josephus disobeyed, having ordered his bodyguards to keep their daggers, and thus – if we take him at his word – barely escaped alive (302 ff.).

As I have mentioned, Josephus's appointment was finally confirmed by some sort of vote in Jerusalem, and he even managed to incite in the capital, with the help of his agent, an outburst of popular anger against both Simon and Ananus – a public episode, difficult to invent. That he succeeded in isolating all four envoys through trapping them one by one, and dispatching them back home (317 ff.), must be similarly historical (whatever can be argued about his rhetoric, agenda or narrative details), which is confirmed by the fact that he continued staying in his office until his surrender to Vespasian at Jotapata.

The fiasco suffered by the Jerusalem authorities in the Josephus affair is telling: it reflects the exceedingly tenuous grasp of the 'first regime' over the situation, not only *vis-à-vis* the radicals, such as zealots, but also other groups within and without the city. It also betrays their lack of judgment. After all, a bitter irony lay in the fact that, by introducing John b. Levi of Gischala into the power struggle at the capital, Simon b. Gamaliel had signed, in a sense, a death warrant to the very government he himself so prominently represented: it was John's turnaround and alliance with zealots which triggered the series of events ending in the overthrow of Ananus's and his own 'moderate' leadership. Of Simon's fate nothing is known.

There remains a man whose reportage serves as our main, and for the most part the only, source for these events – Josephus b. Matthias, an aristocrat and ambitious rebel general, later to become the Roman citizen Flavius Josephus, companion of three emperors (cf. *Vita*, 428 ff.). According to him, having freshly returned from Rome upon the successful accomplishment of a diplomatic mission to Jerusalem, he "already found the start of the revolution and many of those who were much minded to secede from Rome", and attempted some pro-Roman campaign ("to check these men of sedition and make them change their mind") on the grounds that the revolt was doomed to fail (ibid, 17 ff.). But he failed: "Their senseless mania proved much stronger" (19). He insists that as a result his very life was threatened:

> Now afraid that by continuously saying this I might run into hatred and suspicion of favoring the enemy and that I would be at risk of being seized by them and put to death, / ... / I withdrew into the inner Temple.
>
> (20)

Only with the dispatch of Menachem b. Judas and his *sicarii* did he feel safe enough to emerge from the sanctuary, consorting with "chief priests and Pharisees", and having thereupon, under pressure and because of the immediate exigencies, joined the revolution (21 ff.). How much truth lies behind these statements is difficult if not impossible to ascertain, except that his hiding in and the exit from the Temple must have been on public record. In any event, he earned enough of a reputation (though it is left unclear why or how) to be chosen by the 'first regime' as their official representative in Galilee (*BJ*, 2, 568).

It appears that, in contrast to Josephus, enmeshed in the complicated troubles in Galilee, as well as Niger the Peraean and John the Essene, who were summoned to lead the expedition against Ascalon, no other regional commanders, appointed at the Temple meeting, either left their posts or engaged militarily with the Romans.[8]

III.

Josephus's activities in Galilee, as described in both the *Bellum* and the *Vita*, cannot receive detailed discussion here. This subject requires its own book; and such treatment, taking in the complexities of the problem, has been already provided. The difficulties are indeed formidable and sometimes insoluble: they concern the internal inconsistencies in each account, confused chronology and omissions; the contradictions between two texts, which only in part can be explained by the difference of the author's agenda, respectively, in A.D. 70s and A.D. 90s; the multi-vectored character of his polemics and apologetics – against Justus of Tiberias and various other detractors, on behalf of himself, his coreligionists, and his Roman masters; the matter of the audience he sought to win; the effects and failures of his rhetoric, and so on. Add to this the remarkable overall incoherence, fraught with numerous confusions, of the *Vita*, one of the sloppiest literary products that came down to us from Antiquity. So far scholarly efforts succeeded in elucidating some of these issues, while others remain as controversial – or incomprehensible – as before. Perhaps it will be wise to let the latter rest by admitting that any further debate is idle unless new and sensational documentary evidence is discovered.

I will thus limit myself to the basic survey of those developments that can be established with greater or lesser certainty, and comment at some length only on those known elements, admittedly few, of the predicament that may *implicite* pertain to the matter of religious dissent. It will also provide us with an opportunity of looking into what went on in people's minds elsewhere than Jerusalem, or at the very least that might have been considered believable by the public whom the author addressed, Jewish and gentile. One further caveat – as regards our historian's *factual* reliability: unlike the events at Jerusalem, which were witnessed by multitudes of people, Josephus's doings in Galilee would have appeared for most of his readers largely obscure, especially in view of the 30 or so years' interval between them and the publication of the *Vita*. This allowed him larger room than in the *Bellum*, if he wished, for inventing and manipulating his material. Still, one assumes that the chief target of his polemics, Justus of Tiberias, was in full possession of knowledge about what had actually happened in his very homeland, and his informed and demonstrable rebuttal of Josephus's fictions was bound to cause the latter a major embarrassment he would have tried to avoid. In other words, there was still a limit, on Josephus's part, to polemical fictionalizing, and omissions or obfuscations rather than inventions made a better apologetic strategy. This means, as is generally true of Josephus, that one should not concentrate on questioning or denying the actions covered by his reportage, but inquire into his *orchestration* and *interpretation* of them, all too often self-serving, rhetorical and politically biased.

Josephus's two accounts seem to diverge on the purpose of his mission in Galilee: the *Bellum* clearly implies that his chief aim was to fight the Romans (2, 566 ff.); but in the *Vita* it is stated that he was sent (with two colleagues) to pacify the populace and make it subordinate to the revolutionary government in Jerusalem (28 ff.). This discrepancy created scholarly controversy, perhaps for no compelling reason – the two tasks could have been considered complementary, and the historian chose to place different emphasis in each work for whatever reasons of his own. Be that as it may, we do not hear for quite a while of his direct engagement with the national enemy: the *Bellum* (3, 59) places his first such confrontation only upon Vespasian's entering Sepphoris in the spring of

A.D. 67; the *Vita* (394) dates it earlier (allegedly, still at the time of Cestius Gallus), but this latter account is, as is often the case, somewhat incoherent, whereas the earlier episodes are described as virtually non-encounters (115 ff., 121, 215). Instead, both narratives concentrate on the internecine fighting in and between various Galilaean groups and cities, bloody conflicts with their gentile neighbors, and intrigues as well as counter-intrigues conducted by Josephus, his rivals and the ruling council in Jerusalem.

The impression created by the texts is that – whatever might have been his original mandate – Josephus acted and thought during his six-month tenure as governor in terms of his personal rather than collective authority, thus giving substance to the charges of 'tyranny' leveled against him (*BJ*, 2, 626; cf. *Vita*, 193). His two priestly colleagues, portrayed as corruptible, were soon dismissed by him back to the capital and were not heard of any more. In fact, one cannot entirely rule out that his ultimate ambition might have been to become one of the war lords, acting largely on their own, as often happens at the time of socio-political upheaval.

In any event, Josephus's portrayal of the situation in Galilee upon his arrival amounts to a state of anarchy: two major cities, Sepphoris and Tiberias, compete for the status of capital and are prepared to take up arms against each other; the gentiles attack Jews and vice versa; the 'brigands' are bent on plundering those who are rich; the 'Galilaeans', countryside population, are unruly and willing to perpetuate the trouble. As regards the Romans, major cities seem to have developed substantial pacifist and collaborationist factions, which bitterly opposed the revolutionary movement. In turn, the radicals showed no scruples in killing their fellow Jews, motivated not only by excessive zeal, one of the constituents in religious dissent, but also by what we would now call 'class envy', rooted in socio-economic factors. This picture, although undoubtedly biased by minimizing anti-Roman sentiments, nonetheless cannot have been altogether untrue, since otherwise a series of ascertainable facts would remain inexplicable. All of this, however, may undermine the popular vision of the revolt as one spontaneous and virtually unanimous uprising of Jews in Palaestina against the Roman oppressor – as well as the possibility that the entire (or even the majority) of the Jewish elite (in this case, outside Jerusalem) came to join the struggle for liberation.[9]

During Josephus's tenure as the revolutionary general, at least three important cities in Galilee – Sepphoris, Tiberias and Gischala – and at least one beyond its borders, Gamala, repeatedly turned into scenes of violent public turmoil, fraught with the repercussions *vis-à-vis* all participants in the hostilities. These events are narrated by Josephus with varying degree of detail, some of it perforce authentic. Consequently, this evidence, however confused, merits brief examination in our search for the possible influence of religious dissent.

The city of Sepphoris was in various periods recognized as Galilee's capital. Officially, it regained this status in A.D. 54, after the rivaling Tiberias had been transferred under the jurisdiction of King Agrippa II. It is true that Sepphoris had a substantial gentile population, but on the other hand, in the past it also was the scene of the revolutionary activities by Judas b. Ezechias (*BJ*, 2, 56), who may or may not have been that archetypical religious dissenter, Judas the Galilaean; and, one assumes, it provided for at least some of his following. Josephus reports that Sepphoris remained pro-Roman for the duration of the revolt. This is also supported by numismatic evidence. Nonetheless, Josephan narratives concerning that city strike as less than coherent. The descriptions of the events are fragmentary, and even their sequence may not be recoverable. According to the *Bellum*, the residents of Sepphoris happily submitted before Beth-horon to the legionary force sent by Cestius Gallus (2, 510 f.; cf. *Vita*, 30); the *Vita* also mentions in passing their hostages taken by the Romans and kept at Dora (31). Nonetheless, upon his appointment as general, Josephus came to visit it first (*Vita*, 30, 64). This means that at the early stage, and despite its display of pro-Roman sentiments, Sepphoris was prepared to receive an emissary from Jerusalem's revolutionary council. Josephus's assertion that he protected its inhabitants against the rage of the 'Galilaeans', bent on plunder as punishment for their collaborationism (30 f.), may or may not be a piece of self-advertisement. It is similar with the statement in the *Bellum* alleging that he 'allowed' the Sepphorites to fortify the city walls on their own (2, 574): one cannot know at what points the latter might have been willing to recognize or ignore his authority. In any case, what we hear next is the attempt on the part of its citizens to protect it against Josephus through the agency of an 'arch-brigand', one Jesus, a curious character, who (if we trust the historian on this matter) was offering his services for hire to both pro-Roman and anti-Roman groups. The plot, we are told, was foiled by Josephus's dexterity: he had entered the city with his cohorts, ordered its inhabitants to recant, but did not proceed beyond threats (*Vita*, 104 ff.).

The Sepphorites are consistently portrayed as seeking Roman aid and obtaining it in the end, but only after some period of self-reliance (ibid, 394, cf. 373). Meanwhile, they must have resorted to maneuvering, which may account for at least some inconsistencies in Josephus, although he states that they officially forbade their fellow citizens to side with the rebels (346). It seems nonetheless noteworthy that, despite their declaration for Rome, they were repeatedly approached by other revolutionary agents, such as the delegates from the 'first regime' in Jerusalem, and John b. Levi of Gischala, but with no success (*BJ*, 2, 629; *Vita*, 124; 203, 232), which suggests a residual hope on the part of the insurgents that they may rectify their political course. Josephus claims that, in his role as general, he twice captured Sepphoris by storm (*Vita*, 82); but his own accounts do not fully support this statement. He may well have repeatedly attacked it, but whether he could have actually taken possession of the city, and if he did, then how many times, and for how long, remains uncertain (cf. ibid, 103 ff., 373 ff.), and much of what he says about this may well be the product of wishful thinking.

To sum, it appears that in the case of Sepphoris, nationalist propaganda as well as religious dissent, active at the time as they may have been, exercised little or no impact upon the popular mind. This can arguably be explained in terms of the local situation, such as the sense of threat from the hostile Galilaean environment. One presumes that this pro-Roman stand, in itself remarkable, was taken at the expressed wish of the upper class, as well as with the substantial support by the masses, and eventually it came to be rewarded by the Romans.[10]

The developments in Tiberias, Galilee's other major city (but formally under the royal jurisdiction), must have been even more complex, and their accounts found in Josephus are not only convoluted, but exceedingly suspect for at least two reasons: his own deeper involvement in those affairs (he does not attempt to conceal his prejudice) and the prominent role of his antagonists, John b. Levi of Gischala and Justus b. Pistus, known as Justus of Tiberias. The matter is aggravated by his polemics, the purpose and details of which are not always easy to grasp, against history (or histories) published by the latter.

In the course of the revolt, Tiberias sought several times to change sides, depending on the politics of the faction prevalent at the moment. The existence of competing factions in the city cannot thus be doubted, although it does not follow that their portrayal by Josephus is in any sense accurate: in fact, it is thoroughly confused. In view of the subsequent events, however, one cannot deny that pro-Roman and anti-Roman forces in Tiberias must have engaged in a bitter conflict, which may have betrayed some social characteristics: one need not be a Marxist to realize that at the time of revolutionary upheaval the havenots tend to rise up against the haves, and political issues become blended with economic and material concerns. This is implied by Josephus's reference to collaborationists as "respectable" or "refined" (a clear equivalent to the Latin *optimi*), headed by a Roman citizen Julius Capella and his associates (*Vita*, 32 ff.); and to their opponents as "insignificant" (34). It is their party that is apparently labeled elsewhere as one of "the sailors and the needy" (66); at some point it must have been taken over by one Jesus b. Sapphias, an elusive figure, alternatively described as a 'brigand chief' (*BJ*, 2, 450) and as the president of the city council (*Vita*, 134, 278, 294, 300). The reality of the third faction, allegedly, the following of Justus b. Pistus (36 ff.), on whom Josephus places most blame for the troubles at Tiberias (cf. 41, 341), is questionable, owing to the enmity between two men, and the historian's uncanny ability to obfuscate the factual account, if this serves his immediate interest, and to the detriment of those whom he personally hated.

In any event, the choice the citizens of Tiberias faced was not merely between collaborationism and revolution: even having joined the insurgents, they needed to ally with one or another of two revolutionary leaders active in the land – Josephus and John b. Levi of Gischala, with the latter enjoying the support by the Jerusalem delegation, and looking towards the former's impeachment. Josephus claims that twice the Tiberians tried to change their allegiance and invite royal force: in the first case, he thwarted their plans through the ruse of the sham fleet (*Vita*, 155 ff.; cf. *BJ*. 2, 632 ff.); in the second, he prevented the destruction of Tiberias by the Galilaeans (*Vita*, 381 ff.). The account of at least the earlier episode seems reliable, since it must have been the matter of common knowledge.

It appears that Josephus's style of governance was resented by several groups in the city: the radical faction of Jesus b. Sapphias, the supporters of John b. Levi and – later on – of the Jerusalem delegation (which may or may not have been the same people) and, last but not least, the resilient royalists. It is not surprising then that despite his initial attempt to establish control over it at the outset (ibid, 64 ff.), and his complex maneuvers *vis-à-vis* his various opponents, Tiberias twice rose against him. On each occasion Josephus could, in his own words, barely escape with his life (ibid, 87 ff., 94 ff.; 271 ff., 299 ff.; cf. *BJ*, 2, 614 ff.). Nonetheless, his assertion (*Vita*, 82) that he captured it four times by storm is not supported by his narrative, which speaks of only two restorations of his authority over Tiberias, neither time implying any such takeover: first, after the failure of the royalist coup at that city, which he had reportedly quelled with the above-mentioned ruse (ibid, 165 ff.; *BJ*, 2, 635 ff.); and, second, upon its declaration for John b. Levi and the delegates – again through the use of deceit (*Vita*, 327 ff.). The divisions among the Tiberians seem to have persisted until the very end. By the time of Vespasian's approach, the dominant radical party and its leader Jesus b. Sapphias made a show of resistance, but were soon compelled to withdraw from the city. Meanwhile, the collaborationists succeeded in obtaining what is portrayed in the *Bellum* as a general pardon from the Roman general, with the result that upon its surrender it was not pillaged (3, 455 ff.).[11]

As is often his practice elsewhere, in his treatment of the Galilaean campaign Josephus de-emphasizes the religious factor. This makes it difficult to ascertain the role of religious dissenters, if any, in the events he describes. Still, on three occasions the material he offers, largely concerning the region of Tiberias, allows us to consider such possibility – or, at the very least, it may betray attempts at exploitation of these particular sentiments by individuals or groups. One episode pertains to the destruction of Herod Antipas's palace in Tiberias on the pretext of animal representations decorating the building (*Vita*, 65 ff.). Josephus's insistence that he was instructed to proceed thus by the popular assembly at Jerusalem (65) sounds suspect: the issue was minor and would have hardly counted much among the immediate revolutionary agenda. Furthermore, despite some resentment of the Jewish purists (cf. *AJ*, 19, 65), these images were left untouched for the duration of decades (tellingly, King Agrippa I, often sensitive to religiosity of his subjects, did not bother to remove them) and must have become a customary feature of the cityscape. It seems more likely, therefore, that the idea of doing away with them came from Josephus's personal initiative and his wish to demonstrate *zeal* – which, as we know, belongs among major characteristics of religious dissent – and thereby cater to the expectations of the groups or masses appreciative of any such attitude. We learn, however, that the action planned by Josephus was pre-empted by the radical party under Jesus b. Sapphias, and the palace was not only set on fire, but also plundered (*Vita*, 66 f.). Again, the historian's imputation of pillage as the sole motive for burning down the building

(66) may conceal some display of religious fervor: after all, the tetrarch's palace symbolized one man's rule, the notion hateful to the practitioners of the "fourth philosophy", with their slogan "No lord but God."

Another affair, which seems to have caused Josephus substantial trouble, evolved over the issue of forced circumcision. This time, he must have acted according to a view of his reputation as 'moderate' rather than radical. We are told of two gentile dignitaries from Trachonitis, the area under royal administration, who arrived as refugees to Josephus's headquarters at Tarichaeae, with the reason for their desertion of the Roman cause unexplained (*Vita*, 112 ff.). It appears that they were repeatedly pressured by the 'Galilaeans' to undergo circumcision and thus formally convert to Judaism (113, cf. 149) so that they would live "in accordance with the customs of those, among whom they sought safety" (149). One remembers a similar demand reportedly imposed by the religious dissenters who massacred the Roman garrison in Jerusalem on its surviving commander Metilius (*BJ*, 2, 454). Josephus insists that, in this case, it was prevented because of his protests to the effect that it was everyone's choice to worship God as one pleases, but not under duress, and that the newcomers' trust in Jewish hospitality should not be abused (*Vita*, 113). Later on, it transpires that despite his efforts at pacification, popular outcry against those aliens, prodded further by the charge of sorcery, continued to mount, and even their lives came to be threatened (149 ff.). We read that Josephus felt secretly obliged to smuggle them back into the territory controlled by the king, where they received pardon from the latter (152 ff.)

Lastly, if Josephus is to be trusted, a religious issue was employed by his opponents for the purpose of trapping him at one point during the deliberations in Tiberias. Reportedly, one Ananias ("a villain and evildoer" – 290), member of the Jerusalem delegation, proposed a public fast to be held and attended by the worshippers unarmed, thus "making it clear before God that, without divine aid, they thought no weapon was useful" (ibid). According to traditional practice in Judaism, fasting was required only once a year, on the day of Yom Kippur (*Lev.* 23: 26 ff.; cf. *AJ*, 3, 240 ff.). It could, however, sometimes be invoked as a voluntary move under emergency, and this is what Ananias and his associates had in mind. Predictably, Josephus denies his foes any pious motives (ibid), which may or may have not been the case, but as an ostensible exercise of zeal it was certain to attract the sympathies of those taken by, or bordering on religious dissent, with their emphasis on the exceptional, and even excessive acts of devotion. Josephus, on the other hand, admits that he complied with this motion, albeit recognizing the intent to catch him defenseless, for fear of looking impious (291) – but still taking precaution against the possible assault on his person (293), which, as we are made to believe, ultimately saved his life (302 f).[12]

The reasons and motives behind the polemics between Josephus and Justus of Tiberias remain elusive. Justus b. Pistus apparently belonged among that city's distinguished residents. Josephus grudgingly recognizes that he "was not incompetent as regards Greek education" (*Vita*, 40), which must have been common enough within the semi-Hellenized royalist camp. On the other hand, and almost by definition, this would have made him impervious to the irrational tenets of religious dissent. From Josephus's biased account it is difficult to understand what exactly happened to Justus in the course of the revolt: nonetheless, it appears that at some point he chose to leave Tiberias and join the king at Berytus (390 ff.; cf. 357). Several times throughout the *Vita* Josephus contends that Vespasian intended Justus's execution on the grounds of complaints by the gentiles about his raids on Syria's territory earlier in the revolt (343, 355, 410), and handed him for that purpose to King Agrippa; but the latter only imprisoned him and, upon his release, even appointed him his secretary *ab epistulis* (356). We are further told that Queen Berenice kept intervening on Justus's behalf (355, cf. 343), which did not, however, prevent his eventual disgrace for some unexplained misconduct (357). This sequence of statements is very obscure, confused and suspect: it lacks specifics and seems less than coherent, providing no firm data for even cautious speculation. Consequently, it is better to have it left on Josephus's conscience.

We know that the ninth-century Byzantine Patriarch Photius read some historiographical text of Justus of Tiberias and summarized it briefly in his famous *Bibliotheca* (33 = *FGrH* 734). The Patriarch was not impressed: "He has a very succinct style and skips over the majority of most important events." From Photius's sketchy notes much remains unclear and subject to debate, including the number and titles of works, presumably written by Justus, their scope, and their relation to the Jewish revolt. In any event, his attack on Josephus was published, the latter tells us, 20 years after the suppression of the great uprising (*Vita*, 360). Josephus's own *Bellum* does not mention Justus at all, so at least in that respect it could not have given him any cause for offence. Their political and personal quarrels in the course of the war might have supplied the Tiberian with the inspiration for his attack; but if so it remains unclear why he chose to wait for so long. An attractive modern suggestion links this to the attempt by his city at regaining its former prominent stature in the region. This would have necessarily involved exculpating Tiberias of any active part in the insurrection. Hence what seems to have been the thrust of Justus's attack: the claim, irrespective of what we may think about its veracity, that it was Josephus and his Galilaeans who had instigated sedition at Tiberias in the first place (340). It is not surprising that in his polemical apology Josephus repays him in kind (36 ff., 341 ff.). I believe the issue is complicated enough not to be simplistically judged one way or the other.

Both Josephus and Justus insist that, despite their revolutionary activities, they in truth remained royalist and pro-Roman. Any such claim can be easily dismissed as a post-factum attempt at self-justification; but the closer scrutiny of the facts makes one pause. At the same time, I am not persuaded by a certain tendency in scholarship, altogether exculpating Justus of the insurrection charges on the grounds that his role in the raids against Decapolis at the early stage of the revolt (which constitutes a historical fact – cf. *Vita*, 42, 341 f., 410) did not mean any conscious involvement in the war with the Romans: by invading the territory under the jurisdiction of Syria's governor (even if this was done in retaliation for the Jewish pogroms in the area), he had clearly violated the *pax Romana* and must have been well aware of that. This accounts for Vespasian's initial verdict sentencing him to death (343, 355, 410), which could have hardly been invented by Josephus. On the other hand, King Agrippa's choice to rescue him from execution (ibid) suggests that in the course of the war Justus had rendered the royal cause some form of service, for which in the end he was granted – as eventually was Josephus – pardon and promotion.

In terms of apology *vis-à-vis* the Romans, Josephus's own predicament, owing to the scale of his operations in Galilee, was considerably harder. As we remember, he wrote in the *Vita* that, at the very outset (before Beth-horon), he made every effort to prevent the revolt by persuasion (17 ff.), and finally desisted only from fear for his life. Similarly, he insists that the members of the Jewish establishment to which he belonged only pretended to have sided with the militant masses for the same reason:

> There was considerable fear among us, when we saw the populace in arms and we were at a loss regarding what to do, since we were unable to restrain the revolutionaries. Having found ourselves in obvious danger, we said that we were in agreement with their ideas, but advised them to stay as they were and allow the enemy to withdraw so that we might be believed to have risen only for the sake of a just cause.
>
> (22)

In fact, they were secretly waiting for the Romans to bring relief (23). All of this could be (and often is) disregarded as self-serving, but one should consider some factual evidence for the historian's argument about the 'double game', which the circumstances had forced on him (and, by extension, on others of his ilk).

Apart from the unsubstantiated protestations to that effect (e.g. *Vita*, 175 ff.), two instances in particular are to be briefly examined. We learn, first, of Josephus returning to the rightful owner – who was in one version the royal procurator Ptolemy (*BJ*, 2, 595), and in another his wife (*Vita*, 126) – the loot seized, in the manner of brigandage, by some "daring young men" (ibid) from the village Dabaritta. The leakage of this information enflamed even his hitherto Galilaean supporters to the extent that he was charged, at his own headquarters at Tarichaeae, with treasonous behavior. His Tiberian opponent Jesus b. Sapphias, whom we had already heard of, this time characterized in the *Vita* as "by nature prone to disrupt important matters and, like no one else, a sedition maker and revolutionist", acted as the accuser (134; cf. *BJ*, 2, 599). The text says that this man:

> ... holding the copy of Moses's laws in his hands and stepping into the center, said: "Citizens, if you cannot hate Josephus for your own reasons, then observe your ancestral laws, which our foremost general

plans to betray. For their sake, hate the evil and punish the man who dared such acts."

(134 f.)

Although it remains somewhat unclear how exactly Josephus's handling of the situation pertained to the violation of the Mosaic code, this rare acknowledgement of a directly religious attack on him is noteworthy even if – as the narrative implies – this could be a mere display of demagoguery. According to the historian, his very life was twice endangered at Tarichaeae during this turmoil, and his salvation ultimately was owing (as in other cases) to his own quick wit (132 ff.; *BJ*, 2, 597 ff.). This may or may not have been so. But what seems significant is that the Dabaritta affair is narrated not only in the *Vita*, but also in the *Bellum* – the work read and approved by several participants in the hostilities, King Agrippa among them. This suggests that Josephus's story about his restoration of the plundered loot, as a gesture of good will, must reflect some historical truth.

Another case relates to Josephus's dealings with one Crispus, the king's trusted servant and intermediary in the clandestine negotiations with the collaborationist group among the Tiberians. This man had been seized by the revolutionary Galilaeans at the time of the second attempt on the part of Tiberias to desert their cause, but Josephus, then staying at Asochis, arranged personally and in secret for his escape (*Vita*, 382 f., 388 f.). This cannot be dismissed as another piece of apologetic fiction, since Justus b. Pistus is also said to have employed the same services as Crispus as a go-between in his effort to obtain a safe-conduct for his own projected flight from the city into the Herodian camp (393). Much of the *Vita* is written to refute Justus, and it is hardly conceivable that this particular episode, which he must have been intimately familiar with, was invented.

In the final analysis, Justus and Josephus represent – in some respects – mirror images of each other. Both were the upper-class *bona fide* Jews, who received a degree of Greek education and dabbled in local politics, being naturally inclined towards collaborationism and the preservation of the status quo. Both were lured, for whatever reasons, into joining the revolution (one to the lesser, another to the greater extent), while at the same time they harbored doubts about the wisdom of that course. Both sought to exculpate themselves vis-à-vis the Romans by protesting their implicit loyalty and writing the necessarily biased accounts of their activities in Galilee. Each one made a name as a historian. Finally, both managed to ingratiate themselves with the victors and to enter, in Justus's case, the royal and, in Josephus's, the Imperial circle.

The phenomenon of divided loyalties is nothing new. There always exist, especially at times of trouble, individuals feeling torn between two or even more causes or allegiances, which in some instances result in fervent and contradictory activities, and in others may lead to a sort of paralysis. As I have argued elsewhere, for a self-conscious political dissident this requires the practice of dissimulation, while a religious dissenter *par excellence*, owing to his sense of mission ordained by God, is altogether immune to any such experience. Consequently, one must not (though this is often being done) discount Josephus's – or, for that matter, Justus's – claims of their invariable pro-Roman sympathies as simply part and parcel of their apologetic strategies. Furthermore, one should qualify, by the same token, the impression that the majority of the Jewish elite sided with the revolutionaries out of genuine commitment to their nationalist or religious agenda. In reality, at any time of political upheaval (and apart from the few intransigents) individual behavior, as the examples of Justus and Josephus illustrate, is by no means always consistent. It is changeable and depends, for the most part, on the whole spectrum of factors or circumstances, from crude self-interest to lofty wishful thinking.[13]

It appears that of all Galilee's cities, which are discussed by Josephus in any detail, Tarichaeae most consistently displayed the anti-Roman and revolutionary stand, although the account in the *Bellum* implies the existence of a loyalist opposition within its walls from the outset (3,492 ff.). This enthusiasm mirrors that of the countryside's populace and might have related, even if only in part, to the tensions between local communities of which we know next to nothing. It seems that for the entire duration of Josephus's campaign in Galilee, he succeeded in holding this city under his own authority and even managed to survive the potentially dangerous repercussions of the Dabaritta affair. Given the recurrent protestations of his latent pro-Romanism, this apparent support of him by the arguably most radical groupings in the area constitutes a major paradox in the *Vita*'s narrative. In any event, whether or not we give credit to Josephus as regards some political dissension in Tarichaeae (loc. cit.), its residents persisted in their insurrection against Rome until Titus captured the city. This happened not without substantial effort on the latter's part because of the resistance shown by the rebels under Jesus b. Sapphias of Tiberias (*BJ*, 3, 462 ff.). Although Vespasian had originally released the revolutionary defenders of Tarichaeae (most of them fugitives from elsewhere, according to Josephus), he subsequently broke his own promise of safe conduct and attacked them on their way out, killing some and enslaving most (537 ff.): a typical Roman treachery, one may say, unless one also recalls the massacre of the Roman garrison in Jerusalem by the insurgents at the outbreak of the hostilities, likewise performed in violation of the sacred pledge.

Altogether, the record makes very clear the range of uneven attitudes across Galilee towards Rome and the revolt. This was by no means a spontaneous national uprising of the popular imagination. For that matter, we are informed that even John b. Levi of Gischala, Josephus's arch-enemy and the future revolutionary protagonist, earnestly sought at first to suppress the agitation in his native city: "seeing that some citizens were intent on secession from Rome, he tried to hold them back and urged them to observe their loyalty" (*Vita*, 43). (This information is very telling, given the fact that in the *Bellum* Gischala's secession is squarely blamed on John's own thirst for power – 4, 85). But his initially loyalist policies failed, according to the *Vita*, because of the attack on Gischala, mustered by its gentile neighbors, with the result that the city was burned and razed to the ground (44). It is said that John, "angered at this", mounted and led the Jewish retaliation, having upon his return fortified the walls of his native place (45). This development must have prompted him to embark upon the career as revolutionist – in sharp contrast with Justus b. Pistus of Tiberias, who found himself, at the early stage of the hostilities, under not dissimilar circumstances, but ultimately chose to associate with the collaborators. Following Gischala's capture by the Romans, John b. Levi and his cohorts fled to Jerusalem (*BJ*, 4, 106 ff.). This eventually brought about the major turn in his own fortunes as well as in the revolution over which he sought to preside.

The last of Josephus's relatively detailed accounts of urban revolts deals with the events at Gamala (*Vita*, 46 ff., 58 ff.,177 ff., 185 ff.), the city outside Galilee, and under formal jurisdiction of the king (*BJ*, 4, 2). The narrative is again confused, although it relates to the vicissitudes of an already familiar figure, Philip b. Jacimus, as well as the family of Justus b. Pistus. It has been seen that the residents of Gamala had supported Philip b. Jacimus against the usurper Varus/Noarus (59 ff.). The *Vita* claims that the former had consequently secured that fortress, with the adjacent countryside, for the Romans (61), which does not square well with the implication in the *Bellum* that Gamala staunchly resisted surrendering to the loyalist forces (4, 4). Still, one may accept the reliability of the *Vita* in a sense that, at least for a brief time, Philip succeeded in keeping the affairs under control; but the situation obviously continued deteriorating. This accounts for Agrippa's preventive measures: upon their encounter at Berytus, we are told, he ordered Philip to evacuate the royal household from Gamala and resettle the "Babylonian Jews", who had earlier found refuge there, back at Batanea (*Vita*, 184). The revolt broke out shortly after, under the leadership of one Joseph, the historian namesake, supported, as the text says, by "many audacious young" (recklessness of the youth being one of the Josephan favorite motifs) and followed with an inevitable bloodshed: "they coerced some, and others, who disagreed with their views, put to death" (185). It seems that (at some point) the relatives of both Justus and Philip fell prey, which may in part explain why Josephus chose to devote so much space to the latter. We are also told that the rebels approached Josephus in writing to request reinforcements and help in fortifying their city's walls, and that he, in his capacity as revolutionary general, provided for both (186; cf. *BJ*, 2, 574; 4, 9).

Gamala did survive the onslaught of the royal troops for the duration of seven months (*BJ*, 4, 10), and Josephus's lengthy description of its ultimate seizure by Vespasian, which cost the latter considerable loss in effort and manpower (11–53; 63–83), makes one of the dramatic points in his entire narrative. The defenders refused to negotiate (14), relied on divine interference (26) and stood their ground till the very end. Their courage is emphasized, and likewise is their penchant for self-immolation (79 ff.), reportedly committed by many: these are attitudes often signifying psychology of religious dissent. The text says that the entire population was massacred by the conquerors, except two nieces of Philip b. Jacimus, who went into hiding and thus stayed alive (81 f.).[14]

The siege and fall of Jotapata, as narrated in the *Bellum* – a dramatic coda for Josephus's Galilaean campaign – perhaps provide for a surer glimpse into the operation of religious dissent. But before turning to that material, it seems in order to take a brief note of the historian's report on the developments at Samaria (*BJ*, 3, 307 ff.). We have seen that throughout the Roman period, the Samaritans hitherto never rose up against the occupier, despite a few disturbances, and maintained a consistently hostile attitude towards Jews. The evidence suggests their involvement with the Roman authorities on two occasions: the one under Pontius Pilate, in the context of religious agitation, caused by the unnamed Messianic or quasi-Messianic figure, which *may* imply some sort of religious dissent, but our knowledge is insufficient to judge; the second, under Ventidius Cumanus, resulting from the Jewish–Samaritan conflict over the murder of Jewish pilgrims. Although in this second case Claudius had ultimately pronounced in favor of the Jews, it does not seem that Samaria consequently suffered any substantial negative repercussions. In any event, this happened two decades prior to the outbreak of the Jewish war, and in the interval the Samaritans appear to have enjoyed comfortable relations with Rome, as they traditionally used to. This is why their subsequent behavior looks surprising: Josephus claims that, though militarily very weak, they nonetheless "were keen on making trouble" (*BJ*, 3, 308). His language is somewhat ambiguous; but if the gist of what he says was correct, it meant that the Samaritans abandoned suddenly, and for unstated motives, their hereditary feud with the Jews and proceeded to fight the Imperial power, the patronage of which they had enjoyed for decades. The alternative view – namely, that Josephus's account is willfully misleading, that no sedition was contemplated at Samaria, and that Vespasian ordered its residents be massacred merely as a preventive measure – cannot hold: a prudent general like him would not have acted in such a manner against the traditionally loyal subjects, unless he was aware of serious reasons to do so. On the other hand, the whole episode may be plausibly explained, I believe, by the wave of religious dissent (in whatever form) and the resultant public hysteria, infecting the minds of the Samaritans with the hope of divine intervention and enabling them to overcome the vastly superior enemy. Without further evidence, however, this should remain speculative. Nevertheless, we read that after a short siege Mount Garizim was taken by the Roman force under Sextus Cerialis in July A.D. 67 and its 11,600 defenders put to the sword (315).

The story of Jotapata (3, 150 ff; 316 ff.) belongs among the *Bellum*'s narrative peaks. But even when it is stripped of all rhetorical embellishments and reduced to the matter of public knowledge, one must recognize that, having taken command of the small fortress during its heroic 47 day siege, Josephus came to demonstrate considerable generalship, perhaps better than any other revolutionary leader. That he did not invent, or even much exaggerate, his own exploits is also supported by the Imperial imprimatur, which would have otherwise been inconceivable, given both Vespasian's and Titus's presence on the scene. Josephus's descriptions, however, of the goings on *within* Jotapata's walls cannot be properly ascertained since they were owing, at least in part, to his strategies of self-interest. For our purposes, two moments regarding the siege and its aftermath are of particular interest: the determination of the survivors to commit collective suicide and the historian's claim of having possessed prophetic gifts.

Given Josephus's remarkable ability for survival, the report of his attempt to depart from the city under siege, prevented by the rebels (193 ff.), must be, in substance, historical. Similarly, one cannot doubt the defenders' determination never to surrender, further manifest in the desire of those who managed to stay alive, to kill themselves rather than capitulate. Such extreme disregard of their lives and the waste, senseless in the eyes of not only an impartial witness, but also as regards a rational participant, characterizes the religious dissent mentality. It informs the harangue that Josephus had allegedly addressed the audience of 40 fellow insurgents (362 ff.), hiding in the cave upon Jotapata's fall, and bent on self-destruction. That any such performance could have hardly happened in reality, and the obviously fictional origin of that speech, are not relevant: what matters is that the argument it contains must have made sense to Josephus's Jewish readership, fully aware of the difference between what may be called 'normative' (or 'common') Judaism, and the attitudes of the sectarian dissenters. Even though the historian's usual practice is to minimize the significance of religious issues within the revolt context, his apologetic agenda, requiring both explanation and exculpation, forced him to emphasize 'psycho-theological' aspects of the ordeal visited upon him at that point in his turbulent career.

Josephus's argument against suicide (362 ff.) implied a double frame of references, blending the Judaic tradition and some tenets of Greek philosophies. His contention that 'dying in war' is honorable when one dies not by taking his own life, but being killed by the enemy (363) finds support in the Old Testament, with Samson as a primary example, whose choice of death was worthy of praise since it involved a massive destruction of Jewish foes. This concurs with Josephus's approval of dying in struggle for liberty, provided "that one dies fighting, and at the hands of those who rob us of freedom" (365) – and with the patterns of Jewish martyrdom, from the Maccabean time onwards (cf. *2 Macc.*, 6–7).

What follows is a theological rather than moral point, familiar from both rabbinic and patristic commentaries: suicide is unnatural and an offence to God:

> There is no animal that dies intentionally or by its own agency: in all the law of nature holds strong, the wish to live / ... / And do not you think that God is outraged when man abuses his gift? It is from him that we received [the right] to exist, and to him we must give back [the right to decide] that we exist no longer.
>
> (370 f.; cf. 369, 379)

Within the perishable mortal bodies, the text adds, is concealed the "portion of God", our soul that lives forever (372) – a view which was shared, according to Josephus, by both the Pharisees (*BJ*, 2, 163) and the Essenes (ibid, 154 ff.) and, as he surely knew, by the philosophers of Greece. This must have been intended to exploit the interest of the *Bellum*'s gentile readers. Conscious that Stoicism, popular at the time, did approve of suicide as the escape from life's hardships, Josephus circumvents the problem by resorting to the Platonist vocabulary of metempsychosis:

> Do not you know that those who exit life according to the laws of nature and pay in full the debt they had been given, whenever the giver wishes to collect it, will gain the eternal glory / ... / their souls, remaining pure and obedient, will share the holiest place in heaven, from which, through the revolution of the eons, they will return and again inhabit chaste bodies?
>
> (*BJ*, 3, 374)

In contrast, the suicides are doomed to "the darkest underworld", and "God, their father, will take vengeance on their posterity for the acts of hubris by their parents" (375). The notion of the descendants' hereditary responsibility for sins committed by their ancestors is, of course, un-Greek (unless the latter had committed some particularly heinous crime, which involved a divine curse), though this is one of the leitmotifs in the Hebrew Bible. Conversely, the Platonic belief in the transmigration of the souls (rather than the bodily resurrection), although Josephus appears to associate it with the Pharisees (*BJ*, 2, 163), was basically foreign to traditional Judaism. It finds little or no support in the Old Testament and scarcely figures in the rabbinic writings, but it seems to have acquired, throughout the Second Temple period, a degree of notice in both Judaea and the Diaspora, as is evidenced in some texts by Philo. In other words, Josephus cunningly blends Jewish and Greek attitudes, which is characteristic of his procedures in rhetorical philosophizing and psychologizing. (Another prominent example is his treatment of the massacre at Masada.) On the other hand, Jewish and gentile views on suicide are next explicitly compared and found similar: we are told that the wisest legislators – presumably, on both sides – punish it as the crime "against God" (3, 375). The subsequent mention of the allegedly Jewish custom to leave a suicide's corpse unburied until sunset (376) is, however, a puzzle, since anything of the sort is absent in the Torah. Still, Josephus could have hardly invented this, given his concern with the Jewish audience in the Diaspora that was bound to include learned scholars. I think it not implausible that some such *halakha* may well have existed early enough within the oral tradition, and eventually found its way, in modified form, into the rabbinic material.

In the contexts of his moral and theological arguments, Josephus's attempts at pragmatic reasoning sound lame and conceited, such as: slavery should not be feared, since at the moment freedom does not really exist (367); or that he wants the Romans ultimately to kill him upon his surrender and thus downgrade their own victory (382) – this last exemplifies the abuse of rhetoric close to absurd. Be that as it may, this entire discourse, fictional as under the circumstances it must have been, puts into sharp relief – one is almost tempted to say 'apophatically' – the mental and emotional operation of religious dissent.[15]

Josephus makes it no secret that his ultimate surrender had been negotiated with the Romans: furthermore, he speaks of the whole affair in a manner that is remarkably frank. This means that he had grounds to believe that his life might be spared. Not surprisingly, the fact of his survival created a major scandal in Jerusalem (*BJ*, 3, 438 ff.). We cannot know, of course, what had actually taken place in the famous cave – that is, whether Josephus happened to benefit from an extraordinary coincidence ("is it to be called luck or God's providence?", as he puts it; 391), or whether this was the result, on his part, of some clever mathematical trick. If the latter had been the case, he was a sort of genius. His companions killed each other, while he succeeded in persuading the only other survivor to surrender. The latter might have known a thing or two we would also wish, but never will: it seems likely that the Romans simply had him crucified. Be that as it may, two unspoken points call for attention: that the occupants of the cave (similarly to their eventual imitators at Masada) did not entertain an option to follow Samson's precedent – namely, by rushing out and perishing – but dragged with them into death as many enemies as they could; and that their chosen method of taking one another's life by drawing lots technically amounted not to suicide, but murder. In a strict sense, these were Jews murdering other Jews, which is in clear disagreement with the spirit and the ethno-centric tenets of Judaism.

Even more significant than his next-to-miraculous survival in the cave is arguably the best-known episode of Josephus's career: his prediction to a Roman general of modest social extraction that he will become emperor. The narrative of the *Bellum* carefully prepares the reader for appreciating this extraordinary feat. We are told that even prior to the siege of Jotapata, Josephus came to fear for the outcome of the war (3, 131); but he claims that it was during his time of anguish in the cave when this recognition reached in him a higher, one may call it theological, plane:

> He recalled the dreams through the night by which God foretold to him the events regarding the Jews and Roman monarchs, which were going to occur. He was competent in interpreting the dreams and what God utters in ambiguous manner; and he was not ignorant of the prophecies from the sacred books, being himself a priest, and of priestly descent. Inspired at that hour, and in convulsions at the awful images of his recent dreams, he addressed God in a secret prayer, saying: "Since it pleases you, who had founded it, to destroy the nation of the Jews, and since all fortune has gone over to the Romans, and since you have chosen my spirit to announce the things to come, I give myself up willingly into the hands of the Romans to live, but I call you to witness that I will go not as a traitor, but as your minister."
>
> (351 ff.)

It must be pointed out that, despite the objections of some modern scholars, this makes sense in psychological terms. One may describe the 'conversion mechanism' as a leap from one 'biographical narrative' into another as the result of the 'border situation' (as it used to be called by the existentialists) the subject finds himself or herself in, fraught with exceptional physical or psychological torment. This helps to explain what must have happened to Josephus in the cave. His profound religious faith cannot be doubted. The instinctive belief in dreams was common in the Graeco-Roman world – witness, for instance, Artemidorus's *Oneirocritica* and the *Orationes Sacrae* of Aelius Aristides. Within Judaism, it found support in the Old Testament and numerous pseudo-epigrapha. Add to this the extraordinary anxiety that must have been his permanent emotional state while in the cave: it is known that our daytime concentration on a particular set of thoughts and hopes may result in their re-emergence at night in the dream imagery. All in all, here we are dealing, I believe, with the effects of self-persuasion and, in this sense, an authentic psychological experience. It allowed the future historian to preserve moral integrity upon his abandoning the rebel cause at the moment of a double jeopardy and of the resentment against him in both camps: by the Jews, who predictably considered him a traitor, and by the Romans, angry at the protracted siege of Jotapata he was felt to have been responsible for (cf.: "having escaped the war with the Romans and his own kin ... "; 392). Thus, the belief in, or remembrance of, some nightly visions, coupled with psychological processes known as 'defense mechanisms', worked to mediate between unbearable inner tensions, which might have otherwise brought about his total mental and emotional collapse. And if so, Josephus's subsequent behavior should be interpreted not in terms of calculated gamble, or particularly clever dissimulation, but just as he says – acting on behalf of God and the world.

It is true that in contrast with the material on the value of dreams in Aelius Aristides or Artemidorus, which largely pertains to the aspects of daily routine, Josephus interprets his oneiric experience on a grand scale, relating it to the fates of Israel and the human race. This was bound to have invited a comparison with biblical personages, further fortifying his sense of self-importance and the will to survive: not only with his namesake, the dreamer from the book of Genesis, or another famous dream reader Daniel, but more pointedly with the prophet Jeremiah. In this last case, the parallel, even objectively, makes some sense: in each event, a prominent individual is called by God to deliver dire tidings, obeys the summons, but is disbelieved, mistreated and ultimately rejected by his own people, suffers hardships, finds his predictions fulfilled and earns the respect and decent treatment from the enemy. At this point, Josephus does not compare himself directly to Jeremiah (as he does later on; *BJ*, 392 f.), but no literate Jewish reader would fail to appreciate the resemblance. In a similar manner, although perhaps less compellingly, the historian's portrayal of his clever generalship earlier in the *Bellum* (and even more so in the *Vita*) might have made his gentile audience evoke in their minds the familiar image of Odysseus, man "of many tricks and turns". From the modern reader's perspective, Josephus had succeeded in (whether or to what extent consciously we do not know) representing himself against the background of the Galilaean warfare as an individual who possessed both charisma and the capacity for dissimulation, which – so long as he managed to outmaneuver his rivals – must have been, at least in part, true.

His implicit posture as Jeremiah Redivivus, however, could also work to Josephus's disadvantage, for we read that, unlike him, the great prophet did not turn collaborator or follow the conqueror in Babylon (cf. *Jer.*, 39: 14; 40: 5 ff.). The historian might have thought that his subsequent efforts at peacemaking justified his choice and will ultimately compensate for his course of action in the eyes of those who mattered.

A closer scrutiny of Josephus's text clarifies the twofold origin of what he claims to have been his predictive inspiration: the direct message from God conveyed in dreams (plural, visiting him in recent past), and his skill for interpreting the obscure passages from the Scripture. How these two components ultimately interacted remains uncertain. The immediate heavenly communication through dreams may have been concerned, as often happens in the Bible, with the divine anger at his people for sins they had committed, which made God abandon the revolutionary cause and side with the Romans. This is, of course, Josephus's chief contention, both historical and theological, running through the entire *Bellum*. It should be stated that, on its own terms, and within the perspective of the Old Testament historiography, the argument is cogent and must have been found sensible by at least a part of his Jewish audience. Indeed, the abuse of the Law, crimes and acts of sacrilege, performed by the last Hasmoneans, Herodians, corrupt high priests and, last but not least, the insurgents are meticulously listed across the narrative, with an emphasis on the recurring defilement of the sanctuary by bloodshed, the Temple being for Josephus, a priest, the subject of particular concern. The inevitable inference is that all of this must have sorely tried God's patience and then provoked his retribution in the same form as at the time of Jeremiah: the second Temple was to perish, as did the first, with Israel's subsequent oppression by the conqueror and Vespasian in the role of the Babylonian Nebuchadnezzar.

The reference to scriptural interpretation, on the other hand, seems to have signified the 'Messianic' passages in the Hebrew Bible (for example, *Isa.*, 9:7) and thus pertained to Josephus's specific foretelling of Vespasian's Imperial accession. He claims to have told the Roman general upon their personal encounter in no uncertain terms:

> You suppose, Vespasian, that in Josephus you have got a mere captive, but I come to you as a messenger of greater things / ... / You will be Caesar, Vespasian, and Emperor, you and this son of yours. Put me now in even more secure chains and keep watch for yourself over me: since you, Caesar, are master not only of me, but of land, and sea, and the

entire human race, and I ask for custody more severe as punishment if I misuse the name of God.

(*BJ*, 3, 400 ff.)

As we know, this was one of those rare occurrences when a prophecy proved correct.

Sources other than Josephus also attest to the belief (apparently misreading and distorting the tenets of Jewish Messianism), spread wide throughout the Roman Near East, in a powerful ruler to emerge from Judaea (Tac. *Hist.*, 5, 13; cf. 1, 10; Suet., *Div. Vesp.*, 4; cf. *Or. Sib.*, 3, 652 ff.). The bitter irony, unintended and (presumably) unnoticed by Josephus transpires, however, in the fact that he came to construe some visionary passages about the leader, who will deliver Israel from all sorrows, as meaning the elevation of Israel's enemy and conqueror, which strikes one as quite an extraordinary exegetical twist.

Even if one allows that Josephus's gesture towards Vespasian contained an element of pragmatic calculation, in political terms any such gamble was bound to be exceedingly risky. It is true that by predicting his Roman captor the Imperial purple he could delay being dispatched, as the custom required, to Nero, who would have most likely put him to death. On the other hand, the very fact of that announcement, with the current emperor still in power, constituted treason, the *crimen maiestatis*, and could have caused the self-styled prophet his head, if any of his listeners, for whatever reason, played a *delator* – as well as potential trouble to all who were present. Finally, if Vespasian is suddenly recalled and executed (as happened, for instance, around this time to the great general Domitius Corbulo), or dies while still in command, the author of the prediction would not only have lost his life but also been ridiculed and abused as a charlatan.

The recent scholarship has challenged the traditional view that in the post-exilic time the phenomenon of prophecy ceased to exist. It undoubtedly continued, but in a sense quite different from its descriptions in the Old Testament – a complex matter which cannot be discussed in detail within the confines of this book. It is sufficient to point out that during our period we do not see any more grand figures of the recognized authority addressing the public on moral and religious issues, sharply criticizing those in power and/or, in virtue of their direct communication with God, predicting the future events on a national scale. This kind of activity was largely reduced to those on the fringes of society or within sectarian groups, such as the Essenes, who can by no means be considered part of the religious establishment, or even part of 'common' (or 'normative') Judaism. The priestly elite clearly disapproved of the 'prophetic' activities of single individuals, who were continuously harassed by the Jewish as well as Roman authorities. Nor is there evidence that they were appreciated by the mainstream Phariseism. Even the missions of such powerfully charismatic individuals as John the Baptist and Jesus of Nazareth seem to have affected a relatively small following. It is not an accident that numerous pseudo-apocryphal texts containing prophetic passages, and written throughout the Second Temple period, are invariably ascribed to biblical characters. In consequence, the claims of prophetic powers came to characterize not so much the Jewish faith *per se*, but rather the carriers and promoters of religious dissent as understood in this book.

Against this background, Josephus's status, with his forecasts about "the Jews and Roman monarchs" (*BJ*, 3, 351) delivered, appears nothing but paradoxical: a hereditary priest, and in his own words a Pharisee (*Vita*, 1 f.), he himself thus emerges as a religious dissenter in a double sense: *vis-à-vis* the establishment, to which he belonged, by assuming a dubious (in their eyes) role of the quasi-biblical prophet; and *vis-à-vis* the revolutionary movement he had joined, fraught as it was with eschatological optimism, by playing the prophet of doom. As regards this last point, he compares, which is ironic, with the man in every other respect his opposite – the peasant and street preacher Jesus b. Ananias.[16]

IV.

It must be recognized that the material on Josephus's Galilaean campaign (other than the siege of Jerusalem by Titus and a few isolated episodes, such as Masada, a major block of information we possess about the Great Revolt) defies the popular picture of it as the whole nation's unanimous and universal rise against the foreign conqueror, which is largely the product of wishful thinking and literary imagination. In fact, any such thing rarely, if ever, happens in history, whether at the time of revolution, struggle for national liberation and even defensive warfare. Due to the propensities of human nature, various groups and individuals tend, more often than one would expect, to be motivated egotistically by their conflicting (and shifting) interests, such as survival, safety, ambition, power and gain, rather than by the common cause – even when they are supposed to be acting for the sake of patriotism or religious solidarity. All history would otherwise have looked differently, with offensive wars either invariably lost, or ending in a total physical destruction (Assyrian style) of the defeated.

This point also applies to the Jewish War. In Galilee, the rivalry of the revolutionary leaders – Josephus, John b. Levi of Ghischala, Justus of Tiberias, Jesus b. Sapphias and others – made impossible any concerted effort directed at the Romans, who suffered virtually no harm at all. (As will be seen, the same trouble plagued the rebel policies in Jerusalem under both the 'first' and the 'second' regimes.) Masses of people, who made their following, or competing factions within and without Galilaean cities, were engaged in internal strife, with little regard for the broader consequences, and the populace at large showed little desire to unite against the foreign oppression. The momentum of Beth-horon was irretrievably lost, which not only allowed the enemy to recover, but also provided for the unhindered arrival of an able general, who proceeded to reduce this part of the province with ruthlessness and remarkable speed. The same must be largely true for the rest of the country. The situation in Idumaea will be treated in the next chapter. Episodes of spontaneous popular resistance to

Vespasian's progress certainly occurred throughout the land, but there is no evidence that it was organized in any significant sense. Although Josephus states that each of several generals appointed by the 'first regime' to engage with the Roman foe in toparchies, or districts "pursued their entrusted task with as much energy and intelligence as he possessed" (*BJ*, 2, 569), he does not offer a single detail to support this claim. The only leader of whom we learn acting in the toparchy of Acrobatene, Simon b. Giora, was clearly independent from Jerusalem. Altogether, at this point of the revolt, an informed outside observer could have indeed concluded that from now on it was doomed. The inordinate length of time taken by the subsequent siege of the capital owed more to psychological rather than military factors.

As we have seen, there is no evidence to the effect that any of the major three sects within Judaism took an anti-Roman or pro-Roman stand as a group. Both the radical movements and the collaborationists numbered persons belonging to different sectarian persuasions. Furthermore, to draw the line between them, based on the class principles, will be equally inaccurate: one hears of all sorts of people belonging to various societal strata, who took part in the struggle of liberation or in factional fights, or abstained from either. The same is true as regards sensibilities characteristic of religious dissent – as we had seen, they crossed over social as well as doctrinal boundaries. In the final analysis, this was all a matter of individual choice.

In appearance, religious attitudes of the 'first regime's' leadership, at least, in their outward (that is, public) manifestations were those of conventional piety. Whatever might have been an initial response by some among them to the abolition of the Imperial sacrifices, it seems very rapidly to have ceased being an issue. Their concern with proper observance of the Temple worship must have played some role in their acquiescence, even though at the outset they had clearly felt antagonistic to the zealots' occupation of the sanctuary's grounds. The uneasy truce was the only means to provide for an uninterrupted Temple service that allowed free access for those willing to attend it and signified the continuity of the covenant between Israel and God.

To reiterate: Josephus tries to persuade the reader that, upon taking over the 'provisional government' at the Temple meeting, his fellow aristocrats, whom he calls 'moderates' in their pursuit of the revolutionary agenda, at the same time harbored hopes of achieving some sort of accommodation or 'honorable peace' with the Romans (cf. *BJ*, 2, 651; 4, 320 ff.; cf. *Vita*, 22 f.). This contention seems both logically and politically implausible, and on these grounds it has been increasingly challenged by modern scholars, who saw in it the deceptive strategy of personal apology as well as an attempt to conceal the *en masse* participation of the Jewish élite in the revolt. I have argued earlier in this chapter that the last proposition is untenable; but even if we accept the arguments for Josephus's apologetic purpose, we cannot dismiss a strong impression of a peculiar paralysis suffered by the 'first regime', which cannot be fully explained by the growing tensions, or even a conflict, between the 'moderates' and the radicals.

After all, it stands to reason that precisely by embarking on some meaningful offensive directly against the Roman enemy the tensions and conflict could have been, if not resolved, at least mitigated. By ordering zealots under Eleazar b. Simon to engage with the occupier elsewhere, whether an open field, guerrilla warfare or whatever, the aristocratic leadership would have, first, satisfied their opponents' fervent aspirations; second, made them leave the capital and cease being a threat; and, third, demonstrate energy and vigor *vis-à-vis* both their compatriots and the occupier. Nothing of the sort, however, happened. The Jews largely failed to exploit their first and only victory over their foe, and the resultant disarray within the Roman military command during the prolonged interval between Beth-horon and Vespasian's arrival the following spring. We saw that there has also occurred little, if any, national liberation struggle throughout Galilee; as regards an anti-Roman initiative taken in other regions by the commanders appointed at the Temple meeting (altogether seven individuals – *BJ*, 2, 566 ff.), we do not hear at all. The only operation attempted by the 'coalition' was a failed attack on Ascalon, a Greco-Phoenician city of no immediate importance and, in Josephus's words, "nearly destitute of defenders" (3, 12), and the reasons for it, rather than strategic or tactical, seem to have been traditional animosity and longstanding grievances that had nothing to do with Rome.

Thus the puzzle remains, which bring us back to the matter of 'divided loyalties', which can also be viewed, at least theoretically (empirical evidence being largely absent), from yet another angle. In this regard, two notions must be taken into account. The aristocratic leaders of the 'first regime', given their previously considerable experience in politics and dealings with the Imperial authorities, must have learned and practiced – not unlike their Roman senatorial counterparts – the skills of *dissimulatio* as regards both their Jewish subjects and their Roman masters. They were presumably conscious, in pragmatic terms, of the insurmountable odds faced by the tiny and divisive Judaea confronting Rome's monumental military machine (cf. *BJ*, 2, 357 ff.), supported, as it was, by the entire gentile population of Palaestina. It follows that their reasons for presiding over the revolution, apart from the need to control the masses of which Josephus speaks (*Vita*, 22), would have been some sort of irrational hope, or wishful thinking, they may have been infected with, in one sense or another, by the carriers of religious dissent – the condition further enhanced by the public euphoria that burst out upon the Roman defeat at Beth-horon (cf. ibid, 24): after all, what seems logically implausible often proves compatible psychologically. This potential mixture, however, of dissimulation and wishful thinking strikes us as unhealthy, even though it may help to account for some idiosyncrasies in the picture Josephus paints. The said two patterns of response to reality could invalidate each other. Admittedly, the 'coalition' leadership was bound to realize that by having beaten the enemy in a major battle, the insurgents passed the point of no return, and that Rome was known for not sparing those who challenge its power. This is what Josephus makes the former high priest Joseph b. Gamala rhetorically proclaim in his failed attempt to negotiate with the revolutionary

Idumaeans: "And what may influence us to sell ourselves to the Romans now? For us it was open either not to rebel in the first place – or, having rebelled, make prompt concessions while our surroundings remained unravaged?" (*BJ*, 4, 248). This sounds sensible, but – I repeat – psychology happens to defy logic, and wishful thinking may work both ways: as aspiration for the divinely ordained triumph, or as hope against hope for some sort of compromise with Rome and the latter's subsequent clemency; in both cases it would further contribute to one's emotional and mental confusion.[17]

It is not easy to penetrate behind the rhetoric of 'freedom', 'tyranny' and 'moderation' that pervades Josephus's war narratives, both in his own voice and in the pronouncements he attributes to the leaders of the coalition, and ascertain their desiderata regarding the form of government they might have envisioned in case (however improbable) of their eventual and conclusive victory over the Romans. This question must remain largely unanswered.

In part, the type of rhetoric he employed derives from the historian's own immediate agenda as double apologist, *vis-à-vis* both the Romans and his own people; but in part it might have indeed reflected the public performance of such experienced politicians as Ananus b. Ananus and Jesus b. Gamala. In the latter's exchange with the Idumaean captain Simon b. Cathlas (referred to above) the word 'liberty' and its derivatives are used in the sense of freedom from the Roman yoke. At the same time, both speakers accuse the opposite faction of establishing tyranny, which implies internal suppression of freedom. Not surprisingly, Simon b. Cathlas is made to call such rhetorical display "irony of words" (*BJ*, 4, 279). One is reminded of the Thucydidean caveat (3, 82), that in times of revolution the words acquire different and even contrary sense depending on the particular agenda within the factional context.

Even more patently the double meaning of 'freedom' transpires in a skillful peroration Josephus ascribes to Ananus b. Ananus addressing the inhabitants of the capital on the eve of his decisive showdown with the radicals who took over the Temple (*BJ*, 4, 163–92). In fact, freedom from the zealot tyranny is proclaimed as no less vital than that from the Roman rule: the two 'freedoms' are conceived as virtually inseparable and a prerequisite for the nation's welfare. After ascertaining that the desire of liberty caused the revolt against Rome, the speaker is made to ask a rhetorical question: "If we do not tolerate the masters of the inhabited world, will we be then put up with tyrants who are our own kin?" (178), and then to specify that if subjugation to those from the outside might result from ill fortune or luck, any surrender to domestic villains is a matter of one's character and one's choice (179; cf. 166, 172).

It remains questionable whether this rhetoric of liberty as found in the *Bellum* did, in fact, reflect any genuine feelings or attitudes on the part of aristocrats such as Ananus b. Ananus – especially if liberty is taken in a larger sense more consonant with the meaning of Greek *politeia* or Roman *res publica*. The evidence and common sense suggest that it did not, even though Josephus makes occasional attempts to employ concepts and terms alien to the Jewish tradition for the purpose of conveying to the non-Jewish audience some ideas of what he has in mind. This is not dissimilar (*mutatis mutandis*) from his comparing Jewish sects, such as Pharisees and Essenes, with Greek philosophical schools of Stoics and Pythagoreans (*Vita*, 12; *AJ*, 15, 371), and more often than not such procedure results in misnomer. Jewish literature centuries before and during the Second Temple period did not provide any body of texts on the art of politics or forms of government resembling or comparable to the writings on these subjects by Plato, Aristotle, Cicero or Seneca. The Jewish thought about human condition ran along religious and moral rather than political lines; at times, it burst out into eschatology, which – by its very nature – prevents any meaningful theorizing on conventional politics. Consequently, what mattered was the praxis of the government, and not any speculation on its form or structure; the moral character of a ruler or rulers, their ability (and desire) to observe the Law, and their obedience to God, but not such issues, familiar in the classical world, as the relationship of *civitas* and *dignitas*, and so on. As has been mentioned, the Jewish elite, both priestly and lay, was accustomed to governing their people for extended periods of time, even under foreign occupation, and was not willing or prepared to yield this privilege to any other claimant or group. All of this must be kept in mind when one reads, for instance, Josephus's description of the "famous and noble" (*BJ*, 4, 358) Gorion b. Joseph, executed by the zealots, as "democratic" (ibid). This certainly could not mean that the man entertained sympathy for democracy in a classical sense, or aspirations to introduce it among Jews; the actual meaning of the phrase would connote, most likely, a person notably devoid of social snobbery and exhibiting benevolence towards the common folk.[18]

The historical experience suggests that in the time of a revolutionary turmoil the idea of 'democracy' (in any broad sense) has little, if any at all, relevance to reality. It remains, at best, a slogan, a catchword, a piece of wishful thinking; at worst, it turns into an instrument in the hands of demagogues. In such periods all sorts of conflicts sharpen, and passions run dangerously high. It is usually a time fraught with terror and with a potential for bloody excess, from individual lynching to mass murder, when an orderly process, associated with the notion of democracy (that is to say, the procedures to establish, with any accuracy, the will of the people) becomes impossible. What begin to matter are charisma, eloquence, influence, a power base of single leaders, and their ability to drive masses into a frenzy with the purpose of achieving their own political agenda.

Among the most exasperating features of Josephus as a writer of history is his failure to provide any clear picture of the patterns on which the successive rebel leaderships operated or were structured. From his narrative it is by no means apparent what particular body of citizens was or might have been understood (and by whom) as a source of legitimate authority, or whether there did exist any reliable hierarchy for the transmission of command. It is true that by the very nature of the upheaval, things must have been in flux and, at times, close to anarchy. It also has to be assumed that many arrangements were made *ad hoc*, and the whole situation might have appeared exceedingly blurred even to an inside observer. Much depended on the balance of power between factions and individuals at any given moment. We certainly cannot expect Josephus to play an institutional historian. Still, one would wish him at least to be consistent in the use of institutional terminology, which he is not. He is known to apply different terms to what appears the same body of people, and conversely to call distinct vehicles of power by one and the same name; in addition, he seems often to assign the burden of decision-making to this and that person or group in an arbitrary manner. Some of this might have pertained to his need of handling and presenting such material for the consumption of the foreign audience and/or his inadequate mastery of Greek. Nevertheless, his practice results in a terminological conundrum that can hardly be unraveled. This is particularly regrettable as regards the circumstances of the 'first regime' under Ananus b. Ananus, when Josephus was himself an active participant in the events. On the other hand, the very fact of his activities at the time might have been responsible (especially in the *Vita*) for some deliberate obscurities or confusion on his part, when it could have suited his apologetic intent.

There is no evidence that the leadership of the 'first regime' was elected through the agency of anything that would have resembled a popular assembly in a sense familiar to the Graeco-Roman world. Josephus's account of the Temple meeting (*BJ*, 2, 562 ff.) clearly implies that, convoked as it was after the defeat of Cestius Gallus, it was attended by the victorious rebel leaders and the influential members of the Jerusalem elite whom the former persuaded to join the revolt. Judging by its membership and character, it was not a large gathering of crowds, but rather a relatively small group of individuals, met within the confines of the sanctuary to deliberate so that they would be able to adopt a more or less orderly course of action in decision-making and appointments. It can be easily surmised, or imagined, that at the end of their proceedings, the results, including the names of the appointed, were announced to the masses of people assembled outside of the Temple's walls for the purpose of approval which, under the circumstances, could have hardly taken form other than acclamation by shouts and cheers. It appears, despite Josephus's attempts to suggest the opposite, that the capital's populace retained, for the most part, a passive attitude towards factional strife and policy decisions through the duration of the 'first regime' and even later, perhaps until the very end of the siege. The fighting took place between tightly held bands loyal to a particular cause or leader. Each of them might have enlisted some support from the men on the streets, but there is no evidence of any sweeping enthusiasm on the part of the common people for whatever person or program – except, naturally, the widespread commitment to defeat the Romans. It does not seem surprising then that at the final stages of the siege Jerusalem was dominated by three rebel leaders, presiding over three groups of militants, engaged in mutual destruction and unable, almost to the very last moment, to unite their forces against the Roman foe.

It is difficult, if not impossible, to envision under these conditions any meaningful activities by a standing popular assembly of citizens in the capital which would have required from the participants some proof of local residence (at a time when the city was teeming with refugees) and a reliable method of vote solicitation. On this score, the vague quasi-constitutional language employed by Josephus should deceive no one. It is true that the latter must have been concerned with his narrative's credibility. In fact, this very concern may account for his persistent use of the Greek word to indicate different groupings of individuals – from the actual government (that is to say, the executive authority in charge of dispensing orders) to the 'general public' or 'commonwealth'. This allowed the historian to manipulate the exigencies of his discourse and the expectations of his readers depending upon the context, to create implicitly an impression that the persons or groups he approved of also enjoyed the general or at least predominant favor from the Jewish people. The prime example of this is, of course, Josephus's description of the outrage, reportedly displayed by the Jerusalemites, who even threatened the culprits with violence, upon the news of the attempts, on the part of the ruling faction under Ananus b. Ananus, to remove him from Galilee "without asking an opinion from the 'general assembly'" (*Vita*, 309 f.). It seems much more likely that in reality no such general body was in existence; rather, there must have often occurred the *ad hoc* public gatherings or rallies (in some respects, such as the urgency of purpose, resembling what the Romans called *contiones*), indeterminate in their number of participants, and summoned by the agents of various parties in order to receive an immediate (and informal!) approval of their own conduct and intentions or, conversely, a disapproval of their antagonists. Likewise, this might have provided an opportunity for a leader to address a crowd and to incite it to some kind of action – as, we are told, Ananus b. Ananus did on the eve of the zealots' coup (*BJ*, 4, 163 ff.). In the present case, Josephus's own partisans would have had to convoke such a rally, with the consequences (even if overstated) he describes. There is no need to believe what he wants to imply: namely, that the men in authority were bound by any moral or legal obligation to inform the citizenry of every decision they chose to make. From the accounts in both the *Bellum* and the *Vita* it clearly follows that Ananus b. Ananus and the rest did not bother to consult the world outside about most of their plans (which was sensible, given the fact that the rival zealot faction occupied the Temple grounds) unless, owing to some moment of a particularly delicate power balance, they needed a show of popular approval. Thus, they did not shrink from sending a four-member delegation to remove Josephus from his post in Galilee, and that at considerable public expense – even though the mentioned amount of 40,000 silver pieces (*Vita*, 199) appears inflated; furthermore, if we believe the author (and it might have been a matter of record), ordering numerous citizens (in a time of military emergency!) to accompany the envoys, as well as hiring Jesus the Galilaean and his band to provide an armed escort (199 f.). None of this could have passed unnoticed, but it acquired political significance only when the scandal caught public attention through the efforts of Josephus's network. The moment seemed well chosen indeed: his detractors, fearing the spread of disturbances, and perhaps even a possibility of his alliance with zealots, decided to leave Galilee's recalcitrant governor in peace. We learn that, "much pressured by their own populace" (310), Jerusalem's leaders (ibid) produced official papers to confirm Josephus in his office and recalled the delegation sent to organize his impeachment.

The historian's use of the word *boule* is equally inconsistent and vague, in part owing to his habitual carelessness and, in part, one might again argue, to his tendency of obfuscating issues when they concern his personal predicament and behavior. Depending on the context, this word may connote councils of various kinds, broad and narrow, formal and informal, starting with the *de facto* government led by Ananus b. Ananus (as, for example, in *Vita*, 204). The relationship of this latter to the regular city council of Jerusalem, or to what is in Hebrew called *Sanhedrin* and in Greek *synedrion* (provided that these bodies continued to exist during the upheaval) constitutes – given the current state of our evidence – an insoluble quandary.

As I have repeatedly pointed out, the coalition government, created at the Temple meeting, became ridden with inner tensions from the very outset, and there can be little doubt that this proved the ultimate cause of its collapse. Perhaps it will be fairer to describe the 'first regime' not even as a coalition, but as an uneasy coexistence of two factions, differing in the degree of radicalism, that of Jerusalem nobles and of the militant commoners, fresh from the victory over the Romans – who hated each other and were drawn together, only for the reason of practical exigencies, by a shaky truce that was bound to explode. It has been mentioned that zealots, who were occupying the Temple grounds, were excluded from the actual exercise of power, and their leader Eleazar b. Simon, despite his considerable financial resources (he is said to have possessed spoils taken from the defeated Cestius Gallus and a large portion of the public treasury – *BJ*, 2, 564) received no official appointment (ibid). It is then of little surprise that the latter, paraphrasing Josephus, made good use of his money and, by means of what the historian calls "beguilements" (presumably, meaning 'intrigues'), proceeded to work on the popular mood with the purpose of turning the tide of events to his own benefit (565). It was thus inevitable that the initial tension between two groups was to develop into open conflict, an outbreak of violence leading to the 'egalitarian' dictatorship of zealots.

As a general principle, it must again be pointed out that at the time of trouble, of revolutionary turmoil, political allegiances and alliances are shifting, constantly in flux and often short lived. The old ties, hereditary, traditional or customary, run risks of crumbling, and people tend to associate not only on the basis of mutual interests, membership in a particular social group, or of what it is now fashionable to call 'ideology' (that is, common belief), but also, and more often than not, owing to the requirements of the moment – which may change dramatically – if they hope that it would result in an immediate increase of power to the detriment of their rival or rivals. The old group arrangements may be transformed by policies of personal aggrandizement, and these latter may even cross over family lines, as we know happened in the case of the first rebel leader

Eleazar b. Ananias, who defied his high priestly father Ananias b. Nedebaeus and became, even though indirectly, responsible for his murder.

This is why one should resist the temptation to envisage a political landscape, in times such as the Jewish revolt against Rome, in accordance with the modern notion of 'party membership' and think twice, unless there exists direct and irrefutable evidence, before one attempts to reconstruct the configuration of alliances from occasional mention in our source of two or more names together in the same phrase or paragraph. Such a procedure, although sometimes found in modern scholarship, is unreliable, and the project itself, in particular, when the evidence is scarce, is ultimately futile. It becomes even more problematic when applied to an author such as Josephus, with his penchant for carelessness, inconsistencies and vagueness.

In any event, the reader of the Josephus narratives observes manifest signs of tension among the aristocratic ruling group itself – even apart from their conflict with zealots. This is by no means strange: Ananus b. Ananus must have caused animosity within some quarters of the upper class, which is evidenced in the complaint laid against him by prominent Jerusalemites before the king and the procurator regarding his role in the execution of James the Just – a move that led to his impeachment as high priest. A clear indication of those inner problems may be further found in the account of the Josephus affair: it appears that Ananus b. Ananus and his entourage only reluctantly yielded to the pressure exercised on them by Simon b. Gamaliel; while Jesus b. Gamala, explicitly identified as Josephus's friend, informed the latter, via his father, on the progress of the intrigue. This did not, however, prevent the historian from mentioning all three of them (that is, Simon, Ananus and Jesus) in one and the same passage which portrays the first regime's leaders urging the people of the capital to suppress the zealots (*BJ*, 4, 159 f.).

There is only one other known example of an action by the aristocratic leadership (before their final showdown with the radicals) directed against other Jews: namely, their persecution of Simon b. Gioras and his following whom they refused a share of power despite their major role (cf. *BJ*, 2, 521) in the defeat of Cestius Gallus. According to Josephus, that man, who was to become one of three dictators in Jerusalem during the siege, even at the early stage of his career, proceeded to harass the wealthy, "clearly showing that he embarked on the pass of tyranny" (ibid, 652) In any event, we learn that Ananus b. Ananus sent a military force against this group of insurgents, active in the toparchy of Acrabatene, and drove them to seek refuge at Masada (653), which was by that time in the hands of the *sicarii*, the adherents of the slain Menahem b. Judas.[19]

What remains is to examine what is often called the 'ideology' of the 'first regime' – an unfortunate use of the word since its modern underpinnings necessarily, even if subtly, distort mental and psychological aspects of the human phenomena from the distant past. The issue might be better described as a sort of mindset, a set of attitudes towards such themes as social inequality, property rights or recourse to violence. In our case, this can be practically narrowed to an inquiry into the meaning and ramifications of the Greek word for 'moderates' – a term that Josephus consistently applies to the government formed at the Temple meeting and its individual members. The immediate impression is that it denotes those among Jewish groups or leaders who were more inclined than others to negotiate peace with the Romans. This is presumably what the historian would have sought to impress on his audience. It results from his deliberate strategy, which largely seeks to exculpate himself and the individuals whom he thought appropriate in the eyes of the non-Jewish readership. The logic of Josephus's narrative, however, undercuts this picture: whatever private doubts or aspirations this group of rebel leaders might have entertained, whether they did or did not regret at various moments, and under the pressure of adversities, the political choice they have made, the configuration of the events required them to keep waging war against the Romans. The charge of "Romanizing" seems to have often been thrown at them by their radical opponents, based as it was on their earlier public record, to wit, their years' long policies of collaboration with the occupier. This means that Ananus b. Ananus and his associates could not afford dismissing accusations of treason, however false, lightly: these were fraught with the whole gamut of trouble, from simple embarrassment to the outbursts of popular wrath. As a result, the members of the 'first regime' were compelled to tread on the thin line in what they did and spoke.

The closer reading leads me to believe that, within the Josephan discourse, the meaning of the word "moderate", which makes better sense, derives not from the individual or collective attitudes *vis-à-vis* the Romans, but from what is presented as the contrast in domestic politics – between the ways of the Ananus b. Ananus's faction and zealots under Eleazar b. Simon in their interaction with fellow Jews. For Josephus, as one should expect from a person of his class and background, the degree of 'moderation', on the one hand, and 'radicalism', on the other, must have depended, first and foremost, on the willingness of various individuals or groups to engage in violence and plunder. It is not an accident that he uses the word 'bandit' or 'brigand' to indicate both the outlaws and the revolutionaries or lumps them together in one sentence (for example, *Vita*, 28). The 'moderates', on the other hand, are presented (largely through silence) as respecting both the life and property of their compatriots, and the historian endeavors carefully to demonstrate that their eventual, and failed, assault on zealots was both inevitable and justifiable, since the latter had been perpetuating pillage, atrocities and sacrilege.

To conclude: any attempt at historical assessment must fully take into account both the unstable foundation of the aristocratic 'first regime' and its self-destructive dynamics. Its leaders were undoubtedly experienced politicians who found themselves, however, caught by the predicament, which – in the long run – they proved unable to manage. In part, this owes to the external circumstances, such as the character and agenda of their temporary zealot allies, and the general disorder or confusion throughout the land, especially outside Jerusalem, that at times came close to anarchy and presented a major obstacle for any consistent military effort. Against this background, one obviously has to appreciate the fact that the group around Ananus b. Ananus succeeded in exercising power for a little less than two years while enduring pressures from within and without that rapidly accumulated. It is further to their credit that they at least tried to implement certain measures to achieve national unity, in terms of both organization and propaganda, which also found some manifestation in their coinage. One even imagines that owing – for the most part – to their policies of military preparation and buildup of material resources in Jerusalem, the capital later became able to survive many months of Roman siege.

At the same time it must be recognized that the 'first regime' was not undone by the Romans, and not even by its zealot rivals and their Idumaean allies, but fell prey to corrosive factionalism within their own class that constituted a deeply entrenched tradition in the politics of the period's Jewish elite. Its leaders were compelled to learn and practice dissimulation (of the sort not unlike that of the senatorial dissidents) when dealing with Roman Imperial officialdom as well as, *mutatis mutandis*, with their own domestic rivals. But that was a feature largely alien to Jewish temperament and attitudes (once again, note Josephus's praise of 'speaking freely' in his judgment on Gorion b. Joseph). At the same time, as I have speculated, psychological aspects of dissimulation, conjoined with the need for wishful thinking (although to a smaller degree than among typical religious dissenters) may have further crippled their course of action.

In any event, it was due to the power struggle inside the ruling clique, aggravated by the ambience of the revolutionary upheaval, that its members failed miserably in controlling their individual passions, fears and ambitions. The Josephus affair makes one prominent – and ugly – example of how inordinate energies could have been wasted for no other reason than gratification of petty personal rivalries instead of having been directed towards the support of the common cause and the struggle against the national foe. One feels amazed to realize that in the time of bitter warfare, with the Roman enemy (not mentioning gangs of brigands) at large, men in command could dispatch a small army, supported by substantial sums of money, for the only purpose of removing, on dubious grounds, a capable and duly appointed general from his office. In other words, multiform divisions – on the societal, factional, even individual or psychological level (that is, within one and the same person) – reinforced each other. The result was the near paralysis of political will vectored outwards, in the direction of Rome. This provided, on the one hand, the critics of the leadership with the grounds for the charges such as treachery, or "Romanizing"; and, on the other, allowed the author of the *Bellum* to play their apologist and argue for their (and his own) political 'moderation'. We will see that the same policy and the same set of attitudes (although this time with no room for inner doubts) were inherited by their successors: the factional strife only intensified and continued to run rampant – a proof that the beliefs of many modern political scientists notwithstanding, both individuals and groups are all too often motivated not by calculations and rational pursuits of their interests, but by a variety of uncontrollable desires.

What has been said elucidates yet another aspect of the Jewish revolt: it was largely by the people of Jerusalem that the war against Rome was waged with extraordinary perseverance and zeal, their resolve strengthened with the awareness of defending the sacred city and the seat of the Temple. The centrality of Jerusalem in their concerns as revolutionary headquarters and – I think – more importantly, as the heart of the Jewish world, emphatically transpires in the legend on the coinage issued by the 'first regime': JERUSALEM THE HOLY. Since Ascalon, no further offensive action had been undertaken by the insurgents, and the episodes of their determined defense such as Jotapata and Gamala – are, on balance, altogether few, of local origin and apparently occurring outside Jerusalem's control. The intransigent resistance at Massada provides a famous example, but it was conducted by the militant sect of the true believers; in Galilee Josephus behaved as a fairly independent actor, motivated by the exigencies of the moment, and we have learned of citizen groups and entire communities seeking to change sides or remain neutral.

It is true that at the early stage of the 'first regime' there existed a balance of power, however fragile, which proved both the source of its short-lived stability and the cause of its eventual collapse. In the final analysis, however, it becomes clear that its key figures, despite their potential as 'professional' politicians, failed to meet the expectations of their followers. Even aside from partisan politics (the conflict of the 'moderate' and 'radical' camps), which might have been inevitable, the members of the ruling clique used to place their individual or group advantage above the interests of the nation. Josephus did attempt to exculpate, through rhetorical or narrative devices, and obfuscating their competence and motivation, his erstwhile colleagues (some of whom he must have despised) from blame by posterity. But a closer inquiry undercuts any such strategy with the result that one cannot accept the historian's ultimately favorable judgment on their political performance.[20]

5

THE ZEALOUS STORM

I.

With zealots we arrive closer to that type of religious dissenters who challenge or defy reality if it does not accord with their beliefs. The circumstances and date of their origin remain uncertain. An inquiry into their attitudes and activities is further aggravated by a feature of Josephus's narrative that we are already familiar with: namely, his tendency for applying same terms to different phenomena or, conversely, using different terms to denote one and the same. This may be described as the divergence between the *usage* and the *focus*, when the coherence (and accuracy) of the narrative, as well as the narrative's perspective, are sacrificed for the advantage (whatever it might be) – or lack thereof – at the moment. We have seen it in discussing Josephus's institutional vocabulary. It equally pertains to what may be called his 'political' language. Thus, on the one hand, he sometimes treats zealots as a distinct politico-religious movement – most visibly, in his final overview of the Jewish revolutionaries (*BJ*, 7, 253 ff.), where they figure as a particular 'breed' (268); on the other, he often does not seem to distinguish those commonly understood as 'zealots' proper – namely, the radical group of fighters and priests around Eleazar b. Simon who led the coup against the 'first regime', from the wave of "brigands" who broke into the capital (cf. *BJ*, 4, 135 ff.), or from (at least) some in the following enjoyed by John b. Levi of Gischala (cf. ibid., 389 ff.). On one occasion, he employs the same word to indicate the adherents of Menahem b. Judas (*BJ*, 2,444), the leader of the terrorist *sicarii*, whose rise and practices he tends to represent as yet another distinct development. It seems conceivable therefore that in various contexts the term, as handled by Josephus, may cover several rebel groups, or constituents, whose boundaries were vague or intentionally obfuscated.[1]

As a consequence, the debate continues as to whether the word *zelotai*, as it appears in the *Bellum* (Hebrew *kanaim*) implies an identifiable political faction (party), or whether it just describes revolutionary individuals with a certain politico-religious temperament and agenda. The word itself derives from the Greek *zeloun*, which means 'emulate', 'imitate', 'adore'. In contrast to the Greek usage, politically or religiously neutral, in the ambience of Jewish dissent – and, by extension, beyond it within a broader spectrum of Judaism – the concept of 'zeal' (Hebrew *kana*) directly pertained to the realm of the Divine: Israel's zeal for God and God's zeal for Israel ("For I am the Lord thy God am a jealous [= zealous] God" – *Exod*: 20), individual and collective zeal for God, for the Law and for the Sanctuary. The Torah provides several example of 'zeal for God' (even though they often seem misguided from the modern, and sometimes even from the late rabbinic, viewpoint), such as Simeon and Levi, exterminating all men of the city Shechem on the grounds that the Shechem prince had seduced their sister Dinah – even though the latter did not mind marrying her, and both he as well as all males among his people consented to undergo circumcision (*Gen*: 34). Moses himself, at God's command, ordered the tribe of Levi to decimate those who had worshiped the golden calf: "Put every man his sword by his side, and go in and out from gate to gate throughout the camp, and slay every man his brother, and every man his companion, and every man his neighbor; and the children of Levi did according to the word of Moses: and there fell of the people that day about three thousand men" (*Exod*: 32,27 f.); and – most prominently – Phineas (Pinhas), who is described as 'zealot' in the Septuagint (*Num*: 25,11: the word *zelos* and its derivatives appear three times in one verse; cf. ibid, 13), and is similarly referred to in the Pseudepigraphic and Tannaitic writings. The biblical episode in question occurred in the context of Israel's involvement with the worship of Baal-peor, following their intercourse with Moabite women:

> ... and the anger of the Lord was kindled against Israel. And the Lord said unto Moses, "Take all the heads of the people, and hang them up before the Lord against the sun, that the fierce anger of the Lord may be turned away from Israel" and Moses said unto the judges of Israel, "Slay ye everyone his men that were joined unto Baal-peor." And, behold, one of the children of Israel came and brought unto his brethren a Midianitish woman in the sight of Moses, and in the sight of all the congregation of the children of Israel, who were weeping before the door of the tabernacle of the congregation. And when Phinehas, the son of Eleazar, the son of Aaron the priest, saw it, he rose up from among the congregation, and took a javelin in his hand; and he went after the man of Israel into the tent, and thrust both of them through, the man of Israel, and the woman through her belly. So the plague was stayed from the children of Israel. And those that died in the plague were twenty and four thousand. And the Lord spake unto Moses, saying: "Phinehas, the son of Eleazar, the son of Aaron the priest, hath turned my wrath away from the children of Israel, while he was zealous for my sake among them, that I consumed not the children of Israel in my jealousy. Wherefore say, Behold, I give unto him my covenant of peace. And he shall have it, and his seed after him, even the covenant of an everlasting priesthood; because he was zealous for his God, and made

an atonement for the children of Israel." Now the name of the Israelite that was slain, even that was slain with the Midianitish woman, was Zimri, the son of Salu, a prince of a chief house among the Simeonites. And the name of the Midianitish woman that was slain was Cozbi, the daughter of Zur; he was head over a people, and of a chief house in Midian.

(Num. 25, 3 ff.)

One further biblical champion of 'zealotry' for Yahweh and for the law from the later period (that of the Kingdoms), compared and – in a higher sense – sometimes identified with Phineas, was the prophet Elijah, one of the most popular figures in the Old Testament, who was even believed (as, within certain circles, was Phineas) to have been taken by God, for the reason of his zeal, into the heaven alive (*2Kings*: 1, 11). He is said to have entered the religious contest with 850 false prophets ("the prophets of Baal four hundred and fifty, and the prophets of the groves four hundred" – *1Kings*: 18,19), won it over through direct divine intervention and thereupon performed their wholesome execution at the brook Kisson (ibid, 40). In his benevolent and infinitely more attractive aspect (as an intercessor for Israel before God, a healer and a resurrectionist – cf. ibid, 17, 17 ff.), Elijah is widely revered in today's Judaism.

From what has been said, it should cause no surprise that in the ambience of Jewish radicals and dissenters, the Greek word *zelotes* was given passionate religious overtones which were bound to affect the populace at large. The term, given its intentionally positive import, must have been a self-designation chosen by its bearers. This is emphatically confirmed and commented upon by Josephus in his survey of the revolutionary groups intended as a sort of a final judgment:

> Throughout they committed consummate lawlessness, this breed of so-called zealots. By their deeds they proved true to their name, since they were thorough in imitating every evil act, and they did not fail to emulate any wicked precedent for which there was a record. Yet they took their name from zealotry in pursuit of virtue, in mockery of those whom they wronged, whether in sarcasm, owing to their beastly nature, or because they regarded the greatest of their evils as good deeds.

(BJ, 7, 268 ff.)

All sarcasm notwithstanding, Josephus here in a masterly way pinpoints the inherent and crucial contradiction in their whole enterprise, which made it vulnerable to moral, political and religious attacks, although obviously disregarded, or glossed over, by the zealots themselves (as well as by some modern interpreters bent on justifying, or exculpating, their conduct), namely: a conflict between their strict commitment to law and ritual as established by God and their willingness to perform sacrilege and violence in God's name. What Josephus (and many moderns) failed, however, to recognize was the psychology behind this predicament, when religious dissenters vastly privilege their own individual or collective 'zealous' interpretation of God's will above everything else (which includes, to their credit, their own lives as is witnessed by their readiness for self-sacrifice or for suffering martyrdom) – a vision that takes precedence in their minds even over God's explicit and unambiguous moral commandments found in the sacred texts. That is the situation when such injunctions as "thou shalt not kill", "thou shalt not steal" or "thou shalt not take the name of the Lord thy God in vain" (*Exod*: 20,13; 15;7) lose their relevance: killing even a co-religionist and compatriot becomes a virtue if the latter is suspected of a different attitude vis-à-vis God and God's plans; the same is true in plundering such person's estate. As we have seen, this could have allowed, or justified in their eyes, the massacre of the Roman garrison on the holy Sabbath day by the rebels after their solemn pledge (which should have surely involved an oath by God's name) to save the enemy lives. This subordination of all things sacred and profane to the superior purpose of wishful thinking about their role in the divine scheme of things, which – as this book argues – largely motivates the bearers of the religious dissent, is a theme to which I will repeatedly return.[2]

By now it must be evident that dealing with an author so negligent about formalities, precision and details as Josephus, an *argumentum ex silentio* must be applied with particular caution. That he makes zealots, although not yet identified as such, first to appear in the context of the Temple meeting after Cestius Gallus's defeat at Beth-Goron does not mean at all that they were hitherto nonexistent.

The major question is whether they related, and if they did, in what sense, to the revolutionary outlook called by Josephus the "fourth philosophy" and which originated, according to him, in A.D. 6 in a rebel leader Judas the Galilaean and a Pharisee named Saddok (*AJ*, 18, 4 ff.; cf. 23 ff.; *BJ*, 2, 118; 433; 7, 253 f.). This particular story properly belongs to the discussion of the *sicarii* and will be treated in some detail at a later stage. It cannot, however, be doubted that there was substantial convergence, in terms of attitudes and ideas, between the adherents of the "fourth philosophy", aimed at national liberation, theocratically understood, and zealots, such as the contempt for the existent religious authority and the belief of being in direct communication with the divine. The difference seems to have lain in organization (or lack thereof) and tactics, and perhaps in stricter attention to the ritual on the part of some zealot groups rather than by other freedom fighters such as the *sicarii*. In contrast to the latter, who emerge in Josephus as the ultimate offshoot of the "fourth philosophy", zealots apparently abstained from terrorist policies against other Jews until the events leading to their actual takeover of Jerusalem. Nor do they appear a well-defined and tightly knit group – unlike the *sicarii*, who were governed on a sort of dynastic principle.

It must be emphasized that Josephus does not treat zealots as a separate 'sect', unlike his description, both in the *Bellum* and in the *Antiquitates* (*BJ*, 2, 118 ff.; 162 ff.; *AJ*, 13, 171 ff; 297 f.; 15, 371; 18,11 ff.; 23 ff.; cf. *Vita*, 10), of Sadducees, Pharisees, Essenes and the "fourth philosophy". Moreover, we have seen that he sometimes mixes the zealots up, not bothering to differentiate, with other rebel constituencies, which – at least initially – must have been of different origin. This speaks, in my judgment, against constructing zealots as a party, in any sense close to modern – that is, endowed with a *sui generis* 'ideology' and 'program'. One may assume that every radical Jewish group of the period was affected, in various degrees, by the doctrine of national liberation and theocracy preached by Judas the Galilaean and his followers, but it does not mean that, during the revolutionary turmoil, they were prepared to accept the latter's specific agenda, their leaders, or style of leadership (witness the early murder of Menahem b. Judas and the subsequent flight of the *sicarii* from the capital). Furthermore, in times of trouble, borders between radical factions tend to become blurred: what would matter had been not so much differences in outlook or in doctrinal subtleties, but in individual backgrounds, personal loyalties and connections. Thus, if as it is often argued, most zealots who, upon the downfall of the first regime, with Eleazar b. Simon as their chief, took over the Temple and attempted ruling the capital and conducting the war, were priests, this could have provided them, similarly to their insistence on their exceptional piety, with yet another claim for distinction. Yet, it remains uncertain (and hardly ascertainable) whether those zealots thought of themselves (and if they did, in what sense) as a faction, *vis-à-vis* other radical factions, other than by bearing this name and following a particular leader or leaders. Rather, they seem to have represented one, however influential, strand within the spectrum of the more or less like-minded religious dissenters: since the stated aim of them all was an achievement of national independence as ordained by God, in their view, the dimensions of politics and religion must have ultimately merged. It is perfectly conceivable, on the other hand, that – apart from the priestly confederates of Eleazar b. Simon – any person of fitting temperament, attitudes and behavior could assume the appellation of 'zealot' or be called thus by friends or foes alike.

Thus, a member of any Jewish radical religious dissent movement might have thought of himself, first and foremost, as an instrument of divine will; as a person of great piety (zealot in a narrow sense); as a fighter for national freedom; as a supporter of some particular individual within the same ambience – but perhaps least of all as a participant in politics of any conventional style. This, of course, would not have prevented the outsiders from perceiving zealots, in a variety of ways, as a distinct group (which, for the most part, Josephus does), not only on the grounds of their self-publicized 'zealotry', but also in terms of their relationship with this or that factional leader. It was primarily by this latter feature that in the ensuing mayhem up to and even into the siege, the zealot adherents of Eleazar b. Simon could have been differentiated from the equally militant followings of John b. Levi and Simon b. Giora.

The material, found in Josephus, does not establish whether the zealot movement, centered in the capital, spread beyond the confines of Jerusalem, and if it did, then how far. The impression made (and perhaps intended) by the text is that zealots, similarly to the *sicarii*, comprised a relatively small group. This assumption allowed some of the modern interpreters *implicite* to conclude that because of their small numbers they were not able to exercise any substantial impact upon the course of the revolt. One must not, however, be deceived on this score, even if Josephus was correct: the historical experience amply demonstrates that a radical militant group need not always be particularly large to incite the masses and create, or exploit, a revolutionary situation: witness the French Jacobins, Russian Bolsheviks or contemporary Islamic terrorists.[3]

II.

Before taking up an inquiry into the circumstances, which provided zealots with an opportunity for toppling in Jerusalem the government of Ananus b. Ananus and installing their own (however short-lived) 'second regime', I find it imperative to digress on one characteristic tendency, bordering on prejudice, in Western historiographical tradition. What I mean is the persistent trend to privilege revolutionary movements and their leadership on the mere grounds that they claim to be – or are perceived as – fighters against all sorts of oppression, irrespective of other motives they might have harbored and notwithstanding the terror they introduced, or bloodshed they perpetrated, sometimes on a monumental scale, in the course of their enterprise. This attitude, by and large the product of the Enlightenment, was upheld and further developed by the liberal political theoreticians, and subsequently usurped by the Marxists with the purpose of justifying, in ethical terms, their doctrine of class struggle and beneficent socio-economic upheaval. Despite their sophistication, often considerable, most of these authors avoid inquiring into a major problem of revolutionary psychology and motivation. It is all too often uncritically assumed that the rhetoric and activities of the revolutionists always reflect their true (and honorable) beliefs rooted in their desire of social or political justice for their people. Any other possible considerations, such as thirst for power and vengeance, contempt for human life, the destructive and self-destructive potential of hatred (even if it might seem justified), and – in general – the spirit of *anomie* which, to a greater or lesser degree, is present in the ambience of any revolt, are preferably ignored. That all these and similarly reprehensible motives, conscious or not, may coexist in one and the same mind with genuinely lofty aspirations does not help much – witness the behavior of most revolutionary regimes upon their seizure of power. With few exceptions, their policies prove much more ruthless and oppressive than those of their predecessors, however tyrannical the latter might have been. This becomes painfully obvious when we examine seriously and without prejudice the course and outcome of the French Revolution, Russian Revolution, Chinese Revolution and so forth. It must be recognized that national liberation movements are not immune from those same deficiencies, especially when their leaders pursue their own interests and self-aggrandizement at the expense of people's welfare. The examples from recent history might include such personages as Zimbabwe's Robert Mugabe or Saparmurat Niiazov (Turkmenbashi) of Turkmenistan.

If one accepts that a compassionate humanist should venerate sanctity of human life above all other values, it follows that the concept of any violent revolution or rise to power cannot be regarded as morally permissible. That this position is not particularly popular even within liberal democracies testifies to an ironic paradox inherent in modern liberalism, and to the human propensity for wishful thinking. Only by allowing the latter, one may explain how creative intellectuals of great personal integrity, such as Heinrich Böll and Günther Grass, could have sympathized with the wave of political terror in Germany of 1970s, or the sentiments of many in the present-day American academia favoring Palestinian, or Chechen, murderous practices against innocent civilians. The above-mentioned paradox of contemporary liberalism consists, therefore, in simultaneous promotion to the utmost of the individualist agenda and callous disrespect (by justifying some forms of violence as necessary) for single individuals' lives. One is tempted to suspect that none of today's (even after September 11) terrorist sympathizers ever tried to imagine themselves in the role of their victims.

What has been said applies, *mutatis mutandis*, to the issue of modern judgments – in moral and political aspects – on the zealots of the revolutionary Jerusalem. The problem is aggravated by the widespread perception of the Jewish War as one of glorious episodes in Jewish history – not the least, one assumes, owing to the story of the heroic resistance against the Romans by the defenders of Massada and their subsequent collective suicide.

To be sure, the zealots at Jerusalem presided over the popular effort at national liberation from Rome – but it is less often than one might wish properly appreciated that at the same time they were waging war on their own people, and perhaps as relentlessly as against the common enemy. As a result, even sober-minded scholars tend to minimize the scale, or even the very fact, of their atrocities. From what has been said, however, on the interpretation of 'zeal', inherent in the mindset of the religious dissenters, and their total belief that their mission was in full agreement with the divine intent, it follows with iron inevitability that the policy of terror made a natural course in their attempt at accommodating the reality to their beliefs – a tool directed against any individual construable as God's foe, both within and without the people of Israel, and prevailing over any further considerations, moral, legalistic, ritualist, pragmatic, exegetic, or any other; and given human propensity for iniquity, it must be equally clear that terror and any form of terrorism, in the ambience of revolutionary upheaval, could have easily gone out of hand and turned out practically unrestrained, irrespective of whether we moderns may like this or not.

A related and equally important question is how reliable and historically accurate may be the portrayal of the reign of terror instituted by zealots upon their seizure of power as found in the *Bellum*, which is virtually our sole source on these events. One cannot doubt, of course, that Josephus belongs among most tendentious ancient historians and had to pursue not only what may be called nationalist agenda (that is, the defense of Jews and Judaism in front of the

Roman conqueror), but also personal and apologetic *vis-à-vis* both the gentiles and the fellow Jews. Yet, in his case (as in the case of Tacitus, who also wrote about many events still within living memory, and who is all too often accused by scholars of anti-Imperial bias), there existed a major factor that I have repeatedly cited: the requirement of credibility so far as the immediate audience was concerned. Josephus's readership consisted of people, in and outside Judaea, who were contemporaneous with the events he described, many of them having been their witnesses or participants. A show of integrity was critical for his success, particularly *vis-à-vis* members of Rome's Jewish community, his closest environment, who must have been in touch on a regular basis with both the Holy Land and the Diaspora. This placed the historian in a dire need to produce a narrative sufficiently persuasive, that is to say, the one, which – his own multiple biases notwithstanding – would not have too far deviated from the truth. As we have already seen, he was fully conscious of the predicament he faced by formulating it in the very proemium to the *Bellum*: the ancient historians, who wrote history of their own times, he says, had to proceed in such a way "that their own involvement with the events enhanced their narrative, while lying means to fall into disgrace in the eyes of those who know" (I, 14). The depth of this concern on his part is further testified by Josephus's persistent attempts to solicit approval of his text from various quarters that mattered, including the members of the Herodian family (*Vita*, 361 ff.), and by his heated polemics against Justus of Tiberias. It follows that in order to achieve, and not defeat, his purposes, he had to implement a variety of narrative strategies, such as omission and obfuscation, while not inventing any fact of genuine importance, or even exaggerating it beyond the limits of probability, which would have defied common knowledge and been decidedly counterproductive.

Modern scholarship has demonstrated that the events leading to the zealot coup against Ananus b. Ananus and his regime in winter A.D. 67/68, and of the coup itself, were not narrated by Josephus in proper chronological order. He might have structured this narrative as he did for the purpose of greater thematic and dramatic effort; alternatively, he might have been simply lacking more precise chronological information.

Be that is it may, in the broader sense Josephus's portrayal of the status quo in Jerusalem on the eve of the coup is altogether believable. It may be described as a 'diarchy' (that is, the situation when two centers of power exercise a roughly equal control over different groups). This is by no means unusual at the time of cataclysm: the immediate example coming to mind would be an uneasy coexistence in the revolutionary Russia, upon the overthrow of monarchy, of the Provisional Government and the Soviets of People's Deputies – for a few months, until all power was violently seized by the Bolsheviks in October 1917.

In revolutionary Jerusalem, this was an inevitable outcome of an artificial arrangement achieved a year and a half earlier at the Temple meeting. The determinant factor at the time must have been an apparent inability of either side to suppress the other, a stalemate that could continue for long. The ruling faction of Ananus b. Ananus possessed no military force to contend with their opponents, while zealots under Eleazar b. Simon must have failed in arousing enough popular support for striking first. This last point is of some interest in assessing the mood of the masses: at least at this stage, the city's residents did not demonstrate any marked preference for the radical agenda. As we will see, many of them supported the 'moderates' to the very end.

On the other hand, by having occupied the Temple grounds, zealots did acquire strategic advantage, both in political and military terms. Furthermore, with gradual Roman conquest of Galilee, their prestige grew while that of the aristocratic regime declined, given the fact that divided and paralysed as they were, its leaders proved unable to stop the Roman progress: no doubt, this proved one of the factors that precipitated their downfall. At the same time, manpower on the side of zealots kept increasing, since the waves of escapees from the countryside repeatedly broke into the capital, multiplying the number of discontented. Josephus predictably treats these hordes and their leaders (cf. *BJ*, 4, 135) as 'brigands' (*lestai*). I find it idle to speculate, with any precision, on the meaning of this word in Josephus: it is clear that in his texts it covers the whole spectrum of troublemakers – rural, or urban, revolutionaries and/or religious dissenters, as well as actual bandits, but there is hardly any reasonable way to specify his treatment of these groups by analyzing specific passages. Furthermore, at the time of historical upheaval it is often similarly difficult to discriminate between genuine revolutionists (that is, motivated by clear social or political ideals) and all sorts of bandits or marauders: each category is active, sometimes they intermingle, and many individuals or groups can be described as belonging to both. Thus, Joseph Stalin, during his revolutionary youth, also presided over a criminal gang engaged in a number of bank robberies.

In any event, the influx of the countryside refugees into Jerusalem emphasized by Josephus was bound to enhance the prospects of the zealot faction for eventual takeover and tightened their hold over their adherents. By then it must have become apparent that the regime of 'diarchy' proved even less stable than the original coalition, and that the showdown was bound to happen, sooner or later. As it follows from Josephus, preparations were already under way on both sides.

It would be, however, simplistic (and ultimately mistaken) to analyze the situation that we now deal with exclusively in terms of politics (that is to say, power struggle) as many interpreters tend to do. The factor of religious dissent among zealots, with its psychological repercussions, played no lesser, but perhaps even greater role in this standoff and the subsequent violence than any practical, tactical, political and similar disagreement, or the difference in social standing.

The claim by zealots of being the instruments of divine justice could alone have antagonized the 'first regime's' largely Saducean leadership. According to Josephus, the tenets of their sect denied God's intervention in human affairs, so in their view, this particular form of self-proclaimed 'zealotry' must have signified presumptuous and dangerous nonsense. Furthermore, they must have entertained no illusions as regards zealots' attitudes towards them and their role as religious establishment: the dissenters regarded it as illegitimate, betraying not only the people's interests (through the decades' long collaboration with Rome) but also the very foundations of the Jewish faith – which position they graphically demonstrated soon after in electing by lot a high priest of their own.

Nor could zealots trust the members of the high priestly elite by the very definition of their dissent: the persistent propaganda they launched, charging their opponents with treasonous intent or secret negotiations with the Romans, which Josephus tries to explain away as the work of calumny or demagogy (e.g., *BJ*, 4, 146, 218, 227 ff., 245 ff.; 280f., 336 f.), in fact must have reflected their genuine anxieties and beliefs. Those who, in the pursuit of their wealth, power and self-aggrandizement, were content to tolerate the foreign yoke against God's will, in the eyes of the radicals, looked towards the restoration of the *status quo ante* so that they could continue enjoying the fruits of treacherous opportunism, their current rhetoric of liberty notwithstanding. Furthermore, one still cannot rule out a possibility that the charges brought out against the members of the 'first regime' by their foes may not have been entirely unfounded, and that even within the ruling clique there still existed some individuals who considered seeking an accommodation with Rome for a variety of reasons – or in order to escape the imminent harassment or slaughter at the hands of zealots. In other words, the showdown was inevitable, and not only for the reason of power politics, but – more importantly – owing to the incompatibilities of the worldviews held by both sides. The factors which kept them together for a span of more than a year included, in the first place, the common threat of the Roman enemy (with whom they failed to deal efficiently); the changing balance of power in the capital; and the resemblance of diplomatic game, exercised, on the one hand, by Ananus b. Ananus, who – after years of handling the Romans – must have learned much about the ways of dissimulation, and – on the other – by Eleazar b. Simon, a somewhat unusual case of dissenter, as portrayed by Josephus. The latter ascribes to him, at one point, an inordinate capacity for intrigue (*BJ*, 2, 565; cf. 4, 150). This man must have understood at least something about politics (in contrast to such fellow radicals as the *sicarii*, whose leaders were apparently motivated by their own vision of things human and divine), although his behavior, as we will see, later became inconsistent, contradictory and even enigmatic.[4]

The bold move, on the part of zealots (namely, their decision to elect the rival high priest by lot, and certainly not invented by Josephus, being a matter of public record), which gave a novel dimension to the quandary already in existence, should not surprise the student of religious dissent in the least. It had been argued that their lack of legitimacy constituted the chief concern of the zealot faction especially since they chose to shut off the Temple grounds, turning it, in Josephus's phrase, into their fortress (*BJ*, 4, 151). After all, the leadership of the 'first regime' was elected, or appointed, at the Temple meeting, however dubious that procedure might have seemed. According to one viewpoint, this unique high priestly election was undertaken precisely out of the desire to rectify that very predicament. To assert their own legitimacy must have indeed been a part of the zealots' intent; but I submit that with an equal, if not even greater, urgency they felt the need to make a statement exposing the *illegality* of their opponents, presided over for the past few centuries by the high priestly families who had no legitimate right, so far as zealots were concerned, for that position: after all, during the last several decades, their members were at the time both appointed to and dismissed from the office at whim by the Herodian puppet rulers or their Roman masters. Of the last in that line, officially holding the post during the revolt, Matthias b. Theophilus (cf. *AJ*, 20, 222), we know literally nothing, and perhaps not by accident: the man might have been an utter nonentity, or so compromised, in one sense or the other, that Josephus did not deign to provide us with any further information on him.

The historian reports the election by lot with a sense of outrage and, in order to emphasize its significance, discusses it twice within a very short narrative space (*BJ*, 4, 147–149 and 153–157). It is, of course, arguable that it was not this episode (despite Josephus's claim: "Their audacity the people did not tolerate; rather, all of them hastened, as if for the overthrow of a tyranny" – 158), but subsequent judicial murders which prompted Ananus b. Ananus and his supporters to finally launch an attack on zealots. But it does not follow that Josephus's angry emphasis should be explained away as mere rhetoric or dramatics. On the contrary: in these passages he pinpoints a major feature in mentality, attitudes and behavior of religious dissenters, within the framework of an established religion, to whom zealots belonged: namely, repudiating the currently established hierarchy viewed as disloyal to the very foundation of their own faith, and creating a supreme priestly authority to rival the one already in existence. This was a quintessential gesture generated by the dynamics within that form of dissent: in various manifestations, the same psychological characteristic is repeatedly found among Christian medieval heretics, Protestant sects and militant Islamic groups.

In his account, Josephus both highlights and obfuscates some aspects and repercussions of this particular phenomenon. As I have repeatedly observed, one clear tendency he displays is to politicize the events he narrates at the expense of their often-religious character: Josephus's strategy was to minimize the role of religion (but not of what he considered deviations within it!) in the Jewish revolt and internecine warfare. Thus he insists that, by electing a high priest of their own, zealots intended further to test and humiliate people of Jerusalem, who had been already reduced to "most abject fear" (4, 147). "Mockery was added to the horrors ... even more painful thing than their doings" (ibid, 152). One must look beyond this mixture of politics, moralism and what we might now call 'pop psychology', favored by Josephus. An earlier example is his pronouncement that zealots elevated unremarkable and low-born men (148) to the highest office so that they could "gain accomplices in their impiety"; ibid) since "those who happen to arrive at the highest honor not by merit, need to obey those who granted it to them" (149). This last point is, of course, a rhetorical cliché, which does not make it *eo ipso* wrong: the element of pragmaticism might have been present in the way zealots conducted their affairs, but it was by no means dominant. What mattered was their urge to defy the established religious powers and, preferably, in the most offensive manner.

It is significant that zealots chose to select a high priest by lot (4, 153). This was obviously a gesture pointing to the time of the Judges, before the advent of kingship, when God was supposed directly to communicate with Israel (cf. 1 *Chron*: 24, 5). This is again a feature that recurs in religious dissent of this type, to wit, a desire to reverse history and reinstate the faith in its pristine purity. Josephus reports that, in justification of their measure, zealots referred to the ancient custom arguing, that "in the old days the high priesthood was decided by lot" (ibid, 154). Predictably, the historian hastens to disprove not their claim (which he treats as a pretext) but yet again their motives by proposing that "in truth, it was dissolution of what was firmly established and the device to achieve their own domination by taking over these appointments" (ibid). The very need of this comment suggests that there were many who did not share the author's opinion. In fact, a genuine belief that the return to the allegedly primordial practices is in agreement with God's will is consistent with what we know about the outlook of religious dissenters in different historical periods and within other creeds.

One further charge against zealots, proffered by Josephus in connection with the same episode, represents, however, an intentional deceit on his part. The historian portrays as unprecedented their choice of candidates for high priesthood outside the cluster of the privileged priestly clans from whose ranks a succession of high priests used to be drawn (*BJ*, 4, 148). But that was by no means the case: the continuous hereditary line of high priests came to an end in 152 B.C., when Jonathan Maccabaeus, his brother Simon, and then the Hasmonaean royal dynasty usurped the office (cf. *AJ*, 13,46; 20, 239; BJ, 1, 50 ff.; *Vita*, 3 f.). Herod, after his accession to power and his murder of the last Hasmonaean high priest Aristobulus III (*BJ*, 1, 437), proceeded, for his own political purposes, to appoint as high priests men of no personal distinction, even from the clans unacquainted with Judaea's political scene (*AJ*, 20, 247; cf. 15, 22). One has to assume that it was merely the fact of an attempt by zealots to subvert the principles of succession within high priesthood (hereditary or by appointment) and create an alternate unorthodox procedure which so deeply offended Josephus's sensibilities: we know that he was proud of his own Hasmonean, that is to say, high priestly descent (*Vita*, 1 ff.).

Josephus narrates the *modus operandi* chosen by the zealots with undisguised sarcasm. He tells us that they summoned the members of a priestly clan, called Eniachin, presumably one of the least influential (this is the only mention of it in the available sources), and cast the lot for a high priest (*BJ*, 4, 155), which fell to a certain Phineas b. Samuel from the village Aphthia. This man, writes the historian, due to his rustic habits, "did not understand exactly what the high priesthood was" (ibid, 155): there hardly can be any doubt nonetheless that this person must have belonged among genuine descendants of Aaron, which the historian chose conveniently to omit. But in Josephus's eyes, even the accident of this choice seems to prove the zealots' perversity (155). He continues with relish:

> ... they actually dragged him against his will from the countryside and, putting the sacred vestments on, as if an actor on stage not up a strange mask, and then explained to him what he should do to fit the occasion.
>
> (ibid, 156)

Resorting to a familiar device, Josephus denigrates their motives through insinuation by a claim that the zealots treated "so great an impiety" (157) as a matter of "joke and game" (ibid). One can state with confidence, however, that nothing could have been further from the truth: the historical experience strongly suggests that in any age the religious dissenters of this particular kind exhibit a lack of humor and strive to perform what they consider their multiple – and divinely ordained – duties in earnest. Nor does Josephus even try to support his rhetorical contention.

Neither should his next statement – that the priests other than zealots, watching from afar the ridicule of the law (ibid) lamented and bemoaned the debasement of their sacred honors; ibid.) – be taken fully at face value. No doubt, there were in attendance those who shared the sentiments described; after all, zealots could not have represented the entire priestly constituency. Still, one cannot dismiss altogether the favorable tradition, sharply contrasting with the satire of the *Bellum*, on the election of Phanni (Phinehas or Pinhas) b. Samuel, found in the Tannaitic writings, and perhaps even traceable close to the time of the actual episode. Thus the Tosefta says (*tYom*, 1, 6):

> They say about Pinhas of Habbata, on whom the lot fell to be high priest, that the revenuers and supervisors came along and found him cutting wood. So they filled up his woodshed with golden *denars*.

The most patent point about this man, however, is that he, not unlike the 'official' high priest Matthias b. Theophilus, exercised apparently no impact whatsoever upon the course of events. An inadvertent irony lay in the fact that these two individuals, one legitimately, the other not, became the last high priests in Jewish history. With the destruction of the Temple this office, like some other important features of Jewish social and religious life, ceased to exist.[5]

Among many things, Josephus accuses zealots of stirring up, by means of intrigue or slander, jealousies and enmities within the government of Ananus b. Ananus (*BJ*, 4, 150). It may or may not have been so. Or this could signify the historian's desire to explain away clashes among the members of the ruling faction he documented earlier in connection with his own predicament in Galilee. It is easy to imagine Ananus b. Ananus trying to achieve greater consensus between his followers in the face of the growing influence enjoyed by zealots. One would expect him and his colleagues, for some period of time, to have been engaged in propagandistic measures which Josephus happens to mention only on the eve of the showdown, when he tells us that the reputable leaders, such as Gorion b. Joseph and Simon b. Gamaliel, began publicly to address citizens at the gatherings (ibid, 159) of the sort I have earlier compared with the Roman *contiones* or modern rallies; they are also said to have privately visited important individuals, urging the need "to punish the defilers of freedom and to cleanse the sanctuary from the polluted" (ibid). These activities, adds Josephus, were reinforced by the most eminent (160) of the high priests, Jesus b. Gamala and Ananus b. Ananus himself, who "vehemently chastised the people at the 'meetings' for their sloth and incited them against zealots" (ibid)

In Josephus's order of events, the election of the high priest follows the account of judicial murders perpetrated by zealots – anticipating the reign of terror they were to launch upon their subsequent takeover. It has been reasonably argued, however, that in reality it must have happened the other way around. Perhaps the historian reversed the order of the events to present religious blasphemy as their (so far) uppermost crime. Be that as it may, his narrative on the incipient stage of terror leaves much to be desired. Josephus's procedure is primarily rhetorical rather than informative, as for instance:

> They did not limit their daring to robberies and plunder, but went on even to murders, not at night or clandestinely, but openly in daylight, and beginning with the most prominent citizens.
>
> (*BJ*, 4, 139)

It is by no means clear, on the other hand, how zealots managed to seize and then put on trial three members of the royal family, one of whom was in charge of public treasury, which must have been an official appointment within the government; what might have been their reasons for prosecuting these particular individuals; and why the ruling 'moderate' faction allowed this to happen. The whole affair might well have been the result of accidents and mixed motives. Antipas (III), the most prominent of the captured Herodians, was mentioned by Josephus on an earlier occasion as a member of the embassy sent, upon the cessation of the Imperial sacrifices, from Jerusalem to King Agrippa with the request to interfere (*BJ*, 2, 418). The same delegation included Saul and Costobar, apparently Antipas's relatives. Later on, all three of them were reportedly besieged by the rebels in the royal palace; as we know, Saul and Costobar succeeded in escaping to the Romans and went subsequently to Greece, carrying Cestius Gallus's report for Nero. But Antipas chose otherwise: he stayed in the capital, as Josephus phrased it, "disdaining to take flight" (2, 557). His motivation is impossible to ascertain: it is not very likely, however, that he felt any serious concern for religion or patriotism, neither having counted for special interest among the Herodians. Rather, he might have been worried about his possessions, whether urban real estate or some other form of investment. Finally, he could have provoked enmity in the Herodian clan, plagued as it was with bitter family feuds, and – conversely – relied on his connections within the aristocratic rebel camp to insure his personal and material safety. In any event, Antipas's choice to stay seems initially to have paid off. He was appointed to administer public treasury (*BJ*, 4, 140), although we do not know whether this occurred at the Temple meeting or at some later point. On the other hand, this very appointment may have proved the major cause of his subsequent ruin: the position Antipas came to occupy was the one to which, as can be inferred from Josephus (cf. *BJ*, 2, 564), the leader of the zealots, Eleazar b. Simon, aspired.

We are left ignorant as regards the circumstances of Antipas's arrest. Under the conditions of 'diarchy', with two competing centers of authority, anything might happen and much depended on chance. Antipas could have been detained during one of his visits to the sanctuary – that is, before the Temple grounds were shut off by zealots; or through a special raid to the part of the city zealots did not control. Two other Herodians (a Levias and one Syphas b. Aregetes – 4, 141) whom Josephus cites in the same context as arraigned by zealots are otherwise unknown; more persons of high reputation are mentioned (ibid), but not specified. The aristocratic faction apparently did not attempt to negotiate their release, or if they did, they must have failed: on this, as on other related matters, our source chose to keep silent. Nor did they try to liberate the prisoners by force, either recognizing their lack of power or, perhaps, for more sinister reasons. After all, Ananus would have felt little sympathy for the members of the royal house, given the king's role in his own deposition from high priesthood. It may even not be too far-fetched to allow that he intentionally abstained from any action, believing that this arbitrary exercise of (in)justice on the part of the radicals may serve (as it actually proved so) a further incentive for his followers within the populace to take arms and attack zealots at their Temple stronghold.

Be that as it may, the three Herodians, reports Josephus, were first put in prison (ibid), presumably, in the city's territory held by zealots. The latter, we are told, still considered it unsafe merely to keep them in jail (4, 143) – which implies that they were not certain for how long they would have been able to control this situation. Josephus specifies that the prisoners were influential (141), with numerous families ready to avenge them, and besides, he says, the radicals feared that "the people angered by their lawlessness will rise against them" (144). (At this point, however, his own logic betrays itself: the common sense suggests that by the murder of the prisoners, the anger of the "people" and, consequently, the probability of their rising up against the perpetrators would increase rather than diminish.) The narrative graphically portrays what must have subsequently happened: a commando of ten, led by one John b. Dorcas, "the best expert in murder among them" (145), entered the jail with drawn swords and butchered the prisoners (ibid).

It is not stated whether the execution of three Herodians resulted from any formal trial, which may or may not have been the case; but the reasons for it, as provided by the zealots, are spelled out: three men were put to death for treason and negotiation with the Romans planning to betray the city, that is to say, as "traitors to common liberty" (146) – a charge that Josephus predictably finds "a false pretext for so great a crime" (ibid). He must have been right: for a public figure such as Antipas (or any other) enjoying the position of authority, to undertake at this stage of the revolt a move towards peace with the Romans, risking exposure, would have meant an act of folly. The historian uses this opportunity rhetorically to depict an atmosphere of growing terror that stands in dramatic contrast with the claim by zealots to have been "benefactors and saviors of the city" (ibid): "Dreadful panic seized the people, as if the city had been taken by the enemy, and each man desired his own salvation" (142).

According to Josephus, it was a peroration, addressed by Ananus b. Ananus to the people of Jerusalem, which proved a turning point in the standstill. It is true that the historian chose to call that gathering *ekklesia* (*BJ*, 4, 162) rather than, more habitually, *koinon*; but given the lack of precision or consistency in his use of terminology, and owing to the emergency of the moment, it must have been yet one further rally of sympathizers – perhaps on a bigger scale than before – rather than a properly constituted assembly of citizens as the Greek word might imply. There is no reason, however, to deny the fact of Ananus's speech to the masses (162–192), or even the gist of the argument (that is, the need to fight zealots) as presented by Josephus, since its contents, under the circumstances, would have been predictable. Its rhetoric (at some points, as we will see, counterproductive) reflects, on the other hand, the agenda of the historian, who at the time of the event languished in a Roman jail.

I have already touched upon Ananus's speech in connection with the rhetoric of liberty as employed by Josephus and (likely) practiced by the leaders of the 'first regime'. Indeed, the opposition between 'freedom' and 'tyranny' is the crux of the speaker's presentation, where the tyranny of zealots (*BJ*, 4, 166; cf. 185; 175) is portrayed as even worse than that of the Romans. Those latter, Ananus is made to say, respected the Temple's sacred grounds and "never went past the boundary of the profane, nor violated any of our religious customs, but trembling, observed the enclosures of the sanctuary from a distance" (4, 182), while the fellow Jews, that is, zealots, born and brought up in accordance with the Law, trod upon holy places "with their hands still hot from the murder of their compatriots" (184). The point is admittedly specious and deceitful: it was on record, and known to any educated person among the Jews, that upon his conquest of Jerusalem (63 B.C.), Pompey did in fact desecrate the Temple and even penetrate the Holy of Holies (*BJ*, 1, 152; *Ap*., 2, 82,). As regards Ananus's claim that the Romans, if victorious, would have spared the Jewish nobles whom zealots did not (*BJ*, 4, 181), this is apparently a piece of Josephus's own retrospective wishful thinking: we remember how Gessius Florus, on the account of personal slight, put to death without trial even those Jews who achieved the rank of Roman knights.

The historian's immediate concerns are no less patent in the rhetorical innuendo he has the speaker employ regarding the current war: "As for the war with Rome, I refrain from investigating whether it is profitable and appropriate and to our advantage, or the opposite" (177). It is most unlikely that the real man would have made any such statement, however qualified, at that point of the developments, since it would have only confirmed popular suspicion about his collaborationism.

On the other hand, this obviously served Josephus's conception of the war when writing the *Bellum*, in which he sought to persuade his audience that the members of his own class, that is, the Jewish aristocracy, and their leaders were reluctant to participate in the military effort, having been compelled to do it only by the force of circumstances. Side by side with the theme of liberty – from zealots' tyranny rather than Rome's – the motif of sloth and apathy shown by the residents of Jerusalem towards radical factions runs in the speech, allowing them to grow in numbers (cf. 166 ff.). This inertia is treated as contrary to the very idea of freedom and as tantamount to the predilection for servitude:

> Has the most honorable and most natural of passions, the desire of liberty, perished among you; have we become enamored of slavery and masters [e.g. zealots – V. R.], as if we have inherited submission from our forefathers?
>
> (175)

It is predictably answered with the references to the exploits of the heroic past – the resistance to the Egyptian and Persian yoke (176). This, in turn, starts the line of reasoning that leads to the conclusion: subservience to the external foe may owe to ill fortune, while an acquiescence in the face of internal tyranny betrays the debasement of national character (178 f.). Altogether, this oration seems curiously to reflect on the 'paralysis' and 'schizophrenia' of the 'first regime': it is addressed to the plebs, but emphasized nobility; it calls for arms, but implicitly praises the Romans; it expresses concern for people's safety, and at the same time attacks their complacency – in sum, it betrays psychological contradictions shared by many among the nobility whom I have previously discussed.

Finally, although the occasion must have certainly required that the orator refer to matters divine, it is not possible to ascertain what exactly Ananus b. Ananus could have said in reality on that subject. The version, provided by Josephus, starts with a highly rhetorical lament: he is described having wept (162). The author makes his speaker deplore the fact of his being still alive since he has to watch the House of God (163) laden with so much outrage, and its "inaccessible and holy terrain afflicted upon by the feet of murderers" (ibid). He proceeds then to announce that, even if he remains alone (164), he is prepared to devote his life to the cause of God (ibid) because life among the people who had lost their stamina is worthless (165). The same pledge not to spare his own person is reiterated at the end of the peroration (192), after the statement that "to die at the sacred gates and give up life if not for wives and children, but for God and for the sanctuary" makes a noble end (191).

Interestingly, this final coda is preceded by an expressed wish, perhaps reminiscent of some biblical precedent regarding Israel's foes, that the Deity whom they offend may turn the missiles of the rebels upon themselves "so that the impious be destroyed by their own weapons" (190). Taken together with the earlier reference to the Romans' piety (their votive offerings, it says, are still on view at the Temple courts – 181), this comes close to Josephus's favorite argument to the effect that, appalled by the blasphemies his own people had committed, the God of Israel, as he also used to act in the past, once again came to side with their enemy, the Romans.

Nothing in this largely fictional rhetoric is able to offer any insight into the speaker's genuinely religious sentiments, whatever they might have been. It would be, of course, the same even if it were a literal transcription of what Ananus b. Ananus had to say. One may, however, reiterate that, having been experienced politicians of the Sadducaean persuasion, he and his ilk were unlikely to feel the same intense anxiety over the issues of faith as did the religious dissenters who rose up against them. This is not to say that the establishment was not disturbed by doctrinal and ritual deviations, characteristic of the latter; but it stands to reason that their chief concerns lay with their political and military predicament, vis-à-vis the Romans, on the one hand, and the revolutionary radicals, on the other.

Josephus's account does not place responsibility on any one side for initiating the showdown: it suggests that it was the ruling group that urged people to take up arms and began the preparations, but the zealots moved first by launching an attack from their stronghold at the Temple (*BJ*. 4, 193 ff.). The motives ascribed by the historian to the radicals – that they despaired of obtaining pardon for their crimes (ibid, 193) – sounds indeed shallow, betraying his own agenda and wishful thinking rather than the truth: most certainly, zealots went on fighting fully convinced of the righteousness of their cause.

I will only briefly dwell on the actual developments of the coup, which Josephus describes at length (4196–4236); it also must have been well remembered by his readers in Judaea. It is worth noticing, however, that zealots could not have won until the arrival of the Idumaeans, which seems to confirm the historian's contention that the city populace largely supported the 'first regime' – despite the arrival *en masse* of the fugitives from the outside. One point his account persistently makes is the numerical superiority of the 'moderate' forces versus the better weapons and military training within the radicals (cf. e.g., 197 f., 202). It appears that upon the first skirmishes, the latter were driven back into the Temple's inner court by men loyal to Ananus b. Ananus (204 ff.). What followed is somewhat confusing. We are told that the Temple grounds were polluted with the blood of the wounded zealots, who sought refuge therein (201), and this is why Ananus abstained from assailing the "sacred portals" (205; presumably of the inner court) "under their [zealots' – V. R.] missiles falling from above" (ibid). The claim is that he thought it unlawful, even if he might win, to "lead the multitude [of his followers – V. R.] in, without first performing purification" (ibid). It was the outer court, one assumes, which had already been occupied by the 'moderates' that stood in need of purification: Ananus would not have been able to purify the inner court without invading it and slaughtering its defendants, and at the same time, he could not have invaded it before it were purified – the conundrum known to us as 'Catch 22'.

Be that as it may, he reportedly chose a temporary measure: select 6000 men by lot and post them, on the basis of rotation, to guard the porticoes (206; presumably, of the inner court). One can only speculate whether this decision was made on the grounds of Ananus's genuine piety, his desire ostentatiously to display it, or simply for the reasons of sound strategic considerations. Subsequent to this success, Josephus asserts, the fortunes of the 'moderates' began to deteriorate due to the intervening intrigue by John b. Levi, who was, as we well know, the historian's personal and bitterest enemy. It was he who created multiple obstacles for Josephus during the latter's campaign in Galilee, and then fled with his followers to Jerusalem upon the capture of his native city Gischala by Titus in the fall of A.D. 67 (*BJ*, 4, 106 ff.; 121 ff.).

This personage plays a major role in the narratives of both the *Bellum* and the *Vita*, and I will keep returning to him and his activities. At this stage it suffices to emphasize that, having languished at the time in Roman captivity, the historian could have witnessed in person none of John's allegedly treacherous dealings with the 'moderates' or zealots, which he describes with an air of confidence. Indeed, he must have largely relied on hearsay, but the public character of what had happened placed some limits to his misrepresentation of the facts. Still, one suspects that much of what he says, which certainly includes the speech he makes John b. Levi address with the leaders of the zealots, belongs among historical fiction.

Josephus portrays John b. Levi as primarily responsible for a subsequent debacle, a skillful manipulator and accomplished practitioner of dissimulation. According to the historian, his old foe, upon his arrival to Jerusalem, engaged in an insidious double game, first by ingratiating himself with the ruling faction of Ananus b.Ananus (at one point, we are told, even swearing an oath of allegiance to their cause – *BJ*, 4, 214), and then confiding their secrets to zealots. By virtue of his oath and perhaps for the reason of his known contacts with the radicals, we read, he was chosen as a delegate to negotiate the treaty with the latter. Josephus explains this initiative on the part of the 'moderates' in terms of pious considerations: they sought, he states, to preserve the Temple (presumably, its inner court, since the outer had been already occupied by their forces) from pollution "so that no one of their compatriots could have perished there" (215). This claim notwithstanding, it seems likely that their ultimate motive for seeking truce must have been neither piety nor charity but rather knowledge of their insufficient strength at the moment and strategically adverse circumstances for any immediate or decisive action. Be that as it may, John is said to have betrayed his mission and indulged in deliberate misinformation by telling the zealots that Ananus intended to purify the premises in order to undertake yet another assault on them, and that he persuaded people to send an embassy to Vespasian with the request to come at once and take over the city (218 f.). Furthermore, Josephus makes John imply that his very choice as an envoy was a manifestation of God's will (219), and then warn zealots against the treachery supposedly planned by their opponents. They must remember, goes the argument, that their earlier "daring deeds" (221), such as murders and "dissolution of laws and law courts" (223), will be neither forgotten nor forgiven. This is evidently a rhetorical device on the part of the author who, by placing his own favorite contention, namely, the fear of punishment (rather than their belief in their divinely ordained cause), as the chief reason for zealots' perseverance in their crimes in the mouth of his own antagonist, seeks to double its persuasive effect. Finally, the speaker is shown as advising his audience to ask for external help (220), to wit, the Idumaeans (224) and – almost as an afterthought ("in order personally to provoke the leaders of zealots" – ibid) – informing two zealot chiefs, Eleazar b. Simon and Zacharias b. Amphicalleus, that they are specifically targeted by Ananus b. Ananus for destruction (ibid).

There is no valid way to determine whether, or to what extent, the charges raised by Josephus against John b. Levi were in any sense legitimate. Judging by the man's remarkable and proved ability for self-aggrandizement as well as survival, none of them sounds beyond belief. Still, one must recognize that the historian's treatment of him in this episode bears a close enough resemblance to the account in Thucydides (who was Josephus's implicit model – cf. *Ap.*, 1, 18; note also *BJ*, 1, 5) of Alcibiades betraying the Athenian cause to the Spartans (6, 88 ff.): in both cases a turncoat offers advice detrimental to the fortunes of his homeland, former friends or allies.[6]

Whatever might be said about the status of the Idumaeans *vis-à-vis* Judaea's Jews, it is clear that Josephus – and therefore his contemporaries – considered them a separate entity. Even though converted to Judaism under the Hasmonaean King John Hyrcanus I, they apparently did not fully integrate into Jewish society and tended to be looked upon, at least by some, as not *bona fide* members of Israel. It cannot be established to what extent, if any, the Idumaean descent of Herod the Great and his royal house might have affected Jewish attitudes towards their race and vice versa. Although Josephus emphatically labels the origin of Herod's family "half-Jewish" (*AJ*, 14, 403), it is not unlikely that the widespread popular view of him owed more to his despotic policies than to his non-Jewish extraction. At the same time it seems that some among the Idumaeans, however few, might have continued adhering to their ancient pagan cults, such as that of the god Cos, which is also reflected in the nomenclature. Nor is it possible to ascertain, for the lack of meaningful information, what motives might have prompted the Idumaeans (more accurately, their tribal leaders) to side with the extremist zealots against the 'moderate' supporters of the 'first regime'. It is true that converts often happen to exhibit even greater religious zeal than any average believer; but in this case the conversion had occurred

200 years earlier, so that by the time of the revolt it must have ceased being any significant factor to account for the Idumaeans' behavior. Furthermore, their break with zealots in the aftermath of the coup indicates that they did not share the latter's agenda as proponents of religious dissent, nor their belief of being specially chosen to accomplish divine will. Their decision might or might not have pertained to tensions between the urban and rural populace in Idumaea, or any other social problems; but of this we have virtually no evidence. So it seems safest to assume that they were primarily motivated by animosity against the Roman conquerors and their collaborators, real or imaginary, which is in agreement with Josephus's overall portrayal of the Idumaeans as ardent patriots (e.g. *BJ*, 4, 281; cf. 233, 278).

Upon the reception of the letter from zealots besieged in the Temple, the Idumaean leaders, we are told, called for action and, having amassed the force of "no less than twenty thousand" marched to the capital (*BJ*, 4, 235). This number looks suspect and its veracity was repeatedly debated. For some, this signified a fundamental unreliability of Josephus's narrative, to the point of arguing that he invented the whole episode of the Idumaean intrusion in Jerusalem to aid zealots and their participation in the subsequent reign of terror. It is true that in many cases figures proffered by Josephus do not seem plausible. It must be remembered, however, that the ancient historians' approach to numbers was far from statistical in any modern sense of the word. Furthermore, as regards, say, the count of casualties on a battlefield, more or less precise calculation could have arguably been made; not so in a sudden and spontaneous outburst of violence under discussion. In fact, even today, in the events of political rallies, public protests and such, the official and unofficial figures of participants sometimes differ vastly, in terms of thousands. Finally, we know, of course, that Josephus could not have been present on the scene and had to rely on the rumors, which by their very nature exaggerate. The number he employed serves to convey an impression of huge multitudes breaking into the city able to overcome those whom the historian (and undoubtedly many of the locals) saw as defenders of law and order. It seems sensible to suggest that it was exactly how the populace must have felt during that night of the massacre.

Josephus mentions four Idumaean leaders whose first names are unmistakably Jewish: Simon, son of Cathlas; two brothers, John and James, sons of Sosas; and one Phineas, son of Clusoth (*BJ*, 4, 235; cf. 5, 249). Of them all, Simon b. Cathlas seems to stand out: Josephus makes him object in a sharp rejoinder to the lengthy arguments proffered by the high priest Jesus b. Gamala before the gates of the capital, calling the Idumaeans to desist from joining forces with the zealots (4, 273 ff.). Irrespective of the specific reasoning the historian ascribed to either party, this occurrence could well have been historical, in which case Simon b. Cathlas must have enjoyed among his people not only the authority of a commander but also a reputation for eloquence. Equally, it appears that he was endowed with physical prowess: later in his narrative, Josephus singles him and James b. Sosas out of ten Idumaean commanders under Simon b. Giora

(5, 249 f.), and two of them are again praised as playing heroes during the fight with the Romans at the time of the siege (6, 148). Of the gallant James b. Sosas (cf. also 6, 92) we learn, however, that only few weeks before the fall of Jerusalem, he entered a secret complicity with other Idumaean chiefs with the purpose of entering negotiations for surrender and even agreed to serve as one of five envoys to Titus. But the plot was reportedly detected by Simon b. Giora, which led to his arrest and imprisonment (6, 379 f.). His subsequent fate, as well as that of Simon b. Cathlas, remains unknown. Finally, John b. Sosas, brother of James, is mentioned as having perished in the aftermath of the Jewish attack on the Romans, while he tried to burn their engines and entrenchments some time between Titus's laying siege to the capital and his capturing the first (Agrippa's) wall in May A.D. 70. The historian reports that he was pierced by the Arab arrow and died on the spot. He is the only Idumaean rebel whom Josephus graced with a short eulogy: "This left both the Idumaeans as well as the insurgents with great sorrow and anguish since he was distinguished by the strength of both his hand and his mind" (5, 290). The name of the fourth Idumaean commander, Phineas b. Clusoth, is never mentioned again.

The subsequent course of the zealots' coup can be briefly summarized. The Idumaeans encamped at the city gates, closed to them by the 'moderates', and at night (we are not told how long after their arrival) they suffered from a violent thunderstorm, on the meaning of which Josephus seems theologically confused (*BJ*, 4, 286 ff.). In his view, it foretold "the destruction of mankind", a calamity of no small proportions (287). On the one hand, the thrust and tenor of his narrative imply that by this God made manifest his wrath (288) at the radicals (zealots and Idumaeans) in support of Ananus b. Ananus with his cohorts (and, the historian fancifully claims, it was exactly thus interpreted by both warring sides – 288); at the same time, the (literally) 'strategy' of Destiny (297) made it work otherwise so that the 'moderates' became doomed to perish. How the two notions were to be reconciled, the reader is not told.

Be that as it may, it appears that the same night, after some deliberations (which Josephus fictionally elaborates upon, without, of course, having been present at the proceedings – cf. 292 ff.), some zealots, besieged in the Temple, managed clandestinely to open the city gates (they cut through the bars with the Temple's saws) so that their Idumaean allies could enter the capital (298 ff.). What followed Josephus describes with some real dramatic skill (301 ff.). According to him, those zealots who allowed the Idumaeans in restrained their fury and desire for rampage by entreating them first to liberate their comrades, still inside the Temple, which they did upon having successfully overcome the 'moderate' guards. This done, they are portrayed as seeking out and then slaying the leaders of the 'first regime' – Ananus b. Ananus and Jesus b. Gamala (314 ff.) – and, as always happens under such circumstances, no doubt numerous others. On the historian's encomium of both men I have already commented. Josephus insists that their corpses were cast out without burial, "naked, to be eaten by dogs and beasts", emphasizing that this ran contrary to the Jewish law which requires that even the crucified criminals should be buried before the sunset of their execution day (317; cf. *Deut.*, 21, 22 f.).

Josephus's contention of ignominy, visited on this and other occasions (cf. *BJ*, 4, 343, 360) by the revolutionaries upon their victims' dead bodies, was objected by hyper-criticist scholars on the grounds that Judaism considered such treatment a sacrilege while in Greece it was a just punishment of traitors, with the inference that Josephus willfully used the foreign model to distort the truth. This argument betrays a failure on the part of the moderns to comprehend the dynamics of self-justification inherent in the psychology of religious dissent, which has been obvious to Josephus: he knew that such individuals, by committing sacrilege or mass murder, were perfectly capable of claiming it to have been an act of duty in the fulfillment of divine will, thus regarding "the greatest of their evils as good deeds" (*BJ*, 7, 270). This, of course, is a contradiction in terms; but the fanatical behavior never stops at being irrational. (The "rationalist" and "scientific" Marxists, even when perpetrating genocide, as in Kampuchea, were quite capable of explaining it away in terms of their pseudo-humanist "dialectics"). Not even a biblical precedent lacked: one recalls the body of Queen Jezebel left for the dogs (*2 Kings*: 9, 30 ff.), which fulfilled the pronouncement of no lesser figure than Prophet Elijah (*1 Kings*: 21, 23). Finally, Josephus's contention is enhanced by his several further references to similar practice (*BJ*, 4, 331 f.; 343, esp. 382 ff). I find it inconceivable that so significant a leitmotif within his narrative was nothing but fiction. That would have seriously undermined the value of his account in the eyes of his Jewish contemporaries who were bound to know better, an eventuality the historian could not afford.

For those endowed with the mentality and temperament of religious dissenters, violating God's commandment in order to implement (as they believe) God's will is nothing uncommon: in this respect, they are as relativistic as any postmodernist. Thus, for instance, Islam – which insists on the obedience to the law of the Koran as thoroughly as Judaism in its commitment to the law of the Torah – explicitly prohibits Muslims killing the faithful even in the case of hostilities (see, e.g., 4, 92 f.). As we now know so well, this did not and does not prevent Islamic radicals from destroying countless lives of their innocent co-religionists by the acts of terrorism, including blowing up the holy mosques with the attendant worshipers, in Pakistan, Indonesia or Iraq. That the radicals in Jerusalem, during their ascent at and stay in power, performed multiple blasphemies, there can be no doubt: they ranged from the defilement of the Sabbath day (when they massacred the Roman garrison despite the pledge for their safety), to the abuse of the Temple's treasure, to murders perpetrated on the sacred territory. Against this background, what happened, in the words of Josephus, to the corpses of the two leaders as the objects of hatred should not cause a particular surprise, but represents yet another atrocity by those who feel chosen for an exceptional achievement in service to their God, where and when everything is allowed.[7]

III.

The new dispensation, which emerged as a result of the coup, can be called the 'second regime' only in a very loose sense. Not unlike its predecessor, it began as a manner of a 'coalition', this time essentially tripartite, consisting of zealots under their leader Eleazar b. Simon, allied with the contingent from Idumaea and John b. Levi, who brought his followers from Galilee to Jerusalem upon the fall of Gischala (with the 'brigands' from the countryside, who might – or might not – have comprised a separate or fourth element). For the most part, however, it was no 'regime' at all: shortly thereafter, when the allies of zealots seceded at some point in the spring of A.D. 68 (*BJ*, 4, 389 ff.), a centralized control of the capital broke apart. This triggered the eruption of civil warfare within and without Jerusalem, now presided by a two-way faction of Eleazar and John; as for the Idumaeans, some of them withdrew from the city, and those staying, although they originally sided with John, seem to have sympathized with Simon b. Giora, who sought meanwhile to occupy their homeland. It was this man, and not the Romans, whom both city factions attacked next (4, 514; 538 ff.), an enterprise which eventually led to his entry into the capital in April A.D. 69. This was reportedly achieved by means of an unlikely alliance between the local aristocrats and the remaining Idumaeans, who must have been disenchanted by the continuous inner strife, or by their own failure to acquire a share of power (ibid, 566 ff.), or for any other reason. In consequence, two-way rivalry was replaced by three-way fighting (Eleazar–John–Simon). As Tacitus puts it, "there were three leaders, and as many armies" (*Hist.*, 5, 12 – *tres duces totidem exercitus*). This dismal state of 'triarchy' continued up to the arrival of Titus on Passover A.D. 70 with the intention of laying siege to the capital. Thereupon John b. Levi took over Eleazar with his zealots (*BJ*, 5, 99), as if restoring the earlier form of 'diarchy' (cf. Tac., loc. cit.: *ita in duas factiones civitas discessit* – "thus the state broke up into two factions") – this time, his own and Simon's (*BJ*, 5, 99), while the quarrel between those two as well as their refusal to join forces under a single command continued virtually until the end.

Even this very brief outline of events seems to justify Josephus's emphatic claim (ibid, 4, 318) that the victory of the radicals over the 'first regime' became the ultimate cause of subsequent disasters, including the capture of Jerusalem and destruction of the Temple. In any event, it should not be dismissed lightly as merely self-serving or biased, which certain scholars tend to do. Despite their professed, and obviously genuine, anti-Roman fervor, the new leaders utterly failed in directing any military initiative against the enemy – unlike their 'moderate' predecessors, who at least had attempted, even though it proved unsuccessful, an attack at Ascalon. This lack of action seems particularly remarkable given the fact that, after Nero's downfall, the Roman Empire was plunged into a misery of its own civil war, with the rapid succession of emperors; and with Vespasian deciding to suspend hostilities, perhaps in preparation for his own *pronunciamento*. The radical factions never exploited opportunities offered by this unexpected development – not even by raising a guerilla force to engage with the Romans, or by taking measures in anticipation of an inevitable siege. To an impartial, or rational, observer the political behavior of this kind would seem almost incredible; but it must signify, on the one hand, their faith in an imminent divine aid and, on the other, the extent of their absorption in mutual undoing, which cannot be denied. It is, however, increasingly difficult to inquire into, or interpret, their conceivable motives for this fratricide tantamount to suicide.

But before making any attempt at this, or at discussing the leadership and membership of the revolutionary groups, it is imperative to return to the scene at the capital in the aftermath of the zealots' coup and to Josephus's controversial account regarding the campaign of terror they are said to have launched.

As I have repeatedly argued, any adequate judgment on Josephus's narrative requires appreciating his concern with the credibility of his reportage. The events he described in the *Bellum* were very much within living memory, having been witnessed by the masses of his contemporaries, both Jewish and gentile. This means that he was not at liberty, whatever his bias or rhetorical preferences might have been, merely to fictionalize their portrayal, as it is now increasingly argued, or to distort it, in terms of exaggeration or omission, to the point when it becomes unbelievable. Josephus's ardent polemics in the *Vita* with Justus of Tiberias patently testifies to the anxiety he must have felt about the credibility issue. It is true that from the moment of his surrender to Vespasian and until the siege of Jerusalem by Titus (whose retinue he had joined) began, the historian was not present at the capital and therefore could not bear direct witness to the misdeeds, which he describes with genuine gusto, perpetrated by the zealots, their allies and their rivals. This information he must have received either at the time by hearsay from the individual refugees who attempted to reach the Roman camp, or later on by talking to or interrogating the survivors. This may account for faulty chronology, some minor implausibilities, and for obviously exaggerated figures of the victims. The text of the *Bellum* often exhibits inaccuracies and similar signs of neglect, perhaps engendered by the author's sense of urgency in completing his project. It is likely that in a number of cases he lacked either the time or desire, or both, to undertake a deeper inquiry. To this must be added, of course, the quality of his imagination and his undisputed desire to malign his personal and political enemies as much as the circumstances (that is, the need for credibility) allowed.

None of this justifies, however, modern arguments, which seek to deny the basic historicity in Josephus's treatment of zealots and, in particular, the reign of terror upon their seizure of power. It does not befit a modern observer to repudiate the evidence found in an ancient source simply because, for whatever reason, one does not like it, or because it does not suit one's own ideological agenda. As I have pointed out, what Josephus had written must have been considered sufficiently trustworthy by his immediate readers, many of whom were directly implicated in the events, saw them unravel or suffered their burden – otherwise, his whole enterprise would have proved useless. It also must be taken into consideration that in his narrative strategy he followed the established practices of Graeco-Roman historiography by making a general statement about the horrors and killings that took place under tyranny or revolution, and then by illustrating them with one or two prominent examples. This does not naturally mean that the victims had been only those named in the source. The classical analysis of the *stasis* in Corcyra by Thucydides (3, 70 ff.; 4, 46 ff.), Josephus's implicit model, does not name casualties (except one, the early victim of the oligarchs – 3, 76); but this by no means impinges (notwithstanding the currently fashionable 'metahistorical' arguments) on its essential veracity. Seneca's *Apocolocyntosis* (14) charges Claudius with the murder of 35 senators and 221 knights (the figures at the time obviously familiar to the public); but one could have hardly expected Tacitus's *Annales* (even if the now lost parts of the Claudian narrative would have survived) to list all of those individuals by name.

Back to the point, Josephus starts his denunciation (first among several) of the terror, inaugurated by the victors, upon murdering the 'moderate' leaders, with the picture of indiscriminate massacre: the revolutionary hordes, he says, "butchered people as if they have been the packs of unclean animals" where they were seized (*BJ*, 4, 326 f.) – a behavior expected by the conquerors against the conquered. It is not surprising that many commoners perished on the spot: history demonstrates that in the time of civic upheaval low classes suffer no less than the upper. Nor is there any reason to doubt the historian's report of numerous arrests among the young nobles (327; cf. 333), who were put in jail, tortured and then executed (327 ff.) – all of this must have been a matter of common knowledge. Whether Josephus's claim is justified that this atrocity owed to an attempt by the victors to compel those young men to join their cause (327; not a single one, he asserts, chose to consent: 328), and upon their failure in achieving that, to exercise their vengeance, remains uncertain. One suspects an embellishment on his part. Be that as it may, the figures provided by the historian – 12,000 victims (332) – are, of course, untenable. Unless this round number was an emendation by the scribe, we may only infer that it was based on a rumor (and, in any event, who at the time would have done the counting?), merely signaling a huge waste of human life, and accepted by Josephus without any further check.

Specifically, the notion of terror implies at least two components, which were prominent in the policies of the zealot regime: the combination of extra-legal and quasi-(or pseudo-) legal murders, and the assignment of guilt by association. The imprisonment and slaughter of the young aristocrats without trial is a clear case of an arbitrary extra-legal act. It seems that the same was true regarding the subsequent murder of Gorion b. Joseph (*BJ*, 4, 358; in this passage he is referred to merely as 'Gourion'). Aside from two high priestly leaders, this man is the only victim named ("among many others"; ibid), who took, as we saw, an active part in the 'moderate' government: the text speaks of no formal action against him. His allegedly 'democratic' views I have already discussed.

For an example of a quasi- (or pseudo-) legal charade (we would have called today "a show trial"), Josephus chose to concentrate on an affair of one Zacharias, son of Baris (*BJ*, 4, 335 ff.). In contrast to some other of his reports, the wealth of details suggests that this particular account was based on reliable testimonies, perhaps even from those who were present at the court. We do not know of any relationship Zacharias b. Baris might or might not have entertained with the fallen regime: hitherto his name has not been mentioned, but it is unlikely that he had held any official post – perhaps one reason why his case was chosen by Josephus as an *exemplum*. The latter describes him as the "most eminent" citizen (335), who presumably antagonized the new masters by his hatred of wrongs and love of liberty (ibid). He was also rich, which made Josephus immediately impute that, by destroying him, zealots at once sought to remove an influential person and pillage his property (ibid). As regards his religious sensibilities, it seems fair to assume that this man did not differ much from the others of his ilk, with their conventional piety and lack of sympathy for zealous fervor manifest in radical dissenters, or for their revolt against the established priestly order.

Next, we learn that 70 men of some authority were summoned by command to serve as a court at the Temple (the method of selection or the principles of its composition remain unexplained) – and were assigned, adds the historian with an emphasis, as if in a play, the role of judges deprived of any real power (ibid, 336). Predictably, zealots indicted Zacharias b. Baris for an alleged intent to deliver the state to the Romans and conducting treasonous communication with Vespasian (ibid). Similar charges were earlier laid against Antipas (III) and two others executed Herodians, as well as – by means of a whispering campaign – the fallen leaders of the "first regime". Similarly to those other cases, claims of this sort lack plausibility: at that stage of the revolt, any such move would have been both dangerous and senseless. The historian insists that no evidence for the defendant's guilt had been adduced (337). Not unlike his account of the high priest's election by lot, Josephus's treatment of this episode is stylized, both angry and sarcastic, with a touch of satire, and cannot be entirely taken at face value. One is entitled to skepticism reading that *all* 70 'judges' exhibited the same defiance in repudiating the charges and voted, as a body, says the text, for the acquittal of the accused, "preferring to die with him rather to take on responsibility for his ruin" (341). Surely there were enough of them to include opportunists, or perhaps even genuine supporters of the coup. Furthermore, Josephus indulges in his habit of unwarranted speculations as to what might have been going on in the heads of others. Thus, he makes Zacharias realize that he was summoned "to a prison rather than a court", with no hope for delivery left, but did not allow the defendant's sense of despair to affect his *parrhesia* (freedom of speech) by ridiculing the charges against him, expanding on the enormities committed by his foes, and lamenting the confusion in public affairs they had caused (338 f.). Likewise, the narrative alleges that zealots, in an uproar, "barely managed not to draw out their swords", but wished to bring this "pretense and mockery of the trial" to a close, so that they could test the willingness of the 'judges' to place a just cause over personal danger (340). Despite his apparent taste for dramatization, it cannot be doubted, however, that the proceedings ended by what the historian reports: zealots, annoyed at their failure to procure a quasi-legal verdict, must have slain Zacharias b. Baris on spot, – very much in the Phinehas-like style, but at the same time desecrating the sacred Temple grounds – and thrown his body into a ravine (343). The man was prominent enough to have been well known to Josephus's audience (another reason for the choice of his case as an *exemplum*), which would have precluded any attempt on his part at fictionalizing the place or circumstances of his death. Other details (as, for instance, Zacharias's display of bravery) may or may not be authentic, although nothing really speaks against their historicity. The episode concludes with the author's sarcastic comment on the impotent 'judges' driven by the zealots from the Temple precincts at sword's point, their lives spared for the sole reason that to all the rest they could play heralds of their own enslavement (344).

The last individual, cited by Josephus as victim at this stage of terror, Niger the Peraean, must have suffered through guilt by association. As we know, he was the 'first regime's military hero, although never a member of the ruling clique. His anti-Roman stand and personal valor could not be impeached (a fact emphasized by Josephus – *BJ*, 4, 359), which must have immunized him against the charge of 'Romanizing': with distinction, he fought Cestius Gallus at Bethhoron; for a time governed Idumaea (but subordinate to two other men); twice he led attacks on the Roman garrison at Ascalon and, when defeated, performed a miraculous escape. The historian implies that zealots feared him as a figure capable of bringing them down (363), but given their full control at the time over the capital, this does not sound realistic.

As portrayed by Josephus, Niger's execution resembles an act of lynching: we read that he was dragged throughout the city, "howling and often pointing to his scars" and killed outside the gates (359 f.). Dying, he is said to have been calling on the heads of his murderers Roman vengeance, famine, pestilence and fratricide (361). The author seizes the opportunity to declare from hindsight that God ratified those curses upon "the impious", and among them "the most just one, the frenzy of their fellow rebels they were soon bound to taste" (362). Once again, some embellishments notwithstanding, Josephus's account seems credible enough, including one other pathetic moment – Niger's plea to provide him at least with a decent burial and his foes' refusal to do so (360). As I have earlier argued, no custom or tradition, however sacred, could prevent religious dissenters who believe they are the instruments of divine will from satisfying even their basest passions. In practical terms, Niger's removal might well have been, in addition to an atrocity, a blunder: the man was apparently one of few able Jewish generals and, as his record shows, he knew how to obey a higher command. Staying alive, he was likely to continue fighting the Romans no less loyally under the new masters than he was before.

Josephus rounds up his narrative of terror, perpetrated by zealots following the coup, in the grand style of classical rhetoric, reminiscent both of Thucydides, his model and Tacitus, yet to come:

> There was no portion of the populace for whom they did not labor to provide a pretext. Anyone with whom there had been a difference was

put to death; the man who in peacetime had had absolutely no dealings with them was suspected as arrogant, the man who had approached them with candor as contemptuous, the toady as a conspirator. There was a single punishment for the most serious or most charges, death, and no one escaped, except the very humble, whether by low birth or by accident.
(363 ff.)

In itself, this – and similar broadly painted pictures of human suffering – are at once true and false, that is to say, they invoke some facts, known (or credible) to the reader, but play on the latter's emotion, eliciting a desirable response. Nor should this rhetoricization be treated according to whatever criteria of impartial report: of this, both the author and his audience must have been fully conscious. But it does not follow that it was intended as fiction, or was accepted as such – rather, it must be considered an effort to convey in words a sense of anguish, alien to our habitual daily experience, at the time when the customary routine is crumbled by forces whose meaning or conduct seem unpredictable, as the presumption of innocence ceases to exist.[8]

Eleazar b. Simon and 'a certain' Zacharias b. Amphicalleus, both of priestly descent, are named (*BJ*, 4, 225) as zealot leaders who presided over the perpetration of the coup. Of the latter nothing else is known from Josephus, although his father's name suggests that he came from a family sufficiently Hellenized to have adopted Greek nomenclature. Priestly origin does not necessarily imply membership in the Jewish elite: the existence of poor priests is well attested, as is the fact of their exploitation by the rich and the powerful (cf. *AJ*, 20, 206). The very zealotry those two were famous for suggests their Pharisaic persuasions, perhaps following the school of Shammai, which insisted on stricter commitment to the rules in accordance with both the Torah and the 'ancestral traditions'.

In contrast to his colleague Zacharias, Eleazar b. Simon, the "most influential" man (*BJ*, 4, 225) among zealots, is given more attention throughout Josephus's narrative, although in the typically incoherent manner; still, his personality remains almost as elusive as that of his namesake Eleazar b. Ananias. We remember him as one of the Jewish heroes at Beth-horon, taking over the Roman spoils and much of public treasure, and as a participant in the Temple meeting, whom Ananus b. Ananus managed to outmaneuver by denying him any real share of power, though he controlled much of the Roman spoils (*BJ*, 4, 564). It is noted that the 'moderates' regarded him as a potential tyrant, surrounded, as he was, by loyal bodyguards (ibid). Still, he must have played some role in the emerging 'coalition', even if informal, at the same time patiently spreading zealot influence among the people: Josephus accuses him of intrigues and cleverly manipulating financial exigencies (565), but what it exactly means remains unclear. The historian's contention that Eleazar's strategy of "beguilements" ultimately made people "obey to his authority in all things" (ibid) may or may not signify that he took upon himself some title or office, before or after the coup: as we have repeatedly seen, Josephus's institutional language and notions are notoriously vague.

He could have been the force behind the idea of selecting the high priest by lot (*BJ*, 4, 153; 155 ff.), an attempt to defy the established religious order, which is a quintessential characteristic of the dissent type he represents: at the very least, this would not have happened without his consent. One cannot doubt, on the other hand, the power of his and his followers' religious ardor, however perverse (or blasphemous) in its results: only a profound sense of piousness explains the fact that, under his command, zealots kept admitting the faithful for worship and sacrifice at the inner Temple they came to occupy (e.g., *BJ*, 5, 15) – a policy that would have impeached upon their own security. In the end this, indeed, served to their detriment: we learn that on Passover A.D. 70 John b. Levi of Gischala, who by then held the outer Temple, used the opportunity to invade the inner court with his men in the guise of pilgrims, and thus subdued Eleazar and his following to his will (5, 98 ff.).

Although, apparently, a man of strength and purpose, credited by Josephus with the ability both "to plan what should be done and implement his plans" (*BJ*, 4, 225), Eleazar b. Simon proved, in the final analysis, an inadequate leader. Except for a short period after his immediate accession, he never succeeded in uniting the rebel forces in the capital or inflicting any sizable damage on the Romans: for instance, no effort was made to exploit, to the benefit of the insurgents, the pause in warfare provided by the fall of Nero and the outbreak of civil warfare in Rome. Josephus chose to emphasize this point by attributing to Vespasian a comment that, at this stage of their revolt, "the Jews were not busy with preparing arms, fortifications, or levying men to fight with them / ... / but strangling each other in internecine was and discord, each day suffering worse misery than they [the Romans – V.R.] could have inflicted on them by attack and capture" (4, 375) and, consequently, the best course to be taken against them would be allowing them "to proceed with their own destruction" (ibid).

Furthermore, Eleazar b. Simon failed to prevent the secession of John b. Levi (4, 389 ff.), a major blow to his leadership. Later on (presumably, late A.D. 68 or early 69), he attempted to consolidate his own faction and split resolutely from John's by occupying the inner court of the Temple and leaving the outer to his rival, but this only led to the renewal of infighting (5, 5 ff.). According to Josephus's order of events, at some point Titus's Legion X encamped on the Mount of Olives (70). This, we read, made the factions at the first time temporarily join forces in "evil unity" (72), which did not prevent, however, John b. Levi from exploiting an opportunity and driving zealots under Eleazar into submission (98 ff.). One suspects that the latter's grasp over his own adherents was tenuous, which may account for the infrequency of his direct appearances in Josephus's narrative: the historian prefers to speak of 'zealots' in plural, rather than of their recognized chief, which stands in contrast to his individual treatment of two other rebel leaders, John of Gischala and Simon b. Giora.

Around the same time, both Eleazar's and John's factions lost whatever military or diplomatic game they played against Simon: in spring A.D. 69 the latter took over the capital, except for the Temple Mount, where he laid siege to them both (4, 577 ff.), who even then did not cease attacking each other. A year later John b. Levi prevailed over Eleazar and his men through a ruse, which was bound to diminish further the latter's stature (5, 98 ff.). It is difficult to ascertain their motives: speaking of his decisive break with John, Josephus dismisses any moral considerations, such as a sense of outrage at the policies of terror (cf. 5, 5), and makes it result from Eleazar's refusal in obeying "a tyrant younger than himself", coupled with "his thirst for power over all and for a despotism of his own" (5, 6). But, as often happens, this malicious imputation does not square with the historian's own subsequent report of Eleazar's eventual consent to a secondary role under the man from Gischala (later on he is plainly called "a former chief" of the zealots, subordinate to John – 5, 250). This fact – as well as his occasional capacity for maneuver – suggests that, despite much of the behavior, which characterizes religious dissenters discussed in this book, Eleazar b. Simon, not unlike his rival John of Gischala, differed from other rebel chiefs, such as Simon b. Giora or Eleazar b. Jairus, and (one assumes) from most of his own following by some flexibility and recognition of political necessities when they arise. This is not unknown in similar religious dissent movements throughout history, when certain leaders come to develop, in one sense or another, a conception and practice of politics as a *craft*, while others, in their mental rigidity, prove unable to do so: Luther and Savonarola, respectively, provide good examples.

Nevertheless, it would perhaps still be fair to allow Eleazar b. Simon, however obscurely drawn in our source, the benefit of doubt and to propose that misguided zealotry, clothed in patriotism, rather than mere ambition, by shaping priorities, might have governed his behavior – after all, he *did* place common interests (as he understood them) above personal ones when he agreed to become a subordinate of John b. Levi. After the reference just cited (5, 250) we never hear again about the "former chief" of zealots: not unlike his namesake, the son of Ananias, he vanishes from Josephus's narrative; it seems likely, however, that he perished, along with other zealots, during the capture of the Temple by the Romans.

Of other prominent zealots only a few names randomly survived. It is written that when Eleazar b. Simon broke from John b. Levi and occupied the Temple's inner court, he was supported by three comrades-at-arms, "men of power" as Josephus puts it, each one enjoying "not a little following" among the zealots (*BJ*, 5, 6). They are referred to as Judes b. Chelcias, Simon b. Esron and Ezechias b. Chobari, the last one described as "not an undistinguished youth" (ibid). One other individual, Simon b. Arinus (or Ari), is later cited as a zealot leader side by side with Eleazar b. Simon (5, 250), both of them fighting under John of Gischala after the latter's success in subduing the rival faction. Twice in the narrative this zealot is praised for bravery (6, 92; 148), once together with his brother Judas (92). It is worth noticing that, even after their ultimate submission to the leadership of John, zealots continued to function as a distinct group within the rebels' ranks (cf. 5, 250; 358; 6, 92; 148).

The inner structure of the short-lived zealot government in Jerusalem remains largely uncertain. There is a tendency to interpret it as a sort of 'egalitarian democracy', a view supported by such features as the election of the high priest by lot, perhaps reflecting the ideas of men's equality before God propagated by the "fourth philosophy" movement of Judas the Galilaean. There is some evidence for an attempt at equality among the "powerful": as we have just seen, each of three notable zealots who sided with Eleazar b. Simon is said to have acquired followers of their own (cf. 4, 389; 393). Moreover, speaking of the motives he ascribes to some of those who later transferred allegiance from Eleazar to John, Josephus cites their preference to have the "blame for their daring deeds" placed "upon one [person] rather than upon many" (391), which implies some notion of collective responsibility current among the zealots. Still, one should be cautious in drawing any further conclusions. The historical experience suggests that, for the reason of interpersonal – or political – exigencies, the egalitarian principle, in its true literal sense, is not possible to implement, even in a closely knit religious community, like Qumran. Despite the postmodern wishful thinking, human nature simply does not work that way: our conception of the world or ourselves, even if we are reluctant to recognize this, is necessarily hierarchical. It is a matter of empirical observation that any socio-political collective spontaneously stratifies, according to one or more parameters, while a group or, for that matter, a single individual assumes leadership and begins exercising authority, which it often becomes difficult to impeach. This seems to have been the position obtained by Eleazar b. Simon with zealots, at least until their submission to John – notwithstanding whatever eschatological dreams might have circulated among the rank-and-file.

We have already seen that Josephus recognized the paradox inherent in the psychology of religious dissent practiced by the zealots – namely, the commitment to fulfill God's will through violation of God's commandments which are sanctified by the Torah and rooted in tradition. *Prima facie*, it would have provided our author with an easy way out of this predicament to portray them as '*atheoi*', deniers of God, unrelated to, or cast beyond, the confines of Judaism. This could have allowed him to repudiate frequent charges, advanced by the pagan Judeophobes, blaming the Jewish religion for the intransigent spirit of the Jews (e.g., Tac. *Hist.*, 5, 4 f.; 8), and thus minimize Judaism's role in disturbances, an important aspect of his agenda as apologist (cf. *cAp.*, 2, 291). He did, of course, nothing of the sort, and for a good reason: such contention would not have been acceptable to his Jewish audience, who knew perfectly well not only that zealots professed a passionate faith in the God of Israel, but conceived of themselves as true believers, even truer than anyone else. This insight into logical implausibility overruled by psychological drive informs much of Josephus's narrative, which helps him at times to play a keener observer of human behavior than some of his modern critics or many political analysts who proceed on the assumption that *homo sapiens* is to be treated exclusively as *homo rationalis*. Josephus recalls "the predictions of the prophets" (cf. 4, 386) that said "a great deal about virtue and evil, which zealots transgressed, thus achieving the fulfillment of prophecies detrimental to their homeland" (387). He proceeds to claim that one such ancient utterance of "divinely inspired men" had foretold the capture of Jerusalem and destruction of the Temple "by the right of war", brought about by a revolt, specifying that "native hands will first pollute God's precincts" (388). The source of this statement cannot be exactly identified. This is not surprising, given the huge corpus of the pseudo-epigraphic texts with apocalyptic content, circulating in Judaea and in the Jewish Diaspora, of which only a share has survived. Alternatively, Josephus might have contaminated, consciously or not, several such pronouncements (on war, on sedition, on the end of the world) to convey the gist of their message. None of it, however, detracts from the validity of the psychological point he subsequently makes: that although the zealots "did not disbelieve" the prophecies, they "made themselves the tools of their realization" (ibid). On the surface, this does not square with the historian's insistence several lines earlier that the same zealots abused all human and divine institutions, mocking the words of the prophets as "tall tales from the conjurers" (386). But Josephus surely could not have been that insipid, his multiple signs of negligence notwithstanding, as not to recognize a flagrant contradiction within only a few paragraphs of his own writing. What he apparently tried to communicate is that passionate obsession with faith does not exclude equally powerful denying, or reversing, any number of its constituents – a condition not unlike the "carnival mentality" as analyzed by Mikhail Bakhtin. What we deal with here is a psychologically vicious circle in which a sacrilege reinforces religiosity and the other way around. Furthermore, the same entanglement provides what can be called 'existential dimension' in the religious dissenters' minds: a peculiar fusion of belief in their cause's imminent triumph with the sense of doom and their readiness to die.

In his second detour on the rule of terror, Josephus again chose to emphasize (within the context of desertion) the denial of burying their victims and enemies, practiced by zealots – "leaving them dead to putrefy in the sun" (*BJ*, 4, 382). As I have argued – in substance, and his rhetoric of dramatization put aside – this could not have conceivably been a product of the historian's fantasy: rather, such persistence signified the extent to which the issue cut through the contemporary Jewish mindset. We read that some individuals, instead of attempting flight, preferred to stay and die within the walls in the hope of burial (380), but zealots did not allow this, irrespective of whether one found death within or without the capital. If the first part of this claim remains an inference, unprovable, if not necessarily wrong, the second, since it pertains to the observable facts, might well have reflected truth. The same applies to what comes next: "For those who buried a relative, as deserters, the penalty was death, and one who provided a grave for another, immediately needed one himself" (383) – a not unfamiliar principle of guilt by association. The passage concludes with a rhetorical coda: the "impious" zealots, the reader is told, transferred their fury "from the living to the killed, and then back from the dead to the living" (384). This whole sequence obviously follows the patterns of ancient historiography in the treatment of *anomie*, a situation in which all sorts of borders and boundaries, governing human activity, are blurred or vanish. But the emphasis on the prohibition of burial adds to it a specifically Jewish element: one possible explanation of the zealots' attitude is that they might have considered their victims, whether deserters or those in whom they saw real or imaginary opponents, as 'others' – the outcasts in a literal sense who failed in their duties as Israel's members and thus belonged outside the law of the Torah. This provides for a new principle of liminality, replacing the old, rooted in the tradition now recognized as having been corrupted, and constitutes yet one more recurrent phenomenon in the history of religious dissent.[9]

The 'second regime' under Eleazar b. Simon, that is, a short-term coalition of zealots, Galilaean followers of John b. Levi, countryside 'brigands' and the Idumaeans, began to unravel with (at least partial) defection of the latter. This event, since it must have been witnessed both by Josephus's sources and his potential readers, had to be a fact, although one cannot doubt that many details, given by the historian, are fictitious. The reason for the disenchantment between the recent allies remains unclear: Josephus's attempt at explanation, namely, that the Idumaeans took offence at random and judicial murders (*BJ*, 4, 345 f.), is characteristically moralistic and hardly credible: according to the same author, their own conduct early on was in no way better. The story that follows – about an unnamed repentant zealot who secretly contacted the Idumaeans and convinced them, with the help of clever rhetoric, to break off (346 ff.) – was, at best, founded on hearsay, but is more likely a product of the author's imagination: that character's speech, found in Josephus, who would not have known its contents anyway, is too elaborate, and the whole affair, due to the hazards involved (e.g., the speaker's presumed lack of concern for his own safety) makes little sense. (The absence of a name for the turncoat is telling: rumors, even false, tend to bestow names on those allegedly responsible for deeds and misdeeds.) One possible clue comes from the claim found in the argument, ascribed to the nameless repentant, to the effect that zealots continued their murderous policies "disregarding men who had rescued them" (350). This *may* indicate that many Idumaeans felt resentful because they were denied by zealots a share of power to which they thought they were entitled; maybe they also did not appreciate the role of ritual. It was also suggested that they chose to leave since they simply believed they had accomplished their mission. This view holds, however, only if one rejects as unreliable yet further piece of information that, before they departed, the Idumaeans liberated 2000 prisoners, who immediately fled from the city to join Simon b. Giora (354). The figure is, as always, suspect, and if the story is true, we are still left in the dark as to whether these people were put in jail by the 'first' or the 'second' regime: it will be seen that both the 'moderates' and the zealots (whose motives are less easy to fathom) waged war against Simon b. Giora and could have harassed his adherents in Jerusalem.

Contrary to Josephus's implication (e.g., 353), not all of the Idumaeans made the decision to go home: many must have stayed in the capital and joined John of Gischala; we hear of them next when they rose up against the latter and proved instrumental in arranging the admission of Simon b. Giora within the city walls (566 ff.).

Jerusalem's control by the group of zealots around Eleazar b. Simon did not last long. Shortly upon their victory, they were dealt a blow they proved unable to recover from and which put an end, once and for all, to their status as the sole dominant rebel faction. At some point in spring A.D. 68 (probably before the Passover), John b. Levi challenged them with his own bid for power and became an independent leader (4, 389 ff.), predictably called 'a tyrant' by Josephus. The core of his following must have consisted of Galilaean men he brought with him to the capital after their flight from Gischala. The growth of his influence must have been gradual but rapid. The actual mechanics of this secession is not clarified. We merely read that, acting as an autocrat to contravene the decisions taken by others, John b. Levi "made obvious his desire for sole rule" (390). As elsewhere, Josephus credits this particular foe's eloquence (391) and energy, bodily and mentally (392). To these qualities, and not only to John's skill in intrigue or deception, he attributes his success in recruiting adherents (391 f.). Regarding the motives of the latter, the author proposes, in accordance with his penchant for 'psycho-rhetorical' clichés, a mixture of devotion and fear, plus one other alleged feature I have already cited – a belief that it would be in their interests if the blame (or responsibility) rests on one rather than on many.

Be that as it may, John of Gischala ultimately failed to achieve unquestioned supremacy. At this stage of developments, he managed to undermine but not overcome the leadership of Eleazar b. Simon, whose (presumably initial) supporters refused to change sides. In Josephus's view, they resented submitting to a formerly equal fellow insurgent and feared in his rise an encroachment of a prospective monarch (393): it will be more difficult, they are said to have believed, to depose such an individual once in power, rather than oppose him at the outset (394). This last point seems valid enough: similar considerations must have been at work earlier in the revolt, when the group led by Eleazar b. Ananias finished off the autocratic chief of the *sicarii* Menachem b. Judas. As it appears, Josephus adequately captured the independent spirit of an average zealot in writing that each of them would rather endure the agonies of war than "voluntary servitude" and perish by the "fate of slaves" (394). The historian admits, however, that for a time Eleazar and John did not fight each other directly, except perhaps for an occasional skirmish, predictably claiming instead that the two "contended in attacks on the people and in taking more booty from them" (396).

John b. Levi of Gischala is by far the best-developed character in Josephus's actual war narrative. His case is opposite to the two Eleazars, the son of Ananias and the son of Simon, who lack any careful treatment, are given a minimum of particulars, and whose fate is not clarified. As regards John b. Levi, one may even be tempted to consider excessive the amount of attention paid to this figure by the author: the plethora of details, found in the text, tend to obfuscate the fact that they serve Josephus in presenting his personal antagonist in the worst possible light. No reader can doubt the force of the historian's hatred towards this personage, which makes the latter's portrayal arguably the most biased as it is the most elaborate: furthermore, John of Gischala is the only major player in the events, whose moral characteristic – unlike, for instance, that of Ananus b. Ananus – is consistently negative both in the *Bellum* and the *Vita*. At the same time, Josephus's account does not conceal but rather underlines some remarkable qualities of the man. He is drawn as a professional troublemaker and a skillful dissimulator; this last feature provides a contrast with the straightforward types, common among revolutionary zealots. Of all radical leaders in Josephus, he seems the only born politician in Max Weber's sense: one for whom politics was a vocation. He must also have exercised considerable charisma in order to feel at ease with both the aristocratic members of the 'first regime', fanatical zealots, Idumaean chiefs, and the masses of rank-and-file who continued to support him not only versus the more dogmatic priestly Eleazar b. Simon, but against the increasingly influential Simon b. Giora, the latter trying to play what we would now call 'a populist card'. To use Rudyard Kipling's phrase, John b. Levi must have been a man who knew how to "walk with Kings" and keep "a common touch". One is left with an impression (especially after reading the *Vita*) that this was the only opponent whom Josephus recognized, however reluctantly, as being on a par with himself: "of many tricks and turns", and equally resourceful.

The narrative of the *Bellum* is structured, perhaps deliberately, as to emphasize John's role as disruptor of any combined anti-Roman effort (in fact, the *Vita* tells us that at first he attempted to restrain the revolutionary movement at Gischala, thus espousing the collaborationist cause which he subsequently betrayed – 43). In Galilee he obstructs Josephus's strategy (*BJ*, 2, 590 ff.; 614 ff.; cf. *Vita*, esp. 70, 85 ff.; 122 ff.; 189 ff.; 236 ff.; 301) and initiates an attempt at his impeachment (BJ, 2, 626 f.; cf. *Vita*, 189 f.), thus in the end bearing much responsibility for Vespasian's victory there; in Jerusalem, he starts an intrigue, leading to the division in, and the subsequent collapse of, the 'first regime' under Ananus b. Ananus (*BJ*, 4, 208 ff.); he breaks away from Eleazar b. Simon, which was bound to weaken the ability of zealots to engage effectively with the Romans (ibid, 4, 389 ff.); and, finally, he prevents Simon b. Giora from establishing the unified command in the capital during the siege (cf. ibid, 5, 11 ff.; 104).

Perhaps the most extraordinary fact about John of Gischala was his physical survival in Roman captivity, contrasting his fate with that of Simon, who was executed at the Flavian triumph. We learn that upon the fall of Jerusalem, he tried to hide in the underground passages with some followers, but soon, suffering from hunger, sought Roman protection (*BJ*, 6, 433) – a final act of betrayal by breaching the rebels' oath (351, cf. 366) never to surrender – and was sentenced to life imprisonment (433; cf. 7, 118). This outcome appears a minor enigma, and how it was accomplished, regrettably, remains unknown: it was not among Roman customs to spare the enemy's life, particularly if he was the chief of the insurgents. Given his dexterity and *savoir-vivre*, John might have activated some of his old relationships with Jewish nobles who Romanized (which possibly required resorting to bribery or blackmail) and procured their interference on his behalf (we know, for instance, that King Agrippa acted thus in regard to Justus of Tiberias – *Vita*, 410); but all of this naturally belongs to the realm of speculation. One wonder whether his survival, put together with his repeated betrayals of his Jewish allies, could have implanted in the mind of Josephus's contemporary reader a thought that John of Gischala willingly played a role of *agent provocateur*, or double agent; this would make an excellent plot for historical fiction. In reality, the records suggest that he managed to succeed against many odds, and ultimately to survive, owing to his knowledge of human nature and an inordinate gift as tactician: he proceeded against Josephus, playing on fears and jealousies of the latter's superiors; abandoned Ananus, after realizing that the latter's adversaries grow stronger; seceded from Eleazar by exploiting dissensions within the zealot camp; and opposed Simon, conscious of the resentment the latter caused in various quarters, especially among the wealthy. It cannot be ruled out that he exhibited a similar sense of timing at the moment of his surrender, when Titus, for one reason or another, needed to display "a quality of mercy".

The links John b. Levi formerly entertained with the members of the fallen 'moderate' regime might have made him suspect in the eyes of zealots from the very outset as an alien body and a potential turncoat. In his review of the crimes committed by radical groups and their leaders (*BJ*, 7, 259 ff.), Josephus singles him out (immediately after having indicted the *sicarii*) as the most conspicuous example of impiety. Not only did he inflict, writes the historian, multiple evils (263) on the community of his countrymen, thereby daringly blaspheming against God (ibid), but he proved equally impious in private:

> He intruded illicit eating practice and revoked rules of purity instituted by our ancestors, to make it no longer surprising that a man so deranged in his disregard for piety to God as not to observe mildness and fellow-feeling to humans.
>
> (264)

This particular piece of information may well be trustworthy: after all, there must have been too many witnesses of John's public and private conduct for Josephus to try a calumny on that scale, and pertaining to so sensitive an issue, without evidence. If so, John's reportedly open contempt for the law and ritual might, in fact, have contributed to the outbreak of conflict between him and the ostentatiously devout zealots, which – despite the latter eventual submission to the former – does not seem ever to have entirely healed. One is not surprised that the use of the Temple's holy wine and oil by John and his cohorts (5, 565) caused our author to indulge in a particular fit of wrath:

> Nor would I abstain from saying what my feelings dictate: I believe that if the Romans had delayed [proceeding] against these offenders, either

the city would have been swallowed up by the earth in an abyss [the reference is to the punishment of Korah and his following in *Num*, 16:32 – V. R.], or swept away, or receive the thunderbolts of Sodom; for the city had borne a generation far more godless than those who had suffered all such things, since their madness ruined the entire nation.

(566)

Similarly, John is decried for plundering the Temple's treasures (563; cf. 36, for his perusal of sacred timber), although the historian must have recognized, though not approved, the potential rationale behind it by making him remark that the rebels "should not fear employ what is God's for God's sake", and that "those who fought for the Temple must be fed by it" (564).

Elsewhere in the *Bellum*, furthermore, Josephus describes the behavior of John's Galilaean followers as most peculiar and, in the eyes of a Jew, singularly outrageous:

> Murder of men and rape of women was their game / ... /, and from the fearless satiety they turned effeminate, arranging their hair, putting on women's attire, soaking themselves in perfumes and painting their eyes for the sake of beauty. They copied not only the fashion but as well the passions of women, and contrived in excess of their license [to practice] illegal love. They wallowed in the city as if it was a brothel, corrupting it all with their unclean acts. Yet while they affected effeminate looks, they killed with their right hands, and walking with languid step, they would suddenly turn into warriors, stretch out their swords from under their colored mantles and slay whomever they met.
>
> (*BJ*, 4, 561 ff.)

Among other things, this obviously suggests the charge of homosexuality, which the Torah considers an offence, punishable by death (*Lev*.18: 22; cf. *cAp*., 2, 199); and transvestism is called "an abomination to the Lord" (*Deut*., 22:5). The picture drawn by Josephus does indeed recall the doings in Sodom and Gomorrah, or at the very least, at the court of Nero, rather than resemble a revolutionary city in the grips of spiritual fervor. This is no reason, however, to dismiss it, even if it exaggerates, as an outright slander. Once again, as in the case of Josephus's judgment on John's own contempt for the Law, to invent this out of the blue would not have been in the author's best interest, given the existence of numerous survivors who had directly experienced the siege and could impeach his credibility if he strayed too far from the truth. It is known that the mind of a religious dissenter is apt to indulge in all sorts of self-justifications, including the belief in everything to be permitted for one who is engaged in a holy war. In any event, according to Josephus, John made no attempt at restraining or reforming his Galilaeans for the simple reason that he depended on them: "for it was they who had brought him to power" (559). We are told that he allowed everyone to do whatever one wished (ibid), which seems to fit his own lack of true deference towards religion. On the other hand, what Josephus calls (meaning perhaps the disregard of piety) their "conceit in wickedness and audacity" (558) must have tried even more sorely the patience of Eleazar b. Simon and his ilk, drawing them further apart.

There is no way to inquire whether in their activities John or his followers were motivated by wishful thinking, "hope against hope", common among those and similar revolutionary types. Some of his actions suggest rather an adventurer, living from moment to moment, and probably enjoying it in full. At any rate, irrespective of Josephus's patent bias and hyperbole, but judging merely on those facts of his career, which comprised the public record, the man from Gischala emerges as a pragmaticist, not to be hampered in his conduct by considerations other than his own interests and advancement.[10]

Any domestic political upheaval is inevitably fraught with social conflict. The condition of *anomie* permits by definition the fulfillment of the aggressive potential inherent in our nature: envy and hatred (personal or class related), anger, jealousy, vengeance, or just the desire of violence to find easy outlets. Setting on fire the public archives, which housed debt records, at the very outset of the revolt, even if it was merely a propaganda gesture, must have certainly reflected the popular mood. By playing informers, true or false, members of any social group gain an opportunity to destroy their equals or social superiors and thus enrich themselves; even undisguised plunder might go unpunished. All of this undoubtedly occurred in the course of the Jewish Revolt, although the intensity, scale and particulars cannot be established. Even the most high-minded revolutionary regime is incapable of insuring justice or minimizing victimization of the innocent – witness the example of the Jacobins; and there is no reason to believe that the radical factions in Jerusalem were interested in doing any such thing. For Eleazar b. Simon and his comrades, the demarcation line must have been drawn between those, who supported both their anti-Roman drive and particular interpretation of Judaism, and those who did not. Very possibly, they proceeded on the principle that "those not with us are against us", which might have explained, to a certain degree, the continuous factional infighting. It would not be strange, furthermore, if they held the aristocrats, who had *en masse* collaborated with the occupier prior to the revolt, particularly suspect, to the point of considering them their primary targets. As regards John b. Levi, he appears too keen a politician to act in accordance with any strict or 'ideological' guidelines: he may well have been conscious of his own membership in the privileged class, even entertaining some former connections, prospectively useful, and trying to avoid unnecessary harassment.

This means, however, that the ruling groups could indeed materially benefit from pillage and confiscation of property belonging to their foes. Even zealots, despite their supposed egalitarian sentiments, seem to have been susceptible to bribery: Josephus reports that those seeking to escape from the capital needed to pay the price, "and only the one, who did not give money, was a traitor" (*BJ*, 4, 379).

In the end, he concludes, "the rich bought their flight and the poor alone were butchered" (ibid). Perhaps not as consistently as the historian wanted his reader to believe, such practices must nevertheless have taken place: there can be no doubt that he personally conversed with and learned some of their stories from people who fled the capital and chose to join the Roman camp. It is left unstated whether those policies of extortion were official: if that was the case, the resultant money would have replenished the public treasury at the Temple. If not, it found its way into the pockets of the individuals responsible for hunting the deserters.

One has to assume that desertion from Jerusalem began after the slaughter of the Roman garrison by the rebels, or perhaps even earlier, as soon as the latter, led by Eleazar b. Ananias, seized the Temple. Some prominent Herodian collaborationists, such as Saul and Costobar, and later Philip b. Jacimus, left the capital upon the Roman defeat at Beth-horon. The flow of those who changed sides must have continued under the 'first regime', although Josephus, who sought to portray the latter's performance throughout the *Bellum* in the best possible light, keeps silent on this. As could be predicted, desertion dramatically increased after the zealots' coup, with their policies of terror, and further waves of it followed. In time of troubles there always exist multiple reasons to get out of the fray: in the first place, fear for one's life, family or property. I have already commented on the state of *anomie* in Jerusalem, taken over by rival factions, engaged in bloody strife, which encouraged personal vendettas, false charges or mere accidents in which anyone, even those staying aloof from politics, could have easily lost their lives. The feeling of uncertainty and insecurity must have been paramount. Common sense suggests that there were some, however few, who genuinely Romanized or developed a keener, albeit cynical, perception of the events and realized the folly in waging war against the Roman superpower: such individuals must have felt and feared the worst.

It is true that Josephus's statements about the measures taken by the radicals to hamper deserters are inconsistent and sometimes fraught with contradictions. Thus, for instance, he repeatedly and strongly implies that the new rulers surrounded the city with a sort of "iron ring" which made the flight impossible unless the bribe was offered (cf. *BJ*, 4, 378; 410; 490), while elsewhere it transpires that there existed secret routes to leave, and the Romans knew of it (5, 493; 496 f.). This and similar examples do not mean, however, that on the grounds of any such inconsistencies one should repudiate Josephus's main thesis, as some scholars tend to do: the gap, even conflict, between a generalization and the details is a an inherent flaw of rhetoricized discourse, so prominent in the period's literature. That the factions took serious measures to seal the city cannot be doubted: this was the only sound strategy if they wanted to prevent the leaking of intelligence. That it did not fully work is also natural: even the Iron Curtain, of recent memory, was not 100 percent proof. At the same time, there could well have been a division on this subject within the leadership: some could have insisted on tight controls; others argued for the policy of ransom to enlarge public (or their own) funds: once again, modern parallels abound – from the Nazis to the Communists.

Finally, the rivalry between two or more revolutionary groups might have provided additional loopholes to be intelligently used. But it does not mean that all who had succeeded in getting out of Jerusalem would have rushed to the Roman camp, although some certainly did; the famous case of Rabban Johanan b. Zakkai will be discussed later. One assumes, however, that most deserters tried to find safety anywhere beyond the Roman grasp, and even in the wilderness.

As we have seen, the radicals inherited the policies of factional rivalry, which undid the regime of their predecessors and, worse, drove them into virtually permanent infighting. It was evidently the most destructive aspect of the revolutionary situation in Jerusalem, but the underlying causes, for the lack of evidence, remain obscure. Josephus's narrative, taken as a whole, creates an impression that the only reason of internecine strife lay in personal ambitions of the individual leaders, most notably, John of Gischala and Simon bar Giora. This factor must have certainly played a role; but does it suffice to explain the intensity and continuity of this fratricide, strongly disapproved by the law of the Torah (e.g., *Lev*: 19,17; *Num*: 35,33 f.; *Deut*: 19, 11 ff.)?

A few comments that follow largely relate to speculation rather than concrete data, and based on common sense and certain features of religious dissent also known from different periods and different sources. The comparable material (such as the history of Christian heresies and the early Protestant sects) suggests that the abolition or discredit, of the organized church (or priesthood) as the intermediary between the human and the divine, often leads to a widespread belief in the possibility of direct communication with God. This can be achieved both through an individual or a group, in each case conceptualized as a chosen channel – and agent – of divine will. Any such claim naturally results in rivalry within or without a particular collective of the faithful, even when all the claimants belong to one movement, with the same goals and same enemies to face. This creates a psychological predicament, nourishing personal jealousies, power aspirations and tactical disagreements, turning them into what we would today call 'ideological conflicts', sometimes fraught with violent clashes; as we know, this phenomenon, even if it lacks religious contingency, is characteristic of political revolutions which often tend "to devour their own children". After all, the revolutionary wishful thinking has much in common with faith in God.

The zealots in the time of the Jewish War were both religious dissenters and revolutionaries. The texts of the Old Testament provided them with multiple examples of God speaking to numerous individuals, from Abraham and Moses to the succession of the prophets. It is true that the 'official' Judaism in the Second Temple Period and thereafter proved at best skeptical and at worst strongly disapproving towards recurrent prophetic movements. This did not, however, prevent the production and spread of the new prophetic texts, such as pseudoepigrapha, and the appearance of figures claiming divine insight, and capable of rallying crowds. Josephus's declaration that he was visited with and then acted upon a prophetic dream – contravening as it does the 'official' contempt for such prophecies – powerfully testifies that believing them genuine was not a mere superstition among the illiterate, but could be shared by men of his own social and cultural stature.

It seems by no means impossible that the mutual resentment between the factions arose, besides individual rivalries, from partisan beliefs in special relationships with the divine. As a group, zealots, with their firm conviction of doing God's work on Earth and thus, by extension, of carrying a superior truth could easily antagonize a flexible pragmaticist, like John of Gischala, or the populist leader Simon b. Giora, perhaps harboring his own Messianic pretensions. And vice versa: any negligence, for instance, in regard to ritual purity on the part of the other two, would have exacerbated the distrust felt by the *bona fide* zealots under Eleazar b. Simon. Contradictory interpretations of what could have been taken for signs or portents were bound only to enhance the tensions. This balance of relationship was naturally subject to constant, maybe even daily, shifts – but the fact remains that the factions became somewhat reconciled only towards the end of the siege. Regrettably, this set of conjectures cannot be supported by the extant evidence, nor can it be established by a factual link between the circulation of the eschatological texts and the activities of any specific revolutionary group. In part, this scarcity of data owes to Josephus's agenda as apologist: he needed to obscure or suppress whatever role the conflict of religious attitudes might have played in the revolutionary developments in order to repudiate the frequent charges of the pagan opponents, portraying Judaism as *per se* the source of subversion. The defense of Jewish religion is the leitmotif of his writings, most prominently, of course, in the second book of *Contra Apionem*, and it would not have been in his interests to present the Jewish revolt as a religious war, which, to a large degree, it must have been. Josephus's purposes were apparently better served when civil strife was explained away exclusively by the quarrel between the power hungry individual villains; but this obfuscated certain aspects of behavior that religious dissent tends to engender. One may further speculate on the possible features of social warfare, citing, let us say, the policies of expropriation, allegedly pursued by Simon b. Giora; but once again the evidence is insufficient for making any inference on whether such issues could have acquired an 'ideological' dimension and contributed to factional infighting.

The factor of faith, on the other hand, must have been significant in the rebels' conduct *vis-à-vis* the Romans. An utter absence of military initiative by the Jews during the 'second regime' in Jerusalem and the factions' rule that followed is only in part explicable in terms of civil divisions and their paralyzing effect. One strongly suspects that this lethargy resulted from the misreading of political realities, rooted in 'omnipotence of thought', and not unusual among the religious dissenters. Nero's downfall and the subsequent wars of succession, the rapid change of the Emperors in A.D. 69, the general sense of crisis, were bound – given the eschatologically charged ambience in Judaea – to be construed as a clear sign that God finally intervened on behalf of Israel and the divine retribution upon the Roman enemy was at hand.

Nero took his own life on June 9, A.D. 68; upon the arrival of this news, Vespasian postponed his campaign against Jerusalem, waiting for the resolution of affairs in Italy (*BJ*, 4, 497 ff.). Around the same time, Simon b. Giora intensified his activities in Idumaea, which would eventually lead to his entry into the capital, inaugurating the new stage of the conflict between factions and their last stand against Rome. These events, culminating in the siege and capture of Jerusalem by Titus, even though they lay beyond the 'Neronian' chronological confines of this study, will be examined, however concisely, in our final chapter.[11]

6

THE DAGGER MEN

I.

The available evidence makes it clear that the Jewish revolutionary group known as the *sicarii* comes closest to the image of religious dissenters *par excellence*. In contrast to zealots, this is not a self-adopted name, but the one imposed on them by their foes, although it cannot be entirely ruled out that in time they came to carry it with a sort of pride. The word derives from the Latin *sica*, a short dagger they were said to have used in their deadly actions (*AJ*, 20, 186). It is worth noticing, however, that in Latin the word *sicarius* also became a legal term to mean simply 'murderer', at least from the times of Sulla, who promulgated a law specifying an appropriate punishment for homicide – the *lex Cornelia de sicariis et veneficiis* – "the Cornelian law on murderers and poisoners" (82 B.C.; *Dig.*, 48, 8, 3, 5; cf. Cic. *Pro Rosc. Am.*, 8; 39; 103). Be that as it may, it appears that what this word did signify in the context of the Roman Judaea was not too far removed from our modern notion of 'terrorist'.

In the writings of Josephus the *sicarii* figure in several episodes, more or less extended, and we are given some information as regards their origin or methods (*BJ*, 2, 255 f.; 7, 254 ff.; *AJ*, 20, 186, 208). In the *Bellum*, they show up prominently at the start (2, 254 ff.; 433 ff.) and at the end (7, 253 ff.; 275 ff.) of the actual war narrative (with the brief interlude regarding their activities in the meantime – 4, 400 ff.): in the first instance, the emphasis is placed on the emergence of their leader Menachem b. Judas at Jerusalem, with his subsequent assassination; in the second, they are emphasized as the defenders of the fortress Masada against the Romans and collective suicides, with the final reference to them as troublemakers in Alexandria and Cyrene (7, 409 ff.) The Masada episode, by far the lengthiest, is justly famous, given the dramatism of its treatment by the historian and the powerful rhetoric in the speeches he ascribes to their leader Eleazar b. Jairus. (In the *Vita*, Menachem and his cohorts are mentioned, but the appellation *sicarii* is not – cf. 21, 46.) The text of the *Antiquitates* tells us, on the other hand, about the events, involving the *sicarii*, which took place prior to the outbreak of the hostilities, namely, their killing of the archpriest Jonathan b. Ananus under the procurator Antonius Felix (20, 162 ff.; cf. *BJ*, 2, 256) and their kidnapping of the secretary employed by Eleazar b. Ananias, the future initiator of the revolt (*AJ*, 20, 208). It will be seen shortly that there is sufficient evidence for linking this 'sect' (the word I use for the sake of convenience) directly to the revolutionary enterprise, half a century earlier, of the man known as Judas the Galilaean and his "forth philosophy", thus offering our discussion a convenient starting point.

Perhaps the most striking feature of the entire development is the dynastic character of the sect's leadership. This is never explicitly spelled out by Josephus, most likely owing to his tendency for occasional incoherence; but the narratives of the *Bellum* and the *Antiquitates* combined to make this fact transparent. The defenders of Masada are emphatically called by the historian *sicarii*, and their chief Eleazar b. Jairus identified as a descendant of Judas the Galilaean (*BJ*, 7, 253; cf. 4, 400 ff.). Elsewhere he is referred to as the relative of Menachem (ibid, 2, 447), the early claimant for the revolt's leadership, who was (as a son or a grandson) Judas's descendant. Although none of Menachem's adherents are directly referred to as the *sicarii*, there is no doubt that it was what they must have been: it is also telling that Masada served both for Menachem (2, 434; cf. 408) and Eleazar (7, 252 ff.; cf. 4, 400 ff.) as the key base of operations. Finally, a decade earlier two sons of the Galilaean, James and Simon, sought to continue their father's revolutionary work, presumably at the head of some following, and were crucified on the orders of the procurator Tiberius Alexander (*AJ*, 20, 102).[1]

I have already commented briefly on the ideas and activities of Judas the Galilaean, that "redoubtable sophist" (*BJ*, 2, 433; cf. 118), and his Pharisee colleague Saddok. (Of this latter, however, nothing is known but the name, and one may infer that he must have played a secondary role.) The revolt under Judas's leadership is firmly placed in the aftermath of Archaelaus's deposition and in the context of the census (A.D. 6–7), conducted by P. Sulpicius Quirinius, who was at the time the governor of Syria (cf. *Acts:* 5, 37). The man from Galilee proved ready to seize the opportunity: we read that he "persuaded not a few among Jews / ... / not to take part in the assessment when Quirinius was sent as censor to Judaea" (*BJ*, 7, 253; cf. 2, 118, 433; *AJ*, 18, 4 ff.; 20, 102). The fact was that, besides economic or legal problems involved, such as taxation, census proved a highly controversial measure from the Jewish religious perspective: the *Book of Numbers* makes it clear that it is entirely legitimate if directly commanded by God (*Num*:1 ff.); when, however, it was performed on King David's own initiative, the divine retribution promptly followed (*2 Sam*: 24, 1 ff.). The census under discussion must have been regarded at the time in some Jewish quarters as an infinitely worse transgression since it had been undertaken not even by a native ruler, but by the order of the hated Roman occupier.

An influential argument, although by no means conclusive, links Judas the Galilaean to the famous 'archbrigand' Ezechias (*AJ*, 14, 159 f.; 167; cf. 17, 271; *BJ*, 1, 204 f.; cf. 2, 56), making him the latter's son, and thus identical with the other rebel figure cited by Josephus, one Judas b. Ezechias, active around 4 B.C. in Sepphoris, the capital of Galilee (*BJ*, 2, 56; *AJ*, 17, 271 f.). The 'archbrigand'

Ezechias (*BJ*, 2, 56; cf. *AJ*, 17, 271) was suppressed by young Herod (ca. 47 B.C.) on the order from his father Antipater, a strongman – or 'vizier' – at the court of the last Hasmonean King (whom the Romans recognized as an 'ethnarch') Hyrcanus II.

As regards Ezechias's son Judas, he is said to have enrolled a considerable body of adherents, broken into the royal arsenals, and attacked some unspecified contenders to power (*BJ*, 2, 56). At the time, the disturbances in the area were largely suppressed by the governor of Syria P. Quintilius Varus (ibid, 68 ff.); but the fate of Judas b. Ezechias remains unknown, which allowed some scholars to postulate that he went underground, to re-emerge after the next ten years at the time of the census, as Judas the Galilaean.

In any event, we are told that this latter came from the city of Gamala (not to be confused with Gamala in Upper Galilee) in the district known as Gaulantis (*AJ*, 18, 3). In the *Bellum*, Josephus merely states that he "incited his compatriots to insurrection, castigating their patience in paying tribute to the Romans and tolerating mortal masters next after God" (2, 118; cf. 433; 7, 253). In the *Antiquitates*, however, the historian expands on Judas' and Saddok's anti-census propaganda:

> They said that this assessment carries nothing but flat out slavery and called for people to seize their freedom; that if [Jews] gain it, they would provide the foundation of their welfare, while if they fail to obtain this great good, they will achieve honor and renown due to their lofty spirit. And that the Divinity would not but support their wishes and aid to their implementation, the more so if they stayed firm in their intent as lovers of great things and did not abstain from murder.
>
> (*AJ*, 18, 4 f.)

The language is apparently tuned to fit the usage of the Graeco-Roman audience, but the gist of the message must have been preserved their claim to be doing God's work and thus enjoy God's support, even while destroying their human fellows - a quintessential feature in psychology of violent religious dissent. Josephus's comment is predictable, reaching as it does beyond the context of Judas's revolt into the future (to wit, the author's own time). Saying that "men gladly listened and responded to what they were told" by the agitators, and thus "a huge and daring conspiracy" (ibid, 6) developed, he charges them of sowing every evil, which affected the nation beyond description (ibid). It makes him indulge in habitual laments, denouncing civil strife, and imitating Thucidides:

> When wars break out, fraught with uncontrollable violence, friends who might have helped in hardship are killed, huge bands of robbers attack, eminent men are brought down – the semblance of an enterprise for the benefit of community, while in fact it is done in the hope of private gain.
>
> (ibid, 7)

This last point is clearly meant as intentional deceit: although it is true that brigandage and profiteering is a recurrent aspect of any revolution or civil conflict, Josephus must have been fully aware that alongside what we now call 'nationalism', many Jewish rebels were motivated by the mindset, specific to the bearers of religious dissent within the mainstream, or 'normative', Judaism. It was not, however, in his interests as an apologist to emphasize the former, and especially the latter motive, leaving the Jewish faith, and anything related to it, as far as it was possible, outside his interpretation of the tragic events. This also seems to explain the discrepancy between his comments on the "fourth philosophy" in the texts of the *Bellum* and the *Antiquitates*. If the earlier work, written in the immediate aftermath of the Roman victory, unequivocally states that Judas the Galilaean founded the "sect, which has nothing in common with others" (*BJ*, 2, 118), at the quieter times two decades later he could afford to acknowledge that his teaching resembled that of the Pharisees "in all other respects, except their unbeatable love of freedom, because they held God for their sole leader and master" (*AJ*, 18, 23). This implies a strong possibility that at least some radical Pharisaic groups, in particular those adhering to the school of Shammai, might have converted to Judas's "fourth philosophy"; but it is still a far cry from a contention that Pharisees as a movement played a larger role in the revolt than any other popular constituency.

Of the attitudes shared by the followers of the "fourth philosophy", the historian emphasizes their willingness to sacrifice both themselves and their neighbors in the name of the cause: "They think little of suffering death in different forms, even of vengeance taken on relatives and friends, as something preferable to addressing any man as master" (ibid) – a feature, prominent enough, as the long historical experience demonstrates, among religious dissenters of various stripes. Josephus hardly exaggerates by saying (he cites the existence of many witnesses) that nothing he might report on this would sound incredible. Rather, he adds, the narrative should not diminish their contempt for pain and torture (ibid, 24). He never hesitates – and this appears to reflect his genuine belief – in placing fault on their doctrine and activities for the disastrous course of events through several decades, which culminated in the destruction of the Temple:

> They sowed the seed, out of which grew strife and political slaughter; some were killed in civil bloodshed owing to the madness of men regarding each other, led by the desire not to be left undone by those who opposed them; others perished in war with the enemy. Next famine arrived, with the utmost show of shamelessness, the takeover and destruction of the cities, until finally this revolt gave God's sanctuary to enemy's fire.
>
> (ibid, 8)

The immediate inference he makes, many times found in the writings of conservative authors through the centuries, is – predictably – that any novelty and change in "things ancestral" (9; any echoing here of the Roman *mos maiorum* concept?) leads to the harm and ruin of the community (ibid). The irony lies, of course, in the fact that the rebels saw their aim in the return to the pristine purity of the Jewish faith as, in their view, it had been practiced by their forefathers. Josephus concludes that Judas and Saddok, by spreading such ideas, not only enlisted the support of many, but also "infused the polity with turmoil, and instantly planted the roots of the evils to overwhelm it by means of these previously unexperienced philosophies" (ibid) And finally: "The resulting folly began to infect the nation at the time of Gessius Florus who, as a procurator by his abuse of power caused the desperate uprising against the Romans" (ibid, 25). This last statement is patently misguiding: Josephus's own account makes it clear that the Jewish revolutionary activities, even though sporadic, and aimed at national liberation, began more than half of a century earlier and grew with time; furthermore, he surely must have realized that the resistance to the occupier, manifest in a variety of forms, should be traced as early as Pompey's outrage at the Temple in 63 B.C.: it was bound to leave a permanent imprint on the popular mind.

The anti-census agitation, undertaken by Judas and Saddok, did not, however, win overwhelming approval among the Jews. We read that the high priest Joazar b. Boethus (who originally owed his position to Herod the Great – *AJ*, 17, 164; cf. 207) managed to persuade many to submit (ibid, 18, 3). Naturally, this was hardly due to that man's mere eloquence, or the force of his arguments; one assumes that those who mattered (most of whom we would nowadays call "the middle class") chose to cooperate, either out of fear, or self-interest, or due to the apprehension they felt towards the anarcho-theocratic doctrine propagated by the insurgents. This lack of mass support must have been the chief reason for the revolt's failure. Another loser, interestingly, proved to be the high priest Joazar: in the course of his career, he may well have played some sort of double game which would explain, perhaps as a result of the source confusion, Josephus's contradictory statements on him. His performance seems to have dissatisfied both sides: we read of what appears a mounting popular pressure to remove him. The Romans, for whatever reason, did not mind. As result, Joazar was made to leave his office for good. He was replaced by Ananus b. Sethi, the New Testament's Annas (ibid, 26).

The fact remains that Rome eventually succeeded in suppressing the abortive revolt the man from Galilee had sought to stir up. On the latter's subsequent fate Josephus is silent, which, as we know by now of his procedures, is nothing exceptional. We do learn, however, about Judas's end from the *Book of Acts*, in the speech ascribed to the Hillelite R. Gamaliel, a member of the Sanhedrin:

> For before these days Theudas arose, giving himself out to be somebody, and a number of men, about four hundred, joined him; but he was slain and all who followed him were dispersed and came to nothing. After him Judas the Galilaean arose in the days of the census and drew away some of the people after him; he also perished, and all who followed him were scattered.
>
> (5: 36 f.)

The chronological conundrum, baffling in this passage (Judas antedates Theudas), may perhaps be resolved by a supposition that, given the divergent manuscript readings, the order of the verses on Judas and Theudas had been inadvertently reversed.

The scale of Judas's movement, or the actual spread of the "fourth philosophy" at the time, is difficult to fathom: but one assumes that the number of his followers was large enough to ensure a vivid memory about the event decades later. Some within their ranks might have even then called themselves 'zealots', feeling prepared to rise up again when the opportunity arrives. But a narrower, even more extremist group – the *sicarii* – eventually crystallized under the leadership of Judas's family and proceeded, without further ado, towards the policies of terrorism so that they could disrupt the attempts by the authorities at maintaining civic peace. A reasonable question is why the *sicarii*, professing not to recognize any human master, seem nonetheless to have accepted, or tolerated, the supremacy of Judas the Galilaean and his descendants. Most likely, they considered them the conduits of divine will, in the same sense as had been the leaders of Israel at the time of the Judges. Another possibility is that they were perceived by the rank-and-file as teachers, rather than rulers, whose task was to interpret, according to the circumstances, God's will as manifest in word and addressed to them all: this might further clarify Josephus's usage of the term *sophistes* applied both to Judas and Menachem (sophists, after all, were professional teachers), although it will be seen that the latter, through his royal and quasi-Messianic pretensions, obviously overstepped those limits.[2]

II.

The next time we hear of disturbance that might be directly associated with the carriers of the "fourth philosophy" under Tiberius Alexander (ca. A.D. 46–48), the only procurator of Judaea (and later the prefect of Egypt), who was an ethnic Jew and whose administration Josephus considers among the most reasonable and successful (*BJ*, 2, 220; cf. *AJ*, 20, 100). It was he, however, who is said to have captured and crucified two sons of Judas the Galilaean, Simon and James, presumably, owing to their revolutionary practices (*AJ*, 20, 102). What the latter consisted of, or regarding the actual number of their adherents, one can only speculate; as well as to whether it was they who might have been responsible for the new tactics of individual terror by a smaller group labeled *sicarii*, or it was the development which occurred later. From Josephus, we learn about the existence of two other individuals, who must also have been Judas's sons (or, as proposed by some, his grandsons) – Menachem and Jairus, father of Eleazar, who defended Massada. On Jairus, nothing is known except his name: the historian does not speak of him separately or mention him in any other context. As for Menachem, he must have survived Simon and James's execution and perhaps gone underground; he was dramatically to re-emerge at the outbreak of the Great Revolt.

In Josephus's narratives, the *sicarii* first appear under that name at some point during the procuratorship of Antonius Felix (ca. A.D. 52–60) – that is, most likely, already after Nero's accession (*BJ*, 2, 254 ff.; cf. *AJ*, 20, 163 ff.), though when they acquired the appellation remains uncertain. The picture the historian attempts to draw of the activities, undertaken by this "other kind of bandits" (*BJ*, 2, 254) "who murdered people in daylight and in the midst of the city" (ibid) does indeed resemble some of our present notions regarding political terrorism:

> Most of all, they would mix up with the crowds during festivals, concealing short daggers under their clothing, with which they stabbed their enemies; when their victims fell, the perpetrators were among those expressing indignation, and by the plausibility [of their imitation], evaded detection.
>
> (ibid, 255; cf. *AJ*, 20, 164 f.; 186 f.)

And, in the next few lines, he chose dramatically to elaborate on the psychological effects:

> The fear was even harder to deal with than the trouble itself: as in the times of war, one expected death any time. People watched their opponents at a distance and would not extend trust even towards their friends as they approached.
>
> (*BJ*, 2, 256 f.)

But even when the victims were suspicious, Josephus adds, and were on guard, it still might not warrant their protection. The killers would also not have been apprehended, which, in his judgment, owed to the operational "swiftness" of the 'sicarian' conspirators and their "skill" in making themselves scarce (257).

The question, of course, arises as to the extent of possible exaggeration. At one point the author claims that "many people had been killed daily" (256), which certainly does not ring true. On the other hand, there is no reason to doubt the basic historicity of what he wrote on the terrorist methods, or the fact that a number of individuals must have fallen prey. At the same time, it should be forcefully pointed out that within the tradition of Judaism, the very fact of committing murder on the festive day – as it was repeatedly done by this breed of religious dissenters – would have meant nothing but dire blasphemy.

In any event, the impression created by Josephus is not exactly of random killings to provoke popular panic, with a hope of perhaps turning it into chaos. The experience shows that even one or a few targeted political murders may have far-reaching consequences in terms of popular sensibilities and spread the sense of fright and instability throughout the society. In contrast to many modern-day terrorists, who slaughter innocent citizens at random, the *sicarii* seem to have been attacking designated public figures on political or personal grounds: as always happens with any similar enterprise, it was bound to provide the participants with ample room for individual vendettas. Furthermore, as it seems implicit in Josephus's narratives, at that stage they avoided direct action against Roman officials (at least no such episode is mentioned), focusing their violence on the Jewish collaborationists with the occupier. Elsewhere Josephus alleges that they even did not shrink from offering their services for hire (*AJ*, 20, 165) – again, not an unknown phenomenon within terrorist groups: as we will see shortly, there must have been evidence to support this charge.

Josephus's report of the multiple killings performed by the *sicarii* notwithstanding, their only victim he cites by name was the high priest Jonathan b. Ananus (brother of the 'first regime's' future leader, and son of the New Testament's Annas). The *Bellum* merely states (2, 256) that he was first to be assassinated by this new type of 'bandits'. In the *Antiquitates*, however, the story is revealed as considerably more complex. In the first place, the murdered man belonged to one of the most powerful families in Judaea, with his father and four brothers having occupied the high priesthood (cf. 20, 198) in the course of more than three decades; as we already saw in one previous chapter, he had been heavily involved not only in public politics, but no less in various intrigues at both Imperial and royal courts. In the second, his career seems to have suffered several reversals, some of which are difficult to interpret. Within less than a year he was first appointed and then deposed as high priest by the Syrian governor P. Vitellius, on the latter's two visits to Jerusalem (late A.D. 36 and spring A.D. 37) – succeeding his brother-in-law Joseph Caiaphas (of the Gospels' memory) and, in turn, being replaced by his own brother Theophilus b. Ananus (*AJ*, 18, 55 and 123). The reasons on the part of the Roman authority for this particular reshuffle are left unexplained. We then learn that in A.D. 42, upon the accession of Claudius, King Agrippa I offered to reinstall Jonathan b. Ananus in the high priestly office, but the latter is said to have declined, this time in favor of another brother, Matthias (ibid, 19, 313 ff.). The motives Josephus ascribes to him – that God judged him unworthy of the honor (314), while Matthias b. Ananus altogether was a better person (315) – sound rather shallow, although they might have reflected, in distorted form, some obscure aspects of the family's politics. (The fifth brother Ananus b. Ananus, who also was made high priest only to quarrel with both Roman and Jewish powers, and came later into prominence as a result of the revolutionary turmoil, was extensively treated earlier in this narrative.) Perhaps Jonathan's most crucial experience pertained to his stay in Rome around A.D. 52: he was sent there, together with yet another high priestly colleague, Ananias b. Nedebaeus and the latter's son Ananus, by Syria's governor Ummidius Quadratus to account for the recent disturbances between the Jews and the Samaritans (*BJ*, 2, 243). It is known that in the end Claudius ruled in the interests of the Jews, so the men must have returned home with their prestige enhanced.

It appears that during his stay in the Empire's capital Jonathan b. Ananus built the relationship which ultimately led to his destruction with the Imperial freedman Antonius Felix, brother of Pallas, Claudius's powerful 'financial minister' (a *rationibus*). In any event, we have Josephus's explicit statement that it was the former high priest who persuaded the Emperor to appoint Felix the next procurator of Judaea (*AJ*, 20, 162). After the latter's arrival to the province, however, the rapport between them supposedly soured: we hear that, on the one hand, Jonathan tried to pressure the new administrator to improve upon the status quo (ibid). On the other, he is said to have been anxious about the potential reprisals from the revolutionaries for his all-too-close collaboration with the occupier (ibid) – in other words, he suffered the not unusual fate of an opportunist. At this point the interests of the Roman procurator and the Jewish dissenters coincided, which helps to explain an unlikely, albeit temporary, alliance between them of which Josephus speaks as a fact. After having remarked that "constant rebukes are taken hard by those who wish to do wrong" (ibid), the historian reports of Felix's move to contact the *sicarii* – they are not given that name in this context, but the relevant passage from the *Bellum* (2, 255) leaves no doubt of who they were – through the agency of Jonathan's own close associate named Doras, whom the procurator had reportedly bribed (163). According to Josephus, the assassins made it into the city with hidden daggers on the pretext of religious worship, mingled with the locals, surrounding their prey, and stabbed him on the spot (164). Even if the procurator's complicity in this crime was nothing but slander (which cannot be fully ruled out), Jonathan b. Ananus, a major collaborationist, proved an obvious target for a terrorist attack.

That no other victim by the *sicarii* is specifically mentioned or discussed in the Josephan texts should not lead to the inference that there were none. Once again, it was not the practice of the ancient historians to supply such lists, nor could their author afford the luxury of sweeping pronouncements on so sensitive an issue unless they were substantiated by common knowledge and memory of the events within his immediate audience, both Jewish and Gentile. In the *Antiquitates*, written at least two decades after the *Bellum*, upon commenting that the high priest's murder went unpunished, which made it possible for the 'brigands' to carry on their terrorist activities, Josephus reiterates his earlier description of the 'sicarian' *modus operandi* (concealment of weapons under their clothes, attendance of public festivals and killings in the midst of the crowds – 20, 165), but adds a few significant details. Thus the historian insists that, along with destroying their own political and personal enemies, they also were used as hired assassins, and in some cases did not shrink from shedding blood even in the Temple (loc. cit.). For this last claim Josephus offers an explanation which fits well what we know by now about psychology of religious dissent: "they dared to do killings there since they did not even consider it a sacrilege" (ibid). The telling passage that follows – with its implicit reference to the biblical prophets' view of history in terms of Israel's sins and punishments – squarely places on such desecrations the fault for subsequent catastrophes, which were caused, in the author's judgment, by divine wrath:

> This is why, I believe, even God, hating their impiety, turned away from our city, considering the Temple no longer a clean place to dwell, and he imposed the Romans on us as well as a fiery purification on the

city, and our enslavement, together with our wives and children, because he wished to sober us up by these disasters.

(166; cf. *BJ*, 4, 323)

Although it is obvious that the assassination of Jonathan b. Ananus, and presumably some other similar acts during Antonius Felix's tenure, had been perpetrated by the *sicarii*, in the text of the *Antiquitates* they first appear under this name somewhat later (and are said to have by then become very numerous – 20, 186), where Josephus describes a more successful administration of the next procurator Porcius Festus. In fact, it is then that the origin of their appellation is at last explained (ibid). Some parts of the *Antiquitates* are notoriously repetitive: thus we read once again of the daggers, festivals and crowds, which allowed the assassins to "kill easily whomever they pleased" (187). The new piece of information, however, states that the *sicarii* were active not only in the capital, but also throughout the countryside: they would, we are told, "often appear armed in the hostile villages, plunder and burn them up" (ibid) – a matter to be dealt with later.

Josephus credits procurator Lucceius Albinus (ca. A.D. 62) with a major attempt at suppressing the terrorists: we are told that he "exercised every effort and foresight with regard to the pacification of the land, destroying many among the *sicarii*" (*AJ*, 20, 204). Whether, or to what extent, this claim is reliable, it is difficult to assess: Albinus's campaign may help to account for the limited role they were to adopt in the upcoming revolt, which could have owed to a drastic decrease of their numbers as result of this persecution. Still, shortly after the text speaks of yet another bold stroke on their part that would today sound very familiar due to regular newspaper reports about kidnappings or taking hostages, with the purpose of political demands, throughout the world. Close cooperation with the procurator (whom he was allegedly bribing day by day with gifts – 205) did not help the high priest Ananias b. Nedebaeus and his household to escape trouble – rather, the relationship might have prompted it: we learn that, entering the city by night at the time of the festival, which by then, one presumes, has become their habit, the *sicarii* abducted the secretary of his son Eleazar, the future originator of Judaea's secession from Rome, and demanded the release of their ten imprisoned comrades for his return (208 f.). Ananias and Albinus's eventual compliance with the blackmail, says the text, led only to the recurrences of similar episodes on the increased rate, and to the further deterioration of the *status quo* (210). There is no reason to question the factuality of the kidnapping episode, although it hardly squares well with the picture Josephus tries to create of Albinus's successful measures against the terrorists. In chronological terms, it seems to be his last specific mention of the *sicarii* until the actual outbreak of the hostilities with Rome a few years later.[3]

III.

As is often his habit, Josephus proves annoyingly imprecise or incoherent about details, including his 'political vocabulary' when describing the events that led to the outbreak of the revolt. Thus, he first ascribes the initial capture of Masada to the insurgents "who were most insistent on waging the war" (*BJ*, 2, 408): they banded together, it is said, attacked the fortress, took it over by guile, slaughtered the Roman guards and replaced them with their own garrison (ibid). Only the subsequent narrative (434) makes it clear that this feat was performed by the *sicarii*, although it still remains uncertain who led the enterprise. Later on we read that their recognized chief, Menachem b. Judas, at some point, "taking his acquaintance with him, went back to Masada, where he broke into King Herod's arsenal and armed the town's commoners as well as brigands" and thereupon entered Jerusalem in 'regal style' (ibid) – which implies that at the previous stage he was not present on the scene. This information is characteristically confusing: perhaps the exact relationship of the incidents simply proved beyond Josephus's grasp.

According to the historian, the takeover of Masada occurred at the same time as the cessation of the Imperial sacrifices (409); this may or may not have been accidental. In the former case, one has to assume that successful negotiations between Eleazar b. Ananias and Menachem b. Judas must have been secretly conducted for some time across the country prior to this whole development. It would have involved substantial agreement not only regarding the final goal – liberation of Israel – but also on the matters of strategy, tactics and, most sensitively, the leadership. As I have earlier suggested, none of this seems likely given the vast and violent disagreements between the revolutionary factions which plagued their efforts from the beginning to the very end – nor is there any evidence to think otherwise. The coincidence of the actions by the radical Temple priests in Jerusalem and the *sicarii* in Masada could have easily arisen from the nationwide sense of outrage at the brutal policies of Gessius Florus – there is no need to postulate a conspiracy or prearrangement.

Josephus insists that the rebels, who burned the archives housing the debt bonds, on the Festival of Wood-Carrying (this wood presumably provided for some of the combustible) were joined by the *sicarii* ("thus they called the bandits, who kept a dagger in their bosom" – 425); who "undertook an assault" (ibid) and, one is tempted to speculate, might have been an inspiration behind the whole idea. It follows that at least some 'dagger men' must have infiltrated the capital even before the arrival of Menachem b. Judas with his cohorts.

We know little about this man from Josephus – who explicitly refers to him as the son of Judas the Galilaean (433); nevertheless, we can still envision a vivid picture of his personality and behavior. Like the latter, Menachem is called a "teacher" (445), which means, at the very least, that he was in the habit of making pronouncements on law, morals and, perhaps, divine matters. How strictly he followed the precepts of the "fourth philosophy" is uncertain; he seems, for one thing, to have sought the royal status, while the sect, as we know, held that Jews must be governed by no man but God, suggesting that his doctrinal commitments were not very strong. Josephus's text also provides the definitive proof that the family of Judas the Galilaean and Menachem did *not* belong to Judaea's establishment: one of the reasons cited why the group around Eleazar b. Ananias so strongly resented Menachem's claim to supremacy was his much inferior social origin (443).

Of the man's ambition to assume national leadership, the historian leaves no doubt: Menachem entered Jerusalem, he says, "like a king" (434), surrounded by spear-bearers (ibid) and emerged as the leader of the revolution (ibid), directing the siege of the palace, with the Roman garrison and chief collaborationists inside – an achievement that must have largely owed to superior military skills and the discipline of his troops. Josephus's charge of royal pretensions is confirmed by this 'sicarian' leader's public style. Even at the moment of his murder, he was reportedly attired as a monarch (444), which, one imagines, the founder of the sect would have found impious, and attended by the retinue of armed fanatics (ibid). This portrayal predictably led the majority of scholars to ascribe Menachem b. Judas 'messianic' aspirations: after all, within the period's ambience, saturated with eschatological sentiments, any contender for kingship, contravening the Roman masters, necessarily took on, or was endowed with, the aura of the potential Messiah.

Whatever expectations, or illusions, of grandeur Menachem and his group might have entertained, the realities quickly cut them short. The siege of the palace proved only partially successful: it is true that the Roman garrison tried to negotiate for safe-conduct, but the rebels had granted it solely to the king's troops (438), which consisted largely of Jews, perhaps in the hope that most of them would join their ranks. Left alone, the Romans fortified several of the palace's towers and continued desperately to resist. Menachem's next move, however, undermines any view of him as an able, or even intelligent, politician: it is hardly a statesman-like act to attack the family of his own chief ally. We read that soon thereafter the collaborationist, former high priest Ananias b. Nedebaeus, and his brother Ezechias – Eleazar's father and uncle – were captured and killed by the sicarian 'brigands' (441). This time, Josephus's psychologizing, despite his customary rhetoric, provides an occasional insight into the mindset of his personages. The recent successes, he writes, so much deluded Menachem into cruelty that he "thought he had no rival in the conduct of things and became an unbearable tyrant" (442) – a predictable feature in a religious dissenter who conceives of himself as a direct instrument of God's will and is capable of almost boundless wishful thinking: Menachem's personal brand of piety (however, arguably, perverse or misguided), cannot be doubted. After all, he was attacked by his foes while worshiping in the Temple – "pompous" and "in royal garb" (443 ff.). This strongly suggests his belief in a personal relationship with God – as portrayed in the Hebrew Bible – was King David's. It surely would not be the first, or only occasion when he behaved in such manner, which must have further deepened a sense of outrage within the Temple priests, who initiated the revolt. Josephus, who was at the time in the capital and being aware of the current talk and rumors, reports:

> The associates of Eleazar opposed him [i.e., Menachem], passing word to each other that it was no good, after having risen against the Romans for love of freedom, to abandon it before a domestic executioner and endure a despot who, even if he would not practice violence, was still far below than they; and if they need a person to lead them, anyone would fit rather than he.
>
> (443)

One recalls the future historian's confession that during these events, presumably to hide from Menachem and his henchmen, he sought and found asylum in the inner court of the Temple (*Vita*, 20), which implies that the rebellious priests were willing to protect him. As regards Eleazar b. Ananias, it was an insult added on injury that the man who was responsible for his father's and uncle's death endeavored so ostentatiously to impose on them all his version of autocracy – even against the egalitarian beliefs originally held by his own sect.

The plot to kill Menachem b. Judas during the religious service in the Temple was, however, a serious blunder, suggesting that Eleazar proved hardly more adroit in political terms (nowadays we might call it PR) than his 'Messianic' rival. Hitherto we could attribute Josephus's statement that the *sicarii* shed human blood on the sacred grounds, even prior to the revolt's outbreak (*AJ*, 20, 165 f.), to an exercise in rhetoric or chronological confusion. But now a prominent figure was assaulted on the same premises in full public view, and at the moment of devotion, which was bound significantly to damage the prestige of the perpetrators among the pious, who must have after all constituted the majority of Jerusalem's populace. Some citizens are said to have also taken part in the massacre by throwing stones "out of anger" and, as Josephus willfully puts it, "in the belief that this man's downfall would put an end to the whole revolution" (*BJ*, 2, 445) – this last clause a clear case of authorial deceit. After futile resistance, Menachem sought to escape into the city and "disgracefully" hide (448) in the locality known as Ophlas, but was caught, dragged out, tortured (a pointless, albeit telling atrocity) and executed (448); his 'deputies' apparently shared his fate (only one name is mentioned, a certain Absalom, "the most significant supporter of tyranny"; ibid), the rest of his followers having been hunted down and slaughtered, with the exception, we are told, of only a few who managed to take flight to Masada under the leadership of the murdered man's relative (presumably, nephew), Eleazar b. Jairus.[4]

Whether all of the *sicarii* left Jerusalem in the aftermath of Menachem's murder cannot be said with certainty – a few may have split and stayed in the city or dispersed to continue operating elsewhere. But those who went to Masada seem to have cut off any ties with the factions ruling the capital almost as decisively as did the Qumran schismatics with the priestly establishment centuries ago. They apparently considered Jerusalem as tainted by the blood of their comrades and perhaps even doomed. In consequence, they had disengaged from the national effort (if it can be called so) to fight the occupier. We do not hear from Josephus about any further activities on their part for the bulk of the war, except their raid on Engaddi (*BJ*, 4, 400 ff.).

They did not seem to have been particularly inclined to receive other rebel groups into their midst. In a telling episode one reads of Simon bar Giora, outlawed by the 'first regime', and seeking at one point to join his forces with theirs at Masada (503 ff.). At first, they reportedly treated him with suspicion, "admitting him with his suite of women only to the lower part of the fortress, while themselves residing in the upper" (505) – a detail that is hardly invented by Josephus. But eventually he, "being of kindred morals", was allowed to participate in their raids, for the sake of loot, against their neighbors (506). The text says that Simon failed, however, to bolster the sense of enterprise among his new allies and, upon hearing the news about the zealot *coup d'état* in Jerusalem, left for good (507 f.). Their inactivity was bound to surprise Josephus, as well as some modern interpreters. The former ascribed it to a sort of inertia ("they became habituated to the fortress and feared to venture all too far from their lair" – 507); the latter even questioned their fighting spirit. But the natural explanation would be, in tune with what we know about the mentality of radical religious dissent, that these passionate rebels looked forward in full trust to God's beneficent aid at the hour of utmost need, as it had happened many times in the past, so that they could complete God's work and crush the enemy once and for all.

Josephus placed the only military venture he mentions, undertaken on a broader scale by the *sicarii* at Masada before its fall to the Romans in A.D. 73 – namely, their assault on the town of Engaddi – around the same time when in Jerusalem John b. Levi of Gischala seceded from Eleazar b. Simon as an independent faction leader. In the words of the historian, the capital came to suffer from three evils: war, tyranny and faction (4, 397), while these new activities of the Masada fighters (given, presumably, their effect on the rest of the country) constituted the fourth, "hastening the nation's ruin" (398). Earlier we are told they plundered only neighborhoods with the only purpose of procuring supplies; the author postulates fear (of what?) as the factor of restraint (400), adding that upon learning of the recent developments, such as inactivity of the Roman army and the faction fighting ("sedition and tyranny") in Jerusalem, they "proceeded with greater vigor and daring" (401). Josephus's psychology is, of course, shallow, but the motives behind the Engaddi episode remain uncertain: perhaps the simplest explanation is the *taedium* they must have suffered from because of their self-imposed inertia, while war and violence reigned elsewhere. One must admit, though, that this expedition provides for a rare concerted effort on the Jewish rebels' part – one may also recall the attack on Ascalon under the first regime, or Josephus campaign in Galilee – in conducting at least some sort of regular warfare rather than spontaneous actions in the cities or countryside. The question remains whether the inhabitants of Engaddi belonged among the enemy, that is, 'the Romanizers'. Josephus's silence on the matter serves as an innuendo, implying that they were not; by the same token, however, the reader may suspect that they were.

Be that as it may, on Passover night A.D. 68 (note again the fact of sacrilege in perpetrating violence during the major religious festival), Masada's *sicarii* stormed into a town of Engaddi, located some ten miles North from their fortress (402); this event must have been on public record. They are said to have dispersed or driven out those able to resist before the latter could arm and gather together; those who failed to escape, women and children, were allegedly massacred, totally up to 7000. One wonders why the sectarians chose to slaughter women and children rather than men whom they reportedly allowed to leave, which casts doubt on whether this part of the story is actually true, regardless of the obviously much exaggerated figure. Upon plundering the houses and the fields – the text proceeds – they withdrew to Masada with their spoils. Whether Josephus's next statement that they subsequently ravaged the villages and whole countryside around that fortress, daily joined by "not a few corrupt characters from every side" (405), or his implicit contention that those deeds came to influence similar disturbances elsewhere (406 ff.) are reliable cannot be ascertained.[5]

IV.

The tragic episode of the *sicarii* at Masada, their last stronghold in Judaea, culminating in self-destruction of 960 men, women and children (*BJ*, 7, 400 f.) in May A.D. 73, strikes one as virtually beyond compare in the history of Antiquity. It seems so, even if one takes into account other known cases of collective suicide, or the tradition of the Jewish martyrdom as arisen during the Maccabean revolt (*2 Macc.*, 7; *4 Macc.*, 1:8 ff.), which, arguably, transpired in tragic precedents, like the one in the cave upon Jotapata's capture, that Josephus managed remarkably to survive (*BJ*, 3, 355 ff.). The historian's intentional juxtaposition of this last event with Masada (including the set speeches, respectively, by the author himself and Eleazar b. Jairus) seems clear, but the major contrast should not be missed: the defenders of Jotapata were all men fighting the foe, and they chose to die by their own hand rather than be killed or enslaved by the enemy; at Masada, however, the *sicarii* slaughtered not only themselves, but also all members of their families, who were the majority, and whose life the Romans were likely to spare. Given, further, the scale of the massacre (compared, for instance, with only 40 suicides after the fall of Jotapata – 3, 342), one seems still able to justify the claim that in the annals of classical history it stands out as no other. The only way to comprehend it is once again attempting an inquiry into the mindset of religious dissent, however bizarre it may seem to us in retrospect, and thus trying to envision what could have happened in those people's heads; nor must it be forgotten that subsequent history, and in different contexts, saw repeatedly the recurrence of a similar behavior among those who shared the mentality under discussion, whether that self-conflagration *en masse* of the Russian old believers in the seventeenth century, or – within the recent memory – the voluntary death chosen in Guyana by the followers of the cult leader Jim Jones (1978).

It must be acknowledged with regret that for the purpose of this study, Josephus's treatment of what had taken place at Masada is not particularly helpful. According to his usual procedures, the historian endeavored to minimize those aspects of the Jewish religious ambience which might have been conceivably interpreted by his gentile readership as the source of political subversion. It seems telling that in two speeches he attributes to the leader of the *sicarii*, Eleazar b. Jairus (*BJ*, 7, 323–336; 341–388), the argument is couched in the language of Greek philosophy as much, or perhaps even more, than it concerns Israel's relations with God. It is no less patent that the text contains statements the historical Eleazar would have never uttered. Nonetheless, as I will try to demonstrate, a thorough scrutiny may not only specify Josephus's own anxieties, bias and agenda, but also provide us with an additional insight into the workings of the 'sicarian' mind.

The archaeological evidence shows that the description of the Masada and the conduct of its siege by the Roman general L. Flavius Silva Nonnius Bassus found in the *Bellum* are fairly accurate. The stronghold, which was barely accessible to military attack, is said to have been erected by "the high priest Jonathan" (7, 285), most likely, Jonathan Maccabaeus. Herod the Great took considerable care to fortify it, with a view of using it, if the need arrives, as a place of refuge either against his own rebellious countrymen or foreign invaders (ibid; cf. 300). The fortress was apparently well stocked by Herod in terms of both food and weapons: we read that the goods could last for years and that at the time when the *sicarii* took over the place, they found the supplies in perfect condition, even though a century or so had passed since they had been prepared (297; cf. 331). Indeed, Josephus makes Eleazar b. Jairus insist in his first 'suicide' speech that although their voluntary exit from life must culminate in burning the whole of Masada, the provisions should be spared: "For they will testify, after we are dead, that it was not any shortage, which had overpowered us, but – as we did resolve at the outset – we have chosen death over servitude" (336).

In the overview of the revolutionary groups (*BJ*, 7, 254 ff.), which precedes his Masada narrative, the historian comes up with a charge, intended to apply, as it seems, to the original promoters of the 'fourth philosophy' under Judas and Saddok, as well as to the former's descendant Eleazar with his cohorts. He argues that their high-minded sentiments of freedom and 'theocracy' (in the latter's true sense, the rule solely by God), in the name of which they waged war against all, who accepted Rome's rule (254), meant nothing but hypocrisy:

> This was in fact a mere pretext used as a cover for their atrocities and greed, which became obvious from their deeds. Those who made common cause with them in insurrection and undertook war with Rome, suffered at their shameless hands; and with the falsehood of that pretext

repeatedly proved, they only increased the maltreatment of anyone who reproached their villainy in his righteous pleading.

(256 ff.)

History has richly demonstrated that in revolutionary times of trouble, the motives of all too many individuals may have little in common with their stated purposes of national or collective welfare. This said, the subsequent analysis will make it clear that the Josephan generalization just cited is yet another instance of his deceptive rhetorical psychologizing: it is undercut in multiple ways by his own treatment of the Masada episode and, in particular, through the interplay of subtext and context within two crucial discourses on death and suicide ascribed to the terrorist leader Eleazar b. Jairus.[6]

Even the place as inaccessible as Masada, we are given to understand, could not resist the Roman military machine for long: the wall was breached, and the second one, built of wood by the defenders, set on fire (309 ff.). Once again, one observes a lack of vigor among the besieged: they never made even defensive forays against the enemy as, for instance, the Jews of Machaerus (7, 193 f.) repeatedly did. It is very unlikely that the historian chose to suppress some such episode because of political bias, or in order to undermine the reader's appreciation of Jewish valor. Rather, in order to enhance the import of Rome's victory, bravery shown by the defeated should have been emphasized, as indeed we see it throughout the *Bellum*, where the heroism of the rebels is more often than not described and extolled. The original reason for the passive attitude taken by the *sicarii* at Masada may well have been the same as in the earlier case (to be discussed in this book's last chapter), with many among the Temple's defenders who fell under the spell of a self-styled prophet after the Romans broke into the sanctuary, setting it on fire: the faith in God's salutary intervention at the 13th hour.

When that moment finally arrived, and God did not interfere, we read that Eleazar b. Jairus (instead of contemplating flight, writes Josephus, or even allowing others to do so) addressed "the manliest" (322) among his comrades with the first of his 'suicide' speeches (323–336). There is no reason to doubt that Eleazar did speak to his following – this would have been required by practical exigencies; or, for that matter, that he spoke to them twice. The text states that seven individuals, including a family of six, managed to escape the subsequent massacre, hidden in the underground aqueducts (399), and were led out by Eleazar's woman relative. She is singled out and praised as "differing from most women in her intelligence and upbringing" (ibid). Allegedly, it was also she who reported the details of what was spoken, and then acted upon at Masada, to the Romans (404), "who listened to her uneasily, not believing in audacity that great" (405). Although the historian was not present at the siege, or perhaps never even visited the place, one cannot altogether rule out that he knew the women survivors personally and thus learned the substance of what Eleazar had, in fact, to say; at any rate, he could have read the interrogation notes made by the Romans and, knowing well the man and his ambience, tried to recapture its possible content. To what extent that substance, or content, is discernible within the elaborate multi-layered compositions ascribed to the 'sicarian' leader by Josephus is a different question. In these impressive rhetorical artifacts the historian has intricately interwoven, in terms of concepts, imagery and vocabulary, the strands owing to both Judaic and Greco-Roman religious/philosophical traditions.

It is imperative, even though problematic, to make at least an attempt at distinguishing between Josephus's own projections and the historical Eleazar's agenda which might have affected both the form and the argument of his delivery. This means, of course, the specifically Jewish (rather than gentile) perspective on the predicament he and his comrades-at-arms found themselves in. Its plausible reconstruction requires a creative effort for imagining the state of mind, under the circumstances, of both the speaker and his audience. During many years of their struggle, these people felt convinced that they were indeed implementing God's will on Earth and God's plan for the salvation of Israel. They inevitably experienced tremendous perplexity and mental anguish upon realizing that this may have not been the case, since their God seems to have turned against them while, apparently, through no fault of theirs: the predicament, which defied any common logic. We might now call it 'cognitive dissonance'. Given the traditional tenets of Judaism, especially of its Pharisaic branch, the resolution was to be sought, first, by looking back to the sacred history of God's relationship with God's chosen people, in terms of the latter's obedience to God or lack thereof; and, second, in the mystery and inscrutability of God's ways. The two aspects were intimately interwoven: God's will, whatever it may be, is to be obeyed without questioning, even if it was incomprehensible. This is the crucial leitmotif in the Old Testament, made poignantly manifest in the stories of Abraham and Isaac, Jephthah and his daughter, and in the *Book of Job*. All of it constituted the material thoroughly familiar to the *sicarii*, immersed, as they presumably were, in the study of the Scriptures and inspired by the legends of the past. It was, in particular, the *Book of Job*, which deprived the notion of God from much of 'psychological anthropomorphism', endowing it instead with the sense of – in Rudolf Otto's memorable words – 'something Other' (*'etwas Anderes'*) and 'something Terrible' (*'etwas Scherkliches'*), when we read:

> Then the Lord answered Job out of the whirlwind: "Who is this that darkens counsel by words without knowledge? / ... / Where were you when I laid the foundation of the earth? Tell me, if you have understanding. Who determined its measurements – surely you know! Or who stretched the line upon it? / ... / Or who shut in the sea with doors, when it burst forth from the womb / ... / Have you entered into the springs of the sea, or walked in the recesses of the deep? Have the gates of death been revealed to you, or have you seen the gates of deep darkness? Have you comprehended the expanse of the earth? Declare,

if you know all this / ... / Do you know the ordinances of the heavens? Can you establish their rule on the earth? / ... / Shall a faultfinder contend with the Almighty? / ... / Will you even put me in the wrong? Will you condemn me that you may be justified? Have you an arm like God, and can you thunder with a voice like his? Deck yourself with majesty and dignity; clothe yourself with glory and splendor / ... / Then will I also acknowledge to you, that your own right hand can give you victory.

(BJob, 38–40, abridged)

What follows are the incredible descriptions of Behemoth and Leviathan (41 ff.). Job's only answer to this is: "Wherefore I abhor myself, and repent in dust and ashes" (Job, 42:6). This is to say that outside his obedience to God's will, Job's ordeal had no meaning at all. In the customary ethical terms, this is inexplicable, even despite the epilogue, in which the sufferer is given by God in reward "twice as much as he had before" (42:10), intended precisely to have the whole unfathomable affair rationalized and moralized.

I find it indeed possible that this vision of the mysterious Deity from the *Book of Job* constituted at least one strand within the construable mindset of the 'sicarian' religious dissenters at Masada. Furthermore, it might have provided not only a subtext for Josephus, but perhaps, given their feelings at the moment of despair and injustice, even the context for the argument pursued by the historical Eleazar, of which the former could have been aware. Likewise, Josephus was bound to realize that the 'theology of inscrutability' as propounded in the Hebrew Bible, especially in the *Book of Job*, made little or no sense for his contemporary pagan audience. In making it intelligible, he needed to operate within a different set of references and translate one conceptual framework into another: that is to say, one must recognize in Eleazar's orations *both* Judaic and Hellenistic aspects, as clearly the author's own contributions.

Josephus's rendering of the first harangue contains at least one line of argument that must have been taken up by the original speaker, namely: "Long ago had we resolved / ... / to serve neither the Romans, nor anyone else, but God who is alone true and just Lord of humankind" (*BJ*, 7, 323). As we know, this was, according to Josephus, a view common to all adherents of the 'fourth philosophy'. Similarly, Eleazar might well have emphasized what the text says he did: that the *sicarii* were the first to revolt (presumably, by capturing Masada at the outbreak of the hostilities) as well as the last to continue their resistance (324) – and even claimed that God had granted them a particular favor: an opportunity "to die beautifully and in freedom" (325; cf. 336), which was not the case with others, who had perished unexpectedly.

Eleazar is made to proclaim that the rebels should have recognized from the outset (and the question remains why would they have done it so early on) that God's real purpose was to doom the Jewish race, once chosen and beloved, to perdition (327), "since if He continued to be benevolent, or just moderately angry at us, He would not have disregarded the death of so many men, nor left his holiest city to fire and destruction at the hands of the enemy" (328). This, as we know, is one of Josephus's own favorite ideas – that owing to the infamies and atrocities, committed by the revolutionaries, God of Israel – as it also happened at the time of the Babylonian captivity – has changed sides and allied with the Romans and adopted Vespasian as the chosen instrument of retribution. Within the context of Eleazar's speech, however, – which is likewise the case in the story of Job – the moral, or theological, perplexity is not resolved since (the speaker states this at the beginning) the insurgents, in fact, did fight *for* God's cause as their only Lord, which sharply distinguishes them from those who witnessed the destruction of the First Temple as the punishment for their sins *against* God's commandments. It is true that the author ascribes to Eleazar an attempt at placing the blame for God's anger on their own acts of crime towards their compatriots (as the mediatory means, aimed at moral rationalization, this serves, *mutatis mutandis*, a function similar to the speeches of Job's friends, trying to make sense of what had happened to him, cf. *Book of Job*: 4–5, 8, 11,15, 18, 20, 22, 25, 32–37):

> Did we indeed hope that we alone of the entire Jewish nation would survive, protecting our liberty, as if we were guiltless before God, and took no part in lawlessness, we who in fact taught the others?
> (*BJ*, 7, 329)

And the speaker keeps emphasizing that the reason for God's wrath must have been "many injustices that we in our madness dared to inflict on our compatriots" (332; cf. "when desiring to reassert our liberty, we suffered from one another so much pain" – 327).

All of this does not, however, sound psychologically and historically plausible or persuasive: the leader of the *sicarii* would have hardly thought, and even less spoken, along these lines, in their utmost hour of need, and urge them to repent. If he did in reality address the moralist issue of guilt rather than leaving it open, he would have most likely cited the collaborators with the occupiers, not his own cohorts of true believers, as having been responsible, both on the earthly and divine plane, for the disaster. One must conclude then that at this point Josephus imposes his own mode of argumentation upon his worst 'ideological' enemy.

Be that as it may, the author makes the speaker conclude, in agreement with the biblical tradition, that it is God who administers mercy or punishment, and thus should be unconditionally obeyed: "Let us pay the penalty for [what we did] not to the Romans, our worst foes, but to God and [do it] by ourselves" (333). Eleazar's first speech ends with an appeal for those who were present to "let their women die without knowing dishonor, and with their children not knowing slavery" (334) so that they could all thereupon "do each other a noble favor" by killing each other and in doing it "preserve our liberty as a beautiful shroud" (ibid).[7]

The most conspicuous feature of the second speech (341–388, more than three times longer than the first) that the historian attributes to Eleazar b. Jairus is indeed the discourse on immortality of soul in an argument, for the most part borrowed from Plato, and much better fitting a Stoicizing dissident senator, like Thrasea Paetus, than the Jewish nationalist and religious dissenter at Masada. As regards the latter, who must have shared strong and anti-gentile bias akin to the Shammai's school, and was hardly well versed or even interested in Greek literature and philosophy, any such display is inconceivable, speaking not of the fact that, under the circumstances, it would have been both counterproductive (one does not resort to the ideas engendered by a hostile culture in an hour of need) and absurd. That Eleazar had to address his companions twice seems believable: fear of death, creed or 'ideology' notwithstanding is an essential human trait. Knowing this, Josephus seizes an opportunity to psychologize: although some, he admits, were "eager to heed [the words of the speaker – V. R.] and were all but filled with pleasure in belief that this was noble death" (337), others, the weaker ones, "were moved by pity for their wives and families, and certainly by the clear prospect of their own end, looking at each other with tears, which signaled the unwillingness in their minds" (338). It would have been only natural if Eleazar were trying to embolden them with the promise of a great reward for their valor in the afterlife. It could easily be done, for instance, through the reference to the Pharisaic doctrine on the resurrection of the dead, and to the vision of God's last judgment on the righteous and the wicked, which might well have been the actual case (and if so, any possibility of the speaker blaming the revolutionaries for the divine wrath must be definitely ruled out). Possibly, Josephus even knew of it from the interrogation of the survivors by the Romans, but realized that reproducing such specifically Judaic arguments would only baffle that reproducing such specifically Judaic arguments would only baffle his Greco-Roman readership and contribute to the confusion in their heads on the subject of his compatriots. (One recalls an episode in the *Book of Acts*, where Paul is questioned by the procurator Porcius Festus and King Agrippa on his beliefs and, after mentioning Christ as "being the first to rise from the dead", is told by the Roman in "a loud voice": "Paul, you are mad; your great learning is turning you mad" – *Acts*: 23, 26 f.).

This accounts for the historian's decision to replace whatever Eleazar might have said regarding the soul's immortality in terms of Judaism, with the Greek-like philosophical disquisition as coming from a Jewish nationalist leader. It was a clever stroke, even though it seems incongruous, or bizarre, to us moderns. Above all, it was intended to further narrow the gap between them and the Jews in the eyes of the gentiles by stressing the common (or construed as common) themes and patterns of thought. Much of the *Contra Apionem* is devoted to the same project in order to promote Josephus's agenda as his people's apologist. (The similar aim is obviously served by yet another equally peculiar device in making Titus extol the God of Israel as an ally of the Romans – e.g., *BJ*, 6, 38 ff.; the Flavians, who had read the *Bellum*, may not have objected because of their effort to propagate among the Jews the notion of Vespasian being a Messianic figure.) Even more ingenious was the author's implicit fusion of Job's incomprehensible Deity with the Greek concept *anagke* ('necessity' or 'destiny') – no less perplexing and still more impersonal: at the same time, vague and polysemantic, and thus well suited to direct – or misdirect – the response of the gentile audience, allowing each reader an opportunity for one's own interpretation. In Greek, this word has a variety of meanings (literal, philosophical and poetic), which include 'necessity', 'compulsion', 'distress', 'destiny' or 'fate', and is often employed to signify the relation to, or the agency of, the divine. It turns up as an aspect of God's punishment in the rebel leader's first speech: "Look, how He exposes the vanity of our hope by inflicting an ordeal (*anagken*) upon us worse in horror than we could anticipate" (7, 330); it looms larger in the second. At any rate, within this context, any promise of posthumous comfort, arising from the belief in resurrection or in eschatology (rather than Greek philosophy posited by Josephus) would seek the same effect as the beneficent epilogue to the *Book of Job*: the fulfillment of our moral and emotional needs.

The historian makes the speaker begin the second peroration by reproaching his listeners with pusillanimity: "I was much deceived in belief that I have chosen as comrades in our contest for freedom good men, who resolved to live nobly or to die" (*BJ*, 7, 341), and further on: "but you did not in virtue or daring excel the run of humankind, since you fear the death that would deliver you from the worst evils, when you should not have, as regards this, or wait for an advisor" (342). This is the rhetorical device, intended to convey the opposite to what is the ostensible meaning, namely, that the *sicarii* were indeed 'good' and 'noble', provided that they follow their leader's advice. One may regard as forced Eleazar's subsequent insistence on the Jews having been continually taught "since the dawn of intelligence" and by "the deeds and thought" of their forefathers the truth found in "ancestral and divine precepts" on the preference of death to life (343); but this might reflect, at least to some extent, the pessimistic vision manifest in the Ecclesiastes, and in certain strands within the tradition of Judaic wisdom (*khokhma*).

The speech proceeds with an argument on the soul's immortality and its separation from the body, given largely in Greek philosophical and poetic terms (344–348), with the reference to sleep as clinching proof, when souls "converse with God and travelling to your kin in every direction foretell the future" (349). The rhetorical questions that follow thus become predictable: if we welcome sleep, why indeed should we be afraid of death (350); and is it not senseless, while we live for the sake of liberty, to resent what is eternal (ibid)?

This part of Eleazar's argument concludes, somewhat unexpectedly, with the discussion of the beliefs and practices among the Indians, both illustrating and enhancing the point about human ability to despise death (351–357). This excursus appears superfluous due to the claim it starts with, that the Jews, trained by the law of their forefathers in readiness to die, should provide a model for other nations (351), which implies that no other analogy is needed. In any event, the choice of the Indians as an example again follows the patterns of Greek historiography and ethnography rather than Judaic tradition, which was not that much interested in the customs of foreign peoples unless they entered direct relationship with Jews threatening to infect them with their pagan vices such as idol worship. This material on the Indian ascetics, whom the Greeks called 'gymnosophists', and their voluntary self-conflagration, drawn as it seems from the writings by the historian Megasthenes, must have been outside Eleazar's own intellectual concerns, but – as some other passages testify (e.g., c*Ap.*, 1, 144; 178; *AJ*, 10, 227) – not those of Josephus. By a circular procedure, the digression ends with the same point as it begins: they must be ashamed of their lesser courage as compared with that of the Indians and, through their cowardice, of disgracing the ancestral laws "which the entire mankind came to envy" (357).

Eleazar is portrayed as insisting, however, that the Jewish doctrine (allegedly) privileging death over life is ultimately irrelevant. Even if they were taught otherwise, it still would not matter: they should brace themselves, since at the moment it was "by God's Judgment and of necessity (or 'destiny' – *anagke*)" that they were to die (358). Placing side by side 'God' and 'necessity' (or 'destiny') is, of course, Josephus's ploy, hardly Eleazar's: there is little doubt that this Greek notion would have proved more palatable to the *Bellum*'s gentile readers than the enigmatic Deity of the Jews. The latter's motives remain, as with Job, largely inscrutable:

> For a long while, as it seems, God passed this judgment, in common, on the entire Jewish people that we must depart from this life if we do not intend to use it rightly.
>
> (359)

This resumes the argument of the first speech, although what is meant by 'wrong use of life' is still uncertain: cooperating with the Romans, or acting in the spirit of 'fourth philosophy' by not recognizing any human master. The next sentence seems to clarify: "Do not put blame upon yourselves" (360), which directly contradicts Eleazar's earlier oration, where it is announced that the revolutionaries are declared guilty for having initiated civil bloodshed and thus provoking God's wrath. It appears that here the author, if not the speaker, was unable to bring the ends together. Nor should the Romans, we are told, be given credit for their success, since "it was achieved not by their strength, but there was at work a far mightier cause that has produced what appears to be their victory" (360).

The historian must have thought it important to assign to the radical leader, despite all obvious probabilities, the vision of things closest to his own. The author's thesis that, in chastisement for Israel's sins, God sided with Israel's oppressors runs against the optimism prevalent in contemporary Jewish apocalyptic writing and, although both sides recognized that the nation had sinned, they would have certainly disagreed on what constituted sins in question.

The statement made in the speech under discussion that neither Jews nor Romans but God decided the issue is implicitly illustrated by the series of flashbacks, each time demonstrating that the Jewish victims suffered innocently: in Caesarea, even before the outbreak of the war, they were attacked on the day of the Sabbath by the locals, who disregarded public order the Romans sought to maintain (362; cf. 2, 457 ff.); in Scythopolis, even though opposing the revolt, they were nonetheless betrayed by their pagan neighbors and butchered by them (364 ff.; cf. 2, 466 ff.); similarly, unprovoked massacres occurred in Syria (367 f.; cf. 2, 559 ff.) and Egypt (369; cf. 2, 487 ff.). On the other hand, although everything, in the speaker's view, both material and spiritual (arms, walls, supplies, fortresses, fortitude, the passion for freedom), seemed at the outset to have favored the insurgents, the enterprise – after a brief season of hope – still ended in ruin (7, 369 ff.).

Therefore, Eleazar's audience needed to reconcile with the fact that God had turned against God's own people, and only those who fell in battle, "defending, and not betraying liberty" (372), could be congratulated. The ones still alive, but languishing in Roman slavery, on the other hand, merited only pity: "Who would not, rather than to endure the same, hasten to die?" (ibid), knowing that the Jewish captives were tortured and thrown to the wild beasts as a "source of laughter and entertainment for their foes" (373). The inference must be obvious: most miserable are those who often pray for death, but in vain (374).

The major proof that God had indeed abandoned Israel was the destruction of the sacred city, Jerusalem. It was thoroughly fortified, says the text (much in agreement with historical truth), by ramparts, towers, plenty of ammunition, and defended "by myriads of men" (375). This raises the obvious, albeit most painful, question: "How did it happen to us who believed that God was its founder?" (376). There remained only desolation (other manuscripts read "the camp of its [i.e., the city's] destroyers") like a memorial, and the wretched old men sitting near the ashes of the sanctuary, with a few women picked by the enemy for rape and shame (377) – the ultimate reversal of any optimistic eschatology. This bleak picture must have become as impressed upon the Jewish historical memory as the lament on the rivers centuries earlier during the Babylonian exile. The sense of poignancy, obviously shared both by the author and the speaker, accounts for the particular force in Eleazar's subsequent exhortation:

> Oh, would we have all died before seeing the holy city torn down by the enemy's hands and the sacred shrine thus blasphemously destroyed. But since it was a not ignoble hope that beguiled us, that perhaps we could take vengeance on the city's enemies, and that hope is gone and abandoned us to necessity [or destiny], let us hasten to die honorably.
> (379 f.)

One notes again an emphasis on the rebels' noble aspirations, which is at variance with Eleazar's alleged initial recognition that they were guilty of instigating and perpetrating crimes (329); and with the reference to the *anagke* as responsible for their present predicament.

The rhetorical pitch intensifies by portraying helpless women and children, led into slavery towards torture and shame, owing to the cowardice of those who could have prevented this by a lethal act (381 ff.). This inaugurates the crescendo built up in the final coda that sums the most persistent leitmotifs of Eleazar's speeches, including the need for the fulfillment of the divine will, which is ultimately the same as destiny or necessity (with, however, the theme of the soul's immortality tellingly absent):

> Un-enslaved by the enemy let us die free, with our children and wives, let us depart together from this life! This is what our laws command, our wives and children beg us to do this. God provided for necessity of this, the Romans desire the opposite and fear that even one of us might die before capture. Make haste, so that instead of joy at our arraignment, we could leave them with the amazement at our death and admiration for our boldness.
>
> (386 ff.)

It remains open to question whether Josephus's treatment of Eleazar might have betrayed any grudging admiration by the historian, or even a secret regret that he himself had failed, when faced with the same alternative, to act likewise and die in glory. Be that as it may, throughout the war narrative, the son of Jairus, alone among the radical leaders, is shown as a person of integrity, endowed with genuine, even if perverse, virtue and thus worthy of remembrance.

Within the structure of the *Bellum*, Eleazar's speeches clearly gesture towards at least three earlier orations composed by Josephus: most prominently the latter's own, given in the aftermath of Jotapata's fall (3, 362–382), where the argument against suicide that he develops is rational and pragmatist (it is honorable to die from the enemy's hand, not one's own) as well as theological (suicide is an act of impiety, a crime hateful to God, who created us), and in every respect opposite to the idealistic emotionalism and fatalist theology professed by Eleazar. It is true that the idea of the soul's immortality is touched upon in both cases; but Josephus's speech, contrary to Eleazar's, couches it in the language of the Torah and the rabbis, rather than Greek philosophy, with the repeated references to God, not man, as responsible for one's own life.

Two other harangues, relevant in one sense or another to Eleazar's performance, are Titus's addressing his soldiers at the siege of Jerusalem (6, 34–53), in which case the Roman commander's digression on the soul's separation from the body and its subsequent itinerary (46–48) may seem to some readers almost as bizarre as when it is similarly placed by the author in the mouth of the Jewish revolutionary figure; and, finally, King Agrippa's admonitory lecture in Jerusalem to the people upon the outbreak of the hostilities to counter their chosen course of action (2, 344–407): the King is made to predict, with the author's deliberate accuracy, the very series of disasters that Eleazar has presented.[8]

The leader's oratory (irrespective of its version found in the *Bellum*, the very outcome suggests that he must have been an able speaker) apparently worked to create a collective hysteria among his comrades. Their subsequent self-immolation is described in detail and with dramatic power, not only exhibiting Josephus's rhetorical abilities, but also, as it seems, betraying some genuine emotion: "Wretched in the grip of necessity (*anagke*), they considered slaying their wives and children with their own hands the lightest of evils" (7, 393). On the one hand, they fell prey to "some uncontrollable urge" (389) and acted "in so great passion" (ibid); on the other, under the spell of Eleazar's argument, each of them "thought it a display of courage and prudence" (ibid). Under the circumstances, this might well have been a correct psychological description. It accounts for the poignant scene that follows:

> Thus while they caressed and embraced their wives and took their children in their arms, implanting on them, in tears, those last kisses, at the same time they did fulfill their resolution, as if doing it with the hands not their own, persuaded by the thought of the ills coming to them from the enemy, taking it as a consolation for the necessity [yet another use of the word *anagke* – V. R.] to kill them.
> (392)

As at Joptapata, the men, who were left, proceeded to slaughter each other by lot and in a manner reminiscent of a ritual as described by the historian, whose source may have been a few women who survived:

> Having chosen by lot the ten as the slayers of the rest, they stretched themselves out, each one at the side of his wife and children and, putting their arms around them, offered their throats readily to those who rendered this wretched service. The latter, who un-hesitantly finished them all and then applied the same rule of lot to themselves, so that the one on whom it fell was to kill the other nine and in the end himself.
> (395 f.)

The last survivor, unknown by name, before taking his own life, was to ascertain that all were dead, and then set afire the royal palace, where this self-sacrifice *en masse* had been performed, and so it was done (397). It happened on the 15th day of the month Nisan (401; Greek Xanthicus, April–May), three years after the fall of Jerusalem.

In any attempt at appraisal, historical or moral, of the tragic Masada episode one enters heated and contested ground, which requires a thoughtful and delicate balance of judgment. It cannot be denied that the account in Josephus is emotionally powerful. This power is amplified by its popular version within mainstream Jewish tradition, especially in Israel, and sometimes referred to as 'the Masada myth'. This version tends to modify Josephus's narrative by emphasizing, or exaggerating, some of its features while suppressing or obfuscating some others. The official reports of the excavations, especially at their initial stage, were colored by patriotic enthusiasm, occasionally excessive, and also contributed to the spread of that 'myth', with help from the media.

Given the known facts of Israel's history, however, the important role Masada came to acquire in terms of ideology and national consciousness is understandable and in no way surprising. The Jewish state, which for half a century was compelled to fight off the attacks of an implacable enemy, including suicide bombers, bent on its destruction, naturally developed a siege mentality and found in the defense of Masada a perfect emblem for its own predicament. The inspirational worth and the appeal of heroism it implies are considerable and, due to the passional component of human nature, one should not wonder that, in the eyes of modern Jewish and Israeli patriots, those factors overshadowed the fact that the fighters at Masada were themselves terrorists and performed a massacre of their own kin, women and children, numbering in the hundreds.

The humanist perspective, on the other hand, privileges an individual life as supreme value. One should not expect, of course, to find the same recognition across the ancient world, although such humanitarian concerns were not entirely alien to the enlightened Stoicism of Seneca and Epictetus. But on the subject of suicide, ancient Judaism held firmer views, largely negative, unless one is forced to it *in extremis* as, for example, by the demand to renege on one's own faith. As we have seen, Josephus even tells us that to the Jews suicide was forbidden by Law: "Among us it has been ruled that the suicides are to be cast out unburied until sunset, while we regard it righteous to bury even our enemies" (*BJ*, 3, 377). This statement equates a suicide with a hanged criminal (cf. *Deut*: 21, 22 f.), although in contrast to the latter, no direct pronouncement, as referred to by the historian, can be found in the Torah. Still, it is most unlikely that Josephus could have invented any such prescription, since among his intended audience were many Jews, who would include experts in Law, fluent in Greek. I find it plausible that, given the associative and increasingly intricate character of the Torah exegesis, practiced throughout centuries, the ruling on suicides quoted by Josephus became recognized early enough as a *halakha*, at least within the Pharisaic circles, as a part of tradition, derived by the established interpretative procedures from some now unidentifiable verse in the Pentateuch. This would explain why in the preceding sentence the historian attributes the punishment for suicides to the "wisest legislator" (loc. cit.), that is, Moses.

The piety of the Masada *sicarii* cannot be doubted. Archaeological findings, including the texts of the Essene, and perhaps even Qumran provenance, attest to this. Still, within the 'theology' (if the term is appropriate) of the 'covenantal' (or 'common') Judaism at the time, their piety strikes as distinctly perverse. It seems telling that the later rabbis chose to debate the legitimacy of self-sacrifice. In their treatment of political 'zealotism', they were obliged to proceed cautiously in order to neither condemn the rebels *explicite* – and thus *implicite* supporting the Roman occupier – nor to approving of them, in view of the historical catastrophe that ended in the destruction of the Temple, and brought about by their attitudes and behavior. They preferred to elide the issue altogether, and refer to it, if needed, indirectly or by means of equivocation. Thus, in the Tannaitic texts the event at Masada is not altogether mentioned. It is more significant that even on the issue of noble self-sacrifice, such as for the sake of another person, their views remained divided, including a disapproval of any such act.

None of this apparently bothered the *sicarii* at Masada. Eleazar's exhortations must have fallen on the psychologically prepared soil: he played on the sentiments already in place. In the end, his audience responded in the manner typical of religious dissenters who do not require an intermediary, whether a priestly establishment or the mainstream legalist tradition, in their relations with God, to interpret what they consider God's will and to decide on the appropriate course of conduct. We have seen that for persons of this mindset, customary precepts, unless they are in agreement with their own vision and intent, turn irrelevant. They are propelled by the latter to dispense not only with their own life, but those of their families, perhaps suffering – at least some of them – from pity, or self-pity, but not on the grounds of moral or metaphysical remorse. This offers a patent contrast with the mentality of political dissidents within the Roman upper class who were, for the most part, prepared to kill themselves only when ordered to do so by the Imperial authorities.

I am by no means certain that such concepts as 'heroism' or 'martyrdom' are in fact applicable to Masada's suicides. After all, the heroes are those who perish fighting the enemy and, preferably, killing as many of them as they can in process. The Old Testament provides a quintessential example of heroism in the figure of Samson, whose exploit was to destroy at once both himself and the hateful Philistines (*Judg.*, 16:23 ff.). Josephus's own *Bellum* includes many and manifold portrayals of similar heroism on the part of the Jewish insurgents. Likewise 'martyr' means a person who underwent torturous cruel death at the hands of the oppressor for refusing to renege his convictions, religious or other. The eminent cases in point would be the martyrdom of seven brothers and their mother under Antiochus IV Epiphanes (*2 Macc.* 7) or, in later times, of the great Rabbi Aqiba.

Eleazar's speeches, as constructed by Josephus and in so far as they reveal characteristically Jewish thinking, imply – at the very best – that God has ordered the *defeat* of the *sicarii* (and other rebels), not their *death*. The suicide they chose to commit thus represented the ultimate rejection of reality, more radical and extreme than a mere withdrawal from it, practiced – for instance – by the sectarians at Qumran. It is the same twisted religiosity that was responsible for a terrible irony inherent in their performance, which was actually the perversion of *a holocaust*, a Greek word employed in the Septuagint to signify a voluntary sacrifice (literally, burning of sacrificial victims or offerings) to God – a perversion, since the very archaic practice of sacrificing humans had been centuries since abandoned in Jewish worship.[9]

I find it useful to compare and contrast the 'sicarian' last stand and self-immolation at Masada with Josephus's account (not famous at all) of the events leading to the Roman capture of yet another Herodian fortress, Machaerus, which – if it is taken at face value – displays some extraordinary features. It was one of several strongholds fortified by Herod (*BJ*, 7, 171 f.), and Josephus describes its location as "to offer a secure hope for safety, and for those who attacked it, hesitation and fear" (*BJ*, 7, 165). The fortress fell into the hands of the revolutionaries early in the revolt (2, 485 f.; cf. 4, 555) and endured, as Masada did, far beyond Jerusalem's capture and destruction. Only in A.D. 72 did the forces of the legate Lucilius Bassus, including Tenth Legion (Fretensis), march against it and put it under siege (7, 163, 190 ff.). At no point in the subsequent narrative does Josephus suggest that Machaerus was held by the *sicarii* or zealots, and the behavior of its occupants as reported makes it clear that they had not belonged to either group. We read that the Jewish rebels seized the citadel, having forced the rest of the residents to stay in the lower town and wait for Roman assault (191 f.). The author's imputation that the defenders did this not only for practical military reasons but also with a view of being able to bargain with the enemy for surrender (192) is not very persuasive, though it will be seen that this was exactly what happened in the end: no such thing would be possible, of course, among typical religious dissenters. In any event (and this must have been on public record), the men of Machaerus, unlike their sectarian comrades in Masada, rather than waiting for intervention from above, or preparing to take their own life, repeatedly – Josephus says daily – engaged in fighting with the besiegers, with "many of them perishing, but also killing many Romans" (193). The success varied:

> It was the chance that gave the advantage to the one side or the other: to the Jews if they fall upon those [the Romans], when they were off guard; to the latter – mounting a good defense when stationed on the mounds in anticipation of an assault.
>
> (194)

It is the eventual outcome of these sallies that seems striking – and is properly considered such by Josephus. He recounts the story of Eleazar, a popular young man, who actively participated in the raids outside the fortress and was, the text specifies, a member of a "great and very numerous family" (204). We learn that on one such occasion he was surprised by a Roman soldier and taken captive. This supposedly provided the legate with the means to intimidate and emotionally blackmail the defenders: the youth was stripped and scourged in full view of the rebels, which was followed with preparations to have him crucified (199 ff.). This spectacle, the reader is further told, has proved so pitiable, augmented by poor Eleazar's own reported pleas to save his life through negotiation, that the insurgents finally consented, surrendering on condition that they "could leave without fear and take Eleazar with them" (205). According to Josephus, Lucilius

Bassus honored this agreement, which, however, did not include those who remained in the lower town, some having attempted flight, by most slain by the Romans (the given figure is seventeen hundred), their women and children enslaved (208).

Irrespective of Josephus's rhetoric or the veracity of his description, I cannot imagine any reason for him to make up this elaborate episode, even if he desired to contrast it with the subsequent and tragic Masada narrative. Its character was virtually unique, and for this reason inevitably known to and discussed by both the author's Jewish and Roman contemporaries; of the latter, military officers and the rank-and-file taking part in the action would have been eyewitnesses. As a result, we must recognize its basic historicity.

The uniqueness – and not only within Jewish ambience and tradition, but also as regards models of attitudes, or patterns of behavior, which characterized the ancient world at large – lay, of course, in the public response that privileges individual life over collective cause (national or partisan, political, social or religious). Even today this problem constitutes a subject of the often passionate moral and philosophical debate. For the purpose of this study, it is important to underscore the disparity, or behavioral gap, between the motives and conduct, on the one hand, of the conventional religious believers (that the Jewish garrison at Machaerus seems to have been) and those entrapped within the religious dissent mentality. The former prove capable of compromise, whether owing to fatigue or, as in this case (apparently), to compassion, while most among the latter consider any of this, at best, weakness and, at worst, betrayal: it will be seen that the factions in Jerusalem under siege remained unmoved by many Jewish captives tortured and crucified on Titus's order before their very eyes.[10]

One might expect that the story of the *sicarii* ended at Masada. This, however, was not to be: an epilogue followed. According to Josephus, an apparently sizable group of them, perhaps some of those who may have stayed in the capital during the siege, or had been active elsewhere in Judaea, managed to escape the country and provoke minor disturbances in Egypt (*BJ*, 7, 410–419) and Cyrenaica (437–451). The latter event strangely came to interlock with Josephus's own story. We read that those who fled to Egypt resumed their "revolutionist schemes" (410), trying to pressure the establishment and the commons at Alexandria "to claim their liberty, treat the Romans no better than themselves and regard only God as their Lord" (ibid) – the latter phrase known as a major tenet of the 'fourth philosophy'. Some of their adversaries, "by no means obscure", who objected, they are said to have killed (411). It is hard, however, to ascertain their ultimate purpose.

As we know, the tension between the Jewish community and the gentiles in Alexandria went back to the Ptolemaic period, largely relating to the issue of *isonomia*: the interpretation of their respective rights before the law that governed the land of Egypt, and the equality in the matters of the city's governance. Sometimes this conflict broke into Jewish pogroms, most notably under Caligula in A.D. 38, as described in detail by the philosopher Philo (*In Flaccum*), and again at the time of the Great Revolt. It does not seem likely, on the other hand, that the 'sicarian' exiles in Egypt were interested in any legalistic or administrative problems. As religious dissenters, they must have been obsessed with the same desperate wishful thinking that became their motivation from the outset: although angered with the sins of Jewish people, and having taught them a lesson, God would ultimately raise them from the utmost misery to glory, if needed, by the means of miracle, provided they also would not spare any effort, however reckless, to implement his will. And it was in Egypt after all that the greatest – and foundational – miracle for Judaism as a whole, the Exodus, had been performed. In their eyes, it must have justified hope against hope, also concurring with the 'theology of history' as made manifest in the texts of the Old Testament prophets: God's relationship with Israel was always passionate, with alternating threats of punishment for disobedience with promises of blissful victory. But in practical terms, Josephus is right in calling the Egyptian schemes of the *sicarii*, whatever they could have been, "madness" (7, 412). Given Egypt's crucial role in the Empire's economic and political system, its strict supervision by the central government, the fact that Vespasian chose it as one of his operational bases in his drive to power, and that even in Alexandria the Jews represented a relatively small minority living within the hostile environment – it left not a slightest chance for success of any attempt at their insurrection, but a certainty of yet another vast slaughter by their foes.

It is not surprising, then, that the Elders (the members of the Jewish council at Alexandria, the *gerousia* (ibid)), although reluctant to act on their own authority so that they could avoid potential trouble, succeeded in persuading the Jewish residents of the need to deliver the newly arrived agitators into Roman hands (414 f.). As a result, Josephus says, 600 of them were arraigned on the spot (415), and those who escaped inland were also subsequently arrested (416). Their persecution culminated, contrasting with what had happened at Masada, in the authentic martyrdom, as Josephus eloquently states:

> There was no one who was not stunned, whether by their perseverance, or madness; or whether we should say 'strength of resolution'. Despite every torture and outrage upon their bodies, the only purpose of which was to make them acknowledge Caesar as lord, not one of them yielded or was even on the brink of saying that he would do so; no, all stuck to their conviction against the inevitable, keeping it triumphant over the torture, as if their bodies felt no pain, all but rejoicing in their spirits in the face of torment and fire.
>
> (417 ff.)

The historian singles out especially the endurance shown by the young and concludes that in the case of them all "the strength of their daring overcame the weakness of their bodies" (419). This behavior fits the Jewish tradition of martyrdom for faith and also, as it responds to the earthly authority, clearly resembles the attitudes shown by the early Christians, even though the latter did not altogether reject temporal power in the manner of the *sicarii*, but thought it subordinate to the power of God. One unfortunate offshoot of this whole affair was the closure by the Roman prefect T. Julius Lupus, on Vespasian's order, of the Temple in Leontopolis, which was founded over 300 years earlier (ca. 170 B.C.) through the efforts of Onias b. Simon (Onias IV), the last Jewish hereditary (and legitimate) high priest, who fled to Egypt during the turmoil prior to the rise of the Hasmonaeans (*BJ*, 7, 433 ff.; cf. *AJ*, 12, 387 ff.; 13, 62 ff.).

As portrayed, the developments in Cyrenaica look different. Josephus writes that "the madness of the *sicarii* struck, like a disease, the towns around Cyrene" (*BJ*, 7, 437). But the subsequent report centers on the commotion worked by one individual, Jonathan the Weaver (438–450; cf. *Vita*, 424 f.). The logic of the narrative suggests that this man, "the worst scoundrel" (*BJ*, 7, 438), was an associate of the *sicarii* and then took refuge in Cyrene, where he, after having incited some among "the lowest" (ibid) with the promises of "signs and apparitions" (ibid) led their exodus into the desert – all of this make elements of the 'Messianic Complex', in the style of 'false prophets', who were earlier active in Judaea. Denounced, we are told, by the city's prominent Jews to Catullus, the governor of the Lybian Pentopolis, this new movement was quickly suppressed (the *Vita*, 425, says that 2000 of its followers had perished) and their leader Jonathan eventually seized (*BJ*, 7, 441). But what is described next seems exceedingly obscure: allegedly, the governor Catullus pressured Jonathan and some of his 'sicarian' partisans into conspiracy to destroy, through false charges of sedition, Alexandria's wealthy Jewish residents (3000 in all, according to our author – 445) and, furthermore, trying to implicate even those who by then came to live in Rome, Josephus included (447 ff.; a shorter parallel account in the *Vita* specifies that Jonathan accused him of providing arms and money to the troublemakers – 424 f.). Upon Catullus and Jonathan's (in chains) arrival to the capital, Vespasian ordered, however, a special inquiry, which – on Titus's intercession – ended in the acquittal both of the historian and his co-defendants (450; cf. *Vita*, 425). The unfortunate weaver, on the other hand, who started the whole trouble, was tortured and burned at the stake (*BJ*, loc. cit.). These latter events must have been well known within Josephus's immediate audience, the Jewish community of the capital.

In itself, the connivance of a Roman official with Rome's enemies was nothing unusual. As we know from both Josephus and Tacitus, Judaea's procurators, Ventidius Cumanus and Antonius Felix (the *Bellum* also adds Lucceius Albinus), were patently suspected of making deals with the revolutionaries. In this Cyrenean matter, though, the motives of the principals remain far from clear. Josephus insists that Catullus overblew the affair in order to appear a winner in the Jewish war (*BJ*, 7, 443), but given the fact that this ambition might have intruded upon the jealously guarded Imperial prerogatives, this appears unlikely. And Jonathan, we are to understand, acted as he did merely out of desire to survive; but why either of them sought to impeach Josephus is left unexplained.

Although Catullus, "due to the Emperors' leniency" (451), reportedly escaped the consequences with only a reprimand (ibid), the historian found it imperative to conclude the episode with the punishment that visited him in the form of a terrible and terminal illness: "And so he died, offering a proof, no lesser than any other, that God's providence brings justice to the wicked" (453). Perhaps Josephus saw this comment a fitful ending for the story of his own nation, which – as he came to believe – fell under the spell of the wicked and was thus plunged into ruin.[11]

7

THE FATEFUL SIEGE

I.

It is not my intent to discuss at any real length all events following Nero's downfall, and constituting the last stage of the warfare: the siege of Jerusalem by Titus, its final capture and the destruction of the Temple. Rather, I will focus in this chapter on those aspects and developments that were, in one sense or another, relevant to our chief concern, the inquiry into psychology of religious dissent.

Within Josephus's chronology, Nero's suicide (June 9, A.D. 68) roughly coincided with the rise of Simon bar Giora, who soon came close to taking over sole command over the rebel forces in Jerusalem, although in the end he never managed it. This must not have been accidental: the growth of Simon's power was facilitated at that point by the situation both within and without the capital. The collapse of the 'first regime', which had been openly antagonistic to Simon, even trying to suppress him by force, provided him with some respite. The attitude towards him on the part of zealots under Eleazar b. Simon, as it later transpired, proved no better; but for the moment the latter were confined to the city, having been first preoccupied with their campaign of terror, and then with the factional strife, initiated by John b. Levi of Gischala.

On the other hand, Vespasian (who by that time had successfully reduced most of the country, including Galilee, Samaria, Peraea, as well as large parts of both Judaea and Idumaea), upon learning the news about Nero, chose to suspend hostilities and postponed a march he is said to have planned against Jerusalem, now standing fairly isolated (*BJ*, 4, 497; cf. 490). This behavior was constitutionally correct: Vespasian's authority had to be confirmed by the new emperor and, always a cautious politician, he sent over his own son Titus to Galba, obviously with the purpose of securing a reappointment (ibid, 498). That mission came, however, to nothing, since Galba was killed on January 15, A.D. 69, even before the young man reached Italy, and he made his way back ("under divine influence", says Josephus), to join his father at Caesarea Maritima (499). It seems telling that neither made a move to approach Otho (perhaps in the belief that the latter's chances were doomed), and it is unlikely that Galba's successor, pressured as he was by the revolt of the German legions, had an opportunity throughout only three month of his rule (he took his life on April 17) to consider the affairs in Palestine or to issue any pertinent instructions. What is more significant is the fact that Vespasian moved to resume his offensive by invasion of Judaea in June (ibid, 550 ff.), without apparently waiting for a word from the new emperor Vitellius. To my mind, this suggests that by then he was already entertaining Imperial designs of his own. In any event, the turmoil in the West of the Empire offered the Jewish rebels a whole year of relative tranquility to mobilize, which, as we know, neither the 'second regime' nor later the factions in Jerusalem, nor the *sicarii* at Masada put militarily to good use.

This does not seem to have been the case with Simon bar Giora, who – despite his ultimate failure and disastrous involvement in factional conflicts – proved the most dynamic rebel leader and might have pursued, in contrast to, say, John b. Levi of Gischala, larger interests than mere personal ambition. Josephus may have recognized this when writing:

> There was one Simon, son of Giora, a young man from Gerasa by origin, a lesser knave than John – who had already taken over the city – but surpassing him in bodily prowess and audacity.
>
> (*BJ*, 4, 503)

As it appears, he was not of purely Jewish blood: 'bar Giora' means 'son of a proselyte', which makes his espousing of the nationalist cause all the more noteworthy. There is no compelling reason to ascribe to him membership in the ruling class as has sometimes been done. The fact that some aristocrats eventually sided with him means nothing in particular: a phenomenon, common enough in history, when socially prominent individuals joined, for various reasons, leaders or movements intent on breaking the power of the groups to whom they originally belonged. As most leaders in his position would do, Simon widely welcomed and sought support.

According to Josephus, he first came to prominence through his participation in defeating Cestius Gallus. The historian writes that Simon had attacked the Romans while they were mounting Beth-horon, destroyed much of their rearguard and took over their provisions (the text says "many baggage mules"; ibid, 521). This feat should have made him hopeful for a legitimate award in terms of sharing substantial authority. But he apparently fared even less well at the Temple meeting than Eleazar b. Simon: although the *Bellum* does not explicitly spell it out, the narrative suggests that he was removed from Jerusalem by an appointment in the toparchy of Acrabetene, north of Jerusalem and close to Samaria (ibid, 653), the area traditionally fraught with trouble (cf. *BJ*, 2, 235): the Ananus regime felt wary regarding the presence of the military, especially other than those of unimpeachable loyalty within their midst. Josephus reports, and there is no means to prove him right or wrong, that on that territory, Simon: "having banded together many revolutionaries, he [Simon] turned to plunder, and not only ravaged the houses of the wealthy, but inflicted violence on their bodies, clearly showing that he had embarked on the path of tyranny" (*BJ*, 2, 652).

Even if this picture is exaggerated, Simon's show of independence provided sufficient reason for Ananus and his colleagues to undertake his eviction from the toparchy with the help of an army (diplomacy either failed or was not even tried), a reminder of their vain attempt to unseat Josephus in Galilee. With Simon, however, they proved successful: we are told that they made him withdraw and join, with his followers, the *sicarii* at Masada, where he remained until the zealot coup and the murder of his principal foes (653; cf. 4, 504 ff.). Together with a similar move against Josephus and the attack at Ascalon, this seems to have been the only other military action the 'first regime' was able to perform. It is worth pointing out that the historian ends this particular account by mention of subversive activities that Simon and his friends carried out from Masada in the neighboring Idumaea (2, 653), where they reportedly compelled the local authorities – whose political allegiance at this point in time remains unstated – to levy the army "on the grounds of many people killed and regular pillage", and place garrisons in the villages (654). This area was to become Simon's power base in his drive to conquer Jerusalem.

We saw that, while at Masada, Simon and his following resided separately from the *sicarii*; he is said to have felt disaffected by the latter's inertia, although he would join in their raids within the region, presumably, for the sake of plunder (4, 505 ff.). One may speculate as regards any further reasons for this somewhat uneasy relationship. One of them must have been a general tendency among all Jewish rebel chiefs not to unite; otherwise, Simon may have felt resentful of the tight disciplined lifestyle practiced by the *sicarii* under their dynastic leadership, or personally of Eleazar b. Jairus; and, perhaps, even of some idiosyncrasies in their religious attitudes on which, however, our source is habitually silent. In any event, we read that upon his failure to persuade those temporary allies to attempt "greater things" (507) – and Josephus never misses an opportunity in referring to the man's high ambitions and tyrannical aspirations (cf. 508) – Simon left Masada for the hills as soon as he had heard about the 'first regime's' downfall in Jerusalem, and embarked on the path of war (508). It is at this point that Josephus speaks of Simon's "proclaiming liberty for slaves" (ibid), but – tellingly – in the same breath (and sentence) as of his promise to reward the free (ibid), perhaps thus suggesting that the former enactment should not be taken as anything exceptional in terms of class struggle or social revolution (which some, especially the Marxists would like to believe), but rather as a measure aimed at the increase of one's own military strength.

The scholarly controversy on the character, membership and goals of the movement, or faction, created by Simon b. Giora once again betrays Josephus's specific inadequacies as a historical source, owing not so much to distortions (which he is so often charged with), but rather omissions and lack of subtlety. In modern times, Simon was portrayed as a nationalist leader, a heroic freedom fighter, a social revolutionary, an unscrupulous adventurer, a brutal dictator, and another failed Messiah. Even though the *Bellum* seems to offer more information on him than on any other rebel chief, except John b. Levi of Gischala, he still remains, in regard to his personality and outlook, as elusive as any. The ultimate impression of him one arrives at is that of an able (but not outstanding) charismatic leader without any special, uniform or permanent social base, whether nobility, peasantry or, for that matter, "brigands" (whoever those might have been), but relying on all sorts of supporters, provided they sought, or claimed to seek, national liberation and were ready to recognize his authority. Even Josephus, who would have otherwise loved to represent Simon bar Giora as no more than a bandit chief, had to concede that his following was socially diverse. The historian tells us that after his departure from Masada, and with his force substantially augmented "by the villains from everywhere" (*BJ*, 4, 508), he made his descent into the lowlands (509), with the following results:

> He was soon the source of dread to the towns, and many notable men were lured [to join] him because of his might and the flow of his achievements. Thus his army no more consisted only of slaves and brigands, but included not a few commoners, who obeyed t him as if he were a king.
>
> (510)

Later I will return to the tangled issue of Simon's probable claim at kingship; it is now sufficient to observe that he did succeed in enforcing his unquestioned command among all his followers.

Simon's progress continued unchecked not only through subjugating the toparchy of Acrabetene, which had been formerly under his command, but also by extending, as Josephus specifies, into the district North to the Idumaean border, where he erected a sort of fortification "for the sake of security" (511), and it is further said that he made use of numerous caves in the area to provide repositories of supplies and temporary quarters for his troops (512 f.) It was obvious, the text concludes, that he was busy "exercising his army and making preparations" (513) for an offensive – not, however, as one would expect, to fight Vespasian, who had reconquered by then most of the rebel territories – but (and this is telling as regards the factional character of this liberation warfare) against zealots in Jerusalem (ibid).

It is not possible to credibly establish the reasons for the enmity between the zealot faction (and later John b. Levi of Gischala) within the capital, on the one hand, and Simon bar Giora, on the other. Sheer power struggle, and a clash of individual ambitions, entertained by the leaders, undoubtedly played an important role; but this still does not fully explain their failure to create a united front in face of the growing menace from the national enemy, which threatened to crush the 'independent Jewish state' with consequences no one would have been able to predict. As previously stated, even under harsh conditions of the siege, John and Simon's factions could not achieve a unified command, but chose to fight the Romans separately by means of loosely coordinated sallies. Josephus's silence on the subject may (or may not) suggest that the religious factor, in one sense or another, might have also been in operation to perpetuate the discord. Each of the factional leaders could have practiced their own brand of religious dissent that would have only deepened their conflict, affecting their desire, or ability, for negotiations. In this context, one recalls the contrast between Eleazar b. Simon and his zealots, with their strict ritualism and radical rejection of the priestly establishment (including the current high priest); John's relativist attitudes towards the rules of the Law and the Torah, aggravated by his opportunistic shifts of allegiance and his former connections among the religious elite, now seen as treacherous, impious or corrupt; and the Messianic elements implicit in the behavior of Simon bar Giora. It seems plausible to assume that each of the three (and perhaps others) considered themselves to enjoy an immediate relationship with the divine (an acceptable notion in biblical Judaism), proper for God's chosen instruments and the legitimate interpreters of God's will: a view shared by each of their following, with predictably different results. This would conform, in psychological terms, with the patterns in religious dissent found elsewhere. One regrets, however, that this contention cannot be directly supported by the extant evidence, despite the profusion of apocalyptic literature at the time: at present, we possess no firm data showing that any known revolutionary group proceeded in their activities on the grounds of either a singular scriptural exegesis, or some prophetic, revelatory text. Still, given the nature of our main source, Josephus, his very silence on religious preferences between the factions may prove significant.

Be that as it may, the hostilities between Simon bar Giora and the zealots in Jerusalem seem especially perplexing since, besides national liberation, they had yet another common cause in opposing and fighting against the 'moderate' regime of Ananus b. Ananus. One could think that, upon the success of the zealots' putsch, they would have welcomed in Simon as a strong ally, harassed and hurt as he was by their predecessors: the relationship between the two groups (unlike that of the zealots with the *sicarii*, who became permanently alienated from Jerusalem after Menachem's murder) so far as we know did not suffer from any mutual grudge and major 'philosophical' or practical disagreements. The rapid growth of Simon's power might have justified in his and his followers' eyes his claim for supreme command of all rebel forces, which was, of course, strategically prerequisite for any serious attempt to defeat the Romans. He was, after all, the only foremost Jewish leader who continued to fight in the field, while Eleazar and John at the capital kept settling accounts between themselves; it is also conceivable that he and they varied on the tactics *vis-à-vis* the Romans. If either party had ever tried to negotiate with the other prior to Simon's march on Jerusalem, it remains unknown. Josephus's silence, perhaps deliberate, leaves the original cause of their differences unexplained.

In any event, the *Bellum*'s narrative, flawed though it is, suggests that the 'second regime' (similarly to the 'first') was quick to recognize in Simon a threat to their authority, "fearing his designs and wishing to anticipate his growth to their detriment" (4, 514). Jerusalem's zealots chose to go ahead and attack him outside of the city's walls (ibid), although the details, such as at what stage of his own preparations it happened, are withheld by Josephus. We are only told that Simon succeeded in repelling the assault, killed many of the attackers and drove the remainder back into the city (ibid), but felt his force inadequate for taking the capital by storm (515). Instead, says Josephus, he set his mind to invade Idumaea (ibid), a substantial part of which had been already recovered by Vespasian (cf. 4, 446 ff.), while the latter – if the narrative's sequence of events is to be trusted – had stayed idle until he resumed hostilities in June, A.D. 69.[1]

As it transpires from the historian's narrative, both the leadership and people of Idumaea at the time remained divided, although no explanation for it is offered. One reason might have been the conflict of loyalties: even though the main bulk of the Idumaeans withdrew from Jerusalem after their split with zealots under Eleazar b. Simon, there could remain those who felt allegiance to the revolutionary cause as envisioned by the latter, and looked on Simon bar Giora with suspicion. One cannot even rule out the existence of the Romanizers, however few, especially among the well-to-do; but in reality they would not matter. All in all, the initial Idumaean resolve to resist Simon perhaps largely depended on the condition of the area: the land had suffered much during the recent incursion by Vespasian, and was not given time to recover: it is not surprising that many among the populace objected at allowing in yet another military force, with the prospect of further havoc. This resistance accounts for Simon's failure to gain a speedy victory: the daylong battle apparently reached an impasse, and he temporarily retreated (4, 516 f.).

It seems that the crucial role in Simon's eventual success belongs to the core group of the Idumaeans, who left Jerusalem upon their break with zealots, but now saw in him a worthier ally in the shared struggle for national liberation. One assumes that they expected him to be devoid of prejudices they might have thought offensive, such as zealots' insistence on ritual strictness (and, conceivably, on ethnic purity), which was likely to alienate the Idumaeans in the first place. Nevertheless, the story, explaining this sudden turnaround in Simon's favor, found in Josephus, may be questioned for its basic veracity, or its details, and it certainly simplifies what must have been the result of numerous factors.

The historian ascribes Simon's subsequent triumph exclusively to the machinations by the Idumaean leader (521), one among several named James, who is almost certainly identical with the resourceful James b. Sosas of whom we have already heard. This man is said to have secretly conspired with Simon, on the promise of some honorable office to be held lifelong (523), in securing the country for him (ibid). The text claims that, to fulfill this pledge, he proceeded, first, with pro-Simon propaganda, "hugely exaggerating" (524) the invader's numerical strength, thus intimidating his compatriots, then by ingratiating himself with the local officers, persuading them to comply (525), and finally by having committed treachery on the battlefield. As a result, the Idumaean army reportedly dispersed in panic even before the engagement began (525 ff.). Simon's next step was to crown his subjugation of Idumaea with taking over the one-time royal residence of Hebron (529), a feat sure to remind his compatriots of King David's remarkable career. This must have made him feel that he had at last achieved, in the public eye, the stature of a legitimate contender for power with the masters of Jerusalem.

Josephus takes pain to impress upon the reader the description of Idumaea's sorry fate under Simon: even though he acknowledges (534) the need of provision for his troops and numerous supporters (40,000, according to the historian), he insists that "apart from his needs, his cruelty and fury against the nation played a major part in completing the pillage of Idumaea" (535). Simon's progress is compared to the plague of locusts that leaves nothing behind but a desert (536): his soldiers, we read:

> ... burned some places, others razed to the ground; all vegetation in the land disappeared, either trodden upon, or consumed; with their march, they made the fertile soil harder than the infertile. In short, whatever they did destroy, no sign was left of its [previous] existence.
> (537)

This is, of course, one of the author's many hostile hyperboles. Simon was not so stupid, or fanatical, as to antagonize his potential allies. It may be safely taken that during his stay in Idumaea the local non-combatants suffered no more than they would have in the case of any war waged on their territory. It seems likely, in fact, that the Idumaeans, with whom he attacked Jerusalem, provided him, for a long while, with the cluster of closest supporters, resembling in that function the Galilaean contingent around John b. Levi of Gischala.

Those developments predictably put Jerusalem's ruling factions on alert (cf. 4, 538). Rather than meeting the victorious Simon in a pitched battle, zealots (but perhaps – *ex silentio* – not John) captured his wife by means of an ambush (ibid), in expectation, says the historian, that to get her back he would come to terms and disarm (539). Josephus's portrayal of Simon's response is a rare example, where the author allows for some human dimension in the characters he disapproves: he compares the bereaved Simon to "some wounded beast", unable to reach its tormentors and therefore attacking whomever it meets on the way (540). As it appears, the ruse employed by the zealots misfired: Simon began seizing, torturing and killing those who had ventured outside the walls (a fact that must have been publicly known); in Josephus's phrasing that extends the earlier hyperbolic simile, in "the excess of his fury almost gnawing their dead bodies" (541; cf. 6, 373). Some of his prisoners he allegedly sent back with their hands cut off (an atrocity also practiced by Titus at a later stage – 5, 455), ordering them to convey an ultimatum to their masters: he threatened breaking into the city and, unless his wife was restored to him, inflicting similar injury on everyone, irrespective of their age, guilt or innocence. The reference to God, "the overseer of all" (543), by whose name the text makes him swear – if authentic – suggests that he might indeed have considered himself a divine tool. Simon's message spread fear among the citizenry and forced the zealots to comply (544).

Simon's eventual entrance into Jerusalem was facilitated by a new outbreak of turmoil at the capital. Josephus speaks of an unlikely alliance of the high priests (4, 572) and those Idumaeans who stayed in the city after most of their countrymen had departed, – a concurrence reached in order to overthrow the zealots and, especially, John b. Levi, with his promiscuously abusive Galilaean cohorts. Upon deliberation, the two groups agreed (the historian predictably treats this as God's punitive interference with their judgment) on requesting Simon's aid, and thus, Josephus says, "imploring that they [be allowed] to impose a second tyrant upon themselves" (573): "a remedy worse than a ruin" (ibid). We read that this move was supported by those citizens of Jerusalem "who were in flight from zealots, wishing back their homes and property" (574) – a statement which is characteristically vague. Still, one can allow that a substantial proportion of the city's populace, suffering at the hands of zealots and John, but continuing to believe in the cause, could have eagerly placed their hopes on another charismatic revolutionary, Simon bar Giora.

As is often his habit, Josephus leaves the narrow motives unexplained: apart from the rhetoric about the evils, perpetrated by zealots and John, one is not told why the Idumaeans, who were the first to secede from John (566), and – in particular – the high priests, chose to do what they did. In the case of the former, the reasons are easier to imagine: the historian's efforts to paint Simon's atrocities in Idumaea notwithstanding, it is clear that he enjoyed there considerable support. This fact alone could account for the change of heart among the Idumaean constituency at Jerusalem: after all, with him Simon was bringing many who must have been their kin and some, like James b. Sosas, their own and esteemed former comrades-at-arms. The complicity of the high priests is harder to comprehend: the 'first regime', one of their making, placed Simon beyond the pale, and his subsequent acts, such as emancipation of the slaves and attacks on the rich, would have antagonized the majority within the establishment even further. The dire reality, however, as Josephus seems to imply, might well have reduced the matter to the choice between two evils: on the one hand, there were John, vile traitor to their cause, and the upstart Eleazar, with their peers' blood on his hands, and, on the other, Simon, who for the lack of their direct experience with him, still remained a somewhat unknown quantity. Under the first two, their existence, speaking not of their welfare, looked very precarious; under the third, with luck, and if they acted intelligently, they could even have arrived at some chance of resurgence. It seems conceivable that the informal leader of this group, Matthias b. Boethus, the member of a major high priestly clan, reasoned along these or similar lines when personally negotiating with Simon. (If so, he was fated to miscalculate and, as we will shortly see, soon himself fell victim to the newcomer's vicious display of cruelty.) It should not surprise us that Josephus rounds up the episode by emphasizing Simon's arrogance ("haughtily consenting to turn despot" – *BJ*, 4, 575) and self-interest: although acclaimed by the people as their 'savior' and 'protector' (ibid), when safely with his troops inside the walls "he was concerned only with his own power and regarded those who called him in as no lesser enemies than those whom he was called to oppose" (576) – a theme the historian would not forget. In any event, at some point during April to May A.D. 69 (cf. 577) Simon bar Giora gained control over most of Jerusalem, except the Temple grounds, and became a dominant factor in the factional rivalry plaguing the city: elsewhere it is stated that he presided over the largest rebel force of 10,000 plus 5000 of the Idumaean contingent (*BJ*, 5, 248 f.).

Simon's arrival was bound to intensify the internecine strife (cf., e.g., *BJ*, 5, 4, 22 f.) and helped in perpetuating the reign of terror. Josephus's descriptions of the latter (5, 27 ff.; 424 ff.; 439 ff.; 516 ff.; 6, 195 f.), despite his evident skill in rhetoric and drama, would have become monotonous were they not enlivened by the accounts of further miseries that began afflicting the rebels with the advent of the famine. Again and again, we read of murders or executions, atrocity, torture, fear, despair, lamentations and neglect of burial. For the most part, Josephus does not discriminate between Simon's and John's role in plunder and harassment, treating persistently both of them, as well as their followers, in plural as 'brigands'. It is curious that, while emphasizing their bitter enmity, the historian asserts, with no fear of contradiction, that they also used to share their victims and their loot:

> One who was stripped by Simon was sent to John and Simon took over the one robbed by John; they both jointly drank the blood of the commoners and shared the miserable corpses. As regards gaining the upper hand, those two were in conflict, but in their impieties they were of one mind: for he who would not allow the one to take part in the evils of the other was thought of as a singular scoundrel, and he who did not partake in the outrage suffered as if he was denied a good thing.
> (5, 440 f.)

The 'cannibalistic' imagery of this 'partnership in crime' looks like a literary *topos* rather than a factual reportage, although one cannot entirely rule out that it might contain at least some grain of truth.

In his final overview of the rebel groups and their misdeeds (*BJ*, 7, 253 ff.), the historian writes of Simon bar Giora that there was no crime that he did not commit (265), which is followed with a series of rhetorical questions and an inference:

> What violence did he not inflict on the bodies of those very persons who, free that they had been, appointed him a tyrant? What sorts of friendship or kinship did not make these men [i.e., the followers of Simon – V. R.] even bolder in their daily killings? For doing evil thing

to the others to whom they were not related they considered villainy, while they thought that by subjecting their closest kin to cruel treatment they would appear glorious.

(265 f.)

This passage, confusing as it is, does not, however, say much. The last statement may or may not be understood literally; rather, it appears a mere metaphor for civil fratricide. The reference to those who made him a tyrant, on the other hand, seems to concern the sole act of political murdering ascribed by Josephus specifically to Simon – the execution of Matthias b. Boethus together with his three sons and their associates (*BJ*, 5, 527 ff.). The man in question must have been an experienced politician, pragmatically inclined, and – as many in his social group – not incapable of dissimulation. His religious views hardly differed much from the rest of his (one presumes) Saducean colleagues, that is to say, lacking any particular ardor, and not dominating his politics, except his natural self-consciousness as a Jew and a subject to the Mosaic law. His family had fared well under the Romans, irrespective of whether they did or did not serve as high priests. We cannot know the reasons for his choice to stay in Jerusalem upon the revolt's outbreak: he could have done so for sheer patriotism, for private or financial reasons, or he might have been affiliated with some members of the 'first regime'. If so, his ties with them could not have been close given the fact that he and his relatives were able to survive the zealot coup unscathed. He even managed to exercise a certain amount of public influence. Josephus insists that Matthias enjoyed "a great trust and honor with the people" (527), which may be an exaggeration; but he must have amassed sufficient clout to become a chief negotiator with Simon: after all, there surely existed other claimants for that role, such as the Idumaean officers, who by then broke away from John b. Levi. We read, on the other hand, that one of his sons had earlier escaped to the Romans (530). Although it is true that during times of trouble political divides often run through families, this fact is telling and, despite the historian's efforts to downplay its significance, must have been at the root of Matthias's prosecution. The actual charge is succinctly described as "sympathizing with the Romans" (530); there could well have been more. One need not disbelieve Josephus (such facts had to be known to the survivors among his own intended readers) on the lack of proper judicial procedure: the accused was denied an opportunity of defense (ibid), and even the request to be killed before and not after his three sons (ibid). All four were condemned to death. We are told that Matthias was first forced to witness the execution of his sons; thereafter, on Simon's order, he was led out by the latter's own guardsman (the cruelest of them all, the author specifies) Ananus b. Bagadatus – who played in this case the role of executioner – and slain in full view of the Romans (531). The rebel leader is reported to add in mockery: "Let him find out whether those whom he sought to reach will help him" (ibid) – a remark that may be authentic or a *locus communis*, typifying the behavior of a tyrant. Similarly to the earlier precedents of impiety, the bodies were left without burial (ibid). The same fate, according to Josephus, was visited upon the priest Ananias b. Masbalus, "a notable person" (532); one Aristeus from Emmaus, who was a secretary of (supposedly) the city council; and 15 more "prominent men from among the people" (ibid). All of them must have been thought of as Matthias's associates.[2]

Regarding Simon's social policies, or attitudes, little can be added to what has already been said. It is true that he seems to have acted against the rich more persistently than Eleazar or John, but this does not warrant any radical conclusions. As we have seen, his appeal was broad enough to attract people of standing who would have hardly joined him if they knew that he intended such measures as an overhaul of the existent socio-economic system or redistribution of property. Similarly to many rebel leaders throughout history, the indiscriminate plunder he came to practice owed more to greed, hatred and the need for supplies rather than any 'ideological' or 'eschatological' persuasions: in this respect, Josephus might have been justified in calling him 'brigand'.

On the structure of Simon's command we only know that he appointed 50 officers (5, 248); a few of them are later mentioned by name. To these must be added ten Idumaean chiefs (249), the two we have already heard of, James b. Sousa and Simon b. Cathlas, having attained the highest reputation. Within his following, Simon's authority, as it appears, carried on largely unshaken for the most part of his supremacy: even after he was driven into the mine upon the destruction of the Temple, those who stayed with him continued their loyal support (cf. *BJ*, 6, 370, 430). The only exception, until very late in the siege, must have been the attempt at his betrayal by his lieutenant Judes b. Judes (5, 534 ff.). Josephus's account sounds somewhat confusing. Although he connects the episode with the affair of Matthias b. Boethus (Judes is said to have witnessed the latter's execution – 534), the historian is unsure about the man's motives: this commander of the garrison in a tower is supposed to have acted "perhaps out of pity for those savagely slain, but chiefly out of foresight regarding himself" (ibid), which means that he foresaw the eventual Roman victory. The speech, addressing his ten most trusted subordinates, as ascribed to Judes by Josephus (and, almost certainly, in its entirety, the latter's fabrication since it is difficult to imagine what might have been his source) is not especially coherent, despite the rhetoric: it mentions the "evils" Simon has perpetrated (535); a threat to their own safety if they continue supporting the "villain" (ibid); the advent of both famine and the Romans (536); Simon's treachery towards his benefactors; a fear that they will also suffer punishment at his hands, while the Romans can be relied on their fairness (ibid). The harangue ends with an appeal: "Let us hand over the walls and save ourselves and the city! Nothing terrible will happen to Simon, if he gives up sooner and is given justice" (537 f.). How exactly this last was to be achieved remains unclear, and John b. Levi, by then in full possession of the Temple, is not even mentioned. In any event, the plot unraveled, for which the Romans were largely to blame (a fact that may bear some responsibility for Josephus's tendency to obfuscate): nowadays we would call it an intelligence operation failure. In order to prevent exposure, we are told, Judes dispatched his warriors, apart from the trusted ten, on various pretexts and then spoke from the tower to the Romans (538). The latter, however, chose to ignore him for all sorts of reasons: contempt, disbelief or caution (539), and when Titus finally arrived with the body of troops, it was too late. Simon came to discover the ongoing treason, occupied the tower, "arrested and slaughtered the men in the sight of the Romans and threw their mutilated corpses over the ramparts" (540).

It was only at the very last stage of the siege that Simon's grasp over his entourage began seriously to slacken, making some of them desert. According to the narrative, it was after the Romans set the Temple's gates on fire (late August, A.D. 70) that Simon's two close associates changed sides – the man whom we heard of, Ananus b. Bagadatus of Emmaus ("the most bloodthirsty of Simon's guardsmen"; cf. 5, 531), and one Archaelaus b. Magaddatus (*BJ*, 6, 229 ff.). Josephus suggests that they had hopes for pardon on the grounds that they had defected at the moment of temporary success by the Jews (229), who just managed to repel the Roman assault on the walls, the enemy siege engines, such as rams, crowbars and ladders notwithstanding (220 ff.). This reasoning seems unlikely and if it nonetheless was the case, unwise. By then, anyone would have known that the Temple's defenders were doomed, with no means (other than supernatural) to save them from imminent destruction. Josephus expands, without really saying much, on Titus's motives for sparing the lives of these two deserters, even though he knew they were guilty of atrocities against their compatriots (230). One reads that he saw through their conceit and thought first before putting both to death since "those do not deserve survival who abandon from the homeland which burns through their own fault" (ibid). Titus's 'trustful disposition' (231), a strange phrasing, is then cited as the reason for his eventual change of heart. In reality, his purpose must have been entirely pragmatic, such as encouraging even more prominent rebels to defect.

Finally, even the Idumaean contingent which, on Josephus's own admission, played an important role in the war (6, 379) began to waver – but not before the Romans won the fight over the Temple and were preparing to attack the upper town (ca. September 8, A.D. 70). The situation was now, indeed, desperate, so the Idumaean chiefs (378), apparently upon secret consultation, decided on negotiating their surrender and sent five envoys to Titus, "seeking his assurance" (378), who obliged – but not without hesitation, the historian says, in hopes to precipitate the capitulation of the rebel leaders and their partisans (379). The plot, however, fell short: it is reported that Simon apprehended the plotters at the point of their departure. He put five emissaries to Titus to death, and imprisoned the conspiring chiefs, among them the reputable James b. Sosas, formerly his close associate (380). That man's subsequent fate is unknown: *ex silentio*, one infers that Simon spared his life, perhaps fearing that the rest of the Idumaeans might revolt: we are told next that "perplexed by the removal of their chiefs", they were placed under close surveillance (381). As a whole, the episode may – or may not – suggest that the Idumaeans, or at least their leaders, continued to regard themselves as a separate body within the revolutionary forces, not bound by the oath, earlier pledged by the rest of the rebels never to surrender.

Josephus carefully avoids providing details on the religious sensibilities of Simon bar Giora, and perhaps not without reason. The only hint directly conveyed is the report, on the earlier occasion, while he still lingered outside Jerusalem, of his swearing by God mercilessly to punish its inhabitants unless zealots restore to him his wife (*BJ*, 5, 543). It can be concluded that, in contrast to John b. Levi, Simon did not abuse the basic ritualist requirements of the Law – otherwise the historian would have surely mentioned any such transgression. Whether anything else about his faith can be gleaned from the *Bellum*'s narrative, for instance, a possibility that he posed as a Messianic monarch, is a matter of controversy, which reveals, in some respects, a clash between positivist hermeneutics and the efforts to illuminate the unfamiliar mindset or behavior in terms of historical and religious psychology. The issue largely hinges on the interpretation of Simon's last public act as described by Josephus, namely, a singular manner he chose to effect his surrender (*BJ*, 7, 26 ff.). We learn that upon the fall of the upper city to the Romans, and accompanied by his most loyal companions, Simon descended into the underground passages in hope of escaping imminent captivity (26): the plan apparently was to follow the existent tunnels and then cut through the rock until they could reach, one presumes, some area outside Jerusalem, at the moment unoccupied by the enemy (27), and then act as circumstances demand. Apparently, events had shown that it was not impossible to leave the capital unhindered: Josephus writes of numerous rebels who made it from Jerusalem and were later butchered by the legate Lucilius Bassus in the forest of Jardes (7, 210 ff.); but in the case of Simon and his entourage it eventually went wrong. They reportedly survived until Titus left Jerusalem, first to Caesarea Maritima and then to Caesarea Philippi (7, 20, 23), but then proved unable to make progress with further mining, while their supplies became nearly all used up (28). And this was what is said to have happened next:

> Simon "so that he could trick the Romans by shock, put on white tunics, fastening upon them a purple mantle, and appeared from under the earth at the exact spot where the sanctuary used to stand. At first, amazement struck those who saw it, where they stood, but then they came nearer and inquired who the man was."
>
> (29 f.)

This account must be historically reliable since there were many witnessing the event, but Josephus's explanation of the motives for this performance, even though it is sometimes taken at face value, leaves much to be desired. The question is what Simon would have achieved through 'tricking the Romans by shock' in the middle of the Temple enclosure, which must have been closely watched by the occupying force. Could he seriously have entertained the possibility that his sudden emergence from the underground would force all Romans present to disperse in fright and thus provide him with some sort of escape route? None of this seems likely. Furthermore, by giving himself up, even as spectacularly as he chose to do so, he followed in the steps of John b. Levi, while betraying the pledge never to surrender collectively sworn by his comrades-at-arms (cf. *BJ*, 6, 351, 366). The irony was not lost to Josephus, who remarks that it was an act "for which he cruelly killed many by pressing false charges of desertion to the Romans" (7, 33). The historian also observes that the manner of Simon's capitulation allowed them to discover the tunnels, which served as his place of refuge and to apprehend his followers still hiding there (35). Finally, Simon must have known about the Roman custom of ceremoniously putting to death an individual whom they considered their enemy's supreme commander. His grand gesture's only practical effect was that it sealed his fate, making his execution unavoidable, especially given the fact that the purple he clothed himself with pointed unmistakably to his claim of royal status. As a result, the Romans were bound to endow Simon bar Giora with the highest military rank among the insurgent leaders, even superior to John of Gischala, whose life this episode might have helped to save.

Most of these objections, however, are removed, and Simon's behavior becomes comprehensible if we assume that his motives were, in fact, not pragmatic, like 'frightening' the Romans, but derived from the belief in his special destiny. In reality, things are always more complex than they sound in theoretical formulation: like other psychological conditions, any such belief fluctuates, alternating with moments of doubt or despair, even if one accepts the validity inherent in the Nietzschean concept of '*amor fati*'. An attempt to penetrate the workings of Simon's mind (with a view of what we know about the attitudes of religious dissenters active in other historical periods) should involve the caveat that his self-conceptions might have wavered at various stages of his career; that he could have fallen prey to self-persuasion and even self-hypnosis or, to the contrary, only half-heartedly believed in what he did, hoping against hope that in the 13th hour God would beneficently intervene and make him prove to be the Deliverer of Israel, as foretold by the prophets. One should again be reminded of the power exercised on our psyche by wishful thinking sometimes leading to what the experts call 'the omnipotence of thought'.

It may seem debatable whether Simon's mentality and posture could be called 'Messianic', but there are some indications that this was the case; or, at the very least, that it revealed the elements of the 'Messianic complex' as defined earlier in this study. That a purple mantle was considered an attribute of royalty by both the Jews and the Romans is a matter of record: it is sufficient to recall its use as an instrument of mocking Christ's alleged 'kingship' cited in the Gospels (*Mk*: 15,17 ff.; *Mt*: 27,29 ff.; *Jn*: 19,2 ff.). We have seen that Simon's claim for royal status is implied by Josephus when he wrote that his adherents "were obedient to him as to a king" (*BJ*, 4, 510). The historian could have hardly spoken of it more explicitly: the issue was delicate, owing to the continuous existence of the legitimate King Herod Agrippa II, with whom he entertained personal relations. On the other hand, with any such proclamation Simon would have followed the earlier precedents, among which we can be certain about at least two that took place shortly after the death of the first Herod (*AJ*, 17, 273 ff.): one, Simon's namesake, a former royal servant, "dared to *don diadem*" (273) and was suppressed through the joint effort of the Herodians and the Romans; another, a shepherd Athronges, who wanted kingship, the text says (a typical Josephan slander!), "so that he could delight in greater outrage" (ibid, 278 ff.) – this one was put down, along with his four brothers, after a period of the surprisingly long resistance (281). It has been reasonably observed that in all these instances, including Simon bar Giora, the Jewish historical imagination could easily recognize an ulterior model from the past, at this point, of particular urgency – David, son of Jesse. Some similarities are, indeed, unmistakable: humble origin, physical prowess, leadership of warrior bands gathered elsewhere in the land, and confrontation with the powers to be. Within the context of eschatological turmoil, and given the fact that the Jewish mindset, trained throughout the centuries in associative interpretation of the Torah, was more than adept at linking the words, concepts and phenomena, sometimes quite remote from each other, it seems certain that any hint at King David was bound to engender in the popular mind the thought of the Messiah. The strongest argument, however, for Simon's Messianic aspirations, predictably obfuscated by Josephus, lies precisely in his ultimate appearance within the Temple area as described: the motive behind it, if one follows this line of reasoning, was twofold: on the one hand, Simon sought to prove the reality of his 'Messianic' role to himself; on the other, he sought to achieve a sort of 'epiphany', not only recognized as such by those present, but resulting in a miracle, namely, his own and Israel's salvation – a state of mind not dissimilar from the one felt by 6000 persons who had gathered, after the Romans set the sanctuary afire, on the still standing Temple portico, in hope for immediate supernatural deliverance (*BJ*, 6, 283 f.) – this I will comment on later.

At any rate, if Simon did, in fact, entertain any such hopes, they must have quickly vanished since nothing happened. Josephus's report that he first refused disclosing his identity to anyone but the commanding officer makes sense given the rage (7, 34) the Romans exhibited in his regard: he had reasons to fear being slaughtered there and then. In due course, Simon bar Giora was handed over to Titus in chains (36), paraded during the triumphal procession in Rome, scourged and ritually executed at the Mamertine prison (154).

Josephus's final judgment on Simon (7, 265 f.) has already been cited. It is predictably harsh, as were all his previous pronouncements. Nor is it surprising as the name of God is repeatedly invoked, for instance, in his assertion that it was God's power over the "unholy men" (6, 399) which drove the rebel chiefs down from the upper city's towers, otherwise impregnable, "wherein they could not have been conquered by force but only reduced through starvation"

(399, cf. 401). With Simon's capture, the historian indulges in yet another, typically quasi-theological, generalization:

> The wickedness does not escape God's wrath, nor is divine justice feeble; and though the wicked may have at first thought they escaped since they were not punished immediately, with time justice reaches those who contravene it, and inflicts on the wicked worse vengeance than any they expected. This Simon learned after he fell prey to the Romans' anger.
>
> (7, 34)

Due to the fact that Josephus constitutes our only source, any 'objective' appraisal of Simon's personality and conduct, despite some modern attempts at it, is not possible. But even within the biased narrative of the *Bellum*, he strikes us as a straightforward, albeit brutal, character and thus different from the wily John of Gischala. One must take into account that his rise had occurred largely outside Jerusalem, and that – in contrast to John – he was not involved, until a much later stage, in the oppressive power play, which required a skill for intrigue and compromise so typical of the Jewish political elite; nor was he devoid of the elemental humanity, as his intense attachment to his wife testifies. In sum, Simon bar Giora might have been more, as an individual or public figure, than Josephus was willing to admit; but it remains true that in the end he impressed on the Jewish historical memory much less than did his formidable namesake, who was to emerge half a century later: Simon bar Kokhba.[3]

II.

Among the most objectionable behavior on the part of the factions, reported in the *Bellum*, is the destruction of city provisions prior to the siege. We know that under the 'first regime' large amounts of food were stored in Jerusalem in anticipation of the imminent shortages, one of that government's few wise measures. At the time of the three-way faction, however, the activities began which, as described by Josephus, proved ultimately suicidal:

> Those of Eleazar's party, who were guarding the Temple's offerings, carried off the wine to spite John, while those with John, who were plundering the citizens, gathered against Simon. For the former the city became the source of supplies vis-à-vis his rebel competitors. / ... / And all the time, to whatever quarter of the city he [John – V. R.] turned, he would burn the buildings stored with corn and other necessities, and upon his withdrawing, Simon moved in and did the same; as if in the interests of the Romans, they were intentionally demolishing what preparations the city had made in the event of a siege, and cutting off the sinews of their own might. The consequence was then that everything around the Temple was burned to cinders, the city had

become a desolate and disputed land between the domestic battle lines; and, with little exception, all corn, that would have sufficed for several years of siege, had been destroyed by fire. In fact, the city fell because of the famine, which would have been hardly possible, if they were not themselves contriving towards that end beforehand.

(5, 21 ff.)

This is by no means a slander: such facts were known to Tacitus (*Hist.*, 5, 12: *magna vis frumenti ambusta* – "great amount of corn [was] burnt"), and their echoes are preserved in the rabbinic writings, which followed traditions other than Josephus. If the latter's explanation of the motives for this particular outrage (that is, a mere power struggle and personal animosity exercised by the faction leaders) is accepted, then any debate over the moral appraisal of their whole revolutionary enterprise must come to an end. That would mean that these individuals were bent solely on their own self-aggrandizement and cared not at all about national liberation, welfare or salvation of Israel (in other words, must have indeed been the unscrupulous villains the historian portrays). Against this, however, speaks quite an extraordinary intransigence they had shown in resisting the Roman besiegers, despite Titus's repeated offers to negotiate: it suggests an ulterior motive, which transcended any individual ambition, self-interest or even self-preservation. Given the paradoxes and perplexities embedded in the psychology of religious dissenters whom we know, the intentional destruction of the food supply in a city threatened with an imminent siege would imply an urge to precipitate the long hoped for eschatological event, implementing the principle that "the worse is the better". Thus a belief, or wish for believing, that only the utmost sufferings of God's people could prompt God beneficently to interfere, as God was reported to have done in the past, was manifest, for instance, in the fervent expectation, still shared by many of them shut at the Temple, to be saved through some miracle, although the entire enclosure had been already set afire (*BJ*, 6, 284 f.). (This might apply even to characters such as John b. Levi, who were not particularly concerned with the display of piety: even the most perverse religious dissenter is never an atheist.) In one of his few insights into such matters, Josephus inadvertently grasped at least something pertinent to this ambivalent mindset. The historian thus reports the response from the rebels to Titus's *demarche* aimed at intimidating them and making them surrender (he had sent several Jewish prisoners, their hands cut off, to the faction leaders, promising them, it is said, that in case they repented he would preserve "their lives, their fatherland and that great sanctuary unshared by others" – 5, 456):

To this they blasphemed from the walls both against Caesar and his father, howling that they despised death, that they have nobly chosen it rather than slavery, that they will inflict as much evil on the Romans as they could and as long as they breathed; that since, as he himself said, they were going to perish, they did not care for their fatherland, and

that the cosmos was for God a better temple, than this one. And they
added that the latter will yet be saved by its Dweller, whom they have
for an ally, and that the they would mock all boasts while the action
lagged behind; for the issue lay with God.

(458 f.)

Apparently, neither the author, nor those who, one presumes, entertained any such sentiment felt bothered by flagrant contradictions between the expressive disregard for the fate of the Temple (and of the land, and their own), the conviction that God would save it in any event, and the implied inscrutability of God's ways.

Josephus's accounts of the famine in Jerusalem under siege (especially in *BJ*, 5, 424 ff. and 513 ff.) belong among the most powerful passages in his entire war narrative, revealing the inordinate literary skills, descriptive and dramatic, he was occasionally capable of. Rhetorical exaggeration may not be doubted, which does not impinge, however, on the essential reliability of what he has to say. Even though the historian was not personally present within the city walls, he was provided with an opportunity for interviewing both the deserters and the survivors – and, as ever, he needed to be careful in not undermining the credibility of his reportage. Moreover, nothing in the scary pictures of physical suffering, moral degradation and widespread *anomie* he portrays contradicts what we know about similar experiences throughout history.

In this case, the wretchedness and horror of starvation were amplified by the ruthless policies of the factions who apparently appropriated most of the food supplies, as well as by mere marauders harassing individual households – although the two groups, as usually happens, would have been intermingled. The *Bellum* contains several famine notices, strategically placed. For the purposes of illustration, it is sufficient to condense the lengthiest:

> As the famine grew worse, the madness of the rebels rose to a peak with it, and both terrors raged more fiercely every day. For grain was completely unavailable, and the rebels would burst into and thoroughly search private houses: if they found food, they would abuse [the residents] for having denied that there was any, if they did not find food they would torture them for having hidden it more carefully / ... / Many secretly exchanged their belongings for one measure – of wheat if they were wealthy, barley if they were poor. Then shutting themselves up in the innermost parts of their houses, some in the last stages of starvation ate the grain uncooked, others cooked it to the extent the necessity and fear obliged / ... / The nourishment was pitiful, the sight worthy of tears as the stronger took more than their share and the weak were left to wail. Famine overcomes all emotions, but it destroys shame above all; what is otherwise deserving of respect is treated contemptuously during famine. Thus wives snatched food from the mouth of their husbands, children

from their fathers and, most pitiable of all, mothers from their infants / ... / Yet eating even such meager fare they did not escape notice, and everywhere the rebels were upon their pickings / ... /. Old men clinging to food were struck, women hiding their food in their hands had their hair torn. There was no pity for gray hair or infancy: they lifted up and flung to the ground children who clung to bits of food. To those who had anticipated their entry and swallowed down beforehand what would have been plundered, the rebels were even more cruel as if they had been wronged / ... / The torturers were not hungry (it would have been less barbarous if they had done it out of necessity), but they were practicing their madness and laying up for themselves provisions for the future.

(5, 424 ff.)

The extraordinary scarcity of food and the effects of starvation described by Josephus here and elsewhere (e.g., 6, 194: "In every household, if there appeared even a shadow of food, it was war happened, and the dearest persons would fight with fists to snatch from each other the miserable sustenance of their life"; cf. 197 ff.) were still remembered centuries later as the rabbinic texts testify. The populace was forced, for obvious reasons, to disregard the dietary laws and consume not only the forbidden food but also what could have hardly counted for food at all; Josephus goes as far as to report a particularly shocking episode of cannibalism (6, 201 ff.). So long as anything like food remained available, even if scarce, possession of money could still have eased the extent of one's misery, and the black market must have thrived. As inevitably happens during times of trouble, the poor suffered most.

Eventually, every opportunity became exhausted, and the starving people were doomed to die in huge numbers. The deserter called Mannaeus b. Lazarus, who joined the Roman camp at some point during the siege, and whom the rebels had previously entrusted with guarding one city gate, claimed that through that gate alone, and within the span of two and a half months (between the 14th of Xanthicus and the new moon of Panemus – *BJ*, 5, 567; i.e., May – 20 July A.D. 70), 115,880 corpses were carried out to be left outside of Jerusalem's holy grounds (5, 567); other refugees believed, according to the historian, that the dead bodies, thrown out through the gates, and consisting only of the poor, amounted to 600,000 (569; 6, 420 cites the total number of casualties during the siege as 1.1 million). Those figures, as for the most part in Josephus, are of course suspect; but this does not mean that they should be ignored, or too drastically minimized: the scale of human losses must have still been enormous. If during the zealot reign of terror the victims were left unburied for what may be called 'political reasons', under the siege, and with the advent of the famine, this became a matter of practical expediency. Writes Josephus:

The roofs were filled with women and dying babies; the alleys with the corpses of the old; children and youths, swollen, reeling like ghosts in

> the marketplace, fell whenever their suffering overcame them. The sick did not have the strength to bury their relatives, and those who did have the strength hesitated because of the large number of corpses and the uncertainty of what was in store for themselves. Many fell dead over those whom they were burying, and many set out for their graves before it was time. In these straits there was neither weeping nor lamentation; the famine countered emotions, and those who were lingering in death looked with dry eyes and grinning mouths at those who had already gone before them to eternal rest. Deep silence and death-laden night embraced the city / ... / The rebels originally had the dead buried at public expense, the stench being unbearable, but later when they were unable to do this they threw the bodies from the walls into the ravines.
>
> (5, 513 ff.)

The purpose of this must have been twofold: not only to prevent an accumulation of the decaying corpses (the ancients knew that it could lead to the spread of plague), but also abiding to the requirements of the Law, which prohibited any burial within Jerusalem's holy confines.

One cannot ignore sincerity in Josephus's expression of outrage at those consequences of what he saw as a criminal catastrophe brought about by the revolutionaries: his famine notices belong perhaps to the most reliable portions within his war narrative and concern the events deeply imprinted on the national memory. Nor should one doubt that the psychology of religious dissent contributed to the misery experienced by the besieged: the profusion of optimistic prophecies and eschatological expectations made them reluctant to negotiate with the Romans even at the most desperate moments, or raise up against the self-destructive policies of the rebel leadership; and the latter's faith in 'being chosen' helped them to disregard and further aggravate the sufferings among the fellow Jews.[4]

The opportunity for desertion, already narrow under the zealot regime, must have further diminished with the advent of the siege. The *Bellum* offers no evidence on social stratification among those who sought to join the Roman camp: one assumes that least of all they were represented by the urban poor, even though some of the latter, as we have seen, were allowed by the rebels to venture beyond the wall in their quest for food. History shows that, more often than not, the lower classes tend to manifest remarkable loyalty to any revolutionary cause, the growth of their own misery notwithstanding. Since the factions controlled the exit from the capital, it is tempting to infer that a number of establishment figures named by Josephus as having escaped to the Romans could have done so only by offering bribes to the guards. One such gatekeeper, as stated above, also chose to take on the path of defection (*BJ*, 5, 567). An alternate method would be to use the knowledge of secret passages and caves and go into hiding, but there is evidence that the insurgents had been searching such places, too.

Be that as it may, at least one person of consequence, the unnamed son of Matthias b. Boethus (the latter having been, as we know, subsequently executed), reportedly left the capital, perhaps even prior to the siege (cf. 5, 530). It was, however, the cessation of the *tamid*, the daily sacrifices at the Temple, for the lack of sacrificial victims on the 17th of Panemus (June/July A.D. 70 – *BJ*, 6, 94), that brought about a spate of the upper-class defectors (6, 113 ff.), which the historian unabashedly ascribes to the effects caused by his own words (93–110) addressing the besieged:

> The speech moved many of the wellborn, but some, dreading the rebel guards, stayed in place, although they recognized the [imminent] ruin both of themselves and the city, while there were others, seizing the opportunity for an escape into safety, fled to the Romans.
> (113)

Josephus lists the chief priests Joseph and Jesus (identifiable as Joseph Kabi b. Simon and Jesus b. Damnaeus), three sons of an Ishmael, most likely Ishmael b. Phiabi, who belonged among the most prominent holders of that office, and four of one Matthias (114), perhaps the same as the last official Jewish high priest Matthias b. Theophilus, with a number of unspecified nobles (ibid) in their wake.

The legitimate question would be, of course, why those ranking individuals, if they in fact had opposed the activities and purposes of the factions, did not secede earlier and side with the Romans? The motives first to remain and then to defect must have been multiple and ranged from opportunism to patriotism, even if they disagreed with the revolutionary goals. The opportunists change sides by definition, depending on the opportunities they are able to seize; as for patriots, history shows that they often defend the regime they hate against the foreign occupant. It should also be recognized that in order not to yield to the prevailing public sentiment at any historical point, whether during times of oppression or liberation, reaction or revolution, and to act 'politically incorrect', one requires an inordinate stamina and capacity for what we now call non-conformism. Otherwise, the drastic change in one's politics, on the basic psychological level, could be engendered by desperate circumstances, when the instinct for self-preservation defeats 'dissident' or 'dissenting' mindsets, as well as any 'ideological' agenda, so that even the staunchest resistants, in hope or delusion, ultimately to survive, throw themselves at the mercy of their victors. The cases in point are episodes which have been earlier discussed: the surrender, or attempts at surrendering to Titus, undertaken towards the end of the siege by Simon's close associates, such as Ananus of Emmaus, Archaelaus b. Magaddatus (*BJ*, 6, 229 ff.) and, finally, James b. Sosas with his Idumaeans (378 ff.).

Titus's treatment of Jewish deserters clearly pursued pragmatic goals, such as public relations and propaganda, and the need for cooperation on the part of Judaea's elite in the future. Even though it is true that a number of the upper-class figures did take a more or less active part in the revolt, the majority must have stayed, at the very least, neutral and had to be reaffirmed in the hope that Rome's victory will result not only in a return to law and order, but also in protection of their interests. What would matter included one's earlier credentials (that is, political attitudes taken prior and through the war, presumably to be backed up by reliable witnesses), social rank, the time of one's desertion (the sooner the better); and one's potential use in terms of influence upon those in Jerusalem who kept hesitating: thus we hear that a group of defectors was made to parade before the city walls and entreat the inhabitants to cease the resistance (6, 118 ff.). Josephus reports that the Romans discriminated between those whom they considered deserters and captives (5, 449 ff.; cf. Dio-Xiph., 65, 5, 3). Of the latter, we are told, around 500 were taken daily (*BJ*, 5, 450), to be enslaved or, worse, tortured and crucified (449), either – says the historian (obviously trying to exculpate this cruelty) – for the lack of accommodation, or as he has himself to admit, with the purpose of deterrence (450). The distinction between two groups must have been, of course, arbitrary as exercised solely by Titus and his staff, and one assumes that most of those deemed 'captives' belonged among the have-nots.

All in all, it seems that, presumably in response to the immediate exigencies, Titus's policy on deserters, recognized as such, underwent certain changes. At the earlier stage of the siege, according to Josephus, he allowed most of them to disperse into the country, wherever they wished, which "encouraged still others to desert, as they would be saved from the evils inside the city and not be enslaved by the Romans" (422). Later on, the group of nobles, including the sons of the high priests named above, after receiving assurances that their property will be restored to them upon the end of the war, was relegated on Titus's orders to the town of Gophna (6, 115 f.) – perhaps to have their behavior suitably supervised: after all, it took them much too long for changing sides to make Titus put full trust in their newly found loyalty. In practical terms, it was sensible policy; but it prompted the factions to spread rumors that the noble deserters were all killed (*BJ*, 6, 116; with the result, claims Josephus, that "their ruse / ... / did work for a while, desertion being restrained by fear" – 117; cf. 5, 453 f.). This caused Titus to bring them back and display before the city's walls, and we read that thereupon "many more fled to the Romans" (118).

Josephus did not shrink, which gives him credit, in view of his pro-Roman bias, from reporting truly abominable facts of disembowelment perpetrated by Titus's (allegedly allied) troops on many Jewish defectors in search of gold the latter were rumored to have swallowed before their flight (*BJ*, 5, 550 ff; cf. 421). "No harsher affliction, in my view – writes the historian – fell upon Jews than this: during one night, in fact, no less than two thousand were thus ripped apart" (552). This, of course, has not and could not have constituted official Roman policy: Titus is described as strongly reprimanding both the officers and the rank-and-file (548 ff.), but abstained from carrying out executions of the guilty due, as Josephus implies, to the great number of offenders (553). Such half-way measures did not, in fact, suffice altogether to stop the outrage: the historian admits that, however secretly done, some foul acts continued (560 f), which drove back many of the deserters.

One further factor that must have affected Titus's attitudes is glossed over in the *Bellum*, but preserved by Cassius Dio (Xiph., 65, 5, 3): some of the Jewish deserters (and captives) kept in his camp were found to have been secretly destroying the Romans' water supply and slaying Roman soldiers, whom they could isolate and cut off from the rest: "Hence Titus would no longer receive any Jewish deserters" (ibid).[5]

The issues of burial and desertion directly relate to a famous tradition, found, however, not in Josephus, but in the Talmud, about one of the period's most celebrated sages, Rabban Johanan b. Zakkai, and his escape from wartime Jerusalem. Although it exists in four recensions, with some divergences in detail, the gist of the story concerns the great man, pretending his own death, to be carried out in a coffin by his disciples beyond the city's walls, as well as his subsequent meeting and negotiations with Vespasian. The confines of this study do not allow an extensive involvement in the convoluted debate on whether anything of the sort did, in fact, happen or – even less – on the historicity and reliability of the factual references in the rabbinic writings. Still, the matter requires a restatement of the methodological position I have adopted at the outset. Modern scholarship provides the full spectrum of opinions, including the extremes, as regards the applicability of the material in the Tannaitic texts to the period before the completion of the Mishnah under Rabbi Judah the Prince (late second century A.D.). On the one pole, its information is treated as no less reliable than anything supplied by the classical historiography and is used for reconstructing not only recurrent exchanges of ideas, or complex developments in politics, but also the basic elements for individual biographies and aspects of person-to-person relationships among the sages; on the other, any scrap of reference to any "fact" is altogether dismissed as deriving from the agenda seen as relevant by every next generation of rabbinic scholars, the structures and strictures of their environment, their intellectual or religious requirements and so forth. Pursued to its logical conclusion, this last approach leaves us with no knowledge whatsoever, except their names, about men such as Johanan b. Zakkai and his peers, who – outside of the Talmud – virtually do not exist.

I firmly believe, nonetheless, that in history, as in nature, nothing happens out of nothing. This means that even the strangest myth, or the most fantastic legend, are ultimately grounded in reality, however insignificant the linkage might appear, at the very least in the reality of our consciousness. For the most part, however, the external factors, even if their role in the myth or legend-making process was infinitesimal, can and should be recognized: the worst excesses of hypercriticism are to be avoided, even when dealing with so idiosyncratic a source as rabbinic scholarship. This means that however fictionalized and delightful the anecdotes may be in the Haggadah; however questionable is the ascription of rulings and sayings to the particular persons in the Mishnah or Gemara – by the very fact of being transmitted across the generations, orally or written down, all of this must have still maintained a link, albeit distorted and far remote, to the past realities it purports to describe. The sages, as portrayed in the Talmud, frequently exhibit distinct human personalities: one cannot confuse, for instance, the soft-spoken Rabbi José with the stern Rabbi Meir or the passionate Rabbi Aqiba. To my mind, this suggests, in the final analysis, some true features of their disposition echoed and reflected.

Nor is the attribution of judgments and pronouncements, however questionable as regards their authenticity, to one sage rather than another entirely accidental: it had to depend on the impact their individual characteristics and outlook had originally made upon popular memory. The closer the correlation between their portrayals as they emerge piecemeal from the (largely Haggadic) texts and the views they are said to have promoted, the greater is the probability that the customary affiliation is correct.

Rabban Johanan b. Zakkai is extolled in the Talmud as a great personage, the "tall pillar, eternal light, mighty hammer" (*ARNa*, 25, 1), a man of massive learning and brave action. The continuous controversy over the details of his life and thought notwithstanding, one major feat by him can hardly be denied: namely, his successful diplomacy *vis-à-vis* Vespasian, which resulted in establishing the rabbinic Academy at Yavneh. Irrespective of one's view on whether the tradition about him can be relied upon, there is an irrefutable fact that the Yavneh Academy came to function in the aftermath of the revolt, which could not happen without the explicit permission of the highest Roman authority – that is, the emperor. This, in turn, must have involved direct negotiations undertaken, on the Jewish side, by person or persons possessing, from the Roman viewpoint, impeccable credentials. Given this, and the paucity of influential leaders, who both survived the war and met those criteria, I find no compelling reason to doubt that R. Johanan not only proved instrumental, but played the crucial role the Talmud credits him with in the whole development:

> He [Vespasian] said to him, 'Are you Rabban Johanan b. Zakkai? Indicate what should I give you.' He said to him, 'I ask from you only Yavneh, to which I shall go, and where I shall teach my disciples, establish prayer, and carry out all religious duties.' He said to him, 'Go and do whatever you want.'
>
> (*ARNa*, 4, 6; cf. *ARNb*, 6; bGitt., 56b)

R. Johanan's masterful personality must have strongly impressed itself on the memory of his and successive generations. The alleged circumstances, however, of his encounter with Vespasian are another matter, to which I will shortly return.

The legends claim that R. Johanan studied directly under the great Hillel, which is scarcely possible on the grounds of the chronological gap between the two. This is no reason, however, to doubt that he must have been Hillelite in his persuasions and outlook, 'liberal' and compassionate, in contrast to the often excessive strictness preached by the school of Shammai. This would also account for his commitment to non-violence, in accordance with Hillel's own pronouncement: "Be of the disciples of Aaron, loving peace, pursuing peace, loving mankind, and drawing all men to Torah" (m*Avot*, 1, 12). Consequently, prior to the revolt, as the Talmud suggests, he might have pursued a moderate line, both in religious and political affairs, and upon the outbreak of the hostilities distanced himself from the revolutionary cause. It seems obvious that, in order for him to be later accepted by the Romans as a legitimate emissary of the loyal forces, R. Johanan's persistent pacifism must have been a matter of public knowledge.

The rabbis preserved the echoes of his periodic conflicts with the priestly establishment over the ritualist and social issues; and in the wartime, of his efforts to resist senseless destruction as regards both lives and the materials, waged by the radical factions. It does not seem plausible that these latter stories of confrontations, relevant as they were at the time to the most passionate discords, had been totally made up. They testified to R. Johanan's *humanitas*, which was bound to require, in his situation, an inordinate exercise of courage and non-conformism: it is sufficient to recall what had happened to the father and uncle of Eleazar b. Ananias, the very architect of the revolt, both killed by the latter's own allies, the *sicarii*. Paradoxically, within the revolutionary environment, dominated by religious discontent, when groups and individuals thought to be fulfilling God's will through all-permissive violence, R. Johanan's Pharisaic orthodoxy, rooted in the careful study of the Scriptures, itself acquired a form of 'constructive dissent'. One assumes it was his despair about his influence, failing to end fratricide, that was responsible for his eventual escape to the Romans.

In all four extant Talmudic recensions dealing with that episode, the narrative falls into two parts: the story of R. Johanan's flight from Jerusalem in the coffin, and that of his encounter with Vespasian. The escape accounts, despite many divergences, present a set of salient features: the Rabban first attempts in vain to reason with the insurgents in order to cease popular suffering and random destruction; next he resolves to get out of the capital; then by his own design, or on the advice of other parties, the ruse how to do it is decided upon; and, finally, after some bickering on the part of his companions with the guards, he is taken out in the coffin outside the walls to re-emerge alive and well before Vespasian. The second part in each recension, describing his interview with the latter, is even more elaborate and divergent, albeit less coherent. The common features consist of their actual encounter, R. Johanan's prediction of his interlocutor's Imperial accession, and the latter's offer to ask for a favor. With the passage of time, this thematic cluster became further diversely embroidered as well as interspersed with new, and sometimes even unrelated, material.

There is no doubt that the entire tradition on R. Johanan b. Zakkai is thoroughly fictionalized: the stories about him evolved across several centuries until they finally took the form that we know. As they now stand, they largely constitute a late Amoraic product, the embellishment and contamination of oral and/or written sources, revised and compiled to meet social, political or ideological exigencies within Jewish communities at various stages of their history, which does not mean at all, however, that some particular elements or components of what eventually became legend did not exist from the very start.

The story of the escape in the coffin certainly strikes a familiar chord: it reminds us of literary or folkloristic plots, and is, in this sense, paradigmatic. Still, it does happen, however seldom, that 'life imitates art', so one should not perhaps necessarily dismiss it out of hand as inconceivable, or total invention, despite the current tendency to do so. This point aside, I find no compelling reasons, if the rabbinic narratives are reduced to their essential elements, to question the historicity both of R. Johanam's flight from Jerusalem and his encounter with Vespasian. He had to leave the capital, probably, by some unorthodox, even if less adventurous, method, when the hostilities still were under way, since otherwise the Yavneh settlement could not have been negotiated. Furthermore, if he emerged only after the capture of Jerusalem, the Roman authorities would not have looked on him kindly. Nor was it likely that he had not stayed in the city at all, which is to say, sided with the Romans at the outset: his role in the Yavneh academy and the high prestige he apparently enjoyed testify that his reputation as a *bona fide* patriot and man of courage could not have been impeached, even by his opponents.

Reasoning backwards, one must conclude that, since the emergence of the Yavneh academy after the war's end cannot be doubted, then R. Johanan's interview, at some point in between, with Vespasian leading, as one must assume, to that result, was almost certainly grounded in historical fact. Any closer dating constitutes, however, a problem: the traditional narratives emphasize famine in the capital, measures against desertion and problems with burial, all of which seem to indicate the conditions under the A.D. 70 siege. But by that time Vespasian had already left Judaea, entrusting the capture of Jerusalem to Titus, and some scholars' attempts to replace Vespasian with Titus in the rabbinic escape stories remain unpersuasive. In other words, we have to deal with two temporalities, which is difficult to reconcile. Still, the adjustment is possible: as has been argued by some, the escape and encounter might have taken place in late June or early July A.D. 69, shortly before or after Vespasian's Imperial proclamation. It does not follow, however, that the report about the Rabban's prediction of his interlocutor's forthcoming emperorship, and its almost immediate fulfillment, should be equally taken at face value: most likely, it was fashioned on the model of Josephus's earlier similar feat, although in this case, characteristically, it is made to result from scriptural knowledge rather than the divine dream.

The significance of the Rabban's conference with Vespasian and their outcome, irrespective of the exact circumstances they might have occurred under, cannot and should not be minimized. In taking the decision he did (that is, by responding favorably to R. Johanan's request about Yavneh), Vespasian took upon himself responsibility for, as the subsequent developments came to demonstrate, the entire future of Judaism. This he could have done only in his capacity as emperor, or – at the very least – after having made up his mind to become one: even if the town of Yavneh did not belong to the Imperial domain, though it very likely did, the issue at hand involved matters of grave political import – namely, the appropriate treatment for the rebellious and reconquered nation. The options were either proceeding with relative leniency, as the Flavians, despite their destruction of the Temple and the massive enslavement of the populace, eventually chose to; or attempting altogether to suppress Jewish religion and nationhood as Antiochus IV Epiphanes had done before them, and Hadrian after. The permission to establish the Yavneh academy, negotiated, presumably, by R. Johanan b. Zakkai, thus sent one of the early signals that the new Imperial regime considered pursuing in future pragmatic rather than strictly punitive policies towards Jews.

It seldom happens in history, in the final analysis, that a prominent individual's reputation across centuries, for good or for bad, is entirely undeserved, despite the present-day fashion of debunking those earlier deemed virtuous and exculpating those thought to have been wicked. More often than not, any such procedure is not based on the newly discovered evidence or the valid reinterpretation of the old; rather, it hinges on the mood and sensibilities within a particular scholar, whether an urge for originality (sometimes with the purpose of self-promotion), a sense of protest, 'political correctness', or just a wish to have fun. It is usually disregarded, however, that our sound judgment must depend not on the moral characterizations regarding a historical personage written by our sources, nor on their blatant rebuffing as fictional or biased, but on the undeniable facts, associated with his name (that is, policies of terror, murders, plunder, and so forth; or, conversely, the acts of foresight, clemency and moderation). This means that in the absence of the strong evidence to the contrary, it is idle to challenge the traditional records whether in respect to good or bad guys, so that the current efforts to whitewash tyrants such as Caligula or Nero – just because one feels displeased with what our authorities say about them – are not merely fanciful, but testify to the deep crisis of postmodernist historiography. It is, of course, another matter if the contradictory material is preserved in the tradition itself to the extent sufficient for questioning the dominant view, or is found in the hitherto unknown document: one successful example of such revision as regards ancient history is the late Arnaldo Monigliano's work on Claudius.

It follows that, despite having been demonstrably fictionalized, the tradition about Rabban Johanan b. Zakkai – the escape, the interview and its outcome – still reflects on the real man's character and achievements. These include his major role in the synagogal reform and, consequently, in reformulation of Judaism as we now know it. As organizer and diplomat, he thus merits comparison with St. Paul; as apologist for his faith, to Josephus, but unlike the latter, having never been a partaker in the revolution, he became immune to the charges of cowardice and betrayal. Similarly to both Paul and Josephus, he strikes us as a consummate politician capable of overcoming considerable odds, whose pragmatic and constructive approach to problems represents an alternative – recognized, regrettably, only with hindsight – to the suicidal course taken by the radical dissenters, with their failure to comprehend politics, other than in crude terms of personal or power struggle. In short, I find this man's quiet heroism, centered on the hard task to restore the nation's spiritual welfare, and which required a fine balance of integrity and adjustment, more impressive than the glamorous collective suicide at Masada.

One difficult, if not insoluble, question that remains is the total absence of R. Johanan's name in Josephus, even though, as has been shown, their views virtually coincided on the most pressing matter – that is, the policies of the radical factions; nor is there any word about the foundation at Yavneh. This is particularly enigmatic since the Rabban's pro-Roman stand would have made a welcome and respectable parallel to the historian's own collaborationism. Furthermore, the neglect was mutual: Josephus is equally unmentioned in the entire rabbinic corpus. This latter fact is perhaps easier to account for: first, many, even among the moderate Pharisees, would have considered a former revolutionary general, collaborating with the occupier, a double turncoat and thus quite different from the famous sage, who opposed the revolt; second, his account of the war, written to satisfy – even if only in part – the needs of the Imperial propaganda, and with a passionate emphasis on the outrages perpetrated by the rebels, must have been found inopportune by the rabbis, who were consistent in altogether avoiding issues politically – and emotionally – explosive. As regards Josephus's own silence, we must admit that it is difficult to explain, especially given his hazardous and at times incomprehensible choices of what to say or not to say. After all, it might well have owed to the historian's annoyance at the rumors (if they already circulated at the time) ascribing his famous prophecy of Vespasian accession to someone else - and to the man more prominent than he. Whatever its cause, Josephus's neglect should not interfere, of course, with our appreciation of Rabban Johanan b. Zakkai and his work.

A Hillelite and a humanizer, whose commitment to nonviolence recalls – *mutatis mutandis* – Erasmus or even Gandhi, he is often considered the founder of Judaism as it came to survive through many centuries since, having thus ensured the perpetuation of the Jewish faith: after all, it was the labors begun by his colleagues at Yavneh which with time brought about the codification of the Mishnah and, centuries later, reached their fulfillment in the Talmud.[6]

III.

Returning to Jerusalem in revolt, one finds it remarkable that the factional conflict continued even into the siege. At first, it seemed that a sort of reconciliation was achieved after Titus had encamped at three different localities around the capital and began preparations for the siege. We read that the insurgents, "watching with dismay the Romans at work in three camps, entered an evil alliance" (*BJ*, 5, 72) and, as a result, joined forces, successfully routing the tenth legion, which was barely rescued, Josephus says, by Titus's personal intervention

(75 ff.). This concord proved, however, short lived. According to the *Bellum*'s order of events, John b. Levi of Gischala, upon his taking over by ruse the zealots under Eleazar (14 Xanthicus), resumed hostilities against Simon:

> Having somewhat sobered briefly after their first sally, they suffered a relapse of the disease, so that the partisans [of the factions] once again began to fight among themselves, [thus] fulfilling every aspiration of their besiegers. Nor did they indeed suffer worse at the hands of the Romans than they inflicted upon each other; and in the aftermath of all this, the city did not experience any novel torment, but the harshest disaster occurred prior to its fall, and those who captured it set the balance straight.
>
> (255 f.)

Josephus's pro-Roman stand and rhetoric in this passage are, of course, obvious, but this must not prevent us from recognizing that – suicidal as this must have been – factional enmities even then took priority over the national liberation cause, as it must have been witnessed by the survivors within the historian's audience: a fact most reasonably explained, at least to my mind, not only through their leaders' naked ambition, but also by the willful disagreements among the groups of religious dissenters about the meaning and methods of their mission seen as divinely ordained. It was only when the Romans proceeded with building earth works and constructing the siege engines that the two parties must have realized the primacy of common danger and the urgent need for common defense (277). Whether Josephus's insinuation that they placed the blame for their discord on God (278) is just another piece of his dubious psychologizing – or yet one more insight into the mindset of these men – cannot be known. In any event, after the decision was reached to postpone their strife (ibid) and unite *vis-à-vis* the Romans, Simon b. Giora made an offer of free passage to all insurgents between the wall and the Temple, and John b. Levi reluctantly – as it is alleged – consented (ibid); we read that ever since, "having thrown their hatred and private quarrels into oblivion, they became one body" (279). There is no mention, however, of a sole military command, so it must be assumed that the two leaders had compromised on sharing it until the very end.

It must have been at some point during the siege that the *sui generis* religious dissenter and self-appointed prophet of doom, Jesus b. Ananias, found his end when – the historian tells us – to his monomaniac Jeremiad about the coming ruin of the people, the city and the Temple, he added: "And also woe to me!", only to be struck by a stone from the Roman ballista and died "with that ominous utterance" on his lips (*BJ*, 6, 309). His apocalyptic message stands, of course, in stark contrast with the eschatological optimism, possessing most of the insurgents, many of whom, as it will be seen shortly, clung to it tenaciously to the very last. Josephus seizes an opportunity to pronounce on what he regards as largely responsible for the war: namely, the "ambiguous oracle", obviously meaning the Messianic prophecies, that "at this time, someone from their land will rise to rule the inhabited world" (ibid, 312). In accordance with his own prediction, upon his emerging from the cave at Jotapata, he again reinterprets the sacred texts in favor of the Romans, thus betraying his own idiosyncratic form of religious dissent:

> They took this to mean someone of their own, and many of their sages were misled in this judgment; but the oracle revealed in fact the authority of Vespasian, proclaimed Emperor in Judaea.
>
> (313)

During the siege Josephus himself made numerous attempts to act as mediator and negotiator, presumably, with Titus's permission and sometimes on his direct instructions (*BJ*, 5, 114; 361 ff.; 541 ff.; cf. 261; 325; 6, 94 ff.; 118; 129; 365). There is no reason to question the sincerity of Josephus's wish for preventing the final ruin of his fellow Jews, not without some risk to his own life: at one point, while arguing their surrender, he was hit by a stone and barely escaped captivity at the rebels' hands, and was even rumored to have died (5, 541 ff.; cf. 362, 375; 6, 112). These must have been facts, since his narrative, as we know, was approved by the Flavians, who had no interest in Josephus's personal agenda – but his reports on the allegedly powerful effects of his exhortations (5, 420 f.; 543; 547; 6, 113 f.; 6, 98) are obviously exaggerated. Two speeches of his, found in the *Bellum*, are in part products of subsequent rhetoricization; but the gist of their message, although predictable, would have made sense, under the circumstances, both at the time of their delivery, and later to Josephus's readership at large. The first, and lengthier, speech addresses the rebel constituency as such (5, 362–420); the second, upon the cessation of the *tamid*, aims primarily at John b. Levi of Gischala (6, 96–112). All the elements of his argument, however varied, are familiar: the sins of the Jews and the futility of their resistance; the piety and clemency of the Romans; and, of course, the strongest point – that God, in divine righteousness, sided with the latter. Although in the first oration the emphasis is placed on the Roman might and penchant for clemency, and, in the second, on the Jewish crimes, the leitmotif, variously expressed, remains the same: "You are waging war not only against the Romans, but also against God" (5, 378).[7]

The siege of Jerusalem lasted over six months (*BJ*, 5, 67 – 6, 434). For soberminded observers on both sides, it must have been clear that the city was doomed, although Josephus is keen on listing and interpreting, with hindsight, a variety of portents (289 ff.). Titus marched against the capital from Caesarea Maritima on about 8 Xanthicus (Nisan = March/April A.D. 70; – *BJ*, 5, 40 ff.). The third outermost wall, begun by King Agrippa I and hastily completed upon the revolt's outbreak, fell to the Romans on 7 Arthemisius (= Iyyar, ca. May 25 – ibid, 301 f.); the second was captured, after two attempts, on the 16th of the same month (ca. June 3 – ibid, 347). The inner first wall, built at the time of the Old Kingdoms (142 ff.), resisted the longest. This forced the enemy to start constructing the siege wall around the city, which effectively sealed it, cutting off even the secret routes of the food supply. Despite a major setback (the first set of the earthworks the Jews tore down almost immediately upon their completion – 466 ff.), this labor was carried out, having taken as long as three weeks (*BJ*, 6, 5), by the 1 Panemus (= Tammuz, ca. July 20). Within the next week the Romans took over not only the first wall, but also the makeshift one, which the rebels erected behind it (ca. July 24 – ibid, 68 f.), thus inaugurating the battle over the sanctuary that was to last for more than a month: both sides, and especially the defenders (albeit still in two separate contingents), are described as having fought with exceptional ferocity (cf. 6, 74 ff.): the first engagement alone went on for 12 hours (79). The Temple's destruction occurred, in fact, gradually: its porticoes were reportedly set on fire first by Jews, who tried to hamper the advance by the Romans, and then finished off by the latter (165 ff.; 180 ff.; 233 ff.). It was atop the one such portico, which stood still untouched, that 6000 dissenters came to perish in the belief that God would deliver them at the final moment (283 ff.):

> A certain false prophet proved the cause of their destruction, who on that day had announced to those in the city that God ordered them to ascend the Temple and there receive the signs of their salvation.
>
> (285)

This tragic episode (historical, since its public character cannot be doubted) belongs among the clearest manifestations of the religious dissent mentality, which constitutes this book's subject. For opportunistic and self-serving reasons, Josephus denies individuals, whom he calls "false prophets", any genuine faith in their visions, which they certainly possessed, but one of his comments (even though a rhetorical cliché) makes perfect psychological sense: "In misfortune man is quickly convinced, and when the liar pledges a release of current horrors, the sufferer becomes wholly filled with hope" (287).

The great sanctuary was finally burned to the ground after six days of fighting, on 10 Loos (= Av, ca. August 30, A.D. 70 – *BJ*, 6, 249 ff.). This was followed by the sack of the lower town (353 ff.), but it took the Romans yet another month to master the upper city. Their victory became complete only by 8 Gorpiaeus (= Elul, ca. 26 September – 403 ff.). As a result, the holy Jewish capital was systematically destroyed.

Throughout the siege the rebels came to display quite an extraordinary gallantry, which Josephus reports on numerous occasions. At one point he observes that "daring, assault, the mass charge, and not turning back even when defeated" (6, 17) are among the Jewish people's innate characteristics.

The following passage, celebrating the exploit of three warriors – Gephthaeus, Magassarus and Ceagiras – illustrates what he must have meant:

> No more daring men arose from the city in the course of the war, nor more terrifying: for, as if running towards friends, not the enemy array,

they never slowed down or turned away, but rushed through the midst of their foes to set fire to the machines. Struck with swords and pressed from every side, they withdrew from danger no sooner than the fire got hold of the engines.

(5, 475 ff.)[8]

The tragic irony lies in the fact that it was this intransigent bravery on the part of the rebels which ultimately doomed the Temple. There are reasons to believe that otherwise it could have been spared. Vespasian and Titus, in contrast to the likes of Caligula or Nero, were first and foremost pragmatic politicians. Their chief agenda was restoring law and order in the rebellious province, with the least possible loss, or negative effects for Roman rule (the concern fully appreciated by Josephus), and subsequent stability, best to be achieved through soliciting cooperation, as broad as possible, within the populace. This accounts for Titus's initiatives, as the *Bellum* reports, to negotiate the rebels' surrender, even offering them the promise of life: the logic of the situation suggests these to have been true facts, rather than the historian's further attempts at whitewashing the Romans. His narrative has it that on five separate occasions the Roman commander urged the insurgents to give up: by sending the captives with their hands cut off (5, 455 f.); thrice – reportedly – through the agency of Josephus (5, 361 ff; 6, 95 ff; 124 f.) of whose speeches two are reproduced at length, as we have seen; and finally in a personal parley with the rebel leaders, after the Temple's fire (6, 323 ff.). One is entitled to disregard much in the unlikely rhetoric, attributed by the historian to Titus, with the references to the God of Israel; but it does not follow that the Romans did not try to avoid committing what the Jews would have considered the utmost sacrilege, and some points, such as reference to Roman religious tolerance and protection of the Jewish faith prior to the revolt, might have actually been made.

It is only towards the end of Josephus's war narrative that the reader learns what might have been the ultimate, although formal, reason for the insurgents' refusal to give up: they are said to have rejected Titus's proposal to surrender and his pledge to spare their lives owing to the oath they had earlier taken never to do so (6, 351; cf. 366). The time and circumstances under which that event did occur remain unknown, although it could hardly happen before the end of the factional strife. This apparently intractable stand betrays, apart from the factor of emotions, the profoundly 'counter-political' constituent inherent in the religious dissent mindset, the same 'theological' hope against hope.

Historically, similar disposition in some cases endures till the very end; in others, it does not: the strength of passion and belief varies in individuals and groups. Anyhow, the rebel leaders reportedly made an attempt, despite their oath, to negotiate at that very parley for a free passage from Jerusalem with their wives and children so that they could withdraw into the desert (yet another trace of eschatological expectations?) and leave the city in the hands of the victors (ibid). This characteristic request, dubious in moral terms (disregarding, as it did, at the price of their safety, the fate of the civilians to be slaughtered and plundered by the conquerors), was predictably denied (352) and followed by Titus's order against further acceptance of deserters (ibid). Moreover, we have seen that both Simon b. Giora and John b. Levi chose eventually to capitulate, while still alive, breaching the very oath they had sworn, and the latter even managed to escape execution. Eleazar b. Simon, on the other hand, seems to have perished fighting.

The conduct of the Temple priests, who were bound to cooperate with the rebels, resembled (as described) that of the two faction leaders. They offered at first violent resistance, "tearing up the spikes from the sanctuary, with their leaden sockets and hurling them at the Romans" from the outer portico, but – with their efforts being frustrated – retired on the wall to meet their doom (278 f.). Only two of them, Meirus b. Belgas and Josephus b. Dalaeus, are cited as having self-destructively plunged into the flames (280). The rest were arraigned a few days later and put to death despite their plea for mercy before Titus (318 ff.), who – according to Josephus – told them that it was too late, and that the only good reason he could have pardoned them for was gone: "It becomes the priests to perish with their Temple" (322).

The exceptional fortitude with which the Jewish rank-and-file defended their Temple is also conveyed in the excerpts we have from Cassius Dio, emphasizing, unlike Josephus, who sought, for the most part, to downplay any such issue, the role that sensibilities, fostered by faith – and, in this book's terms, also by religious dissent – could play in the inspiration for and character of their resistance:

> Then the Jews defended themselves much more vigorously than before, as if they had discovered a piece of rare good fortune in being able to fight near the temple and fall in its defence / ... / And though they were but a handful fighting against a far superior force, they were not conquered until a part of the temple was set on fire. Then they met death willingly, some throwing themselves on the swords of the Romans, some slaying one another, others taking their own lives, and still others leaping into the flames. And it seemed to everybody, and especially to them, that so far from being destruction, it was victory and salvation and happiness to them that they perished along with the temple.
>
> (*Dio-Xiph.*, 65, 6, 2 f.)

To my mind, the most patent explanation for this degree of enthusiasm is to assume that it was motivated by the fervent belief that meeting their death as the champions of God's cause, and on sacred grounds, would secure their membership among the righteous in the glorious afterlife.

Lastly, we learn of numerous rebels, including the zealot commander Judas b. Ari, who managed to escape from Jerusalem, in part, through underground passages, and tried continuing resistance (cf. *BJ*, 7, 215). They were rounded up by the legate Lucilius Bassus, after the fall of Machaerus, in the forest of Jardes, and killed to a man after a ferocious fight in the manner appropriate for true heroes (ibid, 210 ff.) – in contrast to the *sicarii* of Masada, with their choice of taking their own life rather than dying in battle.

The evidence thus suggests that on practical grounds, had the psychological factor (that is, the mindset typical of religious dissenters and shared by too many insurgents) not interfered, the Temple could have been saved. Admittedly, Josephus's narrative is compressed, rhetorically inconsistent and at some points confused in detail; but this is not the reason to deny it a basic historicity in terms of what actually happened.[9]

The *Bellum* reports that, prior to the final assault on the Temple, Titus convoked his *consilium* (*BJ*, 6, 236 ff.), which indicates that, as regards its fate, no decision had yet been made. The mainstream scholarly view holds that at that meeting it was resolved to destroy the sanctuary. Josephus says the opposite: although the opinions of his advisors differed, his text insists, Titus declared that, even if the Jews continued to wage war on him from the Temple, he "would not revenge himself on inanimate objects rather than men, nor ever put to flames so great a structure, since it would mean damage done also to the Romans, but when preserved, it would be an ornament to their power" (241). Consequently, the final disaster – the Temple's burning – proved, according to Josephus, to have been an accident, owing to the misconduct on the part of the insubordinate soldiers (249 ff.). There had been persistent attempts to impeach his account on the grounds, first, of his excessive flattery to the Flavians, and – more persuasively – in view of the statement by the later Christian historian Sulpicius Severus (ca. 363 – ca. 425), who asserts that the Temple of Jerusalem was burned on Titus's explicit orders (*Chron.*, 2, 30 6 f.). It had been proposed that this was not the Christian distortion of Josephus, but derives either directly from Tacitus or from the latter's reliable source. This argument is based, however, on a set of suppositions and should be treated cautiously. Perhaps the most reasonable approach to the issue is to consider it in pragmatic terms, which was a prominent characteristic of Flavian policies. The Roman commander must have indeed realized the political repercussions on the Jewish people of the monstrous blasphemy which the Temple's deliberate destruction would mean in their eyes. This had to be carefully balanced against the argument for deterrence, saying that the sanctuary's very existence constitutes the focus of the Jewish discontent and, when eliminated, it would not only teach the recalcitrant a terrible lesson but also help to pacify the land. Still, to do so could run the risk of yet further and further uprisings, this time not only in Judaea, but also in the Diaspora, which – at that politically still precarious moment – the new dynasty was hardly able to afford.

Josephus might have witnessed the deliberations; but even if he did not attend the meeting, he surely knew of its main thrust, and it seems unlikely that he willfully distorted the outcome, or that this distortion found approval from his Imperial censors, the more so since it would have resulted in cross-purposes – namely, if the Flavians decided that the Jews must be punished with destroying their holiest place of worship, it made no sense to claim that it had happened by accident. So far as Josephus was concerned, that accident fit well his major thesis of God pronouncing a sentence on his own shrine (cf. *BJ*, 6, 250). Thus we read that the Roman soldier, who first flung a fiery branch inside of it, acted as he was under some "heaven-sent impulse" (252).

Be that as it may, the scholarly debate on this matter continues to the present day.

The burning of the Temple, and the moment when it occurred, are fraught with historical ironies capable of impressing a pessimistic mind with the futility of human endeavor: only a few years earlier, during the procuratorship of Lucceius Albinus (A.D. 62–64), its construction was finally completed by King Agrippa II (*AJ*, 20, 219). Another ominous coincidence, even though perhaps fictional, is claimed by Josephus – namely, that both the month and the day proved the same as when the first Temple of Solomon suffered a similar fate at the hands of the Babylonian Nebuchadnezzar (586 B.C.; cf. *BJ*, 6, 250, 268). This final disaster was followed with the wholesale massacre of Jerusalem's population by the Romans: the Jewish capital was later razed to the ground, with only three high towers allowed to remain standing, we read, as a monument to the victor's Fortune "in alliance with whom he was able to conquer the unconquerable" (*BJ*, 6, 413).[10]

CONCLUSION

The suppression of the Great Revolt and the destruction of the Second Temple by the Romans clearly belong among the major national disasters in the history of the Jewish people. In terms of its political, cultural, religious and psychological repercussions, it compares with such catastrophes as the Babylonian captivity, Hadrian's desecration of Jerusalem prohibiting Jewish residence in their own capital, or their expulsion from Spain under Ferdinand and Isabella, and is superseded only by the horrors of the Nazi genocide. Obviously, the whole tragic development was caused by the variety of factors, from social problems to the incompetent decisions, on the part of the Roman administration, Jewish priestly authorities and their revolutionary leaders. In this book I have attempted, however, to demonstrate that, despite the inadequacy of our sources on this theme, it is possible to ascertain the significant role played by the militant religious dissent mindset and its carriers. It was a complex and fluid phenomenon, not at all homogeneous, encompassing groups and individuals often elusive, demonstrating various degrees of radicalism, from the fringe elements, such as, arguably, the 'cave people' exterminated by Herod, to the Temple faction under Eleazar b. Ananias, who provided the pretext for Rome's Jewish War. My purpose was to uncover and discuss, wherever possible, its characteristic components and manifestations in the behavior of historical agents under the Roman rule, starting with the earliest identifiable example, the "fourth philosophy", and ending with the drama of the last 'eschatological' prophet at the doomed Temple, who promised his followers salvation in the 13th hour, having led them instead to fiery death.

The non-violent resolution of any crisis primarily depends on the ability of all sides involved to adjust their interests. But if within an organized monotheist religion its established hierarchy, mainstream membership or single individuals (such as Josephus and Philo) *often* achieve some sort of compromise with outside cultures and even conquerors, as has been repeatedly proved in the history of Judaism, Christianity and Islam, this is *never* the case among militant religious dissenters. A religious hierarchy acts wisely when it recognizes or protects the non-violent forms of dissent, but it is often difficult to ascertain the latter's potential for violence. The official response to such movements depends on whether they are or are not considered a major threat, and on the extent of their belligerence towards the establishment, as well as their leverage within the latter. Ultimately, the demarcation line between violent and non-violent dissent lies in an attitude to the issue of power, involving 'politicization'. If for the recognized priesthood (Judaic, Christian, Islamic) such involvement is needed in order to maintain the status quo, for their radical opponents under the spell of the militant 'dissent mentality', it is the other way around: they deny the current hierarchy the very right to continue as spiritual authority, which amounts, in the final analysis, to the denial of a given religion in its concrete historical form. When a dissenting group or movement becomes, for whatever reason, imbued with revolutionary enthusiasm that inevitably calls for violence and succeeds in producing mass hysteria, the historical upheaval, which leads to the loss of countless lives, is already underway. As a consequence, in Judaea the militant carriers of religious dissent were largely responsible both for how the revolt broke out and how it collapsed, even though other political and military factors were bound to interfere.

It was not my intention in the slightest to exculpate the Romans: their Imperial regime (as many other Imperial regimes throughout history) was bad enough even in the best of times. But I believe it is essential for a deeper understanding of the historical process to recognize violent, or potentially violent, forces within a particular culture and society (in our case, the promoters of militant religious dissent), and indict them as the tools of their own and their nation's self-destruction. Unfortunately, history does not operate along the lines of political correctness. It is rare that historical and socio-political organisms or arrangements deserve to be interpreted exclusively as 'black' (most examples are modern: Hitler, Stalin, Mao, Pol Pot): too many factors of different coloration are usually at work. Even under foreign rule, the oppression of the natives (although from the humanist point of view, which I morally share, always reprehensible) may or may not become intolerable to the point of making its subject feel desperate enough and to justify the massive violence of revolutionary upheaval. It is patent that the Roman administrative policies in Judaea prior to the Great Revolt, however noxious at times, did not threaten in any significant sense the existence of the Jewish people, Jewish faith or Jewish culture – in contrast to the policies of Antiochus IV Epiphanes, whose purpose was to abolish Judaism, policies which triggered (and justified) the Maccabean insurrection two centuries earlier. Even though the communication gap between the conquerors and the conquered was never bridged, attempts at accommodating had been made on both sides; some worked, others did not, but a *modus vivendi*, imperfect as it was, was achieved and lasted for a span of several generations.

Methodologically, it would be an error to minimize the spread of pro-Roman, or neutral, sentiments on the eve or even in the course of the revolt, throughout the land and in various societal circles: there occurred, for instance, little anti-Roman activity in Galilee, but rather a conflict between the urban and rural populace, or infighting among various revolutionary groups. Above all, it was folly to rise up against the colossal Roman military machine, and it would be defying common sense to deny that there must have existed many (not only among the privileged) who realized this at one point or another, having been all the time perfectly pious and patriotic Jews; eventually, so did Josephus himself, rather too late, and in hindsight. This could even have been rationalized in accordance with biblical theology and on the basis of biblical precedents. As Josephus never ceases to remind us: God is omnipotent, and the Roman yoke would never have occurred against God's will. The defiance of the political and military reality betrays powerful irrationalism and wishful thinking, which characterizes militant religious dissent in a qualitatively different sense than the religious mainstream, the latter being better equipped to deal with exigencies, and to avoid catastrophic outcome by a variety of means, such as non-violent civil disobedience. The former is rooted in the belief (conscious, semi-conscious or unconscious) that its proponents represent God's chosen instruments, that they wage war for the sake of God's cause, that they may confidently rely on God's aid and – if necessary – supernatural intervention. It is true that this psychological cluster was bound to affect, in one way or another, the mentality and behavior of mainstream groups and individuals; but it is a variable that does not impinge on the basic distinction between the two phenomena, the importance of which is this book's underlying argument.

I also suggested that militant religious dissent and its irrational character must have played some role in the bloody factionalism that ultimately doomed the Great Revolt, Jerusalem and the Temple. There is no way to evaluate the extent of human losses on each side throughout the hostilities. Given the insurgents' perseverance, especially when under siege in Jerusalem and elsewhere, Roman casualties must have been substantial; but the most tragic aspect of the situation was that, on the Jewish part, they also consisted of Jews killed by Jews – in considerable numbers. To this must be added countless (even if we dismiss Josephan figures as unreliable) civilian victims of the famine. It must be clearly understood that what is often called a national liberation war against a foreign occupier proved to involve, at the same time, and on no lesser scale, civil, religious and social warfare. It is telling that even a century later or so, the concern with and the memories of fratricide made the compilers of the Mishnah, despite the new Roman terror in the aftermath of the Bar Kokhba uprising, go so far as to pray for the Imperial government: "For if it were not for fear of it, one man would swallow his fellow alive" *(mAvot,* 3:2).[1]

The relentless brutality perpetrated by the conquerors on the defeated nation cannot be doubted. It was part and parcel of the traditional Roman military ethos that Virgil euphemistically calls *debellare superbos* – "battle down the proud" *(Aen.* 6, 851): recall the fate of Carthage. The land of the Jews was devastated and depopulated, its economy ruined, masses of ordinary people slaughtered or enslaved. It is known that numerous Jewish prisoners of war were forced to work on the construction of the *Amphitheatrum Flavianum,* known as the Coliseum. Likewise, it is amply documented that the Flavians took every opportunity in using their victory to inaugurate and enhance their new upstart dynasty as legitimate: Vespasian and Titus's joint grandiose and pompous triumph, which Josephus describes in great detail (*BJ*, 7, 123–57), dedicating the Temple of Peace (patently reminiscent of Augustus's *Ara Pacis*) that was to house the golden vessels seized from the Temple (ibid, 161), minting the commemorative coinage in gold, silver and bronze with the legend *JUDAEA CAPTA* ("Captive Judaea"). One oppressive novelty was the institution of the "Jewish tax", *fiscus Judaicus* (218; *Dio*, 66, 7, 2). It is true that, in economic terms (and apart from its mandatory character), it was hardly an additional burden since it constituted the same amount as the earlier and traditional Temple tax voluntarily paid by all Jews. But it was obviously intended – and felt – as an added and painful humiliation since the money thus raised was meant as "Jewish annual tribute of two denarii to Jupiter Capitolinus" (*Dio*, loc. cit.). History shows that psychological injury of this kind may inflict a greater damage on a national psyche than a major material or even human deprivation.

This said, it must be recognized that, for practical purposes, the Flavian regime learned the lesson. In Judaea the incompetent and rapacious equestrian procurators were replaced with senatorial governors as *legati pro praetore*, members of the Empire's wealthy, educated ruling élite, who valued their status and reputation, the *dignitas*. For a few decades we stop hearing of extortions, persecutions or maladministration in the land. The factors that prompted and contributed to the uprising of the Jewish Diaspora under Trajan (which failed significantly to affect Judaea) and of Judaea's Bar Kokhba revolt under Hadrian (not supported by the Diaspora) appear different in each case and, owing to the insufficient data available, often a subject to conjecture. The operation of militant religious dissent, as understood in this book, may or may not have proved equally important; but this requires special investigation. Any student embarking on that quest, however, will confront a formidable task in the absence of a narrative source comparable to Josephus. This should make us properly appreciate the latter and cease blaming him for his real and imaginary shortcomings, many of which are not even, in the final analysis, his own fault but due to the historical predicament and cultural context in which he lived. Irrespective of their numerous flaws, which I have consistently taken into account, the author of the *Bellum* and the *Antiquitates* produced narratives that not only attempt to represent and interpret (rightly or wrongly) a terrible upheaval suffered by his people and his homeland, but also reflect the complexity embedded in the historical process, a virtue not always found among modern theorists and practitioners of the same craft.[2]

In recent times, so-called 'counter-factual history', for a long time considered a province of fantasy or science fiction, has acquired intellectual respectability at the hands of several prominent scholars and, especially, Niall Ferguson. As an analytical instrument, it allows for an indeterminate or incidental dimension in what historically happens, and thus helps more adequately to elucidate the observable dynamics, which include both the potential and realization of various developments and events. I find counter-factual arguments persuasive when they demonstrate that a different set of accidents *might* have indeed dramatically changed the course of history. If one attempts, however, with this in mind, and on a strictly theoretical basis, to apply the same technique in the context of Roman Judaea, the results are not likely to diverge from the extant historical record, except in some, perhaps even critical, details. Two relevant issues arise: first, did there exist even a slight possibility that the Great Revolt might have ended up, like the Maccabean precedent, in a gradual emancipation from Rome's rule; and, second, what could have happened if in A.D. 66 the militant religious dissent mindset had not spread that far and that deep across societal boundaries to provoke the passionate public outburst, which upset the power balance within the Jerusalem establishment so that things got out of control. In other words, would it have been possible for the Second Temple to survive if the Jewish War had never occurred? As regards the first, I cannot envisage the success of the rebels against the enemy 'superpower' unless the Empire began to deteriorate and disintegrate as it did two centuries later. There was no sign at the time to indicate anything of the sort, despite the civil war in the West during A.D. 69 – the 'year of four emperors'; but even this latter fact, which must have increased their chances, the insurgents chose not to exploit. The factional infighting blocked any major cooperative effort, and none of the revolutionary leaders showed qualities to be compared with the military brilliance of Judas Maccabeus, or the skillful statesmanship of his brothers Jonathan and Simon. Under the circumstances, the Great Revolt was doomed even before it broke out. The second question is more complex. The likelihood of Judaea's avoiding an eventual clash with the Roman occupier depended on too many 'ifs': the ability for self-restraint through another two years of the Neronian regime (with or without Gessius Florus still in charge); the continuous improvement of the province's administration during the next century and a half; and its non-involvement in any trouble concerning Jews elsewhere in the Empire. This implies, of course, that the Bar Kokhba revolt had never taken place.

If these conditions were observed, with the emergence of Sassanian Persia by the 230s as Rome's major and militant rival, Judaea *might* have bettered its political status and eventually become one of the semi-independent buffer states between the two. But this scenario's prospects for fulfillment were slim: a rebellion, such as a Great Revolt, could have broken out anytime within the interval for a plethora of reasons, but it does not follow – and this is the crux of the matter – that its defeat, perhaps again unavoidable, was fated to turn equally disastrous, with Jerusalem destroyed and the Temple burned. By extension, this means that historical Judaism would have acquired some alternative form, different from the one we know.

In any event, it remains true that, despite the reprisals, inevitable after the suppression of two subsequent Jewish uprisings, for another 200 years the Imperial government continued to abstain from pursuing consistent policies directed against Jews: in this regard, it followed practices established upon the initial conquest. It was not until the Christian Church's rise to power under Constantine that the situation drastically changed, and religious anti-Semitism, in its ugly aggressive shape, entered the scene. The 'Church triumphant' committed a double betrayal of its own faith shortly after it achieved official status: it betrayed Jesus, a Jew, as a man by encouraging and approving the anti-Jewish imperial legislation; it betrayed Christ as God by rendering unto Caesar what is God's. This was the original sin the Church still needs to have fully acknowledged and expiated.

One major result of Roman victory in the Jewish War was the formation of rabbinic Judaism. It has continued evolving to the present day without major setbacks, tolerating non-violent internal dissent, enriching itself intellectually, despite frequent persecution and significant isolation in both Christian and Muslim worlds, and gradually moving towards the universalist humanism that now distinguishes mainstream Jewish religious thought. Above all, for two millennia Jews never engaged *en masse* in warfare, and thus had no blood on their hands. This makes them unique as *ethnos*, having contributed to the profoundly ethical core of the Jewish philosophical tradition, from Maimonides to Buber. Ironically, against the background of modern Judaism, religious dissent is now represented by the ultra-Orthodox, which is of little concern until they turn violent, as in the case of Yitzhak Rabin's assassination.[3]

While it is a historian's duty to divest oneself, so far as possible, from intellectual and psychological accoutrements typical of one's immediate environment, it is no less clear that similar phenomena, even though they take specific manifestations, kept recurring throughout history and continue doing so. The reader of this book can easily discern both similarities and differences in the activity of religious dissenters then and now, separated as they are by 2000 years. The Romans found it next to impossible to penetrate the minds of the zealots, *sicarii* and their ilk. They proved impervious to the familiar arguments, such as Rome's military might, its providential conquests, and its supposed clemency, sparing the defeated: *parcere subjectis* (Virgil). None of this, and not even the very real threat of annihilation, helped to convince their antagonists that they should yield to a superior force and give up. Likewise, the Western public in bewilderment mixed with fear now watches the jihad undertaken by the Islamic Al-Qaeda, the Taliban and the rest, who represent the carriers of the militant religious dissent in contemporary Islam, against the most powerful civilization, from the material and military viewpoint, that history ever saw. And we similarly lack arguments based on our values capable of persuading them to stop. This is a tough predicament, and it is difficult to see what can be done if we want to avoid yet another violent upheaval. One can wait, of course, for the Moslem militant religious dissent somehow to die out, but there are no signs that this is going to happen anytime soon. Two thoughts, however, come to mind. First, it would be good if the West, by an imaginative effort, could revitalize the notion of the 'sacred', at least so far as to appreciate its meaning and importance for those faithful, irrespective of their religion or denomination, who are passionately concerned with it. And,

CONCLUSION

second: the only discourse, or dialogue, it seems to me, which has a potential, however small, for changing the attitudes of the Islamic extremists must be conducted solely within their own mental and spiritual framework, focusing on the premise that God does not support violence, is ready to punish them for the sin of fratricide, and even sides with their foes. This was, as we know, the line of reasoning taken up by Josephus, and later adopted by the rabbis. One may only hope against hope that this and similar arguments, if persistently and intelligently applied both within and without the world of Islam, may win over the critical mass of those who matter – and prevent a catastrophe on a global rather than national scale, but in kind not dissimilar to the one which visited Judaea under Roman rule at the end of the Second Temple period. I am fully aware of how meager this sounds *vis-à-vis* the threat from what is called "the clash of civilizations"; but it may still be true that, as one Abrahamic religion claims, "In the beginning was the Word."

SELECT BIBLIOGRAPHY

This bibliography lists only book-length publications in English. The full bibliography that includes works in other languages, specialized studies, and articles from collective volumes and journals to cover all references found in the endnotes is located on the website.

Primary sources

Flavius Josephus [*Works*, English and Greek], transl. by H. St. J. Thackeray, Ralph Marcus, L. H. Feldman vols. I–IX, The Loeb Classical Library, Cambridge, MA, and London, 1926–1965

Philo of Alexandria [*Works*, English and Greek], transl. by F.H. Colson and G.H. Whiaker, vols. I–XII, The Loeb Classical Library, Cambridge, MA, and London, 1929–1953

The Dead Sea Scrolls Translated: the Qumran Texts in English, ed. by Florentino Garcia Martinez, Leiden, New York and Grand Rapids, MI, 1996

Jerusalem Bible, general ed. Alexander Jones, Garden City, NY, 1968

The Old Testament Pseudepigrapha, ed. by James H. Charlesworth, vols. I–II, Garden City, NY, 1983–1986

The Mishnah, transl. by Jacob Neusner, New Haven, CT, 1988

The Tosefta, transl. by Jacob Neusner, vols. I–II, Peabody, MA, 2002

Greek and Latin Authors on Jews and Judaism, ed. by Menahem Stern, vols. I–III, Jerusalem, 1974–1984

Cornelius Tacitus [*Histories* and *Annals*, English and Latin], transl. by Clifford H. Moore and John Jackson, vols. I–III, The Loeb Classical Library, Cambridge, MA, 1956

C. Suetonius Tranquillus [*Works*, English and Latin], transl. by J.C. Rolfe, vols. I–II, The Loeb Classical Library, Cambridge, MA, and London, 1914–1930

Cassius Dio Cocceianus [*Roman History*, English and Greek], transl. by Ernst Cary and Herbert Baldwin Foster, vols. I–IX, Cambridge, MA, and London, 1914–1927

Secondary literature

Philosophy of history and history writing

Appleby J., Hunt L., Jacob M. *Telling the Truth about History*, New York and London, 1994
Bal M. *Narratology: Introduction to the Theory of Narrative*, Toronto and Buffalo, 1985
Bloch M. *The Historian's Craft*, New York, 1953

Carr E. H. *What Is History?* New York, 1961
Collingwood R. G. *Autobiography*, Oxford, 1939
Collingwood R. G. *The Idea of History*, Oxford, 1956
Danto A. C. *Narration and Knowledge*, New York, 1985
Evans R. *In Defense of History*, London, 1997
Fergusson N. (ed.) *Virtual History: Alternatives and Counterfactuals*, London 1997
Gaddis J. L. *The Landscape of History: How Historians Map the Past*, Oxford, 2002
Gleick J. *Chaos: Making a New Science*, New York, 1987
Howard M. *Lessons of History*, New Haven, CT, 1991
Jenkins K. *Re-thinking History*, London and New York, 1991
Jenkins K. (ed.) *The Postmodern History Reader*, London and New York, 1997
Kuhn T. *The Structure of Scientific Revolutions*, Chicago, IL, 1962
MacMullen R. *Feelings in History, Ancient and Modern*, Claremont, CA, 2003
Popper K. *The Poverty of Historicism*, Boston, MA, 1957
Ricoeur P. *History and Truth*, Evanston, IL, 1965
Rose G. *How Wars End: A History of American Intervention from World War I to Afghanistan*, New York, 2010
Spitzer A. B. *Historical Truth and Lies About the Past*, Chapel Hill, NC, 1996
White H. *Metahistory: The Historical Imagination in Nineteenth-Century Europe*, Baltimore, MD, 1973
White H. *The Content and the Form: Narrative Discourse and Historical Representation*, Baltimore, MD, 1987
Winks R. (ed.) *The Historian as Detective*, New York, 1968
Woodman A. J. *Rhetoric in Classical Historiography: Four Essays*, London and Portland, OR, 1988
Woodman A. J, Kraus C. S. *Latin Historians*, Oxford, 1997

Religious psychology and psychology of violence

Arendt H. *On Violence*, New York, 1970
Buckser A., Glazier S.D. (ed.) *The Anthropology of Relgious Conversion*, Lanham, MD, 2003
Bakhtin M. *Rabelais and His World*, Bloomington, IN, 1984
Besançon A. *The Intellectual Origins of Leninism*, Oxford, 1981
Bjorgo T. (ed.) *Root Causes of Terrorism: Myths, Reality, and the Ways Forward*, London and New York, 2005
Bromley D. G., Melton J. G. (ed.) *Cults, Religion and Violence*, Cambridge and New York, 2002
Claster J.N. *Sacred Violence: The European Crusades to the Middle East, 1095–1396*, Toronto, 2009
Cohn N. *The Pursuit of the Millennium: Revolutionary Millenarians and Mystical Anarchists of the Middle Ages*, London, 1970
Dickson G. *Children's Crusade: Medieval History, Modern Mythistory*, New York, 2008
Eagleton T. *Ideology: An Introduction*, London and New York, 1991
Eliade M. *The Sacred and the Profane*, New York, 1959
Ellul J. *Violence: Reflections from a Christian Perspective*, New York, 1969
Festinger L. *A Theory of Cognitive Dissonance*, Evanston, IL, 1957
Gallagher E.V. *Expectation and Experience: Explaining Religious Conversion*, Atlanta, GA, 1990
Girard R. *Violence and the Sacred*, Baltimore, MD, 1977
Girard R. *The Scapegoat*, Baltimore, MD, 1986
Hauerwas S., Jones L. G. (ed.) *Why Narrative? Readings in Narrative Theology*, Eugene, OR, 1997

SELECT BIBLIOGRAPHY

Hindley G. *The Crusades: A History of Armed Pilgrimage and Holy War*, London, 2003
Hoffer E. *The True Believer: Thoughts on the Nature of Mass Movements*, New York, 1951
Jones J. W. *Blood that Cries out of the Earth: The Psychology of Religious Terrorism*. Oxford, 2008
Kressel N. J. *Bad Faith: The Danger of Religious Extremism*, Amherst, NJ, 2007
Maloney H. N., **Southard S. D.** (ed.) *Handbook of Religious Conversion*, Birmingham, AL, 1992
Moghaddam M., Marsella A. J. (ed.) *Understanding Terrorism: Psychological Roots, Consequences, and Interventions*, Washington, DC, 2004
Otto R. *The Idea of the Holy: An Inquiry into the Non-rational Factor in the Idea of the Divine and Its Relation to the Rational*, London and New York, 1931
Otto R. *Mystical East and West: A Comparative Analysis of the Nature of Mysticism*, New York, 1970
Phillips J. *Holy Warriors: A Modern History of the Crusades*, London, 2009
Reich W. (ed.) *Origins of Terrorism: Psychologies, Ideologies, Theologies, States of Mind*, Baltimore and London, 1998
Ricoeur R. *The Symbolism of Evil*, Boston, MA, 1967
Riley-Smith J. S. C. *Crusades: A History*, New Haven, CT, 2005
Stein R. *For Love of the Father: A Psychoanalytic Study of Religious Terrorism*, Stanford, CA, 2010
Tyerman C. *Crusades: A Very Short Introduction*, Oxford, 2005
Victoroff J. (ed.) *Tangled Roots: Social and Psychological Factors in the Genesis of Terrorism*, Amsterdam and Washington, DC, 2006
Weber M. *The Protestant Ethic and the Spirit of Capitalism*, New York, 1930
Weinberg L., Pedahzur A. (ed.) *Religious Fundamentalism and Political Extremism*, London and Portland, OR, 2004
Zahn M. A., Brownstein H. H., Jackson S. L. (ed.) *Violence: From Theory to Research*, Newark, NJ, 2004
Zizek S. *Violence: Six Sideways Reflections*, New York, 2008

Second Temple Judaism and related issues

Aberbach D. *Jewish Cultural Nationalism: Origins and Influence*, London and New York, 2008
Alon's G. *Jews, Judaism and the Classical World: Studies in Jewish History in the Times of the Second Temple and the Talmud*, Jerusalem, 1977
Anderson R. T., Giles T. *The Keepers: An Introduction to the History and Culture of the Samaritans*, Peabody, MA, 2002
Anderson R. T., Giles T. *Tradition Kept: The Literature of the Samaritans*, Peabody, MA, 2005
Applebaum S. *Jews and Greeks in Ancient Cyrene*, Leiden, 1979
Barclay J. M. G. *Jews in the Mediterranean Diaspora: from Alexander to Trajan (323 BCE – 117 CE)*, Edinburgh, 1996
Barton J. *Oracles of God: Perceptions of Ancient Prophecy in Israel after the Exile*, London, 1986
Baumgarten, A.I *The Flourishing of Jewish Sects in the Maccabean Era: An Interpretation*, Leiden, 1997
Bickerman E. J *Jews in Greek Age*, Cambridge, MA, 1988
Binder D. D. *Into the Temple Courts: The Place of the Synagogues in the Second Temple Period*, Atlanta, GA, 1999
Beall T. S. *Josephus' Description of the Essenes Illustrated by the Dead Sea Scrolls*, Cambridge and New York, 1988
Boccaccini, G. *Beyond the Essenic Hypothesis*, Grand Rapids, MI, 1998
Borgen P. *Philo of Alexandria: An Exegete for His Time*, Leiden and New York, 1997

SELECT BIBLIOGRAPHY

Boyarin D. *A Radical Jew: Paul and the Politics of Identity*, Berkeley, CA, 1994
Callaway, P. R. *The History of the Qumran Community: An Investigation*, Sheffield, 1988
Cappelletti S. *The Jewish Community of Rome: From the Second Century B.C. to the Third Century C.E.*, Leiden and Boston, 2006
Cargill R. R. *Qumran through Real Time: A Virtual Reconstruction of Qumran and the Dead Sea Scrolls*, Piscataway, NJ, 2009
Cohen S. J. D. *From the Maccabees to Mishnah*, Philadelphia, 1987
Cohen, S. J. D. *The Beginnings of Jewishness: Boundaries, Varieties, Uncertainties*, Berkeley, CA, 1999
Collins J. J. *The Sibylline Oracles of Egyptian Judaism*, Missoula, MT, 1974
Collins J. J. *Apocalypticism in the Dead Sea Scrolls*, London and New York, 1997
Collins J. J. *The Apocalyptic Imagination: An Introduction to Jewish Apocalyptic Literature*, Grand Rapids, MI, 1998
Collins, J. J. *Beyond the Qumran Community: The Sectarian Movement of the Dead Sea Scrolls*, Grand Rapids, MI, 2010
Collins, J. J. *The Scepter and the Star: Messianism in Light of the Dead Sea Scrolls*, Grand Rapids, MI, 2010
Davies, P. R. *Scribes and Schools: The Canonization of the Hebrew Scriptures*, Louisville, KY, 1998
Davies, P. R. *Sects and Scrolls: Essays on Qumran and Related Topics*, Atlanta, GA, 1996
Davies, W. D., Finkelstein L. (ed.) *Cambridge History of Judaism*, vols II–III, Cambridge and New York, 1990, 1999
Delia D. *Alexandrian Citizenship during the Roman Principate*, Atlanta, GA, 1991
Dibelius M. *Studies in the Acts of the Apostles*, London, 1956
Eisenman, R. *James the Brother of Jesus: The Key to Unlocking the Secrets of Early Christianity and the dead Sea Scrolls*, New York, 1997
Eylon D. R. *Reincarnation in Jewish Mysticism and Gnosticism*, Lewiston, 2003
Feldman L. *Jew and Gentile in the Ancient World: Attitudes and Interactions from Alexander to Justinian*, Princeton, NJ, 1993
Fitzmyer J. A. *The One Who Is to Come*, Grand Rapids, MI, 2007
Frend W. H. C. *The Early Church*, Philadelphia, PA, 1982
Frend W. H. C. *The Rise of Christianity*, London, 1984
Freund, R.A. *Digging Through the Bible: Understanding Biblical People, Places, and Controversies Through Archaeology*, Lanham, MD, 2009
García Martinez, F., Terbolle Barrera, J. *People of the Dead Sea Scrolls*, Leiden and New York, 1995
Glick L. B. *Marked in Your Flesh: Circumcision from Ancient Judea to Modern America*, Oxford and New York, 2005
Golb, N. *Who Wrote the Dead Sea Scrolls? The Search for the Secret of Qumran*, New York, 1995
Goodman M. *Mission and Conversion: Proselytizing in the Religious History of the Roman Empire*, Oxford, 1994
Goodman, M. *Judaism in the Roman World*, Leiden and Boston, MA, 2007
Grabbe L. L. *Judaism from Cyrus to Hadrian*, vols. I–II, Minneapolis, MN, 1991
Grabbe, L. L. *Judaic Religion in the Second Temple Period: Belief and Practice from the Exile to Yavneh*, London and New York, 2000
Grant M. *Saint Peter*, London 1994
Gruen, E. S. *Diaspora: Jews amidst Greeks and Romans*, Cambridge, MA, 2002
Hengel M. *The "Hellenization" of Judaea in the First Century after Christ*, London, 1989
Helyer L. R. *Exploring Jewish Literature of the Second Temple Period: A Guide for the New Testament Students*, Downers Grove, IL, 2002

SELECT BIBLIOGRAPHY

Hirschfeld, Y. *Qumran in Context*, Peabody, MA, 2004

Horbury W. *Messianism among Jews and Christians: Biblical and Historical Studies*, London and New York, 2003

Horsley R. A. *Scribes, Visionaries, and the Politics of the Second Temple Judea*, Louisville, KY, 2007

Hunt A. *Missing Priests: The Zadokites in Tradition and History*, New York, 2006

Johnston P. S. *Shades of Sheol: Death and Afterlife in the Old Testament*, Leicester and Downers Grove, IL, 2003

Kampen J. *The Hasideans and the Origins of Pharisaism*, Atlanta, GA, 1988

Kasher A. *Jews in Hellenistic and Roman Egypt: The Struggle for Equal Rights*, Tübingen, 1985

Keresztes P. *Imperial Rome and the Christians*, vols I–II, Lanham, MD, 1989

Laato A. *A Star Is Rising: The Historical Development of the Old Testament Royal Ideology and the Rise of the Jewish Messianic Expectations*, Atlanta, GA, 1992

Lucass S. *The Concept of Messiah in the Scriptures of Judaism and Christianity*, London, 2011

Magen I. *The Samaritans and the Good Samaritan*, Jerusalem, 2008

McConville J. G. *God and Earthly Power: An Old Testament Political Theology, Genesis–Kings*, London and New York, 2006

Mendels D. *The Rise and Fall of Jewish Nationalism*, New York, 1992

Neusner J. *A Life of Yohanan ben Zakkai*, Leiden, 1962

Neusner J. *From Politics to Piety: The Emergence of Pharisaic Judaism*, Englewood Cliffs, NJ, 1972

Neusner J. *The Idea of Purity in Ancient Judaism*, Leiden, 1973

Neusner J. *First-Century Judaism in Crisis: Yohanan b. Zakkai and the Renaissance of Torah*, New York, 1982

Neusner J. *Reading and Believing: Ancient Judaism and Contemporary Gullibility*, Atlanta, GA, 1986

Neusner J. *An Introduction to Judaism: A Textbook and Reader*, Louisville, KY, 1991

Neusner J. *Judaic Law from Jesus to Mishnah: A Systematic Reply to Professor E.P. Sanders*, Atlanta, GA, 1993

Neusner J. *Rabbi Talks with Jesus*, Montreal and Ithaca, NY, 2000

Neusner J., Chilton B. D. (ed.) *In Quest of the Historical Pharisees*, Waco, TX, 2007

Nickelsburg G. W. E. *Jewish Literature between the Bible and the Mishnah: A Historical and Literary Introduction*, Philadelphia, PA, 1981

Paget J. C. *Jews, Christians, and Jewish Christians in Antiquity*, Tübingen, 2010

Painter J. *Just James: The Brother of Jesus in History and Tradition*, Columbia, SC, 2004

Pummer R. *The Samaritans in Flavius Josephus*, Tübingen, 2009

Rajak T. *The Jewish Dialogue with Greece and Rome: Studies in Cultural and Social Interaction*, Leiden, 2001

Rajak T. *Translation and Survival: The Greek Bible and Jewish Diaspora*, Oxford, 2009

Rowland, C. *The Open Heaven: A Study of Apocalyptic in Judaism and Early Christianity*, New York, 1982

Russell D. S. *The Old Testament Pseudepigrapha: Patriarchs and Prophets in Early Judaism*, Philadelphia, PA, 1987

Russell D. S. *Divine Disclosure: An Introduction to Jewish Apocalyptic*, Minneapolis, MN, 1992

Safrai S., Stern M. (ed.) *The Jewish People in the First Century. Historical Geography, Political History, Social, Cultural and Religious Life and Institutions*, vols I–II, Philadelphia, PA, 1974

Sanders E. P. *Judaism: Practice and Belief, 63 BCE – 66 CE*, Philadelphia, PA, 1992

Saldarini A. J. *Pharisees, Scribes and Sadducees in Palestinian Society*, Wilmington, DE, 1988

Saperstein M. *Essential Papers on Messianic Movements and Personalities in Jewish History*, New York, 1992
Schäfer P. *Judeophobia: Attitudes toward the Jews in the Ancient World*, Cambridge, MA, and London, 1997
Schams C. *Jewish Scribes in the Second Temple Period*, Sheffield, 1998
Shanks, H. *The Copper Scroll and the Search for the Temple Treasure*, Washington, DC, 2007
Schenck K. *A Brief Guide to Philo*, Louisville, KY, 2005
Schifmann, L. H. *From Text to Tradition: A History of Second Temple and Rabbinic Judaism*, Hoboken, NJ, 1991
Schiffman L. (ed.) *Texts and Traditions: A Source Reader for the Study of Second Temple and Rabbinic Judaism*, Hoboken, NJ, 1998
Scholem G. *Major Trends in Jewish Mysticism*, New York, 1961
Scholem, G. *The Messianic Idea in Judaism and Other Essays on Jewish Spirituality*, New York, 1971
Schur N. *History of the Samaritans*, Frankfurt am Main and New York, 1989
Schürer E. *The History of the Jewish People in the Age of Jesus Chris*t, revised and ed. by G. Vermes, F. Millar and M. Black, vols. I–III, Edinburgh, 1973–1987
Stemberger G. *Jewish Contemporaries of Jesus*, Minneapolis, MN, 1995
Stone M. E. *Ancient Judaism: New Visions and Views*, Grand Rapids, MI, 2011
Taylor J. E. *Immerser: John the Baptist within Second Temple Judaism*, Grand Rapids, MI, 1997
Thomas, S. I. *The "Mysteries" of Qumran: Mystery, Secrecy, and Esotericism in the Dead Sea Scrolls*, Leiden and Boston, 2009
Tso, M. K. M. *Ethics in the Qumran Community: An Interdisciplinar Investigation*, Tübingen, 2010
Ullmann-Margalit, E. *Out of the Cave: A Philosophical Inquiry into the Dead Sea Scrolls Research*, Cambridge, MA, 2006
VanderKam, J. C. *The Dead Sea Scrolls Today*, Grand Rapids, MI, and London, 1994
VanderKam J. C. *An Introduction to Early Judaism*, Grand Rapids, MI, 2001
Vermes G. *The Story of the Scrolls: The Miraculous Discovery and the True Significance of the Dead Sea Scrolls*, London and New York, 2010
Watson A. *Trial of Jesus*, Athens, GA, 1995
Webb R. L. *John the Baptizer and Prophet: A Socio-Historical Study*, Sheffield, 1991
Wiederkehr-Pollack G. *The Jewish Festivals in Ancient, Medieval and Modern Sources*, Brooklyn, NY, 1997
Wise, M. O. *The First Messiah: Investigating the Savior before Jesus*, San Francisco, CA, 1999
Yerushalmi, Y. H. *Zakhor, Jewish History and Jewish Memory*, Seattle, WA, 1982
Zerbe, G.M. *Non-Retaliation in Early Jewish and New Testament Texts*, Sheffield, 1993

Judaea and the Roman Empire: Politics, culture and relationship

Alvar Ezquerra J. *Romanizing Oriental Gods: Myth, Salvation, and Ethics in the Cults of Cybele, Isis and Mithras*, Leiden and New York, 2008
Barrett A. A. *Caligula: The Corruption of Power*, London, 1989
Bickerman E. J. *Maccabees: An Account of Their History from the Beginnings to the Fall of the House of the Hasmonaeans*, New York, 1947
Bickermann E. J. *God of the Maccabees: Studies on the Meaning and Origin of the Maccabean Revolt*, Leiden, 1979

SELECT BIBLIOGRAPHY

Bond H. K. *Pontius Pilate in History and Interpretation*, Cambridge and New York, 1998
Bowersock G. W. *Roman Arabia*, Cambridge, 1983
Brandon S. G. F. *Jesus and the Zealots: A Study of the Political Factor in Primitive Christianity*, Manchester, 1967
Burr V. *Tiberius Julius Alexander*, Bonn, 1955
Dabrowa, E. *The Governors of Roman Syria from Augustus to Septimius Severus*, Bonn, 1998
Droge, A. J., Tabor, J. D. *A Noble Death: Suicide and Martyrdom among Christians and Jews in Antiquity*, San Francisco, CA, 1992
Everitt A. *Augustus: The Life of Rome's First Emperor*, New York, 2006
Farmer W. R., *Maccabees, Zealots and Josephus: An Inquiry into Jewish Nationalism in the Greco-Roman Period*, New York, 1956
Freyne S. *Galilee from Alexander the Great to Hadrian, 323 B.C.E. – 135 C.E*, Wilmington, DE, 1980
Garnsey P., Saller R. *The Roman Empire: Economy, Society and Culture*, Berkeley, CA, 1987
Gnuse R. K. *Dreams and Dram Reports in the Writings of Josephus: A Traditio-historical Analysis*, Leiden and New York, 1996
Goldhill S. *The Temple of Jerusalem*, Cambridge, MA, 2005
Goodman, M. *The Ruling Class of Judaea: The Origins of the Jewish Revolt against Rome, A.D. 66–70*, Cambridge and New York, 1987
Goodman, M. *Rome and Jerusalem: The Clash of Ancient Civilizations*, London and New York, 2007
Grant M. *Herod the Great*, New York, 1971
Gray R. *Prophetic Figures in the Late Second Temple Jewish Palestine: The Evidence from Josephus*, Oxford and New York, 1993
Greenhalgh P. *Pompey, the Republican Prince*, London, 1981
Griffin M. *Nero, the End of the Dynasty*, London and New York, 1984
Grünewald T. *Bandits in the Roman Empire: Myth and Reality*, London and New York, 2004
Hadas-Lebel, M. *Jerusalem against Rome*, Leuven, 2005
Hoehner H. W. *Herod Antipas*, Cambridge, 1972
Holum K. G., Hochfelder, R. L. *King Herod's Dream: Caesarea on the Sea*, New York, 1988
Horsley R. A. *Jesus and the Spiral of Violence: Popular Jewish Resistance in Roman Palestine*, San Francisco, CA, 1987
Horsley R. A. *Galilee: History, Politics, People*, Valley Forge, PA, 1995
Horsley R. A., Hanson J. S. *Bandits, Prophets and Messiahs: Popular Movements at the Time of Jesus*, San Francisco, CA, 1985
Jensen M. H. *Herod Antipas in Galilee: The Literary and Archaeological Sources on the Reign of Herod Antipas and Its Socio-Economic Impact on Galilee*, Tübingen, 2006
Kasher A. *Jews, Idumaeans, and Ancient Arabs: Relations of the Jews in Eretz Israel with the Nations of the Frontier and the Desert during the Hellenistic and Roman Era (332 B.C.E. – 70 C.E.)*, Tübingen, 1988
Kasher A. *Jews and Hellenistic Cities in Eretz Israel: Relations of the Jews in Eretz Israel with the Hellenistic Cities during the Second Temple Period*, Tübingen, 1990
Knoblet J. *Herod the Great*, Lanham, MD, 2005
Kokkinos N. *The Herodian Dynasty: Origins, Role in the Society and Eclipse*, Sheffield, 1998
Landau T. *Out-heroding Herod: Josephus, Rhetoric and the Herod Narratives*, Leiden and Boston, 2006
Levick B. *Tiberius the Politician*, London, 1976
Levick B. *Claudius*, London, 1990

SELECT BIBLIOGRAPHY

Levine L.L. *Caesarea under Roman Rule*, Leiden, 1975
MacMullen R. *Enemies of the Roman Order: Treason, Unrest and Alienation in the Empire*, Cambridge, MA, 1966
Marshall B.A. *Crassus: A Political Biography*, Amsterdam, 1976
Martin R. *Understanding Local Autonomy in Judaea between 6 and 66 CE*, Lewiston, NY, 2006
McLaren J. S. *Power and Politics in Palestine: The Jews and the Governing of Their Land, 100 B.C. – A.D. 70*, Sheffield, 1991
McLaren J. S. *Turbulent Times? Josephus and Scholarship on Judaea in the First Century C.E.*, Sheffield, 1998
Millar F. *The Emperor in the Roman World: 31 BC – AD 337*, London, 1977
Millar F. *The Roman Near East, 31 B.C. – A.D. 337*, Cambridge, MA, 1993
Miller S. S. *Studies in the History and Traditions of Sepphoris*, Leiden, 1984
Myers E.A. *The Itureans and the Roman Near East: Reassessing the Sources*, Cambridge and New York, 2010
Paltiel, E. *Vassals and Rebels in the Roman Empire: Julio-Claudian Policies in Judaea and the Kingdoms of the East*, Brussels, 1991
Pucci Ben Zeev M. *Jewish Rights in the Roman World: The Greek and Roman Documents Quoted by Josephus Flavius*, Tübingen, 1998
Richardson P. *Herod: King of the Jews and Friend of the Romans*, Columbia, 1996
Rocca S. *Herod's Judaea: A Mediterranean State in the Classical World*, Tübingen, 2008
Rudich V. *Political Dissidence under Nero: The Price of Dissimulation*, London and New York, 1993
Rudich V. *Dissidence and Literature under Nero: The Price of Rhetoricization*, London and New York, 1997
Schwartz D. *Agrippa I: The Last King of Judaea*, Tübingen, 1990
Sievers J. *The Hasmoneans and Their Supporters: From Mattathias to the Death of John Hircanus I*, Atlanta, GA, 1990
Smallwood E.M. *The Jews under the Roman Rule: From Pompey to Diocletian, A Study in Political Relations*, Leiden, 1976
Udoh F. E. *To Caesar What Is Caesar's: Tribute, Taxes, and Imperial Administration in Early Roman Palestine (63 B.C.E. – 70 CE)*, Providence, RI, 2005
Zeitlin, S. *The Rise and Fall of the Jewish State: A Political, Social and Religious History of the Second Commonwealth*, vols I–III, Philadelphia, PA, 1962–1978

Flavius Josephus

Bilde P. *Flavius Josephus between Jerusalem and Rome: His Life, His Works, and Their Importance*, Sheffield, 1988
Cohen S. J. D. *Josephus in Galilee and Rome: His Vita and Development as a Historian*, Leiden, 1979
Feldman L., Hata G. (ed.) *Josephus, Judaism and Christianity*, Detroit, 1987
Feldman L., Hata G. (ed.) *Josephus, the Bible, and History*, Detroit, 1989
Hadas-Lebel M. *Flavius Josephus: Eyewitness to Rome's First-century Conquest of Judea*, Toronto and New York, 1993
Mader G. *Josephus asnd Politics of Historiography: Apologetics and Impression Management in Bellum Judaicum*, Leiden, 2000
Mason S. *Flavius Josephus on the Pharisees*, Leiden and New York, 1990

SELECT BIBLIOGRAPHY

Mason S. *Josephus and the New Testament*, Peabody, 1992
Mason S. (ed.) *Understanding Josephus: Seven Perspectives*, Sheffield, 1998
Mason S. *Josephus, Judea and Christian Origins: Methods and Categories*, Peabody, MA, 2009
Rajak T. *Josephus, the Historian and His Society*, Philadelphia, PA, 1984 (reprint London 2002)
Schwartz S. *Josephus and Judean Politics*, Leiden, 1990
Shutt R. J. H. *Studies in Josephus*, London, 1961
Thackeray, H. St. J. *Josephus, the Man and the Historian*, New York, 1929
Villaba i Varneda, P. *The Historical Method of Flavius Josephus*, Leiden, 1986

The Great Revolt

Aberbach M., Aberbach D. *The Roman–Jewish Wars and Hebrew Cultural Nationalism*, New York, 2000
Ben-Yehuda N. *The Masada Myth: Collective Memory and Mythmaking in Israel*, Madison, WI, 1995
Ben-Yehuda N. *Sacrificing Truth: Archaeology and the Myth of Masada*, Amherst, NY, 2002
Berlin A. M., Overman J. A. (ed.) *The First Jewish Revolt: Archaeology, History, and Ideology*, London and New York, 2003
Bohrmann M. *Flavius Josephus, the Zealots and Yavneh: Towards the Reading of 'The War of the Jews'*, Bern, 1994
Brighton M. A. *The Sicarii in Josephus's Judean War: Rhetorical Analysis and Historical Observations*, Leiden and Boston, 2009
Faulkner N. *Apocalypse: The Great Jewish Revolt against Rome*, Stroud, 2004
Furneaux R. *The Roman Siege of Jerusalem*, London, 1973
Hengel M. *The Zealots: Investigation into the Jewish Freedom Movement in the Period from Herod I until 70 A.D.*, Edinburgh, 1989
Jones, B. W. *The Emperor Titus*, London and New York, 1984
Kadman L. *The Coins of the Jewish War of 66–73 C.E.*, Tel-Aviv, 1960
Levick B. *Vespasian*, London and New York, 1999
Price J. J. *Jerusalem under Siege: The Collapse of the Jewish State, 60–70 CE*, Leiden and New York, 1992
Rhoads D. M. *Israel in Revolution, 6–74 CE: A Political History based on the writings of Josephus*, Philadelphia, PA, 1976
Yadin Y. *Masada: Herod's Fortress and the Zealots' Last Stand*, New York, 1966

SUBJECT INDEX

Achaia 135
Acrabatene 199, 206, 289
Acrabeta 287–88
Actium 93
Acts of the Pagan Martyrs 134
Adiabene 39, 70, 84
afterlife 16, 18, 23, 26, 273, 318
Alexandria 116–17, 120, 121, 134, 155, 253, 282, 283
Al-Qaeda 326
'ambiguous oracle' 314–15
am ha-aretz (rustic) 21
Amphitheatrum Flavianum (Coliseum) 323
anagke 274, 275, 277, 278 *anomie* 215, 242–43, 248, 249, 303
anti-Jewish policy 107–8, 116–17
anti-Jewish sentiment 326
Antioch 163
anti-Semitism 134, 326
Aphthia 221
apocalypse 56, 60, 61–62, 66, 314
Apostolic Council at Jerusalem, first 38
Apostolic generation 37
aqueduct 113
Arbela 94
Armenia 70, 109
Ascalon 164, 166, 172, 173, 179, 200, 209, 233, 236, 266, 288
asceticism 28
assassins 261, 262
Assyrians 35
Athens 45
atheoi 241
atomist gods 17

Baal-peor (god) 211–12
Babylonian exile 17, 35, 53, 62, 272, 276, 321

bandits *see* brigands
Batanea 163, 190
beguilements 205
Behemoth 65, 271
Berytus 97, 163, 186, 190
Beth-horon 88, 129, 153, 157, 161, 162, 182, 187, 198, 200, 213, 236, 238, 249, 287
blackmail 6, 87, 101, 246, 262, 281
blasphemy 90, 102, 118, 128, 150–51, 232, 259, 319
Book of Acts 21, 37–38, 56, 122, 123, 126, 133, 135, 138–39, 141, 143, 176, 257, 273
Book of Daniel 64
Book of Genesis 195
Book of Isaiah 56
Book of Job 270–71, 272, 274
Book of Kings 53
Book of Numbers 254
Book of Revelation 31; *see also* apocalypse
brigands 72, 94, 96, 103, 126, 129–31, 136, 137–38, 151, 165, 175, 178, 207, 210, 218, 255–56, 259, 260, 289, 296
Britannia 108
burial 231–32, 242–43, 295–96, 304–5, 311

Caesar Augustus *see* Augustus Caesar
Caesarea Maritima 39, 76, 76–88, 98, 106, 109, 111, 112, 123, 129, 131, 138–40, 142, 152, 155, 276, 286, 298, 315
Caesarea Philippi 160, 163, 298
'cannibalistic' imagery 294
capital punishment (*ius gladii*) 104, 106–7
Carrhae 91, 92
Carthage 84, 323

SUBJECT INDEX

Cathars 29
celibacy 26, 28
census (A.D. 6–7) 110, 127, 254, 255, 257
Chalcis 125
children's Crusade 6
Christian church, nascent 24, 32, 35, 37–38, 66, 86, 141, 169, 284, 326; as 'new superstition' 8–9; persecution by Nero 8–9, 56, 148–49
Chronicles 53
'Church triumphant' 326
circumcision 21, 38–39, 185, 211
citizen rights 76
civil disobedience 111–12, 118, 151
civil warfare 155, 233, 239, 251
civitas 6
coalition government *see* 'first regime'
Coele-Syria 91
coercitio 78, 106
cognitio extra ordinem 106, 139
coinage 208–9
Coliseum 323
collaboration 106, 109, 153, 159, 161, 162, 182, 183, 188, 196, 199, 245, 261, 272, 313; *see also* pro-Roman sentiment
collective historical memory 54
Commentarii (*Hypomnemata*) 42
composition criticism 47–49, 56
compromise 166–68
confiscation 248–49
contiones 204, 223
Corcyra 235
Corinth 135
corruption 108, 137, 150, 152, 181
Cos, god 229
cosmic apocalypse 61
counter-factual history 152, 324–26
crimen maiestatis 79, 97, 112, 142–43, 197
Crusades 5, 6
Cyrenaica, *sicarii* in 282, 284
Cyrene 253, 284

Dabaritta 187, 188, 189
Damascus 28
Day of Atonement 90
Dead Sea Scrolls 24, 27–29, 49, 56; *Book of Hagi* 34; *Book of Jubilees* 59; *Community Rule* or *Manual of Discipline* (1QS) 26, 28, 29; *Copper Scroll* (3Q15) 35; *Damascus Document* or *The Zadokite Fragment* (CD) 26, 28, 29, 30, 34;

The Halakhik Letter (4QMMT) 34; *Horoscope:* 4Q186*Cryptic* 34; *Songs of the Sabbath Sacrifice* (4Q) 35; *Temple Scroll* (11QT) 26, 30–31, 34; *War Scroll* (1QM) 30–33, 34, 60
death over life, privileging 274–75, 276
debellare superbos 323
Decalogue ('Ten Commandments') 37, 75, 98, 99, 241
Decapolis 39, 186
defection 109, 156, 158–59, 163, 164, 243, 297, 305–7
delator 197
democracy 202, 240–41
desertion 249–50, 305–8, 311, 318
Deuteronomy 17, 53
diarchy 217–18, 224, 233
Diaspora 11, 12, 14, 17, 18, 23, 45, 76, 84, 97, 99, 102, 108, 116, 121, 135, 150, 155, 193, 217, 242, 319, 324
dietary laws 22
dignitas 6, 80, 324
diminutio dignitatis 6
dissimulatio/dissimulation 6–7, 149, 159, 160, 188–89, 196, 200, 208, 219, 228, 295
divided loyalties 45, 165, 188–89, 200, 214, 291
dogmatism xxii
Dora 182
dreams 194–96, 311
Druidism 7
'dying in war' 192

Ecclesiastes 274
Egypt 23, 27, 276; *sicarii* in 282–84
Eighteen Halakhoth 70–71
ekklesia 225
Elders 283
Emmaus 173
emperor: sacrifices to 8, 20, 34, 68–76, 71, 73–74, 77, 81, 85, 87, 108, 115, 154, 157, 158, 162, 175–76, 199, 263; as state incarnate 6
Engaddi 266–67
Eniachin, priestly clan 221
Epicureans 16, 17
eschatology 26, 28, 31, 37, 52, 56, 60, 61, 62, 66, 202, 251, 264, 276, 300, 302, 305, 314, 317
esotericism 26, 33–34
Essa 173

SUBJECT INDEX

Essenes 12, 14–15, 16, 22, 23–28, 30, 32, 34, 37, 49, 66, 173, 192, 197, 202, 213, 279; theology 26
ethnography 275
ethos 326
Exodus 17, 64, 77, 126, 283
extortion 82, 86, 87

factionalism: Imperial court 96, 109, 127, 132, 134, 160, 161–62; rebels 46, 52, 67, 72, 103, 144–45, 162, 163, 167, 168, 171, 173, 174, 175, 176, 181, 183–84, 198–99, 201–5, 207–8, 210–11, 214, 215, 218–19, 226, 228, 233–34, 239–340, 244, 248–52, 263, 266, 282, 286–87, 289–90, 292, 294, 301–3, 305, 306, 307, 310, 313–14, 323, 325
famine 39, 119, 127, 237, 256, 294, 296, 302–5, 311, 323
fasting 185
Fate 16, 18
Festival of the Tabernacles 147
Festival of Wood-Carrying 74, 263
'first regime' 13, 159, 164–79, 182, 199–210, 214, 218, 219, 225, 226, 231, 233, 236, 245, 249, 266, 286, 288, 290, 293, 295
Fortune (Luck) 84, 320
'fourth philosophy' 14, 19, 38, 52, 56, 73, 94, 104, 110, 113, 117, 119, 127, 151, 152, 185, 213, 241, 254, 256–58, 263, 268, 271, 275, 282, 321
fundamentalism 4, 6

Gadara 209
Galilaeans, and Samaritans 72, 130
Galilee 39, 45–46; Josephus and 43, 48, 164, 170–71, 172, 176–98, 208, 209, 228, 245, 266, 288
Gamala 163, 181, 190, 209, 255
Gaul 108
Gaulantis 255
Gemara 308
general assembly 204
Gischala 181, 189–90, 228, 244
God: ally of Romans 271–72, 273, 275–76, 315, 320; appeals to 84; as cause 4, 8, 14, 51–52, 56, 60–61, 70, 147, 172, 194, 195, 256, 282, 290, 292–93, 298, 318, 323; Christ as 326; commandments of 37, 75, 98, 99, 241; communication with 2, 11, 32, 59–60, 65–67, 75, 110, 194, 196, 197, 213, 221, 250; covenant with 11, 29, 34, 38, 199; does not support violence 327; evil, exempt from involvement with 16–17; and human soul 192–93; intervention in human affairs 16–17, 31–32, 53, 62–63, 84, 118, 138, 143, 147, 155, 172, 190, 196, 218, 234, 236, 252, 269, 276, 283, 293, 299, 300–301, 302, 316, 323; justice/judgment of 218, 273, 275; Kingdom of earth 148; nature of 50–51, 323; obedience to 202; ordination by 214; punishment from 274, 283, 285, 293; relationship with Israel 270, 283; relationship with zealots 211–12, 250–52, 264; residence 36–37, 60, 93, 99–100, 114, 172; secular authority established by 56; and the Torah 31, 39; union with 34; will of 2, 5, 10, 16, 17, 22, 55, 66–67, 73, 213, 219, 221, 230, 232, 236, 241, 250, 258, 264, 270–71, 277, 280, 283, 290, 323; wrath of 261–62, 271–72, 273; zeal for 211–12
God-fearers 39
gods, pagan 8, 17, 21, 39, 51, 75, 108, 115, 123, 211–12, 229, 324
golden eagle, affair of 98–100, 101, 112
Gomorrah 247
Gophna 307
Gospels 16, 22–23, 55–56, 107, 111, 115, 169, 260, 299
Grace 38
Greco-Syrians 39–40, 156, 172
'gymnosophists' 275

Haggadah 308, 309
Halakhas 21, 55, 70–71, 279
Hebrew Bible (*Tanakh*) 37, 43, 53, 56, 58, 61, 196, 264, 271
Hebron 292
heresy 14, 37, 38
hermeneutic triangle xxi–xxii
heroism 280
hierarchy 10–11, 241
high priest/high priesthood 21, 105–6, 109, 110, 127, 144, 169, 196, 260, 290, 293; election of by lot (zealots) 219–23, 236, 239, 241
Hillel school 19, 20, 26, 51, 70–71, 309–10, 313

SUBJECT INDEX

historical causality xii–xiv
historical determinism xv
historical imagination xxii
historical narrative xxi–xxii, xxiii
historiography xiii, 20, 25; classical 308–9; composition criticism xxi; configuration xvii; ethical dimension xv–xvii; Greek 275; historian's socio-political-cultural environment xii–xiv ; literary-critical approach xix–xxi; objectivity xiii–xv; postmodern approaches xii–xxii, xix, xxiii, 312; and scholarship xix; 'virtual reality' outlook xxiii
history: interdisciplinary approaches to xxi; theology of 17, 283
holocaust 280
Holy of Holies 13, 90, 129, 225
homosexuality 247
hostages 45, 101, 126, 142, 182, 262
hypercriticism 13, 46, 232, 308

ideology 1, 33, 205, 206–7, 250, 251, 279
Idumaea 39, 76, 104–5, 166, 167, 198, 230, 252, 288, 289, 291–93
Idumaeans 95–96, 173, 174, 175, 229–31, 233, 243–44, 245, 293, 294, 295, 296, 297–98, 306
Imperial cult 8, 20, 34, 68–76, 71, 73–74, 77, 81, 85, 87, 108, 111–12, 115, 154, 157, 158, 162, 175–76, 199, 263
impiety 69, 102, 220, 222, 246, 261–62, 277, 295
impositionist interpretation 137
impostors 136, 141
indeterminism 17
Indians 274–75
Institutum Neronianum 8–9, 56, 148–49
isonomia 282

Jamnia 117
Jardes, forest of 298, 318
Jericho 103
Jerusalem: defensive wall 122, 141–42, 315, 316; desertion from 249–50, 305–8, 311, 318
Jerusalem garrison, slaughter of 46
Jewish elite, and Roman officialdom 106–9
Jewish-Gentile debate, Caesarea Maritima 139–40

Jewish identity 11–12
Jewish tax (*fiscus Judaicus*) 324
Jews: as chosen people 21, 305; equestrian rank 6, 80; expulsion of 135; monotheism 8; nationalism 67, 70, 73, 279, 287, 290; religious affairs 106–8, 117
Joppa 173
Jordan river 126
Jotapata 43, 164, 178, 191–92, 209, 267, 277, 278, 315
Judaism 241, 270; attitudes to human condition 202; attitudes towards kingship 105; covenantal nomism 12; as exclusivist 22; future of 311–12, 325–26; Hellenistic influences 12; missionary dimension of 38–39; normative 256; 'official' 250; purity of 256–57; rabbinic 326; religious establishment 12–13; Roman tolerance of 317; status of 8; tolerance of 107–8
'Judaizers' 111
Judah, tribe of 63
Judges 110, 221, 258
Jupiter Capitolinus (god) 21, 115, 324
Jupiter, priest of (*flamen Dialis*) 21

kidnappings 72, 146, 254, 262
kingship, Jesus of Nazareth 142–43; in Judaism 105; Simon b. Giora 289, 299–300
Kisson 212
Kittim 31
koinon 225
Koran 16

Law *see* Mosaic Law 225
Legion X 239, 281, 313
Leviathan 65, 271
Levites 13, 14, 62, 63, 69
lex Cornelia de sicariis et veneficiis 253
liberalism xiv, 215–16
liberty 201–2
life over death, privileging 282
liminality 243
Luke, Gospel of 115
Lydda 131, 173

Maccabean Revolt (167 B.C.) 10, 36, 39, 64, 115, 155, 192, 322, 325
Macedon 84
Machaerus 269, 281–82, 318

SUBJECT INDEX

Mamertine prison 300
marriage 26, 28, 29, 31
martyrdom 192, 213, 267, 280, 283–84
Masada 35, 74, 193, 194, 198, 206, 216, 253, 254, 258, 263, 265–85, 287, 288, 313, 319; see also *sicarii*
'Masada myth' 279
Masoretic Text 36
massacres 79–80; Roman garrison 75–76, 154–55, 164, 167, 185, 189, 213, 232, 249; *see also* Masada
Mauretania Caesariensis 145
Messianic complex 63, 64, 66, 74, 103, 299
Messianic movements 114, 115
Messianism 17, 33, 38, 52, 56, 60, 62–66, 126, 191, 196–97, 251, 258, 264, 274, 289, 290, 298, 299, 314–15
metempsychosis 193
millenarianism 63
Mishnah 13, 18, 20, 21, 40, 54–55, 113, 176, 308, 313, 323
Moabite women 211–12
'moderates' 140, 154, 159, 167, 170, 172–76, 179, 185, 199–200, 207, 209, 218, 223, 227–28, 229, 229–30, 231, 233, 235, 238, 243, 246, 290, 310, 313
monotheism 5, 8, 16, 38, 50, 321
Mosaic Law 35, 38, 39, 58, 75, 77, 84, 98, 100, 139, 161, 176, 187–88, 202, 279, 290, 295, 298, 305
Moslem militant religious dissent 326–27
mos maiorum 6
Mount Asamon 157
Mount Gerizim 35, 36, 37, 82, 113, 191
Mount of Olives 138, 239
mysticism 34, 56–62

Nabataeans 114–15
Narbata 77
nationalism 67, 70, 73, 279, 287, 290
Nazi genocide 321
necromancy 16
neutrality 167, 175, 209, 307, 322–23
New Covenant *see* Dead Sea Scrolls, *Damascus Document* or *The Zadokite Fragment*
New Testament 17, 18, 21, 22–23, 33, 40, 47, 49, 52, 54, 105, 110, 122, 126, 143
Numidia 108

oaths 68, 75, 98, 317, 318
Old Testament 33, 43, 56, 58, 61, 147, 192, 193, 196, 197, 250, 270, 280, 283
'omnipotence of thought' 299
Ophlas 265
optimi 183
Oral Torah/tradition 13, 15–16, 21, 193

Passover (Pesah) 13, 101–2, 128, 267
pax deorum 8
pax Romana 187
Pentateuch 36–37, 279
Pentecost (Shavuot) 13, 102–3
Peraea 103, 125
Persia 325
Pharisees 12, 13, 14, 14–16, 17–23, 26, 27, 51, 63, 69, 71, 98, 105, 106, 109, 172, 173, 175–76, 177, 179, 192, 193, 197, 198, 202, 213, 238, 254, 256, 270, 273, 279, 310, 313
Philadelphia 125
Philistines 280
pilgrimage 5, 13
pillage 86, 140, 184–85, 207, 236, 248–49, 288, 292
Platonism 193
pogroms 79–80, 116–17, 155, 187, 282
politeia 201
political science xvii–xviii
politicization 322
polytheism 8
Prague school xxii
prayers 13, 14, 134
priesthood/priests 7, 13–14, 15, 18–19, 30, 31, 37, 63, 67, 132, 238, 322
priestly vestments 114, 125, 134
profiteering 256
prophecies and oracles 16, 25, 26, 60–66, 113–14, 194–98, 231, 241–42, 305, 310, 311, 314–15
prophet(s) 113–14, 147, 250–51, 261, 299, 314; false 32, 33, 137, 141, 284, 316; Josephus as 192, 194–96
pro-Roman sentiment 155–56, 162, 166, 167, 178, 179, 182, 183, 189, 322–23; *see also* collaboration
proselytes 12, 21, 38–9, 134, 287
Providence *see* Fate
provocatio 106, 142
Pseudepigrapha 17, 31, 33, 40, 54, 56–62, 211, 250, 273; *Apocalypse of*

341

SUBJECT INDEX

Baruch (2 **Baruch**) 58; *Book of Jubilees* 59; *Psalms of Solomon* 58, 59, 64; *Second (Syriac) Baruch* 65; *Testament of Levi* 62; *Testament of Moses* 58
Ptolemais 39
public archives 74, 248, 263
public worship, as mandatory 8
purity, ritual 21–22, 28, 31
Pythagoreans 16, 23, 202

Qumran 13, 14, 15, 24–25, 28, 59–60, 241, 265, 279; archaeology 28–29; cemetery 28–29, 30; history 28, 30; luxury items at 28, 29; Messiahs 63; pottery production at 28, 30; toilets 28, 31
Qumran community 24–25, 37, 55, 280

rabbinic Judaism 326
rabbinic writings 193; Herod Agrippa I in 121–22; Josephus absent from 313
rabbinism 20
rabbis: and Pharisees 17; and purity 21, 22; on self-sacrifice 279–80
radicals 62, 69, 76–77, 117, 123–24, 141, 144, 146, 155, 159, 165, 167–68, 172–73, 175, 178, 181, 184–85, 189, 199–200, 201, 205, 206, 207, 209, 256, 263, 266, 275, 277, 280, 290, 296, 310, 312–13, 321–22; *see also* zealots
reductionism xxiii
relativism xxii
religio antiqua 8
religio illicita 8
religion, political agenda 3–4
religious extremism 6
religious freedom 7, 8, 107–8, 117, 133, 134, 141, 150
religious toleration 7–8, 317
res republica 201
resurrection of the dead 16, 18, 273
rhetoric xix–xxi, 24–25; Josephus's use of 100, 101, 201–5, 270, 272–77, 278, 281–82, 293–95, 296, 303, 314, 315, 316, 317
Rhodes 94, 96
Roman Church 6
Roman garrison, massacre of 75–76, 154–55, 164, 167, 185, 189, 213, 232, 249
Romanizing 207, 208, 236, 246, 249, 266, 291

Romans Jewish policy 317, 322; law 79; legionary *signum* 99; officialdom, and Jewish elite 106–9; religion 7–8; treatment of deserters 323–24
Rome: civil warfare 233, 239, 251; expansionism 89; Great Fire of 9, 85–86, 148

Sabbath 14, 75, 84, 108, 154, 167, 213, 232
sacred/sacredness 5, 36–37, 77, 90–91, 118, 128, 326; animals 113; of birds 77; of humans 280; Imperial 8, 20, 34, 68–76, 71, 73–74, 77, 81, 85, 87, 108, 111–12, 115, 154, 157, 158, 162, 175–76, 199, 263; sacrifice 141; *tamid* (daily sacrifice) 306, 315
sacrilege 19, 77–78, 90–92, 93, 116–17, 129, 134, 167, 212, 232, 261–62, 265, 267, 317
Sadducees 12, 14–17, 18, 19, 21, 22, 27, 51, 69, 105, 106, 109, 169, 172, 173, 213, 218, 295
sages 23
Samaria 36, 76, 98, 128, 131, 191, 287
Samaritan Book of Joshua 37
Samaritanism 35–37
Samaritan problem 14
Samaritans 39, 72, 76, 104, 111, 123, 130–32, 260; Pilate and 113–14
sanctuary *see* Temple of Jerusalem
Sanhedrin 13, 20–21, 54–55, 92, 94, 98, 105, 106, 143, 165, 205, 257
scribes 14, 22–23
Scriptures 25, 36–37
Scythopolis 155–56, 276
Sebaste 36, 76, 97, 98, 123
Sebastenian troops 36, 76, 109, 131
secessio 7
'second regime' 215, 233, 238, 243, 251, 287, 290–91
secret knowledge 34
seditio/sedition 78, 139
Seleucids 36
self-justification 7, 186, 232, 247
self-sacrifice *see* suicide
semantic breakdown 142–43
senatorial governors 324
Sepphoris 103, 155, 178, 254
Septuagint 211, 280
Shammai school 19, 20, 26, 51, 70–71, 73, 152, 238, 256, 273, 309

Shechem 35, 62, 211
Sheol 16
sicarii 27, 72, 73, 127, 137, 138, 141, 145, 146, 148, 152, 167, 179, 206, 210, 213–15, 219, 244, 246, 253–54, 258, 259, 261, 262, 281, 284, 290, 310, 326; in Cyrenaica 282, 284; in Egypt 282–84; at Masada 263, 265–85, 287, 288, 319; piety 279–80; shed blood in Temple 261–62, 265; study of Scriptures 270, 310
Sidon 119
signs (*semea*) 32
Sinai, revelation at 11, 17
Sodom 247
'sons of Belial' 31, 58
'Sons of Darkness' 26
'sons of Hamor' 62
'Sons of Light' 26
'sons of Zadok' 30
sophists 254, 258
soul, the, immortality of 16, 18, 26, 192–93, 273, 274, 277
sources: argument from silence 40–41, 52; composition criticism xxi, 47–49, 56; fictional component 47–48; Flavius Josephus 42–54; form and style 37, 41–42, 47–48, 56; inductive reasoning 41; Josephus' treatment of 48–49
spirits 32
Stoicism 193, 273, 279
Stoics 16, 18, 202; *summum bonum* 17
Strato's Tower *see* Caesaria Maritima
suicide 7, 84, 156, 192–94, 213, 216, 253, 267–68, 277, 278–82, 313, 319
synagogues 121; sacrilege against 116–17
synedrion see Sanhedrin
Syria 107, 276
Syrians 76, 139–40, 155, 163

Taliban 326
Talmud 55, 153, 308, 309, 310, 313; Simon b. Gamaliel in 176–79
tamid (daily sacrifice) 306, 315
Tannaim period 54
Tannaitic works 17, 22, 40, 49, 52, 55, 70, 211, 222, 280, 308; *Sanhedrin* 106
Tarichaeae 136, 185, 187, 188, 189
Temple in Leontopolis 284
Temple meeting 168, 174, 175, 176, 179, 203, 205, 207, 213, 217–18, 219, 238, 287

Temple Mount 89–90, 239–40
Temple of Jerusalem 14, 28, 31, 32, 38, 63, 64, 67, 72, 101–2, 141–42, 150, 294; blood shed in 261–62, 265; Caligula's personal cult 107, 112, 115–20, 134; completed under Herod Agrippa II 149; Court of the Gentiles 81; cult of 13, 25; desecration of 19, 74–75, 77–78, 90–92, 93 115–20, 196, 225, 236, 257; destruction of 22, 40, 53, 65, 256, 269, 280, 296, 297, 300, 302–3, 312, 316, 317, 319–20, 325; and Herod 98; Holy of Holies 13, 90, 129, 225; holy wine and oil 246–47; Imperial sacrifices 8, 20, 34, 68–76, 71, 73–74, 77, 81, 85, 87, 108, 111–12, 115, 154, 157, 158, 162, 175–76, 199, 263; money for 108; new and perfect 26; survival of 325–26; *tamid* (daily sacrifice) 306, 315; treasure 78–79, 80, 90, 91, 102–3, 160, 223, 224, 232, 238, 247; wall 85; worship 199; zealot occupation of 239, 240, 296, 298–99
Temple of Peace 324
Temple of Solomon 320
Temple tax 113, 324
terrorism 234–35, 249, 259, 261, 262
Thamna 173
theocracy 10, 110, 268
theocratic aristocracy 105
theology 277, 279–80, 323; Essenes 26; of history 17, 283; of inscrutability 270–71; Sadducees 16
Therapeutae 23
third faction 183
Thrace 108, 109
Tiberias 115, 118, 123, 136, 161, 163, 172, 178, 181, 183–89
Torah 13, 14, 15–16, 18, 20, 21, 22, 31, 35, 38, 39, 51, 55, 129, 193, 211, 241, 243, 247, 250, 277, 279, 290, 300, 310; removal of 77–78; sanctity of 11
Torah scrolls 108
Tosefta 71, 144, 222
Trachonitis 185
tradition 18, 256–57, 279; oral 13, 15–16, 21, 193
transvestism 247
treason 79, 97, 142–43, 197
tribute payments 71, 73, 78, 85, 91, 255, 324
Tyre 131
Tyrians 163

SUBJECT INDEX

visionary 30–31, 33, 40, 43, 54, 56–62, 197

wishful thinking 18, 22, 23, 30, 48, 54, 56, 66, 67, 106, 159, 182, 189, 198, 200–201, 202, 208, 213, 216, 225, 227, 241, 248, 250, 264, 283, 299, 323

xenophobia 156

Yavneh Academy 13, 20, 22, 52, 309, 311–12, 313

Yom Kippur (Day of Atonement) 13, 185

Zadokids 15
Zadokite priests 30

zeal 38, 52, 62, 73, 181, 184, 211–12

zealots 145, 148, 155, 161, 164, 167–68, 172, 173, 205, 207, 233, 258, 281, 286, 289, 290, 291, 292, 293, 298, 305, 326; campaign of terror 234–35; *coup d'état* 13, 174, 238, 249, 266, 295; election of high priest by lot 219–23, 236, 239, 241; government of Jerusalem 240–41; in historiographical tradition 215–16; occupation of temple 239, 240, 296, 298–99; relationship with God 250–52, 264; use of term 210–15

zelotai 210–11

NAME INDEX

Aaron 15, 211, 309
Abraham 250, 270
Absalom 265
Aelius Aristides, *Orationes Sacrae* 195
Aequus Modius 163
Agrippina 132, 134
Akiba, rabbi 55, 63, 280, 309
Alcibiades 92, 229
Alexander Jannaeus 101
Alexander, son of Herod I 96, 104
Alexander the Great 54
Alexandra, mother of Mariamne I 96
Aliturus 136
Ananias, a 'villain and evildoer' 185
Ananias b. Masbalus 296
Ananias b. Nedebaeus 68, 71, 72, 73, 75, 132–33, 144, 146, 162, 206, 260, 262, 264
Ananias, son of Sadok 177
Ananus b. Ananus 15, 72–73, 132, 143, 144, 164, 167, 168–73, 174, 175, 176, 177, 178, 179, 201, 203, 204, 205, 206, 207, 208, 215, 217, 218, 219, 220, 222–23, 224, 225–27, 231–32, 245, 246, 260, 287–88, 290
Ananus b. Bagadatus of Emmaus 295, 297, 306
Ananus b. Jonathan 157
Annas (Ananus b. Sethi) 169, 257, 260
Annius Rufus 110
Antiochus IV Epiphanes 10, 64, 115, 280, 312, 322
Antipater I 89, 92, 94, 255
Antipater III 96–97
Antonia 134
Antonius Felix 77–82, 124, 127, 128, 130, 132, 133, 136–40, 144, 149, 152, 253, 259, 260–61, 284

Aquila 135
Archaelaus b. Magaddatus 297, 306
Aristeus from Emmaus 296
Aristobulus III 221
Aristobulus IV 96
Aristotle 41, 202
Artemidorus, *Oneirocritica* 195
Athronges, a shepherd 103, 300
Augustine, St., *De civ. Dei* 5
Augustus Caesar 68, 76, 78–79, 91, 92, 93–94, 96, 97, 99, 104, 107, 112, 117, 121, 125, 149; *Ara Pacis* 324

Bakhtin, Mikhail xxii, 242
Bannus 24
Barrabas 111
Barthes, Roland xxi–xxii
Berenice, Queen of Chalcis 80, 81, 143, 161
Beryllus 140
Bloch, Marc xv, xvi, xix
Buber, Martin 326
Burckhardt, Jacob xx

Caligula *see* Gaius Caligula 160
Carr, E. H. xiii
Cassius Dio 42, 134–35, 318
Cassius Longinus 92, 125
Catullus, governor of Lybian Pentopolis 284–85
Ceagiras, warrior 316–17
Celer 132
Cestius Gallus 81, 82–83, 87–88, 129, 152, 157, 158, 160, 162, 163, 172, 181, 182, 203, 205, 206, 213, 223, 236, 287; *consilium* 157, 319
Chariton, *Chaereas and Callirhoe* xx
Christ *see* Jesus of Nazareth

NAME INDEX

Churchill, Winston xviii
Cicero xvii, 202
Claudius 73, 82, 96, 120, 121, 122, 123, 124, 126, 127, 128, 132, 140, 151, 191, 235, 260; Jewish policy 133–35; *Letter to the Alexandrians* 121, 134, 141; 'new imperialism' 125
Cleopatra 85, 93, 95
Collingwood, R. G., *The Idea of History* xiii
Constantine 326
Coponius 104–5, 110
Costobar b. Antipater 144, 158, 162, 173, 223, 249
Costobar I 95
Crassus 91–92
Crispus 188
Cuspius Fadus 125–26

Daniel 195
Darius, the hipparch 74
David, king 63, 64, 103, 254, 264, 292, 300
Deliverer figure 56, 62, 63, 299
de Tocqueville, Alexis xx
Dinah 62
Dodd, Eric 57
Doetus 131
Domitius Corbulo 197
Doras 261
Drusilla 159

Egyptian adventurer 141
Egyptian 'false prophet' 56, 138
Eleazar b. Ananias 52, 68–69, 71–76, 75, 133, 146, 154, 157, 167, 168, 169, 206, 210, 238, 240, 244, 249, 254, 262, 263, 264, 265, 310, 321
Eleazar b. Deinaeus 127, 130, 137
Eleazar b. Jarius 74, 240, 253, 254, 258, 265, 267, 268, 269, 288; first suicide speech 268, 269, 271–72, 275, 280; second suicide speech 273–77, 280
Eleazar b. Simon 74, 167–68, 200, 205, 207, 214, 218, 219, 224, 229, 233, 238–41, 243, 244, 245, 246, 248, 251, 266, 286, 287, 290, 291, 293, 296, 301, 314, 318
Eleazar, Machaerus rebel 281–82
Eliade, Mircea 5, 36, 57
Elijah 212, 232
Epictetus 279
Epicurus 16, 17

Erasmus 313
'eschatological prophet' 63, 321
Evans, Richard, *In Defense of History* xii
'exiles of the wilderness' 31, 32
Ezechias, 'archbrigand' 74, 94, 133, 254–55
Ezechias b. Chobari 240
Ezechias b. Nedebaeus 264
Ezra 13, 35

Ferdinand of Aragon 321
Ferdowsi, *Shahnameh* 54
Ferguson, Niall 324
Flavius Josephus *see* Josephus
Flavius Silva Nonnius Bassus 268
Florus *see* Gessius Florus
Fukuyama, Francis xviii

Gaddis, John Lewis xv
Gaius Caligula 8, 19, 107, 108, 109, 115, 117, 120–21, 124, 129, 130, 134, 142, 149, 150, 151, 160, 282, 312, 317; Agrippa's banquet 122–23; personal cult 107, 112, 115–20, 134
Gaius Marius 92
Galba 161, 286
Gamaliel I (the Elder) 21, 126, 257
Gandhi 313
Gephthaeus, warrior 316–17
Gessius Florus 71, 72, 77, 87, 129, 139, 140, 145, 146, 148, 150, 152, 153, 154, 161, 162, 225, 257, 263, 325
Girard, René 5
Gorion b. Joseph 202, 208, 223, 235

Hadrian 312, 321, 324
Hanania b. Hezekiah b. Garon, rabbi 70–71
Hasmonaean family 10, 12, 15, 64, 161, 196, 221, 284
Helena, queen 39
Herennius Capito 117
Herod Agrippa I 108, 112, 115, 116, 119, 120–24, 121–22, 134, 151, 159, 160, 184, 223, 231, 246, 260, 273, 315; banquet 122–23; death of 123–24; lecture at Jerusalem 277–78
Herod Agrippa II 68, 71, 73, 74, 78, 80, 81, 82, 91, 108, 125, 126, 127, 132, 134, 143, 149, 151, 162, 163, 181, 186, 187, 188, 190, 300, 320; authority 159–60; palace in Jerusalem 141–42;

NAME INDEX

religious sensibilities 160–61; speech 83–85
Herod Antipas 102, 115, 122, 124, 160, 172; fall of 115, 223, 224–25; palace at Tiberias 184–85; trial of Jesus 115
Herod Antipas III 236
Herod Archaelaus 101–2, 104, 124, 125, 160, 254
Herod I (the Great) 18, 27, 36, 39, 58, 66, 76, 84, 89, 105, 109, 120, 121, 122, 123, 124, 159, 162, 221, 229, 255, 257, 263, 268, 281, 300, 321; accession 92–94; affair of the golden eagle 98–100, 101, 112; building project 97–98; cultural and religious attitudes 97–98; death and legacy 101; extermination of Jewish notables 100–101; foreign policy 95–96; Massacre of the Innocents 101; murder of family 93, 95, 96–97; protectionist policies 97–98; and the Temple of Jerusalem 98
Herod V of Chalcis 125, 127
Herodian family 10, 12, 62, 78, 159–60, 161–62, 196, 217, 220.223–25, 229, 236, 249; monarchy abolished 105
Herodias 115
Herodotus 47
Homer 16

Isaac 270
Isabella of Castile 321
Isaiah 53
Ishmael b. Phiabi 142, 144, 306
Izates II 39

Jacob 44, 62
Jairus b. Judas 258
James b. Judas 127, 254, 258
James b. Sosas 230–31, 291–92, 293, 296, 297, 306
James b. Zebedee 143
James, St 122
James the Just 107, 143, 169, 206
James, William 57
Jephthah and his daughter 270
Jeremiah 53, 147, 195, 196
Jesus b. Ananias 147–48, 198, 314
Jesus b. Damnaeus 144, 162, 169, 306
Jesus b. Gamala 144, 162, 169, 173, 173–75, 206, 223, 230, 231
Jesus b. Gamaliel *see* Jesus b. Gamala

Jesus b. Sapphias 183, 184, 187–88, 189–90, 198
Jesus of Nazareth 37, 55–56, 63, 126, 135, 148, 197, 273, 299, 326; as king 142–43; trial and Crucifixion 111, 115, 169
Jesus, the 'arch-brigand' 178, 182
Jesus the Galilaean 204
Jezebel 232
Joazar b. Boethus 257
Joesdrus, son of Nomicus 177
Johanan b. Zakkai 22, 52, 71, 106, 117, 158, 250, 308, 309–13
John, apostle 56
John b. Dorcas 224
John b. Levi of Gischala 52, 171, 174, 176, 177, 178–79, 182, 183, 184, 189–90, 198, 210, 214, 228–29, 233, 239–40, 241, 243, 244–45, 250, 251, 266, 286, 287, 289–90, 292, 293, 294–95, 296, 298, 299, 301, 302, 314, 315
John b. Sosas 230, 231
John Hyrcanus I 15, 36, 39, 95, 229
John Hyrcanus II 89–90, 91, 92, 93, 94, 255
John the Baptist 55, 63, 115, 126, 138, 147, 197
John the Essene 27, 173, 179
John the tax collector 77
Jonathan b. Ananus 131, 132, 133, 137, 253, 260–62
Jonathan Maccabaeus 30, 221, 268, 325
Jonathan the Weaver 284
Jonathan (*Vita*) *see* Joesdrus, son of Nomicus
Joseph b. Gamala 200–201
Joseph b. Gorion 168
Joseph b. Matthias *see* Josephus
Joseph Caiapha 169, 260
Joseph Kabi b. Simon 169, 306
Joseph, revolutionary 190
Josephus: absent from rabbinic corpus 313; address at Jotapata 277; *Antiquitates Judaicae* (*Antiquities of the Jews*) 19, 42–43, 48, 49, 51, 72, 86, 94, 98–99, 100, 103, 113–14, 116, 118, 125, 128, 129, 131, 132, 136, 137, 138, 140, 141–42, 144, 146, 149, 153, 159, 162, 165, 169, 170, 173, 174, 213, 253, 254, 255, 256, 259, 260, 261, 324; apologetic agenda 20, 70, 186–87, 199, 201, 203, 208, 217, 241, 251, 256, 268, 273, 312; approach to numbers 230,

347

NAME INDEX

234, 235, 267, 304, 307, 323;
audience/readership 44–45, 48, 50–51, 72, 156, 164, 180, 192, 196, 203, 207, 217, 241, 243, 246, 247, 268, 271, 273, 279, 284, 314; *Bellum Judaicum (The Jewish War)* 19, 25, 26, 27, 28, 42, 44, 46, 48, 49, 51, 53, 56, 68, 76, 80, 81, 86, 88, 94, 111, 116, 125, 128, 129, 131, 135, 136–38, 140, 145, 146, 149, 153, 154, 158, 159, 162, 163, 165, 166, 171, 173, 174, 176, 177, 178, 179–81, 180, 182, 184, 186, 188, 189, 190, 191, 193, 194, 195, 196, 201, 204, 208, 210, 212, 213, 216–17, 222, 223, 226, 228, 236, 245, 246–47, 249, 253, 254, 255, 256, 259, 260, 261, 262, 268, 268–69, 272, 275, 277, 278, 280, 284, 287, 289, 290, 298, 301, 303, 305, 308, 313–14, 315, 317, 319, 324; *Bellum Judaicum (The Jewish War)*: Aramaic version 45; biblical discursive procedures 53; character of 44; Christian interpolations 40, 319; *Contra Apionem (Against Apion)* 43, 50, 251, 273; in Galilee 43, 48, 164, 170–71, 172, 176–79, 179–98, 208, 209, 228, 245, 266, 288; as historian xx, xxii, xxiv, 19, 45–47, 48, 83, 95, 100, 101, 112–13, 128, 132, 136, 164–66, 170–71, 176, 179–80, 191–92, 193, 206, 209, 210, 216–18, 220, 223, 225, 229, 230, 232, 234–35, 236, 241–42, 243, 267, 268, 269–70, 271, 281–82, 288, 291, 303, 305, 313, 319–20; impeachment 170–71, 176–77, 204–5, 245, 284; literary techniques 49–54; as mediator and negotiator 45, 315; mental processes 54; narrative strategies 47–48, 234–35; obfuscation 40–41, 46, 48, 51, 167, 180, 183, 205, 209, 210, 217, 220, 244–45, 251, 279, 296, 300, 313; polemical reversal 51–52; political bias 157–59; political vocabulary 210, 262–63; as prophet 192, 194–96; psychologizing 51–52, 269, 273, 314; in Rome 136, 149, 284; as source 42–54; speeches 315; survival in cave 194, 315; treatment of sources 48–49; use of rhetoric 100, 101, 201–5, 270, 272–77, 278, 281–82, 293–95, 296, 303, 314, 315, 316, 317; *Vita (The Life)* 19, 43, 45–46, 48, 49, 76, 149, 163–64, 165, 170–71, 174, 176–79, 179–81, 182, 186, 187, 188, 189, 190, 195, 203, 204, 228, 234, 245, 246, 253, 284
Josephus b. Dalaeus 318
José, rabbi 309
Joshua b. Gamaliel *see* Jesus b. Gamala
Jozar 'of the priestly family' 177
Jucundus 77
Judah the Prince 308
Judas Aristobulus II 89–90, 92
Judas Aristobulus III 93
Judas b. Ari 318
Judas b. Arinus 240
Judas b. Chelcias 240
Judas b. Ezechias 103–4, 182, 254, 255
Judas b. Judes 296–97
Judas b. Sariphaeus (or Sepphoraeus) 99–100
Judas Maccabaeus 63, 325
Judas, son of Jonathan 177
Judas the Galilaean 19, 56, 63, 73, 94, 104, 110, 111, 126, 127, 182, 213, 214, 241, 254, 255, 256, 257–58, 263, 264, 268
Julia Berenice 159
Julius Caesar 54, 92, 107, 117, 149
Julius Capella 183
Julius Lupus 284
Junius Gallio 135, 139
Justus b. Pistus *see* Justus of Tiberias
Justus of Tiberias 43, 163, 165, 180, 183, 185–87, 188–89, 190, 198, 217, 234, 246

Kerenyi, Karl 57

Levi 211
Levias 224
Lucan 7, 49
Lucceius Albinus 72, 86, 143, 144, 145–47, 162, 262, 284, 320
Lucilius Bassus 281–82, 298, 318

Magassarus, warrior 316–17
Maimonides, Moses 326
Malthace, wife of Herod I 101
Manasseh, king 53
Mannaeus b. Lazarus 304
Man of Lie (the Liar) 28
Marcellus 114
Marcus Ambibulus 110
Mariamne I 92, 93, 104

NAME INDEX

Mariamne II 96
Mark Antony 92, 93
Marx, Karl xviii
Mattathias Antigonus 92
Matthias b. Ananus 260
Matthias b. Boethus 293, 295–96; unnamed son of 306
Matthias b. Margalothus (or Margalus) 99–100
Matthias b. Theophilus 68, 220, 222, 306
Matthias, father of Josephus 174
Megasthenes 275
Meir, rabbi 309
Meirus b. Belgas 318
Menachem b. Judas 73, 74, 158, 167, 179, 206, 210, 214, 244, 253, 254, 258, 263–66, 290
Messiah of Aaron 63
Messiah of Israel 63
Metilius 185
Michelet, Jules xx
Monigliano, Arnaldo 312
Moses 31, 114, 126, 211–12, 250

Napoleon Bonaparte xvii
Nathan 53
Nebuchadnezzar 196, 320
Nehemiah 13
Neopolitanus 81, 87
Nero 6, 7, 8, 66, 70, 77, 79, 82, 83, 84, 85–86, 87, 96, 108, 124, 133, 135–36, 140, 142, 145, 150, 151, 153, 160, 162, 164, 197, 223, 233, 239, 247, 251, 252, 259, 286, 317, 312; persecution of Christians 8–9, 56, 148–49
Neronias 160
Nicolaus of Damascus 50
Niger of Peraea 164, 166, 173, 179, 236
Noarus/Varus 161, 163, 164, 190

Octavian *see* Caesar Augustus
Odysseus 44, 195–96
Olympian Games 98
Onias III 15
Onias IV 15, 284
Otho 161, 286
Otto, Rudolf 5, 270

Pallas 124, 128, 132, 133, 140, 260
Paul, St. 21, 38, 106, 135, 138–39, 142–43, 147, 148–49, 273, 312
Peter, apostle 56, 122, 135, 148

Petronius 7, 49, 114, 116, 118–20, 121, 122, 129, 131
Phasael 92
Pheroras 96
Philip b. Jacimus 74, 158, 162–64, 190, 249, 265
Philip, son of Herod I 102, 115
Philo 12, 23, 24, 25, 27, 32, 40, 111, 112, 116–20, 127, 130, 193, 282, 321; *Legatio* 118, 119, 150
Phineas b. Clusoth 230, 231
Phineas (Pinhas) 211–12
Phineas b. Samuel 221–22
Photius, *Bibliotheca* 186
Pilate *see* Pontius Pilate
Plato 11, 193, 202, 273
Pliny the Elder 25
Polybius xx, 45, 46
Pompey 58, 64, 84, 90–91, 92, 93, 115, 129, 150–51, 225, 257
Pontius Pilate 19, 82, 110–14, 118, 121, 124, 125, 126, 129, 130, 132, 151, 191; aqueduct project 113; Crucifixion, role in 111; military standards in Jerusalem 111–12, 113; and the Samaritans 113–14
Poppaea Sabina 83, 85, 86, 87, 136, 142, 144, 149, 160
Porcius Festus 85, 124, 141–43, 151, 262, 273
Priscilla 135
Ptolemy 187

Quinctilius Varus 102–3, 104, 109, 124, 255

Rabin, Yitzhak 326
Ranke, Leopold von xix, xx
Ricouer, Paul xxii, 5
Rose, Gideon xviii
Rufus, Faenius 7

Sabinus 102–3
Saddok the Pharisee 19, 213, 254, 255, 257, 268
Salome Alexandra 15, 18, 89
Salome I 95, 96
Samson 192, 194, 280
Samuel 16
Saul b. Antipater 144, 158, 162, 173, 223, 249
Saul b. Bitnit 144

349

NAME INDEX

Saul, king 16
Scholem, Gershom 57
Sejanus 111
Seneca 7, 49, 135, 149, 202, 279;
  Apocolocyntosis 235
Sextus Cerialis 191
Silas the Babylonian 164, 166, 173
Simeon 211
Simon b. Arinus 240
Simon bar Kokhba 55, 63, 301, 323, 324, 325
Simon b. Cathlas 175, 201, 230–31, 296
Simon b. Erson 240
Simon b. Gamaliel 19, 171, 206, 223; *Rabban* 176–79; in Talmudic tradition 176–79
Simon b. Giora 199, 206, 214, 230, 231, 233, 239–40, 243, 244, 245, 246, 250, 251, 252, 266, 286, 287–301, 301, 314, 318; claim to kingship 289, 299–300; command structure of 296–98; execution of 300; religious sensibilities of 290, 292–93, 298–99; surrender of 298–99, 300–301; wife of 292, 301, 398
Simon b. Judas 254, 258
Simon b. Saul 156–57
Simon Maccabaeus 221, 325
Simon, son of Jonathan 177
Simon, son of Judas the Galilaean 127
Simon the Peraean 103
Simon the Zealot 55
Sosius 92, 93
Stephen, Christian martyr 107, 143
Suetonius 42, 50, 135
Sulla 92, 253
Sulpicius Quirinius 105, 110, 124, 127, 254
Sulpicius Severus 319
Syphas b. Aregetes 224

Tacitus xix, xx, 9, 25, 42, 45, 50, 86, 103, 114, 128–32, 130, 131, 133, 135, 136, 137, 138, 145, 233, 236, 284, 302, 319 ; *Annales* 148, 235
Teacher of Righteousness 28, 30
Theophilus b. Ananus 260
Theudas 56, 63, 126, 138, 141, 257, 258
Thrasea Paetus 7, 8, 273
Thucydides xix, xx, 20, 25, 45, 46, 52, 53, 54, 77, 152, 175, 201, 229, 235, 236, 255

Tiberius 82, 96, 108, 110–11, 114, 115, 125, 126, 134
Tiberius Alexander 124, 126–28, 133, 141, 145, 151, 155, 254, 258
Timothy (St Paul's disciple) 21
Tiridates 70
Titus 45, 53, 65, 70, 80, 92–93, 161, 189, 191, 198, 228, 231, 233, 234, 239, 246, 252, 273, 282, 284, 286, 292, 297, 300, 302, 311, 313, 315, 317, 324; address at Jerusalem 277; *Commentarii* (*Hypomnemata*) 42; *consilium* 319; policy on deserters 306–8, 318; treatment of captives 292, 302, 317, 318
Tolomaeus 126
Trajan 324
Trotsky, Leon xvii
Tyrannius Priscus 88

Ummidius Quadratus 73, 82, 131–32, 260

Valerius Gratus 110
Varus *see* Noarus/Varus; Quinctilius Varus
Ventidius Cumanus 72, 82, 128–32, 132, 133, 134, 140, 191, 284
Vespasian 45, 52, 53, 155, 161, 164, 178, 180–81, 184, 187, 189, 190, 191, 196–97, 199, 200, 229, 233, 234, 236, 239, 245, 252, 272, 274, 283, 284, 286–87, 289, 291, 308, 309, 310, 311, 315, 317, 324 ; *Commentarii* (*Hypomnemata*) 42
Vibius Marsus 122, 123
Virgil 323, 326; *Aeneid* 90
Vitellius 82, 114–15, 125, 131, 132, 260, 287
Vologeses I 70

'wanton king' 58
White, Hayden xx, xxii, 47
Wicked Priest 30
Witch of Endor 16
Woodman, Anthony J. xx

Xistus 83, 160

Yosé b. Yokanan 144

Zacharias b. Amphicalleus 229, 238
Zacharias b. Baris 235–37
Zadok 15
Zamaris 162